Steven Caney's Kids' America

Steven Caney's
KIDS'
AMERICA

Workman Publishing
New York

Library of Congress Cataloging in Publication Data

Caney, Steven.
  Kids' America

  Includes index.
  SUMMARY: Introduces aspects of American life from the colonial period to the present. Suggests such activities as handicraft projects, genealogy searches, and games.
  1. United States — Social life and customs—Juvenile literature. 2. Handicraft—United States—Juvenile literature. 3. United States — Genealogy — Juvenile literature. [1. United States— Social life and customs. 2. Handicraft. 3. Genealogy. 4. Amusements] I. Title.
  E161.C33   973   77 27465

ISBN 0-911104-79-8
ISBN 0-911104-80-1 pbk.

Art Director: Paul Hanson

Designer: Robert Fitzpatrick

Illustrations: Ginger Brown

Photographs: Steven Caney

Workman Publishing Company, Inc.
1 West 39 Street
New York, New York 10018

Manufactured in the
United States of America
First printing May 1978

10 9 8 7 6 5 4 3

DEDICATION

To Shelly

THANK YOU...

Ruth Baxter
Ginger Brown
Susan McCaslin

RESEARCH AND INSPIRATIONS

Gail Farrell
Betsy Groban
Joan Klickstein

GENEROUS KNOWLEDGE

Bernard Barenholtz
Stanley Briskman
Himan Brown
Paul Butterfield
Mary Fraser
Nathan Plafker
Karen Robinson
Walter Salmon
Mel Simons
John Sitaris
Arno Szegvari
Art Turco
Anne Zevin

TALENTED SKILLS

Arthur Boehm
Peter Derderian
Jean D'Urbano
Michael Fein
Diana Peppel
Suzanne Rafer
Shirley Sauer
Lauri Stokes

AND KIDS

Chrissy and Billy Belanger
Mindy and John Berman
Heather Cameron
Jennifer and Noah Caney
Lee and Leslie Caney
Kate Carpenter
Tom and Tod Crowell
Nicole Driscoll
Suzanne and David Dubroff
Carol Eresian
Ted Farnham
Andy Forsberg
Wyman Fraser and friends
Kermit King
Kim and Jamie Klickstein
Cindy Liessner
Peter Milliken
Ted Read
Becky Shepardson
Luis Sierra
Michael and Niki Soforenko
Derek and Allison Stokes
Karen Terrey
Sean Williams
Carlisle Public School kids,
  Carlisle, Massachusetts
Sea Pines Academy kids,
  Hilton Head, South Carolina

AND DOGS

Guenie Dog
Nelly Dog

CONTENTS

INTRODUCTION 21

Chapter 1 AMERICAN HERITAGE

GENEALOGY.. 26

DISCOVERING
YOUR PEDIGREE.. 26

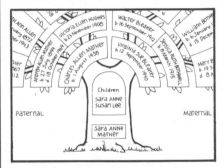

*I'm My Own Grand-
paw* 30

WHAT'S IN A
NAME? 30
Surnames A–Z 31

YOUR COAT OF
ARMS 34

Family Treasures 36

Knock, Knock Names .. 37

Chapter 2 AMERICAN KNOW-HOW

LIVING AMERICAN .. 40

BETTER BUTTER 42
Making a Butter Churn 43
Making Butter 43

MILKING A COW 44
How to Milk a Cow.... 45

REALLY GOOD SOAP................. 45

Grandma's Lye Soap .. 46
Making Soap............ 46
Ivory®, The Soap That Floats................ 47

CANDLES 48
Making Molded Candles................ 48
Making Dipped Candles................ 50
Making a Tin Lantern 51

Making a Candle Clock 52

VALUABLE ROPE ... 52
Making Rope 53

FORECASTING WEATHER 54
Weather Folklore 54
Weathervanes 55
News to Me............. 56
Making a Weathervane 56
Hygrometers 57
Making a Hygrometer . 57
Cricket Thermometer .. 58
Weather Clues 58

PANNING FOR GOLD 59
The Panning Method .. 59
Staking a Gold Claim.. 61

LOTIONS, POTIONS, AND STRANGE NOTIONS 61
Hiccups 62
Warts 62
Freckles................. 62

Insect Bites, Stings, and Itches 62
Sunburn................. 62
Bangs and Bruises 63
Pains and Sprains 63
Small Cuts.............. 63
Splinters and Thorns... 63
Poison Ivy 63
Athlete's Foot.......... 63
The Common Cold..... 63
Coughing 63
Sore Throat............. 63
Sneezing 63
Toothache 63
Earache 63
Nosebleed 63

Chapter 3 AMERICAN HOMES

HOME SWEET HOME 66

What Has Changed? ... 72

GUESS WHAT'S 74

How Nails Are Made .. 76

HEX SIGNS FOR YOUR HOME 77

Making a Hex Sign 78

STENCILED WALLS 79

Making Stencil Prints 79

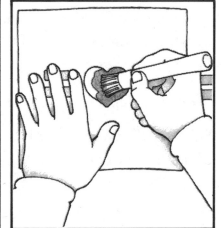

FOUR-POSTER CANOPY BED 82

Making a Four-Poster Canopy Bed 82

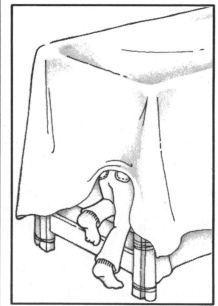

ROCKING CHAIRS .. 84

Fan Rocker and Fly Chaser 84

The Shakers 85

GREAT PLAINS INDIAN TEPEE 85

Making a Five-Pole, Two-Kid Tepee 87

THE GETAWAY TREE HOUSE 89

Building a Tree House 90

Deed to the House 93

Chapter 4 AMERICAN BACKYARDS AND GARDENS

BACKYARD FUN 96

AN AMERICAN
GARDEN 96

Kitchen Gardens........ 97
Planning the Garden .. 98
Making Compost 100
For Potatoes and Tomatoes, Thank You, Thomas Jefferson! ... 100

SCARECROW 101
Making Your Own Scarecrow............. 102

PEANUTS 103
Grow a Peanut Plant ... 104
Recipes for a Peanut Dinner 106

NATURE GAMES 107
Daisy Chains........... 108

Burr Building 108
Acorn-top Finger Puppets 109
Seed-head Shooters 109
Grass-blade Whistle ... 109
Maple-seed Claws and Noses 109

Why Leaves Change Color 110

FROG JUMPING 110
How to Catch a Frog .. 111
The Frog-Jumping Contest 111
From The Celebrated Jumping Frog of Calaveras County, by Mark Twain 112
Make a Fly Catcher 113

FAMILY PETS 113
Pets You Don't Own ... 114
Dog Happy 115

America's Pets 118

BIRD FEEDERS 119
Making Bird Feeders .. 119
Birdhouse Pointers 120

TIME CAPSULES 121
Your Own Time Capsule 122

DIGGING FOR BOTTLES 123
Poison Bottles 125

DOWSING FOR WATER 126

Chapter 5 AMERICAN FASHION

FASHION: PLAIN AND FANCY 130

DRESSING UP......... 135

COLOR DYEING 136

CHILDREN'S FASHION............. 138

WHERE DID YOU GET THAT HAT? ... 139

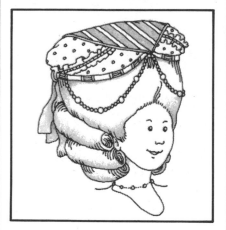

Making Hats 142

The Basic Cap 144

WALKING STICKS... 144

Chapter 6 EATING IN AMERICA

AMERICAN DIET 148

All-American Dishes .. 150

USING THE
  KITCHEN 151

APPLES 152
American Apple Pie ... 152
Golden Delicious 153
Candy Apples 153
Dried Apple Rings 154

Johnny Appleseed 155

AMERICAN CHEESE 155
Three Kinds of Cheese
  to Make 156
"Big Cheese" 157

HAMBURGERS, THE
  PEOPLE'S CHOICE 157
The Best Burgers 158

HOT DOGS 159
Batter-dipped Corn
  Dogs 159

SUBMARINE
  SANDWICH 160

SPICY KETCHUP 162

CRISPY POTATO
  CHIPS 163

POPCORN 165
Make a Corn Popper ... 165
Corn Popping 166
Popcorn Balls 166

DOUGHNUTS 167
Fried Dough............ 167

Lunch Counter Lingo .. 167

PEANUT BUTTER.... 168
Making Peanut Butter . 168

GRAHAM
  CRACKERS......... 168
S'Mores................ 169

PRETZELS 169

Philadelphia Soft
  Pretzels 170

AMERICA'S SWEET
  TOOTH 171
Soft Drinks 172
Ice Cream 172
Vanilla Molasses Taffy 173
Chewing Gum 174
Getting Off the Gum ... 175
*Does Your Chewing
  Gum Lose Its Flavor
  on the Bedpost Over
  Night* 176

FORAGING 177
Day Lilies 177
Acorns 178
Dandelions 178
Rose Petals 179
Cattails................ 179

Chapter 7 AMERICAN SCHOOL DAYS

THE THREE R'S 182

INK 184
Nut Ink 184
Berry Ink 184

FANCY PENS 185
Make a Wood-Nib Pen 185
Make a Quill Pen 185

HOW TO WRITE
    FANCY (LIKE
    JOHN HANCOCK) 186

Primers 188

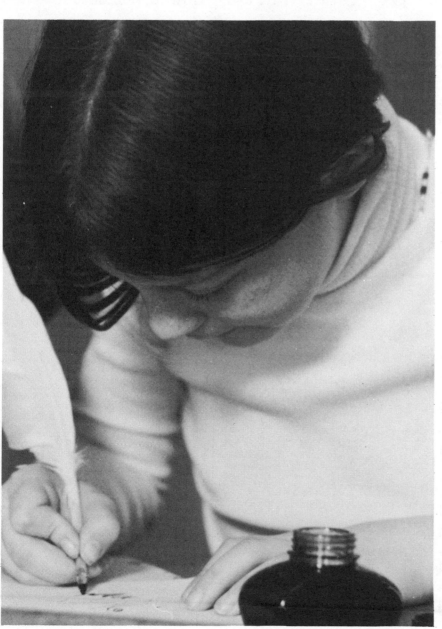

SPELLING 189
Spelling Bee 189
*100 Words Commonly
    Misspelled in the
    English Language* ... 190

REBUS 190
Rebus Dictionary 192

TONGUE TWISTERS 193

AUTOGRAPH
    VERSES 194

ETIQUETTE 196
The Formal Afternoon
    Tea 196
Invitations and Replies 197
What to Wear 197
Setting the Table 197
How to Make
    Good Tea 198
Serving the Tea 199
Table Accidents 199

Chapter 8 MADE IN AMERICA

UNDERSTANDING ART 202

SHAPE 203
Project 203

COLOR 203
Project 204

LINE 204
Project 205

LIGHT 206
Project 206

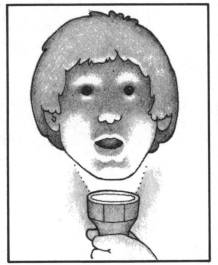

TEXTURE 207
Project 207

MOTION 207
Project 208

COMPOSITION 209
Project 210

FRAMING 210
Project 210

MODERN ART 211

MIXED MEDIA 215
Project 215

ACTION PAINTING .. 216
Project 216

COLLAGE 217
Project 217

POP ART 217
Project 218

ENVIRONMENTAL
SCULPTURE 219
Project 219

OP ART 220
Project 220

MOBILES 220
Project 221

American Kitsch 221

HAPPENINGS 222

ARTS AND CRAFTS 223

GRAVE ART 223
Gravestone Rubbing ... 224

WHITTLING 225
How to Whittle 227

SILHOUETTE ART ... 228

Making a Silhouette
Portrait 230
Paper Doll Chains 231

FLOWER DRYING ... 231
Air Drying.............. 231
Sand Drying............ 232
Press Drying 233
Flower Arrangements.. 233
Plants to Dry........... 234

SCRIMSHAW 234
Plastic Scrimshaw 235

Chapter 9 TOYS, PUZZLES, PLAY-PRETTIES, AND GAMES

PLAYTHINGS .. 238

NEWSPAPER TOYS .. 242
Paper Snake 242
Paper Tree 243

FLYING TOYS 244
Flying Propeller 244
Ring Wing Glider 245

SNOW GLOBE 246
Making a Snow Globe . 246

Noah's Ark 247

PUNCHBOARDS 248
Making Punchboards .. 248

MARBLE RACEWAY 250
Making a Marble
    Raceway 250

DOLLS 252
Yarn Doll 253
Roly-Poly Dolls 254
Life-Size Doll 256

Dress-Me Paper Dolls . 258
Teddy Bears 260
Ventriloquism 262

CRYSTAL RADIO 263
Making a Crystal
    Radio 264

PUZZLES 266
Ox-Yoke Puzzle 266

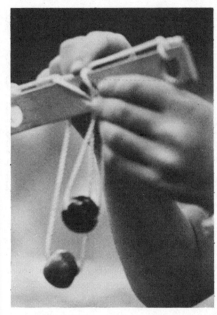

Button Hole Puzzle 268
14-15 Puzzle 269
Knots-and-Not-Knots .. 270

Four Color Cubes 271

PLAYPRETTIES 272
Finger Trap 272
Domino Trains 273
Soggy Ring 274
Sky Hook 274
String Figures 275
Target Shooting 278

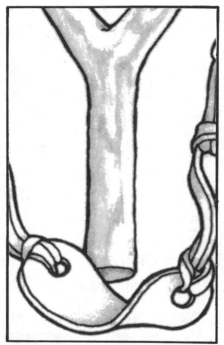

GAMES 280
Fox and Geese 280
Indian and Rabbits 282
Solitaire 282
Triangle Solitaire 283
How Many Moves 283
Point Tic-Tac-Toe 284
Tabletop Olympics 285
Calculator Games 288

Chapter 10 SATURDAY NIGHT

THE CIRCUS .. 292

CIRCUS TALK 294

SIDESHOW TRICKS
EXPLAINED......... 294
Sword Swallowing 294
Sword Walking 295
Fire Eating 295

ROPE SPINNING 295
How to Spin
a Flat Loop 296

BE A STRONGMAN . 297
Break a Deck of Cards 297
Tear a Telephone Book 298

BE A CLOWN 298
*You Really Can Join
the Circus* 299
Putting On a Clown
Face.................... 299
Clown Clothes 300
Clown Pantomime 300

FORTUNE-TELLING 301

Palmistry 302
Card Reading 305
Graphology............. 307
*How Do You Cross
Your T's?* 310
The Fortune Cookie.... 310

JUGGLING 311

MAKING MUSIC 314

MUSIC FOR ALL
OCCASIONS 316
Mother Goose.......... 316

JUG BANDS 317
Playing the Jug 317
Making a Washtub
Bass.................... 317
Playing the Washboard 318
Playing the Musical
Comb 319
Playing the Spoons..... 319

Playing the Tin Can,
Flower Pot, Wastepaper
Basket, Cooking Pot,
and Cake Pan......... 320

MUSICAL GLASSES. 321

YOU CAN PLAY THE
HARMONICA 322

PUSH-BUTTON
TELEPHONE
SONGS............... 323

AMERICA DANCES . 324
Tap Dancing 325
Dance the L.A. Hustle 327
Dance the New York
Hustle................. 329

AT HOME 332

COMIC BOOKS AND
FUNNY PAPERS.... 332
Making Shuffle-Deck
Comics 334

AMERICA'S FUNNY
BONE 335

PARLOR GAMES 338
Charades................ 338
Grandmother's Trunk.. 339
Alphabet Sentences 340
Twenty Questions 340
Botticelli or The Nope
Game 340
Geography............... 341
Ghost 341
Whist.................... 342

GHOST STORIES 342
The Ghostly Rider 343

Nobody Here But You . 344
The Haunted House.... 345
Homemade Ghost
Stories 347
White House Ghosts ... 347

OLD-TIME RADIO ... 348
Radio Plays 349
Making Sound Effects . 350

Chapter 11 LAND OF OPPORTUNITY

AMERICAN FREEDOM.... 354

It's the Law! 356

HOW TO BE A POLITICIAN........ 358
The Campaign 358
The President Wants to Hear From You....... 360
Presidents Come in All Shapes and Sizes..... 361

HOLIDAYS AND CELEBRATIONS ... 361
Make Your Own Official Day of Celebration 362
Guide to the Well-Decorated Bike or Doll Carriage 362
Official Whatever Days 363

FIRECRACKERS...... 364

Making Paper Firecrackers........... 364

NEED INFORMATION?................ 365

SYMBOLS OF AMERICA............ 366
American Flag 367
Flag Code 368
The Donkey and the Elephant.............. 368
The Great Seal of the United States 368
The American Bald Eagle.................. 369
Uncle Sam.............. 369
The Pine Tree (Liberty Tree).................. 370
American Symbols to Draw.................. 370
The Rattlesnake 371
The Buffalo 372
Cigar Store Indian 372
Bumper Stickers 373
Hobo Sign Language .. 374

AMERICAN MONEY 376
Coins 377

COIN COLLECTING . 379
Valuable Change 380

BORROWING MONEY 382

SAVING MONEY 382
Piggy Banks............. 382
Make a Piggy Bank 383

INVESTING MONEY 384

GOING INTO BUSINESS.... 386

CHOOSING A BUSINESS 386
The Business for You... 387
Making a Business Plan 388
Business Books and Records............... 391
Phone Tabs.............. 391

NEWSPAPER LOGS .. 392

BABY-SITTING 392
The Preliminaries 392
On the Job.............. 393
What to Do If 394

HOUSE PAINTING ... 394
Paints.................... 394
Paintbrushes............. 396
Paint Rollers 397
Preparing the Surface .. 397
Using Ladders 398

GARAGE SALE 398

Overworked Children.. 401

INDEX 402

INTRODUCTION

Kids' America is a book about America's spirit, its history, ingenuity, and life-styles; of how this country came to be, and how to translate all of this information into things you can make and do.

As a kid in America, whether born here or not, all its heritage belongs to you. But, this is not a history of events and dates; rather it is a rich and exciting social history of the American people, from the early days right up to the present time, and with an occasional glimpse into the future. If you have ever spun a cowboy lasso, dowsed for water, cured hiccups with a home remedy, started an afterschool business, raced a jumping frog, built a tree house, ate a soft pretzel, or tried to play a musical jug, then you have already experienced a bit of the history you have inherited, and a small piece of Kids' America.

Each generation of Americans is unique, with its own styles, fads, attitudes, and inventions. Kids' America is a rediscovery of those bits of America's past that are fun to know today. It includes what people wore, studied, ate, and played; their superstitions, crafts, inventions, and the American spirit they created.

Although not everything that is typically American was actually invented by an American or even in America, all the subjects and projects in this book have earned the reputation of being a solid part of our heritage. Many were once considered the chores and drudgery of every day life—making butter, soap, candles, rope, concocting remedies, building homes, and planting gardens—but now they can be enjoyed as crafts and hobbies because we no longer *have* to do them. Many have always been fun—tap dancing, playing charades, inventing clown faces, building a tree house, making the best submarine sandwich, and being a ventriloquist. By sampling the hundreds of games, recipes, crafts, toys, and ideas in Kids' America, you may gradually begin to understand just why America is so special.

The Early American, by necessity, was a generalist. He could do almost anything using his ingenuity, and whatever materials were available. But, America passed quickly from a pioneering farm economy to an industrial economy in which machines could produce hundreds and thousands of a product, and every one the same. With each new invention and mass-produced product, the generalist, so necessary in Early America, became more of a specialist and hand skills, once a part of daily life, became obsolete and part of our history. As we abandoned the tasks and inconveniences of an earlier, more demanding life-style, and depended on others we didn't even know for nearly everything we needed or wanted, we Americans had to remember not to lose the spirit and knowledge that helped create this country. Do you know how to milk a cow, make your own soap, stop the itch of an insect bite, build a tepee, dress a scarecrow, or cook your own ketchup?

There are plenty of museums throughout this country that have preserved most of the artifacts from all periods in our history, but a museum cannot collect or display the American spirit. You can see a museum exhibit of hand-whittled objects, read the history of whittling, and even watch someone demonstrate the technique, but you cannot really understand the enjoyment and pride of the whittler until you whittle a piece of wood for yourself. Pride in what you do, and a sense of accomplishment and self-worth, are feelings that you give to yourself and no one else can do that for you.

The spirit of this country is reborn with each new generation. Children instinctively make life an adventure, and the more opportunities you have to use that spirit, the better equipped you will be as an adult to understand and use the rich resources of this country. You can still be a pioneer in America.

I began writing *Kids' America* by researching the life-styles and attitudes of the American people and looking for crafts and any other products that could be considered typically American. Ideas came from a variety of sources—public and private libraries, museums, public relations pamphlets from manufacturers, newspapers, magazines found on waiting room tables, stuff in old barns and at garage sales, brainstorming sessions, and my own memories of childhood and travel throughout America.

One evening while watching a TV talk show I saw a guest set up a long chain of standing domino pieces, then knock over the first causing the rest of the line to fall over one by one in a rhythmic chain reaction. I remembered that a lot of kids I used to play with made "domino trains" especially on sick days when they were home from school. The domino idea seemed to fit my definition of a typical American pastime but now I wanted to try it again myself, and then see if kids today would still enjoy knocking down a line of dominoes. I was pretty sure they would, and so with a few neighborhood kids, I began making domino trains in every imaginable configuration: sometimes spelling out names, sometimes up and down propped-up books, with the last domino in the chain dropping off the edge of a table into a cup. The kids thought making domino trains was great—and so did I.

In much the same way every interesting and typically American idea was tested with typically American kids, and then we decided exactly what was to be a part of *Kids' America*.

When one of us would suggest an interesting idea but I could not find any reference material on the subject, I searched out those people who did know. I was able to get a few trade secrets from food companies so that I could present authentic recipes. And I not only interviewed a dance teacher, but ended up taking a few lessons in tap dance so I could write about it better. I was taught how to milk a cow by an old dairy farmer, and got to see a calf being born while I was there. My research took me to the Harvard Business School for a lesson on kids going into business. I was fascinated to learn about old-time radio shows and how to make sound effects from a man who had been in radio broadcasting since the beginning. And in meeting these people, and several others, I also developed a few new friendships.

I like the feeling of knowing how to do things for myself even if I don't need to do them and among several other things, I have become an amateur tree house architect and graphologist, stand-up comedian, fortune-teller, forager, weather forecaster, art critic, fashion designer, snack food chef, circus clown, and a gold mine of American trivia.

Some of the recipes and a few of the projects in *Kids' America* are presented in instruction just as they were probably originally done in America. However most projects, or parts of them, are presented as my own 'goof proof' designs. The construction materials are usually scraps and discards found around the house and the tools are mostly your hands, kitchen utensils, the sewing box, and sometimes a hammer and saw.

However, even though I have designed these projects to be constructed simply, at little or no cost, they are also designed without sacrificing function. My design for a clothes hanger weathervane is just as sensitive to the changing wind as a big old brass New England rooster weathervane. The projects to make and do really work and you don't have to be a kid to try them!

You can read *Kids' America* as a story book, crafts book, recipe book, practical reference, and even a history book. Just thumb through these pages to sample the various flavors of America and see what tickles your curiosity.

Kids' America was written in the true spirit of Early America—with dedication, hard work, and without haste.

Frank Derby Family. Photo taken by Alfred Hosmer (1851–1903). Courtesy of the Concord Free Public Library, Concord, Massachusetts.

Chapter 1

AMERICAN HERITAGE

GENEALOGY

You might have heard your parents talk about your Great Aunt Betty whom you have never met, or your Uncle Harry who moved to Arizona when you were a baby, or your mother's brother-in-law who had a cousin who was once a famous actor. Who were these people and exactly how are they related to you? Who was your first family ancestor to come to America and when? Do you have any relatives in your past who fought in wars? It is interesting to learn about your relatives and the many ancestors and generations that preceded you—where they lived, what work they did, who their children were, what their names were, and when they died. Of course, not everyone's ancestors helped to found America, but most Americans can find some ancestors that helped America to grow.

A study of your chain of ancestors is called "genealogy"—a word meaning "family knowledge." Genealogy has always been a popular hobby of Americans, and today there are hundreds of genealogy clubs and organizations that swap information and help each other locate facts about long-ago relatives. You can trace your own roots and learn about your heritage, but you will probably need to do some detective work in gathering information.

Searching through the family photograph album.

DISCOVERING YOUR PEDIGREE

Your pedigree is your direct line of heritage—or "bloodlines"—starting with yourself and working backwards through your parents, grandparents, great-grandparents, and so on. A person's pedigree is often shown as a chart, Fig. 1. Another way to show your heritage is to make a "family tree" or "family circle," Figs. 2 and 3. Before setting out to make your own pedigree chart it is often helpful to first fill out a "family group sheet" listing your own family, the families of both pairs of your grandparents, your great-grandparents, and so on. Try to do a family group sheet for each generation until you discover your first relative to have come to America. Some people may not need to go back further than their parents or grandparents; the descendants of an original settler may need to trace his pedigree back more than fifteen generations.

Family facts

You can do family group sheets on notebook paper, filling in the categories shown in Fig. 4. Put your father's name in the space next to "husband" and your mother's name in the space next to "wife." Fill out as much information as you know about your parents. Put your own name and the names of any brothers and sisters under "children." Children's names should be listed in the order of birth; if you were the third child to be born in your family you would be listed next to the number 3. Fill in as much information about you and your brothers and sisters as you know.

Fig. 1

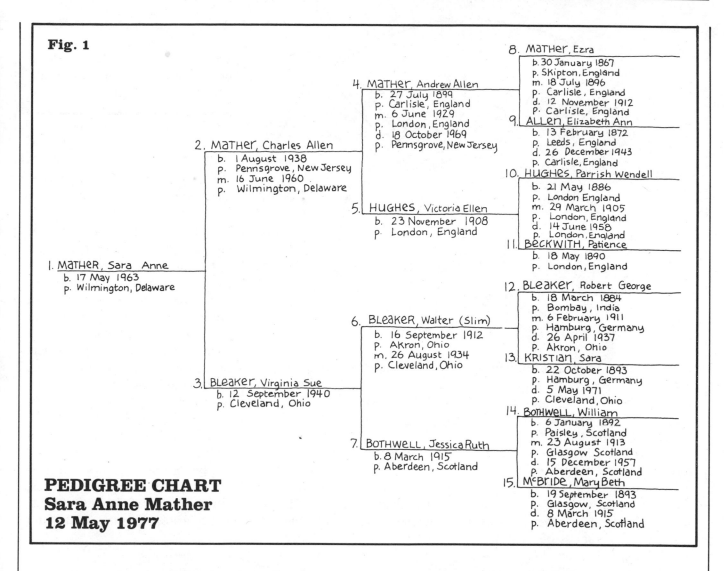

8. MATHER, Ezra
   b. 30 January 1867
   p. Skipton, England
   m. 18 July 1896
   p. Carlisle, England
   d. 12 November 1912
   p. Carlisle, England

4. MATHER, Andrew Allen
   b. 27 July 1899
   p. Carlisle, England
   m. 6 June 1929
   p. London, England
   d. 18 October 1969
   p. Pennsgrove, New Jersey

9. ALLEN, Elizabeth Ann
   b. 13 February 1872
   p. Leeds, England
   d. 26 December 1943
   p. Carlisle, England

2. MATHER, Charles Allen
   b. 1 August 1938
   p. Pennsgrove, New Jersey
   m. 16 June 1960
   p. Wilmington, Delaware

10. HUGHES, Parrish Wendell
    b. 21 May 1886
    p. London England
    m. 29 March 1905
    p. London, England
    d. 14 June 1958
    p. London, England

5. HUGHES, Victoria Ellen
   b. 23 November 1908
   p. London, England

11. BECKWITH, Patience
    b. 18 May 1890
    p. London, England

1. MATHER, Sara Anne
   b. 17 May 1963
   p. Wilmington, Delaware

12. BLEAKER, Robert George
    b. 18 March 1884
    p. Bombay, India
    m. 6 February 1911
    p. Hamburg, Germany
    d. 26 April 1937
    p. Akron, Ohio

6. BLEAKER, Walter (Slim)
   b. 16 September 1912
   p. Akron, Ohio
   m. 26 August 1934
   p. Cleveland, Ohio

13. KRISTIAN, Sara
    b. 22 October 1893
    p. Hamburg, Germany
    d. 5 May 1971
    p. Cleveland, Ohio

3. BLEAKER, Virginia Sue
   b. 12 September 1940
   p. Cleveland, Ohio

14. BOTHWELL, William
    b. 6 January 1892
    p. Paisley, Scotland
    m. 23 August 1913
    p. Glasgow Scotland
    d. 15 December 1957
    p. Aberdeen, Scotland

7. BOTHWELL, Jessica Ruth
   b. 8 March 1915
   p. Aberdeen, Scotland

15. McBRIDE, Mary Beth
    b. 19 September 1893
    p. Glasgow, Scotland
    d. 8 March 1915
    p. Aberdeen, Scotland

PEDIGREE CHART
Sara Anne Mather
12 May 1977

There are certain recommended procedures used by genealogists to keep the recorded information organized and understandable when listing names and dates on your family group sheets and family pedigree chart. Write each name with the last name printed first in capital letters, followed by the first name, then the middle name. If a person has a nickname it can be listed in parenthesis after the given name. Dates are listed by printing the day of the month, then the month and year—for example, 5 May 1897. Always use a woman's maiden name (her last name before she was married) and not her married name. Some genealogists like to list a brief biography of each

parent on the back of the family group sheet.

Rooting out clues

Most people have trouble completing their group sheets beyond their own immediate family without having to search for more facts than they know. To get "unknown" family information, start by asking questions of your oldest relatives and non-immediate family members. Longtime residents of your town and friends of your family may be able to give you information. If after asking your parents and relatives you still have unanswered questions and blanks in your family group sheets, you will probably need to start searching old

records for clues.

Look for clues written in family Bibles. The Bible was often used to record births, marriages, and deaths in the family. Also look for clues in family scrapbooks, diaries, and baby books.

If your family has lived in the same city or town for many generations, the public library may have genealogical records to help you. You might also get good clues from church records and cemetery gravestones.

County records kept at the county courthouse include property deeds and wills that often list relatives names. Your city hall or town office usually keeps records of births and marriages as well as

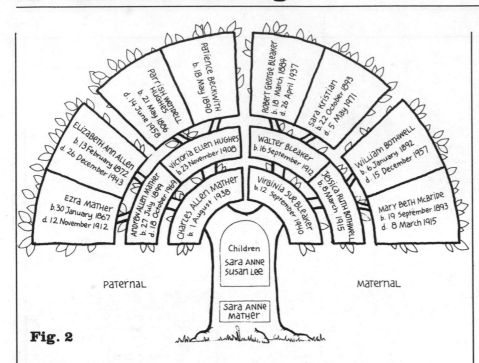

Fig. 2

PATERNAL   MATERNAL

Elizabeth Ann Allen
b. 13 February 1872
d. 26 December 1943

Parrish Wendell Hughes
b. 21 May 1886
d. 14 June 1958

Patience Beckwith
b. 18 May 1890

Robert George Bleaker
b. 18 March 1884
d. 26 April 1937

Sara Kristian
b. 22 October 1893
d. 5 May 1971

William Bothwell
b. 6 January 1892
d. 15 December 1957

Ezra Mather
b. 30 January 1867
d. 12 November 1912

Andrew Allen Mather
b. 27 July 1899
d. 18 October 1969

Victoria Ellen Hughes
b. 23 November 1908

Walter Bleaker
b. 16 September 1912

Jessica Ruth Bothwell
b. 6 March 1915

Mary Beth McBride
b. 19 September 1893
d. 8 March 1915

Charles Allen Mather
b. 1 August 1938

Virginia Sue Bleaker
b. 12 September 1940

Children
Sara Anne
Susan Lee

Sara Anne Mather

death notices. You may even find a genealogical society in your town that can help you. Some queries may have to be made by mail. When writing for family history, be complete but concise about your question, and enclose a self-addressed, stamped envelope for the reply.

As you do your investigations try to keep accurate written notes—don't rely on your memory. List not only information you have found, but also give the source. Try to get as much information as possible about each person on your family group sheet:

Name of person
Born when and where
Parents' names
Married who, when, and where
Lived where
Occupations
Children, born when and where
Died when and where

People who make genealogy their hobby or even their profession insist that they have proof in at least three written records for each entry on the family group sheet.

However, unless you find conflicting clues, verbal information should be acceptable.

Chart it

Now that you have completed your family group sheets, you can transfer the information to your own pedigree chart, see Fig. 1. Copying the format of the chart, put your

name on line number one. Underneath each name line there is a space for additional information to be listed; each category is abbreviated by a small letter:

b=born	d=died
m=married	p=place

Under your name, and for each name you list on the chart, include the information that is relevant.

You will find that your name line on the pedigree chart branches out to two lines, one for each of your parents. On line number two list your father's name, and put your mother's name on line number three. As you continue to fill out your pedigree chart, you will find men's names will always be written on even numbered lines, and women's names on odd numbered lines. A father's number on the chart will always be twice the number of his child, and his wife's number will always be one less than her husband's. After listing your parents, list your parents' parents—that is, your grandparents. List your

Fig. 3

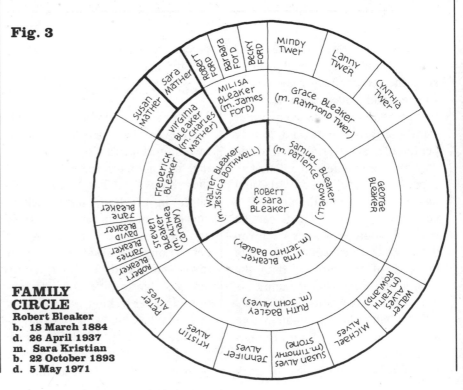

FAMILY CIRCLE
Robert Bleaker
b. 18 March 1884
d. 26 April 1937
m. Sara Kristian
b. 22 October 1893
d. 5 May 1971

Robert & Sara Bleaker

Walter Bleaker (m. Jessica Bothwell)

Grace Bleaker (m. Raymond Twer)

Samuel Bleaker (m. Patience Sowell)

Irma Bleaker (m. Jethro Bagley)

Mindy Twer
Lanny Twer
Cynthia Twer
George Bleaker
Walter Alves (m. Faith Rowland)
Michael Alves
Susan Alves (m. Timothy Stone)
Jennifer Alves
Kristin Alves
Peter Alves
Ruth Bagley (m. John Alves)

Susan Mather
Sara Mather
Robert Ford
Barbara Ford
Becky Ford
Milisa Bleaker (m. James Ford)
Virginia Bleaker (m. Charles Mather)
Frederick Bleaker
Steven Bleaker (m. Althea Canady)
Jane Bleaker
David Bleaker
James Bleaker
Robert Bleaker

FAMILY GROUP SHEET

HUSBAND *Mather, Charles Allen*
b. *1 August 1938*
p. *Pennsgrove NJ*
m. *16 June 1960*
p. *Wilmington DE*
d.
p.
FATHER *Mather, Andrew Allen*
MOTHER *Hughes, Victoria Ellen*

WIFE *Bleaker, Virginia Sue*
b. *12 September 1940*
p. *Cleveland OH*
d.
p.
FATHER *Bleaker, Walter*
MOTHER *Bothwell, Jessica Ruth*

CHILDREN	born/place	married/place/who	died/place
1. *Susan*	*6 June 1961/Wilming. DE*		
2. *Sara*	*17 May 1963/Wilming. DE*		
3.			
4.			
5.			
6.			
7.			
8.			

Fig. 4

father's parents on lines four and five and your mother's parents on lines six and seven. Continue to fill in your pedigree chart until you have gone through all your family group sheets and you reach the family generation that first arrived in America.

Look at the illustrated pedigree chart. What can you tell about Sara Mather's family from the information given? Sara's first relatives to have come to America seem to have been her great-grandparents, Sara (Kristian) and Robert Bleaker. William Bothwell's wife, Mary, died on the same day her daughter (and Sara Mather's grandmother, Jessica Bothwell) was born. If you study the chart even closer, and use your imagination, there are several clues about where Sara Mather's ancestors lived during their lives and why.

Family trees and family circles

Another way of drawing a pedigree chart is in the graph style of a branching tree in which each fork of a branch represents an individual's parents, Fig. 2. The "family tree" does not need to be as complete as the pedigree chart, and if you make one you may want to list only names and possibly dates of birth and death.

Still another way to show your family ancestry, and to better understand family relationships, is to make a "family circle," Fig. 3. In this diagram you begin with an ancestor—for example, your first ancestor to arrive in America—and list him and his wife in the center of the circle.

In the next ring list the children of that ancestor, in the third ring

list *their* children, and so on. When listing a name on the family circle, include marriages by writing the husband's or wife's name in parenthesis, after *m*. Each ring of the circle then represents the children of the next generation.

After you have completed the family circle up to your own generation, you can "read" the circle chart to see the relationships between family members. But just in case you are confused about second cousins, first cousins once removed, or grandnephews, here is an explanation of most family relationships that are sometimes difficult to figure out.

Sorting out relations

The parents of your father or mother are your grandfather and grandmother and you are their grandchild.

The parents of your grandfather or grandmother are your great-grandparents and you are their great-grandchild.

The parents of your great-grandparents are your second great-grandparents and you are their second great-grandchild, and so on.

The children of your brothers and sisters are your nephews and nieces, and you are their uncle or aunt.

The children of your nieces and nephews are your grandnieces or grandnephews, and you are their granduncle or grandaunt.

The children of your grandnephews and grandnieces are your great-grand-nephews and great-grandnieces and you are their great-granduncle or great-grandaunt, and so on.

Your parents' brothers and sisters are your uncles and aunts and you are their nephew or niece.

The children of your uncle or aunt are your first cousins and you are their first cousin.

The children of first cousins are second cousins to each other.

The children of second cousins are third cousins to each other, and so on.

The children of your first cousins are your first cousins once removed and you are the same to them. "Once removed"

always implies a different generation.

The children of your second cousins are your second cousins once removed, and you are the same to them.

The grandchildren of your second cousins are your second cousins twice removed, and you are the same to them.

The great-grandchildren of your second cousins are your second cousins three times removed and you are the same to them, and so on.

I'M MY OWN GRANDPAW
by Dwight Latham and Moe Jaffe

Many, many years ago when I was twenty-three
I was married to a widow who was pretty as could be
This widow had a grown up daughter who had hair of red
My father fell in love with her and soon they too were wed.

This made my dad my son-in-law and changed my very life
For my daughter was my mother 'cause she was my father's wife
To complicate the matter even though it brought me joy
I soon became the father of a bouncing baby boy.

My little baby then became a brother-in-law to dad
And so became my uncle though it made me very sad
For if he was my uncle then that also made him brother,
Of the widow's grown-up daughter who, of course, was my
  stepmother.

Father's wife then had a son who kept them on the run
And he became my grandchild for he was my daughter's son
My wife is now my mother's mother and it makes me blue
Because although she is my wife she's my grandmother too.

If my wife is my grandmother then I'm her grandchild
And every time I think of it, it nearly drives me wild
For now I have become the strangest case you ever saw
As husband of my grandmother I am my own grandpaw.

Chorus
I'm my own grandpaw
I'm my own grandpaw
It sounds funny I know
But it really is so
Oh, I'm my own grandpaw.

WHAT'S IN A NAME?

There is a greater variety of surnames—also called family or last names—among people in America than anywhere else in the world. This is because the ancestors of all Americans (excepting American Indians) immigrated from literally every country in the world. The immigrants brought their "foreign" names with them.

Many immigrants arrived in the United States unable to speak English. Often the pronunciation of their names was misunderstood or simplified by others—it was easier for newcomers to accept their Americanized names than to correct people continually. Different pronunciations of surnames lead to different name spellings. Some names were changed to suit the English language alphabet and its methods of spelling. Some "strange" names had letters or whole parts removed to make them easier to pronounce. Some people just didn't like their names and changed them to something else. America ended up with a lot of last names.

A meaning all its own

But do names have any meaning? Every person's surname was at one time most likely a word-picture of themselves. Several hundred years ago; and in some Early American villages, whatever you reminded people of was likely to become your last name. A man's profession, his heredity, or his most noticeable and striking characteristic, quirk, or physical trait soon became what people called him and that became his name. So a name often gives clues to its meaning.

Some people in Early America

might have referred to certain tradesmen as "Bill Weaver" or "Fred Carpenter" or "Eli Mason." Most names ending in *ing, kin, sin, sohn, son, uez, poulous, i, ian, ben, ski, sky, ich,* or beginning with *Mac* or *O* usually mean "son of." It was once common to refer to someone as his father's son "John, the son of Richard" or as it was more easily pronounced, John, Richard's son. And so Richardson became a last name.

Thomas who lived by the water might have been called Thomas Atwater or Susan who lived in the house on the large rocky meadow might have been referred to by others as Susan Rockland.

Sometimes saints' names were taken as last names for children born on holy days. For example, Saint Claire could become Sinclair, or Saint Paul might become Sample. Some people adopted names with no apparent meaning, just whatever sounded pleasing to them. And although by tradition, and a sense of family pride, we usually keep and use the name that our parents gave us, Americans have the right to give themselves whatever first and last name they like.

Since most surnames had a specific meaning at one time, you can probably discover the meaning of your own name. But many names have changed through generations, so if you think that your name might have been different at one time you may need to do some investigation. Ask your parents, grandparents, and other relatives.

SURNAMES A-Z

Below is a list of some of the more common surnames in America and their meanings. If your name is not included you can still use the list to look for name clues. First try to determine the "root word" in your name. Many names contain recognizable root words like *water, man, field, wood,* etc. Then read through some of the listed names and their meanings to see if you find clues to the rest of your surname. For example, in many names *ley* means meadow, *shaw* is forest, *ville* is town, *stein* means stone or rock, and *burn* is brook or stream.

Although you may not be certain that you are absolutely correct, it is interesting to find out the meaning of your surname; you might also learn something about the life of your ancestors.

Abel noble
Abercromby home at the mouth of a crooked river
Ackerman owner of a field or a farm
Adler noble warrior
Adrian dark one
Agostino majestic and proud
Alden old friend and protector
Alderman judge or jurist
Aldrich; Eldredge wise and old ruler

Alexander defender of men
Allen fierce one
Altman wise old man
Alvarado wall made of small stones
Alvarez noble and brilliant
Ames beloved one
Andrews strong and manly
Anthony the priceless one
Arman; Armand army man
Armstrong strong-armed warrior
Arnett young eagle
Ash home by an ash tree
Ashburn ash tree brook
Ashley ash tree meadow
Atwood home by the forest
Auerbach marshy brook
Augustus majestic and exalted
Avery elf-ruler
Ayer inheritor
Babcock youthful and proud
Bach; Bachman lives by the brook
Bacon bacon seller
Badger grain dealer
Bailey caretaker
Baird ballad singer
Baker bread baker
Baldwin bold friend
Ball bald person
Ballard bold and strong
Bamberg mountain forest
Bancroft bean field
Bannister basket maker

Banks river bank dweller
Barclay; Berkley birch tree meadow
Barker stripper of bark
Barlow bare hill
Barnes owner of barley
Baron nobleman
Barret strong as a bear
Bartholomew farmer
Bass; Basset short of stature
Baum tree
Baxter village bread baker
Beal the handsome one
Beatty food merchant
Beaumont beautiful mountain
Becker bread baker
Beckett little stream
Bellamy good friend
Bells; Belli handsome one
Beltz fur clothier
Bemis place of trees
Benfield bean field owner
Benjamin son of the right hand
Bennett young blessed one
Benson son of the bear
Bentley; Benton bent-grass meadow
Berg; Bergen mountain dweller
Berman hunter
Bernard; Barnhart brave as a bear
Bernstein amber or brown stone
Berry hill dweller
Biggers small piece of land

Blaine   thin man
Blair   field
Blake   the pale-complected one
Blankenship   small valley
Bliss   joyful one
Block; Blocher   block of wood
Bloomfield   field of flowers
Blumberg   flower-covered mountain
Blumenthal   valley of flowers
Blyth   the joyful one
Bogart   powerful with a bow and arrow
Bolton   manor house
Booker   the author
Boone   good man
Booth   messenger
Boswell   forest estate
Bowden   young messenger
Bowles   bowl and pot maker
Bowman   an archer
Boyer   bow maker
Bradbury   broad hill
Brandt   bad tempered
Brenner   brick baker
Brewer   brewer of beer
Bridges   home by a bridge
Brinkley   sloping meadow
Butcher   seller of meat
Butler   wine cellar keeper
Byrd   catcher of wild birds
Cahill; Cain   descendant of a warrior
Calder; Caldwell   forest stream
Calvert   calf herder
Cameron   hooked or crooked nose
Campbell   man with a crooked mouth
Cantrell   young singer
Carnes   rocky hill
Carpenter   worker with wood
Carr   swampy land
Carrillo   owner of a small cart
Carroll   champion warrior
Carter   cart hauler
Cartwright   cart maker
Carver   wood carver
Cassidy   descendant of a curly-haired person
Caswell   house by a spring
Cavanagh   descendant of a handsome person
Chambers   steward of an estate
Chandler   candlemaker
Chaplin   chapel keeper
Chapman   salesman and merchant
Chase   home in a hunting forest
Chavez   key maker
Chiang   home by a river
Chin   the diligent one
Clayborn   clay bottomed brook
Clark   scholar
Clemens; Clement   kind and gentle person

Coffin   the bold headed one
Cohen   priest
Collier   charcoal maker
Colombo   dove or pigeon keeper
Conte   member of nobility
Conway   descendant of the intelligent one
Cook   chief cook in a castle
Cooper   barrel maker
Corbett   young raven
Corey   descendant of a fluent talker
Cornell   blonde-brown hair
Cornett   trumpet blower
Corregio   leather craftsman
Counter   accountant and book-keeper
Coward   cow herder
Cox   roosters
Crocker   maker of pitchers
Crockett   small, bent one
Croft   small farm owner
Crook   bend in the river
Crosby   home by a shrine or cross
Culver   dove
Cummings   stranger
Cunningham   resident of a royal house
Curry   champion
Curtis   courteous one
Cutler   knife maker and seller
Dahl; Dale   valley dweller
Dallas   field by waterfall
Dalton   valley farmstead
Damon   down the river
Danforth   valley river crossing
Daniels   God be my judge
Darling   favorite one
Darrell   young spearman
Davidson   Son of the beloved one
Davis; Davies   beloved one
Day   dairy owner
Decker   house roofer
Dennis   sacred to the God of Wine
Denton   valley farmstead
Dewar   brave hero
Dewilde   son of a ruthless one
Diamond   shining protector
Dick   powerful ruler
Disney   place of iron mines
Dobbins; Dobbs   shining with fame
Domingo   born on Sunday
Dorman   gate keeper
Draper   seller of cloth and clothing
Dreyfuss   three-footed man with a crutch
Driscoll   interpreter of languages
Dumas   isolated country home
Dumont   home on a high place
Dunn   dark brown complexion
Eames   an uncle's son
Eastman   man from the east
Eaton   wealthy man's farm
Eberhard   strong as a boar

Eckhart   powerful with a sword
Ecklund   the owner of an oak grove
Edelstein   precious gem
Eden   prosperous one
Edmond   prosperous protector
Edwards   prosperous guardian
Egbert   sword maker
Eisenberg   iron mountain
Elder   elder and wise citizen
Elwood   old forest
Emerson; Emory   industrious ruler
Endicott   house at the edge of town
Enriquez   son of the estate ruler
Ernest   the serious one
Espinosa   thornbush land
Eubank   riverbank with yew trees
Evans   the well-born one
Fabian   bean grower
Fairchild   the handsome child
Fairfax   the fair-haired one
Falco   falcon or hawk
Fanta   young child
Farber   dyer of cloth
Farnham   fern-covered field
Faulkner   falcon or hawk trainer
Farrell   great valor
Faust   man with a strong fist
Fazzio   beech tree
Fein   the superior one
Feldman   field owner
Felice   lucky or happy
Fennell   muddy crossroads
Ferdinand   the peaceful and bold one
Ferrari   horseshoer
Ferrar   horseshoer
Fiedler   fiddle player
Fielding   field owner
Filippo   horse-lover
Fillmore   the famous one
Finley   the fair hero
Finney   descendant of a soldier
Fiori   flower
Fisher; Fischman   fish seller
Fisk   fisherman
Flagg   town resident
Fleischer   meat butcher
Fletcher   an arrow featherer
Flores   son of the flower grower
Flowers   arrow maker
Flynn   the red-faced one
Foulks   man of the people
Folsom   cattle enclosure
Forbes   son of the field owner
Ford   the river crossing place
Foreman   overseer of an estate
Forsythe   home in the woods
Fortier   strong man
Fortunato   the lucky one
Foss   waterfall
Fowler   gamekeeper

Franklin   free man
Frazer   strawberry field
Fried   the peaceful one
Frome   violent waters
Fuchs   fox
Fukumoto   good luck
Fuller   shrinker of cloth
Fullmer   the famous one
Furness   iron smelter
Gabel   pitchfork
Gable   young man of God
Gagnon   hog
Gaines   the direct one
Gale; Galland   lively man
Gallup   small boat owner
Gamble   the wise old man
Garcia   the spear man
Garfield   owner of a triangular field
Gavin   dangerous man
Gaynor   fair-faced
Gebhard   gifted and strong
Geiger   the fiddle player
Gerber   leather tanner
Giles   the young one
Glaser; Glassman   the glass maker
Glenn   small valley
Glover   glove maker
Glickman   lucky man
Goff   blacksmith
Goldberg   the gold mountain
Goldsmith   gold craftsman
Gomez; Gonzales   son of a famous warrior
Gordon   small grain field
Gould   golden-haired
Graber   hole-digger
Grace   the fat one
Graf   nobleman
Grange   grain warehouse
Grant   large or great man
Grasso   the fat one
Graves   groves of trees
Griffith   the fierce chief
Grogan   the angry one
Gross   large or stout man
Grubb   the rough one
Haberman   oat farmer
Hafner   potter
Haines   the owner of hedged fields
Haley   hillside meadow
Hallowell   holy spring
Hamlin   the young homeowner
Hamman; Hammett   the well-dressed one
Hammond   the protector
Hardwick   cattle pasture
Hardy   bold and daring
Harlow   rabbit hill
Harmon   soldier hero
Harper   harp player
Harris   ruler of land
Hartman   strong man

Harwood   rabbit forest
Hayden   man of good character
Haywood   enclosed forest
Head   high ground
Heald   sloping land
Healey   clever and inventive
Hearn   horse owner
Hecht   pike fish
Herrera   blacksmith
Higgins   young Richard
Hobart   the brilliant one
Hodgkins   son of young Roger
Holmes   island in a river
Holt   small forest
Honeywell   sweet water spring
Hopper   dancer or entertainer
Horn   hunting horn
Howe   small hill
Hubbard; Hubert   brilliant intellect
Hughes   intelligent one
Hummel   bumblebee
Hyatt   high gate
Inman   innkeeper
Irvine; Irwin   white river
Isaacs   laughing
Iverson   bowman with a yew-wood bow
Ives   great strength
Jablonski   appletree
Jaeger   game hunter
Jarrett   brave spearman
Jason   healer
Jeffers; Jeffries   peaceful one
Jesse   wealthy one
Jones   God is gracious
Joyce   joyful one
Judd   praised man
Kalb   calf
Kaplan   religious chaplin
Kastner   grain weigher
Katz   priest or great speaker
Kaufman   merchant
Keating   cheerful one
Keenan   descendant of a wise old man
Kehoe   horseman's son
Keil   club warrior
Keller   keeper of the wine cellar
Kelly   descendant of a warrior
Kellogg   lake spring
Kendal   the bright valley
Kendrick   clever leader
Kerr   marshy land
Kidder   traveling salesman
Kinsey   the victorious leader
Kipling   waterfall on a mountain peak
Kirk   house by the church
Klein   small man
Knowles   hilltop house
Kohler   charcoal maker
Kovacs   blacksmith
Kraft   strong and courageous one

Kramer   merchant
Krauss   curly-haired
Kruger   maker of pitchers
Lafayette   grove of beech trees
Lambert   owning well-known land
Lamont   man of the law
Lang   very tall man
Langley   owner of a long meadow
Lawrence   the victor
Leach   doctor who used leeches to draw blood
Lederman   leather tanner or seller
Leonard   powerful as a lion
Levin   beloved protector
Light   intelligent man
Lindsey   island of serpents
Link   left-handed
Livingston   stone fortress
Lloyd   gray-haired man
Lockhart   strong fortress
Logan   hillside dwellers
Long   very tall man
Lopez   son of a wolf
Lovell   young wolf
Lowenthal   valley of lions
Lubin   young loved one
Lucas   messenger of wisdom
Machado   hatchet user
Madison   mighty one
Mahoney   descendant of the bear
Mallory   armor maker
Mancini   left-handed one
Mandel   young and joyous
Martin   warlike
Mason   stone mason or stone cutter
Mather   mower of grain
Matsuda   field of pine trees
Maynard   powerful and brave
Mead   owner of meadows
Melendez   young and industrious
Mendez   mountaineer
Mercer   merchant or trader
Mertz   young and famous
Messerschmidt   sword or knife maker
Metzger   butcher
Michaels   man who is like God
Moody   brave and proud
Moore   pastureland
Morales   blackberry bushes
Morgan   shining like the sea
Mosconi   active person
Moseley   home by a marshy meadow
Mulligan   bald person
Mullins   owner of a flour mill
Murphy   sea warrior
Murray   seaside village
Nabors   nearby farmer
Nadell   needle maker
Nagy   large man
Neuman   newcomer to town
Newton   newly planned farmstead
Nichols   victorious army man

Nielson   son of the champion
Norton   village to the north
Novak   newcomer to town
Nutter   nut-seller
Oates   wealthy man
Ochs   bull or ox
O'Donnell   descendant of the mightiest
Ogden   oak tree valley
O'Keefe   the handsome one
Oliver   olive tree
O'Neil   descendant of the champion
Orr   pale complexioned
Otis   young and prosperous
Owens   well-born person
Packer   salesman or peddler
Paine   country dweller
Palumbo   wooden pigeon
Parsons   man of high status
Pastor   shepherd
Patterson   son of a noble man
Paul   the little one
Peabody   finely dressed man
Penny   feather
Perez   son of Peter
Perkins   young Peter
Petty   short or small man
Philips   lover of horses
Plummer   feather seller
Pollard   short-cut hair
Powell   young and alert
Putnam   home by a pit
Quackenbush   noisy trees
Quintero   farmer
Raab   the raven
Rader   wheel maker
Ramos   home in a grove of trees
Rathbone   stump covered meadow
Reagan   the young ruler
Redford   red-soil river crossing
Reid   red-haired man
Reiss   very great man
Renner   runner or messenger
Rhodes   roadside home
Riggs   ridge of hills
Rizzo   curly-haired man

Rogers   famous spearman
Roper   rope maker or seller
Rosenbaum   rose tree
Ross   peninsula of land
Rowe   builder or resident in a row of houses
Royer   wheel maker
Sachs   people of the sword
Sadler   saddlemaker
Sagar   carpenter
Salmon   the peaceful one
Saltzman   miner or seller of salt
Sanborne   sandy brook
Sawyer   sawer or cutter of wood
Schaeffer   shepherd
Schatz   wealthy hero
Scheib   owner of a round field
Schiff   sailor or boat owner
Schroeder   woodworker
Schubert   shoemaker
Schwartz   dark-haired or dark-complected
Seligman   happy man
Sellers   saddlemaker
Seltzer   seller of fish or meat
Sennett   old, wise man
Setzer   tax collector
Sharp   quick-witted man
Sherman   shearer of sheep
Sierra   mountain ridges
Silver   silver merchant
Singer   singer of ballads
Skinner   leather tanner or fur seller
Snook   long-nosed man
Snyder   tailor of clothing
Souza   seaside marsh
Spivak   singer of songs for nobility
Stacy   prosperous man
Stanley   rocky meadow
Steinberg   rocky mountain
Steiner   stone cutter
Stoddard   horsekeeper of an estate
Stringer   string or cord maker
Sussman   charming man
Swift   currier or messenger

Talmage   pilgrim or traveler
Tang   soupmaker
Tanner   tanner of leather
Tauver   dove or pigeon raiser
Taylor   maker of fine clothing
Thatcher   roof thatcher
Thorpe   farming village
Tinker   traveling seller of pots and pans
Todd   fox
Tomaso   son of a twin
Towers   tanner of skins and hides
Trapp   short and stocky man
Traub   bunch of grapes
Travers   crossroads
Trowbridge   wooden bridge
Tyler   maker of roofing tiles
Udall   yew tree valley
Ulrich   wealthy and powerful
Vaccaro   owner of cows
Varga   home and property on a very steep slope
Vicente   conqueror
Wagner   wagonmaker or driver
Walton   walled-in farm or village
Wardell   lookout hill
Washburn   flooding brook
Waterman   ferryboat owner
Weaver   cloth weaver
Weinberg   grape-covered mountain
Wheeler   wheel or cart maker
Willard   powerful one
Wilson   determined man
Winkler   storekeeper
Wong   king
Woodward   keeper of the forest
Wright   carpenter, wheel maker, or cart maker
Xavier   owner of a new house
Yamashita   below the mountain
Zabel   young frog
Zandt   rocky cliff
Zarate   field of corn
Ziegler   maker of roofing tiles
Zimmerman   carpenter or owner of a wooden house.

YOUR COAT OF ARMS

Some settlers who came to America were of noble birth or had achieved great wealth and prestige in the Old World. Some Early Americans had even been admired as heroes for certain accomplish-ments. It was the custom in many Old World countries for such people to have an identifying name shield. The symbols or "emblems" used in a name shield depicted the individual's admirable traits.

There was a specific order and design for all name shields. The actual shield might contain only one emblem or several, depending on the individual's honors. Below the shield was listed the family surname or sometimes a motto such as "Purity of Mind" or "I Remain Strong" or some other inspiring phrase. Above the shield there were often elaborate decorations including wreaths, a helmet, and a crest.

It was the custom for descendants and future generations to continue using the shield of an honored ancestor as a family symbol and as an example for family members to emulate. And so, a few individuals and families who came to America probably brought with them their family shield or "coat of arms," as it was often called.

Although we Americans still use shields with emblems mostly as "official seals" of states, high government offices, and various organizations, not many individuals or families continue to use a coat of arms.

But if you were to have your own personal shield, what would be its design? Below is an illustrated list of common family shield emblems and their meanings. Choose the emblems that best suit you, then copy or trace the shield outline and emblems in an orderly design. In the banner below the shield you can print your surname, or make up a personal motto.

HUMOR

APPETITE

INGENUITY

sincerity

cleverness

peace

courage

WISDOM

PRIDE

strength

valor

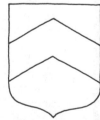

achievement

Beauty

WARRIOR

PRACTICALITY

religion

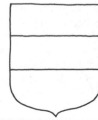

Honor

eagerness

FAMILY TREASURES

Your family does not need to be rich to own treasures. A family treasure is anything that a member of the family wishes to save because it is in some way important to him.

A treasure might be an heirloom that has been passed on to each new family generation—great-grandmother's jewelry, an antique vase, an oil portrait of grandfather, or maybe his pocket watch. A treasure can also be a memento, something of purely personal value that captures an old or fond memory—letters, photographs, handicrafts, clothes, and even records. A treasure does not have to be an object at all. It might be a family secret—a recipe or a secret remedy.

If you ask, you will usually find that most family treasures have a history or interesting story connected with them. Treasures reveal much about a family—where people have been; what they have done; as well as styles, fads, and customs of different periods. Every family has its own special treasures because every family is unique.

Go on a family treasure hunt. Ask your parents about their treasures and the stories that may go with them. Ask about other family objects and if they might eventually become treasures. Look at knickknacks on shelves, scrapbooks, and boxes of letters; look in attic and basement trunks; ask about those deer antlers stored in the garage. Maybe you can get a "tour" through your mother or father's jewelry boxes. Why do your parents keep an old worn out and unused hooked rug or patch-

Uncovering family treasures which have been packed away for years.

work quilt stored in the closet? Does your mother still have her wedding dress, and did it first belong to your grandmother or great-grandmother? Who are the people you don't recognize in the family photo album?

Many items that are no longer practical or decorative and seem useless will take on a new meaning once you have heard their "story." Maybe your father wears a pocket watch, not because it is handier to use than a wristwatch (it isn't), or because it is more accurate (maybe it is), but because it first belonged to your great-grandfather, and has an inscription on the back commemorating his forty years as a railroad engineer. Possibly, one day, that pocket watch will be given to you.

Does your father still have his old army uniform with insignias and medals, and has he ever told you what they mean? What

about the family silverware or china your mother displays or keeps stored in boxes but never uses? Do you know why? What old and interesting books does your family own? Are there inscriptions on the inside covers or maybe pressed flowers or handwritten notes between the pages?

Someday a few of your own possessions might become family treasures—awards you have won, a poem you write, a special collection of shells or buttons, your school report cards, the foul ball you caught at the baseball game, the pigtail you saved when you had your hair cut short, the ticket from a Super Bowl game you went to, or postcards from trips you have taken. Although anything can be a treasure, that does not mean that everything is. The deciding factor is the importance of the item to you.

In a small notebook make a list of your favorite family treasures as well as your own treasures, Fig. 5. Try to give as much information about each object as you know, including interesting facts and stories. When your notebook is complete, it too will likely become a family treasure.

Fig. 5

Family Treasure Notebook

OBJECT *Wood and ivory checker board and checkers*

ORIGINAL OWNER *My great grandfather, John Thomas Atwater*

OTHER OWNERS *My father, Byron John Atwater*

PRESENT OWNER *My older brother, Thomas Harley Atwater*

NOTES *My father told me that his grandfather bought the checkers set on his wedding trip to New York*

KNOCK, KNOCK NAMES

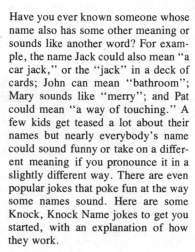

Have you ever known someone whose name also has some other meaning or sounds like another word? For example, the name Jack could also mean "a car jack," or the "jack" in a deck of cards; John can mean "bathroom"; Mary sounds like "merry"; and Pat could mean "a way of touching." A few kids get teased a lot about their names but nearly everybody's name could sound funny or take on a different meaning if you pronounce it in a slightly different way. There are even popular jokes that poke fun at the way some names sound. Here are some Knock, Knock Name jokes to get you started, with an explanation of how they work.

You say: *Knock, knock*

Your friend says: *Who's there?*

You say a name, for example, *"Watson"*

Your friend says the name plus the word *"who"; Watson who?*

You say the punch line: *Not much, Watson who with you?* When said fast, this sounds like "What's new with you?"

Ida who?
I don't know, do you?

Annie who?
Annie body home?

Anita who?
Anita place to stay

Philip who?
Philip my glass please

Sara who?
Sara doctor in the house?

Hugo who?
Hugo to my head

Shelly who?
Shelly dance?

Toots and Theresa who?
Toots company, Theresa crowd

Jimmy who?
Jimmy a little kiss

Abby who?
Abby, C, D, E, F, G

Wendy who?
Wendy moon comes over the mountain

Arthur who?
Arthur any humans living here?

Donna who?
Donna you know me?

Harry who?
Harry up and let me in

Hugh who?
Hugh hoo yourself

Sonny who?
Sonny me

Elsie who?
Elsie you later

Lil who?
Lil Miss Muffett

Olive who?
Olive you, sweetie

Toby who?
Toby or not to be, that is the question

Chapter 2

AMERICAN KNOW-HOW

LIVING AMERICAN

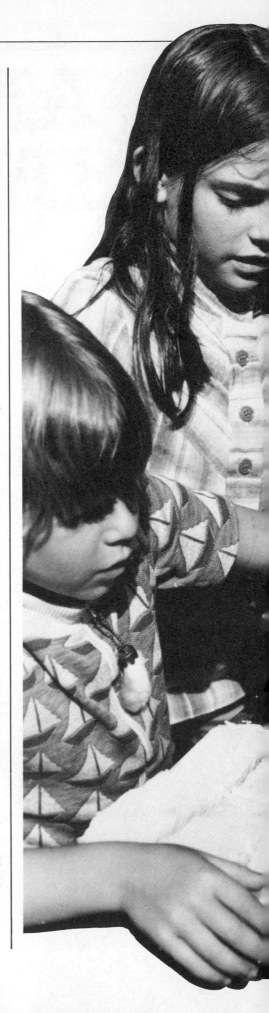

Can you imagine what it would be like if you had to make nearly everything you needed to survive? You would probably have to know how to raise livestock, weave cloth and make clothes, milk cows, pickle and preserve foods, make cheese, butter, candles, and soap, cut lumber and build houses, clear land and plant fields. Almost everything a person had in Early America was the product of his own efforts. To survive, the first settlers had to know how to *do* things.

Most Early Americans lived on farms that were sort of miniature factories producing everything the household needed. With so much work to be done, children were not exempt from household chores. Large families with ten or more members were common, the more children, the more helping hands. As soon as a child was old enough—often as young as three or four—he became an "apprentice" to his parents, assisting in a task until the skill it required was well learned. Then the child took on the chore as his own responsibility.

Boys were their fathers' helpers and girls their mothers', each with specific jobs to do. Most outdoor and heavy work—plowing and planting, pulling stumps, building with rock and timber—was considered a man's work whereas women made clothing, prepared food, and supplied whatever other household products were necessary like soap, candles, and brooms.

All in together

The Early American pioneer families were independent and could do for themselves, but there was a very strong sense of neighborliness too. Certain jobs required great amounts of strength or needed to be done quickly. When building a new house, clearing a piece of land, or constructing a stone fence or in any type of emergency, a settler could expect generous cooperation from his neighbors.

To repay a favor or return a previous loan of help, children were often sent to do work at a neighbor's house for a day, a week, or sometimes even longer.

To make big jobs or laborious tasks seem easier, the work was often organized as a party. For a barn raising or corn husking, entire families within a morning's travel would arrive at a neighbor's house to get the job done. Everyone worked together. To make the work go easier and faster, many jobs were turned into contests—"see who can husk the most corn in one hour," for example. The construction jobs did not require the girls and women usually, so their time was spent helping a neighbor finish a quilt, preserve foods, or in exchanging surplus goods for needed things like candles, soap, foods, or whatever.

The length of the work day was determined by sunrise and sunset. Summer work days were very long— sometimes fifteen hours or more—and on occasion, if the moon was full and bright, work would continue well into the night. Summer was, of course, the preferred time to do the big jobs; in winter, much more time was spent in the house. It was the season for fixing and mending.

When the job was finally finished it was a cause for celebration. Food was served to all the neighbors, a bonfire might be lit, and for those who had any energy left, games of strength and skill would be played.

Hard work but rich rewards

Home life was terribly hard in Early America but it also had great rewards. Being able to make do using whatever was available gave the settlers a rich awareness of life and a great sense of personal accomplishment. Even though many of the daily chores of Early American life seem hard if not boring to us today, there was joy in learning how to do a thing and do it well. Pride of ability and in craftmanship made almost any job worthwhile. In time better and easier ways to do the necessary jobs were discovered or invented. Many of the chores of daily life evolved into specialties. These tasks—like making clothing, for example—were done at first by artisans and tradesmen of the town and eventually by factories and machines. Something was gained but something was lost as well.

To Early American pioneers who were trying to make

Cutting homemade soap into bars.

their way in a practically untouched land, their house, farm, or village was the whole world. Our sense of the world has today grown much larger. No one, least of all kids, is expected to know how to make or produce everything he needs or even how to repair those things he owns. However, anyone can still have the feel and satisfaction of knowing how to do many of the simple life chores of Early America. The knowledge will stay with you should you ever need to use it; it will, in any case, be a fine thing just to know "how."

Part of the fun of butter making is in the tasting.

BETTER BUTTER

Like so many other foods that are now commonplace in American homes, butter was once considered quite a luxury which few American families could afford. For those families that had milking cows, the butter that they made was often traded for simple necessities, such as food or clothing. But as dairy farming expanded across America and milking cows became more plentiful, so did the supply of milk, and the butter churn became a fixture in American kitchens.

Late spring was the favorite butter making season, for that is when cows give the most milk. The women and children of the house were responsible for the task. The children would milk the cows and bring the pails of fresh warm milk into the house. The pails were left to sit until the milk began to sour, then the cream was skimmed from the top of the milk and put into the butter churn.

There were many clever and practical designs for butter churns but two types were most common. The tall wooden bucket with a long pole or dasher was easy to make or inexpensive to buy, but required a lot of tedious arm pumping to use. The "rocking churn" was a wooden box with a tight-fitting cover which sat on rockers so it could be worked by the feet, leaving the hands free to do some other task.

Churning and singing

When enough cream had been collected in the churn, the butter making process began. Butter making was not so hard to do as it was tiresome work, so the job of beating the dasher up and down was usually given to the children. To amuse themselves, the children chanted butter-churning rhymes in time to the up–down pumping motions.

> Come butter come
> Come butter come
> Peter standing at the gate
> Waiting for a butter cake
> Come butter come.

The whole process took about a half hour or more, depending upon the enthusiasm with which the butter maker worked the dasher. At first nothing seemed to happen to the cream, then after a while it would begin to bubble and foam. Only after some more beating with the dasher would the cream slowly turn into floating lumps or curds of butter.

When it seemed as if no more butter lumps would "come," the butter was scooped out of the churn. The white liquid that remained was the buttermilk—a delicious drink that was sometimes given to the children as a reward for their work.

Before the butter was eaten, it was first rinsed in cold water and then shaped into squares using two wooden paddles, or packed into small table-sized tubs called firkins. The color of the butter would vary from light yellow to deep gold, depending upon what feed the milk-giving cow had eaten. The taste of the butter was sweet, although salt was sometimes added for flavor and also as a preservative.

Butter to be proud of

In Early America butter molds were quite popular. These were made of wood with traditional designs of eagles, wheat, or thistle carved into them. The raised design was stamped onto butter squares. Many butter makers were proud of their product. Their butter mold design became their trademark.

As America grew and people developed automated machinery, trades, and special skills, butter became a product of the creamery. The formula for making butter has not changed but modern creamery machines do nearly everything from milking the cow and separating the cream to adding the salt flavoring. As you might expect, though, the butter you make yourself tastes just a little bit better.

Making a Butter Churn

Materials

coffee can, glass jar, or any tall, wide-mouth container with a snap-fit plastic lid
Tinkertoy® parts

Tools

small knife

Fig. 1

1. The barrel or bucket of the butter churn consists of the tall, wide-mouth container with a snap-on plastic lid, Fig. 1.

2. Make the dasher by assembling eight of the shortest (1 inch) Tinkertoy® dowels around the edge of a Tinkertoy® wheel and then use one long Tinkertoy® dowel for the handle, Fig. 1.

3. Cut or punch a hole in the center of the plastic snap-on lid just large enough for the dowel handle to fit through easily. Assemble the butter churn by putting the dasher in the can and snapping on the lid with the handle protruding.

Making Butter

Ingredients

whipping or heavy cream
salt

Utensils

butter churn or a wide-mouth jar with a tight-fitting lid spoon

1. Let the cream stand at room temperature for a few hours and then pour it into the butter churn until the churn is about half-full.

2. Place the lid tightly on the churn and begin beating the dasher up and down at a steady rhythm. Try chanting the *Come Butter Come* rhyme as you do it. If you like, friends can take turns. After twenty or thirty minutes the butter should come as lumps that float on the top and stick to the dasher. Sometimes the cream will turn to whipped cream before the butter curds form—just keep churning with the dasher.

3. When no more curds seem to form, remove the lid and scoop out the butter curds. (You might want to refrigerate and save the buttermilk that remains.) The butter will be quite soft and mushy. Put the curds in a bowl and rinse them under cold running water to remove any milk left in the butter.

A butter churn can be made from Tinkertoys® and a coffee can.

4. Put the butter in the refrigerator to cool. After an hour or so the butter balls will be firm enough to be molded together. While you are doing this, taste the butter. It will probably seem sweet compared to the butter that you usually eat. Just a pinch or two of salt blended with the butter will give you that familiar butter taste.

5. The butter can now be shaped into balls, sticks or pats, or cut into shapes using small cookie cutters. You could also pack the butter into small firkin-like tub containers. If you still want to do more, try carving designs on the butter using the point of a toothpick.

You can make small amounts of butter without a butter churn, using instead a wide-mouth jar with a tight-fitting lid. Although there is no history of "butter jars" in Early America, this technique does work

and also demonstrates the principle of butter making.

After the cream has sat at room temperature for a few hours, fill the jar about half-full and screw on the lid tightly. Hold the jar by the end firmly, and start shaking vigorously, Fig. 2. You can take rests if you tire or alternate shaking and resting with a friend. After fifteen or twenty minutes of shaking, the butter should come. Prepare the butter by washing, chilling, salting and molding as described above.

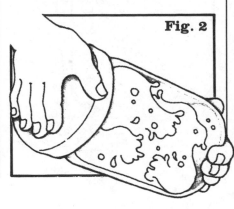

Fig. 2

MILKING A COW

Milk is nearly a perfect food because it contains well-balanced amounts of nearly everything that is necessary for good nourishment. Although milk from goats, sheep, camels, and other animals is quite drinkable by humans, in America we almost always drink milk from cows. In fact, nearly one-quarter of all food consumed in America today is derived from milk.

In Early America the family cow not only supplied milk but was a beast of burden to help with the plowing and hauling. Those people who had cows had security. When it was a poor year for crops or other bad luck befell the family, there was still the cow that contentedly gave milk. Milk is the basic ingredient for foodstuffs such as cheese and butter—and often these products could be bartered for the other necessities of life. A good milk-giving cow could produce nearly thirty quarts of milk each day.

Dairying—the production of milk—was at first done only in spring and summer when the cows could feed in the open pasture. But soon farmers built shelters to protect their cows and began storing corn and hay so the animals could be properly nourished and produce milk through the winter months.

Kids and cows

The task of milking the cow was the responsibility of the farmer's children. Twice a day the cow needed to be milked and fed—once in the morning and again in the late afternoon—and the cow manure collected to be used to enrich the farm soil. This was also the children's task.

As cities grew and it became

impossible for families to keep their own cow, dairy farms were established. Today the production of milk has become highly industrialized. Twice a day the cows are brought to "milking parlors" where they are milked by vacuum machines and fed from conveyor belts. Even the cow manure is removed automatically on a conveyor belt.

From the milking machine the milk is pasteurized to kill any harmful germs, and most of the milk is homogenized to mix the butterfat into the milk uniformly. Then the milk is bottled or placed in cartons and sent off to the food store.

Though you may have never met a cow, it's nice to know how to milk one. You can never tell just when the occasion might present itself.

How to Milk a Cow

Milking by hand (or machine) never hurts the cow. Actually, a cow feels quite contented after it has been milked. To protect the milk from contamination, it is very important that the cow, the milker, and the milking pail all be spotlessly clean. Wash and dry your hands and wash the cow's udder and teats with a clean cloth and warm water.

Place the milking stool on the right side of the cow. There is no reason why the right side is appropriate, other than custom says it's so, and probably because most people are right-handed.

Begin with the two front teats, grasping one in each hand. Squeeze the teats alternately, closing the fingers around the teat and at the same time pulling slightly downward, then relax your grasp on the

Try to avoid getting sprayed when milking a cow by hand.

teat. Before filling the bucket, milk out the first two or three streams from each teat into a container other than the milking pail. This cleans the udder and stimulates the cow's glands so the milk will flow freely. Aim the teat so that the milk squirts into the container. Now milk into the milking pail. Continue milking as long as the milk comes. A good cow milker works quietly and rapidly, and can milk as many as ten cows in an hour!

REALLY GOOD SOAP

Probably the least desirable chore for the Early American household was soapmaking, and it was considered strictly a woman's job. Soapmaking was a long, hot, and smelly task, usually done only once a year before spring cleaning. The ingredients for making soap—animal fat and wood ashes—were common to most farms and were waste that would be normally thrown away. During the winter months all fat from cooking and butchering was saved as well as wood ashes from the fireplace.

Since the job was so smelly, it was always done outdoors. Fortunately the whole process took but one day of suffering. First water was poured through the wood ashes to make a caustic liquid called lye, then the lye and fat were heated in a large kettle until the mixture became soap. And if the mixture of fats and lye was not made just right, the result would be a pot of hot, smelly liquid, no soap at all. It was, therefore, a common custom on soapmaking day for neighbors to wish you good luck and hope that your soap would thicken.

Homemade soap was not exactly the same as the soap of today. Directly out of the kettle the soap was a soft, dark yellow paste. This soap was fine for washing clothes, but much too harsh to use on the skin. By adding certain berries and other ingredients, the soft soap could be made sweet and hard and more tolerable for personal use. But then people of those days did not bathe as frequently as we do today. A bath might be taken only twice a year, and dirty clothes were saved up so the wash need be done only once a month at most.

And you thought it was just for cleaning

Besides cleaning, soap had a number of other important uses around the house. As a lubricant, soap was used to make drawers slide more easily; nails were coated with soap to avoid splitting the wood; and saw blades were soap coated to keep the blade from binding. Soap was also applied to metal surfaces to prevent rusting.

As towns grew, the task of soapmaking was eventually taken over by a tradesman, usually the candlemaker who used a similar rendering process to make his candle tallow. The townspeople would bring their fat and ashes to the soapmaker, who would, for a fee (which might be some of the soap), convert the ingredients into soap cakes.

Eventually soap became a factory product with many different sizes, colors, types, and smells offered. Today there are special soaps for nearly every purpose, yet they all contain the basic ingredients of fat, oils, and lye, and none clean much better than the original homemade lye soap.

GRANDMA'S LYE SOAP

Song portion of the "sermon" It's In The Book, *a spoof on the nursery rhyme,* Little Bo Peep. *Recorded in 1952 on Capitol records by John Standley. Written by John Standley and Art Thorsen.*

You remember Grandma's lye soap
Good for everything in the home.
And the secret was in the scrubbing,
It wouldn't suds and couldn't foam.

Then let us, all sing right out
Of Grandma's
Of Grandma's lye soap
Used for, for everything, everything on the place.
The pots and kettle, the dirty dishes,
And for your hands and for your face.

Little Herman and Brother Thurman
Had an aversion to washing their ears.
Grandma scrubbed them with the lye soap,
And they haven't heard a word in years.

Then let us, all sing right out
Of Grandma's
Of Grandma's lye soap
Sing all out, all over the place.
The pots and kettle, the dirty dishes,
And also hands and also face.

Mrs. O'Mally out in the valley
Suffered from ulcers I understand,
She swallowed a cake of Grandma's lye soap,
Has the cleanest ulcers in the land.

Then let us, all sing right out
Of Grandma's
Of Grandma's lye soap
Sing right out all over the place.
The pots, the pots and kettle,
The dirty dishes and the hands and the face.

Lyric transcription provided by *Record Exchanger,* America's Oldies magazine, Box 6144, Orange, Ca. 92667.

Making Soap

The critical processes of melting the fats and leaching out the lye were quite tedious and often dangerous tasks in making homemade soap. Too much fat or lye, the wrong temperature, stirring too fast or too slow, and even the impurity of the water could cause a would-be batch of soap to be ruined.

Today the task is safe and much easier. Fine soaps can be made using various ingredients found at the grocery store. The specific ingredients used will determine the kind of soap you get—hand soap, laundry soap, cold cream soap, honey soap, rosewater soap, avocado soap, cucumber soap, strawberry soap, and so on.

The following recipe shows how to make Olive Oil Soap, a good, creamy, all-purpose hand soap. Follow the recipe carefully using the exact proportions and procedures shown.

This project should be supervised by an adult.

Ingredients
32 ounces olive oil
14 ounces vegetable shortening
6 ounces lye flakes
16 ounces water

Utensils
newspaper
3-quart pot (or larger)
1-quart pot (or larger)
wooden spoon
cooking thermometer (candy thermometer)
shallow pan or shoe box
waxed paper or plastic wrap
shirt cardboard
rubber gloves

Important information

Both pots should be made from stainless steel, iron, glass or be enameled. Do not use aluminum pots. They are ruined by the lye.

Lye flakes (sometimes called caustic soda) is available at grocery stores in 13-ounce packages. Be sure to get pure lye flakes and not the type of lye used as a drain cleaner. Be careful. Although not very likely, lye can give you a burn. If the lye should come in contact with your skin, wash the affected area immediately with *cold* water and rinse using vinegar or lemon juice. Just to be extra safe, wear a pair of rubber gloves while making soap.

1. Lay newspaper over the area on which you will be working.

2. Put the olive and the vegetable oil in the large pot. Heat, using the lowest setting on the stove. Stir the mixture with the wooden spoon and keep stirring from time to time.

IVORY®, THE SOAP THAT FLOATS

About a hundred years ago, William Procter and James Gamble started the Procter and Gamble Company in Cincinnati, Ohio. They were "makers of candles and fine soaps." Although business was good, it was the accidental discovery of a floating soap that made the company famous.

A forgetful employee, while having lunch, left his soap mixing machine running. When he returned, the machine had beaten air into the soap, much as air is beaten into cream to make whipped cream. Of course, the worker was embarrassed by his mistake, but before reboiling the batch to save it, someone in the company decided to try the whipped soap as it was. He quickly discovered that soap beaten with air would float. It took a few years to perfect the soap, but the result was a pure white soap bar good for bath, kitchen, and laundry, that would float on water.

Because the soap was excitingly different, it deserved a brand name. William Procter's son was inspired at church one Sunday by the reading of the Forty-fifth Psalm:

*All thy garments smell of myrrh, and aloes,
and cassia, out of the ivory palaces,
whereby they have made thee glad.*

And he suggested that the new white soap be named Ivory®.

A few years later the Procter and Gamble Company decided to have Ivory® soap tested against a number of their competitors' products. The test report, in part, stated that Ivory® was $99\frac{44}{100}\%$ pure. Being impressed with the results of the test, Procter and Gamble began to use them in their advertising. Today the slogan "$99\frac{44}{100}\%$ Pure" is an Ivory® soap trademark.

3. Dissolve the lye flakes in the water using the small pot as a container, Fig. 3. Do not heat the lye yet. Lye mixed with water produces its own heat. Soft water is important to making good soap. If the water in your area is very hard, add a half teaspoon of lye flakes to the water at least twenty-four hours before using, or collect rainwater for soapmaking.

4. To make soap happen, correct temperature of the oils and lye mixture is important. Both the oil and lye must be close to 96°F. (36°C.) before they can be mixed.

When mixed at this temperature, the oil and lye "come together" or *saponify* to make soap. Using the cooking or candy thermometer,

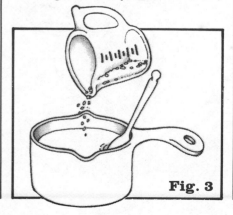

Fig. 3

check the temperatures of both oil and lye mixtures. The lye mixture will have gotten very hot. Don't let it cool below 96°. Adjust heat under the oils as necessary. When oils are the correct temperature, remove from stove.

5. Pour the lye mixture slowly into the oil stirring all the while. This is the trickiest step in soapmaking. The pouring must be slow and even, and the stirring must be steady, not too fast, not too slow!

6. Stir the mixture until it is thick and syrupy, fifteen minutes or more. If the mixture gets lumpy put the pot over the lowest heat and continue to stir.

7. Prepare the soap molds. (You can do this earlier if you wish.) Line a shallow pan or shoe box with waxed paper or plastic wrap. Make sure all surfaces are well covered. The soap is molded in a large "brick" and later cut into bars.

8. Pour the soap mixture into the mold, Fig. 4, and cover it with shirt cardboard. The mixture must cool slowly.

9. Let the soap harden for at least twenty-four hours and then cut the large soap brick into smaller bars. The soap will still be soft at this point as the saponification process is still taking place. Do not use the soap yet, but let the soap age for three or four weeks, allowing plenty of free air to circulate around it.

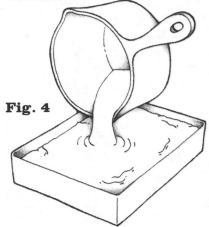

Fig. 4

CANDLES

Before electric lights and gas lamps, candles were used for lighting homes. A single candle in the dark gave just enough light to keep someone from bumping into furniture; for reading or writing, a cluster of several candles was necessary. Candles were difficult to make and expensive to buy so only the more affluent families could afford to light their homes brightly after dark. It is interesting to think about the fact that the writers of many important documents, including the Declaration of Independence, wrote at night by candlelight. And the first evening reception at the White House was lit by a thousand candles.

Collecting fat for candles

At first candlemaking was a home craft done during the fall season so a fresh supply of candles would be ready for the early darkness of winter days. Gradually the job was taken over by tradesmen and eventually by candle factories. Candles were mostly made from tallow, the liquefied fat of any animal. All year round families would save fat from cows, pigs, geese, deer, opossums, bears, and other creatures, and hoard it in a large barrel. The fat was boiled in huge outdoor kettles and skimmed over and over again until only a clear liquid remained. Then a wooden rod hung with lengths of cotton wick was dipped repeatedly into the molten fat and hung on a rack to cool and harden. As the process was repeated the dipped wicks would fatten. Finally, the completed candles were carefully stored in a wooden chest to be safe from breakage and from mice, who are fond of eating tallow candles.

Dipping and molding

Using the dip process even an expert candlemaker could produce only one hundred or so candles a day. Later in the eighteenth century an unknown American invented the candle mold. The fat still needed to be collected and the smelly tallow boiled, but the process of pouring the tallow into the molds was much easier and faster than dipping. Dipped candles were still considered better, though, and gave a brighter, cleaner, and more even light.

As better and more efficient types of lighting were invented, the candle was used more for its pleasant lighting than practical purposes. Candles made from berries of bayberry bushes (appropriately nicknamed candleberry plants) were often lit for visiting company. The smoke would perfume the house with a sweet, spicy fragrance.

Eventually candles for decoration and celebrations came to be made from smokeless, dripless waxes in a great variety of shapes, sizes, colors, and scents. Even today we find the candle a soothing light source and a mood setter. And that is why candles have never really gone out of fashion.

Making Molded Candles

It is considerably easier to make candles today than it was in colonial times. Paraffin wax is readily available at grocery stores and it does not have the terrible smell of tallow, the rendered animal fat used for candle making. Paraffin is very flammable, however, so you must take some precautions. Always use a double boiler to melt the wax, and keep baking soda handy as a fire extinguisher in case the wax should come in contact with a flame. An adult should supervise this project.

Materials

molds such as milk cartons, tea-cups, paper cups, drinking glasses, margarine or yogurt tubs, cigarette boxes, freezer containers or any smooth-sided container

cotton string or store-bought candlewicks

weights—bolts, nuts
    paper clips, etc.

pencil

cooking oil

paraffin wax

stearin (optional)

crayon or lipstick stubs (optional)

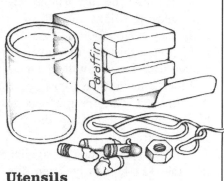

Utensils

scissors

cooking pot

tin can (should fit comfortably in the pot)

knife

wooden spoon

potholder

1. First prepare the mold. Any smooth-sided container that will allow the finished candle to be removed easily will do. At first try not to make too large a candle. The process works better for small candles.

2. Cut a length of cotton string or wick material a few inches longer than the depth of the mold. Tie one end of the string to a small weight and the other end to the middle of a pencil. Hang the weighted string in the center of the mold and twist the pencil to make the string straight and taut, Fig. 5. Smear a light coating of cooking oil on the inside of the mold so the finished candle will release easily.

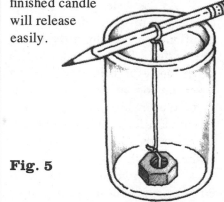

Fig. 5

3. Set up a double boiler by placing a tin can inside a cooking pot. Estimate the amount of wax that will be needed to fill the mold and using a knife cut the wax into small chunks about the size of dice.

4. Put the paraffin into the tin can and fill the pot about two-thirds full of water (the tin can must not float).

5. Melt the paraffin over medium heat, Fig. 6. As soon as the paraffin has melted you can add color, otherwise your candle will be white. Use crayon or lipstick stubs and stir them into the wax mixture until the color is even. Don't overheat the wax. A special chemical called stearin (available at craft shops) may be added to wax now in a ratio of one part stearin to ten parts paraffin. This will make the finished candle much harder and longer burning and eliminate dripping wax.

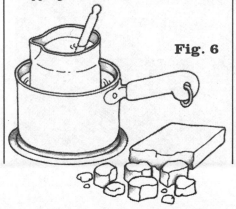

Fig. 6

6. Turn off the heat and remove the tin can using a potholder. Slowly and carefully pour the molten wax into the mold, Fig. 7. Let the wax cool and harden. Depending on the thickness of the candle, the wax should take from a few hours to half a day to harden completely.

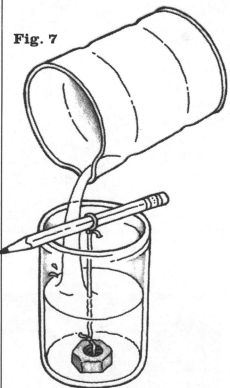

Fig. 7

7. Remove the candle from the mold by tapping the sides and gently pulling on the wick. If you have used a paper or cardboard mold just tear it away. If you have any difficulty removing the candle, put the mold under hot running water for a few seconds and try again.

8. Trim the wick to about one-half inch long and your candle is finished and ready for use. Burn the candle in a saucer to catch any drips. Metal jar lids make good candle saucers. Should your candle not turn out exactly as you like, simply cut it up into small pieces, melt it down, and try again. Any spilled wax or wax left on utensils can be scraped away easily once the wax has hardened.

Making Dipped Candles

Ask an adult to assist you with this project.

Materials
paraffin wax
cotton string or store-
   bought candle wicks

Utensils
newspaper
cooking pot
tall tin can (should
   fit comfortably
   in the pot)
fork
scissors

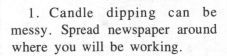

1. Candle dipping can be messy. Spread newspaper around where you will be working.

Hand dipped candles can be made in the kitchen with a fork, wick, and wax.

2. Fill the can about two-thirds full of water and place it in a pot. Fill the pot about half full with water and put it over a medium heat.

3. As the water in the pot and can begins to boil, add chunks of paraffin to the can until the can is nearly full. Wax is lighter than water, and as it melts it will form a layer on top of the water. This method of melting the wax is very economical for candle dipping and saves you the expense of filling the entire can with wax.

4. For candle dipping the melted wax must be at just the right temperature, not too hot or the wax will slide off the wick, not too cool or the wax will be too thick for dipping. You'll have to gauge this by trial and error. In general, turn down the heat to a low setting once the wax has melted or turn the heat off completely. (If you turn the heat off, make sure the wax does not begin to thicken.)

5. Cut a piece of cotton string or wicking material at least twice as long as the can is high and weave the string between the prongs of a fork as shown, Fig. 8.

Fig. 8

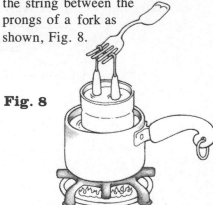

6. Holding the fork handle, dip the dangling wicks into the can until they touch bottom. As the wicks pass through the layer of molten wax, the wax will be deposited on them. Pull the wicks out of the can and wait for the wax to harden. Be sure to keep the two wicks separated.

7. Continue to dip, always letting the wax harden between dippings. After a few dippings the wicks may need to be straightened, but as the wax builds up from continuous dippings, the candles will become quite stiff and straight on their own. Dip the wicks quickly in and out of the wax until the candles are the thickness you want. It takes many dippings—sometimes fifty or more—before the candle is fat. (You may quicken the process by filling a tall pitcher with cold water and alternately dipping the candles between the wax and the water.)

8. When your candles are complete they will have the characteristic connecting wick between them that was typical of all dipped candles in Early America. Snip the loop with a scissors and trim the wicks to about a half-inch long.

Making a Tin Lantern

The tin lantern was used in Early America for carrying a lit candle from place to place. Fires were not that easy to start, and it was important to "keep" a flame once you had it going. Glass lanterns were very rare and quite expensive, but tin was cheap and looked almost like silver when it was new and shiny.

The most common lantern shape was similar to a large round tin can. The tin was punched with many small holes usually in a decorative pattern such as a sunburst or an eagle. This pinpricked or pierced tin not only allowed the heat to escape (keeping the lantern cool) but also emitted a fanciful pattern of light all about the room. In the bottom of the lantern was a candle cup to hold the candle steady, and at the top of the lantern a handle or hook to carry the lantern or hang it.

Not everyone had the knowledge or tools necessary to make their own lantern. The tin peddler would come to town now and then selling tin lanterns, as well as other tin products, from the back of his wagon or from a pack on his horse. Some towns had their own tinsmith. He, was, interestingly enough, called the tinker.

Materials
tin can (coffee can size is best but any size will do)
wire coat hanger, electrical wire, or heavy twine
candle (at least one inch shorter than the can)

Utensils
colored marker or crayon
newspaper or folded towel
nails
hammer
wire-cutting tool or scissors

1. Remove the lid from the can but leave on the bottom. Remove any labels and wash the can thoroughly.

2. Using a colored marker or crayon draw a punch-hole pattern on the can. Make a traditional American eagle design or invent your own design.

3. Fill the can with water and put it in the freezer until the water is solid ice, one or two days depending on the size of the can. The ice will keep the can from collapsing when you make the holes.

4. Remove the can from the freezer and place it on several layers of newspaper or a folded towel. Using a hammer and nail, hammer holes in the tin can following the pattern you have drawn, Fig. 9. You can vary the size of the holes in your design by using different-sized nails. Make holes for the handle at opposite sides of the can rim. When all the holes have been punched, drop the ice out of the can.

A colonial tin lantern with carrying pole.

Fig. 9

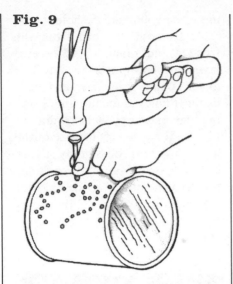

5. If you have a wire-cutting tool, use it to cut a wire coathanger to form a loop handle. Otherwise, tie a loop of bare electrical wire or heavy twine to the handle holes. If you use twine, make sure to keep it away from the lantern candle when the lantern is lit.

6. Drip wax from the candle into the bottom of the lantern and mount the candle in it in an upright position, Fig. 10. The tin lantern may now be carried to transport a flame or hung in a room for decoration or an interesting light show.

Fig. 10

Making a Candle Clock

The most convenient way of telling the time of day in Early America was to listen for the ring of the town bell or church bell which would peal on the hour, every hour. But for those who lived far from town, the bells were too distant to be heard. For the farmer it didn't matter. He got up at sunrise. When the sun was in mid sky it was noon, and he went to bed at sunset. But as life became more involved and time planning more important, better "clocks" were needed, especially after dark when the sun's position could no longer give clues to the hour. Wealthy families might have had magnificent mechanical clocks but the time keeper of the ordinary family was often a burning candle.

The candle clock had regular markings along its side which indicated the hours. As the candle burned down at a constant rate from one mark to the next, the time could be told. There was usually no other indicator of time (like the town clock) by which to set or start the candle so candle clocks were rather crude clocks. They measured the hours rather than actually telling time.

Materials

2 or more fat candles the same length and thickness
2 candleholders, candlesticks, or jar lids

Tools

pencil, crayon, or felt-tipped marker
clock or watch

The candles need to be calibrated or marked off in hour units, each mark representing one hour. In Early America the distance between marks was determined by trial and error or according to a pre-scribed unit of length for a candle of given thickness. You can use a clock or watch to calibrate the first candle.

1. Mount the two candles side by side in candlesticks. If necessary you can use two metal jar lids for candle holders by dripping wax in the centers of the lids and mounting the candles upright in them.

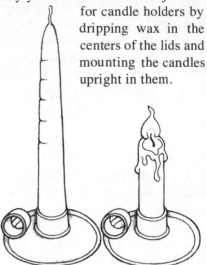

2. Notice the time on a clock and light only one of the candles. After one hour place a mark on the other candle at exactly the remaining height of the burning candle. Make another mark in the same way at each hour until the candle has burned down completely. Number the markings to match the hours.

3. The marked candle is now ready to be burned and used as a clock. Other candles of exactly the same height and thickness as the marked candle can be calibrated using the same spacings for making marks. As the candle clock burns, you'll be able to keep note of the hours as they pass.

VALUABLE ROPE

Although rope was used in many Early American homes for hauling the water bucket from the well, making beds and other household projects, good rope was quite expensive and not commonly available. Ropes were highly valued and treated with care. They were mended, washed, and preserved with oils to extend their usefulness as long as possible.

Because the manufacture of rope required special equipment and skills, it was a task usually left to the ropemaker artisan. Few people could afford all they needed, so it was a custom of the ropemaker to rent his ropes for special purposes such as hoisting beams in construction work.

"Give My Regards to Ropewalk"

Until the nineteenth century, all ropes were made entirely by hand in ropewalks—long, low buildings usually located at the end of town where space was plentiful. The length of a ropewalk determined the length of rope that could be made there. At one time New York City's main street, Broadway, ended as a ropewalk which extended nearly one-half mile uptown into a meadow.

Here the ropemaker would comb hemp or other plant fibers into long continuous threads, soften the threads with oil, then wind the threads around his waist. As the ropemaker walked backward up the ropewalk he would unwind the threads while a boy at the upper end of the walk turned a crank which wound the threads into rope. The more threads added to the

rope, the stronger it would be.

Today ropes are made in any needed length by spinning machines. The fiber strands are continuously and automatically laid or 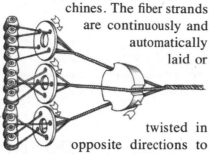 twisted in opposite directions to keep the finished rope from untwisting. Hemp and other fiber ropes are now easily affordable, and ropes for special purposes are made using a variety of different fibers such as plastic, metal, glass, and cotton.

Making Rope

You can make you own rope following a process similar to that used in factories, though your homemade ropes will be much shorter than manufactured ropes, of course. Here is what you need.

Materials	Tools
lengths of string, yarn, or other cord toilet paper or food-wrap tube	pencil scissors

1. Using lengths of string, yarn, or cord—or a combination of these—lay out together a number of strands about three times the length of the rope you want to make. You can tie shorter lengths together, if necessary, Fig. 11. The

more strands you use the fatter and stronger the finished rope will be. Tie strands in a knot at both ends.

2. Hook one end of the tied strands over a doorknob, bedpost, or chair back, Fig. 12. Stretch the cords out straight and put the other knotted end through the paper tube. Slip a pencil through the strands between the tube and the knot, Fig. 12. Holding the tube in one hand and, keeping the strands taut, wind the strands tightly by twirling the pencil, Fig. 12. As the strands twist together the overall length of the rope will shorten, and you will have to keep moving in toward the doorknob. Be sure not to let the twisted strands go slack and kink.

3. When the strands are tightly twisted, have a helper grab them at the center and bring your end around to the doorknob doubling the thickness. Remember to keep the strands taut. The helper should now move his hand a few inches from the folded end and let the end of the folded strands twist together, Fig. 13. As the rope twists together, the helper should slide his hand slowly down the rope toward the doorknob.

4. When the rope is doubled and twisted together all along its length, remove the pencil and tube and cut it from the doorknob. To keep the loose end of the rope from unwinding, tie it in a knot, Fig. 14. Depending on the type you have made, you can use your rope for practical jobs around the house, to hang a flowerpot or as a belt.

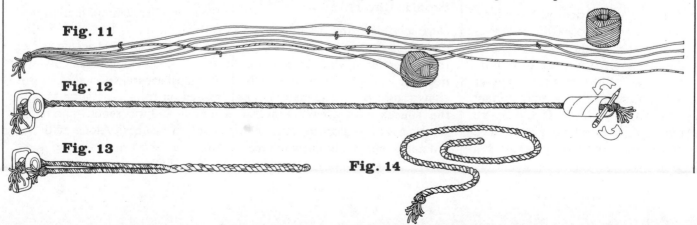

Fig. 11

Fig. 12

Fig. 13

Fig. 14

FORECASTING WEATHER

People talk about the weather because it affects nearly everything—the clothes they wear, the work they do, the mood they're in.

If we are curious about coming weather, we usually listen to the radio or television for the weather report. The forecast is not a certainty, however, and we frequently hear such predictions as "possibility of showers," "rain likely," or "twenty percent chance of snow." Everyone wants to know what the weather will be, but predicting it with accuracy is quite difficult. There are sophisticated instruments for measuring such things as wind direction, air pressure, and temperature. We also have weather radar, space satellite pictures of weather patterns, observations from ships at sea, and instant communication about weather information across the country. But even so, most weathermen can still give us only an estimate of tomorrow's weather.

In Early America, weather forecasts were not so easily had. Predicting the weather was critical to the lives of everyone, especially farmers. "Will it rain tomorrow or will it be sunny?" was an important topic of discussion. If rain came too soon after planting, the seed might be washed away; after a rainstorm the roads were muddy and useless for travel, so trips could not be planned if rain was forecast. The ability to predict was a necessary skill for most people. Benjamin Franklin implied the importance of weather to Early Americans when he said, "Some are weatherwise and some are otherwise."

Weather Folklore

Nowhere on earth is the weather more varied and less predictable than in America, especially New England. The shape of the land and the ocean currents make it possible for the weather to be different in neighboring towns—rainy or foggy in one place while it is sunny just down the road. Mark Twain is supposed to have said, "If you don't like the weather in New England, just wait a minute."

You can imagine the difficulty the Early American settlers had in predicting the weather. Most predictions are based on careful and repeated observations of weather patterns and certain signs over a period of many years. The settlers brought with them some knowledge of weather in the form of folklore but it proved to be unreliable in the New World. The American Indians, having lived on the land, had developed a more accurate weather folklore, and much of it was soon passed on to the new settlers.

Smells like rain

Depending on the traditions of the region, a person might look at the sky, sniff the wind, listen to the trees, or look for the many telltale signs shown by the animals. Even the sounds of a creaking house were signs of weather to come. Although no one really knew the reasons, a reasonably accurate weather prediction could be made about tomorrow's weather—or at least about the weather for the rest of today.

Of course, not all weather signs really worked, and many had no scientific basis whatsoever. One such sign depends on the groundhog. If the groundhog comes out of his hole at noon on February 2 and casts a shadow, winter will continue, supposedly, for another six weeks. If the groundhog casts no shadow, the remainder of winter will be mild and spring will come early. Because of this belief, February 2 has become known as Groundhog Day.

There are many other weather beliefs that are not necessarily true. Here are a few:

> "The higher the hornets build their nests, the higher the winter snow will be."
>
> "Small snowflakes mean a long snow, large snowflakes show the snow won't last."
>
> "A robin is a sign that spring has come."

Among the many weather beliefs are those sayings and stories that are used to explain the weather to children. To comfort a child afraid of lightning and thunder, the story is told that "the Mountain Men are bowling." Children chant, "It's raining; it's pouring; the old man is snoring" to celebrate and "explain" a storm.

Reliable predictions

Weather observations that proved reliable usually had a scientific basis and eventually became part of trusted American weather folklore. The most accurate weather lore was passed on from generation to generation, and was set down in books called almanacs. Along with the folklore, the almanac also gave "scientific" forecasting information based on the phases of the moon, the position of the tides, and an accumulated history of weather patterns from past years. Eventually nearly anyone concerned about the weather—farmers and city folk alike—needed only to refer to their almanac and make a few observations of nature to predict rain or shine.

Even today, weather folklore can prove more reliable for short-range forecasting than the weatherman's prediction. The following are a few of the more scientifically accurate expressions of this lore. Although they will work for the entire country, these sayings and rhymes come mostly from New England and therefore best reflect Northeast weather patterns.

"Flies will swarm before a storm."

"Halos around the moon or sun
    Mean that rain will surely come."

"When forest murmurs and mountain roars,
    Close your windows and shut your doors."

"Moss dry, sunny sky;
    Moss wet, rain you'll get."

"When smoke descends,
    Good weather ends."

"Red sky in the morning, take warning
    Red sky at night, tomorrow's delight.
    Red sky at noon, rain very soon."

"When the bees stay near the hive.
    Rain is close by."

"Sea gulls sitting in sand mean that rain is surely at hand."

"A cow's tail to the west
    Is weather coming at its best.
    A cow's tail to the east
    Is weather coming at its least."

"High clouds bring good weather."

"When the dew is on the grass
    Rain won't come to pass.
    When the grass is dry at morning light
    Look for rain before the night."

"Lightning in the southern sky
    Brings little else but dry."

"Crows gathered around the ground
    A sign that rain will soon come down."

"Ground smells
    Rain it tells."

On hurricanes:

"June too soon;
    July stand by;
    August look out;
    September you'll remember;
    October it's all over."

Weathervanes

One of the most important clues to forecasting the weather is wind direction. Other methods and folklore may have helped Early Americans make or add information to a forecast, but first and always a New Englander would observe the wind direction and apply this saying:

"A wind from the west
Brings weather at its best;
    A wind from the east
Brings rain to man and beast."

Or more simply put, "West wind best, east wind least." The change in wind direction is just as important to forecasting as the actual direction. A wind that changes so that the weathervane has moved clockwise is considered to have "veered," a counterclockwise wind change is called a "backing wind," Fig. 15. With that information all one needs to remember is that:

"A veering wind is a clearing wind and a backing wind brings stormy weather."

Other weather predictions can be made from wind directions:

"When the wind shifts during a storm from east to west, clearing will shortly follow."

"A steady and strong south or east wind will bring rain within thirty-six hours."

"In winter, northeast winds bring heavy snow."

Fig. 15

GOOD WEATHER   BAD WEATHER

Which way is the wind blowing?

There were few weather instruments known or used in Early America, but the first and most basic was the weathervane, which told wind direction. The early weathervanes were quite simple. A strip of lightweight cloth was attached to the top of a pole. The slightest breeze caused the cloth to wave and indicated the wind direction. These weathervanes were called wind flags. They had no north, south, east, or west markings—every farmer knew the exact direction of north.

As villages and towns in America developed, so did the weathervanes. Almost every barn and house was topped with one sort, and by now the typical weathervane contained an arrow of brass or iron on a free-turning pivot. The feather part of the arrow was large enough to catch the wind. The arrow would always point in the direction the wind was coming from. These weathervanes also included letters which indicated the direction of north, south, east, west. As weathervanes continued to be popular they also developed into an art form. The simple arrow was replaced by all kinds of figures whittled from wood or hammered out of metal: cows, horses, fish, eagles, or whatever struck the maker's fancy. The rooster was a favorite weathervane shape because its large tail caught the wind easily, and many people today still refer to a weathervane as a "weathercock." Sometimes the shape or symbol of a weathervane served as

a trade sign for a craftsman or merchant, or marked the location of a firehouse.

The giant grasshopper weathervane atop Faneuil Hall in Boston is one of the oldest and most famous weathervanes in New England. A Boston legend has it that Benjamin Franklin was once asked to prove his identity while traveling away from home. He was asked to describe the weathervane on Faneuil Hall, and when he mentioned the grasshopper, the evidence was considered sufficient. The grasshopper weathervane is still well-known and valued by Bostonians.

Making a Weathervane

Materials
wire coathanger
aluminum foil
tape
pint-size plastic tub and lid, (a sour cream, yogurt, or cole slaw container, for example)
sand

Tools
scissors
colored marker or crayon

1. Bend the loop of a coathanger so that it is as straight as possible, Fig. 16.

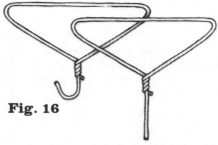

Fig. 16

2. Cover one half of the coathanger with aluminum foil, Fig. 17. Cut the foil an inch or so wider than the wire outline, fold over the edges and tape.

3. Fill the plastic tub com-

Fig. 17

pletely with the sand, packing it down well (in a pinch you might use a glass jar with a screw-on lid). Put on the lid.

4. Poke a hole in the center of the lid using the straightened stem of the coathanger. (If the lid is made of metal, you might need to poke the hole using a hammer and nail.) Put the vane through the hole in the lid and push it down into the sand so the stem touches the bottom of the container, Fig. 18. The weathervane should turn freely. If it does not, check to be sure the hole in the lid is big enough and not binding the stem.

5. Using a colored marker or crayon, mark the locations of north, south, east, and west on the side of the container. Make sure north is opposite south and east is opposite west. Place the weathervane in an open area where it can catch the wind. The higher the location the better. By using a magnetic compass, or asking someone who knows, properly orient the markings on the base to the proper directions. The open-wire half of the weathervane will always point in the direction from which the wind is coming.

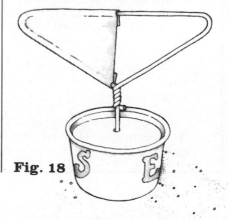

Fig. 18

Hygrometers

The change in relative humidity (the amount of moisture in the air) is still another indicator of the weather to come. As a storm approaches, the humidity increases: a decrease in humidity signals a return to fair weather. Some people find that their bodies react to a change in humidity and they can predict a storm coming when their bones ache or they get a pain in their big toe. But body aches and pains are not necessarily indicators of humidity change and therefore not a very reliable forecasting method.

Other things do reliably react to changes in humidity. An increase in humidity will cause some types of cord to twist tighter and some human hair to curl.

The science of curly hair

> "Curls that kink and cords that bind
> Signs of rain and heavy wind."

Many Early American farmers used this principle to build weather forecasting devices. A length of hemp rope was sometimes hung from a rafter in the barn with a heavy wood pointer tied to it just above the floor. When good weather came, the farmer made a marking on the floor indicating the direction the pointer turned. When bad weather came, he did the same thing. As the humidity changed, the rope would twist tighter or untwist, turning the pointer or forecasting the oncoming weather.

Devices that measure the amount of moisture in the air or the change in humidity are called hy-

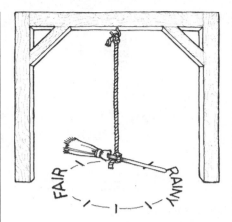

grometers. In later years there was another type of hygrometer that worked on the same principle and was called a weatherhouse. This simple novelty consisted of a small wooden house with two figures inside—usually a boy and a girl. The emergence of one figure or the other from the house indicated an increase or decrease in humidity, and therefore predicted the weather. The figures in the weatherhouse were mounted on a base that was supported in the middle by a length of human or sometimes horse hair. The hair reacted to humidity which caused it to twist and make the pointer turn.

Making a Hygrometer

Materials
strand of human hair
toothpick
glue
pipe cleaner
clear wide-mouth drinking glass or jar

Tools
felt-tipped marker or crayon

1. Find or pluck a single strand of hair at least a few inches longer than the glass is tall. Blonde hair works best. Wrap one end of the hair a few times around the center

This weather house, with its painted figures, predicts sun or rain.

Fig. 19

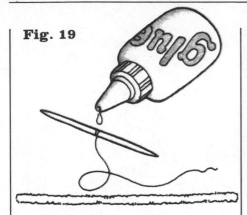

of the toothpick and add a drop of glue, Fig. 19.

2. Bend the pipe cleaner as shown to form a yoke and place it across the top of the glass.

3. Hold the toothpick by the hair and hang it inside the jar making sure the toothpick hangs just above the bottom of the jar and does not touch the sides. Holding the hair in that position, wrap the free end around the pipe cleaner yoke and secure it with a drop of glue, Fig. 20.

4. Over a period of both fair and rainy weather notice the change in

Fig. 20

CRICKET THERMOMETER

The cricket is a reasonably accurate thermometer for determining the temperature. The warmer the temperature, the faster a cricket will chirp; the cooler, the slower his chirps. Using a watch with a second hand, count the chirps of a cricket for fifteen seconds. Add 40, and you will have the temperature in Fahrenheit degrees —at least the temperature will be correct for the location of the cricket.

the direction of the toothpick pointer. Using a colored marker or crayon, indicate the "rain" and "clear" pointer positions on the outside of the jar. You should be able to predict a change of weather.

WEATHER CLUES

What is the weather going to be? Can you predict a change in the weather using the seven clues shown in the illustration?

PANNING FOR GOLD

Although gold was known to exist in many places throughout America, very few people had the patience to prospect for it until, quite by accident, large deposits of gold were found in the riverbed of a California sawmill. The discovery started the great California Gold Rush. Whole families all over America packed their possessions and headed west with great dreams of getting rich. Almost any man, it was said, might earn a good living panning for gold—maybe even make a fortune. A lot depended on luck. A prospector could hit an especially gold-laden riverbed and earn a thousand dollars or more in one day. Another, working nearby, might pan for a week and earn nothing at all.

Panning for gold in a local stream.

The tools of gold prospecting were at first few and quite simple: a shovel with which to dig gravel from the streambed and a gold pan (sometimes just a large frying pan was used) to shake the gravel in and expose the gold ore. Individual prospectors mined the streams of California and Alaska for years, using only shovel and pan. When the streams were exhausted, large gold mining companies moved in. They dug deep tunnels into the hills and mined for gold ore with huge extracting machines.

Fig. 21

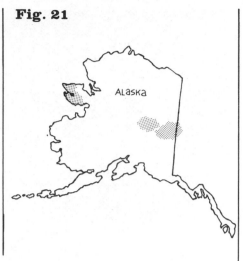

In them thar streams

Although a prospector can no longer walk along the bank of a stream and spot shiny pieces of gold lying along the bottom, there is still much gold to be found by panning. Each year the spring runoff washes new gold down from the mountains. Look at the gold map, Fig. 21. Small amounts of gold can be found in nearly every part of the country. If you live in a "gold region," however, your chances of being a successful prospector are much improved. If you are uncertain about finding gold in your own area, you might try writing to your state Chamber of Commerce to ask for relevant information. Remember that the possibility of finding gold is just as great for you as for the prospector who's been panning "all his life." But you won't know if there's gold in that local stream until you've tried to pan for it.

The Panning Method

Tools
garden spade
heavy metal pie pan
tweezers
empty pill bottle

The running water of a stream breaks loose particles of gold from gold veins that run near or through the stream. The gold is then carried by the water current, but will drop to the bottom of the stream whenever the current is not strong

Tweezers work best for sorting through sand and picking out gold particles.

the stream is hard, you dig it out with the garden spade, otherwise just scoop the pie pan into the streambed, bringing up a panful of gravel. (Avoid using thin aluminum tins that twist and bend out of shape.) Dig as deep into the streambed as possible—the farther down in the gravel you dig, the better the chance of finding gold. Now put the loaded pie pan into the water and stir the gravel until all the dirt and fine particles of material are washed away and only clean gravel, sand, and pebbles, are left. Any stones and pebbles larger than a pea can be picked out and tossed away. By now you should have only a small amount of material in the pan.

The proper rock

Scoop some water into the pan and rock the pan gently in a circular motion so that the remaining gravel spins around. Some prospectors prefer just to rock the pan back and forth. Using either method, let bits of the gravel slowly spill over the edge of the pan until almost all the large particles are gone. For the same reason that gold settles in the stream—its heaviness—any gold particles in the pan will stay put while the lighter gravel spins away. Scoop up more water as you need it. If there is gold in your pan you will soon work the gravel down to a handful of black and colored sand. Whenever gold is to be found in streams, you will also find black sand. If there is no black sand in your pan, pick up and move to a new location—or to a new stream entirely.

All that's yellow

If you find black sand in your pan, finger through it. Look for shiny small grains of gold. The gold particles to be found in streams range in size from that of a pea to smaller

enough to keep it moving. The best part of the stream in which to prospect for gold, therefore, is where the water is slack, where it is not running hard. Look by the edge of streams and around the inside of curves. You might drop a leaf into the stream and follow it to see where it slows down. That will be the most likely place for gold to settle and the best place for you to pan.

Once you have found what seems like a good place to pan, take out your tools and assume the "prospector squat." If the bed of

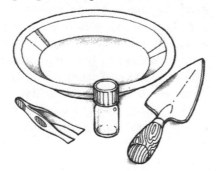

than the head of a pin. Many prospectors sort through the sand using tweezers. Some of the particles in

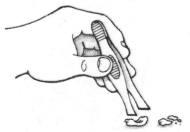

your pan may look like gold, but are probably not. Real gold is quite soft, and you can easily flatten it out with a hammer or press it using your fingernail or tweezers. If the "gold" you've found is yellow mica, it will shatter when poked with the tweezers. "Fool's Gold"—pyrite—is very hard and will not flatten out. Put any particles you think are gold into a capped pill bottle. You will probably want to have your discovery assayed—that it, tested by an expert to see if it is really gold and, if so, how pure it is. Check your telephone directory to see if there is a United States Government Assay Office near you.

If you don't find any gold, don't be discouraged. No one really knows exactly where to look. Keep trying—you may strike it rich!

Staking a Gold Claim

If you are sure you have found gold, you should protect the rights to your discovery by staking a "mining claim." A claim is a temporary right that will allow only you—and those you may wish to have help you—to pan for gold in the area of your claim. The first step is to mark the location of your find. A post with a sign or a pile of rocks will do. Then make a note of the location, the date, your name, and the names of any others who

made the find with you. The next step is to find out from the city hall or town offices who owns the land. If the claim is on privately owned land (owned by an individual or company) you will just have to negotiate and agree to terms with the landowner. He may ask for a certain amount of the gold you find, or maybe just a payment for the right to pan gold on his property. If the land is owned by the state, you will need to write a letter

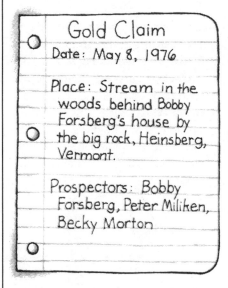

Gold Claim
Date: May 8, 1976
Place: Stream in the woods behind Bobby Forsberg's house by the big rock, Heinsberg, Vermont.
Prospectors: Bobby Forsberg, Peter Miliken, Becky Morton

to the person in charge of state lands at the state capitol. In your letter tell the location of the gold you have found. Laws about mining claims vary from state to state so you will have to wait for a reply that will tell you what to do next. If you find that the land is owned by the federal government, write a letter stating the location of your claim and send it to:

Bureau of Land Management
Department of the Interior
Washington, D.C. 20240

If your claim is considered by a state or federal agency, you will probably need the help of a parent or other adult and maybe even a lawyer.

LOTIONS, POTIONS, AND STRANGE NOTIONS

In Early America nearly all cures were based on home remedies and superstition. Many illnesses of no apparent cause were believed to be the result of spells or evil spirits that had entered the body. The spell could be broken or the spirit chased from the body only if you knew just what to hang around your neck, put in your tea, or apply to the affected area.

American Indians had many cures and remedies using certain herbs and roots. These "medicines" were adopted by the Early American settlers and helped in the development of better medical practice.

Those cures that seemed to work best were passed on from generation to generation, from family to family. Soon hundreds of household "remedies" for every imagin-

able illness were printed in magazines and home doctoring books. School-trained doctors were very scarce, so people treated themselves, or relied on knowledgeable neighbors. Often a barber not only cut hair and gave shaves, but also acted as the town physician.

Did the cures really work? Some did seem to work well for some people but not at all for others. Quite a few remedies made patients even sicker. The cures and remedies that follow are perfectly safe and were all in America at some time. Even today many are still considered effective, but don't take them too seriously: sometimes the cure will work, sometimes not. Remember that for any cure or remedy to be effective it is more important that you *believe* the treatment will work. Of course, for any serious or persistent problem, you should see a doctor—today doctors know a whole lot more.

Hiccups

Have someone stare you in the eye and dare you to hiccup.

Hold an ice cube against the lobe of your right ear.

Hold the tips of your two pointer (index) fingers as absolutely close together as possible without touching.

Put your thumbs in your ears and press your pointer fingers against the sides of your nose while sipping water from a cup that someone holds for you.

Eat a spoonful of peanut butter.

Say "hiccups sticcups" nine times quickly; then quickly stand up straight.

Soak a lump of sugar with vinegar or lemon juice and eat it.

Warts

Put a piece of raw bacon on the wart and keep it there for one day.

Each night before going to bed, rub the wart with a fresh slice of potato.

Wear a straw hat for three days; then burn it in the fireplace.

Rub the wart with the skin of an uncooked chicken; then hide the skin under a rock.

Wet the wart with vinegar; then sprinkle it with baking soda. Let the mixture remain for ten minutes. Repeat three times a day until the wart is gone.

Put a paper bag over the hand with the warts. The person who removes the bag will get your warts.

Rub the wart with a kernel of corn; then feed the kernel to a rooster.

Freckles

Collect a cup of rainwater which drips from the roof. Add to it a squeeze of lemon juice and ten raisins. Stir the mixture every day for nine days, then use it to wash the freckles away.

Apply sap from a grapevine to the freckles.

Rub a mixture of buttermilk and lemon juice on the freckles with a live frog. Let the frog go.

Rub the freckles with a penny, then throw it away. Whoever finds the penny will get the freckles.

Insect Bites, Stings, and Itches

Apply one of the following to the affected area:

camphor	garlic juice
tea	lemon juice
mud	honey
soap	wet salt
slice of onion	
paste of baking soda and water	

Make a wad of seven different types of leaves, twisted together. Tear the wad in half, and rub it on the affected area.

Sunburn

Take a mint-tea bath. To a tub filled with warm water add six tea bags and two cups of fresh mint leaves.

Rub the affected area with cold cider vinegar or charcoal or the juice from an aloe vera plant.

Bangs and Bruises

Make a dough of dandelion leaves and water, and apply.

Rub the affected area with cider vinegar once every hour.

Pains and Sprains

Lift a stone or rock so that one edge remains on the ground. Spit under the rock and let it down exactly as found.

At bedtime turn your shoes upside down and sleep with your feet in a large brown paper bag.

Wrap the sore area in a cloth that you have wet with warm vinegar.

Rub butter on the sore area and have a dog lick it off.

Small Cuts

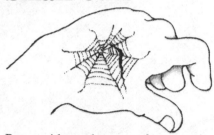

Put a spider web across the wound.

Wet a cigarette paper and place it over the cut.

Apply a wetted mixture of spider webs and brown sugar to the cut.

Put a soft goose feather on the cut and leave it there until it falls off.

Splinters and Thorns

Cover the splinter with a piece of adhesive tape and leave it on for twenty-four hours. When you remove the tape the splinter will come out.

Poison Ivy

Rub the affected area with the inside of a banana peel.

Wash the affected area with a solution of baking soda, then apply cider vinegar.

Apply to the affected area the juice of a green tomato, or used tea leaves, or white shoe polish.

Athlete's Foot

Step in fresh cow manure.

Wrap wool yarn loosely around the affected toe.

The Common Cold

Eat onions roasted in hot coals.

Put fingernail clippings in a bag, tie the bag to a live eel, and let the eel swim away.

Drink a tea made from one of the following:
ginger and honey
white elderberry flowers
roots of a wild rose

Coughing

Mix a teaspoon of black currant jelly in a cup of hot water and drink the mixture before going to bed.

Sore Throat

Wear a necklace of onions baked in a fireplace.

Find a sock that has been worn for several days—its odor should be terrible. Tie it around your neck.

Swallow a mixture made from ground-up rose petals and sugar.

Gargle every hour with a mixture of cider vinegar and water with a pinch of salt and pepper.

Apply uncooked bacon or pork fat to the outside of your throat.

Sneezing

Stop a sneeze by pressing the side of your finger against the area between your upper lip and your nose.

Toothache

Put a drop of vanilla on the painful tooth.

Hold a mixture of warm vinegar and salt in your mouth until the pain goes away.

Earache

Wash all around and in your ear with a warm salt water solution.

Apply a piece of cotton moistened with vegetable oil and sprinkled with black pepper to the ear.

Apply the blood from a broken-in-half Betty bug (whatever that is!).

Nosebleed

Wear a lead fishing sinker around your neck.

Lie down and put a dime over your heart.

Hold your hands over your head for five minutes.

Wrap a piece of ice in a handkerchief and hold it against the top of your nose.

Press a nickel against your upper lip under the bloody nose.

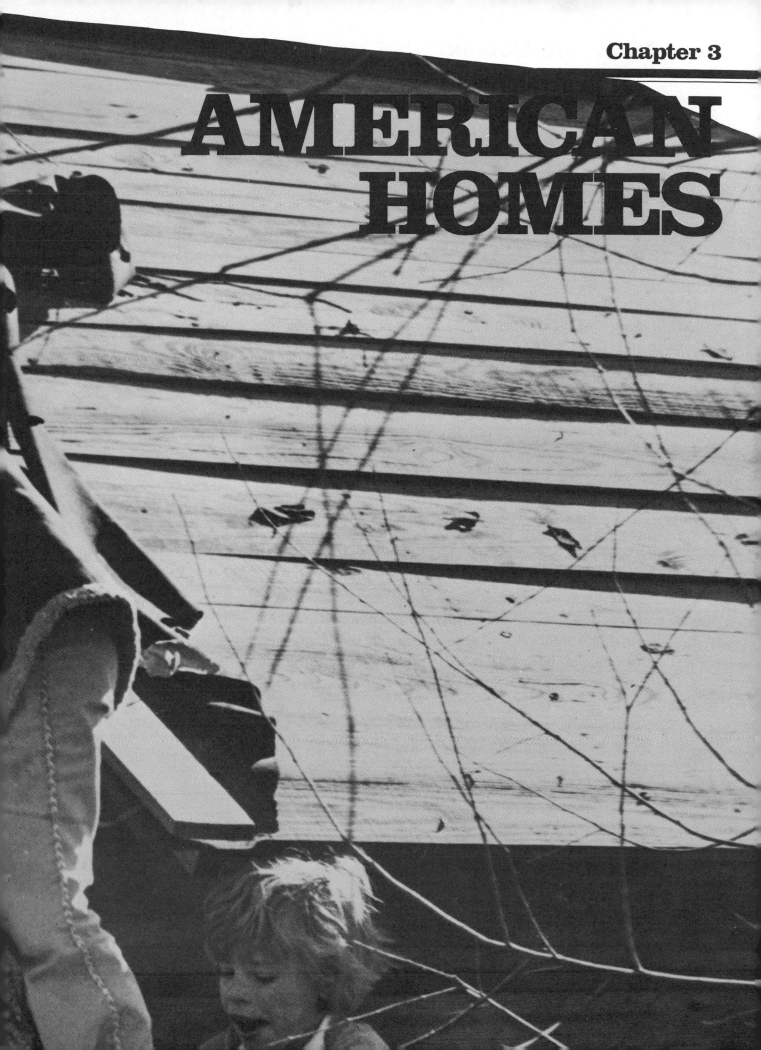

AMERICAN HOMES

HOME SWEET HOME

Fig. 1

When the first settlers came to America, there were no homes waiting for them. In order to survive, the newcomers quickly constructed rough shelters, which would serve until more permanent homes could be built. A site was usually selected near a pond or stream since water was so necessary for drinking, cooking, and washing; for feeding the livestock, watering crops, and—in some cases—turning waterwheels to provide power. Some of the first temporary homes of the early settlers were no more than covered holes dug in the ground, or roughly made huts of piled logs and bark. But as settlers continued to arrive in the New World, real houses began to appear.

The early houses were not designed by architects, nor built by contractors! Everything—including planning, clearing the land, cutting the lumber, gathering the stones, and construction itself—was done by the owner-to-be with help from his neighbors. American climate and materials were often unlike those of the settler's homeland, and tools were hard to come by. Settlers really had to start from scratch.

At first, logs were either used whole, or boards were made by hand-splitting logs into planks, using wedges and a very large, heavy wooden mallet. Where trees were plentiful, log cabins, Fig. 1, were built, using only an ax and handsaw. (The advantage of the log cabin was that it could be constructed quickly by a single man. On the Plains, where there were no trees, the settlers chopped the hard earth into sod "bricks," and used the sod like bricks for building.)

Held together with mud

Without nails, the settlers used clay and mud to fasten wood together, and posts were held to beams by carefully

Fig. 2

fitted wooden pegs. Depending on the climate, roofs were made flat, for easy construction, or steeply pitched to shed the winter snow. Because cut-wood roof shingles needed to age before they could be put up, temporary roofs, made of tree bark or thatched with straw, were erected. Some home builders tried to hurry the process, believing the superstition that newly cut shingles put on in the moonlight would not curl as the wood dried.

Houses were not constructed all at once, but gradually completed and improved as time and resources allowed. As a family grew or acquired wealth, the family home became larger, more elaborate, frequently reflecting the architectural styles of the settler's homeland. Depending on the materials available, the English built what we now call colonial, cape, and saltbox style wooden homes, similar in style to the homes of rural England, Fig. 2. The Dutch built "stepped roof" colonial homes of brick, Fig. 3. Many of the German and Swedish colonists constructed their houses from stones cleared from their farmlands, Fig. 4, and the French and Spanish had their "old country" styles as well.

Fig. 3

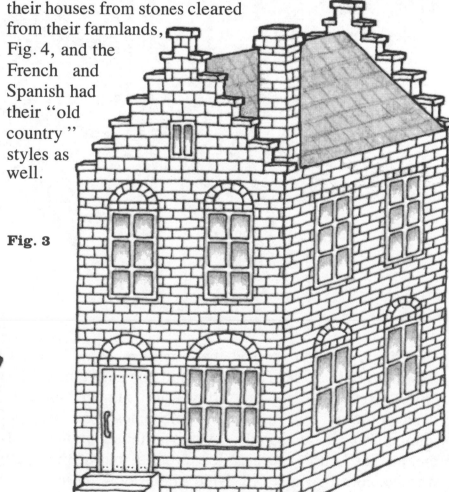

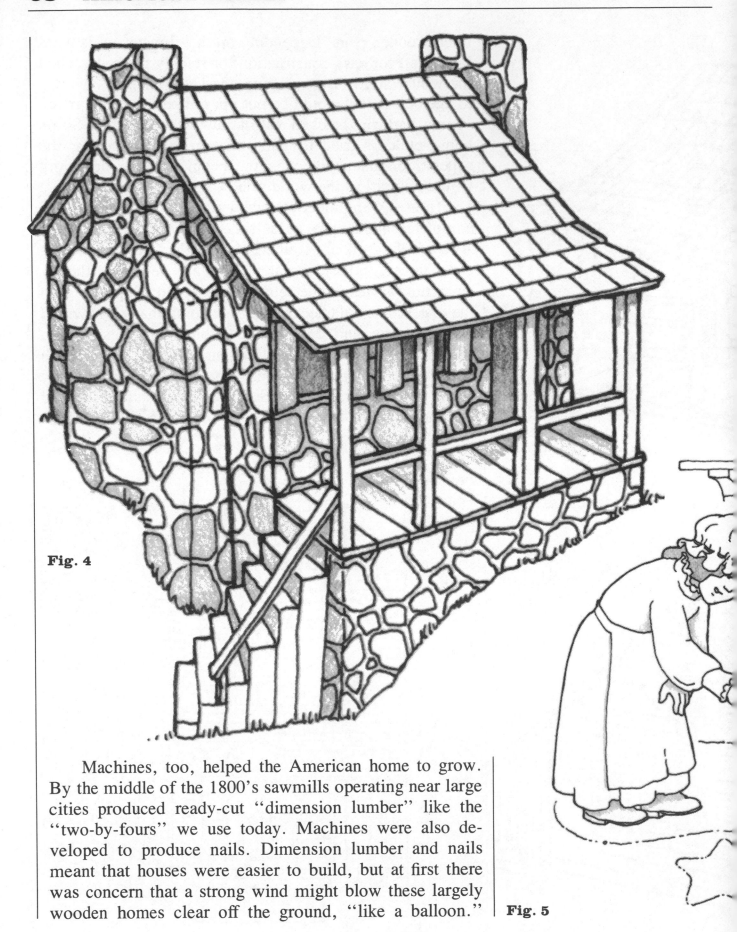

Fig. 4

Machines, too, helped the American home to grow. By the middle of the 1800's sawmills operating near large cities produced ready-cut "dimension lumber" like the "two-by-fours" we use today. Machines were also developed to produce nails. Dimension lumber and nails meant that houses were easier to build, but at first there was concern that a strong wind might blow these largely wooden homes clear off the ground, "like a balloon."

Fig. 5

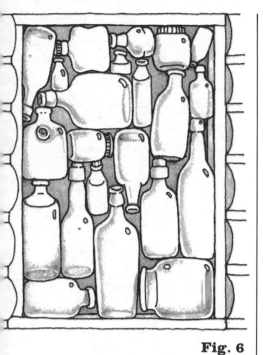

Fig. 6

However, these early "balloon frame" houses, as they were properly called, proved to be sturdy. We still build houses in that way today.

Whatever the building material or style, nearly all Early American homes—the basic American home—followed the same interior plan: one large room with a single central fireplace or two fireplaces, one at either end of the house. The fireplace was the focal point of the house. It provided heat for cooking, warmth from the cold, and some light during the evening hours. The fireplace room was used as the kitchen, the dining room, the living room, and also the bedroom. The fire was so important—and so difficult to re-light if it went out—that it was kept going day and night, summer and winter. Around the fireplace hung gadgets galore. Not only pots, pans, and cooking implements, but homemade devices for cracking nuts, washing clothes, warming cold beds, and many things that look today like abstract sculpture, so difficult is it to recognize their function.

Simple dirt floors

Inside walls in the very early homes were bare structure or structure covered with boards. In the fancier homes the boards were covered with a type of plaster made from ground up seashells, sand, and water. Paint was scarce and used only as decoration. There was no plumbing or running water, so all water used for cooking, drinking, and washing had to be hauled in buckets to the house from a nearby stream or a hand-dug water well.

Before a wooden floor was laid—which might be postponed for years in favor of other more important tasks—the plain dirt floor was pounded hard and swept each day. The dirt floor was especially suitable for scratching out games and drawing plans. When company was expected, fancy designs and patterns were scratched in the floor to make a "dirt carpet," Fig. 5.

At first windows were only open holes in the walls that could be closed with shutters. Some window holes were covered with oiled paper. The oil made the paper translucent so that some light would pass through, and the paper kept out the wind and rain. Before sheet glass became available, some families made "glass" windows by piling up glass bottles in the window hole, Fig.6. Even the glass windows that were available were full of sags and bubbles that made things seen through them appear ripply and distorted. And only ten pieces of glass were allowed in a home before a special tax had to be paid. Glass was so valuable in Early America that when a family moved they took their glass windows with them.

Sometimes a loft or second-floor level was built in the house to make extra room. The loft was accessible by a ladder and was where the children often slept. The loft was a snug, safe-feeling place, and the warmest spot in the house due to the rising heat from the fireplace.

Adding on buildings

The house was built first, but it didn't stand alone for long. Barns were built to keep livestock and provide a working space. Corncribs, mounted off the ground to keep the mice away, stored the corn harvest until it was used, Fig. 7. The smokehouse—which frequently burned down and was, therefore, kept a good distance from the main house—was used to cure meats and give them a good flavor as well as to preserve the meat from spoilage. The cellar of a house was the place to store food. It kept food cool in the summer and from freezing in the winter. The cellar, however, was not necessarily under the house, but beside it—a pit or room-in-the-ground on the sunless north side. Depending on any other trades the farmer was skilled at, he might have a forge barn for shaping iron, a grist mill for grinding grain, or possibly even a ropewalk. And, of course, an outhouse—an outdoor toilet. Even in Early America, and especially at public buildings, there were sometimes separate outhouses for men and women. The half-moon symbol or "luna" meant the outhouse was for women and the sun symbol or "sol" meant it was for men, Fig. 8. In the colder New England climates the outbuildings were attached to the main house. (It is interesting to note that some New England homes built by the sea had a small fenced-in platform perched atop the highest point of the roof called "a captain's walk" or a "widow's walk." The walk was reached through a trapdoor in the ceiling and provided a sea captain, or the wife of a ship's captain who was at sea, with a view of the harbor and all incoming ships, Fig. 9.)

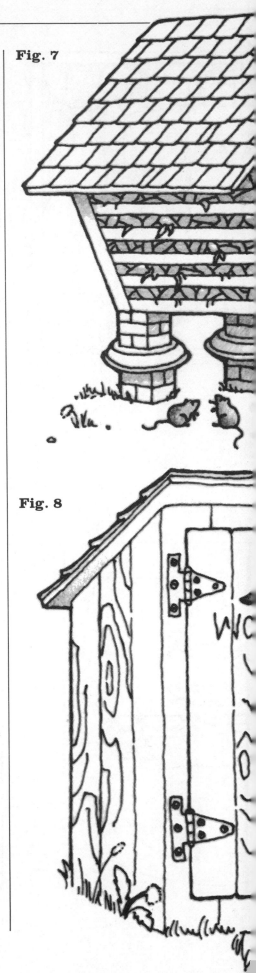

Fig. 7

Fig. 8

Fig. 9

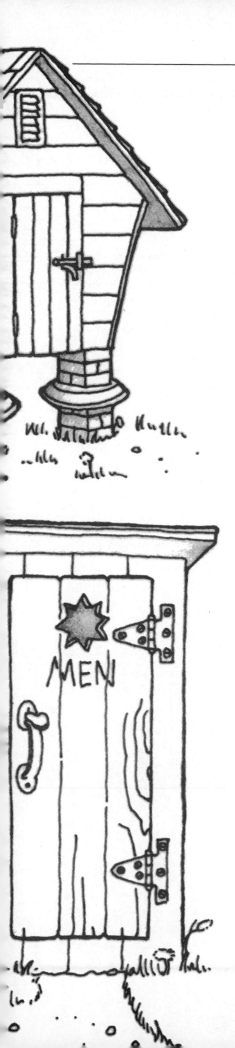

Our homes today still reflect the styles of the Early American builders. Much of the building technology has changed over the years, however. We still use dimension lumber, but we also have the convenience of poured concrete, aluminum siding, plaster wallboard, smooth clear glass, central heating and air conditioning systems, indoor plumbing, and, of course, a slew of electrical conveniences.

The fireplace is no longer a necessity in most homes, but we still like to build them into our homes for the warmth and atmosphere they create. Gone are most of the outbuildings—barns, smokehouses, and so on—because we now buy most of the things we need rather than produce them ourselves. As our life-styles change, so do our houses change to reflect our new habits and ways of life. What will our houses be like in the future? Think about energy, recreation, food production, and safety, and try to imagine your house twenty-five years from now.

WHAT HAS CHANGED?

A house, once constructed, becomes a valuable family asset. Unless it has deteriorated beyond repair due to damage or neglect, it is rarely torn down, but rather improved, enlarged, and made more modern, in keeping with newer life-styles and conveniences. Many homes built by the settlers and colonists over two or three hundred years ago have been refurbished and modernized, and are still comfortably lived in today.

The three illustrations that follow depict a house that might have been built two hundred years ago and show how it has been adapted through the years to reflect our changing way of life. See how many changes you can spot.

GUESS WHAT'S

Life in Early America was quite different from life today and required different tools and gadgets to help make work around the home easier or to provide entertainment. Some of these things could be bought from a local craftsman, but many were homemade and one of a kind.

Sugar came in loaves so there was a device in most kitchens like a pair of big scissors called a sugar loaf cutter. For getting out of bed on cold winter mornings there were boot warmers made of soapstone blocks that were heated by the fire and kept in the boots during the night.

Many odd but ingenious gadgets were in fact necessities to the farmer. When milking the family cow there was a cow tail holder to keep

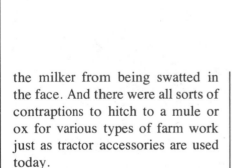

A.

the milker from being swatted in the face. And there were all sorts of contraptions to hitch to a mule or ox for various types of farm work just as tractor accessories are used today.

Ingenious but defunct

Many handmade devices went out of fashion because they were no longer needed. Mass production

meant that affordable labor-saving tools could be manufactured to help the farmer or householder. The newer machinery was, of course, operated by electricity instead of by hand.

But in some ways things haven't changed that much. We Americans are still very much a gadget-conscious society, and in every kitchen, basement workshop, or garage there are bound to be numerous implements and devices to make household chores easier. Some are surprisingly similar in function to those of Early American living while others are unique to today's life-styles.

The following illustrations and photographs show gadgets and things that were once made and used in America. Most seem odd looking and their functions are not readily apparent, but when you do discover to what uses they were put, they will seem quite logical. See if you can guess what they do.

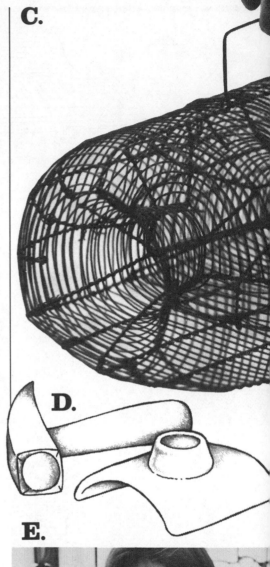

C.

D.

E.

B.

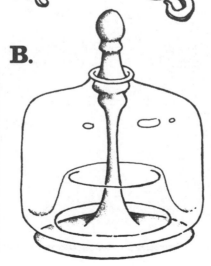

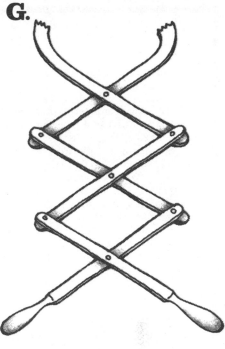

G.

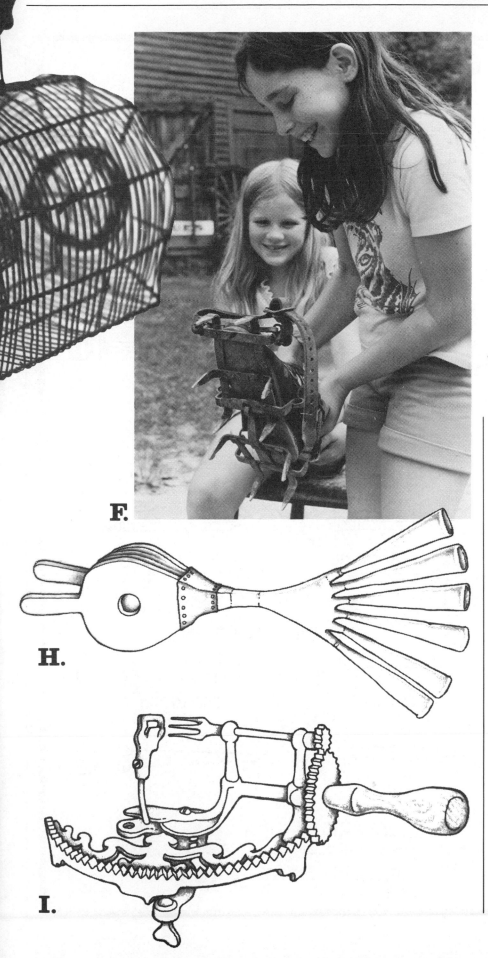

F.

H.

I.

A. Toaster—bread was placed in the wire rack and the entire device put in front of the fire and rotated.

B. Fly Trap—honey or some sweet bait was put inside the jar to attract flies; once inside, the insects were caught.

C. Rat Trap—the rat climbed into the trap to get the bait, but had a hard time finding his way out. This trap advertised that it could catch ten to thirty rats a night and came in both family and hotel size.

D. Knee Nutcracker—the nut was placed in the holder and cracked with the hammer. This was also used as a knee warmer by first heating it by the fire.

E. Snow Shoes—for horses.

F. Ice Shoes—for people.

G. Dog Tongs—although these might have had other functions, they were used chiefly by the sexton to remove noisy dogs from church during services.

H. Hand Bellows Fog Horn

I. Apple Peeler

HOW NAILS ARE MADE

For building homes and other wooden structures in Early America, metal nails were the easiest way of fastening boards together. A family had its own metal forge for making nails of all shapes and sizes, or they bought their nails from a skilled tradesman called the nailer.

Whoever made the nails, the process was the same. First, long thin iron rods were heated in the burning coals of the forge. When the end of the rod was red-hot, it was hammered to a point, then broken off to the length of the nail desired.

Finally, using a hammer and a special holding tool, the nail was given a flat head.

It was during the 1700's that nail making machines were invented that could cut, point, and head a nail all in one operation. Nails were made in all shapes and sizes for specific uses. There were special nails for house framing, floorboards, cabinet building, mounting hinges, making boats, and attaching shingles. Today we have a greater variety of nails designed to do various specific jobs.

When buying nails you will probably not only hear the salesman refer to them by types (common, finishing, roofing, etc.), but by size, using the word penny, as in a two-penny nail or an eight-penny nail. The term penny (indicated by the small letter "d") once referred to the price of the nail. An 8d nail then cost eight cents per one hundred. Today the term refers only to the length.

Nail Size	Length in Inches	Length in Centimeters
2d	1 inch	2.5 cm
3d	1¼	3.2
4d	1½	3.8
5d	1¾	4.4
6d	2	5.
7d	2¼	5.7
8d	2½	6.4
9d	2¾	7.
10d	3	7.6
12d	3¼	8.3
16d	3½	8.9
20d	4	10.2
30d	4½	10.8
40d	5	12.7
50d	5½	14
60d	6¼	15.9

Machine-made nails

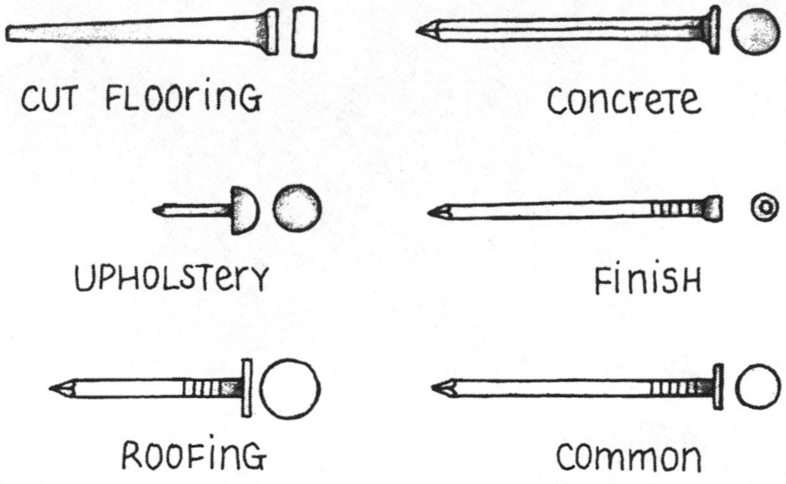

CUT FLOORING   CONCRETE

UPHOLSTERY   FINISH

ROOFING   COMMON

Hand-forged nails

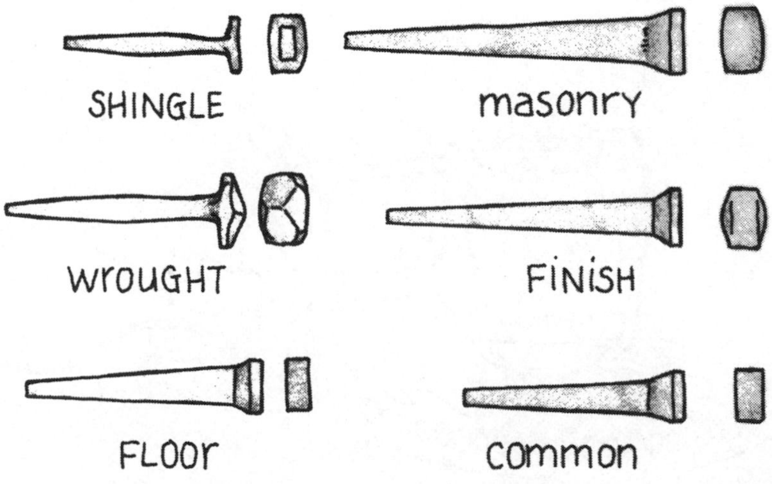

SHINGLE   masonry

WROUGHT   FINISH

FLOOR   COMMON

HEX SIGNS FOR YOUR HOME

In parts of Pennsylvania, Virginia, and West Virginia, barns were, and still are, decorated with hex signs. Although nowadays hexes are purely for decoration, the colorful geometric designs were once thought to be good luck symbols that would ward off sickness, fire, lightning, and all kinds of evil spirits.

The hex sign is attributed to the Mennonites and the Amish people who settled in the southern Pennsylvania area in the seventeenth century. Early hex signs were drawn with mostly straight lines, but later barn artists began using curves and circular patterns. Often the barn owner would paint his own hex signs, but more often he secured the services of a local barn painter who was given the freedom to design and paint symbols of his own choosing.

Typical designs, almost always within a circle, include stars with four, five, six, eight, ten, sixteen, and up to thirty-two points. The stars are usually decorated with symbols and the hex sign painted in yellow, white, red, and black. Many hexes are done in only one or two colors, however. A white stripe painted around a barn door to ward off the devil was another hex "design."

Hex meanings

To some, the number of points on the hex star give different and significant meanings to a symbol:

- A four-pointed star supposedly brings good luck.
- A five-pointed star protects barns from lightning and demons and represents the five senses and good health.

Hex signs on barns supposedly ward off evil and bring good luck.

Photo courtesy of Mel Horst.

- A double five-pointed star is a sign of the sun or good weather.

- A six-pointed star represents love or good marriage.

- A seven-pointed star is a ward against all evil.
- An eight-pointed star is a sign of good will, freedom, and land ownership.

- A twelve-pointed star represents knowledge, wisdom, and sincerity.
- A sixteen-pointed star is the symbol of justice.

Making a Hex Sign

Using simple tools—a circle compass, a ruler, and crayons or markers—you can make hex signs to ward off bad spirits or to bring good luck. Below are directions for drawing a six-pointed star design, but you can easily design any other hexes you like, or you may need.

Materials
plain paper

Tools
circle compass
ruler
pencil
crayons or felt-tipped markers

1. Using a circle compass, draw a circle as large as possible on a plain sheet of paper, Fig.10.

2. Generally following the proportions in the example shown in Fig. 11, draw three more circles within the first circle using the compass. Using the same center point for drawing these circles as you did the first circle.

3. With a pencil and ruler, draw eight evenly spaced spokes in the doughnut-shaped part of the circles, Fig. 12. An easy way to do this is to lay the ruler across the circles, lining up the straight edge with the center compass dot. Draw the two horizontal spokes. Now line up the straight edge vertically,

and draw two more spokes. The "doughnut" is now divided into four equal sections. Continuing to use the ruler and center compass dot, evenly divide each of the four sections with a spoke line to complete all eight spokes.

4. Make a dot mark on the larger inner circle at a point halfway between each two adjacent spokes. To make the star points, draw lines from the outer tips of the spokes to the dots on the inner circle, Fig. 13.

5. Finish the hex design by adding circles or other decorations between the star points, and adding color to the drawing using the felt-tipped markers. Fig. 14.

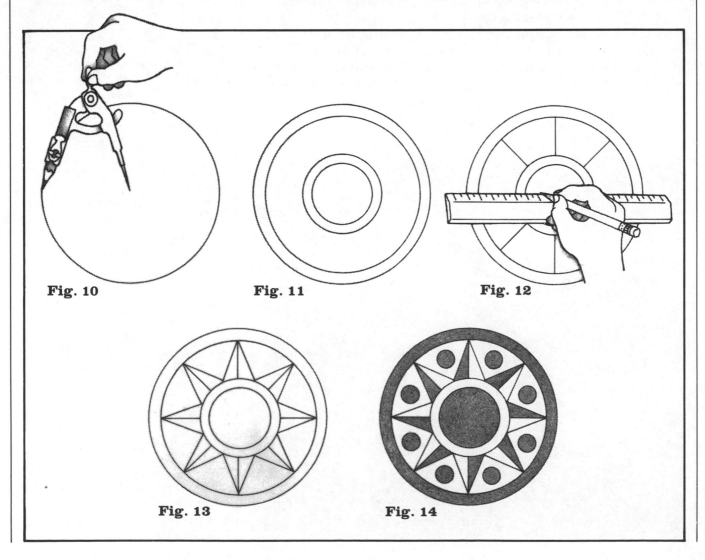

Fig. 10

Fig. 11

Fig. 12

Fig. 13

Fig. 14

STENCILED WALLS

There was no time or place for fancy decoration in the homes of the first settlers. But by the end of the eighteenth century large cities had developed, and many services were available to the family that had once done everything for itself. There was more leisure time, so people could be concerned about interior decoration. Stenciling of walls, furniture, and floors was one of the first forms that this concern took.

For people who couldn't afford wallpaper, or who lived in such a remote place that they had nowhere to buy it (or for those who just preferred hand-done work), stenciling was the answer. Sometimes an artistically inclined housewife would do her own stenciling, but most often the job was done by an itinerant house and barn, wall mural, and portrait painter. The charge for his services was usually room and board plus, perhaps, a small fee.

Early American graffiti

The stenciler would paint samples of his work on the attic walls, and from this selection the homeowner would choose designs. Sometimes a householder would want just one bold stencil over the fireplace, but usually a whole area or border would be decorated with small designs, repeated frequently at regular intervals. The most popular rooms for stenciling were the parlor and the master bedroom. Once a design caught on, however, it might appear on almost everything, anywhere—chairs, picture frames, bedboards, window frames, chests and boxes, tabletops and legs, tinware, lampshades, serving pots, bedspreads, and curtains.

The graphic subjects of the stencils reflected the sentiments of the people: Patriotic eagles, native flowers, fruits and nuts, and baskets and urns filled with flowers and fruits were the usual motifs. Many designs had rather specific significance, which dictated their placement. A hearts-and-flowers design was most likely to be a bedroom stencil. The pineapple motif—a symbol of hospitality—usually appeared in the dining room. The weeping willow (longevity) or thistle design (prosperity) decorated the living room.

Stencil art

The process of stenciling, although not complicated, did require special materials and techniques. The stencils were first drawn or copied on heavy paper. Then the paper was oiled to make it more durable. After the oil had dried, the stencil design was cut. The perforated stencil was then held in position and thick paint—made from a dry powder moistened with soured milk or buttermilk—was applied to the stencil with a stiff stencil brush. The paint got on the surface only where the stencil had been cut, thereby creating the design. After the paint had been applied, the stencil was removed and cleaned for its next application.

The art of stenciling would have probably continued in its popularity had it not been for the Industrial Revolution and the wealth of inexpensive wallpapers and printed fabrics that it brought.

Making Stencil Prints

There are several illustrations below of stencil designs like those used nearly two hundred years ago. You can copy these designs to make stencils or make up your own. Decorate a wall or window shade, or maybe just paint stencil pictures on paper.

Materials
heavy paper such as brown wrapping paper, Manila paper, or file-folder paper
poster paint in various colors

Tools
pencil
small scissors
stiff paint brush

1. Decide on a design, and draw it full size on a sheet of heavy paper. Keep in mind that only the area that you cut out on your stencil will appear painted on the thing stenciled. When drawing, indicate the areas to be cut out by shading

Fig. 15

them with the pencil. Try not to make the design too small or delicate or it might be difficult to cut.

2. Using a small-pointed pair of scissors or a razor-sharp craft knife (if you know how to use one safely), cut out the shaded areas in the design.

3. Thick acrylic paints may be used to stencil permanent designs, but for just making pictures on paper, or for practicing your stencil technique, poster paint will do. Use a stiff bristle brush to apply the paint. Hold the cut stencil firmly and flat against the surface that you want decorated, or tape the stencil in place. Dip the brush into the paint so that the brush is full of paint, but not dripping. Gently dab the brush over the stencil cutouts until the entire cutout area is painted, Fig. 15. The secret of a successful stencil technique is not having the brush so wet with paint that the paint drips behind the stencil; or too dry so that the color is splotchy or uneven.

4. Carefully pull away the stencil taking care not to twist it or you will smear the design. Then clean off the stencil so that it is ready for use again. A stencil can be used repeatedly as long as it does not rip or get a heavy accumulation of dried paint on it. If you want your stencils to keep for several uses, oil your stencil paper with a mixture of boiled linseed oil and turpentine mixed in equal quantities. Rub the mixture lightly on the paper, and then let the stencil dry for at least an hour. The oil makes the paper more leathery and durable and easier to clean.

Here are some sample patterns which you can trace and use as stencil designs.

FOUR-POSTER CANOPY BED

The earliest settlers probably slept on the floor, and close by the fire on cold nights. But in time more comfortable beds were made by stringing ropes across a wooden frame, and placing a mattress stuffed with corn husks, leaves, and straw on top of this rope frame "spring." Under the large bed there was often a smaller "trundle bed" that could be pulled out at night for the children; some beds were hinged to fold up against the wall when not in use. These early beds were not uncomfortable, especially those whose mattresses were stuffed with feathers; but be-cause it was not uncommon to have all of the family sleeping in several beds in a single room, the bed offered little privacy. The four-poster bed offered one solution.

A private place

The four-poster bed, as its name implies, had tall posts, one connected to each corner of the bed, with a framework around the top of the posts. The frame was covered with fabric so that the bed became totally enclosed. In the wealthiest homes, the bed curtains were made of silk, but more commonly they were linen or patchwork, and always decorated. Besides privacy, the bed curtain also held in body warmth and kept out cold drafts and annoying bugs.

Canopy beds are lovely to look at and comfortable to sleep in.

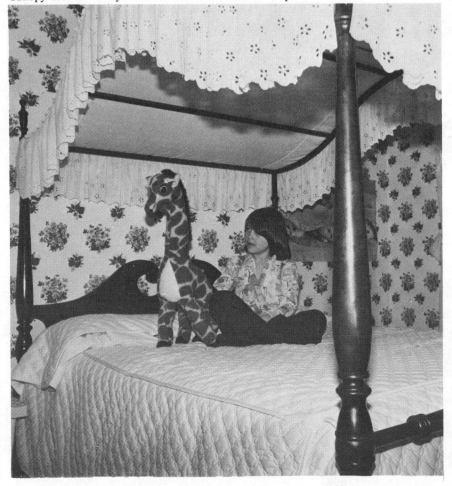

Making a Four-Poster Canopy Bed

With a few common materials you can—at least temporarily—convert your own bed into a four-poster canopied bed, and feel what it might have been like sleeping in Colonial America. Here's how.

Materials
newspapers
tape
large bed sheet
string or yarn

The framework of the canopy bed will be made from rolled newspaper tubes. The exact length you make the tubes depends on the size of your bed, and how high you want the canopy to be.

1. To make the newspaper tubes, first lay out four full sheets of newspaper and stack them neatly, Fig. 16.

Fig. 16

2. Starting at one of the narrow sides, roll the newspapers into a tight tube about as fat as your wrist, Fig. 17. Keep the newspapers from unrolling with two or three strips of tape.

3. To make the tube longer, roll four more sheets of newspaper around the first tube you made, rolling the paper from about half-way up the length of the first, Fig. 17. Tape the newspaper so it doesn't unroll, and tape the two tubes together.

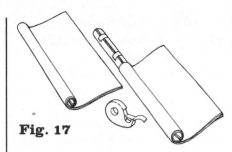

Fig. 17

4. Continue making the structure longer by rolling another newspaper tube separately and narrower than the first, taping it, and inserting it halfway into the longer tube. Tape the new tube to the old. By continuing to connect newspaper tubes you can make the structure any length necessary, Fig. 18.

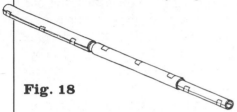

Fig. 18

5. Make four newspaper tubes, all the same length and as high from the floor as you'd like the top of the canopy to be. Attach each tube-post vertically to each corner of your bed. Tie the tubes in place using string or yarn, Fig. 19.

6. Make up four more newspaper tubes, two of them a bit longer than the length of your bed, and two of them a bit longer than the width of your bed. Attach these tubes to the vertical tube-posts to complete the frame, Fig. 19.

7. To connect the tubes at right angles, bend the end of one tube, pinch the bent end together, and insert it into the open end of another tube, Fig. 20. Tape.

8. Carefully drape a large bedsheet over the frame. To add a finishing touch, make draw strings to open an end of the canopy, Fig. 21.

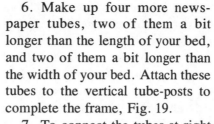

Fig. 19

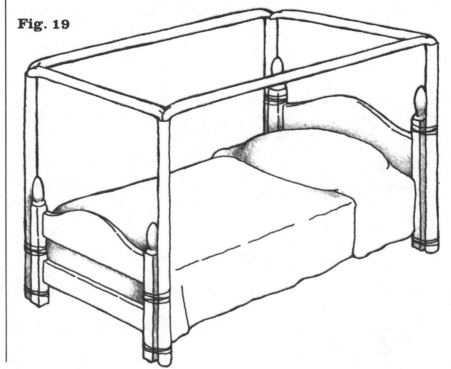

Fig. 20

Fig. 21

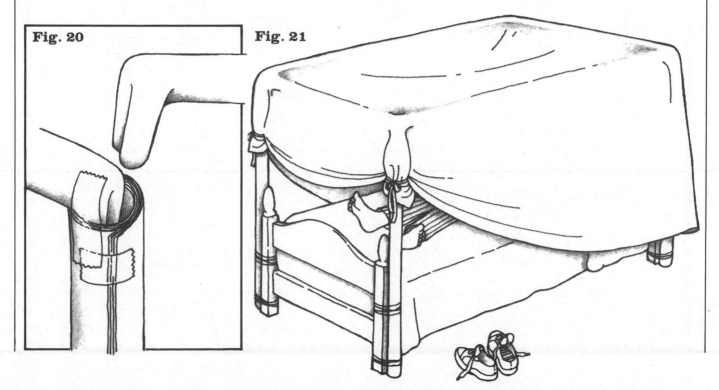

ROCKING CHAIRS

The furniture of Early America—like almost everything else for the house—was homemade. It might appear crude at times, but it was usually very functional, even multi-functional. The ladder-back chair, for example, could be used not only for sitting, but as a ladder. There were chairs designed so that boards might be rested between them to make shelves. And, of course, there was that most "functional" chair of all, the rocking chair.

The rocking chair seems to be an American invention. It was undoubtedly first made by the less-than-wealthy who could not afford large, overstuffed furniture in their homes, but wanted something comfortable nonetheless. The idea probably came from the baby's rocking cradle, and a few historians credit Benjamin Franklin with the invention. The earliest mention of a rocking chair is in a hand-written bill from a Philadelphia furniture maker, dated 1774, in which he charged a woman for "bottoming a rocking chair." So 1774 stands as the time for the invention of the rocker.

Rock in style

Nearly all early rocking chairs were regular chairs that had been converted using wooden rockers attached to the chair legs. But once the rocking chair was widely accepted, even by the wealthy, furniture makers began producing them in a great variety of styles and types. There was the rather stiff and upright ladder-back rocker; the overstuffed Lincoln rocker (named after Abraham Lincoln's favorite rocking chair); a Shaker rocker that also swiveled around; and a Windsor-chair rocker with a writing desk attached. There was also the squeaky, finger-pinching "stationary rocker" or "standard rocker" which rocked on springs. And there was the rockee, a long, bench-type rocker that had a baby cradle mounted on it. The rockee permitted the mother to sit on one end sewing clothes or doing some hand task while at the same time she rocked herself and the baby. Once the baby had grown, the cradle could be removed, and the bench used as a rocker for three people.

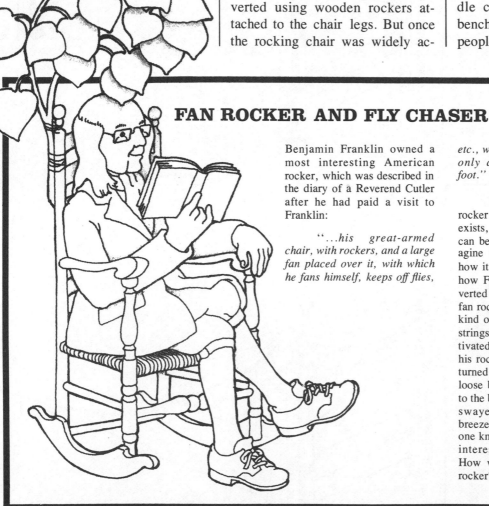

FAN ROCKER AND FLY CHASER

Benjamin Franklin owned a most interesting American rocker, which was described in the diary of a Reverend Cutler after he had paid a visit to Franklin:

"*...his great-armed chair, with rockers, and a large fan placed over it, with which he fans himself, keeps off flies,* etc., *while he sits reading, with only a small motion of his foot.*"

Ben Franklin's fan rocker and fly chaser no longer exists, and no illustration of it can be found, so we must imagine what it looked like and how it worked. Try to think of how Franklin might have converted his rocking chair into a fan rocker. Did he invent some kind of contraption that pulled strings when he rocked and activated an overhead fan? Did his rocking pull a crank which turned a fan? Or did he just tie loose branches with big leaves to the back of his rocker so they swayed and caused gentle breezes when he rocked? No one knows for sure, but it is an interesting design problem. How would you design a fan rocker?

THE SHAKERS

The Shakers called themselves "The Believers," which was short for the "United Society of Believers in Christ's Second Appearing." It was only outsiders who called the sect "Shakers" owing to the Shakers' uninhibited style of worship. The Shakers literally shook in ecstasy while "lifting their hearts and hands to God" at Sunday meetings. Hard work was another form of Shaker worship and prayer, and it was to be practiced to perfection.

The Shakers were some of the best inventors of their time. Credited to them is the flat broom, which was a much better cleaner than the round one which preceded it. The Shakers even cultivated a new species of corn to provide a stronger, more resilient broom bristle. The Shakers discovered ways to breed superior cattle. They were the first to supply packaged garden seed, and in the process they invented a "printing box" to produce seed labels. A Shaker invented the circular saw blade, which soon revolutionized lumber cutting. The Shakers were also inventors of the common clothespin, cut nails, condensed milk, the boat propeller, and an automatic pea sheller.

But the Shakers are probably best remembered for their furniture designs. Not only did they invent new types of furniture—including the revolving chair, fold-up beds, and swivel stools—but the style of their furniture was unique, pleasing, and functional. Other craftsmen in America were greatly influenced by the designs of the Old World, but the Shaker designs were completely their own in-vention. The Shakers produced furniture for their own use, but their designs were so successful that others copied them. The new style was soon offered as "Shaker furniture."

Shaker furniture was completely free of decoration, and the designs always used the minimum amount of material. It was believed by the Shakers that the appearance of an object should reflect its function. A Shaker chair was very sturdy though it weighed little. When not in use, all the chairs in a Shaker home were hung on wall pegs so the room could be easily cleaned or cleared for religious gatherings and ritual dances.

Today only a few elderly members of the Shaker sect remain, but Shaker furniture is still being made. It is considered a true American style, and appreciated for its clean lines and usefulness.

GREAT PLAINS INDIAN TEPEE

The American Indian tepee (the word means "for living in" and the Indians spell it "tipi") is one of the best and most practical homes ever invented. It is roomy and well ventilated, warm in winter, cool in summer. It is easy to build—one person can do the job—and easy to move. The tepee's conical shape makes it structurally sound in high winds and heavy rains.

Not all Indians lived in tepees. They were invented by the Indians of the Great Plains, and did not come into being until the beginning of the eighteenth century. Before that time the Plains Indians were a non-migrant farming people who lived in huts. When they became hunters of the buffalo—after guns and horses had become a part of their lives—the movable tepee was born.

A Great Plains classic

The classic tepee—a cone-shaped tent made of long thin poles with a buffalo-hide covering—was a simple but sophisticated structure. To make it, poles were cut from tall, straight trees or branches; the bark

was stripped from the wood, and the ends of the "sticks" pointed to make them hold in the ground. The poles were then carefully dried so they would not bend and cause the tepee to sag. The basic design utilized three poles, but some Indians used more, as many as thirty poles in a single structure.

To pitch the tepee, a high piece of level ground was found and cleared of stones, roots, and brush. A ditch was dug around the site down to the lowest ground level to drain off rainwater. The three fattest poles were set up in tripod fashion, and wrapped together with cord where they crossed. Additional poles were added to make the structure more secure.

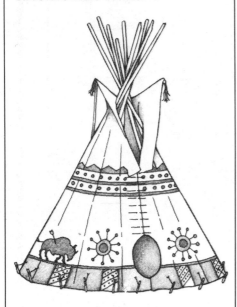

Dressing the poles

The tepee covering was pre-cut from several buffalo hides; wooden pegs or pins were made for fastening closing flaps, and attaching the cover to the ground. The cover was wrapped around the frame and laced tight so that it fit snugly. The door opening was arranged to face east to get the morning sun and protect against the prevailing westerly winds. (In many tepee designs there were two additional poles outside that held and adjusted the

smoke flaps.) The Indians made sure to leave a "smoke hole" at the top of the tepee for venting the inside fire. The hole was covered with a flap to regulate the fire, which would also cover the hole in rainy weather.

Tepee secrets revealed

The secret of a tepee, however, is its inner lining. Decorated cloth was cut to fit around the inside of the poles. The air space between the outside cover and the inside lining created an insulation that made the tepee comfortable all year around. The lining also kept rainwater from dripping off the poles and onto occupants; at night it provided privacy by preventing shadows from being cast on the cover by the fire.

Everything inside the tepee was made to be easily carried. The "floor" was a waterproof ground cloth that was easily picked up. In many tepees, beds were just buffalo hides laid out on the floor at night and rolled up for storage during the day. For sitting in the tepee the Indians used "lean backs" made from a tripod of sticks and covered by a woven mat, or a buffalo skin,

with part of the mat on the ground as a seat. Many of the Indian's belongings—his food, clothing, and tools—were kept in a suitcase called a parfleche. These suitcases were always made in pairs so they could be hung over a horse like saddle bags for traveling.

Tepee etiquette

In Indian culture it was the women who built the tepee and its furnishings. Women also selected the site, decorated the interior, and were in charge of what went on on the inside. Sometimes men would decorate the outer covering and inner lining with colorful pictures of animals, but it was primarily the man's job to hunt and be the warrior. The sign of a well-kept tepee was straight poles. Crooked or poorly made poles gave a woman a "bad reputation." Indian children were taught by their mothers to make small play tepees for "playing house," and sometimes tepee dog houses were built for the family's pets.

There was a code of etiquette for those visiting another's tepee. If the door—a flap of hide—was open, you could just walk in. If the door flap was closed, you had to call out for permission to enter and wait for an invitation. Two sticks crossed against the flap meant the owners were away or didn't want company. Men sat on the north side inside; women on the south side. Men sat cross-legged and women sat either on their knees or with their legs folded to the side.

When entering a tepee it was proper to walk behind not in front of a seated person. When invited to eat, a guest was expected to bring his own dish and utensils. Guests were expected to eat everything served them, or ask another to eat

the remaining food, or take it home with them. A pipe that was smoked inside the tepee was always passed to the left, with the pipe stem pointing to the left, and when the host decided to clean the pipe, it was a signal that the visit was over and that the guests should leave.

Making a Five-Pole, Two-Kid Tepee

With an old bed sheet and newspaper tubes you can build a small one or two kid-sized play tepee. The design is not elaborate or as functional as a true Indian tepee, but the feeling of being inside a cone house is all-Indian.

Materials
old bedsheet
string
newspapers
tape
4 safety pins

Tools
scissors
felt-tipped markers or crayons

1. Find an old bedsheet that no one minds having cut up, and lay it

Tepees can be built indoors as well as outdoors.

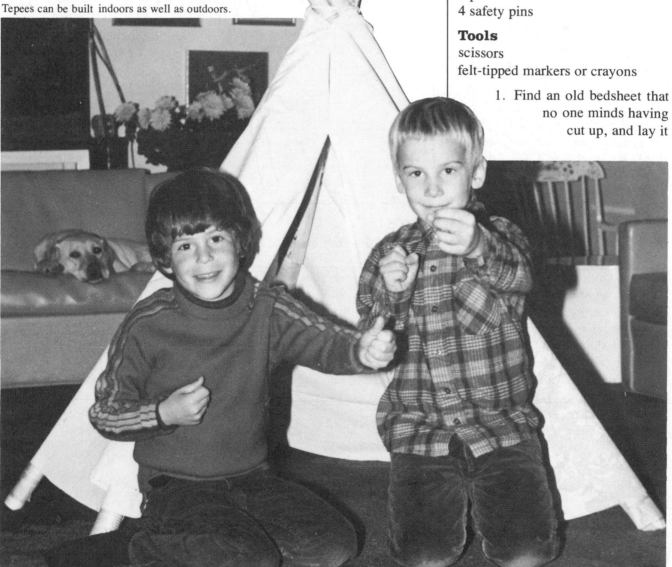

out flat on the floor. Make a large circle compass by tying a length of string to a felt-tipped marker or crayon. Hold the marker at one corner of the sheet, *A* in Fig. 22, and have a friend hold the string taut at the center of a long end of the sheet, *B*. Draw a semicircle on the sheet and cut it out with a scissors.

Fig. 22

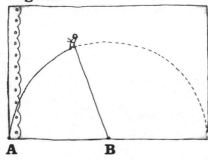

A   B

2. Make five newspaper tubes each about one foot longer than the radius of the circle, the distance between *A* and *B* in Fig. 22. To make newspaper tubes, see the instructions for making a four-poster canopy bed in this chapter.

3. Gather the five tubes and tie them together loosely with several wraps of string, about one foot down from the top, Fig. 23.

4. Spread the tubes at one end to make them stand, Fig. 24.

5. Cover the tepee frame with the cut sheet by placing the center of the sheet's straight edge (*B* in Fig. 22) at the point where the tubes are tied, and then wrapping the sheet around the frame, Fig. 24.

6. Where the sheet comes together, fasten the upper two-thirds with safety pins. The bottom one-third should be left open for an entrance, Fig. 25.

7. Spread the poles out more until the sheet fits taut. Before or after you fit the sheet, you may decorate it with Indian designs using felt-tipped markers or crayons. Copy some of the examples shown, or make up your own.

Fig. 24

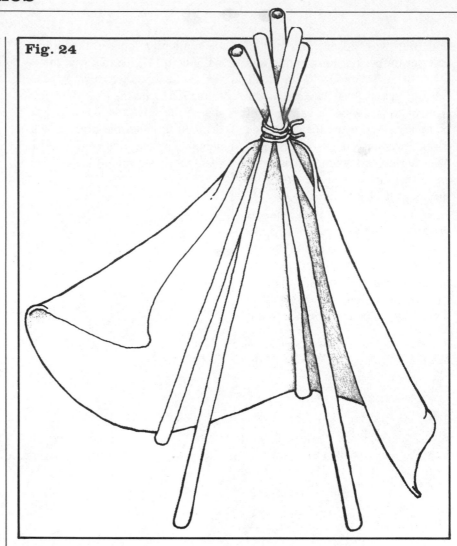

Fig. 25

Fig. 23

THE GETAWAY TREE HOUSE

A tree house is an escape—a place to hide from everyone. It's a good feeling to be up in a tree. When the wind blows and the tree sways, the tree house sways too giving the occupants a feeling of being part of the tree. A tree house is a place to hold secret meetings without being overheard, a peaceful place for anyone to read in, to take a break in, to be contemplative in.

Individual preferences

Like adult homes, a kid's tree house can be constructed in a variety of styles, sizes, and materials, with the spread and size of the chosen tree's branches dictating much of the tree house form. Actually, only limited planning is necessary for building the tree house. The special quality of any tree house is often the result of the builder's imagination and "on site" decisions. A casual tree house erected at a secret spot in the woods can just "grow" from found branches lashed together, or scraps of board nailed between the branches. More elaborate tree houses are often the work of a "handyman" parent and tend to be

A tree house makes a great playhouse.

made using neatly cut planks bolted and nailed. Architects sometimes design complimentary tree houses for their house-client's children. But a kid enjoys his roughly made structures more than one made for him by any adult.

Safety precautions

Whatever tree house you build, there are some precautions that must be followed for your safety and the safety of your tree house

guests. The basic tree house consists of a platform securely fastened to at least three closely spaced trees or tree branches, and a ladder or "steps" to get up to, and down from the platform. If your tree house is built more than a few feet off the ground, you should construct a railing around the platform so no one will accidentally fall off. As an added safety measure, be sure the ground below and around the tree house is free of rocks, tree

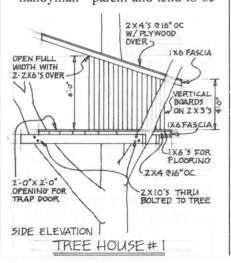

2X4'S @ 16" OC
W/ PLYWOOD
OVER

OPEN FULL
WIDTH WITH
2-2X6'S OVER

1X6 FASCIA

6'-0"

VERTICAL
BOARDS
ON 2X3'S

1X6 FASCIA

1X6'S FOR
FLOORING

2X4 @ 16" OC

2'-0" X 2'-0"
OPENING FOR
TRAP DOOR

2X10'S THRU
BOLTED TO TREE

SIDE ELEVATION
TREE HOUSE # 1

stumps, bikes, toys, or other objects that might cause injury if someone were to fall from the platform. It is a good idea to cover the ground around the tree house with a thick layer of leaves or straw—just in case—and also to have an adult check out the area.

Legal restrictions

State, city, or local town governments are likely to have building codes that include regulations concerning the erection of tree houses. One town in New York State once required that all of them have walls at least forty-two inches high, and at least one-inch thick flooring boards supported by "two by sixes." The code specified that no tree house could be built more than twelve feet off the ground, and that the supporting trees or branches must be at least five inches in diameter if hard wood, and seven inches in diameter if soft-wood trees. Nails were required to be a minimum of sixteen penny, and access to the house had to be by a

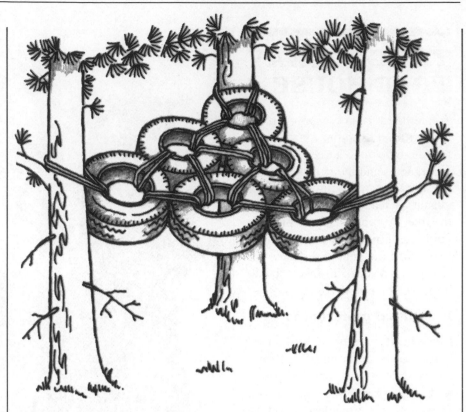

"structurally sound ladder." In spite of the rather formidable requirements of this particular code, many town building inspectors seem to understand the spontaneity involved in building a tree house

and tend not to interfere.

Whether your town has a tree house code or not, here are some universal tree house "regulations":

- Building materials should be scrounged—you should make do with what is available.
- Bent nails can be straightened and reused, but avoid rusty nails.
- Never build higher than you are willing to fall.
- Build a ladder only you and your friends can climb (but little brothers and sisters can't).

Building a Tree House

Because of all the variables—tree types and sizes, materials available, and type of tree house desired—no *special* plans or detailed instructions are given here for building one. A tree house should be built a board at a time with the builder-architect deciding what comes next according to the materials at hand, and what seems

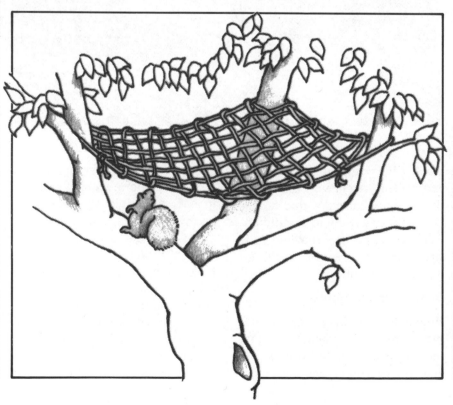

most appropriate. You'll have to use your imagination for design-making and your intuition for engineering. There are some guidelines, however, which follow below. Read them carefully before you begin.

Select the proper tree

Look for a tree in your yard, in a woods, or maybe find a friend who has a good tree-house tree in his backyard. The tree should not be too young (too thin and weak), or so brittle that the branches would break off easily. The best trees are oak, maple, apple, chestnut, beech, and willow. A good tree-house tree should have strong, spreading branches which will support a platform. If one large tree can't be found, find a "stand" of three or more trees close together—pines, birches, or nearly any tree with a strong trunk will do.

Materials and planning

A traditional kid's tree house is built using wooden planks and nails, but many other materials will do, depending on design and the use you intend for the tree house. Tree house platforms can be made from woven rope, old tires mounted together, or heavy fallen branches lashed to the tree with cord. Every tree house will be different and that is as it should be. The design should reflect the materials used, the size of platform desired, and concern for the living tree.

Try to place the platform low in the tree where the main branches leave the trunk. There is less wind-whip there and less chance that the structure will twist and loosen. It is not very important that the tree house be high, at the top of the tree. As long as the platform is at least above your head, the tree house will be high enough.

Fig. 26

Construction

First, it is important to build a sturdy platform. If using planks, attach the support boards around the major branches. The boards might rest in the fork of the branch or be attached with long nail spikes, Fig. 26. If you have a drill, use long bolts and nuts to hold the frame to the tree. Drilling a hole in the tree branch is less harmful to the tree than hammering it full of nails. In either case, it's a good idea to lash the boards to the support branches using heavy twine or rope, Fig. 27. In no case should you cut into or notch the branch because it will harm a living tree.

Place the floor planks across the supports, and nail them to the supports to make the platform, Fig. 28.

Using straight sticks or a length of rope, make a guard railing all along the platform to protect the tree house occupants from accidentally falling. Fig. 29.

Fig. 27

Fig. 28

Fig. 29

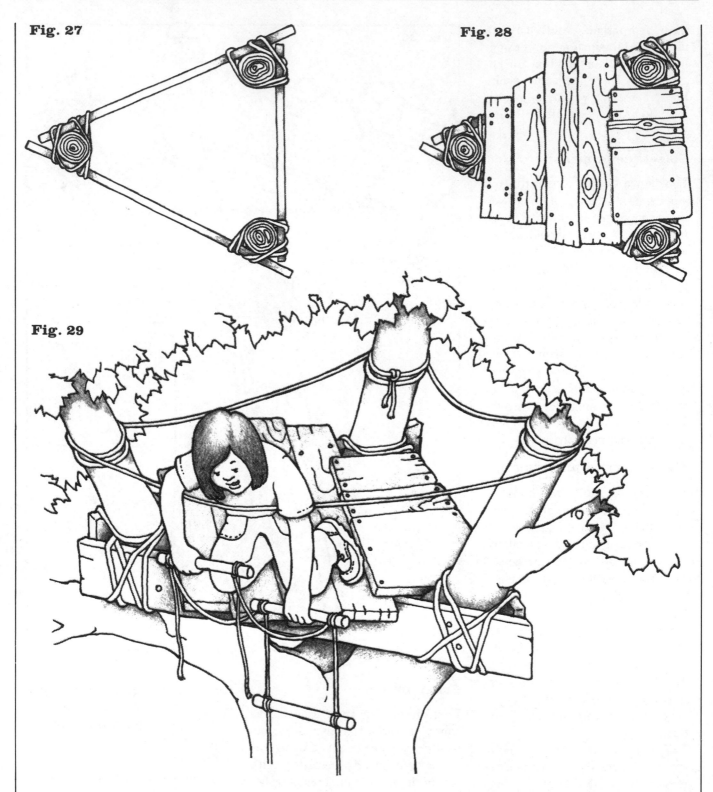

Ladders

There are several ladder types you can use for getting up and down to and from your tree house. For privacy, you can make a rope ladder that can be pulled up into the tree house when you are "at home" to shut out intruders, Fig. 30. A knotted rope will work well also, Fig. 31. The construction of the ladder will again depend on the materials available and the tools you have to work with. A regular wooden-rung ladder can be made easily from two long posts and smaller scraps of lumber, and if the tree house isn't too far off the ground, the ladder can be pulled up into the tree house for privacy, Fig. 32. Or you might just attach a climbing

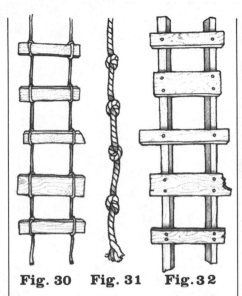

Fig. 30   Fig. 31   Fig. 32

pole or smooth rope to one edge of the platform and shinny up and down. Maybe you can find a way of climbing the tree to get to your tree house, or of making a ladder on the tree trunk itself by securely nailing ladder rungs to the trunk, Fig. 33.

Fig. 33

Once the basic tree house is complete, you can use it as is or continue to build onto the structure with walls, a roof, and maybe a few accessories such as a rope and bucket hoist.

DEED TO THE HOUSE

If you buy or build a house, even a tree house, you should have a "deed" to prove that you own the house. A deed is a legal document that describes the location of the house, the property it is on, and tells who the owner is.

When you buy or sell a house, the deed is given by the seller to the buyer. The buyer's name is then written on the deed and the deed becomes proof that the buyer is now the owner. A deed may have more than one person's name on it if there is more than one owner.

However, to make a deed official it must be recorded by giving a copy to the Registrar of Deeds in your county. Recording a deed is just making known to the public who owns a particular house; it also provides an ongoing history of property ownership.

Entitled enjoyment

A deed not only shows ownership of a house, but entitles the owner to the "enjoyment" of his house—sometimes, however, with certain restrictions. These limitations on house and land use are also listed on the deed. At one time in America a homeowner could do anything that he wanted as long as it was done on his own property or in his own house. Today, however, limitations or "encumbrances" to the deed try to help us be good neighbors. Encumbrances to a deed may prohibit a homeowner from cutting down a beautiful stand of trees, or from damming up a stream that runs across his property.

Sometimes there are zoning restrictions listed as encumbrances that limit the type of structure that can be built on a piece of land. For example, the zoning law may not allow a factory to be built on land surrounded by people's homes. Or a zoning law may limit the height of a house, how close it can come to the road, or the minimum amount of land you need to build each house. Zoning laws are usually decided by town or state government committees, and help protect a homeowner's enjoyment of his property.

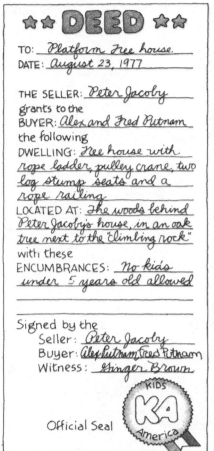

☆☆ DEED ☆☆

TO: _Platform Tree house_
DATE: _August 23, 1977_

THE SELLER: _Peter Jacoby_
grants to the
BUYER: _Alex and Fred Putnam_
the following
DWELLING: _Tree house with rope ladder, pulley crane, two log stump seats and a rope railing_
LOCATED AT: _The woods behind Peter Jacoby's house, in an oak tree next to the "Climbing rock"_
with these
ENCUMBRANCES: _No kids under 5 years old allowed_

Signed by the
Seller: _Peter Jacoby_
Buyer: _Alex Putnam Fred Putnam_
Witness: _Ginger Brown_

Official Seal

KIDS KA America

Draw up a deed

If you build a tree house, draw up a simple deed stating the location of the tree house, who the owner or owners are (and who the seller is if you are acquiring an already-existing tree house) and whatever restrictions that you, the owner, think are necessary.

Make two copies of the deed, keeping one yourself and "officially record" the other copy with the owner of the property on which the tree house is built, or with one of your parents.

Chapter 4

AMERICAN BACKYARDS AND GARDENS

BACKYARD FUN

There are few places in or around the house that a kid can claim as a personal playspace to use for playing alone or with friends. A kid's bedroom or the family playroom often serves the purpose but there is so much you can't do indoors, and besides, when the weather is pleasant it is much nicer to be outdoors.

If you are lucky enough to have your own backyard then you probably have already discovered that backyards too can be one of those special play places.

An apartment house common, a nearby vacant lot, a playground, or maybe even a schoolyard that hasn't been covered with asphalt can become your own backyard where you can plant a garden, have a picnic, set up an overnight tent, dig for whatever might be buried there, or even find a new free pet.

Your backyard may already have several play materials built right in—trees for climbing and holding up a tree house, wild plants for picking and making things, and rocks, dirt, grass, puddles, and mud for playing in. The typical American backyard is very much a special kids' place and here are some typically American ways to use it.

Fun outdoors in the sun
among trees and twigs.

AN AMERICAN GARDEN

The success of home food gardens meant survival to the first American settlers. As soon as the food supplies they had brought with them ran out, the settlers had to depend upon available wild foods and their own abilities to garden the land.

The prosperity of the settlers' first food gardens was quite impressive. The soil was fertile and the plants and seeds the Early Americans brought with them seemed to grow bigger and better in the New World than in Europe. The settlers learned from the Indians, who had cultivated the land for centuries, of new plants and varieties of foods that were unique to America.

Early garden staples

Corn was one of the staple crops for the Indians, and it was widely grown in several edible varieties in three colors, yellow, red, and blue. To be eaten, the corn was cooked over a fire or boiled to soften the hard kernels. The kernels could also be beaten with a mortar to make corn flour for baking. Blue corn was considered a good medicine for aches and certain illnesses.

After corn, pumpkin was the Indian's main garden food. Boiled and flavored, pumpkin was a filling and delicious meal, as well as an Indian cure for stomachaches and other digestive ailments. Another Indian food eaten for both pleasure and its supposed healing power was the exceedingly juicy watermelon. The settlers learned also to cultivate squash, cranberries, and a variety of new beans, berries, and nuts. And there was that non-edible crop, tobacco.

Finally a good smoke

Tobacco plants were grown so the leaves, when dried, could be crumpled up, put into a pipe, set on fire, and the resulting smoke "sucked into the stomach and thrust out again through the nostrils." Smoking tobacco was an enjoyable experience for the settlers who soon found it a pleasant social pastime. The habit was believed by the settlers to be a deterrent and a cure for a variety of illnesses, including ulcers, headaches, animal bites, and spots before the eyes. All this sounds funny today.

Nearly every plant known to the American settlers proved to have multiple uses, not only for eating and medicinal purposes, but also as ingredients in fabric dyes, deodorants, seasonings, brewed drinks, insect repellent, and other household products. The settlers relied upon Indian knowledge and customs as well as their own to "grow up" America.

Kitchen Gardens

Food gardens were not like fancy gardens but, of necessity, practical and neatly laid out for the convenience of the housewife who tended and used the crops for her cooking and other kitchen needs.

These kitchen gardens, as they were sometimes called, were located next to the house so fresh crops could be picked as needed. The garden was square in shape, and fenced to keep hungry unwanted animals out. The growing beds inside the garden were also square or rectangular with walk spaces between the crops for easy tending. The beds were raised for drainage, edged with boards and wood stakes, and filled with the richest soil available. The seeds were planted in straight rows and

sometimes fertilized with fish heads, another practice learned from the Indians.

And garlic 'way over there!

The arrangement of the crops also followed common sense. Sweet

smelling herbs and flowers were planted under the house windows and strong smelling herbs and vegetables (onions and garlic, for example) planted as far from the window as possible. Vine plants such as watermelon, pumpkin, and squash, were planted just outside the garden so the wandering and

unpredictable growth of their shoots would not take over the smaller plants in the garden. Beans were planted next to the fence so the vines had something to climb, and big-rooted plants like potatoes were kept away from the shallow-rooted plants like radishes. Frequently, the lettuce, radishes, and

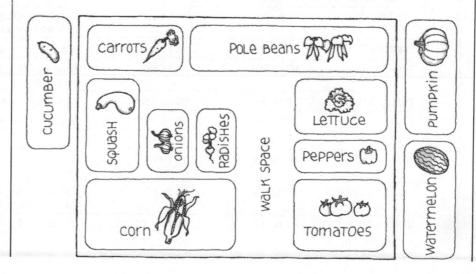

onions were grown in the same bed so they could be harvested together for salads.

Altogether, the kitchen garden was a small but very efficient food factory providing nearly all the vegetable and fruit produce a family needed to survive.

Growing a kitchen garden

Gardening does involve some work, but for most people it is considered pleasant or hobby work. Not only is the activity of gardening healthful in terms of the exercise and fresh air you get, but vegetables picked ripe and eaten while fresh usually taste considerably better and contain more vitamins than crops that have been packed and shipped over great distances.

A small space with rich soil can grow a surprisingly large crop, especially since some vegetables mature from seed in only a few weeks and so repeated crops can be planted throughout the growing season.

The requirements of a successful garden today have not changed much from those of the Early American garden: All plants need good soil, adequate water, sunlight and warmth, proper spacing between plants, and sometimes fertilization. Except for sunlight, everything else can be controlled by the gardener.

Preparing the soil

To some soil is only dirt, but soil suitable for gardening is a natural combination of minerals from rocks, decomposed organic materials, tiny plants and animals, water, and air. Soil is built up gradually, but it may take from over one hundred to nearly one thousand years to add just one inch of new soil to the land.

Your garden crop will be as good as the soil it grows in. Some companies sell soil test kits that tell you exactly what fertilizers and other conditioners your soil may need. But much can be told just by looking at and feeling the soil. If the

---

PLANNING THE GARDEN

Before digging the first spade of dirt, plan the garden. Decide on the size and location, then make a scale drawing showing where you intend to plant what. A kitchen garden of vegetables, fruits, and herbs requires plenty of sunlight, soil with good water drainage, and a minimum of competition from the roots of nearby shrubs and trees. Take care in choosing a proper location.

The following chart will help in planning your garden, but always follow the specific directions on the seed packet for information about your particular region of the country and other helpful planting hints.

Vegetable	Days to Germinate	Days to Harvest	Helpful Hints
CARROTS	7 to 14	65 to 75	
CUCUMBER	7 to 14	50 to 65	grow outside the garden on a fence to conserve space
LEAF LETTUCE	7 to 14	40 to 50	
MELONS	7 to 14	75 to 120	has long vines—grow outside the garden in a sunny area
ONION	10 to 21	95 to 120	plant in loose, sandy soil
PEPPERS	10 to 21	60 to 80	seeds will germinate only in warm soil
POLE BEANS	7 to 14	65 to 100	a pole or fence is needed for support
PUMPKIN	7 to 14	95 to 120	has long vines—grow outside the garden
RADISH	7 to 14	25 to 60	
SUMMER SQUASH	7 to 14	50 to 60	
SWEET CORN	7 to 14	65 to 90	grow in "blocks" of short rows for good pollination between plants
TOMATO	7 to 14	50 to 85	seeds will germinate only in warm soil

soil is hard and doesn't break up easily it probably contains a lot of clay, and that is not good for garden plants. If your soil is mostly clay, add peat moss, manure or compost, and work it well into the soil with a garden rake or hoe. Good garden soil is usually a dark, rich brown color, loose, easy to crumble, and slightly moist.

Most soils will benefit from a treatment of lime worked in well with a spade or rake. However, if you live in California or another far-western state, your soil will probably benefit more from a similar treatment of sulfur.

Prepare the soil for planting by spading it to a depth of about one foot (30 cm.). Break up the loose clods, remove large stones and rocks, and rake the top so it is smooth and level.

Planting the seeds

Use a rake handle to draw in the soil and mark the location of your plantings according to your plan. Then, still using the rake handle, make shallow and straight furrows or grooves in the soil. Sow the seeds of each plant variety according to the instructions on the seed packet, and cover the seeds with a thin layer of soil. Tap the soil firm but don't pack it down hard or the seed sprouts may have difficulty breaking through. Warning: Most seeds that don't come up have been planted too deep.

Caring for the garden

Left alone in good conditions most seeds will germinate and grow to mature, fruitful plants. But growing conditions are not always ideal and you should periodically perform certain garden maintenance tasks:

1. Pull up any weeds that interfere with the growth of your plants or rob them of soil nutrients.

2. Cultivate (loosen and break up) the soil around the plants so it will readily accept water.

3. Fertilize the garden soil once or twice during the growing season using an all-purpose garden fertilizer.

4. If the weather becomes dry and the soil shows signs of drying out, water the garden once a week or more.

5. Some gardeners like to mulch or cover the garden soil to both smother the garden weeds and keep the ground moist. An inch or two layer of grass clippings, straw, hay, peat moss, or old leaves, will make a good garden mulch.

Harvest

This is the big payoff for all your efforts and patience, and by far the easiest part of gardening. Pick off any vegetables as soon as they are ripe, and for best flavor and nutritional content, eat your harvest as soon as possible. If you intend to freeze or can some of your vegetables, process the food as soon as possible.

Giant sunflowers grow to incredible heights.

Making Compost

As plants grow they take nutrients from the soil, nutrients that somehow must be replaced if crops are to be grown in the same soil again. Nature takes care to replenish to some degree through decaying roots, leaves, and animal waste, and the action of worms that burrow holes in the soil to loosen it and allow air and water to enter.

But man can also improve the soil. One of the best ways to replace nutrients and make the soil more workable is to add compost. You make compost yourself from a mixture of organic materials such as grass clippings, weeds, vegetable scraps from the kitchen, dead foliage and flowers, and even shredded newspaper.

The organic material decays over a period of time greatly diminishing in volume and eventually producing a rich soil-like material full of minerals and other chemical foods that encourage good plant growth. Compost alone is too rich for growing most plants, but worked into the garden soil it is an excellent conditioner and fertilizer. Even desert sand can be made into plant-growing soil by mixing with compost.

A place where no one looks

To make a compost pile select an inconspicuous location *away from the house*. Sometimes a compost pile can look like a miniature garbage dump and you would not want to offend anyone's sense of beauty!

Dig a shallow pit in the ground a

FOR POTATOES AND TOMATOES, THANK YOU, THOMAS JEFFERSON!

Two well-known American foods, the white potato and the tomato, were once considered deadly poisonous and therefore inedible. The green potato plant leaves and the round red tomato fruit were grown in home gardens only as ornamental plants, if they were grown at all. The Indians did not eat these foods and that was probably considered proof enough.

The acceptance of both the white potato—or Virginia potato, as it was known in Early America—and the tomato, or tomata as it was then called, is credited to none other than Thomas Jefferson, the third president of the United States.

Jefferson spent much of his time as a botanist, experimenting with various types of unusual plants. It was not until the late eighteenth century that Thomas Jefferson convinced his fellow Americans that the Virginia potato was a healthy food, easy to grow, and quite tasty in various preparations. However, widespread acceptance was slow and even then the custom was to boil the potatoes so the "poison" would be released into the cooking water making the potato safe to eat. The "poisonous" cooking water was, of course, carefully discarded.

It took a while longer for Americans to accept the tomato. After all, no one really wanted to test their belief that the fruit was poisonous and possibly die!

Once again, Thomas Jefferson tried to introduce the tomato, and although he is credited with that, the fruit was not commonly eaten by Americans for at least another hundred years. Actually, as one

legend goes, it was not until a man in Salem, New Jersey, stood in the public square courageously eating raw tomatoes in front of a big audience—without dying or becoming ill—that Americans were truly convinced of the goodness of the delicious fruit.

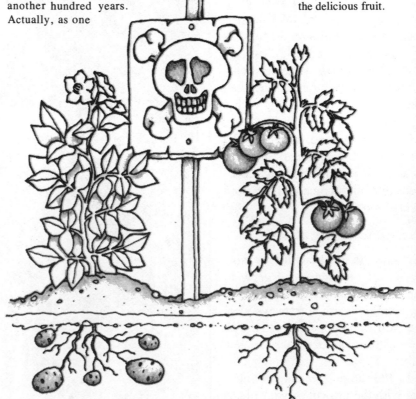

SOIL
FERTILIZER
LIME

ORGANIC
MATERIAL

few feet in diameter and then fill the pit with one or a variety of the organic materials mentioned above. Add a thin layer each of lime and garden fertilizer, cover the pile with a layer of earth, then wet the pile down thoroughly with water.

In a short time the pile will begin to rot, you may then continue to add organic material to it as you wish. To encourage rotting, be sure to keep the compost pile moist— not soggy—and every few months or so turn the pile with a rake or garden fork to be sure any newly added material gets to the center of the heap where decomposition is taking place most rapidly. A compost pile started in the summer will be ripe and ready to be used in the garden the following spring.

SCARECROW

A farmer in Early America had to contend with many enemies to his crops. Although he could do little to control the weather, harmful plant diseases, or insects, the farmer was constantly waging a battle of wits with the birds that would swoop down to his fields and eat the newly planted seed or freshly sprouted seedlings.

Indeed, so bothersome were the birds that a wise farmer would plant four seeds in each hole—one to grow, one for the worms, and two for the birds. By far, the most troublesome bird to the farmer was the crow who was clever enough to scratch out buried seeds and pull up

seedlings. And so most of the farmer's inventions to ward off the birds were called scarecrows.

Scarecrows were not new to Early America. The native Indians would often have a live man stand in a planted field, waving his arms, tossing stones, and letting out loud

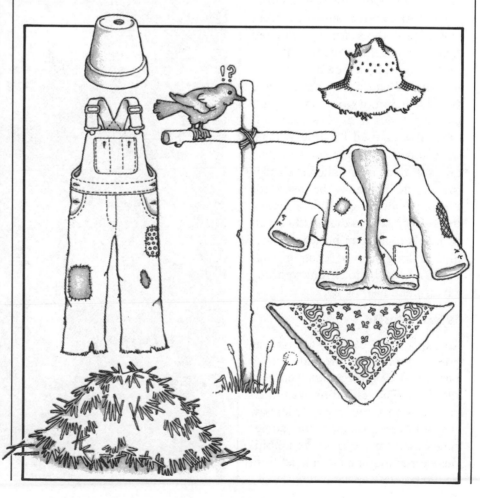

whooping yells to scare off the threatening birds. Of course, most farmers could not afford to use a man only as a scarecrow, so he would erect a stuffed figure of a man. Unfortunately for the farmer, the birds were not so dumb. For a day or two they might be frightened away, but when the lifeless figure did not seem to harm them, the birds would quickly learn to ignore it and go about eating the seed.

The well-dressed scarecrow

The best scarecrows were those who wore bright-colored clothes, streamers, bright pieces of metal, and noise-making bells. There is even a farmer's folktale about a scarecrow so fearsome looking that the birds brought back all the seed they had taken the year before. But most of the time the farmer found it necessary to move his scarecrow to a new location or change its clothes every few days for the stuffed figures to have any effect at all.

The typical scarecrow was an improvised and hastily constructed figure made from worn out, cast-off clothing. Men's clothes were almost always used because women were much more reluctant to give up even their most tattered clothes that could someday be used for making another garment. Usually the scarecrow was dressed in a pair of patched and sun-bleached overalls, a long-sleeved coat or shirt (with all the buttons removed and saved), and a straw hat.

What a build

To support the clothes, a post was pounded into the ground with a horizontal crosspiece attached near the top. The clothing was then stuffed with straw, grass or leaves. An old broom or mop was sometimes used for the head; an ambitious farmer might make a head from an old pot with a face painted on it.

Once in a while a farmer would wake up to find the clothes on his scarecrow missing, and he could only assume that sometime during the night a poor wanderer had found the scarecrow's clothes better than his own and made off with them.

Actually, the familiar farmer's scarecrow has not changed at all since Early America, though his use is now limited for the most part to the family garden. Commercial farmers today use seeds treated with special chemicals that birds find quite distasteful. Blasting loudspeakers and even firecrackers keep pesty birds from pulling up the young plants.

Making Your Own Scarecrow

No two scarecrows are ever exactly alike, and indeed each scarecrow can almost be considered a piece of

Imaginative scarecrows keep birds from eating seeds.

American folk art. Detailed instructions are not necessary for making a scarecrow. All you need are some old clothes and other discards around the house, a bit of stuffing, and a touch of imagination.

First select a location in the garden where the scarecrow will be easily seen. Erect a cross made from two sticks such as fallen branches or broom handles. Pound the longer stick into the ground so that it holds firm and attach the other stick crosswise using twine or strong string.

Depending on what type of clothes you will be using, it is sometimes best to put the upright post through a pants leg before attaching the crosspiece. A few large safety pins (or diaper pins) will come in handy for attaching the pants to a jacket or shirt, or you could make a pair of suspenders to hold up the pants.

If you want the scarecrow to really keep the birds away, try to use bright-colored clothing that will wave with the breeze. Belts, neckties, scarves, play jewelry, pieces of aluminum foil, or any bright accessories will liven up your scarecrow and make him a more visible deterrent to the birds.

Hay, dried grass clippings, or fallen leaves can be used to stuff the scarecrow. In a pinch you can use crumpled up newspaper for stuffing, but you will then have a drooping, soggy scarecrow after the first rain.

Finish off the scarecrow with a head and maybe a face. Some things you might use for the head are an empty bleach bottle, a stuffed plastic bag, a flowerpot, a pie pan, or even an old Halloween mask.

And if you really want a true-blue American scarecrow, top him off with a straw hat.

PEANUTS

Peanuts first came to America via ships sailing from Africa. They were used as a cheap and plentiful food for the slaves. The goober, as the Africans called the nut, was nutritious and easy to grow, especially in the South where most Africans were brought as slaves to work the fields. The peanut is not a nut, in fact, but rather a pea that looks like a nut. And so Americans coined a new name for the goober pea and called it the peanut.

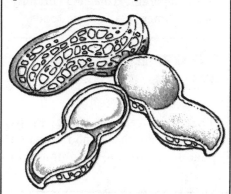

Like the potato and tomato, which took time to find acceptance in America, the peanut was at first very much ignored as a valuable food. Indeed, it was a strange and nearly disastrous turn of events that eventually brought the peanut to American fame.

"When them cotton fields get rotten"

About one hundred years ago cotton was by far the most important crop and industry in the southern states of America. Then came the destructive boll weevil. This small bug feeds on the cotton plant and then infests the soft, fluffy cotton pods with millions of tiny eggs. In quick order, entire fields of cotton were laid to waste and the southern cotton farmers were faced with ruin.

To the rescue came a black

American scientist, George Washington Carver. Carver was fascinated by the seemingly limitless

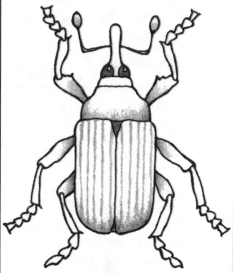

uses of the peanut. In his laboratory at the Tuskegee Institute in Alabama, Carver devised over a hundred ways of preparing the peanut as food, including peanut cheese, peanut fudge, peanut butter, peanut soup, and even peanut ice cream. Carver was motivated by a desire to find ways poor and malnourished people might use the plentiful ground-nut.

With the sudden destruction of the cotton crop by the boll weevil, George Washington Carver urged farmers to burn off their infested cotton and plant peanuts, which were immune to the boll weevil and could restore the land.

It may taste like chicken

At first no one really listened. "Nothing that grows that easily can be very good" was the common attitude. So to dramatize his confidence in the peanut, Carver persuaded another black American, Booker T. Washington, to invite a number of influential southern businessmen to lunch. The meal prepared under Carver's direction consisted of soup, mock chicken, creamed vegetable, bread, salad, ice cream, candy, cookies, and coffee. Everything on the menu had been made from peanuts. When Washington and Carver announced their deception, the guests burst into applause.

Peanuts win out

Faced with continued destruction by the boll weevil, and encouraged by Carver's claims, farmers and whole communities began to abandon cotton and started planting peanuts. The peanut was successfully grown and farmers became anxious to find other uses for it so that the new industry might widen its markets. Carver continued his experiments. He ground, cooked, and squeezed the peanut to make peanut oil, then blended the oil with other ingredients to make peanut margarine, soap, cooking and rubbing oils, and even cosmetics. From the red peanut skin Carver made paper; from the hulls

he made a soil conditioner, insulating building board, fuel briquettes and synthetic marble; and from the nut came ink, dyes, shoe polish, shaving cream, bleach—altogether nearly three hundred products.

There stands today on the main street of Enterprise, Alabama, a monument "In profound appreciation of the boll weevil and what it has done." Almost destroyed agriculturally by the ravages of the boll weevil, Enterprise became prosperous due to the peanut. The peanut is now one of America's most important crops and certainly one of America's favorite foods.

Grow a Peanut Plant

There are several varieties of peanuts, but the Jumbo Virginia peanut is the most common in

America and the type you are probably most familiar with.

The peanut inside the shell is the seed that is planted to grow a new peanut plant, although some farmers prefer to just crack the outer shell and plant the shell and seed together. If you buy peanut seeds, you will get the peanut only. If you can find unshelled raw peanuts (not roasted), you might want to try to plant using the shell-and-seed method.

In either case you have a choice of growing peanuts outside or indoors, depending on the climate of your region and the season. Peanut plants require four to five months of warm, frost-free growing with plenty of rain. If you live in a warm climate, that should be no problem. But for the rest of the country, indoor growing in large deep pots is preferable.

The soil you use should be loose and sandy, but nearly any soil that

will grow other crops will grow peanuts. The particular type of soil in your region will determine the color of the shell, from light tan to dark brown. Spade and loosen the soil, then plant the peanut seeds about two inches (5 cm.) deep. For garden planting, place the seeds about six inches (15 cm.) apart, and separate the rows by three feet (1 m.).

What a way to grow!

Peanut plants are interestingly unusual in the way they grow. From the seeds sprout long, slender, and hairy shoots that develop flowers (like many other plants). As the flower withers, a stalk or peg comes out of the flower and grows

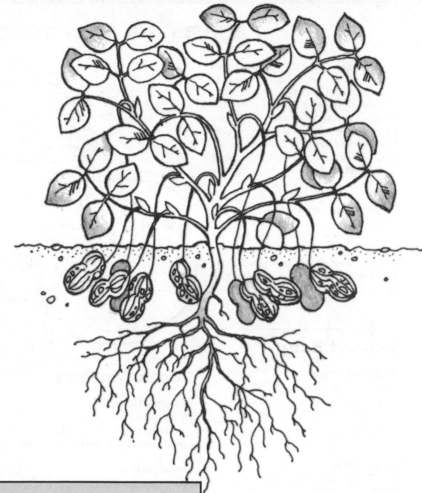

Although most peanuts arrive two-to-a-shell, some come as singles, some as triples, and some in strange shapes.

down into the soil. The "seed" inside the flower travels through the peg where it develops underground into the shell pod with the peanut inside.

After at least a hundred and twenty days of growing, or before the first frost, dig up the entire peanut plant and let it air dry (for a few weeks if you can wait) before removing the shell pods.

Crack open a few shells and eat the peanuts—they will probably taste strange (they may remind you of raw peas). The peanuts in shells that you buy in the food market are roasted to give a crunchy taste. Place the peanuts, in shells, on an oven pan and roast them at 350°F. (175°C.) for about twenty to thirty minutes.

RECIPES FOR A PEANUT DINNER

Below are five selected peanut recipes for a complete peanut meal. They are adapted from George Washington Carver's bulletin suggesting one hundred and five delicious dishes, all using the peanut. It was Carver's wish "that every farmer will learn to appreciate [the peanut] and raise large quantities for his own consumption; and . . . that the city folk will find the diet not only wholesome, satisfying, healthful and appetizing, but very economical."

In preparing these recipes, use only peanuts bought in the shell (you can use roasted, but raw peanuts are preferable) and not the salted cocktail peanuts usually bought in a can.

Peanut Soup

Ingredients
1 cup peanuts (shelled)
1 qt. milk
2 tsp. flour
2 tsp. butter
salt and pepper to taste

Utensils
measuring cups and spoons
2-quart saucepan
blender

1. Cook the peanuts until soft in simmering water. Remove the skins and mash, grind, or blend the nuts until very fine.

2. Let the milk come to a boil and add the peanuts. Cook the milk and peanut mixture slowly for twenty minutes.

3. Add a little of the peanut milk to the flour and stir to make a paste; add the remaining milk and put over a low flame.

4. Add butter to the soup; season with salt and pepper to taste; serve when hot.

Peanut Salad with Bananas

Slice bananas and spread them out on lettuce leaves. Sprinkle liberally with chopped peanuts and serve with mayonnaise or plain salad dressing.

Mock Chicken

Ingredients
1 cup peanuts
1 whole egg plus 1 egg white
rolled bread crumbs or cracker dust
salt
sweet potatoes
peanut oil for frying

Utensils
measuring cups and spoons
nut or meat grinder
mixing bowl
knife
frying pan

1. Blanch a sufficient number of peanuts (drop them into boiling water, allow water to return to a boil and remove the nuts). The amount is a matter of personal judgment; start with about one cup.

2. Grind the nuts until they are quite oily; stir in one well-beaten egg. The consistency of the peanut mixture should be that of a thickish peanut butter. If it is too thin, thicken it with rolled bread crumbs or cracker dust. Stir in a little salt.

3. Boil some sweet potatoes until soft. Peel and cut the potatoes in thin slices and spread generously with the peanut mixture.

4. Dip the slices in white of egg and fry to a nice chicken-brown in hot peanut oil. Serve hot.

Peanut Cookies

Ingredients
½ cup butter
1 cup sugar
2 eggs
1 cup milk
1 tsp. baking powder
1 tsp. vanilla
1½ cups ground peanuts

Utensils
measuring cups and spoons
wooden spoon
mixing bowl
cookie sheet

1. Preheat the oven to 375° (190°C). While it is heating, cream the butter and sugar (beat them together until light and somewhat fluffy). Beat the eggs thoroughly and add them to the butter/sugar mixture.

2. Add the milk and flour alternately by thirds, stirring after each addition. Add the baking powder, then stir in the vanilla.

3. Add the peanuts and drop by the spoonful onto a well-greased cookie sheet. Bake in the oven for ten minutes.

Peanut Candy

Ingredients
2 cups sugar
1 cup roasted, skinless peanuts

Utensils
measuring cups and spoons
frying pan
wooden spoon
shallow dish

1. Melt the sugar slowly in a frying pan, stirring constantly.

2. Butter a shallow dish, and cover the bottom with the roasted and cleaned nuts; pour the melted sugar over them.

3. Set aside. When cool, break into pieces, and serve.

These recipes were adapted slightly from Carver, G.W., *How to Grow the Peanut and 105 Ways of Preparing it for Human Consumption*, Tuskegee Normal and Industrial Institute Experiment Station Bulletin No. 31 (Alabama, Tuskegee Institute, March, 1916) pp. 10, 13, 19, 25, 26.

NATURE GAMES

It is nearly impossible for a kid to walk through a yard, a field, or just a vacant lot without picking a flower, plucking off a leaf, or uprooting a stem. Nature often provides the materials for play; you supply the only tools necessary, your hands and imagination.

Nature games are usually meant to be played only in passing as simple amusements for yourself, then left behind. Many of these games, like certain children's jokes, are spontaneously rediscovered by each new generation. But the joys of these simple crafts are rarely forgotten.

Did you ever spend an hour looking for a four-leaf clover or pulling the petals off a daisy to see if "he loves me" or "he loves me not"? Have you ever been tickled under your chin with a buttercup, sucked the nectar from a honeysuckle, or tried to catch a snowflake to see its pretty design? Have you ever followed a floating milkweed to find where it would go? Just about everyone has done some or all of these things. America's children have always played and been amused with simple nature games. Here are a few.

Leaf collecting in the fall when leaves turn color.

Daisy Chains

These are fun to wear in your hair, around your wrist or neck.

1. Pick a bunch of long-stemmed daisies, say fifteen or twenty. Daisies bloom mostly in early summer, so if that is not convenient, any long-stemmed wild-flower will do.

2. Hold one of the daisies upright in front of you and place another daisy over the first cross-wise, Fig.1.

3. Bend the stem of the second daisy under and around the stem of the first, then up and over its own stem, Fig. 2. Pull the twisted stem so that it wraps knot-like around the first.

4. Now add a third daisy, a fourth, and so on "knotting" each in the same manner as you did the second daisy, Fig. 3, until you have a daisy chain that will fit around your wrist, neck, head, or wherever.

5. Join together the ends of the daisy chain by twisting a few of the loose stem ends around the over-lapping ends and tuck the stem ends into the bundle, Fig. 4.

Burr Building

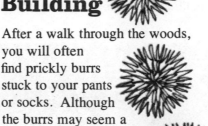

After a walk through the woods, you will often find prickly burrs stuck to your pants or socks. Although the burrs may seem a nuisance and sometimes uncomfortable if the tiny quills stick in your skin, they can be used for play-building all kinds of things. You can build a burr ball, burr stick figures, a burr building, or what-ever looks good to you. Simply press the burrs together and they stay attached, Fig. 5. Add burrs to burrs to make whatever you'd like.

Fig. 5

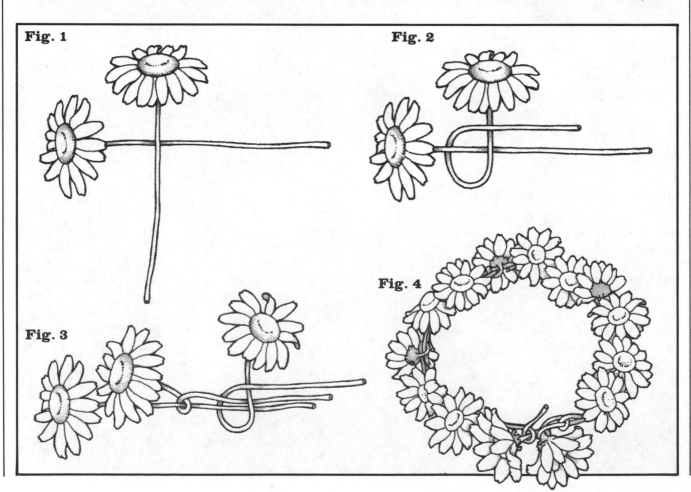

Fig. 1

Fig. 2

Fig. 3

Fig. 4

Acorn-top Finger Puppets

The simplest costume can transform one of your fingers into a play puppet. Put an acorn top "hat" on your fingertip and you have a finger puppet, Fig. 6. Your imagination does the rest. Draw eyes or a mouth on your fingers, if you wish. Make two finger puppets, just to see what kind of conversation they make.

Fig. 6

Seed-head Shooters

Some kinds of wildflowers have seed heads left at the tops of their stems when the petals have fallen off. Pull up a long-stemmed seed head and twist the stem around and over itself as shown, Fig. 7.

Fig. 7

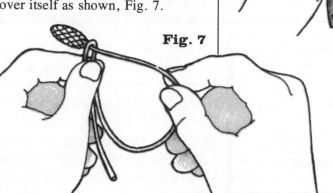

Using the thumb and first finger of one hand, grip the bent stem near the seed head, then in a quick, snapping motion of your other hand, pull the seed head through the bent stem loop. Depending on your skill, the seed head will shoot out a few feet or several yards, maybe even hit a target.

Grass-blade Whistle

Some people can do it and others just cannot, but at least give it a try. Pluck a long, flat blade of grass and hold it tight and taut between the edges of both thumbs, Fig. 8. The blade of grass should be in the middle of the gap created between your thumbs.

Put your lips up against your thumbs and blow hard through the gap. If you do it just right, the noise will sound like anything from a noisy mouse to a squawking elephant.

Fig. 8

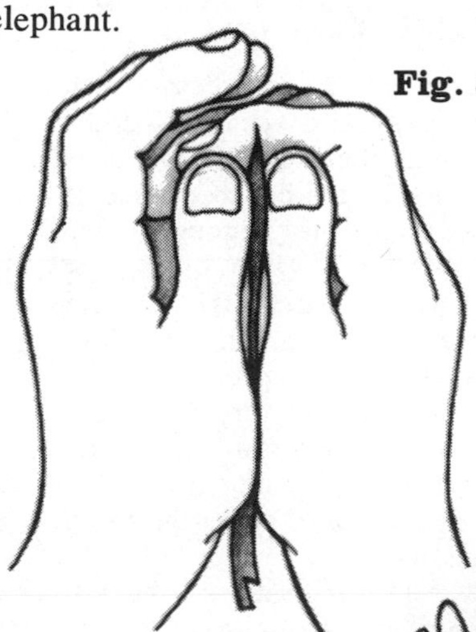

Maple-seed Claws and Noses

Maple seeds are a bit different from most seeds because they have wings! The wing on each seed causes it to fall gently from the tree to the ground. If you drop a maple seed it will spin and float down in a helicopter sort of way, and that itself can be fun. But if you split open the fat end of the pod, Fig. 9, you can attach the maple seed to

Fig. 9

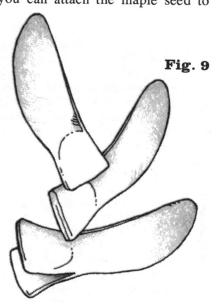

your nose and give it the look of a bird's beak. Or stick maple seeds on the tips of your fingers to make long animal claws, Fig. 10.

Fig. 10

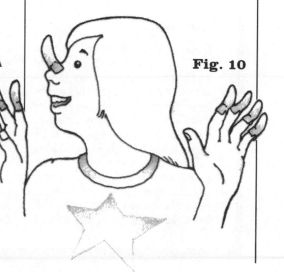

WHY LEAVES CHANGE COLOR

Have you ever wondered why the leaves on trees turn from green to shades of red, yellow, and brown each fall? Why the colors are better some years than others? Or even why leaves are green in the first place? Once each year during the fall season the trees of many regions in America, and especially of New England, produce a spectacular color show that signals the death of the leaves and a dormant winter period for the tree.

Trees, like all living things, need food and energy to live and grow. Leaves are a tree's food factories. Water and minerals are supplied to the leaves through the tree's root system and through a series of veins that go up the tree trunk, out the branches, and into each leaf. All leaves contain a green pigment called chlorophyll, which has the ability to absorb energy from sunlight and turn the water and minerals into a starch food for the tree.

Leaf food

During the summer months when there are long days and warm temperatures, the leaves are busy making food, but as the days of sunlight grow shorter and the weather becomes cooler, the leaf-factories begin to slow down until the process of making food stops completely. The green chlorophyll is no longer needed and slowly disappears from the leaves. The reds, yellows, and browns of fall foliage appear. Where do the colors come from? They were there all the time.

Leaves contain yellow, orange, and brown pigments that are always present in the leaf but remain hidden by the strong chlorophyll green in summer. The colors appear only when the green chlorophyll fades.

As the leaves turn color, the tree pulls any remaining food out of them, storing it to survive during the winter months. The red shades of some fall leaves appear when the sugar produced by the leaves gets trapped in them rather than returning to the tree. The sugar dissolves in the sap of the leaf and turns it red, orange, or purple. Some leaves have no color pigments except for the chlorophyll and just turn a dull shade of brown before drying up.

Subtle shedding

Trees called evergreens—such as pines and spruces—don't drop all their needle-like leaves during the fall but shed some of them continously throughout the year. They grow back new "leaves" during the warmer months. Evergreens, as their name implies, appear green all year round. In very warm climates, many broad-leaved trees drop only some of their leaves at a time and also appear green all year round.

The intensity of the fall colors varies from year to year depending on fall weather conditions. With frosty weather, the colors may not be as varied. Cloudy, rainy weather produces dull shades of red. Warm, humid conditions produce brightly colored but speckled leaves. Dry, sunny, fall weather produces the most spectacular colors of all.

FROG JUMPING

Each June since 1955 a frog jumping contest takes place on the grounds of the Mark Twain Memorial in Hartford, Connecticut. Mostly just for fun, it's also in honor of Mark Twain and his story, *The Celebrated Jumping Frog of Calaveras County*. This is America's "official" frog jumping contest and is complete with regulation jumping arenas, frog stables, judges, and distance measures. Here are the official rules implemented for the purpose of being fair to all competitors and their frogs, and to certify any new distance records that may be set.

1. Contestants may be any boy or girl between the ages of six and sixteen.

2. The frog must be in good physical condition and show no evidence of being caught with a hook and line or of being kept in an inhumane fashion.

3. All frogs must be identified and registered before the jump. Each entry will get a number tag which must be presented to the judges at the time of the jump-off.

4. Frogs may be kept in the frog stable until starting time. There are no stable fees.

5. Each frog will be given three consecutive jumps and the frog's official distance will be measured in a straight line from the starting point to the end of the third hop. The longest distance determines the winner. The record jump, by the way, is held by an unnamed frog at 135 inches (343 cm.).

Other than the official rules, there are certain suggestions regarding the jumping arena as well as a few helpful hints and techniques that those involved in the sport of frog jumping find useful.

The jumping arena should be a grassy (but mowed) area at least 9 feet by 12 feet (approximately 2¾ by 3½ meters) and roped off so spectators can see and the jumping frogs are out of danger of people's misplaced feet.

Of course, you may modify these rules and regulations as you wish for your own frog jumping contest. You don't need fancy equipment, just an area set aside for jumping. And, of course, you need some frogs.

How to Catch a Frog

First you need to know the difference between a frog and a toad, because only frogs should be used for jumping contests. There are many species of frogs in all sizes and colors, but the most common frogs in America are usually some shade of green, whereas toads are brown

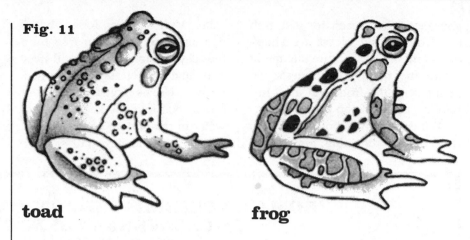

Fig. 11

toad   **frog**

with bumps or "warts" all over their bodies, Fig. 11. Frogs are found in or near water but toads are nearly always found on dry land. And frogs are usually larger than toads, especially the most common frog in America, the bullfrog.

It is most likely that you will spot a frog in or near a pond or stream. Frogs can usually be seen sunning themselves, perched on rocks and fallen trees by the water's edge. It is nearly impossible to sneak up on a frog and try to catch him with your hands without the frog avoiding capture by jump-

ing away at the last moment. Frogs are very smart that way. It is usually best to use a net on the end of a long pole, and even then you will need to work at it slowly and with patience. Frogs are just not that easy to catch.

Nighttime catching

There is another even better way to catch a frog but it must be done at night. Using a flashlight with a strong, bright beam, search the water's edge for a frog. When you spot one, keep the light pointed at the frog's eyes while you slowly

THE FROG-JUMPING CONTEST

At one end of the arena you have chosen for the contest place a launching pad made from a Turkish towel with a bull's-eye starting spot marked in the center, Fig. 12.

To jump a frog, first wet it well with water, then place it on the center-mark of the launching pad. The frog's owner must now encourage the frog to jump, by either dumping water on it, tickling the frog with a feather, or abruptly slapping the ground just behind it. Whichever method you use, make certain the frog is not injured in any way. Distances jumped may be measured or judged by an impartial parent or non-frog-owning kid.

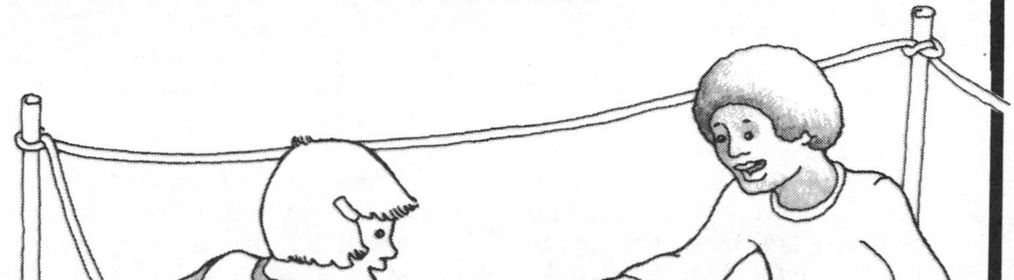

Fig. 12

approach, then reach for and grab him from behind. Never use a hook or any method of capture that might injure the frog! Once caught, be gentle with the frog, and most important, always keep your frog wet.

You can jump and play with your frog before returning him to the water where he was found, but if you intend to keep your frog for a few days or longer, you will need to build a comfortable environment for him. Use as large a container or box as possible and keep a tray of water in the bottom of it, Fig. 13. The box should have tall sides to keep the frog from jumping out or a lid with air holes punched in it so the frog can breathe. Punch holes in the side of the box as well, and keep the frog box out of the direct heat of the sun.

Now you will need some sort of food to feed your frog. Earth-

FROM THE CELEBRATED JUMPING FROG OF CALAVERAS COUNTY BY MARK TWAIN

"...[Smiley] ketched a frog one day, and took him home, and said he cal'lated to educate him; and so he never done nothing for three months but set in his back yard and learn that frog to jump. And you bet you he *did* learn him, too. He'd give him a little punch behind, and the next minute you'd see that frog whirling in the air like a doughnut—see him turn one summerset, or maybe a couple, if he got a good start, and come down flat-footed and all right, like a cat. . . .Why, I've seen him set Dan'l Webster down here on this floor—Dan'l Webster was the name of the frog—and sing out, 'Flies, Dan'l, flies!' and quicker'n you could wink he'd spring straight up and snake a fly off'n the counter there, and flop down on the floor ag'in as solid as a gob of mud. . . .And when it came to fair and square jumping on a dead level, he could get over more ground at one straddle than any animal of his breed you ever see. . . ."Well, Smiley kep' the beast in a little lattice box, and he used to fetch him down town sometimes and lay for a bet. One day a feller—a stranger in the camp, he was—come across him with his box, and says:

"What might it be that you've got in the box?

"And Smiley says, sorter indifferent-like: 'It might be a parrot, or it might be a canary, maybe, but it ain't—it's only just a frog.'

"And the feller took it, and looked at it careful, and turned it round this way and that, and says: 'H'm—so 'tis. Well, what's *he* good for?'

"'Well,' Smiley says, easy and careless, 'he's good enough for *one* thing, I should judge—he can out-jump any frog in Calaveras county.'

"The feller took the box again, and took another long, particular look, and give it back to Smiley, and says, very deliberate, 'Well,' he says, 'I don't see no p'ints about that frog that's any better'n any other frog.'

"'Maybe, you don't,' Smiley says. 'Maybe you understand frogs and maybe you don't understand 'em; maybe you've had experience, and maybe you ain't only a amature, as it were. Anyways, I've got *my* opinion, and I'll resk forty dollars that he can outjump any frog in Calaveras county.'

"And the feller studied a minute, and then says, kinder sad like, 'Well, I'm only a stranger here, and I 'ain't got no frog; but if I had a frog, I'd bet you.'

"And then Smiley says, 'That's all right—that's all right—if you'll hold my box a minute, I'll go and get you a frog.' And so the feller took the box, and put up his forty dollars along with Smiley's and set down to wait.

"So he set there a good while thinking to hisself, and then he got the frog out and prized his mouth open and took a teaspoon and filled him full of quail shot—filled him pretty near up to his chin—and set him on the floor. Smiley he went to the swamp and slopped around in the mud for a long time, and finally he ketched a frog, and fetched him in, and give him to this feller, and says:

"'Now, if you're ready, set him alongside of Dan'l, with his forepaws just even with Dan'l's, and I'll give the word.' Then he says, 'One—two—three—*git!*' and him and the feller touched up the frogs from behind, and the new frog hopped off lively, but Dan'l give a heave, and hysted up his shoulders—so—like a Frenchman, but it warn't no use—he couldn't budge; he was planted as solid as a church, and he couldn't no more stir than if he was anchored out. Smiley was a good deal surprised, and he was disgusted too, but he didn't have no idea what the matter was, of course.

"The feller took the money and started away; and when he was going out at the door, he sorter jerked his thumb over his shoulder—so—at Dan'l, and says again, very deliberate, 'Well,' he says, '*I* don't see no p'ints about that frog that's any better'n any other frog. . . .'"

Clemens, Samuel L., *Mark Twain*, Vol. 23: *Sketches Old and New* (New York, P.F. Collier & Son, 1875, 1899, 1903, 1917).

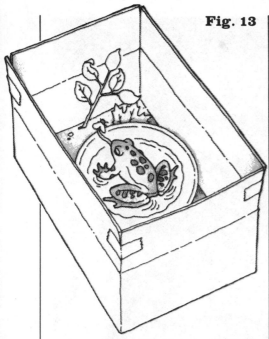

Fig. 13

worms, flies, tadpoles, and small fish are all part of the frog's natural diet. But what a frog actually wants to eat sometimes depends on the season of the year, so if your frog won't eat one of the foods you have provided, just try something else. If you watch your frog eat you can observe his rather interesting and skillful technique. The frog's tongue is very long, attached to the front of his mouth and folded back in his throat. When feeding, the frog flips out its tongue with lightning speed, "grabs" his food, and flips it back into his mouth.

Make a Fly Catcher

Common houseflies are a good food and diet for your frog, but catching flies is not so easy unless you use a fly catcher. Here is how to make one.

Materials

bait (raw meat)
saucer
2 twigs or pencils
widemouthed glass jar
cardboard

1. To attract the flies, put a small piece of raw meat as bait in the center of a saucer.

2. Straddle the saucer with two twigs or pencils, one on either side of the bait, Fig. 14.

3. Place the widemouthed jar upside down over the bait and support it on the twigs.

4. Now wait patiently until a few flies have been attracted to the bait, then "scare" the flies by approaching or touching the trap. The flies will try to get away and a few will inadvertently fly up into the jar. Simply slip a piece of cardboard or stiff paper under the open mouth of the jar and the flies are trapped. To keep the flies captive and easy to handle, put a small amount of water in the jar and shake it up. The flies' wings will become wet and heavy so they cannot fly away when you dump them into the frog box.

Fig. 14

FAMILY PETS

In Early America farm animals became the pets of the children whose responsibility it was to feed them. A farmer might also keep a pet dog that was trained to help in the hunt for wild birds. During the gold-rush days, miners kept pet cats to catch the rats and mice that infested the bunkhouses.

Through the years Americans have kept parrots, goldfish, hamsters, squirrels, parakeets, gerbils, guppies, canaries, even monkeys and skunks (not to mention dogs and cats) as pets. No other people in the world have as many pets as we Americans do. It seems nearly impossible in America for a kid to grow up without having at least one, and probably several pets. We accept all types of living creatures as pets; kids usually want to tame every animal they see or find.

Enjoying your pet

A pet is kept for pleasure, and the pleasure should be mutual. There are, therefore, several considerations to be kept in mind before making your choice.

Some pets are passive and may become boring to their owner after a time. Some pets require more care and time than you may be willing to give. Some pets can be easily trained, and others not at all. Remember, pets cost money to buy, to house, to feed, and to cure if they get sick. Some pets, like fish, usually require a major initial investment in equipment, but from then on the cost of maintaining them is minimal. On the other hand, a St. Bernard dog, for example, is not only expensive to buy, but eats lots of food every day.

Sometimes your pet won't eat the food you have supplied. Try a variety of foods to see what your pet *will* eat. Once you have discovered your pet's favorite food, try to stick with it. Pets, unlike people, are perfectly content to stay with an unchanging diet.

Any pet can be troublesome at times, but if you or your family are willing to spend the time necessary to house, feed, train, and care for

Cats make elegant and furry pets.

your pet, the rewards in accomplishment and companionship will feel very good.

Pets You Don't Own

Some pets you don't own, but you can make their friendship and call them your pets anyway. A wild animal lives in nature where it finds all its necessities like food and shelter. You don't have to "own" a wild animal to make it your pet. You can make friends with an animal by just supplying him food in the same place every day. And if you are careful to hide or stay

motionless, you can watch the animal while it is eating. The animal will learn to expect its feeding, and return to the spot you have chosen nearly every day. But be careful! Some wild animals will bite if you approach them too closely or try to pet them. If you decide to keep a wild animal as a pet rather than for observation only, try to catch an animal as young in life as it is possible for it to live without its parents. Wild animals more easily accept human companionship and training while they are still very young. Some states have laws that prohibit people from keeping wild animals as pets. If you are in doubt, check with your local state game commis-

sion. Sometimes you can get a special permit to keep a wild animal.

A varied selection

If you live in a city where there are pigeons, regular feedings of bread crumbs, seeds, or even popcorn will soon make the pigeons your "pets." You will begin to recognize certain particular pigeons, and maybe even consider one of them a special friend.

Raccoons are very clever and interesting to watch, but be careful that all you do is watch because they are strong biters. Raccoons feed in the evening, often by lifting the lids off garbage cans and rummaging through the contents. Raw eggs are a favorite raccoon meal,

and by leaving an egg on the ground outside of your window in the night, you will eventually attract a raccoon on a regular basis. It is a good idea to leave a pan of water next to the egg as raccoons like to wash their food before eating it as well as to wash their hands afterwards.

Squirrels are good windowsill feeders, and especially like nuts and birdseed. When a squirrel has become comfortable feeding at your windowsill, it will probably want to come in to see if there is more food around. But be careful, squirrels can cause a lot of damage by knocking things over, and by biting if you try to catch them.

What should I call you?

Wild or not, you will want to come up with a good name for your pet. Gone are the days when most dogs were named Spot and Rover, and pet fish were just called "fish." Today pet owners take pride in naming their pets. A pet name can be a reflection of the animal's looks or personality (Frisky, Jumbo, or Slowpoke) or maybe a name that just goes with the animal's breed name (Leonard Lizard, Thomas Toad). Pets are not choosy about what you name them.

Dog Happy

Even with the huge variety of pets available to Americans, the family dog has always been and still re-mains a strong favorite. No other domestic pet offers such a variety of breeds, sizes, colors, and personalities. There are many decisions to be made in choosing the type of dog you want to have: big or small, long hair or short, lazy or active, watchdog or household pet, and so on. Remember that some breeds need more care than others, eat more, or make more noise. Fortunately, there are several common breeds to choose from, and there is usually a breed to fit your exact requirements.

Be careful of choosing a stray dog as a pet. A dog on the loose without the care and upbringing of a human, or those animals that have been neglected by former owners, may at times turn to its wild instincts and bite or attack. It is best to acquire a dog as a puppy, and give it loving care. Dogs enjoy returning the good feelings.

Bringing up puppy

The early upbringing of a puppy—its first few months of life and the first few months you spend with your new dog—will greatly determine the dog's personality. Right from birth, a dog needs warmth and love from its mother, companionship from its littermates, and an as-

sociation with caring people. The most happy dogs tend to be those that have been home-raised, or raised by a breeder for about three months and then sold directly to you. You can ask a veterinarian or other dog owners for information about breeders or the location of newly born litters of the breed you want. Be careful of dogs offered by the local dog pound or pet shops. (All puppies look cute in the pet shop window, but puppies become adult dogs.) Stray dogs or puppies raised in cages often tend to become nervous and in some ways uncontrollable.

Male or female?

One other decision you will need to make, if you have the choice, is whether to get a male or female dog. There are some differences. In general, a male dog tends to be more active and more likely to wander. Males tend to get into more fights than female dogs, who stay close to their home territory. Female dogs are sometimes more gentle and easier to train.

And, finally, when trying to choose a dog from the litter, don't be too hasty. Spend a little time with the puppies. Watch them play awhile, see which comes to you and acts the friendliest. Also observe the puppies' social habits.

Below is a list of common dog breeds with some of each breed's most important characteristics. (The height in each case is given to the shoulder.) Try to decide which personality features are most important to you and your family and which breed comes closest to having them.

Airedale: An intelligent, devoted pet, and unbeatable watchdog with a keen sense of smell. Excellent in police work. A digger, which may cause a problem with the neighbors. Grows to twenty-four inches tall; forty to seventy-five pounds. Has a wiry coat that needs regular clipping.

Alaskan malamute: Affectionate, devoted companion, and good with children. Tireless and powerful, a good sled dog. Grows to twenty-five inches tall; eighty-five pounds. Has a thick coat that sheds.

American foxhound: Not dependent on human companionship and, therefore, not a good house pet. A good pack dog and scent-hunter, but must be strictly trained. Grows to twenty-two to twenty-five inches tall; fifty to sixty-five pounds. Has a medium length coat.

Basset hound: Easy to control with a good disposition, a one-person dog. A good scent-hunter, but noisy when on a scent. Grows to eleven to fifteen inches tall; thirty to sixty pounds. Has a short coat.

Beagle: Affectionate, but not easily trained. A good scent-hunter, but noisy. Grows to thirteen to fifteen inches tall; twelve to twenty-five pounds. Has a medium-length coat.

Bloodhound: Gentle, shy, and affectionate. An excellent scent-hunter. Grows to twenty-four to twenty-six inches tall; eighty to ninety pounds. Has a short coat.

Boston terrier: Gentle, lively, and intelligent. A good house pet and watchdog. Grows to twelve inches tall; twelve to twenty-five pounds. Has a short, smooth coat.

Boxer: Gentle, alert, fearless, and intelligent. A good guard dog, but

can become lethargic and over-weight with age. Grows to twenty-two to twenty-four inches tall; forty to seventy-five pounds. Has a short coat.

Bulldog: Kind, affectionate, and a good companion. A good watch-dog, but can be a fighter. Grows to fifteen inches tall; thirty to sixty pounds. Has a short coat.

Chihuahua: Alert and intelligent. Eats very little. Does not play well with other dogs. Grows to five inches tall; four to six pounds. Has a smooth, short coat.

Cocker spaniel: Clever, bright and happy. A good household companion. Grows to fourteen to fifteen inches tall; eighteen to twenty-four pounds. Has a long-haired coat that needs grooming and clipping.

Collie: Very intelligent and good with children. Grows to twenty-four to twenty-six inches tall; forty-five to seventy-five pounds. Has a long-haired coat.

Dachshund: Lively and alert, clever and courageous. A good apartment dog. Grows to nine inches tall. Fourteen to sixteen pounds. Generally smooth haired.

Dalmatian: Quiet and well-mannered. Intelligent, willing, and friendly; strong and active. Easily trained. Likes to follow horses. Grows to nineteen to twenty-three

inches tall; thirty to fifty-five pounds. Has a short, clean coat that requires no care.

Doberman pinscher: Alert, intelligent, loyal, and obedient. Easily trained. A strong and fearless watchdog. Grows to twenty-four to twenty-seven inches tall. Sixty-five to seventy-five pounds. Has a short coat.

English setter: Lovable and intelligent; a good family pet. An active, outside dog. Grows to twenty to twenty-five inches tall; fifty to seventy pounds. Has a long coat.

English springer spaniel: Friendly, willing to learn, eager to please and obey. A good family pet. Grows to nineteen to twenty

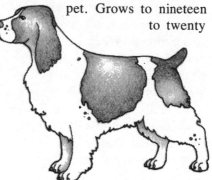

inches tall; forty-five to fifty pounds. Has a medium-length coat and docked tail.

German shepherd: Intelligent, loyal and alert. Strong, fearless guard dog. Easily trained. Grows to twenty to twenty-six inches tall; sixty to eighty-five pounds. Has a heavy coat.

Golden retriever: Alert, gentle, intelligent, and sensitive. Active. A good house pet. Can withstand extreme cold. Grows to twenty-two to twenty-four inches tall; sixty to seventy-five pounds. Long, dense, flat coat.

Great dane: Friendly and affectionate with owners, but difficult to train. Sensitive and resists a change in environment. A one-person dog. Grows to twenty-eight to thirty inches tall; ninety to one hundred and fifty pounds. Has short hair.

Great pyrenees: Faithful, devoted, intelligent, and gentle. Good with children. Good guard dog. Grows to twenty-five to thirty-two inches tall; one hundred to one hundred twenty-five pounds. Has a heavy coat.

Greyhound: Lovable disposition. An excellent house dog and companion if never allowed to chase small animals. Grows to twenty-eight to thirty-one inches tall; sixty to seventy pounds. Has a short coat.

Irish setter: Gentle, lovable, and active. Good scent dog, but difficult to train. Grows to twenty-five to twenty-seven inches tall; fifty to sixty pounds. Has a medium coat.

Irish terrier: Affectionate and very loyal. A good playmate for children and household companion, but a digger. Grows to eighteen inches tall; twenty-five to twenty-seven pounds. Has wiry hair.

Labrador retriever: Alert and active. A good family pet. Can withstand great cold. Grows to twenty-three inches tall; sixty to eighty pounds. Has a short coat.

Maltese: Intelligent and healthy. An active, affectionate lap dog. Eats very little. Grows to five to eight inches tall; three to seven pounds. Has a long, straight coat; needs frequent grooming.

Newfoundland: Intelligent, loyal, and happy disposition. Good with children. A strong swimmer. Good watchdog and easy to train. Grows to twenty-six to twenty-eight inches tall; one hundred and ten to one hundred and fifty pounds. Has a heavy coat.

Old English sheep dog: Intelligent, affectionate, and home-loving. An ideal house dog. Grows to twenty-two to twenty-six inches tall; sixty to eighty pounds. Has a shaggy coat.

Take care of your pet and enter it in a competition.

Pekingese: Good-tempered, calm, and loyal, but stubborn and independent. Grows to six to nine inches tall. Six to fourteen pounds. Has long hair.

Pointer: Alert and even tempered, but not a good house pet. A good scenter. Grows to twenty-four to twenty-six inches tall; forty to seventy pounds. Has a short coat.

Poodle: Active, intelligent, and an exceptionally quick learner. A good companion. Grows to ten to fifteen inches; twelve to twenty-five pounds. Coat needs grooming.

Pug: Alert and affectionate. Requires little care. A good family pet. Grows to eleven inches tall; fourteen to eighteen pounds. Has short hair.

St. Bernard: Intelligent and powerful. A good watchdog and family pet, but frequently drools. Grows to twenty-seven inches tall; eighty to one hundred and eighty pounds. Has a heavy coat.

Samoyed: Affectionate, strong, and a good companion. Grows to eighteen to twenty-two inches tall; forty to sixty pounds. Has a thick coat.

Schnauzer: An intelligent, reliable, high-spirited watchdog and good rat catcher. Grows to twenty-two to twenty-six inches tall; thirty to forty-five pounds. Has tough, wiry hair.

Spanish terrier: Independent and devoted, but a digger. Grows to ten inches tall; seventeen to twenty-five pounds. Has a short, wiry coat.

Siberian husky: Strong and courageous, yet gentle and friendly with children. Clean, no odor, and easy to train. A good watchdog. Grows to twenty-two to twenty-four inches tall; forty to sixty pounds. Has a medium-length coat.

Wirehaired fox terrier: Alert, but often too energetic and playful. A good rat dog, but a digger. Usually not a good family pet. Grows to fifteen inches tall; fifteen to twenty pounds. Has a hard, wiry coat.

Yorkshire terrier: Highly spirited, grows to eight to nine inches tall; four to seven pounds. Long, straight coat that requires frequent grooming.

AMERICA'S PETS

Ants
Bees
Beetles
Chameleons
Canaries
Cats
Caterpillars
Chickens
Chinchillas
Chipmunks
Crickets
Dogs
Ducks
Frogs
Gerbils
Goats
Goldfish
Grasshoppers
Guinea pigs
Hamsters
Horses
Lizards
Mice
Minnows
Monkeys
Myna birds
Parakeets
Parrots
Pigeons
Rabbits
Raccoons
Salamanders
Skunks
Snails
Snakes
Spiders
Tadpoles
Toads
Turtles
Worms

Gerbils reproduce quickly and the babies make cute pets.

BIRD FEEDERS

Wherever you live and whatever the season of the year, there are likely to be several types of wild birds in your neighborhood. And as with so many other wild animals, you can eventually gain the trust of birds and make them your "visiting friends" just by giving them food in the same place every day.

Birds spend much of their time looking for food, so once you have started feeding your neighboorhood birds it is important that you don't suddenly stop, or the birds may not be able to find another source, especially during the winter months. Certain birds will learn to depend on your feeder as their main source of food.

Seasonal diet

There are many foods that birds will eat, but certain foods are better for the bird's diet depending on the season of the year. In the warmer months, a bird meal of bread crumbs or wild birdseed is sufficient. But during the colder months, birds need to eat fatty foods—peanut butter or raw suet—which help keep their bodies warm. Individual birds have food preferences, so it is a good idea to keep a variety of bird foods available year round. In addition to bird seed, bread crumbs, and suet, you might offer berries to your neighborhood birds, or maybe raisins, popcorn, and cut-up pieces of fruit.

Some people who feed the birds just lay the food out on a windowsill or toss it on the lawn. Both locations are good for observing birds feeding, but bird food just tossed outside will probably also attract squirrels and other hungry animals—and the birds will be frightened away. There are several kinds of bird feeders that you can easily make that will keep other wild animals from stealing the food.

Making Bird Feeders

A pine-cone bird feeder can be made by stuffing the cone between its "petals" with a mixture of birdseed and peanut butter and hanging it up by a string, Fig. 15.

Pieces of suet—from the market—can be hung in a plastic mesh bag, Fig. 16.

Fig. 15

Fig. 16

Using a needle and doubled sewing thread, you can string popcorn, raisins, and berries, then wrap the length of threaded bird food around the end of a branch, Figs. 17 and 18.

Place your bird food in a location that is easily visible from a

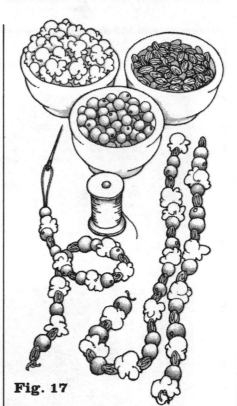

Fig. 17

window. Hang the bird feeder high off the ground so that dogs, squirrels, and raccoons can't get at the food.

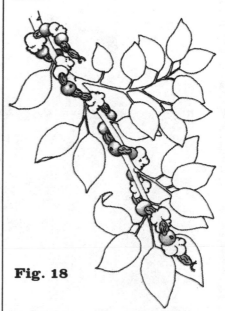

Fig. 18

Sometimes it takes a few days or even a week for the birds to discover your feeder. Be patient, and the same birds that are attracted to your feeder will probably come back every day and even the next season.

BIRDHOUSE POINTERS

If you like the idea of having birds around you but don't care to begin a regular feeding schedule, a birdhouse may be just the thing. A birdhouse becomes a nesting place, which will allow you to watch birds lay eggs, raise their young, and so on.

Not all birds will take to a man-made house, however, and those that do will live in the house for only a few weeks during the spring when they are raising their young. Once the bird has made a nest in a birdhouse and left it, the house must be thoroughly cleaned before another bird will be attracted to it.

The birds don't care what a birdhouse looks like as long as it represents a dry, hollow, safe place from other animals and passing people. But many birdhouses are quite elaborately built to represent castles, log cabins, churches, lighthouses, or even miniature copies of the builder's own home.

The size and number of holes in the birdhouse will determine which type of bird will, possibly, nest there. Single-holed birdhouses will attract chickadees, titmice, bluebirds, house wrens, nuthatches, purple finches, and crested flycatchers, to name a few. Starlings, purple martins, and some tree swallows prefer the apartment-type of house with several homes.

TIME CAPSULES

Although time seems to pass very slowly when you are young and nothing seems to change, everything does in fact change, and we often too quickly forget much of our past. Have you ever looked through the family photo album, or found an old school notebook, and been surprised at how much you had forgotten and maybe how much you have changed? Have you ever spent an afternoon exploring and rummaging through old clothes, furniture, toys, or pictures of your parents or grandparents and tried to imagine what it was like when they were your age? How far back can you remember, and how are things different since then? As all things change in time, we frequently leave behind records or clues as to how it once was. Each of these excerpts of life becomes a "time capsule" to be discovered at some future date.

For future generations

In 1938, at the site of the New York World's Fair (held in 1939), an actual time capsule made of metal was filled with lots of information about our American society at that time and buried fifty feet below the earth, with the specific instruction that it not be opened for five thousand years. A plaque with the following inscription marks the spot:

TIME CAPSULE OF CUPALOY, DEPOSITED ON THE SITE OF THE NEW YORK WORLD'S FAIR ON SEPTEMBER 23, 1938 BY THE WESTINGHOUSE ELECTRIC & MANUFACTURING CO. IF ANYONE SHOULD COME UPON THIS CAPSULE BEFORE THE YEAR A.D. 6939 LET HIM NOT WANTONLY DISTURB IT, FOR TO DO SO WOULD BE TO DEPRIVE THE PEOPLE OF THAT ERA OF THE LEGACY HERE LEFT. CHERISH IT THEREFORE IN A SAFE PLACE.

Cupaloy refers to a metal of almost pure copper from which the capsule was made so it would resist the eroding effects of time. Inside the seven-foot-long time capsule tube is another tube made of glass and covered with wax; inside the glass tube are the objects which were to be preserved. Because the space inside the capsule was relatively small, much of the contents consisted of writing with drawings describing the most advanced products, technological and cultural concepts of the year 1938. There is information about architecture, highways, transportation vehicles, machines and other inventions; facts about the techniques of mass production, our arts and entertainment, games, sports, food, newspapers and magazines; cartoons, descriptions of religions and how the American government works; a history of America; a "key" to reading, speaking and understanding the English language, even diagrams to show what we look like.

But things change quickly

Every age considers itself the most advanced and knowledgeable of any society that preceded it. But only twenty-seven years after the time capsule was buried, such vast changes had occurred in American technology with the invention of home television and space rockets, among many other things, that another and updated capsule was deposited next to the first. And now, today, we could fill yet another capsule with information about America's newest technological and social changes. Even though things don't seem to change very much from day to day, you have only to look back to see that our American way of life does change, and for the better.

A time capsule buried many years ago is filled with lots of surprises.

Your Own Time Capsule

You probably have already collected several "time capsules" from your own past. Maybe you keep an album or shoebox filled with your old report cards, letters, or greeting cards. Maybe your parents have kept some of your baby clothes, a lock of your baby hair, some of the drawings you first made, or what used to be your favorite toy. All of these things can now give you a glimpse of what you were like sometime in the past and how much you have changed since then. If you enjoy remembering and rediscovering your own personal history, you might want to make your own time capsule about your life right now, to be opened up in a few months, or a year, or anytime in the future to see what things have changed. You may want to pick a special day—maybe a holiday or your birthday—on which to make your time capsule.

All about you

First, write a list or just think of the things you would like to put in a time capsule. Which things tell something about the way you and "your world" are now? A photograph of yourself, the ticket stubs from your favorite movie, the newspaper listings of your favorite shows, a list of your favorite things, the newspaper front page of that day, special letters and mementos, and maybe a short message that you write to yourself to be read when the capsule is eventually opened, are some possibilities. The more you include, the more memories you will have later on. And don't forget to write a note to place on the outside of the capsule giving your name, and date, and instructing anyone who finds the time capsule to leave it undisturbed until the day that it is meant to be opened.

Find a good capsule

Now you'll need something to use as a capsule. If you actually plan to bury your time capsule outside somewhere you will need a waterproof container large enough to hold the items you've selected. Glass jars and plastic containers with tight-fitting lids work well, and those egg-shaped pods that hold pantyhose will make a fine mini-capsule if you seal the two halves with tape. Even though the capsule may be sealed tightly, you should still put it into a plastic bag knotted closed before burying the capsule in the ground. If you decide to stash your capsule in the back of a closet, in the attic, the basement, the garage, or any indoor place, just a shoe box or any container with a lid will do. But whatever location you choose, your time capsule should be able to stay undisturbed until the designated time of opening. And finally, so you don't forget about your time capsule or where you put it, make a note or a map to remind you of the location and date of opening. Put the note in a safe place. If your opening date is sometime within the next year or so, you can mark the date on a calendar as a reminder. Now just wait; you'll see just how much you've changed.

Make a hobby of collecting old bottles.

DIGGING FOR BOTTLES

Many of the products of early American industry have been lost due to the natural process of decay and erosion and before their often intriguing histories were recorded. When we no longer have a use for something, we usually throw it away, leave it behind, or get rid of it in some manner. Many things just get lost. But objects don't completely disappear, and eventually nearly everything returns to the surface of the earth. Old houses are torn down, and the leftover old materials are bulldozed into the ground or hauled off to the dump. These "wastes" are buried or used for landfill; many unwanted things are just abandoned in some inconspicuous place (causing a litter problem, unfortunately). Much of what we throw away or loose will naturally decay in time, but some of the materials that man has discovered and learned to manufacture are highly resistant to the effects of time and decay. They just get buried and remain unchanged, waiting to be dug up and found.

One of the most permanent materials to have survived the old and sometimes forgotten trash heaps of Early America is glass, and the most common glass product of Early America was the bottle. Glass may break easily and it may wear down, but it doesn't burn and it won't decompose in the ground. If you want to discover an interesting history of America and go on a treasure hunt at the same time, then try digging for old bottles.

Bottles filled with everything

Glass was one of colonial America's earliest products. Some was made into window glass for buildings, but most American glass factories, or "glass houses" as they were called, molded or blew glass bottles for holding a variety of household liquids. Bottles were used for medicines, wine, water, poison, ink, shoe polish, foodstuffs, fruit, and all sorts of things. But although glass factories did exist in Early America, they were not widespread and their products were somewhat expensive. Each bottle had to be handmade by a skilled glassblower. Initially, families saved their glass bottles and used them over and over again much for the same reason we don't throw away our drinking glasses, cups, and plates after we have used them once. But as glassmaking became an established industry in America and glass bottles became much cheaper to produce, Americans began to develop the habit of buying products already packaged in jars and bottles and throwing away the "empties" when the contents had been used. There were lots of empties, hundreds of thousands of them.

And in so many great shapes

Bottles came in a huge variety of shapes and sizes, each designed for some purpose, or distinctively decorated. There were small perfume bottles with stoppers that could be used as dabbers, bottles shaped flat to be carried in pockets, commemorative bottles with molded designs celebrating historic events, politicians, and famous army officers. There were bottles in the shapes of animals, musical instruments, heads and faces, and bottles to be used as banks when their contents were emptied. There were round bottles and square bottles, bottles as small as your thumb and bottles nearly too large to lift. Bottles were made not only from clear glass but in a variety of colors—mostly blues, greens, amber, and sometimes red.

When you find an old bottle, you may be able to guess what it was used for just by its shape, size, and color, and by whatever patterns are embossed on its sides. A small bottle with a daisy might have held a sweet-smelling perfume, or a bottle in the shape of a coffin probably once contained some type of poison. Old bottles that have survived can give us many interesting clues about the way Americans once lived. Whatever bottle you find, you will discover something of someone's past and you just may be the first person to have touched it since the bottle was thrown away or lost maybe a few hundred years ago. And then maybe you'll just find a familiar Coca-Cola® bottle from not so very long ago.

Where and how to dig

There are no talents needed or "secrets of the trade" to learn to dig for bottles. All you need is a promising site and a little bit of luck. You can start digging in your own backyard and you might find something—but then you might not. You are much more likely to find buried bottles if you've done a little research first. Bottles and other objects are most likely to be found in the places where people have purposely thrown them away. Good digging sites are usually old dumps, in lots, next to buildings, in the "old part" of town, or in the backyard of older homes. If you live in an area that has ghost towns or deserted sections, these too can be good places to dig. Ask the older members of your family where any roadside taverns were once located, or check with the local historical society or in books for other information that might help you choose a good digging site. Also look for areas of new construction where bulldozers and power shovels have already done some of the digging for you. Of course, before you dig anywhere you will need permission from the present owner of the property. You might offer to share some of what you find with the owner for the right to dig on the land. Old bottles can be very valuable.

Some keen sleuthing

Even after you have chosen a site you will need to pick a particular spot to start your digging. You may not be able to see under the ground, but there are several clues to help you find the best spot. Look for pieces of glass and other objects just slightly protruding from the earth's surface where they have been pushed up by the winter frost. Depressions in the ground can also indicate an old compost or rubbish pile that settled over time. Look for sections of a property where the earth has been built up with landfill. If you still can't decide where to start digging, you might try poking around the ground with a long pointed pole. Although a thin steel rod will give you a good clink when you hit glass, a pointed stick or broom handle will also do. Poke around until you strike something curious enough to dig up.

The only tools you need for digging bottles out of the ground are a hand shovel or spade with a rounded tip and a box or pail to carry home your found treasures. Sometimes a rake is also handy to sift through the dirt for small bottles and objects. Wherever you dig, try to be neat. Decide on an area maybe two or three feet square, carefully dig up the sod, if there is any, and put it aside to be replaced when you're through.

Dig in

Start digging but don't be too aggressive with the shovel. Remember that glass breaks—and you also might miss something if you dig too quickly.

The bottles and objects that you do find will probably be dirty and filled with grit. Scrubbing them in water will get most of the dirt off. If the glass has badly caked-on dirt and stains, try soaking it overnight in water with ammonia added. The insides of bottles are a bit tougher to clean. Try filling the bottle with warm soapy water. Then add several small pebbles and shake.

Once you have found an old bottle try to figure out what it was used for. There are several library books with pictures and descriptions of bottles to help you. Finally, display your bottle along with any others you find. Each one probably has an interesting history that you are helping to continue.

POISON BOTTLES

Among the many substances kept in glass bottles around Early American homes were certain poisons that were commonly used in the preparation of various household products including soap, cloth dye, and even medicines. There must have been instances of people mistakenly taking poison rather than the intended substance because early in the nineteenth century the state of New York passed a law requiring that all poison items be labeled with the word "poison" for easy recognition. The skull and crossbones, used by pirates as the symbol for their flag the Jolly Roger, became the "death's-head" symbol adopted for a warning on poison bottles.

Soon many manufacturers began producing bottles specifically designed to hold poisons. The idea was to make the bottle clearly identifiable not only by carrying the word "poison" or the death's-head symbol but by making the poison bottles of colored glass—usually a dark blue and molded in a rough texture so the bottle could be identified if the light were too dim to see the label.

A few manufacturers invented and produced some rather special poison bottles that easily got across the message of danger. They were made in the shape of coffins or skulls and bones; some were completely covered with small, prickly glass pieces; others had caps that could only be removed by someone who knew the special way to push, turn or pull on them—much like the safety caps used on medicine containers today.

Unfortunately, too many poison bottles were so colorful and interesting in shape that they attracted the curiosity of children, thereby defeating their purpose. Within the last fifty years or so, most poisons have been clearly labeled as such and packaged in plain containers with some sort of safety closure. Should you come across these bottles in your excavations, enjoy them for their special past and unusual design. They are really collector's items.

DOWSING FOR WATER

In Early America, as well as today, it was necessary to have a source of clean, pure water close to home for drinking, cooking, washing, and doing many of the chores necessary to survive. Today nearly all homes have plumbing that brings water into them through pipes leading from city water supplies or private wells. But the settlers usually had to rely on nearby freshwater streams, rivers, or ponds, or collect their water in barrels from rain or melting snow as it ran off the roof. The rainwater barrel might have worked fine, but unless a large amount of water could be saved and stored, a long dry spell could leave a family without any water at all. But you can collect rainwater without a barrel.

Much rain and melting snow seeps into the ground and forms pockets of water and streams. The earth is a large storage tank of water, so all that is needed for a steady year-round water supply is to dig a well down to the source and pump the water out. The problem is knowing exactly where to dig. Two wells might be dug only a few feet apart—one might give you plenty of water while the other was nearly dry. Water might be found only a few feet below the surface in one location, while a short distance away you might have to dig or drill a well several hundred feet down.

Locating a well

Those settlers who were lucky were able to dig out a shallow well with a pick and shovel and use a rope and bucket to get the water out. In time well-drilling equipment was designed and built that could dig down to deeper pockets of water.

But finding the exact location of underground water and knowing where to dig without being able to hear, touch, smell, or see the water was still the big problem. Many homeowners and well diggers selected the proper site by using the mysterious technique of "dowsing." The art of dowsing (also called water witching, divining, and doodle-bugging) was accomplished by the dowser who slowly walked across the land holding a Y-shaped twig in his hands. When the twig pointed down it was the sign of exactly where to dig for water.

Just why dowsing worked no one seemed to know. But it did. And many rural American families would not select the site to build their house until the local dowser was first consulted. Even today many well drillers use a dowsing rod to select the best well location. And the art of dowsing is no longer limited to just finding water. Dowsers are now able to locate underground mines, lost objects, and oil. Even large corporations and town public-works departments use dowsers to locate underground pipes, electrical cables, and treasures, as well as water wells.

Dowsing tools and techniques

In any case, the tools and techniques of dowsing are very simple, and while some dowsers claim that it is a gift not everyone has, others say that anyone can learn to dowse successfully. But before you try to dowse for anything, you must know how to make the dowsing stick, how to use it, and what signs or signals to look for.

People have dowsed with all sorts of objects—even a sausage—but the most common dowsing rod is a Y-shaped branch about two feet long and not much thicker around than your little finger. The branch from a willow or fruit tree is most popular although any branch will do so long as it is flexible, though not flimsy. The branch should be smooth, free of knots, with any leaves and small twigs removed.

Now, using both hands, hold on to the two long ends of the stick with the stem of the Y pointed away from you and parallel to the ground. The stick should rest in your hands so that your thumbs point away from you; your fingers are toward you and your palms are turned up, Fig. 19. Hold the dowsing rod firmly enough so that grav-

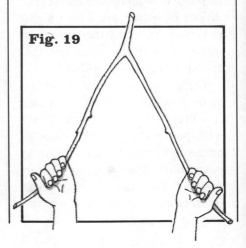

Fig. 19

Dowsing rods are important when looking for water.

and the dowsing rod will pull steadily downward. Continue to walk around the immediate area, and if the rod points down, you will perhaps be standing on the exact spot of what you are looking for. For a few people the rod will point directly up instead of down.

But you must remember that dowsing takes great patience—there isn't water everywhere underground and most amateur dowsers can only detect water to a depth of about fifteen feet. (More experienced and sensitive dowsers can often find water down fifty feet or more.) If you do get a strong reaction to the dowsing rod, you should probably repeat the dowsing several times to convince yourself that it is the underground water causing the stick to move and not you.

Water, yes or no?

Now to prove that the dowsing rod is correct. You would probably find it difficult to dig a well just for proof (if you are looking for water). But maybe someone can tell you if there are water lines or sewer pipes under the ground at that spot. Also, if more than one person is dowsing in the same location, your locations for water should be the same.

There are also many games you can play or invent to test your ability at dowsing. Have a friend line up several containers with only one filled with water. Cover them all with a towel, board, or anything else so long as you cannot see which container has water. Now try dowsing over the containers and see how you do at picking the right one. But there is no reason why you have to search only for water. You might play games trying to find hidden objects under the carpet, or may look for hidden treasure. Will it really work for you? You'll just have to try and see.

ity alone doesn't pull it down, and keep your hands at waist level with your arms at your sides. There are other ways of holding the rod that also work well, but try this method for a while before experimenting with other grips.

Concentration is the key

For the dowsing rod to work properly you, the dowser, must concentrate on water or whatever you are trying to find and let go of any other thoughts in your mind. Relax and breathe evenly. This concentra-tion and calming centers your mind on the task so that it will be receptive to the signals "sent" by what you are looking for.

Now, holding the rod properly balanced and straight in front of you, slowly walk over the area you are checking. Try to be systematic in covering the territory so no spot is skipped. Walk back and forth across an area in strips just as if you were mowing a lawn. When you approach underground water or whatever else you may be concentrating on, you will feel a strong tug

Chapter 5

AMERICAN FASHION

FASHION: PLAIN AND FANCY

The reasons for wearing clothes haven't changed much in the history of America, but fashion has. The first settlers to come were so involved with the hard work of making homes and adjusting to new conditions that they were not concerned with fashion, but they were still very conscious of the clothes they wore. Clothing, plain or fancy, was a symbol of a family's prosperity. If good fortune came to you, you could show it off by what you wore.

Generally speaking, the first American "fashions" were rugged. Early clothing relied heavily on animal skins that provided good protection against harsh winters; men wore leather pants and sometimes beaver hats. Women sewed the pelts and did the spinning. All clothing was made at home except—later on—for a few accessories like hats or buttons that might be purchased from traveling merchants.

For practical reasons, some Early American women carried in their clothes the sewing things they always needed. Simple tools and materials were kept in patchwork pockets, and scissors and pincushions were hung by red ribbons over dresses.

Eventually some Americans had more leisure time and were able to dress accordingly. For example, when good crops made tobacco farmers in the southern colonies prosperous, they enjoyed spending money on fancy cloth and fashion accessories imported by ship captains.

Proper little grownups

Children were dressed to look like little adults! Infants and young children—both boys and girls—were clothed in dresses until they were old enough for family work. Then they were dressed exactly like their adult parents, and expected to act accordingly.

Of course, just as today, tradesmen dressed according to their profession. A butcher wore a long apron and carried his meat cleaver, a blacksmith wore a heavy leather vest or apron to protect himself from burning coals. A traveling merchant's coat had lots of pockets to help carry his wares.

Clothes were not discarded when they became too small or worn out. Holes and rips were mended, or the material was reused to make smaller garments. Hand-me-downs were gratefully accepted. A person's best or newest clothes were saved for special occasions, including church and town meetings. Many favorite clothes became family treasures, and were passed on to new family members in wills.

The Puritans and Pilgrims had their own code of dress which forbade any fancy cloth, ribbons, or lace, and favored only plain and drab colors. Puritan men wore leather vestlike jackets, a large white collar, britches, wool knee socks, and large-brimmed hats. Puritan women wore long dresses with a white cloth apron and a hoodlike hat on their heads.

By the middle eighteenth century, many Americans were wealthy enough to give up homemade clothes and buy their fashions from clothing shops which mostly sold garments imported from England. In this way England began to dictate the styles that people wore. But that didn't last for long. Soon the English taxes on clothing became so great that Americans protested, and gradually returned to wearing their own clothing. The American Revolution forced all families to be economically independent of England and to demonstrate their ability to supply their own needs. There grew a new interest in home sewing and weaving, and ladies' sewing bees became a popular pastime. It was now patriotic to make your own clothes.

Peacocks of fashion

The Revolution brought victory and independence and a feeling of extravagance to Americans. The American people were "proud as peacocks" and they dressed that way. Fancy materials were once again imported from abroad, and more people could afford to dress for show rather than solely for function. Clothing of thin and fancy cloth was not as warm as wools or leather and frequent sickness became the price of high fashion.

Americans became obsessed with the style of their clothes. You could even tell a man's politics by his dress. Republican men dressed according to French fashions—in high collars, big puffy ties, tight-fitting pants, high boots, short-waisted coats with long narrow tails, and cocked hats. Men who followed Federalist politics dressed like the English, which more closely followed the old style of knee britches and shoe buckles.

Until the Industrial Revolution, all clothing whether homemade or tailor made was custom fit to the wearer. But with the invention of automatic weaving machines, cloth-cutting machines, and electric pressing irons, mass produced, inexpensive, ready-to-wear fashions became available to everyone. Ready-to-wear clothing, which came in all sizes and prices, was itself a new invention. New styles could be made easily in great numbers, and fashions changed rapidly. City people could shop in department stores and country dwellers either traveled to the city on shopping trips or bought their clothes mail order.

Dressed to the teeth

By the latter-part of the nineteenth century, well-dressed ladies went on afternoon visits to neighbors' homes wearing gowns, fancy bonnets, gloves, embroidered silk stockings, and high shoes. The style was now the "wasp waist," which necessitated the wearing of tightly laced corsets that caused women to complain constantly of poor health, and often faint. These "mannerisms"—faintness and unhealthiness—were also in fashion. Gentlemen wore white shirts with removable stiff collars so the shirt could be worn for several days—only the dirty collar was changed. Men who labored wore colored shirts with soft collars. The sleeves of men's shirts came in only one

length—long. Sleeve lengths were adjusted by wearing arm bands.

Americans had more leisure time and found activity to fill that time, and fashions reflected that change. On the beach, about 1900, parasols kept women's skins clear of the sun. Bathers wore so much clothing that the heavy wet garments prevented them from swimming—and almost caused some bathers to drown! In time, swimming fashions changed to reflect their function, and arms and ankles were bared.

Special outfits were designed for riding in automobiles that protected fancier clothes from being splattered with mud or soot from the smoking engines. These coats were called dusters.

Finally, we can breathe again

As women began to play sports—mostly bicycling, golf, and tennis—their clothes became less restrictive and elaborate. Shorter skirts, comfortable blouses, and a more tailored appearance became the fashion. The First World War also had a dramatic effect on fashion. Material was needed to make soldiers' uniforms, so styles were fashioned to use less cloth. Steel couldn't be "squandered" on corset bracings, so corsets went out of fashion. But when the war ended, so did its austerity, and American fashion once again turned to the extravagant.

The Flapper Era of the 1920's saw women trying to appear slender, even boyish, in straight skirts and dresses, raccoon coats, bobbed hair, lipstick, and long eyelashes. Men's fashion, although not as changeable as women's styles, still had its extremes. By the late 1930's, some young men favored a style called the zoot suit, made up of a coat which went down to the knees and pants which went nearly up to the chest.

World War II once again interrupted fashion because of its restrictions on cloth. Skirts were shortened and made formfitting. Shirt sleeves were made narrower to save cloth. Women had to work in the factories, so they began wearing pants; soon pants for women were introduced as a fashion. But the end of that war once again brought about extravagance in clothes, particularly in women's styles.

During the past thirty years, many fashions have come and gone, and Americans are still experimenting with the styles that they like the best. Today, we have a great variety of fashions to meet our wide range of life-styles. People can, and do, wear almost anything they like. Women wear maxi-, midi-, or mini-length skirts; pantsuits; and even T-shirts. Men can carry handbags and wear bright colors and patterns. Everybody wears jeans, and at some beaches some people wear nothing at all!

Clowning around in old clothes.

DRESSING UP

Many old pieces of clothing that might be worn-out or found in the attic can be trimmed with scissors or re-sewn in some way to make dress-up costumes like fashions once worn in America.

A costume helps you to "be" the person you are playing, and it also allows the audience to believe the role you are playing. In a ball gown, you can easily play a lady of society attending a grand party, or in a long-tailed coat and walking stick you might suddenly find yourself acting as a gentleman of great wealth.

In addition to the costume, hair-styles, wigs, beards, jewelry, and makeup help create the total effect. A few wrinkly lines drawn on your forehead with an eyebrow pencil will make your face look older, a touch of lipstick, rouge, and perfume will make you feel and look elegant.

Guess who I am

There is usually one article of clothing or one makeup technique that best conveys the idea of who you're pretending to be. For example, a headband with a feather "says" American Indian, a long gown suggests a distinguished lady, and a darkened beard and ragged clothing make you a hobo.

With an apron, you are a peasant girl, but wearing a crown makes you a queen.

You might find some costumes ready-to-wear by searching through attic trunks and storage closets for old or outdated fashions and accessories. Just wearing an over-sized man's sport coat and pants is the beginning of a great zoot suit. Or with a few scissor snips and a bit of sewing, you can transform many of your own worn-out clothes into older-style fashions. Long pants cut short make knee britches.

Darling, you look lovely

Look at pictures of styles Americans once wore and see if you can copy them in a costume that you

make yourself. Here are some suggestions:
● Make a man's cravat by tying a silk handkerchief around your neck, Fig.1.

Fig. 1

● A high stiff collar cut from a piece of cardboard will give you the look of a Victorian gentleman, Fig.2. Or a Puritan collar can be cut from an old bedsheet or pillow-case, Fig. 3.

Fig. 2

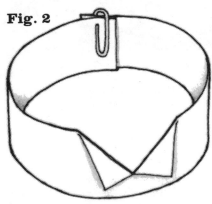

Fig. 3

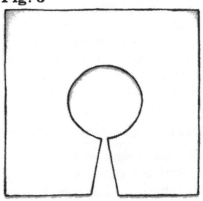

Fig. 4

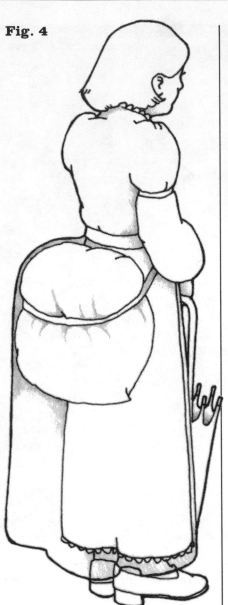

● Make a bustle to fit under a large skirt with a pillow or by stuffing a trash bag with crumpled newspapers. Attach the bustle around your waist with a piece of string or ribbon, Fig.4.
● A cape can be made by just draping a large beach towel over your shoulders and fastening it with a safety pin. A fashionable hand muff is easily made by cutting off the closed end of a pillowcase, Fig.5. An adult-sized silk nightgown with a high-waist tie ribbon looks very much like an Empire dress of the late eighteenth century. And long underwear or "union

suits" don't look much different from the bathing suits of seventy-five years ago.

Fig. 5

COLOR DYEING

Nearly all of the woven fabric in Early America was made of wool or linen. The color of these threads, as well as the fabric they produced, was a drab gray or dull tan. The plain material always looked dirty. To make the fabric more attractive, linen was often bleached white by repeatedly washing it in buttermilk and then spreading the cloth out to dry in the sun. Wool yarn or material was dyed a variety of colors using roots, flowers, leaves, berries, minerals, and even dried insects.

The craft of dyeing was common to all Early American homes. On the floor of every kitchen there was usually one or more clay dye pots for soaking or dyeing small pieces of thread or cloth. Bigger jobs were done outside in large heated kettles. An iron kettle was used for dark colors, and a copper kettle for keeping light colors bright.

The interesting shades these natural dyes produced were never predictable. Each new batch of dye had its own particular hue. Nearly every plant or tree was a source of some dye color, although most plants common to colonial America tended to produce various shades of red, yellow, or brown.

Where the colors come from

These are the colors of Early America and several of the plants once used to make the dyes:

Red: cherries, dogwood bark and root, pokeberries, red onions, strawberry, red oak bark, dandelion root.

Gray: sumac berries, blackberries, rhododendron leaves.

Purple: grapes, raspberries, elderberries, blueberries.

Black: walnut root, black walnut leaves.

Blue: sorrel stocks, roots, and leaves; chestnuts.

Brown and Tan: hemlock bark, walnut shells, sumac leaves, elderberry leaves, maple bark.

Green: lily-of-the-valley stalks and leaves, black-eyed Susan flowers, morning-glory blossoms, bayberry leaves.

Yellow: birch bark, onion skins, grass, marigold flowers, goldenrod flowers, willow leaves, ragweed, sunflowers, beet root.

Orange: sassafras root, bark, and leaves.

Each batch of dye that you prepare will be different. So many conditions affect final dye color that even leaves from the same plant will give different shades of dye at different seasons of the year. The strongest colors are made from plants gathered at the peak of their development. Berries make the best dye when they are completely ripe, but berry colors do tend to fade. Flowers should be picked when they are in full bloom. Roots and barks make the richest colors in early spring, but only small pieces of tree root should be cut off to avoid injuring the tree. Tree bark should be stripped from fallen trees and branches only. Leaves can be used at any time during the growing season, but are best used in late spring.

Preparing the dyes

To prepare a natural dye, choose leaves, roots, fruits, bark, or nuts using the preceding "chart" as a rough color guide (or experiment with local growing things). Chop the plant material into small pieces and soak them in water for half a day or longer. Heat the mixture to boiling, and simmer it for at least an hour. Then strain the resulting dye through a piece of wire mesh or cloth. The plant or berry you use will determine the color you get. The amount of water used to dilute the dye, and how long the material simmers in the dye solution, will determine the shade of the finished material.

To prepare yarn or woven material for dyeing it is frequently first washed in a special bath called a "mordant." An Early American mordant was mixed from various kitchen ingredients that allowed the dye to penetrate more deeply and permanently into the material fibers. Some typical mordants were made by adding rusty nails to the dye (which also made the colors darker) or soaking the material in urine ("chamber lye" as it was politely called). Vinegar was also a popular mordant.

The mordant for you

Each dye requires a different type and ratio of mordant to coloring to give the richest shade and permanence of color. However, many plant dyes need no mordant at all. When mixing your dye and preparing the mordant, you should experiment with different ingredients—even though the resulting color

may be a surprise. A simple home mordant that works well for wool dyes and most cotton dyes is a bath containing one part white vinegar to four parts water.

Heat (but do not boil) the material to be dyed in the mordant for an hour or just leave it in the mordant bath overnight. When the material is removed from the mordant, it should be thoroughly rinsed in water and gently squeezed to remove as much water as possible.

Getting the color you want

Some mordants and dyes can be mixed together and the material soaked all in one operation. In that case, the mordant is first mixed in with the dye solution. The material must still be thoroughly washed before dyeing. The wet material is then immersed in the pot of heated dye and mordant. The dye should simmer but not boil. Add water to the dye mixture as it evaporates. When the material appears dyed, it can be removed from the pot and rinsed in water until the rinse water runs clear. Remember, however, that the color of wet material will appear darker than when it is dry. Gently squeeze out the fabric and let it dry in the shade.

CHILDREN'S FASHION

For a long time, American children were dressed in clothing styles that were exact copies of those of their parents. (The garments were smaller, of course, and sometimes they were dyed scarlet or other hues considered "children's colors.") Yet, children always have had special items of clothing and even clothes which follow their own fantasies.

In Early American infants and toddlers, both boys and girls, wore long frilly dresses—although the dress for a boy was referred to as his "coat." It was a family occasion when a baby boy was of age to give up his coat in favor of britches like those the men and older boys wore.

Another Early American garment was the "pudding cap." This soft, padded bonnet was tied around the head of a baby just learning to walk. It supposedly protected the child's head from serious bumps and bruises if he fell.

What a sweet little boy

In 1886 the author Frances Burnett wrote a popular novel and play about a young American boy, *Little Lord Fauntleroy*, who wore long curls, a velvet suit with a lace collar, a big silk bow around his neck, buttoned shoes, and a wide, flat-brimmed hat. The costume supposedly made little boys look like "mother's darlings." Little boys hated it. The clothes were impractical for play and made the wearers feel like sissies.

Parents' clothing may not fit and that's a good enough reason to put it on.

For the next fifty years or so children's fashions were based more on the attire of hero types. Stories of cowboys and sheriffs produced the children's cowboy suit—complete with holster belt and gun. And sailors who traveled the world became models for the many popular children's sailor suit fashions.

And don't forget your gloves

While some young boys and girls were aspiring to be heroes, others were dressing to be "proper." The well-dressed "young lady" of three years and older wore a colored organdy smock over her dress, Mary Jane shoes with short white socks, and, sometimes, white gloves. Her boy counterpart wore a suit jacket with short pants, shirt and bow tie, long socks, and sometimes a small brimmed cap to match his jacket.

Today children's clothes are mostly practical, being designed for active play. The basic clothing style for both boys and girls seems to be jeans, T-shirts, and sneakers. But kids today like to add their own personal fashion touches to their clothes like tie-dyeing, embroidered designs, "billboard" messages, homemade jewelry and experimentation with outlandish clothes combinations.

WHERE DID YOU GET THAT HAT?

Throughout American history rarely did men, women, or children dress without a hat. Some of the hats that people wore were purely utilitarian. A hat with a wide brim, for example, might protect the wearer from rain or hot sun, and a woolen cap helped to keep in body warmth on a cold day. But most hats were worn purely for fashion, created in tune with the style of dress at the time.

Hat Conformature for taking shape of Heads.

H. DICKSON, HATS, CAPS & FURS, No. 60 STATE STREET, ALBANY.

Fig. 6   **Fig. 7**   **Fig. 8**   **Fig. 9**

One of the most popular hats for men in Early America was the beaver hat or "cap" as it was called, Fig. 6. The best caps were made from beaver pelts that had once seen some other use—maybe as part of a coat or as a suitcase. The dirty and worn-out pelts were fashioned into caps that were believed to have certain curative powers. It was thought that wearing a beaver cap improved a man's hearing and stimulated his memory. That is probably the origin of the expression "put on your thinking cap." A well-worn beaver cap was considered a prized family possession and when not being used was kept in a protective box. It was also common for beaver caps to be bequeathed in wills to other family members.

Early American women wore plain and simple caps or hoods, Fig. 7, but as clothing fashions became more elaborate, bits of lace, ribbon, fur, and other decorations were added, Fig. 8.

Pardon me but is that a rooster

Until the American Revolution, most men and women wore caps in many styles; but with the birth of a new country, and the extravagant fashions that followed, hats also became quite elaborate. Hats for women were the most important accessory of dress. Styles became outrageous. Elaborate and whimsical hats crested the top of high hairdos, Fig. 9. Hats contained all sorts of decorations—bird feathers, flowers, leaves, lace and ribbon. One hat of the time actually had a stuffed rooster on it, Fig. 10. The

high-hair fashion for women brought about a popular hat style called the "calash" that looked like the hood of a carriage, Fig. 11. Because the calash could be pulled down to cover the face, it acquired the name "bashful bonnet."

I used to be short

About 1800, the first high hats or "stovepipe" hats for men appeared, Fig. 12. But the fashionable high hat often proved a nuisance—it was frequently knocked off by low doorways and branches, or blown off by the wind—and so the skull-shaped bowler or derby-style hat was adopted for certain occasions, especially hunting and other informal events, Fig. 13.

In the middle nineteenth century, an American invented a machine for making felt, and the

Fig. 10   **Fig. 11**   **Fig. 12**   **Fig. 13**

Fig. 14

Fig. 15

Fig. 16

Fig. 17

man's soft felt hat soon became the style, Fig. 14. It's still popular today. The straw hat, Fig. 15, and the Panama hat, Fig. 16, were other men's hat fashions that soon followed.

After the large, elaborate hats that women had been wearing, bonnets tied under the chin once again became fashionable, Fig. 17. Various versions of the bonnet remained popular in women's fashion until the twentieth century when hats once again became oversized and elaborate, Fig. 18. A popular women's style of this large-hat revival period was the "merry widow" and some versions were made with large ostrich plumes, enormous bows, and rows of flowers, Fig. 19.

Hold on to your hat

The invention of the automobile brought about its own hat style. Women wore large hats with veils to protect their hair from wind and soot while driving. Men wore snug-fitting caps that wouldn't blow off easily.

When women decided to wear their hair much shorter in the early 1930's, hats became much smaller —often only a cap with a feather or bow for accent, Fig. 20 and 21. In the last forty years hats for both men and women have gone through more style changes from small to large to small, and so on.

Today, hat styles are as varied as the people who wear them. On a typical hat rack of the late twentieth century you will probably find a rain hat, sun hat, a snow cap, or maybe even a contractor's hard hat. Perhaps the biggest change in hat fashion is that today many Americans prefer to wear no hat at all.

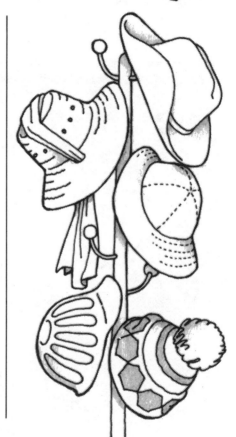

Fig. 18

Fig. 19

Fig. 20

Fig. 21

Making Hats

Considering the great variety of hat styles that have been worn in America, and the various materials and adornments added to them, just about anything around your house that can be worn on your head can be made into a "fashionable" hat.

A paper or plastic paint bucket, half of a basketball, a Frisbee®, small lampshades, round boxes, and even plastic flowerpots can all be the beginnings for making a hat.

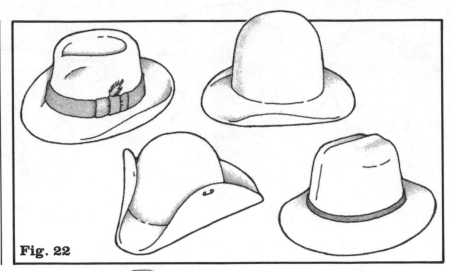

Fig. 22

A stylish hat always puts a finishing touch to an outfit.

Sometimes it is easier to begin with a ready-made hat; by twisting, pinning, cutting, and adding decorations to it, you can convert it into a new style, Fig. 22. A man's felt hat can be pinned up on three sides to make a Colonial tricorn, or the crown or top can be pushed up to give it the look of a "ten-gallon" cowboy hat. And if you pull down the brim and crease the crown, you will have a Panama-style hat.

Designing your own

A large-brimmed woman's sun hat can be decorated with nearly anything to mimic the large, ornate hats American women once wore. Just sew or pin items on the brim and top in an interesting design. You might try using ribbons and bows, feathers, cotton balls, flowers and ferns, buttons, even Christmas tree ornaments or small stuffed animals, Fig. 23.

Fig. 23

A simple colonial cap can be made by cutting a piece of cloth into a circle about two feet (60 cm.) in diameter. Cut small, close, evenly spaced slits around the cap a few inches in from the edge, and thread a length of ribbon through the slits, Fig. 24. Pull the ribbon ends to gather the material. Fit the cap to your head and tie the ribbon in a bow.

Dunce cap

Many hat styles can be made of cut and glued paper, newspaper, or

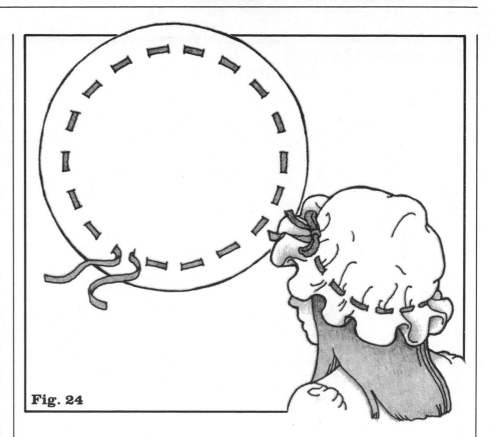

Fig. 24

paperboard. To make a dunce cap, stack several sheets of newspaper, and roll them up together diagonally to make a large cone shape, Fig. 25. Tape the cone so it won't unroll, and with a scissors cut off the base until the cap is the correct size to fit your head.

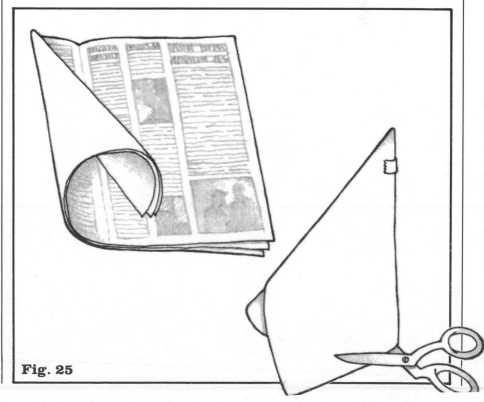

Fig. 25

THE BASIC CAP

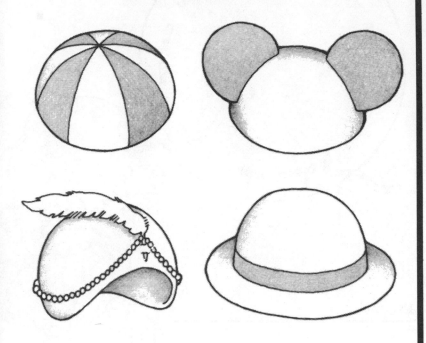

Many American hat styles are based on the cap. You can make a basic cap by cutting away the brim of a sports cap, or by molding papier-mâché over an inflated balloon.

Materials:
large balloon
flour
water
newspaper torn into strips

Utensils:
large bowl

1. Blow up and tie a knot in the stem of a balloon which is about the size and shape of your head.

2. Make the papier-mâché paste by mixing flour and water in a bowl until it is a thick, soupy consistency. You can also use wallpaper paste or white glue thinned with a little water.

3. Tear newspaper into short, narrow strips. Dip each strip into the paste and mold it around the balloon in the shape of a cap. Apply several layers of papier-mâché to build up the thickness, Fig. 26. Let the cap dry and harden for at least a day, then pop the balloon.

The papier-mâché cap is now a beanie that can be painted with stripes, or "ears" can be cut from cardboard and glued in place to make a mouse hat. You can also cut a narrow brim from cardboard and glue it in place to make a bowler or derby hat. By styling the papier-mâché around the balloon or using other differently shaped balloons, you can make a cap for a flapper's hat. Just add a feather or beads for accent.

Fig. 26

WALKING STICKS

One of the proudest possessions an Early American could own was a fine walking stick or cane. Everyone, from "hero" to "villain," carried some type of cane. It became a tradition in Early America

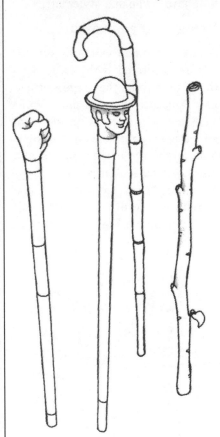

to give the leader of an organization a cane; once owned, the cane was rarely thrown away and usually willed to a good friend. When Ben Franklin died, he willed his "fine crab tree walking stick" to George Washington.

The terms "cane" and "walking stick," although used interchangeably, were once defined in social terms: "a person strolls with a walking stick and swaggers with a cane." "Walking stick" was obviously considered a much more elegant word than cane. The walking stick was carried even by poor men as a sign of leadership. If a man's clothes were drab, the walking stick gave him a feeling of elegance—it made him feel like a gentleman. In some periods it was just as fashionable for women to carry walking sticks as it was for men, and even children in Early America were given miniature canes.

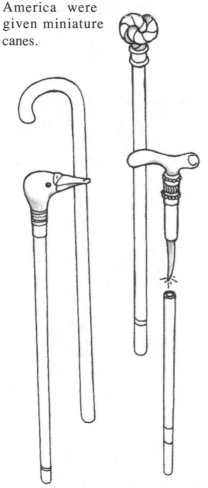

It was not enough just to have a cane, you needed to know how to use it. A code of walking stick etiquette prescribed that the cane should never be carried under the arm, should not be used for leaning when standing, nor dragged behind when walking. And it was unpardonable to use the cane for "writing idly in the dirt." For practical purposes, the cane could be used to help dodge mud puddles or assist in getting down from the high steps of horse carriages.

When walking in the woods, a branch helps you keep a steady footing.

Something to lean on

A walking stick or cane could be made of anything from a piece of tree branch to an elegantly carved piece of wood with a gold or silver handle. There have been canes made from bamboo, ivory, corncobs, shark bones, and even banana stalks. Some canes were hollowed out and held various concealed devices including forks, spoons, knives, rulers, telescopes, saws, flags, flasks, candles, paper and pen, pipes, fans, and umbrellas. A few physicians carried medicinal perfume in their canes to disinfect the room of a patient they were visiting. But the canes of ordinary Americans were quite simple—usually just a straight stick with no handle on top. A few had hooks that allowed them to be attached to the waist by a cord.

When men's briefcases came into fashion and men rode in cars instead of walking, the walking stick went out of fashion. Today a cane is used primarily by those who need it as a walking aid or as a very formal accessory of men's fashion when attending special functions. But walking sticks for serious hikers or those just taking a trek through the woods are still useful tools. It helps set a rhythm or pace, and is handy for dodging branches, pushing aside brush, or testing the solidity of the ground ahead.

There's little more to making a walking stick than simply finding one. Any stick-like part of a fallen branch that isn't too brittle and is cleaned of twigs will do. If you want to be more elaborate, you can whittle a few designs on the stick with a penknife, or paint the stick with a coat of shellac. You might be lucky enough to find a long, straight stick with a sharp curve—a ready-made handle. The proper length depends on your height and what is comfortable for you, but generally the top of the stick should come up to your waist.

Chapter 6

EATING IN AMERICA

AMERICAN DIET

The settlers of Early America did not worry so much about what they would eat as whether they would eat at all. When the food that they had brought with them was gone, the settlers had to rely on the land and their own skill at hunting and growing. After several winters and summers, the Pilgrims began to learn the pattern of America's growing seasons; and in cooking side by side with the Indians they adapted their old familiar styles of eating to the new variety of foods that were available. The settlers learned to use molasses as a substitute for sugar and became adept at recognizing strange varieties of edible roots and plants. And they learned to hunt the woodlands for wild animals that many had never seen or eaten before.

The rich soil of America grew the seeds that the settlers had brought with them, as well as many crops known to them. The Indians introduced the settlers to corn, which could be grown nearly everywhere in the New World, and the colonists soon learned to prepare it in several new and delicious ways. Corn became such a popular food that travelers would always pack some just in case they couldn't get it along their journey. When going to France on a long visit, Thomas Jefferson took corn seeds for planting so that he could grow, pick, and eat right from his own Paris garden; and it is known that Ben Franklin, when he was in England representing the colonies, sent a message to America asking to be sent cornmeal so he could make and eat his favorite corn bread.

Plain and simple cooking

The cooking of Early America was in keeping with the settlers' puritan life-style—plain, nothing extravagant. But their food was nonetheless plentiful and hardy. The colonists prepared seafood chowders, bear and varmint stew, puddings, and once in a while even a few sweet treats. In

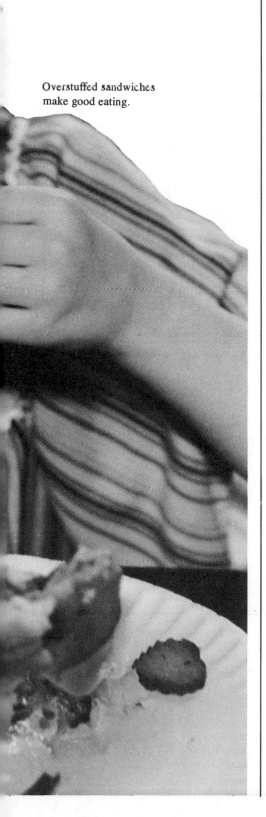

Overstuffed sandwiches make good eating.

their pots hanging over a fireplace flame they cooked baked beans, Yankee pudding, or the still-famous New England boiled dinner. New England farmers raised orchards of apples, cultivated wild grapes for jams and drinks, discovered the cranberry, and made milk into butter and cheese. The sea provided an abundance of tasty codfish, mackerel, haddock, clams, and lobsters which became staples of the coastal settlers' diet. The Indians taught the settlers to cook seafood by first packing it in seaweed along with corn and spices—and the now-famous New England clambake was born.

In the Old World only the very rich had been able to afford to eat meat; but in America the woodlands were full of edible animals—so much so that in time Americans became one of the greatest meat-eating peoples in the world. It has even been suggested that the energy and ambition of colonial Americans was partly attributable to the large quantities of meat protein in their diet.

Traveling food

For a long time the food Americans ate was limited to what was grown in the region where particular groups lived and to their own ethnic cooking traditions. But as the country expanded, eating habits began to change. In the nineteenth century, Gustav Swift began transporting meat across America in refrigerated train cars that prevented spoilage. And sometime later, Philip Armour transported fruits and berries in a similar way, making it possible for a family in Connecticut to eat a fresh California orange. Clarence Birdseye perfected freezing—a method of preserving food for long periods of time that he had learned from the Eskimos. Now Americans could eat the meats, fruits, and vegetables they wanted regardless of where they lived or the season of the year.

As the eating tastes of the many cultures that comprised America blended together, there developed a new cuisine: American food. And although we now have a "melting pot" style, ethnic cooking is still alive and well, flourishing better than ever. In American cities you can choose to eat Italian, Chinese, Greek, Japanese, French, Mexican, Spanish, or American, as well as other foods.

ALL-AMERICAN DISHES

America is a land fabulously rich in a grand variety of food resources. Our oceans, mountains, plains, tropical regions, lakes, and streams all provide unique "raw materials" that Americans, according to cultural heritage and invention, have turned into a countless number of all-American dishes. Each region of our country has its own distinctive food specialties based on both the resources of the area and the background of its people. Here is a partial list of all-American dishes; perhaps you've tried some from your own area.

There must be an easier way to prepare lobster for dinner.

New England

New England Clam Chowder
Boston Baked Beans
Boston Fish Chowder
Vermont Cheddar Cheese
Bar Harbor (Maine) Lobster Salad
New England Clambake
Yankee Pot Roast
New England Barbecued Chicken
New England Cole Slaw
Boston Brown Bread
Rhode Island Cob-Apple Pie
Boston Cream Pie
Boston Black Bean Soup
Boston Horseradish Sauce
Cape Cod Crown Pork Roast
Fall River Grape Soup
Maine Codfish Bouillabaisse
Martha's Vineyard Lobster Newburg
Nantucket Cucumber Soup
New Bedford Clam-Vegetable Chowder
Yarmouth Herring Salad
Indian Pudding

Mid-Atlantic

Manhattan Clam Chowder
Philadelphia Pepper Pot Soup
Jersey Sour Beer and Brown Bread Soup
Maryland Crab Soup
Chesapeake Bay Crab Cakes
Baltimore Crab
Grand Central Oyster Stew
Grand Central Pan Roast
Terrapin à la Maryland
New York Cut Steak (Porterhouse Steak)
Harlem Barbecue Sauce
Chopped Chicken Liver
Chicken à la Maryland
Long Island Duckling
Maryland Ruddy Duck
New York Baked Beans
Wilmington Submarine Sandwiches
Crab Salad Delaware
Waldorf Salad
Adirondack Mulled Cider
Amish Steak
Annapolis Sherried Cheese Spread
Baltimore Oyster Soufflé
Wall Street Tournedos of Beef
Yankee Berkshire Soup
Delaware River Cole Slaw
Baked Alaska
Philadelphia Red Cole Slaw
Lancaster County Cabbage Soup
Lord Maryland Soft-Shell Crabs
Grand Central Oysters Baked In Shell
Lancaster Chicken Loaf
Oyster Maryland au Gratin
Philadelphia Scrapple
Pennsylvania Green Tomato Pickles
Shenandoah Broiled Duck
Virginia Pecan Pie
Virginia Fried Sweetbreads
Susquehanna Green Pepper Omelet

Southwest

Red Snapper Steak Texas Gulf Style
Arizona Jerky with Eggs
Texas Beef Enchiladas
New Mexico Chicken
Arizona Refried Beans
Oklahoma Beans
Arizona Avocado Salad
Texas Toast
Santa Fe French Toast
Arizona Deep-Dish Grapefruit Pie
Oklahoma Pudding
Texas Chile
Texas Beef Stroganoff

Rio Grande Roast Veal
Texas Veal Stew

Pacific Coast

California Olive Soup
San Francisco Halibut Broth
California Dip
California Macaroni
San Diego Omelet
Monterey Jack (cheese)
Baked Portland Salmon
Seattle Salmon Mousse
Monterey Tamale Pie
California Oven-Barbecued Chicken
Pacific Chicken Mousse
San Fernando Salad
California Fruit Salad
California Burger
Chicken California Style
California Guava Shortcake
California Prune Pudding
Barbecued Spareribs San Francisco Style
Grant Avenue Short Ribs
Brook Trout Nob Hill
Malibu Beach Mussels Maison
Spitted Yosemite Pheasant
Santa Barbara Spareribs with Fruit

Alaska

Seal Alaskan
Alaskan Sourdough Waffles
Eskimo Sourdough Doughnuts
Eskimo Ice Cream
Mooseburgers
Whale Steaks
Cranberry Ketchup
Alaska Reindeer Chops

Hawaii

Marinated Raw Fish
Pit-Roasted Chicken
Poi
Macadamia Nuts
Hawaiian Surprise
Hawaiian Rumaki (liver)

South

Georgia Egg Pie
Mobile Imperial Crab
Baked Kentucky Ham with Pickled Peaches
Baked Ham West Virginia Style
Kentucky Burgoo
Old Virginia Chicken Pudding
Brunswick (Virginia) Stew
Florida Seafood Salad
Key Lime Pie
Fried Peach Tarts Georgia Style
Liver Atlanta Style

Royal Street (New Orleans) Filet of
   Beef
Blue Ridge Mountain Roast Venison
Bourbon Street Chicken Gumbo Filé
Carolina Persimmon Jam
Chesapeake Fish Stew
Breast of Chicken Delta Style
Florida Rum Sauce
Virginia Eel
Everglade Fried Bananas
Florida Pork Chops
Georgia Peanut Soup
Maryland Spoon Bread
Mississippi Oxtail Ragout
Red Snapper Biloxi Style
New Orleans White Sauce
Onion Soup New Orleans
Louisiana Court Bouillon
Louisiana Honey Bread
Smithfield Ham
Lady Baltimore Cake

Midwest

Milwaukee Beer Soup
Michigan Black Bean Soup
Indiana Spaghetti
Wisconsin Welsh Rabbit
Planked Michigan Whitefish
Wisconsin Fish Stew
Indiana Potato Salad
Wisconsin Beer Bread
Indiana Corncake
Great Lakes Liver Pudding
Lake Erie Stuffed Veal Birds

Plains

Baked Dakota Pork Pancake
Missouri Kitchen-Barbecued Steak
Iowa Goulash
Kansas Potatoes Fried Whole
Nebraska Herring Salad
Kansas Cracked-Corn Griddlecakes
Missouri Hoecake
Missouri Dakota Honey Custard

Northwest

Baked Columbia River Salmon
Washington Salmon Loaf
Montana Buck Stew
Idaho Lumber Camp Hash
Oregon Beef-Fruit Stew
Roast Lamb Utah Style with Hot
   Minted Applesauce
Montana Baked Corn
Wyoming Bean Salad
Washington Applesauce Cake
Washington State Peach Pie
Idaho Potato Doughnuts
Oregon Apple Pie

Learn how to use a stove properly before attempting any cooking.

USING THE KITCHEN

A kitchen is actually a workshop equipped with many tools, a few of which could be dangerous if not used properly and conscientiously. Kids should always ask permission to use the kitchen, and parents should always be aware of what their children are doing in it, supervising when necessary. Using the kitchen alone requires a sense of responsibility and the ability to follow directions well. And remember that part of the responsibility of kitchen work is cleaning up when the cooking is over.

Whether your recipe turns out well or poorly is not nearly so important as your safety in the kitchen. Here are a few kitchen rules and hints to keep you safe and also help your cooking:

• Wash your hands and protect "good" clothing with an apron.

• Before starting a recipe have all ingredients and utensils organized, and prepare a clean space for working.

• Place the recipe where it can be easily seen near where you are working, and be sure you understand all of the directions.

• Keep a clean sponge handy for unexpected spills and splashes.

• Use a cutting knife on a cutting board, not on the kitchen counter or table.

• All pot handles should be turned to the back or the side of the stove so they can't be easily bumped. Always use a pot holder for lifting and moving pots on the stove.

• Be sure kitchen appliances are turned off after using them.

• Clean up any mess you have made. Wash and dry all utensils and sponge off counters and tables.

APPLES

"As American as apple pie" the saying goes; but although the apple has become a favorite American fruit, its origin goes far back in history, and in legend all the way back to the Garden of Eden. The first apple trees in America were planted in Massachusetts only a few years after the Pilgrims arrived. Because the apple was so delicious and could be used for eating, cooking, and for making cider, apple orchards were planted in every settlement and village. The apple tree could be grown all over America except where weather was extremely hot or cold year-round.

In Early America if you wanted to grow apples you could just plant an apple seed and wait for it to grow into an apple-bearing tree. However, apple trees grown from seed don't always produce fruit of the same quality or variety as the apple you took the seed from. Today apple trees are grown by grafting a bud or a twig of an established variety onto a young apple tree grown from seed.

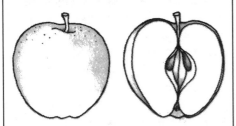

So many varieties

Of the large variety of apples grown in America you will usually find only a few common types at your local food market. Some are tart to the taste, some sweet, some are juicier than others, some best for eating raw, and some are best for cooking. Generally, tart apples are better for cooking and sweet apples are better for eating raw.

Here is a list of a few of the more common apple varieties in America.

Mackintosh—medium in size, dark red with stripes, fragrant, juicy and a bit tart. Best for eating raw and good in salads.

Golden Delicious—medium to large in size, yellow, sweet, firm, and crisp. Excellent for eating raw, in salads, and pies, and good for applesauce and baking.

Red Delicious—medium to large size, deep red color, five "knobs" on the blossom end, firm and sweet. Best for eating raw or in salads.

Cortland—medium to large size, striped red, mildly tart. Good for eating raw, and general cooking. Stays white when cut or peeled.

Winesap—small to medium size, bright red with scattered white dots, juicy, hard, crisp and tart. Fair for eating raw, general cooking or baking whole.

Baldwin—large in size, red, hard, juicy and tart. Best for pies and baking, good for applesauce.

The American health food

We may eat apples because we like their taste, but the apple has also become an American tonic for good health. "An apple a day keeps the doctor away" may not be literally true, but some doctors do say that apples help relieve common colds and the flu, and at least a few dentists claim that chewing on an apple does a better job at cleaning your teeth than a toothbrush and toothpaste.

Americans also give credit to the apple in many other ways. Someone you like might be referred to as "the apple of your eye"; or if you want to impress your school teacher, it has been traditional to bring him or her a gift of a shiny red apple—but then you might be called "an apple polisher." And besides crunching your teeth into a raw apple, there are plenty of apple recipes for making treats such as apple pie, candy apples, apple butter, apple cookies, fried apples, baked apples, apple cider, applesauce, and apple ice cream. All in all, its good looks, sharp aroma, and flavor, besides its being healthful to eat, has made the apple America's "King of Fruits."

American Apple Pie

Bake a delicious pie in the fall when apples come into season.

Ingredients
6 or 7 medium-sized tart apples, the same variety or several different kinds
½ cup sugar
½ tsp. cinnamon
1 tb. all-purpose flour
2 tb. butter
pastry for 2-crust 9-inch pie

Utensils
paring knife
mixing bowl and spoons
9-inch pie tin
fork or spoon

1. Preheat the oven to 400°F. (205°C.). Peel, core, and slice ap-

ples. In a mixing bowl stir together the apple slices, sugar, cinnamon, and flour.

2. Line the nine-inch pie tin with a pastry crust. You can use a ready-made frozen pie crust, a pie crust mix or stick, or start from scratch. If necessary, ask a parent for a pie crust recipe.

3. Fill the pastry-lined pie tin with your apple mixture and dot the top with pieces of the butter.

4. Add a pastry top. Using your finger or a pastry brush, wet the outside edge of the bottom crust with cold water, then place the top crust over the pie. Seal the edges with a fork or spoon, and cut a few slits in the top crust for steam to escape while baking. Some cooks like to make and are known for the designs they mold around the pie edge. Sprinkle a little sugar and cinnamon on the crust.

5. Bake in the oven for fifty to sixty minutes, or until the crust is light golden brown and the apples are tender.

Candy Apples

If you like eating apples and also have a sweet tooth, satisfy your craving by eating candy apples. The giant lollipop-like candy apple has become an American favorite, especially at fairs and around Halloween time. Making candy requires cooking at high temperatures, so kids must have the help of a parent or someone older who is allowed to use the stove. Cooking candy should be done when the weather is cool and dry. When it is hot or humid, the candy might get sticky.

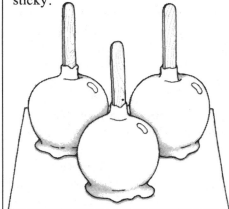

GOLDEN DELICIOUS

Keep Out Protected by Alarm

Literally thousands of varieties of apples have been grown, but not very much is known about exactly how these varieties came about. Nurserymen experiment in cross-breeding apple trees by grafting apple tree buds and branches onto seedlings and young trees; in time a new variety of apple may appear unexpectedly on one branch that is quite different from the rest of the fruit on the tree.

It was by experimenting in this way and by luck that the Golden Delicious apple was discovered. The apple trees on a particular hillside orchard in West Virginia were old, neglected, and produced only small, bitter, misshapen fruit. To save the

stand of trees the orchard farmer tried several grafting experiments. After a few years, one of the trees produced a new apple variety that was large, juicy, sweet, and golden in color. The tree was the only one of its kind in the world, and so valuable that a steel cage was erected around it complete with a guard and a burglar alarm.

The new apple was named Golden Delicious. The following spring grafting buds and branches were taken from the original apple tree to start new Golden Delicious apple trees. Today there are thousands of Golden Delicious apple trees, all directly related to that very first one.

Ingredients
1¼ cup sugar
1 cup light corn syrup
6-8 hard eating apples
ice cream stick for each apple
food coloring (optional)

Utensils
measuring cup
wooden mixing spoon
waxed paper
medium-sized cooking pot
candy thermometer (optional)

1. Mix the sugar with the corn syrup and cook over a medium heat.

2. Stir occasionally until the

mixture begins to boil. Turn down the heat if the mixture threatens to boil over the pot. If you have a candy thermometer, attach it to the pot. Be sure the thermometer bulb is in the mixture but not touching the sides or bottom of the pot. Let the mixture heat until the thermometer reads "hard crack" (300°F./149°C.). Be patient; you may have to wait twenty to thirty minutes for the mixture to reach the correct temperature. If you don't use a candy thermometer, use the water drop method. After the mixture has been boiling for about fifteen minutes, spoon a little of it out and drop it into a cup of very cold water. The candy ball that forms in the water should be hard and brittle—then you know the mixture is ready.

3. While the candy mixture is cooking, prepare the apples by putting an ice cream stick into the stem end of each one. Spread a sheet of waxed paper on a counter near the stove.

4. When the candy mixture is ready, turn off the heat. The mixture should now be a light brown color. If you like, you can add about twenty drops of food coloring to the mixture to get the candy apple color you prefer. Red is most popular. One at a time, hold each apple by its stick and dip and twirl the apple in the mixture until it is entirely coated with the candy. Now put the apple, stick up, on the waxed paper to cool and harden.

Dried Apple Rings

Eating dried apple rings is a totally different apple taste experience. Unlike the juicy crunch of a fresh raw apple, a dried apple ring is rough and chewy with no juice at all, but the apple taste is still quite rich. Dried apple rings are usually eaten as a sweet snack, but they can also be put into cereals, cakes, and other baking recipes. What is also nice about dried apples is that they can be carried and stored safely without refrigeration; this makes them a perfect snack on long car trips or hikes. The rings can be stored for several years even in a jar with a tight lid without losing their flavor.

Ingredients

tart apples, as many as you want

Utensils

paring knife
twine
cheesecloth (if necessary)

1. Start with firm, ripe apples, choosing a variety with a strong, tart flavor. Apples picked at fall harvest make the best dried apple rings. Using a paring knife, peel and core several apples; then slice them across the core into rings about one-quarter inch (6 mm.) thick.

2. Now you must dry the apple rings as quickly as possible before they spoil. String the rings on a length of twine and then hang the string between any two "hooks" in a warm, dry, airy place.

Drying can be done indoors or out. If outside, be sure the weather is dry and sunny; and be sure to bring the apples indoors when the weather is damp or rainy and during the nighttime dew. If flies and insects try to feed on your drying apple rings, try covering the rings with a piece of cheesecloth. Outdoor drying during warm weather may take only a few days, but if you are willing to wait a while longer—maybe as long as two

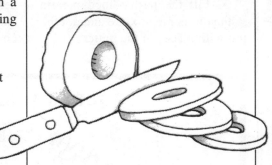

weeks—it is often easier to dry the apples indoors.

For indoor drying, hang the string of apple rings in the driest and warmest place of your house. Depending upon the time of year, that might be in the kitchen, by a radiator or heating stove, in the attic, or even in the basement by the furnace. Don't try to dry the apple rings in the oven. When heated too quickly they form a dry skin which prevents the inside from drying.

3. When the apple rings have been dried enough they will have a leathery texture and taste quite chewy. Remove the apple rings from the twine and put them in a bowl for snacking.

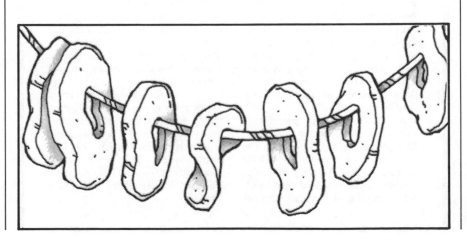

JOHNNY APPLESEED

If there is any name that you associate with apples, it is most probably Johnny Appleseed. Some people think that Johnny Appleseed is only a legend, but he really did exist. When America was just a young country, Johnny Appleseed was born in a part of Massachusetts which was then the frontier. His real name was John Chapman. It is said that as an infant he would scream and yell until his parents let him play with a branch of an apple tree full of blossoms. In any case, John Chapman grew up to be a nurseryman, quite knowledgeable about herbs and flowers, but most of all very much devoted to growing apples.

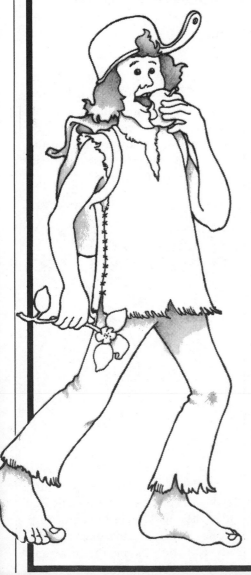

John Chapman would collect the seeds from cider presses so he could grow apple tree seedlings to sell. Although he started the business to earn money, Chapman soon began giving his apple trees to the settlers and pioneers heading west, or trading them for food and other necessities.

As a young man, Chapman went west to Ohio. The country was just being settled, and the only roads to travel were Indian trails. Most pioneers traveled by horse or wagon, but John Chapman walked barefoot leading a packhorse loaded down with sacks of apple seeds. Along the way he stopped at settlements and planted apple tree nurseries. With help from the settlers, he would clear spots in the forest, plant apple trees, and nurture the seedlings until they were trees. Then he would move on to the next settlement. To the people who knew him, and even to those who had only just heard of him, John Chapman was known as Johnny Appleseed.

For nearly fifty years John Chapman traveled about midwestern America planting his apple seeds. A gentle and religious man, he loved nature and preferred to live out-of-doors with the animals and Indians. Indeed, Johnny Appleseed was so tenderhearted that he couldn't prune the branch of an apple tree, since he believed it caused the tree great pain. As much as he was known for his goodness, generosity, cheerfulness, and his respectful relationship with the wilderness and the Indian people, Johnny Appleseed became a legend for the clothes he wore. For a hat, Johnny Appleseed wore a long-handled pot; for a shirt, he cut two armholes in a coffee sack; his pants were ragged and his feet were bare.

Throughout his years of traveling, Johnny Appleseed would often return to the settlements he had once visited to renew friendships and admire the grown apple trees he had helped to plant. The spirit and dedication of John Chapman has become a legend, so that today every apple tree in America is a tribute to Johnny Appleseed and America's love for apples.

AMERICAN CHEESE

There were no cows or goats in America when the settlers first arrived, so there were no dairy products—no milk, cream, or cheese. As America grew, ships from other countries brought not only new settlers but livestock so that the centuries-old art of cheesemaking soon became another colonial home chore.

The first cheesemaking was of a practical nature. Fresh milk could easily spoil, but might be used to make cheeses, which would last considerably longer. Any surplus milk was usually made into cheese.

The hard cheeses and cottage cheese produced at home were good, but the taste and amount of cheese available were inconsistent. It was not until 1891 that the first cheese factory in America—and the world—was established in New York State. The eastern United States remained the cheese-producing capital of America until the early 1900's, when the factory system of making cheese began to move westward. With rolling hills for cow pastures, and a plentiful supply of clear, fresh water, the state of Wisconsin was a natural attraction for cheesemakers. And although cheese is made in nearly every state in America, Wisconsin today produces by far most of the cheese we eat.

When you're hungry, say cheese

Although there are several cheese tastes and varieties, nearly all are made from cow's milk—the difference in flavor and texture coming mostly from the way the cheese is cooked and cured. The odds-on favorite in America is Cheddar cheese. In fact, a mild type of Cheddar cheese has become so popular in the United States that it has acquired the name "American cheese." This is the familiar orange-yellow sliced cheese usually grilled between two slices of bread or melted over a hamburger. Actually, other cheeses besides this one have been known as American cheese, including colby, Monterey, and various other Cheddar-type cheeses. At times American cheese has also been known as store cheese, rat cheese, Yankee cheese, and dairy cheese.

Cheese plus

America is also responsible for the invention of "processed" cheese —a dubious distinction. Processed cheese is a mix of various natural cheeses which have been shredded, blended, and heated so that no further ripening or aging will occur. That is, the process stops the cheese flavor from changing once it has reached a certain point. Although processed cheese lacks the rich taste of natural cheeses, it does have consistency and uniform flavor. It keeps well and melts quickly when used for cooking.

Another type of American cheese that you might frequently see in the food market is "processed cheese food." It is essentially the same product as processed cheese, but with less fat content and more moisture. Sometimes processed cheese food contains other ingredients for flavoring, such as spices or bits of meat.

The next time you are at the food market read the cheese labels so you know what you are buying—a natural cheese, a processed cheese (also known as "pasteurized processed cheese"), or a processed cheese food. To learn the taste of the cheeses and which you like best, you will just have to try them.

Three Kinds of Cheese to Make

Making homemade hard cheese requires a lot of special ingredients, equipment, and careful work. Making soft cheese, however, is quite simple. You probably have all the ingredients you need already in your kitchen. If you like soft cheese on crackers as a snack or if you just want to see how the process works, try one of these soft cheese recipes.

COTTAGE CHEESE

Ingredients
2 cups whole milk
1 tablespoon vinegar
salt

Utensils
measuring cup and spoon
pot or saucepan
mixing spoon
strainer
bowl

1. Pour the milk into the pot and heat over a medium setting until bubbles begin to form on the top. Stir while heating.

2. Remove the pot from the heat and slowly stir in the vinegar. Stir gently and watch for the cheese curds to form. The curds are the cottage cheese and the liquid left is the whey.

3. Empty the contents of the pot

into a strainer held over the sink or a bowl. Gently squeeze the curds with a mixing spoon to be sure all the whey is removed.

4. Put the cheese into a clean bowl and let it cool in the refrigerator. Before eating, salt the cottage cheese to your taste. Be sure to refrigerate any that is left uneaten.

POT CHEESE

Ingredients
1 quart yogurt
salt, pepper, paprika, chopped
    parsley (optional)

Utensils
cheesecloth or kitchen towel
plate
string
bowl

1. Spread out a double thickness of cheesecloth or a kitchen towel on a plate and pour the yogurt into the center. Make the cloth into a bag by folding up the sides and edges and tying them with a piece of string.

2. Hold the cloth bag over the sink and gently squeeze it. The liquid whey will begin to run or drip from the bag leaving only the solids. Now tie a loop in the string and hang the bag from the sink faucet

"BIG CHEESE"

You have probably seen cheese at the food market or delicatessen counter in several different shapes and sizes. A "loaf" of cheese is rectangular in shape so that slices from the loaf will fit the shape of bread for sandwiches. There are also balls, blocks, and barrels of cheese; but the most popular shape for cheeses in all sizes is the cylinder or "cheese wheel." The largest of the cheese wheels (those weighing more than one hundred pounds) is called a "mammoth."

At Thomas Jefferson's Presidential Inauguration in 1801, a group of admirers from Massachusetts gave him the largest mammoth cheese the world then had ever known: sixteen hundred pounds. It took three weeks to haul the cheese to Washington, D.C. on a sled. Other presidents have also been honored in a similar way. President Andrew Jackson once received a fourteen hundred pound cheese that was completely eaten within two hours by visitors to the White House, and Franklin Delano

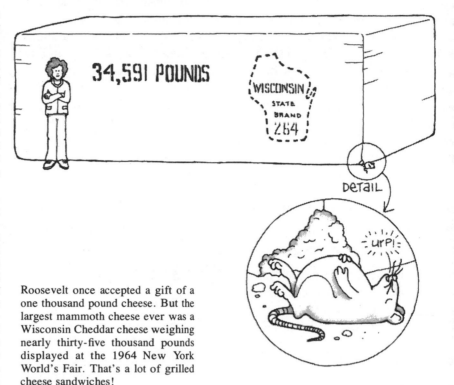

Roosevelt once accepted a gift of a one thousand pound cheese. But the largest mammoth cheese ever was a Wisconsin Cheddar cheese weighing nearly thirty-five thousand pounds displayed at the 1964 New York World's Fair. That's a lot of grilled cheese sandwiches!

---

for several hours allowing any remaining whey to drip out.

3. Remove the cheese, put it in a bowl and taste it. Add salt and pepper, paprika, or chopped parsley to taste. Be sure to refrigerate any uneaten pot cheese.

SOFT AMERICAN CHEESE

Ingredients

1 quart whole milk
¼ cup buttermilk
salt, pepper, paprika, garlic (optional)

Utensils

2-quart pot
mixing spoon
measuring cup
plastic wrap or foil
cheesecloth or kitchen towel
string
bowl

1. Pour the whole milk into the pot and heat it over a medium setting for just a few minutes or until the milk is warm (but not hot) to touch.

2. Turn off the heat and mix the buttermilk with the whole milk. Cover the pot with a piece of plastic wrap or foil and let it stand at room temperature for at least one day or until the milk has turned creamy and thick.

3. Continue as for making pot cheese by putting the thickened milk into a cheesecloth or towel bag, then squeezing out the whey and hanging the bag to drip for a half day or so.

4. Put the soft American cheese into a bowl and add salt or other spices to taste. Be sure to refrigerate any uneaten cheese.

HAMBURGERS, THE PEOPLE'S CHOICE

If someone asked you what the number one favorite food in America is, what would you say? If what we eat the most is any indication, then the hamburger is the people's choice. On the average, every person in America eats more than two hundred hamburgers each year. But this most popular American food isn't a native to our country. The hamburger as we know it is an invention with a long history. Here is one version of how it came to be.

Legend has it that during medieval times German traders took to the Russian custom of eating raw shredded beef. German people learned to like the dish and adopted it for their own, calling the raw beefsteak "Hamburg" in honor of their native city. When German immigrants came to America, they brought the idea of eating raw beef with them. These "hamburgers," as the raw beef patties were called in America, were first cooked and put on a bun at the 1904 Louisiana Purchase Exposition in St. Louis. To Americans who were not accustomed to eating meat raw, the cooked hamburger was an instant success.

Bad times for the burger

The dish has had its ups and downs. The hamburger—or at least its name—disappeared from popularity for awhile during World War I when anti-German feeling ran high. At that time hamburger was renamed "Salisbury Steak" in honor of Dr. James Salisbury, a nineteenth century nutritionist who recommended a diet of ground beef as a cure for all types of illnesses.

The name hamburger did not become popular again until 1921 when America's first chain of hamburger restaurants—the White Cas-

tle—opened. The original White Castle hamburger was square, served in a bun, and cost five cents. The American concept of the fast-food hamburger was born.

Today you can have a hamburger nearly any way you like and eat it nearly any place you go. You can choose a plain hamburger, cheeseburger, pizza burger, pickle burger, bacon burger, soy burger, or one from any of the dozens of hamburger chains, and eat it in your car, at the drive-in movies, at a sports event, in the shopping mall, at carnivals, and even at home in your own kitchen.

The Best Burgers

You might think it unnecessary to explain the simple process of preparing and cooking an all-American hamburger, but you will be well rewarded if you know the fine points of hamburger cookery.

First, you need to buy good hamburger meat. It is difficult if not impossible to know the quality and reliability of meat-market hamburger that has already been ground and packaged. Quality grades and names of hamburger meat vary

from store to store and you probably don't know how much fat, or fillers, or chemical additives may have been added to the beef. To be sure of consistently good hamburger (and don't mind a little extra effort), grind your own hamburger from chuck meat. Select a piece of chuck with just enough fat to suit your taste, or trim off any extra fat. Cut the meat into two inch squares or smaller and run them twice through a meat grinder. For safety, have an adult supervise.

Ingredients

1 pound ground beef
salt, pepper, other favorite seasonings
hamburger buns

Utensils

broiling or frying pan

1. Add nothing else to the ground meat and, above all, don't stir or handle it more than absolutely necessary. Any handling of the ground beef will cause the meat to bind together and be tougher when eating. Using your hands, and without pressing the meat flat, shape the hamburger into patties about one-half-inch thick. One pound of meat will make about four good-sized burgers. Now season the patties to taste; maybe using salt, pepper, garlic powder, soy sauce, chopped onion, butter, or whatever you like.

2. For the best taste, cook the patties under a broiler or over charcoal. If you pan-fry or grill the hamburger, cook it in its own fat over a medium to high heat. Cook the hamburger patties to taste, or about three or so minutes on each side depending on the size. Searing each side over high heat will seal the natural juices inside of the hamburger and actually help the meat to cook better and be tastier.

3. While the hamburgers are

cooking, warm the rolls in the toaster or oven. When pan-grilling or charcoal-cooking the hamburgers, and especially when adding cheese for cheeseburgers, heat the roll by placing the two halves directly on top of the cooking patty after one side of the patty has been cooked and the patty flipped over. After cooking, add ketchup, mustard, lettuce, tomato, onion, or whatever you usually like on your hamburger.

HOT DOGS

There is very little American about the sausage called "hot dogs." Many countries made sausages long before America, but the idea of putting a sausage in a roll and calling it a hot dog is certainly our own. The first sausage on a roll was served at the Louisiana Purchase Exposition in 1904. Legend has it that a sausage seller began giving away white cotton gloves with his sausages which he called "red hots" because they were "too hot to handle." This advertising gimmick was successful but turned out to be quite expensive, so he, as well as other sausage vendors, began serving their red hots in a folded slice of bread or a bun. The hot dog as we know it was born.

The nickname "hot dog" came into being a few years later when a newspaper cartoonist drew a dachshund nestled in a roll. He commented on how a sausage he had eaten at a baseball game resembled the dog's body, and he captioned his drawing "Hot Dog."

The hot dog has certainly become one of America's favorite foods and one of the most popular sausages in the world. We still eat hot dogs at baseball games, as well as on cookouts and parties or anyplace else that appeals to our informal, casual, and often hurried eating habits.

Batter-dipped Corn Dogs

Throughout much of western and southwestern America, people enjoy their hot dogs dipped in a delicious corn-flavored batter and fried until golden brown. These corn dogs are served on a stick like an ice cream pop, and are favorites at roadside restaurants and snack bars. Although most corn-dog eat-

America's favorite "quick" foods often sound and look delicious.

ers prefer their dogs plain, mustard and sometimes ketchup are often used for additional flavor.

Transforming an ordinary hot dog into a corn dog is a bit of a job, so you might make several at a time and freeze those you do not eat. After freezing, the cooked corn dog can be simply reheated in a low oven for about ten to fifteen minutes. Making corn dogs requires deep fat frying at high temperatures, so make this recipe only with the help of an adult.

Ingredients
cooking oil for frying
2 cups all-purpose flour
⅓ cup yellow cornmeal
1 tb. baking powder
¼ cup sugar
1 tb. salt
3 tb. dry milk
1 cup water
12–16 boiled hot dogs

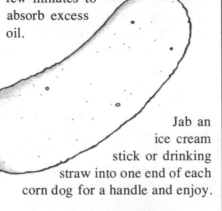

Utensils
deep pot for frying
deep-frying thermometer (optional)
mixing bowl
mixing spoon
paper towels
ice cream stick or plastic drinking
    straw for each hot dog

1. Fill a deep pot with at least two inches of cooking oil and put it over medium heat. Let the oil heat for about twenty to thirty minutes. The oil must reach a temperature of 360°F./182°C. or the corn dogs won't cook properly. Use a deep-frying thermometer if you have one.

2. Mix all the dry ingredients in a large bowl. Add the water slowly until the mixture is of a thick consistency, but not too pasty.

3. Dip each hot dog into the batter so that it is completely coated and then, using a mixing spoon, place each hot dog in the hot oil. Cook for about two to three minutes, or until the batter coating is

golden brown. Be sure the corn dog is completely submerged in the oil. If the breading falls apart while cooking, or if it takes longer than three minutes to brown, the oil is not hot enough.

4. Remove the cooked corn dog from the oil with a mixing spoon, and place it on paper toweling for a few minutes to absorb excess oil.

Jab an ice cream stick or drinking straw into one end of each corn dog for a handle and enjoy.

SUBMARINE SANDWICH

Depending on where you go in the U.S., the submarine sandwich is called either a hero, hoagie, grinder, poor-boy, bomber, rocket, torpedo, or the original "sub." And no one seems to agree on what ingredients you need to end up with a true sub—except, perhaps, a "submarine" roll. Some stores call their sandwiches subs just *because* they're served on a sub roll.

A real sub is more than a mere sandwich—it's an art form to be appreciated in its preparation, enjoyed in its eating, and remembered with a lingering satisfaction until "next time." The specific in-

A correctly made submarine sandwich.

gredients must be carefully chosen and proportions exactly adjusted so that no one flavor—or texture—dominates. In the finest sub shops the ingredients are always freshly cut so that each sandwich can be "custom built." And neatness is not necessarily a plus, the best-tasting subs having ingredients that hang from the sides and ends of the roll. Arrangement of the ingredients cannot be sloppy, however: the sub eater should taste all of the makings on his first giant bite.

Sub city

Subs vary in quality from place to place, but the one and only sub center of the universe—and its home—is Philadelphia, South Philly to be exact. Although, sub experts know that the best subs can be found at nearly any sub shop in Wilmington, Delaware (just a few miles south of Philadelphia). Subs made in Wilmington have been taken as gifts to people all over America. A twelve-foot-long Wilmington sub was once ordered by the House of Representatives in Washington, and a two hundred-foot Wilmington sub was constructed for a charity benefit where it was sold by the slice. The best sub shops throughout the country usually have proprietors, who, when questioned, admit to having received their training in sub-making in the Philadelphia/Wilmington area.

Assembling the best-ever sub

Sub sandwiches must never be prepared in advance, or in the kitchen of a restaurant away from the customer. Each sub must be built to order, in view of the person for whom it is being prepared. That way the customer can make his preferences plain: "Light on the oil, no pickles, and I'd like a little

extra cheese, please," for example. By having his work constantly scrutinized by the customer, the sub maker becomes more and more skilled at his art and "worldly wise" in dealing with people. Of course, every sub maker will tell you that his sub is the best in town, and a lot else you'd probably be interested in knowing. Like the barber and the cab driver, sub makers must enjoy dealing with people, and their customers expect to be able to "shoot the breeze" with them. The regular sub eater enjoys everything there is about coming to

a sub shop, and deep loyalties are quickly formed.

Construction plans

To achieve the best flavor, all sub ingredients should be at room temperature. Have cold cuts and cheese sliced to normal lunch-meat thickness. The completed sub should be eaten soon after it is made or the roll will become soggy. Subs that are going to travel, or won't be eaten for some time, should not have the oil added until just before serving.

The following submarine

sandwich formula is courtesy of John Sitoras of Tom's Sub Shop, 30th and Market Streets, Wilmington, Delaware.

1. Begin with a ten-to-twelve inch long Italian sub roll with a hard (but not too hard) crust and a soft inside. A length of Vienna bread or Italian bread will do, but you may need to scoop out some of the soft bread inside to make room for the ingredients. Slice the roll lengthwise nearly all the way through and open the roll flat.

2. Spread five slices of cooked salami or Genoa salami across both sides of the open roll.

3. Add two slices of Provolone cheese.

4. Tear a handful of lettuce from the head (never cut the lettuce with a knife), crunch it up, and add it to the sandwich.

5. Add sliced raw onion to suit your taste.

6. Add four or five slices of tomato in a row down the middle of the open sandwich.

7. Place five or six round slices of kosher dill pickle over the tomato.

8. Add sliced hot cherry peppers to taste.

9. Spice and flavor the sandwich with salt, oregano (or sage), and soybean oil (not olive oil).

10. Spread five slices of Cappicola ham across both sides of the open roll.

11. Add two slices of boiled ham down the middle of the sandwich.

12. Place the dull back edge of a long kitchen knife along the center of the sandwich to hold ingredients down while you close the roll.

13. Pull out the knife, cut the sub in two (for easier handling) and you're ready to eat.

Weigh your sandwich as a final test of your "submanship"; completed it should weigh at least one pound.

SPICY KETCHUP

Without question ketchup is America's favorite sauce. We put ketchup on almost everything we eat. Just ask someone what foods they like with ketchup and you will probably be surprised. We Americans have been known to put ketchup on potatoes, meats, tuna fish, eggs, peanut butter, clams, onions, salads, pickles, cereals, soups, spaghetti, cheese, cakes, ice cream, and in several beverages.

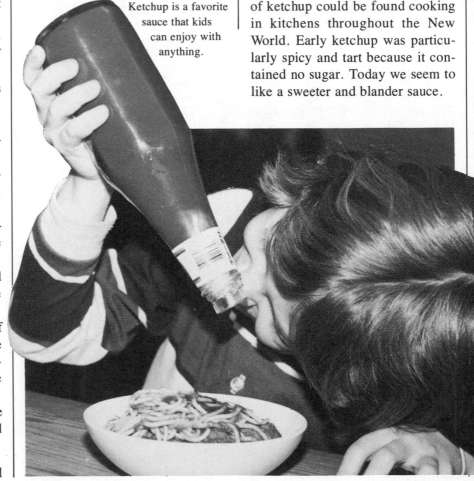

Ketchup is a favorite sauce that kids can enjoy with anything.

Although we may think of ketchup as American, the spicy red tomato sauce has a rather long and adventurous history that began when sailors brought back to America tomato seeds and recipes for a sauce they had eaten in many other parts of the world. The spicy tomato sauce was called *kachiap* in Spain, *kechap* in Singapore, *kai-sup* in China, *kechup* in Malaysia, and the list goes on. (You may have noticed in the food market that several food companies spell *ketchup* either *catsup* or *ketchap*, as well as *ketchup*.) All three ways of spelling are correct; it is only a custom that ketchup companies keep the spelling they started with years ago. Before then the early settlers made another kind of spicy sauce using walnuts and mushrooms or fruits and berries. But once America discovered the tomato, bubbling pots of ketchup could be found cooking in kitchens throughout the New World. Early ketchup was particularly spicy and tart because it contained no sugar. Today we seem to like a sweeter and blander sauce.

Out of the bottle, onto the plate

Ketchup was one of the first factory-produced foods in America and has always been packaged in the familiar eight-sided glass bottle with a tall, narrow neck. The shape of ketchup bottles was designed for holding and pouring and not for appearance, although that might not seem so obvious to you if you've ever tried to coax that first dash of ketchup from a stubborn bottle. To keep the contents from spoiling, the first ketchup bottles were plugged with a cork and soft wax. Thin metal foil was then twisted over the neck of the bottle and a paper band placed around the neck to hold the foil and add a distinctive trademark to the product. By the twentieth century screw-cap closures had replaced cork and wax, but out of custom the neck band on the bottle still remains.

Here is the recipe for a ketchup you can make. The ingredients are the same as those used in Early America, except that sugar has been added. The ingredients below will make one eight-to-ten ounce bottle of ketchup. The entire project from start to cleanup takes about two hours. If you like, you can make larger amounts of ketchup by proportionally increasing the quantity of ingredients; however, the cooking times may be somewhat longer.

Ingredients

4 medium to large ripe tomatoes
1 small onion, peeled
½ sweet red pepper (sweet green pepper will also do)
⅓ cup sugar
¼ tsp. each paprika, salt, allspice, ground cinnamon
dash of clove, celery salt, dry mustard
juice of ½ lemon

Utensils

2-quart pot
small kitchen knife
kitchen blender
measuring cups and spoons
mixing spoon

1. Fill the pot half full of water. Add the tomatoes whole and bring to a boil. Turn off the heat and allow the water to cool. Remove the tomatoes, cut out the stem end, and peel off the tomato skins. Throw away the skins, and dump out the water.

2. Cut the tomatoes, onion, and sweet pepper into small chunks and put them together in the blender at medium speed for fifteen to thirty seconds, or until the mixture is soupy.

3. Pour the mixture into the pot and cook over a low heat. Do not put a lid on the pot. While the mixture is cooking, add all the remaining ingredients except the lemon juice. Stir the mixture at least every ten minutes and cook for about one and one-half hours, or until the ketchup is as thick as you like it.

4. When the ketchup seems thick and ready, stir in the lemon juice and cook for another few minutes. Turn off the heat, and let the ketchup briefly cool. Then pour the ketchup into a storing jar or serving bottle and refrigerate.

Homemade ketchup is darker in color than the store-bought kind and is also a bit more spicy. When making the next batch, you might need to adjust the amounts of the various ingredients to suit your own taste.

CRISPY POTATO CHIPS

About one hundred years ago, an American Indian chief, George Crum, was working as a chef in a hotel kitchen in Saratoga Springs, New York. On one occasion, a few hotel patrons complained that the french fried potatoes served them were too thick. So, to "give them what they wanted," the chef cut the potatoes paper thin, deep-fried them and served his guests his new-fangled "Saratoga Chips." The new, thin potato chips became the specialty of their house, and soon of nearly everyone's house throughout the land.

Ingredients

4 large potatoes
vegetable oil
salt

Utensils

vegetable (potato) peeler
cooking pot
paper towels
slotted spoon

1. Remove the skin from the potatoes using a vegetable peeler; then rinse the potatoes under cool water. Dry them well.

2. Using the vegetable peeler, cut each potato into several wide, paper-thin slices, the thinner the better. Be careful; it is not easy to slice a potato. Make sure the potato is dry and keep your fingers away from the cutting edge of the peeler. If the peeler seems to get stuck on a slice, turn the potato around or over, and slice it in a different direction. Put the potato slices on paper towels and blot them with another piece of toweling to soak up the juices.

3. Put enough vegetable oil in a wide cooking pot to cover the bottom to a depth of one inch. Set the stove burner to medium high and heat the oil. Be very careful! Frying requires very high cooking temperatures and an adult should supervise this part of the chip making. Never let your fingers touch the hot oil, or anything hot, for that matter.

Getting potatoes ready for homemade chips.

Be careful of splattering oil when making potato chips.

4. When the oil is hot, put the potato chips one at a time into the pot until most of the surface of the oil is covered by them. The potato slice will cook up in about thirty to forty-five seconds, so be ready to fish out the cooked chips *as soon* as they start to turn a light golden brown. Do not let the chips turn completely brown before removing them from the pot, or they will overcook.

5. Scoop the cooked chips from the pot using a slotted spoon so the oil will drain, and place the hot fried chips on several thicknesses of paper towel to absorb any remaining oil. Continue to cook up all the sliced potatoes. When the chips have cooled, put them in a closable container or a plastic bag, and add salt to taste. Remember to let the chips cool before touching or eating them.

POPCORN

Corn is a food native to America. At the first Thanksgiving feast, an Iroquois Indian presented the settlers with this novel fare in the form of fluffy popped corn kernels. The settlers did not quite know what it was until it was explained that popcorn was to be eaten—so the settlers put it in their soup! The popped corn kernels quickly caught on as a new staple food. Besides tasting good, popcorn is also nutritious and was soon being served to colonial children as a breakfast cereal. And quite a few Sunday dinners consisted of popcorn served with butter and salt.

In present-day America popcorn is one of our greatest munchies and has almost become a necessity for watching a movie. Americans are the biggest—if not the only—popcorn eaters in the world.

The secret: How popcorn pops

Locked inside every popcorn kernel there is a tiny amount of water. When the kernel is heated, the water turns to steam. The steam expands until it suddenly blasts the kernel to nearly thirty times its original size in volume.

There are basically two kinds of popcorn, white and yellow, with many sub-varieties of each. White popcorn is almost tasteless, while yellow popcorn has a mild, nutty flavor. You might notice that popped corn has different shapes. Two of the most common shapes are described by their names: butterfly popcorn and mushroom popcorn. The common grocery store type is usually a variety of yellow butterfly popcorn.

Make a Corn Popper

Since that first Thanksgiving there have been many types of corn poppers devised. As a pastime and for a snack, Colonial children would throw popcorn kernels on the hot coals and stones of the kitchen fireplace where the kernels would burst open with a sharp pop and bounce around for the children to scramble after. A great variety of kitchen pans and crocks with lids were used as corn poppers, but the favorite Early American popper, and by far the best, was a covered wire mesh basket held over the kitchen fire with a long handle. Not only could you hear the corn popping, but you could watch it! Wire basket corn poppers are still sold at some hardware stores and fireplace shops, or you can make a version of the basket popper yourself.

Materials
piece of *metal* wire window screening, about 2 feet square
wire coathanger

Tools
felt-tipped pen or crayon
yardstick
large scissors

1. Using a felt-tipped pen or crayon and a yardstick, draw an equilateral triangle on the screening (a triangle with all three sides the same length) about eighteen to twenty-four inches per side, Fig. 1.

2. Using a large pair of scissors, cut out the triangle and save a piece of the scrap screening. Fold about a half-inch of each edge of the triangle over. You can do this with your fingers—use the yardstick as an edge guide—but be careful not to poke yourself on the prickly wire ends of the screening, Fig. 2.

3. Lay the triangle flat with the folded edge sides facing up, and with the yardstick and marker draw lines from the centers of each edge to form a smaller equilateral triangle in the center, Fig. 2.

4. Now carefully fold up each of the three large triangles, bending

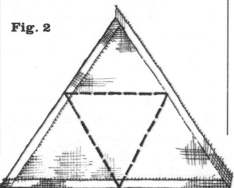
Fig. 2

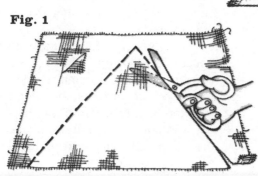
Fig. 1

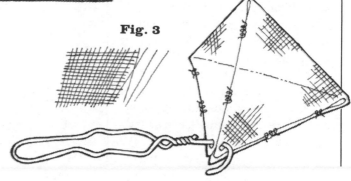
Fig. 3

the screening along the lines drawn to make the second equilateral triangle, Fig. 2.

5. Using lengths of screen wire pulled from the scrap of screening, fasten together the adjoining edges of the three bent together triangles in about two or three places on the edge of each, but not too close to the top. You must be able to pull the points of the basket back to open the popper.

6. Take the wire coathanger and bend it out to make a handle, Fig. 3. Put the hook end of the coat hanger through two of the points, Fig. 3.

7. To add popcorn kernels to the popper, pull back the third point. To pour out the popped corn, remove the handle and open all three points. The popper will cool almost immediately after being removed from the heat and does not need to be washed. Be sure to use a pot holder around the hanger handle when popping corn to prevent burning your hand.

Corn Popping

Ingredients
popcorn kernels
butter
salt

Utensils
corn popper

1. Open the top of the popper and pour in enough kernels to cover about half of the bottom of the basket. Do *not* use any cooking oil. If you are using a gas or electric stove, use the largest burner and set the temperature to high.

2. Attach the handle to the basket and hold it a few inches above the heat. If you are popping over a campfire or fireplace, keep the basket above the flames.

3. Continually shake the basket

gently to keep the kernels moving around so as not to be scorched by the heat—this is very important. In about a minute the first kernel should pop, and within a few more seconds you will see hundreds of kernels exploding in the basket.

4. Continue to shake the basket so that the already popped corn won't burn and any unpopped kernels will fall to the basket bottom.

5. When the popping has slowed down and almost stopped, take the popper from the heat and pour the popcorn into a bowl. The popcorn is now ready to eat, but since basket popcorn is made without oil, you will have to pour melted butter over the popcorn before salt will stick to it. Basket popcorn is the best tasting popcorn you will probably ever eat.

Popcorn Balls

Although there were no candies in Early America, molasses was sometimes used to make food treats. Popcorn balls were one of those treats made especially for kids. When making this, remember that candy requires cooking at high temperatures, so kids must get help from a parent or someone older who is allowed to use the stove. Cooking candy should be done when the weather is cold and dry. When it is hot and humid, the

candy might get very sticky.

Ingredients
1 cup molasses (dark or light)
1 cup sugar
1 tb. butter
8 cups (2 qts.) unsalted popcorn

Utensils
measuring cups and spoons
wooden mixing spoon
medium-sized pot (3 qts. or larger)
candy thermometer (optional)
waxed paper

1. Mix the molasses, sugar, and butter in the pot, and cook over medium heat.

2. Stir occasionally until the mixture begins to boil. You may need to turn down the heat a bit to keep the mixture from boiling over the pot. If you have a candy thermometer, attach it to the pot. Be sure the thermometer bulb is in the mixture but not touching the side or bottom of the pot. Let the mixture heat until it reaches "hard ball" (260°F./127°C.). Depending upon your particular stove or pot, it might take twenty to thirty minutes to get the mixture to hard ball. If you don't use a candy thermometer, use the water method. After the mixture has been boiling for about five minutes, spoon a little out and let it drip into a cup of cold water. If the candy ball that forms in the water is firm, the mixture is ready.

3. Remove the pot from the heat. Add the popcorn to it, stirring and blending with a wooden spoon until all of the popcorn is coated. The candied popcorn should be cool enough to handle after five or ten minutes.

4. Lightly coat your hands with butter or cooking oil. When you are certain the mixture has cooled (don't be too anxious, but don't wait too long or the stuff will harden), scoop out handfuls, shape them into balls, and let them harden on waxed paper.

DOUGHNUTS

The early Dutch settlers and Pennsylvania Dutch Germans introduced to Colonial America a yeasty, deep-fried cake called an olykoeck, which literally meant "oil cake." Oil cake was a festive food often eaten at religious celebrations and especially as a last treat before Lent. The original oil cake was made of a yeast dough shaped into little cakes with raisins or a bit of chopped apple placed in the center. The cakes were deep-fried in hot fat until golden brown, rolled in sugar, and served hot.

Some oil-cake eaters preferred to dunk their cakes into coffee or eat them with a coating of sweet molasses. But the cakes were not yet doughnuts because they had no holes.

The legendary hole

American legend has it that the doughnut first got its hole in 1847 when Hanson Crockett Gregory, a young boy in Maine, complained to his mother that her oil cakes were uncooked and tasted "doughy" in the center. Before the next batch was cooked, Hanson poked a hole with his finger through the center of each of the cakes so they would cook better, and when his mother took the cakes with holes from the hot fat they were fried to perfection. The holes had done the trick. A bronze plaque marks Hanson Gregory's birthplace in Rockport, Maine, honoring the doughnut hole and its inventor.

Today the doughnut is an American institution and is made in a huge variety of flavors. You can eat your doughnuts chocolate-covered, jelly- or cream-filled, sugar-frosted, sprinkled with cinnamon and sugar, coated with nuts, dipped in honey, or just plain. Some doughnut bakers even sell the fried doughnut holes.

In recent years America has once again discovered the taste of the original oil cake or "fried dough." You probably know what a doughnut tastes like, so now try some fried dough and taste the treat our early ancestors enjoyed. (This project uses hot oil and younger children should have an adult assistant with them in the kitchen during the preparation and cooking.)

LUNCH COUNTER LINGO

All over America restaurants, diners, and lunch counters use a peculiar slang language of their own. The foods that are most commonly ordered, as well as other typical restaurant expressions, have "nicknames." Maybe you've been to a lunch counter and heard the waitress yell back to the cook, "Burn a burger all the way, a side of french, and a small cow." If you know lunch counter lingo, you know the waitress was placing an order for a well-done hamburger with all the trimmings (onions, lettuce, and tomato), a side order of french fried potatoes, and a small glass of milk.

For those of you who want to understand lunch counter lingo, or maybe even try to use it the next time you eat out, here are a few of the more common food nicknames and their meanings:

Adam and Eve on a raft: two poached eggs on toast
All the way: with all the regular trimmings
Apple: a slice of apple pie
Black and white: a chocolate soda with vanilla ice cream
Bloody: meat cooked rare
B.L.T.: a bacon, lettuce, and tomato sandwich

Bowl: a bowl of soup, as in a "bowl of chicken"
Bucket of mud: dish of chocolate ice cream
Burn: to cook well-done
C.B.: corned beef
China: a cup of tea
Cow: a glass of milk
Down: toasted, as in "a tuna sandwich down"
Draw one: a cup of coffee
Drop: a scoop of ice cream
Fire: chili, as in a "bowl of fire"
Grade 'A': milk
Hail: ice, as in "a coke, no hail"
O.J.: orange juice
On wheels: an order to go, as in "a burger on wheels"
Over easy: a fried egg done on both sides but soft inside
Patch: strawberry
Set-up: a place setting of silverware, napkin, and water
Side: a side order, as in "side of cole slaw"
Smear: butter
Stack: an order of hotcakes
Stretch: a Coke
Suds: a root beer
Walk: an order to go, as in "a B.L.T. to walk"
Twist: a slice of lemon
Wrecked: scrambled

Fried Dough

Ingredients
2 cups all-purpose flour
2½ tsp. baking powder
¼ tsp. cinnamon
¼ tsp. nutmeg
½ tsp. salt
1 egg
½ cup sugar
1½ tb. shortening (at room temperature)
½ cup milk
32 oz. shortening for frying

Utensils
2 large bowls
sifter
measuring spoons and cups
mixing spoon
rolling pin
spatula
deep frying pan

1. In one of the bowls sift or blend together the flour, baking powder, cinnamon, nutmeg, and salt.

2. In the other mixing bowl beat the egg for about thirty seconds until it is lemon-colored. Add the sugar and 1½ tablespoons shortening to the beaten egg and stir until there are no lumps.

3. Gradually add the flour mixture and milk to the egg mixture, a little at a time. Stir with a wooden spoon until the dough is well-blended. Now chill the dough in the refrigerator for a half hour.

4. In the deep frying pan (don't use a high-sided pot) melt enough shortening so that it is at least one inch deep. Put the heat on medium-low. If you have a candy or pot thermometer, heat the oil until it is 375°F.(175°C.). Oil for deep-frying is very hot and can splatter, so be very careful.

5. Sprinkle a little flour on a breadboard or a kitchen counter top so the dough won't stick. Scoop off a piece of dough about the size of a golf ball or a little larger, and roll out the dough with a floured rolling pin to a thickness of about one-quarter inch. Roll out the rest of the dough in the same way.

6. Lift up the flat dough shapes with a spatula and drop the dough into the frying oil one at a time. Cook the dough for one to two minutes on each side until golden brown. Remove the fried dough from the oil and drain on a few layers of paper towels. Makes six to eight large fried doughs.

If the oil is too hot, the dough will burn and won't get cooked all the way through. If the oil is not hot enough, the dough will become oil-soaked. You might test the temperature by frying a few test pieces of dough before frying the whole batch.

PEANUT BUTTER

Nearly one-half of all the peanuts grown in this country are used for making peanut butter, meaning that peanut butter is one of America's— and especially American kids'— favorite foods. We Americans like our peanut butter with jelly on bread, in celery ribs, with apples, bacon, bananas, ham, and even served as hot peanut butter soup. A United States senator even once claimed to have used peanut butter for shaving when he ran out of his regular shaving cream. Peanut butter is also quite nutritious. There is more protein in a pound of peanut butter than in a pound of sirloin steak. Depending on the process you use, you can make either creamy style or crunchy peanut butter.

Making Peanut Butter

Ingredients
roasted peanuts in shells
corn oil or vegetable oil

Utensils
measuring cup
food grinder (for crunchy style) or
    food blender (for smooth style)
tablespoon
jar

1. Crack open the shells and remove the peanuts. Most shells contain two peanuts, but it is not at all uncommon to find one, three, and occasionally four peanuts in a shell. Measure out about one cup of peanuts.

2. Remove the red skin from the peanuts.

3. If you want chunky peanut butter, put the peanuts in a food grinder and run the chopped mixture through three or more times until the peanut butter is the consistency you like. For creamy style peanut butter, chop up the peanuts in a food blender.

4. Add about one to two tablespoons of cooking oil in small amounts and regrind or blend the mixture until the peanut butter is the familiar paste consistency.

5. Add salt until the taste is just right.

Homemade peanut butter contains no preservatives or other additives, so to avoid spoiling, keep any unused portion in a closed jar in the refrigerator.

GRAHAM CRACKERS

Did you know that the graham crackers you eat today began as one of America's earliest health foods? The original graham biscuit appeared in the early part of the nineteenth century. They were made from whole wheat flour rather than the refined white flour that was popular then, and still is today.

Sylvester Graham, after whom the crackers were named, was a preacher and nutrition expert of the time who studied the eating habits of American people. He concluded that Americans were ruining their health by eating "bad" foods, such as meat, fat, salt, and especially refined white flour. Indigestion, Graham claimed, was a national disaster. The only way to stop it was for families to boycott commercial bakers and make bread at home using only the more nutritious coarse whole wheat. The commercial bakers didn't agree with Graham, of course, and once while preaching the virtues of whole wheat to a gathering in Boston, Graham and his followers were stormed by an angry mob of bakers. Actually, many of Graham's ideas about nutrition that seemed radical during his time have since been acknowledged as scientifically accurate.

Whole wheat treats

By virtue of his firm commitment to convert Americans to his ideas of nutrition, Graham initiated a health food movement that convinced some food stores, restaurants, and hotels across the country to serve breads and biscuits baked from only whole wheat or "graham" flour. Followers of the Graham nutrition movement even formed a Grahamite Society and opened food stores specializing in Graham flour and Graham products—including graham crackers.

The graham cracker is still popular today, probably not because of its nutritional value but because we like the taste. It's likely Sylvester Graham would be amazed and somewhat disappointed if he saw the way we Americans now eat his crackers—with honey, chocolate, cinnamon, pudding, or whatever cracker spread is favored.

S'mores

For many American kids the graham cracker has become an essential ingredient in one of their favorite cookout snacks— s'mores. In fact, the name of this delicious treat, if you haven't already guessed, came from kids always asking for "some more."

To make s'mores, toast a marshmallow on the end of a stick over a campfire flame. The more gooey and burnt the marshmallow, the better. Put the melted marsh-

mallow on a graham cracker square, add a hunk of milk chocolate and sandwich the whole thing with another graham cracker.

PRETZELS

Pretzels were a favorite snack of many people long before they came to America. According to legend, the pretzel got its start when an imaginative European monk baked twisted ropes of dough into tasty rewards for children who had learned their prayers properly—the name pretzel comes from the Latin word "pretiola," meaning small reward. The distinctive pretzel shape is supposed to represent the crossed arms of a child praying.

When the first settlers came to America on the *Mayflower*, the pretzel came along with them. The pretzel quickly became a favorite snack here in America as well.

Pretzels were used as money to barter with the Indians and Colonial children would frequently make a wish on a pretzel before eating it, just as you might do on a wishbone. Two people would each hook a finger through the pretzel loops and pull—the one getting the larger piece was supposedly granted his wish.

Twisters weren't always dancers

In 1861 the first pretzel factory in America was opened in Lititz, Pennsylvania, and is still in operation today. Before the relatively recent invention of pretzel-making machines, factory workers known as "twisters" shaped the dough.

But American pretzels were not always as crunchy as the ones we eat today. All pretzels were once soft and chewy, but, as legend has it, a factory pretzel baker fell asleep while a batch of pretzels was cooking in the oven. He woke up to find his pretzels had overbaked— instead of being soft, they were quite hard and crisp. Before tossing out the batch, a few fellow workers tasted the crispy baked dough and liked them. By accident, America had invented the hard pretzel, and it quickly became very popular.

Pretzels without salt

Since then, American ingenuity has been responsible for many new varieties of the pretzel. Just a few years ago, a leading bakery tried to freeze pretzels, but the salt became damp and didn't taste right. The pretzels were baked and frozen without salt, and a new variety known as "bald heads" was introduced. Bald heads have taken their place as a favorite American snack along with cheese pretzels, pretzel sticks, rods, nuggets, and sticks, kosher pretzels, and light or dark chocolate-covered pretzels. There is even a special pretzel used as a teething ring for babies.

Pretzels are actually very nutritional snacks. They are rich in protein, contain several healthful minerals, and their crispness or chewiness helps to exercise the jaw. For those snackers who are diet conscious, there is less fat and fewer calories in a pretzel than in nearly any other snack.

Philadelphia Soft Pretzels

Nowhere in America is the pretzel more popular than in Philadelphia, Pennsylvania. In fact, Philadelphians eat nearly half of all the pretzels made in America, quite a few of them the original soft variety. On nearly every downtown Philadelphia street corner there is a vendor with a glass box pushcart, carrying soft pretzels and a jar of yellow mustard for flavoring. Here is the pretzel recipe:

Ingredients
1 cup warm water
2 packages active dry yeast
2 tb. sugar
3 cups all-purpose flour
2 tsp. baking soda
butter or shortening
1 egg
coarse salt (kosher salt)

Utensils
measuring cups and spoons
large mixing bowl
mixing spoon
breadboard (optional)
dish towel
large shallow pot
2 cookie sheets
rolling pin
table knife
spatula
small bowl
pastry brush

1. Put the cup of very warm (not hot) water into the mixing bowl and add the yeast. Stir until the yeast is completely dissolved.

2. Add the sugar and stir. Gradually add the flour and stir. As you are adding the last of the flour, the dough will become stiff and dry—that is as it should be.

3. Sprinkle some flour on the counter top or a breadboard and flour your hands. Now knead the dough for about five minutes by pressing it flat with the heels of your hands, folding the flattened dough in half, and then pressing it flat again.

4. Form the dough into a ball, put it back into the bowl, cover the bowl with a dish towel, and place the bowl in a warm, dark place for at least thirty minutes. The rising dough will nearly double in size.

5. While the dough is rising, heat the oven to 400°F.(204°C.). Fill the pot half full of water, add the baking soda, and bring the

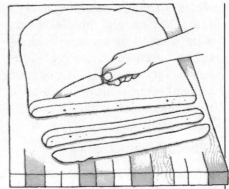

Fig. 4

water to a slow boil. Grease or butter the cookie sheet.

6. When the dough has risen, put it back on the floured breadboard or counter. Flour the rolling pin and roll out the dough into an approximate square about one-fourth to one-half inch (six to ten mm.) thick. Using the dull back edge of a table knife, cut the dough with a back and forth sawing motion into strips about as wide as your fattest fingers. You don't have to be exact, Fig. 4.

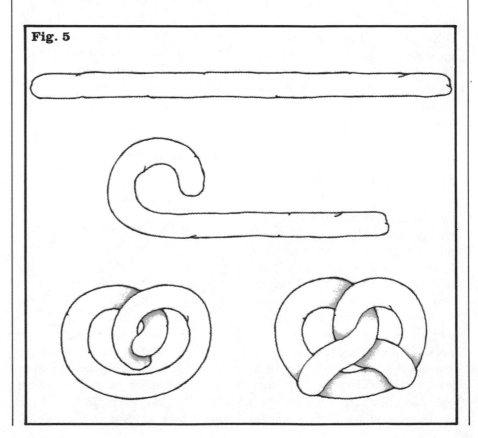

Fig. 5

7. Twist each strip into a pretzel shape, as shown in illustration, and pinch the ends together, Fig. 5. As you handle the long strips of dough, try not to let them stretch too thin.

8. One at a time, place each pretzel on the spatula and lower it into the boiling water for five to ten seconds. Remove the pretzel with the spatula and place it on the greased cookie sheet.

9. Beat the egg in a small bowl for a minute, and with a pastry brush coat the top of each pretzel with the egg. Now sprinkle the salt to your liking over the pretzels.

10. Bake the pretzels for about twelve to fifteen minutes or until they are golden brown.

AMERICA'S SWEET TOOTH

Americans are the world's greatest snack eaters, and our favorite snacks are sweets. Even though we are constantly warned that excess sugar can cause us to become overweight, decay our teeth, ruin our appetites, and disrupt our digestive systems, we still can't seem to get enough. After meals, between meals, at the movies, at parties—wherever we go, we seem to crave that special taste. We sprinkle sugar on our cereals, demand it in our drinks, add it to our non-dessert cooking. Food companies take advantage of our sweet tooth and add sugar to many products where we least expect it, so that we'll return for more. Because of our eating habits, we've become addicted to sugar. We even choose to reward children by giving them sweets.

Just as our bodies need water and nutritional food, we also require sugar for energy. Any good diet including fruits and vegetables should supply our bodies with more than enough. But if we insist on eating candy and ice cream, we can still be healthy—if we don't eat too much. Occasional sweet treats are fine and fun; it's the excess sugar we consume that is bad for us. You should try to be a little more aware of just how much sugar you eat and try to cut down. Then the delicious recipes which follow will be a special pleasure, and doubly good because you make them yourself.

An old-fashioned root beer ad.

Soft Drinks

In Early American homes various teas and berry juices were the common everyday beverages. And although bubbly carbonated water was known then, no one actually thought of drinking the stuff. It was a professor of chemistry at Yale University who first bottled carbonated water—called "mineral water," "belch water," or the more popular name, "soda water"—and convinced people to drink it as a refreshment. Early soda water was clear and unflavored, but it quickly became popular because the makers and sellers claimed that the bubbly stuff made the drinker feel as good as if they were "in love." It was several more years before someone added flavor and sugar to soda water to improve the taste. Flavors then included root beer, birch beer, spruce beer, pepsin, ginger, lemon, cherry, sarsaparilla, and the most popular flavor, cola. Although cola and other carbonated drinks were then believed to be remedies for headaches and other body pains, today "soft drinks" are promoted as just being refreshing; we drink soda solely for pleasure.

Several magazines and cookbooks of the 1850's published recipes for making homemade soda water with a variety of flavors. One of those sodas can be made using ingredients you probably have in your kitchen.

SODA POP

As an experiment you might mix up an old-fashioned soda drink. The taste will not be like the soda we drink today at all, although the bubbles will still tickle your nose. Here is the basic recipe.

Ingredients
fruit drink, punch, iced tea, or juice
½ tsp. cream of tartar
¼ tsp. baking soda
white sugar

Utensils
drinking glass
measuring spoons

1. Into a glass of fruit drink, punch (or any of the other listed possibilities) that is two-thirds full add a half teaspoon cream of tartar and a quarter teaspoon baking soda.

2. If the drink you are using does not already contain sugar, add one teaspoon of white sugar to the glass.

3. Stir for a few seconds until the soda water is bubbly, and then taste the drink quickly—you'll have to decide whether or not to finish the glass. Experiment using different drinks and flavors as well, or different proportions of the ingredients.

Ice Cream

Americans are in love with ice cream. We produce and consume more ice cream than any other country in the world, to the point that we tend to think of ice cream as a typically American food. This is only partly true. The people of many countries had learned the process of ice cream-making long before America was born. It was we Americans, however, who made the frozen treat so widely popular.

George Washington and Thomas Jefferson were both exceptionally fond of ice cream and had it served frequently, especially at formal dinner parties. At that time ice cream was considered a rare treat because it was so difficult to make. There were no home freezers for making ice or for keeping the ice cream from melting. Ice was either cut from frozen streams or ponds, or fresh snow was used. It was not until the 1800's and the invention of the "icebox" and "ice cream freezer" that any family was able to make their own ice cream. All the ice cream freezer required was the ingredients and muscle power. The kitchen icebox kept the ice cream frozen.

I scream, you scream

Ice cream was soon the rage of America. Ice cream parlors became quite fashionable and ice cream street vendors attracted their customers by yelling out, "I scream, ice cream." All kinds of ice cream dishes and concoctions were invented, including the popular ice cream sundae embellished with fruits, syrups, nuts, candies, jellies, and, of course, various flavored ice creams. There are several stories or legends about how the ice cream sundae got its name, but all seem to agree that its name is a purposeful misspelling of the day.

But the greatest boon to the popularity of ice cream was the accidental invention of the ice cream

cone at the 1904 Louisiana Purchase Exposition in St. Louis. An ice cream vendor ran out of dishes and the waffle vendor next to him offered his waffles as a substitute. The ice cream man rolled the waffle into a cone. The combination was delicious and the ice cream cone was invented.

EASY VANILLA ICE CREAM

Although an ice cream freezer makes ice cream quickly and easily, you can make homemade ice cream using only a few kitchen utensils and a little muscle power.

Ingredients

⅓ cup sugar
1 tb. all-purpose flour
dash of salt
1 cup milk
1 egg (beaten)
1 cup cream
1 tb. vanilla
lots of ice
rock salt

Utensils

medium-sized cooking pot
large ice bucket or plastic pail
1 or 2 lb. coffee can with a snap-on plastic lid
wooden spoon

1. Mix the sugar, flour, salt, and milk in the pot and heat over a medium low heat until the mixture thickens. Stir occasionally.

2. Add the beaten egg to the mixture, then cook and stir for about one minute. Turn off the heat and let the mixture cool for ten to fifteen minutes.

3. Add the cream and vanilla to the mixture and stir well.

4. Put a layer of crushed ice in the bottom of the ice bucket or pail and sprinkle rock salt over the ice. Use approximately one part salt to six parts ice. If necessary, table salt can be used instead of rock salt.

5. Fill the coffee can with the cooled ice cream mixture no more than two-thirds full and place the can in the bucket.

6. Add more ice and salt to the bucket around the can until the bucket is full nearly to the top of the can.

7. Using a wooden spoon, stir the ice cream mixture until it becomes frozen mush. You may have to stir for twenty or thirty minutes. Add ice and salt to the bucket to maintain the ice level around the can.

8. Remove the can of ice cream when it has become too thick to stir, put on the lid, and put the can in the refrigerator freezer to "ripen." The ice cream will be ready to eat in a few hours. Makes one pint.

Vanilla Molasses Taffy

An afternoon taffy-pull party was once a popular pastime in America, as much for the making as for eating the candy. Taffy pullers get to pull, twist, stretch, and play with the rubbery candy until it becomes taffy—then the second treat comes in the eating. First try the recipe yourself or with a friend, then some afternoon have your own old-fashioned taffy-pull party.

Remember, making candy requires cooking at high temperatures, so kids must have help from a parent or someone who is older and allowed to use the stove. Cooking candy should be done when the weather is cool and dry. When it is hot or humid, the candy might get very sticky.

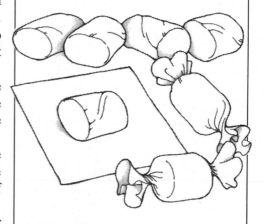

Ingredients

1½ cups sugar
1 cup molasses
¼ cup water
1 tb. vinegar
2 tb. butter
½ tsp. baking soda
1 tsp. vanilla

Utensils

measuring cups and spoons
wooden mixing spoon
medium-size pot
candy thermometer (optional)
large baking pan
knife

1. Mix the sugar, molasses, water, and vinegar in the pot and cook over a medium heat. Stir occasionally until the mixture begins to boil. As the mixture heats, its volume will nearly double. Turn the heat down as necessary to keep the mixture from boiling over. If you have a candy thermometer, attach it to the pot, being sure the thermometer bulb is in the mixture but not touching the sides or bottom of the pot. Let the mixture heat until the thermometer reads "soft crack" (275°F./135°C.). Be patient. It may take thirty minutes or longer for the mixture to reach the correct temperature. If you don't have a candy thermometer, use the water-drop method. After the mixture has been boiling for about fifteen minutes, spoon a little out and let it drip into a cup of cold water. The candy ball that forms in the water should be firm and hard. Then the mixture is ready. Keep testing until you get it right.

2. Turn off the heat and stir the butter, baking soda, and the vanilla into the mixture.

3. Butter the bottom and sides of a large baking pan and pour the taffy mixture into the pan to cool for twenty to thirty minutes.

4. When the taffy is not too hot to be handled (but *not* cool), butter your hands (have any other taffy pullers do the same) and pick up the taffy. Pull the taffy into long strips, and then fold and squeeze it into a large lump. Continue to pull the taffy again and again until it turns much lighter in color and begins to pull apart.

5. Stretch and twist the taffy into long skinny rolls, then cut the rolls into small chewable pieces using a buttered kitchen knife and scissors. Wrap each of the candy pieces in waxed paper.

Chewing Gum

Americans first began chewing gum when the native Indians taught the settlers to chew the gummy resins of certain trees. It seemed as though the act of chewing helped to relieve thirst, tension, loneliness, boredom, sadness, and anger. But even with these relaxing virtues, from the beginning, the chewing of gum was considered by many Americans to be a bad and unmannerly habit. Many people thought that chewing gum caused tooth decay and that swallowing gum would cause your insides to stick together. Early books of etiquette, if they mentioned gum at all, flatly stated that chewing gum was vulgar and unattractive. Even in plays and early movies, it was always the bad guy who chewed gum, never the hero.

Actually, the only thing bad about chewing gum is the unnecessary sugar you get from it. Rather than being bad for your teeth, chewing gum helps keep your teeth clean, strengthens your jaw muscles, and helps your blood circulation. Chewing will make your ears pop clear when they get blocked or start to ring at high altitudes. Many dieters chew gum instead of eating, and American astronauts have chewed gum as a substitute for toothbrushes.

A substitute for rubber

The first gum to be commercially produced and sold in America was made by John Curtis, a Maine logger, who gave up tree cutting to boil down and package spruce tree gum for his fellow chewers. But as spruce tree gum became scarce and difficult to process, it was necessary to find another more plentiful source of gum. Chewing gum as we know it today came about when Thomas Adams, Sr., a New York photographer and part-time inventor, failed in his attempts to make a rubber substitute out of sap from a

The first commerical chewing gum made of chicle. A picture of New York's City Hall appears on the box.

GETTING OFF THE GUM

One of the lesser pleasures of chewing gum is having it get stuck to the bottom of your shoe, in your hair, or anywhere else that's outside your mouth. If you are ever stuck with some misplaced gooey gum, here are a few hints to help get unstuck.

1. If the gum is stuck on fabric, don't wash it! Gum that has been washed into cloth just can't be removed. First try putting an ice cube on the gum to harden it. Then scrape the gum off with a table knife. If that doesn't work, you might try using rubbing alcohol or nail polish remover—but not on synthetic fabrics.

2. If you have a bubble burst on you, simply chew up some more gum and use it to lift off the stuck gum.

type of chicle tree and turned his failure into a chewing gum.

Adams' chicle gum was easy to produce and chewed well; soon there were dozens of other companies turning out chewing gum. One gum company in 1906 produced a new kind of gum, Blibber Blubber®, which could be blown into a bubble. The only problem with this first bubble gum was that the gum was nearly impossible to get off your face if the bubble burst.

Tie your hair back

Although most enthusiastic chewers blow relatively small bubbles, there are a few American champion bubble gum blowers who can reportedly blow gum bubbles larger than themselves. The president of a chewing gum company in Philadelphia even claims to be able to blow a bubble within a bubble within a bubble—three bubbles in all—from the same piece of gum.

Today in America more than half of all the people chew gum, and more adults chew gum than kids. Most gums today are no longer made from resin or chicle, however. The main ingredients are often sugar, a chewable plastic, corn syrup, and flavoring. If you would like to experience the taste and chewiness of America's early gums, here's the simple process for making it.

MAKE SPRUCE GUM

This gum is made the same way the Indians and Early American settlers did it. All you need is a pocketknife, a sharp eye, strong teeth and jaws, and a spruce tree. The best resin for gum comes from the black or red spruce tree, but any spruce will do. Although you can find spruce at any time, the spring season is best because the resin is flowing and is already a good chewing consistency. And since the tree foliage is not full at that time of year, it is easier to see the globs of resin.

DOES YOUR CHEWING GUM LOSE ITS FLAVOR ON THE BEDPOST OVER NIGHT?

Words by Billy Rose and Marty Bloom
Music by Ernest Breuer

Oh! me, Oh! my, Oh! you
I don't know what to do.
Hallelujah! The question is peculiar,
It's got me on the go,
I'd give a lot of dough
If someone here would tell me is it
"yes" or is it "no."

CHORUS

"Does your chewing gum lose its
flavor on the bedpost over night?
If you chew it in the morning will it
be too hard to bite?
Can't you see I'm going crazy,
won't somebody put me right?
Does your chewing gum lose its
flavor on the bedpost over night?"

The nation rose as one,
And sent its fav'rite son,
To the White House,
This mighty country's lighthouse.
He saw the President,
He said that, "I've been sent,
To solve the burning question that
involves the continent."

CHORUS

"Does your chewing gum lose its
flavor on the bedpost over night?
If you pull it out like rubber will it
snap right back and bite?
If you paste it on the left side, will
you find it on the right?
Does your chewing gum lose its
flavor on the bedpost over night?"

Here comes the blushing bride
The "boob" right at her side,
To the altar
As steady as Gibraltar.
The bridegroom has the ring,
It's such a pretty thing,
He puts it on her finger and the choir
begins to sing:

CHORUS

"Does your chewing gum lose its
flavor on the bed post over night?
Would you use it on your collar
when your button's not in sight?
Put your hand beneath your seat and
you will find it there all right?
Does your chewing gum lose its
flavor on the bedpost over night?"

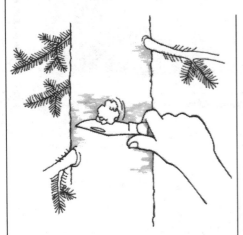

Gum on the end of a stick is used to rescue a key dropped through a grating.

Find a tall spruce tree, one with sap resin coming from the scars where the branches have fallen off or animals have cut into it. With a pocketknife blade scrape off a hunk of the resin that has hardened around the scar. Now just pop the resin in your mouth and begin to chew. At first the resin might be hard and crumbly, but with a little bit of hard chewing it will quickly become just the right consistency for gum.

FORAGING

Foraging—collecting and eating plants from the wild—was a necessity for the Early American settlers. After living through the winter months on dried meats and stored vegetables, the settlers were happy to see the first green shoots and blossoms of spring. Plants, wild as well as cultivated, meant food for the settlers and came just as their stored supplies were running low. A short walk through the woods, along a stream, or just around the house might yield enough edible plants to make an entire meal. It was quite common to see colonial table food, such as day-lily salad, boiled dandelion greens, and biscuits made from the flour of cattail roots, served with wild strawberry jam, and a cup of pine-needle tea.

Forgotten foods

Today with the convenience of food factories and food markets, most Americans have forgotten—or never learned—the simple skills of foraging. That's too bad. We might complain about the cost or freshness of the food we buy when enormous amounts of tasty edible plants are growing all about us, waiting to be picked. You don't have to live in the country or be a farmer to forage food. Wherever there is soil, there will be plants growing from it and the food is free, just for the work of gathering and preparing it. If you define a weed as a plant that grows in a place you don't want it to grow, then foraging the many wild plants around your own property will help you to have fewer weeds. Many places in America are so rich with wild foods that a person knowledgeable in foraging could easily survive eating only what was

picked from the ground.

There are considerably more benefits from eating wild plants than just saving money. Food that you forage is fresh and contains no chemical additives and can add tasty variety to your menu or provide you with food when hiking or camping. But wild foods should not be thought of as taste substitutes for foods you normally eat and like. Each wild edible has its own particular taste, aroma, and texture. You should learn to appreciate a wild food for its own taste.

Make sure it's edible

Foraging is something that *you* can do, something that should make you feel good about your own resourcefulness, knowledgeable about your environment, and just closer to nature. And best of all, you get to eat what you find. However, the one warning to anyone who forages is to *never* gather or eat anything unless you are sure of what it is. Some plants are poisonous and can make you ill. Recognizing the proper plants is the key to successful foraging, and it does take time and experience to learn what is edible—rose petals, cattails, acorns, and dandelions—and what is not. To forage for wild foods, including berries and mushrooms, carry and refer to a foraging handbook or a field guide with clear, realistic pictures, plant descriptions, danger warnings, and suggestions for preparing wild foods. Of course, it is also helpful to have someone along who is experienced in foraging.

Spring and summer from late May to early September is usually the best time for foraging with fall reserved for nut gathering. All you need to take is a small hand spade for digging, a knife for cutting, and a basket for collecting. Your lunch today may be growing outside just

waiting to be gathered. The foraging suggestions that follow are all common plants that most children and adults should recognize.

Day Lilies

The orange day lily so common in gardens and along the roadsides of America during June and July is a naturally tasty plant that is commonly eaten by many peoples around the world. The day lily acquires its name from the fact that each blossom of the plant, of which there are several, blooms for only one day, and then withers and drops to the ground.

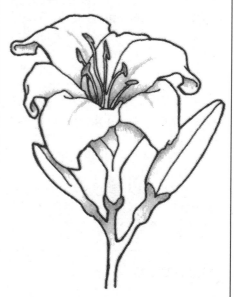

Although most parts of the day lily plant are edible—sprouts, buds, flowers, and roots—the flower buds just before opening are the most delicious. To prepare a vegetable from day lily buds, collect a few handfuls of the large unopened buds, rinse them under cold water, and cut off any stem pieces remaining. Put the buds in a small pot and add just enough water to cover them. Bring the water to a boil and cook for only a few minutes. Drain the buds and flavor to your liking with salt, pepper, and butter.

If you would like to experiment with a spicy wild food taste you can prepare the freshly cooked day lily buds as pickles. Here is what you will need:

Ingredients
¾ cup white vinegar
¼ cup light brown sugar
3 whole cloves
1-inch stick of cinnamon
dash of salt and allspice
1 pint cooked day lily buds (see above)

Utensils
1-quart pot
1-pint jar with tight-fitting lid
mixing spoon

1. Put all the ingredients except the day lily buds into the pot. Bring to a boil over medium heat and cook for a few minutes.

2. While the mixture is boiling, pack the freshly cooked day lily buds into the jar. Let the mixture cool off for a few minutes, and then pour the pickling syrup carefully over the buds until the jar is completely filled.

3. Put the lid tightly on the jar, refrigerate, and let the buds pickle for a few weeks before serving.

Acorns

There is probably no other nut more familiar and common to Americans than the acorn, the nut of the oak tree. And because the acorn was so plentiful and easy to gather, it became the basis for several foods in Early America. The sweet-tasting acorn of the white oak was often eaten raw, but the acorn nuts of many other types of oaks are somewhat bitter and were first boiled before eating, then sometimes roasted also. The acorn nuts were ground into flour or meal to make bread, muffins, and even an Indian acorn stew.

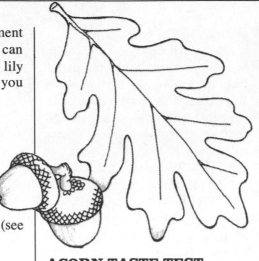

ACORN TASTE TEST

To see whether or not you might like the taste of acorns, try roasting a batch. During the fall season, collect a potful of acorns from those fallen to the ground. Try to find the sweet acorns of the white oak. You can recognize the tree by its scalloped or "lobed" thin green leaves. Look over each nut and reject any with a tiny little hole because there is probably a worm inside. Remove the "acorn caps," then crack open the hull of each nut and remove the shell. To crack the nut you can use a nutcracker, or put the acorn on a rock, pointed end of the acorn up, and hit the nut with a hammer or a stone.

Put the shelled acorn nuts back into the pot, fill the pot with water until the nuts are covered, and boil. When the water turns a dark tea color, pour the water out and reboil the nuts in fresh water. Continue to boil and change the water for about two hours. (It will save some time if the change of water is pre-boiled before pouring it into the pot.) Sample the nuts, and when the bitterness is gone, stop boiling. It is normal for the nuts to darken as they boil.

Drain the water from the pit, and then spread the acorn nuts out on a cookie sheet or shallow baking pan and put them in the oven at 275°F.(135°C.) for about one to

one and a half hours. As soon as the acorn nuts have cooled, they can be eaten. Save any uneaten nuts in a jar or can with a tight-fitting lid.

Dandelions

To the typical American homeowner the dandelion is nothing more than an unwanted weed that crops up on lawns over and over again, no matter how often it is dug out. The forager, however, anxiously awaits the first spring appearance of the persistent plant. The young leaves make a delicious salad. In Early America the settlers and the Indians actually grew the dandelion plant for food, as well as for the beauty of the golden seed head. The dandelion plant contains lots of healthful vitamins and minerals and was often used as an effective cure-all for several illnesses.

Most of the dandelion plant can be eaten raw or cooked, but in either case it is most important that the plant be picked very early in the growing season before it has flowered. As soon as the dandelion starts to send up a shoot and the bud forms, the dandelion eating season is over. Plants that are picked too late in the season will taste very bitter.

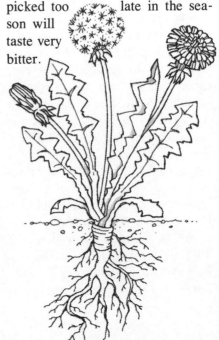

To make a dandelion salad you can use two parts of the plant: the leaves and the crown. The crown is the small white portion where the dandelion leaf meets the root. Wash the plant under cool water to get rid of any dirt and grit. Pull off the individual leaves and slice up the crown into small, pea-sized chunks. Put the greens and the crown parts in a salad bowl and eat plain or add your favorite salad dressing.

If the dandelion green and crown are too bitter for your taste, it may be because you picked the plant a little too late in the season. You can get rid of the bitterness by boiling the plant for five minutes in salty water and then seasoning the greens and crown with salt and pepper or vinegar.

Rose Petals

The leaves, flowers, roots, and bark of several wild plants can be used to make tea. One of the most fragrant teas can be made from the flower petals of a rose.

Gather the petals of several roses and lay them out to dry in a warm

indoor place. In a few days, when the leaves are dry and brittle, crush them into fine pieces and store them in a jar with a tight-fitting lid.

ROSE PETAL TEA

To make rose petal tea, add about one to two teaspoons of crushed leaves to a cup of hot water and let it brew for about five to ten minutes. The actual amount of rose petals you use per cup will depend on your own taste for strong or weak tea. If you wish the tea sweeter, you can add honey or sugar to taste.

Cattails

There are few other wild plants, if any, that can be made into as many tasty dishes as the common swamp cattail. The Indians and the early settlers took advantage of the cattail as a plentiful food source and discovered ways to prepare literally every part of the plant as a delicious food—from the roots to the thousands of tiny flowers that make up the long, sausage-shaped plant head. Today, however, the wild cattail that is such a familiar sight in the swamps, marshes, and along roadsides, is mostly ignored as a source of food.

Cattails first appear in the spring and grow throughout the summer months. When the cattail is ripe it will produce a thick coating of bright yellow pollen on its brown flower head. Even the pollen of the cattail can be eaten and is especially tasty for making pancakes and other baked goods.

To collect the pollen, bend the head of a ripe cattail over an open container or bag and just shake off the pollen or rub it off with your hand. Prepare the pollen for cooking by putting it through a sifter or a fine-mesh strainer.

CATTAIL PANCAKES

To make cattail pancakes, just substitute cattail pollen for one half of the pancake mix, or the flour if you're starting from scratch. Or try this cattail pancake recipe:

Ingredients
¾ cup all-purpose flour
¾ cup cattail pollen
3 tsp. baking powder
1 cup milk
1 beaten egg
2 tbs. salad oil
dash of salt

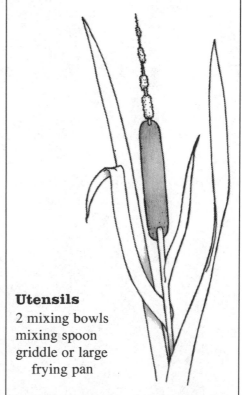

Utensils
2 mixing bowls
mixing spoon
griddle or large
   frying pan

1. In a bowl, mix together the flour, pollen and baking powder.

2. In a second bowl combine the milk, egg, salad oil, and salt, then add the liquid mixture to the dry ingredients. Stir only until the dry ingredients are moistened. It is fine if the batter is lumpy.

3. Pour the batter into pancakes on a hot griddle or pan. Bake until the top side becomes quite bubbly (and the bottom side golden brown), then flip the pancake to cook the other side.

Chapter 7

AMERICAN SCHOOL DAYS

THE THREE R'S

It has been said that in America education opens the door to opportunity. It is a right of every American to receive an education that will lead to a better way of life for him and a better society for all. But the methods and attitudes about education in America have changed greatly. In Early America it was the responsibility of the school to teach the "3 R's"—originally Reading, Writing, and Religion—as well as love of country, nationalism, morality, etiquette, and whatever else was supposed to develop a good "American character."

Since schoolbooks were not common, and those available were quite expensive, the family Bible became the child's textbook. This was most appropriate considering the strong emphasis given in school and school textbooks to the teachings of God. Good penmanship was also considered important and children were often made to practice letters and numerals over and over again. Students used a wood-nib pen and ink, or a small slate chalkboard.

Repeat after me

Learning meant memorization in Early American schools, with little explanation of the lessons provided. After the teacher read an exercise, the class, chanting in unison, would repeat the lesson several times. Each individual pupil would then be made to stand straight and motionless while reciting the lesson from memory. It was not so important that the student understand the lesson as long as it was implanted in his memory. And should a pupil make a mistake in his recitation, or even worse be caught napping, out came the "stick" for a good flogging.

Not every child went to school—most children had no schooling at all. It was for boys only, as it was generally thought that girls had delicate minds and could not easily absorb school learning. Too much education for girls could lead to a troubled mind and even insanity, it was believed.

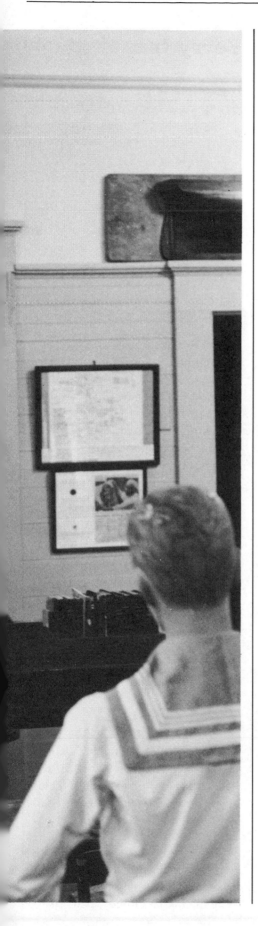

Those children who did get to school did not attend very often. School was open only during the winter months and then only one or two days a week. Children were needed for work around the house or farm during the rest of the time. Only the children of the wealthy had schooling every day—provided, usually, by a tutor. Eventually laws were passed requiring towns and cities to have schools, and compelling children to attend them. Poor families still could not send their children, however, because they were needed at home to work.

Lessons were sometimes held at the teacher's house because no other space was available, and when a town did build a one-room school it was cheaply made and furnished as inexpensively as possible. Early American schoolhouses were painted red because that was the cheapest color of paint that could be bought.

Learning for all in one room

All grade levels of children ages five to sixteen were taught in a single room. A teacher would teach one grade of children at a time leaving the other grades to study. With so many different grades and ages packed into a dingy and small classroom discipline problems were constant. The teacher's role was more often that of an order-keeper than an educator. You can imagine that many towns looked for teachers who were physically big and strong. Sometimes it didn't matter what teachers knew, or if they could teach, just as long as they were willing to take the job. A teacher might be the minister's wife or a visitor passing through the town who had nothing else to do and so spent a few days a week drilling lessons. Teachers were not required to be very educated and were not paid very much.

As you know, schools in America today are much different and much better. Teachers are college educated and well respected, and there are programs and methods of teaching that can make it fun to learn. But most important, the student today is considered an individual. He is taught to think and reason rather than memorize.

Mannequins are used as models in this American classroom of days gone by.

INK

Sometimes the teacher in an Early American school would supply small bottles of ink to the students for their practice writing, but most often each pupil would have to bring his own ink from home. Inks were made at home from a variety of ingredients depending on the color that was wanted. Berries, roots, powders, and even chimney soot were used to make inks of different colors—beautiful blues, browns, reds, and gold. There were even formulas for invisible inks, glow-in-the-dark inks, and ink erasers.

Two of the most common inks used in the schoolroom were made from nut shells and berries. Although the formulas here have been simplified a bit, the inks they produce can be used for writing just as well as any bought in a store.

Nut Ink (brown)

Ingredients
shells of 8 whole walnuts
1 cup water
½ tsp. vinegar
½ tsp. salt

Utensils
hammer
scrap cloth
small saucepan
measuring cup and spoons
strainer
small jar with tight-fitting lid (a baby-food jar is fine)

1. Crush the empty shells into very little pieces by wrapping them in the piece of scrap cloth and pounding them with a hammer, Fig. 1.

2. Put the crushed shells into a saucepan, add one cup of water,

Fig. 1

and bring the water to a boil. Turn the heat down to low or "simmer" and let the pot sit for about one-half to one hour or until the water turns a dark brown. Most of the water will have evaporated leaving a small amount of brown ink.

3. Remove the ink from the heat, let it cool, then pour the mixture through a strainer into a small jar with a tight-fitting lid, Fig. 2.

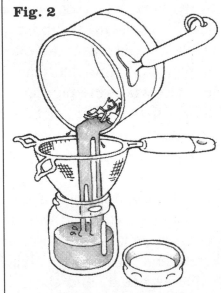

Fig. 2

4. Add a half-teaspoon of vinegar to the ink to help keep the color from fading, and one-half teaspoon of salt so that the ink will not turn moldy.

Try making other inks in the same way, using other kinds of nut shells, bark—birch or willow bark are good—or roots.

Berry Ink

Ingredients
½ cup ripe berries (blueberries, cherries, blackberries, strawberries, elderberries or raspberries are all fine)
½ tsp. salt
½ tsp. vinegar

Utensils
measuring cup and spoons
strainer
bowl
wooden spoon
small jar with tight-fitting lid (a baby-food jar is fine)

1. Fill the strainer with the berries and hold it over a bowl. Using the rounded back of a wooden spoon, crush the berries against the strainer so that the berry juice strains into the bowl, Fig. 3. Keep adding berries until most of their juice has been strained out and only pulp is left. Throw the pulp away.

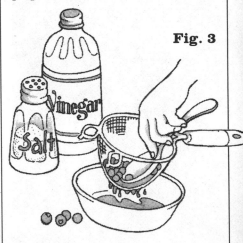

Fig. 3

2. Add the salt and vinegar to the berry juice and stir well. If the berry ink is too thick, add a tablespoon or two of water, but don't add too much or the ink might get too pale.

Store the ink in a small jar with a tight-fitting lid. Make only a small amount of berry ink at a time, and keep the ink jar closed when it isn't being used. (Without special chemical ingredients, the ink may turn to jelly after a while but you should not try eating it.)

FANCY PENS

Before the invention of pencils, fountain pens, ball-point pens, and all the other types of modern writing devices, schoolchildren used rather crude pens made from small carved twigs or feather quills. Quill pens worked best because the quill held the ink better—you didn't have to dip the pen too often. But wood-nib pens were much cheaper and could be carved in a few minutes.

Make a Wood-Nib Pen

Materials
pencil-sized twig

Tools
penknife

Using a penknife, carve one end of the twig to a thin point, Fig. 4. This will be the writing nib. (By the way, that is how the penknife got its name. It was a knife carried just for the purpose of carving a pen nib or keeping a nib pointed.)

Fig. 4

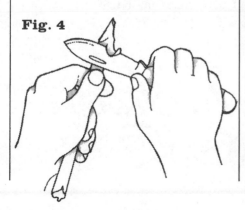

Once you have a thin point, dip it into the ink and try writing. You will probably have to dip the pen into the ink quite often, sometimes for every letter you print. When the nib becomes too soft or flat, just carve the point sharp again with your penknife.

Make a Quill Pen

A quill is the hollow stalk of a bird's feather and the finest quills for writing came from the wing feathers of geese. But if a goose quill wasn't easy to get, the large wing feather of a crow, turkey, or swan would also make a good pen.

Materials
bird's feather

Tools
penknife

1. To make a quill pen you will first need to find a large feather. During the spring and fall when birds molt their feathers you might be able to get several good quills

Writing with a quill pen is not easy work.

from your local zoo. Or you might also ask the neighborhood poultry butcher for a feather.

2. Strip off some of the feather if necessary from the fat end of the quill. This enables you to hold the pen comfortably in the standard writing position.

3. Now form the penpoint by cutting the fat end of the quill at a slant curving the cut slightly, Fig. 5.

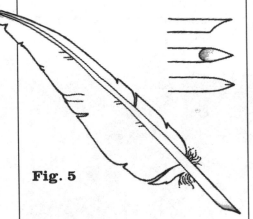

Fig. 5

4. Check to be sure the inside of the hollow quill point is open and smooth so the ink will flow to the point. If necessary you can clean inside the quill point using the end of a paper clip. The pen will now write with ink; the width of the line it draws will be determined by how sharp or blunt the point is. To get a varied line so that the harder you press the heavier the line, cut a small slit in the penpoint—about one-eighth inch (three mm.) right up the middle from the tip, Fig. 5.

Use the ink you've made or regular fountain pen ink of any color and dip just the tip of the pen in. After some practice you will learn just how far to dip without the ink "blobbing" on the paper. Keep a paper towel ink blotter handy just in case. Experiment to find out how a quill pen writes by drawing lines, curves and individual letters. Hold the pen at different angles or try cutting a new point at a slightly different slant.

HOW TO WRITE FANCY (LIKE JOHN HANCOCK)

Just about everyone has seen John Hancock's elaborate signature, which appears on the Declaration of Independence. If you have seen other examples of Early American writing then you have probably found that "fancy writing" was once quite common. Not everyone in Early America knew how to write, but of those who could, fancy writing was often considered the sign of an educated and refined woman or man.

In Early American schools, penmanship was considered one of the most important lessons taught. Teachers were more concerned with how legibly and attractively a pupil wrote than if his words were spelled correctly. After morning prayers and Bible reading, usually the teacher would write a word or phrase at the top of each pupil's paper or slate, and the rest of the morning was spent copying the letter forms over and over again until the pupil's handwriting looked just like the teacher's.

While the students practiced their penmanship, the teacher would go from desk to desk checking everyone's sitting and writing posture. Teachers believed that to write properly a person must sit with his back straight, shoulders square, with the pen in his right hand. Left-handed writing was not allowed.

If a school had an ample supply of writing paper, each pupil might keep a small notebook in which he wrote religious essays or proverbs of the day, such as, "contentment is a virtue" or "procrastination is the thief of time." At the close of the school year the teacher would sometimes have a "community day" at which time parents would come to school to see the fancy writing and virtuous lessons their children had learned.

Schools today still teach penmanship but there is much more freedom, allowing each student to develop his own personal writing style—plain or fancy. Even though you may not want to learn how to write fancy for everyday use it could be fun learning to write your name Early American style—like John Hancock.

You can write your name or whatever else you would like by tracing the fancy letters from the alphabet, Fig. 6. You can write with any kind of pen on tracing paper or thin notebook paper, but first draw a light base line in pencil across the page so the bottom of all the traced letters will be in line. Keep the letters close together so that each letter flows smoothly into the next.

If you want to get more of the real look of fancy writing, you should write with an ink pen having a flexible tip. Fountain pens and

Fig. 6

quill pens write a heavy line when you press down and a thinner line when you ease up a bit. For most fancy writing the pen is pressed down on a down stroke and eased up on an up stroke.

After you have written your name you might add a few distinctive flourishes. These fancy line patterns can be traced onto the first or final letters or under your name as a border.

Now learn to write your name fancy without tracing, the same way early American school kids were taught—copy, copy, and copy again until your freehand signature looks just like the tracing.

PRIMERS

He that ne er learns his A, B, C,
For ever will a Blockhead be ;

But he that learns these Letters fair
Shall have a Coach to take the Air.

If an Early American schoolroom had any schoolbooks at all it probably had a "primer"—and that was most likely to be the *New England Primer*. The primer was a small book that each pupil would copy and memorize.

The primer not only taught reading, writing, and spelling but lessons in honor, friendship, and good moral character. The primer was considered an essential tool with which to mold a child's life according to the Christian Ethic. The moral of the lessons was that if you led a good, considerate life you would eventually be rewarded, and if you led a bad life you would be punished.

Here is a typical school quiz from an Early American *New England Primer*. The purpose of the lesson was to test the student's ability to memorize the answers. You might like to try your hand at it.

QUESTION: What is Sin?
ANSWER: Sin is any want of conformity unto, or transgression of the law of God.

QUESTION: What is the duty which God requires of Man?

ANSWER: The duty which God requires of Man is Obedience to His revealed Will.

QUESTION: What did God first reveal to Man for the Rule of His Obedience?
ANSWER: The Rule which God at first revealed to Man for his Obedience was the Moral Law.

QUESTION: What does every Sin deserve?
ANSWER: Every Sin deserveth God's Wrath and Curse both in this Life and that which is to come.

SPELLING

Of the academic subjects taught in Early American schools, good spelling was considered of prime importance. Before the telephone, radio, and television existed the written word was a most essential tool of communication. If you wanted to send a message over a distance greater than you could holler, it was important to know how to spell.

The spelling of words in the English language is not very easy. There are more written ways than one to make a particular sound. For example, the *"sh"* sound in the word "she" can be spelled more than twenty different ways in other words: ocean, machine, sure, attention, anxious, and so on.

Many words have been borrowed from foreign languages. Although there are some spelling rules and patterns, English spelling is quite irregular. Most words need to be learned by repetition and memorization. And although good spelling has very little to do with intelligence, it is a skill—one which some people have a natural aptitude for while others must struggle along.

From time to time certain words in the English language—those with either complicated spellings or unnecessary silent letters—have been simplified for easier spelling. For example, music was once spelled musick and color was spelled colour (in fact, in England it still is). In years to come, the spelling of many other words will probably be simplified so that spelling will be just that much easier.

Spelling Bee

The spelling bee, or "spelldown" as it is sometimes called, was a popular Early American parlor game and school exercise. Although the spelling bee is still an activity in many classrooms, it is quickly becoming a thing of the past. In a spelling bee, if someone

A school S-P-E-L-L-I-N-G B-E-E.

spells a word incorrectly they are out of the game. It is the good speller who stays in the game the longest who wins.

The rules for holding a spelling bee are quite simple. All the players line up in a row, and then in order, one at a time, each player must correctly spell the word assigned to him by an impartial teacher or leader. The teacher first pronounces the word clearly, uses the word in a sentence, then finally repeats the word. The teacher will say, for example, "Language. We are speaking the English *language*. Language." The player first says the word, then spells it out, then repeats the word again. For example, "Language...

L-A-N-G-U-A-G-E

...Language." A player is eliminated and must sit down if he misspells a word, and the word then goes to the next player. The last player left is the winner, although he must correctly spell the word last missed by his opponent or the game is tied and continues.

Each year in some cities the local newspaper sponsors a spelling bee for schoolchildren under the age of sixteen. The winners of local contests are invited to become finalists in the National Championship held in Washington, D.C.

Here are a few of the tricky, uncommon words that have been used to stump even champion spellers. Try making your own spelling bee word list and include a few of these tougher words:

afflatus	ichthyology
atelier	incandescence
baccalaureate	lavender
badinage	meringue
cedilla	miscible
codicil	mnemonic
condominium	persiflage
dentifrice	quidnunc
encomium	quietus
esoteric	ratiocination
exorcism	sarcophagus

REBUS

Some lessons in Early American schools were actually fun. One of the most popular classroom games was rebus: a representation of words using symbols, pictures, letters, and numbers whose names resemble the intended word. Each rebus is actually a riddle or puzzle to be solved. For example, in the first rebus puzzle, Fig. 7, the letter *A* is added to an illustration of a spire to make the word ASPIRE, the number 2 and the letter *B* are joined to read TO BE, and the letter *Y* is pluralized to make the word WISE. This rebus would then read, ASPIRE TO BE WISE. The other rebuses are decoded in a similar way.

Rebus puzzles were included in many classroom books not as a game of pleasant amusement but primarily as a lesson used by the teacher to "strengthen the brain" and teach "independent thinking,

100 WORDS COMMONLY MISSPELLED
IN THE ENGLISH LANGUAGE

absence	ecstasy	innocent	parallel	sergeant
accommodate	eighth	irresistible	peculiar	sheriff
all right	embarrass	irritable	persistent	sophomore
analyze	exceed	jealousy	phenomenon	subtle
anoint	existence	league	plebeian	supersede/supercede
anonymous	fascinate	leisure	principal	surgeon
benefit	February	license/licence	principle	tongue
boundary	forty	losing	privilege	tragedy
business	fulfill	maneuver	procedure	truly
category	government	marriage	pursue	tyranny
committee	grammar	meant	receipt	undoubtedly
conscience	guarantee	minute	receive	until
conscious	guerrilla/guerilla	misspelled	recommend	vacuum
corroborate	height	necessary	repetition	vengeance
counterfeit	hoarse	ninth	rhythm	vicious
dealt	holiday	noticeable	ridiculous	warrant
definitely	hygiene	occurrence	roommate	weird
despair	icicles	often	schedule	wholly
dilemma	imagine	optimistic	seize	yacht
disappoint	indispensable	pamphlet	separate	yield

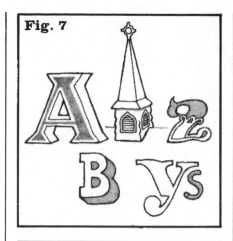

Fig. 7

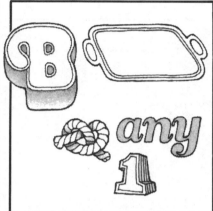

into a rebus, then look at each word individually and see what word or object you can find to stand for the word. For example, in the word STOP is the word TOP: STOP in rebus could be written:

$$S + \text{🪀} = stop$$

Other examples are:

$$T + \text{👒} = that$$

$$L + \text{🂡} = lace$$

Another form of rebus uses the names of letters and numbers only. A familiar American rebus is IOU which stands for I OWE YOU. Combinations of letters can also be used to make words. The word BUSY can be made from the two letters B + Z, or the word CITY can be written C + T. L + F + 8 + R reads ELEVATOR. Here are a few rebus sentences for you to figure out and a simple rebus dictionary to help you decode the sentences and make up your own. As you invent rebus words, add them to the list.

logic, and reason.'' Today the rebus is used to help teach illiterate people to read and write. There are even television game shows and magazine contests that use the rebus puzzle. With a little thought you can make up your own rebus puzzle using cutouts from old magazines and newspapers. Here's a clue to help you. Start by thinking of a simple sentence to translate

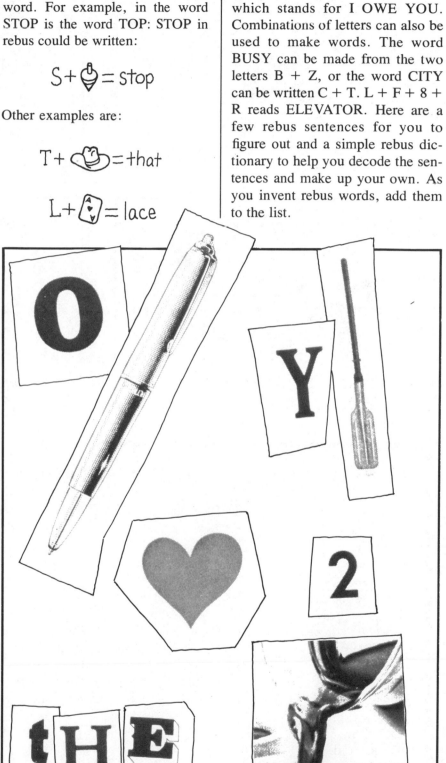

REBUS DICTIONARY

A = a
    hay
    hey
B = bee
    be
B+4 = before
B+Z = busy
B+U+T = beauty
C = see
    sea
C+L = seal
C+N = seeing
C+T = city
D = the
D+R = deer
D+Z = dizzy
E = he
    me

E+R = here
E+Z = easy
F = if
G = gee
G+P+C = gypsy
L+F+N = elephant
L+T = healthy
L+O = hello
L+F+8+R = elevator
M = am
    ham
N = hen
    an
    in
N+Q = thank you
N+M+L = animal
N+E = any
N+M+E = enemy

N+D+N = indian
N+D = indeed
N+6 = insects
O = oh
    owe
    know
O+K = OK
O+T = boat
P+K+N = peeking
Q = you
Q+T = cutie
R = are
S = is
    yes
    has
T = tea
T+S = tears
T+P = tepee

U = you
U+R = your
X = eggs
X+M+N = examine
X+L+N = excellent
X+L = excel
Y = why
Y+N = wine
Y+S = wise
1 = run
2 = two
    to
2+L = tool
3 = tree
4 = for
6 = sex
8 = ate
    hate

TONGUE TWISTERS

In American schools of the 1800's teachers believed that articulate speech was the sure sign of a well-educated person, so one of the compulsory school subjects for all children was "elocution" or proper public speaking. To practice the lessons of good speech, each pupil would stand before the class and slowly recite some difficult sentence or phrase over and over again until each word was clear and crisply spoken.

"Bring me some ice, not some mice."

"Red leather, yellow leather."

"Rush the washing, Russell."

Sometimes the class played an elocution game similar to a spelling bee in which each pupil in turn had to speak some tongue-twisting sentence clearly after correctly reciting each of the sentences that preceded his turn. Whoever goofed was out of the contest. A typical progression of sentences might have gone like this:

Proper speech and clear communication are still important lessons, but elocution as a school subject has nearly disappeared. All that is left are a lot of tricky tongue twisters, to be recited clearly and crisply and as quickly as you can without goofing. Some tricky tongue twisters are meant to be repeated over and over again a number of times in a row while others are difficult enough so that you are lucky to get through them correctly just once. Many of those tongue twisters were once actually school lessons, but now you can try them just for fun.

Some shun sunshine—
Do you shun sunshine?

A big black bug bit a big black bear
And the big black bear bled blood.

A skunk sat on a stump;
The stump thunk the skunk stunk
And the skunk thunk the stump stunk.

Cross crossings cautiously.

Sheep shouldn't sleep in a shack;
Sheep should sleep in a shed.

The swan swam out to sea;
Swim swan swim!

Three grey geese sat on the green grass grazing.

The sixth sheik's sixth sheep's sick.

She's so selfish she should sell shellfish shells
But shells of shellfish seldom sell.

Two tutors who tooted the flute
Tried to tutor two tooters to toot.
Said the two to the tutors,
"Is it harder to toot
Or to tutor two tooters to toot?"

One old Oxford ox opening oysters.

Two tired turkeys trotting to the trolley.

Three tricky tigers tipping ten tall trees.

Four fat friars foolishly fishing for flowers.

Five funny Frenchmen fanning fainting flies.

Six sick sailors sighting sinking ships.

Seven sinister sisters swallowing soothing syrup.

Eight elegant Englishmen eagerly eating eclairs.

Nine nimble noblemen neatly nibbling nothing.

Ten tiny ticks throwing terrible temper tantrums.

Betty Botter bought some butter,
   "But," she said, "this butter's
bitter.
   If I put it in my batter
   It will make my batter bitter.
   But if I buy some better butter,
   It will make my batter better."
So Betty bought some better
butter
   Better than the bitter butter,
   And she put it in the batter
   And it made the batter better.

Esau Wood sawed wood. Esau Wood saw wood. All the wood that Esau saw, Esau Wood would saw. Oh the wood that Wood would saw! One day Wood's wood-saw would saw no wood, but Wood would saw wood with a wood-saw that would saw wood. Wood saw a saw saw wood as no other wood-saw Wood saw would saw wood. Of all the wood-saws Wood ever saw saw wood Wood never saw a wood-saw that would saw wood as the wood-saw Wood saw would. Now Wood saws wood with the wood-saw Wood saw saw wood.

AUTOGRAPH VERSES

Collecting the autographs of friends and classmates is an American custom that began sometime during the 1800's. Rarely was an autograph book signed without the writer including some witty rhyme of love, friendship, success, or maybe even a joking insult.

   Some autograph verses are personal and original to the writer, but most are quite traditional. These two- or four-line rhymes continue to be passed on from one generation (or graduating class) to the next.

   Autographs and verses are still collected in autograph albums and school yearbooks, but through the years America has also invented the autograph stuffed hound dog and autograph jacket, as well as the custom of signing the plaster casts of broken bones. So the next time you are asked to sign someone's book or leg, don't be caught without the appropriate verse for the occasion. Here are some to choose from.

LOVE

Butter is butter
And cheese is cheese—
What is a kiss
Without a squeeze?

Pretty are the flowers
That grow by the brook
And pretty is the girl
Who owns this book.

Our eyes have met,
Our lips, not yet,
But wait and see,
I'll get you yet.

With all my wisdom,
I do declare,
You and (name of a girl or boy)
Make a good pair.

Fall comes after summer,
And you can fall from above,
But the best fall of all
Is to fall in love.

Roses are red,
Violets are blue,
I love me,
And you love you.

I love you bip
I love you bop
I love you better
Than a pig loves slop.

A kiss is a germ,
And so I have waited.
But, kiss me quick,
I'm vaccinated.

I love you once,
I love you twice,
I love you better
Than a cat loves mice.

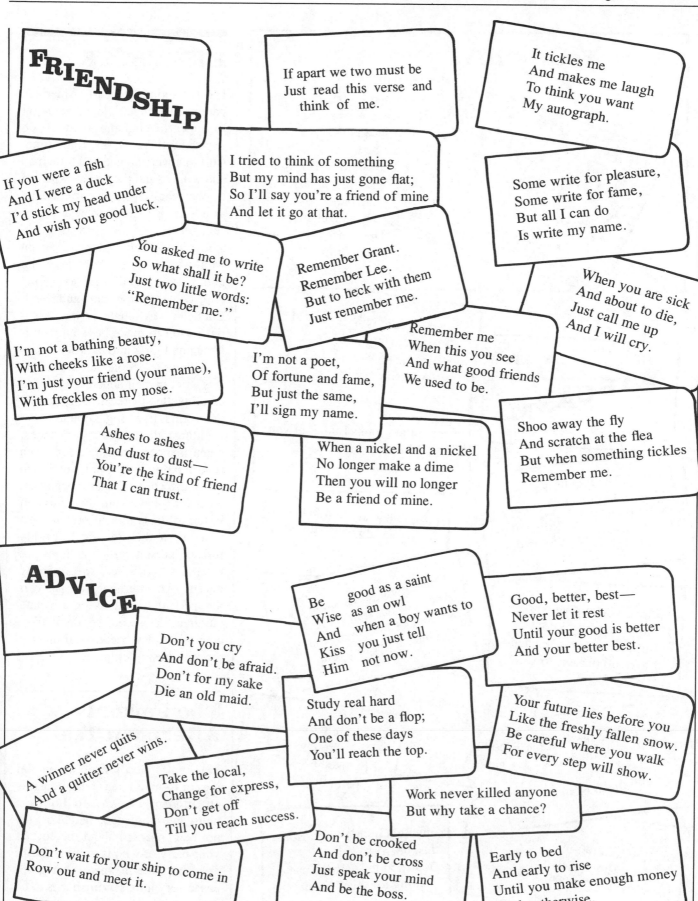

FRIENDSHIP

If apart we two must be
Just read this verse and
think of me.

It tickles me
And makes me laugh
To think you want
My autograph.

If you were a fish
And I were a duck
I'd stick my head under
And wish you good luck.

I tried to think of something
But my mind has just gone flat;
So I'll say you're a friend of mine
And let it go at that.

Some write for pleasure,
Some write for fame,
But all I can do
Is write my name.

You asked me to write
So what shall it be?
Just two little words:
"Remember me."

Remember Grant.
Remember Lee.
But to heck with them
Just remember me.

When you are sick
And about to die,
Just call me up
And I will cry.

I'm not a bathing beauty,
With cheeks like a rose.
I'm just your friend (your name),
With freckles on my nose.

I'm not a poet,
Of fortune and fame,
But just the same,
I'll sign my name.

Remember me
When this you see
And what good friends
We used to be.

Ashes to ashes
And dust to dust—
You're the kind of friend
That I can trust.

When a nickel and a nickel
No longer make a dime
Then you will no longer
Be a friend of mine.

Shoo away the fly
And scratch at the flea
But when something tickles
Remember me.

ADVICE

Don't you cry
And don't be afraid.
Don't for my sake
Die an old maid.

Be   good as a saint
Wise   as an owl
And   when a boy wants to
Kiss   you just tell
Him   not now.

Good, better, best—
Never let it rest
Until your good is better
And your better best.

A winner never quits
And a quitter never wins.

Study real hard
And don't be a flop;
One of these days
You'll reach the top.

Your future lies before you
Like the freshly fallen snow.
Be careful where you walk
For every step will show.

Take the local,
Change for express,
Don't get off
Till you reach success.

Work never killed anyone
But why take a chance?

Don't wait for your ship to come in
Row out and meet it.

Don't be crooked
And don't be cross
Just speak your mind
And be the boss.

Early to bed
And early to rise
Until you make enough money
To do otherwise.

Yours till...

Niagara Falls.
The kitchen sinks.
The ocean waves.
The soda pops.
The butter flies.
The board walks.
The bed spreads.
The radio waves.
The ginger snaps.
Day breaks.
The lemon drops.
The comic strips.

SARCASM

Roses are red,
Violets are blue,
Garlic stinks
And so do you.

Every time it rains I think of you:
Drip, drip, drip.

Twinkle, twinkle little star,
Powder puff and cold cream jar.
A little powder and little paint,
Makes you look like what
you ain't.

I can make any fool in town,
Turn this page upside down.

I love you, I love you,
I love you, yes I do.
But don't get too excited—
I love all turkeys too.

Though your tasks are many,
And your rewards are few,
Remember the mighty oak tree
Was once a nut like you.

God made the rivers,
God made the lakes,
God made you;
We all make mistakes.

Sugar is sweet,
Coal is black,
Do me a favor
And sit on a tack.

Roses are red,
Violets are blue,
If I looked like you,
I'd be in the zoo.

To the handsomest boy
in the world.
From the biggest liar in the world.

Jimmy's in the White House
Just been elected.
You're in the garbage can
Waiting to be collected.

ETIQUETTE

It was important to Early American parents that their children be taught the rules of etiquette—how to do the right thing at the right time. Children were considered little men and women and they were expected to obey the same rules of etiquette as adults. By knowing what to do, say, write, and wear on all occasions, it was believed that a person would learn to be "gentle, calm and patient, and treat everyone with consideration and kindness." Etiquette was taught as the essential lesson to make boys into gentlemen and girls into ladies.

Although people have become less strict in their adherence to rules of etiquette, there are still special occasions like engagements and weddings, dinner parties or dances, when manners are called for, even fun. You don't need an invitation to show off your company behavior, however—have your own party! It is fun to dress up and pretend that you are a distinguished, highly refined person with the finest of manners who is entertaining guests. An afternoon tea party is the perfect occasion for a young cultured "lady" or "gentleman" to entertain a few friends and display the very best of etiquette.

The Formal Afternoon Tea

You really don't need a special reason to give a tea, but often it is an appropriate way to honor a house guest or a good neighbor. Do not be concerned about the cost of your party or who is going to help. Teas are quite inexpensive and because very little serving needs to be done, it is perfectly permissible to

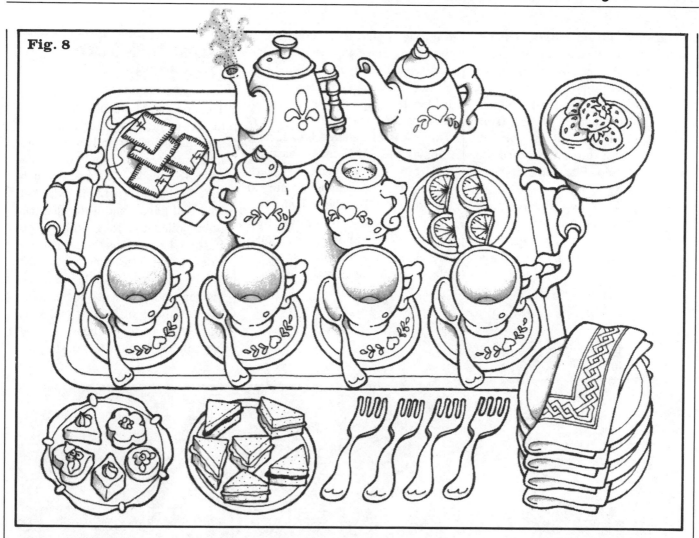

Fig. 8

give a formal tea without the help of servants.

Invitations and Replies

Invitations to a tea can be given personally by the host or hostess, but it is more appropriate to send a note (note cards for teas are smaller than cards used for invitations to grand balls). The notes may be engraved or handwritten but never typed.

Miss Kim Andrews will be home for tea Monday the 17th of May from four until six o'clock Indian River Road.

In accepting an offer to tea a note is sent to the host or hostess repeating nearly all the information on the invitation, but not the address of the hostess.

Miss Jennifer Price accepts with pleasure Kim Andrew's kind invitation to tea Monday the 17th of May from four until six o'clock.

If you must decline the invitation it is not necessary to repeat the day and hour.

Miss Lisa Morton regrets that she cannot accept Kim Andrew's kind invitation to tea.

What to Wear

Tea time is a fashionable time of day, but you may dress according to the neighborhood custom. During the cool months a wool daytime dress or a pants suit is appropriate. In the summer a brightly-colored cotton or linen dress or skirt should be worn. Hats are optional. The host or hostess should greet each guest at the door, say something pleasant about the guest's attire, and if necessary tell the guest where to leave his or her coat.

Setting the Table

Tea is usually served in the dining

room or receiving room but if the weather is mild, tea may be served outdoors. The appearance of the tea table is most important and a host or hostess will take great pride in the compliments received from guests about it. Unless you are using a glass table, a tablecloth should be used. Place an empty tea pot, a caddy of tea or tea bags, a cream pitcher (with milk, *not* cream) a sugar bowl, slices of lemon on a dish, and cups with saucers and teaspoons on a large tray, Fig. 8, and set it at one end of the table. Place the necessary silverware and tea plates at either side of the table, and on each plate a folded tea napkin. Put plates of food on the table in a pretty way. Thin slices of buttered bread, jam, cookies and small cakes, pastries, strawberries and cream, or a variety of dainty sandwiches are all nice to serve. But the refreshments must never be so filling that they will interfere with the dinner appetite. A few flowers in a vase can be placed on the table to add beauty.

How to Make Good Tea

The first rule for making good tea is to use fresh cool water and to be sure that the water boils for three to four minutes first—no more, no less. Tea made with water which isn't boiling temperature will not have full flavor, and water that has been boiled too long will not be fresh. When the host or hostess decides that it is tea time he or she brings the boiling kettle from the kitchen and places it on the tray. The ceremony of making tea is always reserved for the hostess if one is available. Into the teapot she puts

It was once important to learn teatime etiquette.

You can't beat tea parties with sweet snacks.

one teaspoon of tea (or one tea bag) for each cup to be served. She then pours the boiling water into the teapot, puts on the lid, and lets the tea steep (the leaves or bag sits in the hot water) three to five minutes before pouring.

Serving the Tea

Pouring the tea is usually done by a close friend of the host or hostess who has been selected for good manners and friendliness. If a guest should ask, "May I have a cup of tea?", the one pouring should reply, "Certainly. Would you like milk or lemon?" The server need only smile as he or she hands each guest a cup of tea. However, if the guest is alone, the server may make a few pleasant remarks and then move on to serve the next person. The server may also approach a guest and ask, "Would you like a cup of tea?" If the guest refuses, the server should then say, "Would you like anything else?" If the answer is "yes," and there is another server free he or she should serve the drink after it has been made in the pantry—or, if the first server has no help the guest may be asked to pour his or her own drink.

Table Accidents

If a guest drops a spoon, a fork, or a napkin, he or she should let it remain on the floor and ask the host or hostess for another. If a cup or plate is accidentally broken, a simple but sincere word of regret will relieve the awkwardness of the moment, but no further mention or apologies should be made for the accident. A most serious and unpleasant accident occurs when a cup of tea is overturned on the table. Matters are only made worse by fussing about it and making exaggerated apologies. A simple word or two of regret to the hostess is quite satisfactory, but it is most important not to let this happen too often lest the guest acquire a reputation for being clumsy and without manners.

Sun Machine, by Charles Eames. Collection of Charles Eames.

Chapter 8

MADE IN AMERICA

UNDERSTANDING ART

Just as words, sentences, punctuation, and parts of speech make up our spoken language, there is also a visual grammar consisting of shape, line, color, light, texture, composition, motion, and framing that enables us to understand and create art. And just like the writer using written grammar, the artist can combine the elements of visual language to create art that conveys almost any feeling or attitude.

You don't necessarily have to draw well to be an artist. The difference between an artist and someone who is not is that the artist has an ability to express what he sees visually. It is you, the one viewing the art, who interprets the message of the artist and gives the art meaning. To create or "see" art, you must educate your vision and learn to understand visual images. And as with any new skill, you will need to practice "seeing" art to become good at it.

Appreciating the art of one's peers.

SHAPE

Shape can be made using curved and straight lines. Shapes that are curved and smooth we generally find pleasing. They can convey a feeling of calm and peacefulness, while shapes that are angular, harsh, or irregular often seem disturbing and unsettled.

In *Incense of a New Church*, the artist uses angular shapes to present the factory buildings as solid, massive, cold, impersonal objects, while also using gentle and flowing curved shapes to give the feeling of smoke, or the smell of church incense gently and softly wending its way among the buildings.

Project

Using newspapers and old magazines, cut out pictures of various objects: a car, television set, people, furniture, houses, flowers, and so on. Select two images that normally would not go together and mount them with glue on a sheet of paper, so the two objects share an "interesting" relationship.

Incense of a New Church (1921), by Charles Demuth. Courtesy of The Columbus Gallery of Fine Arts, Columbus, Ohio. Gift of Ferdinand Howald.

The more unlikely that the two objects would seem to go together, the stronger the new image. Try to deal with objects of contrasting shapes and scale: a giant flower growing from the roof of a car, or hamburgers as clouds in an outdoor scene. Sometimes by breaking with convention—with what we think are pleasing images that go well together—we can create new and exciting visual images. What can you say about the new image you have made? How do the shapes and their relationships to each other affect you? What would you title the work?

COLOR

Artists use color to bring out the viewer's feelings. A painting that is primarily red will seem exciting or warm, probably because it reminds us of fire or blood. The color green reminds us of nature and "feels" refreshing and alive. Blue is peaceful, sad, or cool like water, and yellow is bright and cheerful as the sun on a summer day.

Although *High Noon* is reproduced here in black and white, you can probably guess what colors the

High Noon (1944), by Arthur Dove. Courtesy of the Wichita Art Museum, Wichita, Kansas. The Roland P. Murdock Collection.

artist used from the title, *High Noon*. The sun is surrounded by a bright, hot-yellow aura, dramatically contrasted against a dark sky.

Project

From a magazine, newspaper, or book, select a drawing or photograph of a person or object, and make three or more copies on an office copy machine. If you can't make copies, try making several tracings of the drawing. Using crayons, felt-tipped markers, or colored pencils, completely color the entire image using a different color for each copy. Now place the colored drawings all in a row and try to describe the different feelings

you get about each one. How does the color change the picture? Does one drawing seem happier or livelier than the others? Which drawing might seem the warmest if you touched it, which the coolest? Which one do you like the best?

LINE

Line can express weakness or strength. All heavy lines are strong, impressive, or powerful, while thin lines suggest a weak, delicate, or fragile feeling.

Bold lines in *Summer Landscape* define and draw attention to the houses; they also give the tree and telephone pole in the foreground a massive feeling. In contrast, the fence, boats and far away buildings appear much more delicate and help to give the scene a sense of depth.

Project

You can easily trace the outline of objects using the technique of shadow drawing. Hold an object under the sun or a bright room lamp, an inch or two above a plain sheet of paper. Hold the object steady in one hand and quickly trace its shadow outline. Make shadow drawings of several types of objects: flowers, rocks, leaves, small toys, tools, or kitchen utensils. Draw each object two or three times—once with a fine, sharp

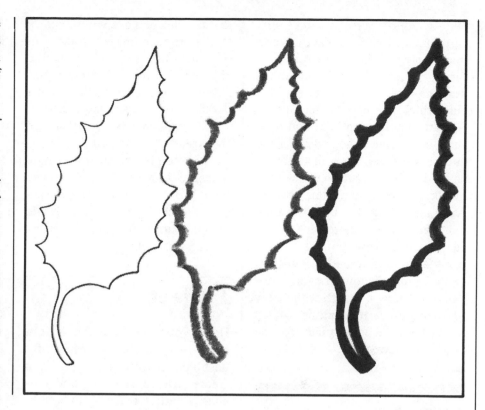

Summer Landscape (1930), by Stuart Davis. Courtesy of The Museum of Modern Art, New York, New York.

pencil, again with a wide felt-tipped marker or crayon, and maybe a third time with yet a different weight line. Compare the drawings of each object, and decide which line best fits the image. A feather will seem light and delicate with a fine line, whereas the outline of a toy car will be bolder and more appropriate with a line made by a marker or crayon. After selecting the best drawing from each pair, compare them to each other. Now you might try using several different weight lines in the same shadow drawing—for example, draw a branch with heavy lines but use a lighter line, which might be more appropriate, for the buds and leaves.

LIGHT

Light is frequently used to create a dramatic effect and to emphasize a part of the picture. Artists know that the viewer's eye will be drawn to the brighter images. Shades of light and dark also create an illusion of depth and dimension. Brighter images seem close, while darker images appear more distant.

Even though only a small area of the scene represented in *Nighthawks* is bright, the artist uses light to isolate the viewer's attention and focus it on the lunch counter, specifically on the counterman rather than the surrounding, mood-setting darkness of night.

Project

Have you ever made a "light mask"? By aiming the beam of a flashlight at your face, you can create strange shadows and emphasize certain features. In a darkened room, hold the flashlight to your chin, aimed up. Look in a mirror and notice what features stand out in the lighted areas, and how the dark shadows create their

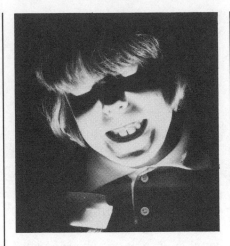

own shapes on your face—especially the dark areas around your eyes. You probably look a bit mean or scary. Now try holding the flashlight to your forehead and aim it down at your face. Do you still look scary? Which areas are now in light and in shadow? Continue making light masks by holding the flashlight to the side of your face and then at different angles. You can see that just by changing the direction of the light, you create different feelings for the same object.

Nighthawks (1942), by Edward Hopper. Courtesy of the Art Institute of Chicago, Chicago, Illinois.

Barns (1917), by Charles R. Sheeler, Jr. Courtesy of the Albright-Knox Art Gallery, Buffalo, New York. Gift of A. Conger Goodyear to the Room of Contemporary Art.

TEXTURE

Texture gives us a sense of what things painted or drawn feel like—or what they're made from. Smooth and soft textures are pleasant and inviting—they make the viewer want to reach out and feel the image. Rough textures can also be interesting, but like angular shapes, they are not so inviting.

Each shape in *Barns* conveys the texture of the material from which it is made: wood, stone, earth, glass. It is the various textures that give interest to the barns and make them look real.

Project

Very often, changing the texture of a single material can create many different feelings. Compare two plain sheets of paper, one smooth and flat, the other crumpled, then opened and laid flat. How would you describe the different textures? Crumple up several more sheets of paper and open them flat again. Try using newspaper, waxed paper, aluminum foil, tissue paper, or paper napkins. For a fine texture, crumple the paper tightly, and for a

rough texture, crumple it loosely. To get the full effect of your texture art, view the paper with a bright light from several different angles. Notice how the texture changes as the light and shadow changes. Understanding how light affects texture, where would you hang or display a piece of texture art?

MOTION

Even a still painting or sculpture can give the feeling of motion. The artist can "freeze" an incomplete action, such as that of a bucking bronco, falling snow, or a tree being cut down. We get a feeling of motion because we can imagine what will happen next and complete the action in our mind. Art that is a mass of line and shape or feels crowded is said to be "busy"

Handball (1939), by Ben Shahn. Courtesy of The Museum of Modern Art, New York, New York. Abby Aldrich Rockefeller Fund.

and that also can convey a feeling of motion. Art that contains several separate images can give the illusion of motion by making our eye follow the various images drawn.

The motion in *Handball* is obvious—the boy in the center is about to hit the ball against the wall, and the players at either side, as well as the person viewing the art, can anticipate what is about to take place. The interrupted motion in this drawing creates a mild feeling of tension, as if the viewer was waiting to return the hit ball.

Project

Here's a simple game you can play with one or more of your friends. Each person in turn starts and continues to wildly wave his hands, twist his body, kick his legs, and shake until someone yells "freeze." At that instant, the player stops and holds the pose he is in, while other players try to guess what he might be doing—throwing pizza dough into the air, dancing the hustle, screwing in a lightbulb, falling out of a tree, running away from Dracula, skiing out of control, itching from a bug in his shirt. It is possible for the image to have several interpretations. The player can select whichever action he thinks describes him best, but then he must continue to perform and act out that action.

COMPOSITION

The way that an artist puts together the parts of his picture—the lines, shapes, and so on—can give the viewer a sense of depth, a feeling of seeing things that are in the distance. (Think of a drawing of railway tracks disappearing far away.) Composition also creates a point of view. It puts us somewhere in relation to what we are seeing. Having to "look up" at a subject focuses our attention and gives the subject an importance greater than the viewer; "looking down" on a subject gives the viewer power and command over the subject. Another as-

pect of composition is balance. If the arrangement of parts in an image feel balanced, then the art seems complete or satisfying. If the elements are not in balance, then the image appears disturbing or incomplete.

The spectators in *Stag at Sharkeys*, as well as the viewer's eyes, are directed up at the two fighters, therefore emphasizing the fighters' power and importance.

The artist has arranged the elements of *Old Models* in a balanced and pleasing pattern. What makes this feel like art has less to do with the subject and the various individual objects, and more to do with the way the objects have been presented in a composition and pat-

Old Models (1892), by William M. Harnett. Courtesy of the Museum of Fine Arts, Boston, Massachusetts. Charles Henry Hayden Fund, 39.761.

Stag at Sharkey's (1907), by George Wesley Bellows. Courtesy of The Cleveland Museum of Art, Cleveland, Ohio. Hinman B. Hurlbut Collection.

tern. The composition does not mean "old models" as much as it means "interesting and pleasing arrangement."

Project

Carefully remove and save the labels from several food cans and jars, and cut out the face panels from empty food boxes. On a large sheet of paper or cardboard arrange the labels in rows as if they were lined up and sitting on grocery shelves. Try putting all of the big labels together on one "shelf" and the smaller labels on another. Step back and look at the composition you have created. Now rearrange the labels so that the ones with similar colors are together. Finally, mix up the labels and place them

randomly on the shelves. Does each grouping present a different feeling? Which patterns seem to have the best balance? Which one do you like best? Continue to rearrange the labels until you like the

The Power of Music (1847), by William Sidney Mount. Courtesy of The Century Association, New York, New York.

composition. Then, if you want, glue the labels in place.

FRAMING

The artist must determine how much or how little of the scene or object he has made he wishes to show. Often the artist will show us more or less than we are accustomed to seeing so that we can view the subject in a new way— somewhat like looking through a microscope or looking out of a window. Framing is sometimes accomplished within the picture itself. The artist might create a picture in which we are looking through a window or doorway into another room.

The barn door in *Power of Music* creates a frame within the picture that helps tell the story. Framing here creates two scenes: the music being played and enjoyed inside the barn, and the person outside the barn also enjoying the music.

Project

Make a small frame from a piece of cardboard by cutting a square or rectangular hole in the center. Look through a magazine to find a large picture, preferably one with several

people or objects in it. Place the frame over the magazine picture and move it around to frame the different parts of the picture. Do you find the meaning or the feeling of the smaller pictures you make different from the whole picture? See how many pictures with different meanings you can make. Then mount your favorite composition to the back of the frame with glue or tape.

MODERN ART

Nearly all the visual art produced in Early America were portraits. Portraits were not so much considered art, as a means of preserving one's likeness in a picture—much as we take family snapshots today. In their struggle to survive the American wilderness, the early settlers had little time for the fine arts. Even portrait painters of the time were self-taught and considered themselves craftsmen rather than artists. Most Early American painters did not even bother to sign their work.

We now refer to these early works of art as "primitives." Primitive art does not mean bad art, but only that the style was simple, original, and a bit flat. In many ways the primitive art style reflected and recorded the rather plain and unpretentious lives of the people pictured in the paintings. *Caverly Family* is a good example of primitive art.

By the nineteenth century, Americans were leading a more prosperous life, and they were feeling proud—and rightly so—about the vast and varied beauty of their country. Artists were inspired by the rolling countryside, the majestic mountains, the lush forests, and the clear rivers; and by now they had begun to develop their own visual style. So while American portrait painters were still considered craftsmen, fine landscape painters such as the painter of *Peaceful Village* were developing into talented artists.

Painters soon became interested in showing everyday scenes of life which depicted the dignity and homespun virtues of the common people. Ordinary men, women, and children going about their everyday chores and pleasures filled many canvases. Paintings portrayed fur trappers hunting the woods, riverboat captains and their

Caverly Family (1836), by Joseph H. Davis. Courtesy of the New York State Historical Association, Cooperstown, New York.

Peaceful Village (1850), by an anonymous American Artist. Courtesy of the Philadelphia Museum of Art Collection, Philadelphia, Pennsylvania. The Edgar William and Bernice Chrysler Garbisch Collection.

vented, and at first it seemed to eliminate the need for portrait artists. A photograph captured a portrait or scene exactly as it was, down to the last detail. All that was missing in early photography was color—photographs then were in black and white only.

Mechanical images

Photography was at first only a mechanical process for reproducing a portrait or scene rather than an art form in which the photographer used skill and technique to create a "feeling" about the subject as well as an accurate picture. The camera was a copying device that nearly everyone could use—the basic skill or technique necessary in the photographer's visual vocabulary was limited to framing: choosing just how much or little of an object or scene to include in a picture.

ships crossing the Mississippi River, farmers working the land, mothers scolding children, and folks just sitting around relaxing or having a merry time—*Flax Scutching Bee*.

By the mid-nineteenth century, the picture camera had been in-

In time the techniques of the painter's visual vocabulary were

Flax Scutching Bee (about 1860), by Linton Park. Courtesy of the National Gallery of Art, Washington, D.C. Gift of Edgar William and Bernice Chrysler Garbisch.

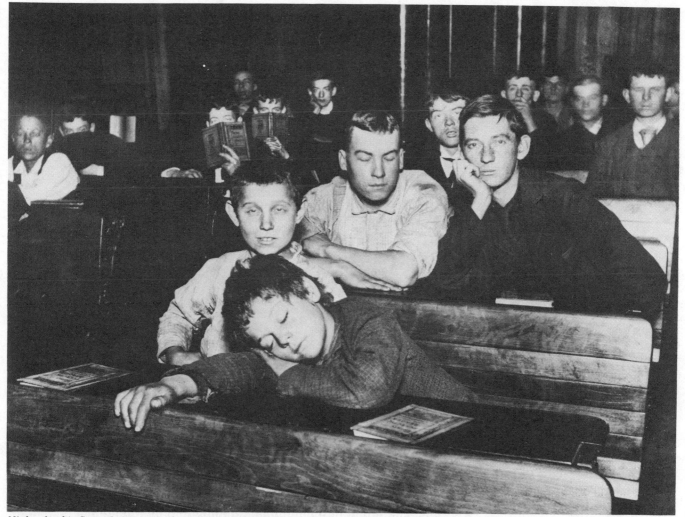

Nightschool in Seventh Avenue Lodging House, Children's Aid Society (1900), photograph by Jacob A. Riis. Courtesy of the Museum of the City of New York, New York.

applied to photography, and the photographer became an artist. By choosing subject, framing, and light, the photographer was able to create pictures with greater appeal and feeling than that of snapshot recordings. Jacob Riis's shows a group of students attending nightschool in this early twentieth century photo.

Although photography nearly replaced portrait painting in America, both artists—the painter and the photographer—continued to create pleasing images in their own ways. Both the painter and the photographer limited their images to what they could see. In their pictures they tried to copy best what the eye had seen.

Painters try new techniques

The painter, no matter how skillful, could not produce images with the accuracy and detail of a camera, however, and so he began to experiment with new and different images—images that looked like nothing actually seen, but were taken rather from the imagination; images that the camera could not create. Artists found them not only in the world of nature and objects around them, but in their minds, emotions, fantasies, and dreams. Because the images of experimental art were often unrecognizable interpretations of the subjects being painted, this new form was called "abstract art" or "modern art."

By using various abstract art forms, the artist found that he could actually better convey his attitude towards and feelings about a subject than by just copying that subject in a realistic way. Abstract art became a pure example of how the elements of visual language—shape, color, line, and so on—could be used by themselves to express a particular feeling. Abstract painting is nothing more than a purposeful combination of the visual elements themselves.

What do we mean by what we've just said? Let's look at three paintings: *Bash-Bish Falls, Smelt Brook Falls,* and *Fall.* Each of these conveys the same image—falling water. But each artist has

Bash-Bish Falls, S. Egremont, Mass. (1855), by John Frederick Kensett. Courtesy of the Museum of Fine Arts, Boston, Massachusetts. M. & M. Karolik Collection.

Smelt Brook Falls (1937), Marsden Hartley. Courtesy of The St. Louis Art Museum, St. Louis, Missouri. Eliza McMillan Fund.

Fall (1963), by Bridget Riley. Courtesy of the Tate Gallery, London, England.

used a different style to create a visual statement. The first painting is clearly realistic and gives the viewer an almost photographic account of the scene. The second painting is abstract, but still quite recognizable as falling water. We get, however, a stronger feeling of rushing water and massive rocks in this painting than we did in the first; whereas the water in the first painting might be making the sound of a soft, gentle roar, the water here seems to be rushing and splashing loudly. The third painting is completely abstract. It uses no recognizable image of a waterfall, but only the elements of visual language. Stare at the picture—especially the lower area where the wavy lines are close together. The line, shape, texture, motion, and composition of this image can also convey the image and movement of falling water.

Interpreting the artist

By not painting the actual image as we are used to seeing it, and using only the visual elements as the subject, the modern artist tries to give the viewer the essence of the subject—in the above case, the feeling of a waterfall. But exactly *what* the essence is, is left largely to the viewer. It is you, the viewer, bringing your own associations, experiences, and feelings to the image, who interprets the message of the modern artist. Often there may be several different ideas about what the artist is trying to show; all ways of seeing the artist's abstract image are valid, all are interpretations of the image. It is the idea that each person viewing modern art can have his own personal feeling about the image that makes modern art different from reality or "look-alike" art. Today modern art is created using several techniques and styles and almost any material as the medium. Here are several popular American art forms now being used by artists.

MIXED MEDIA

An artist may choose to combine two or more different art forms or "media" to create a single image. This mixed media composition, *Covering the Earth*, combines painting and sculpture.

Project

Look through a few old magazines or newspapers and pick out several interesting headlines, or parts of headlines, or even single words, for example, "everyone to pay more," "two stickers for one plate," "call a truck," "one of the world's largest." Now look for objects (or magazine pictures of objects) to which you can apply a headline that will give a new or different meaning to the object.

Covering the Earth (1967), by Larry Rivers.

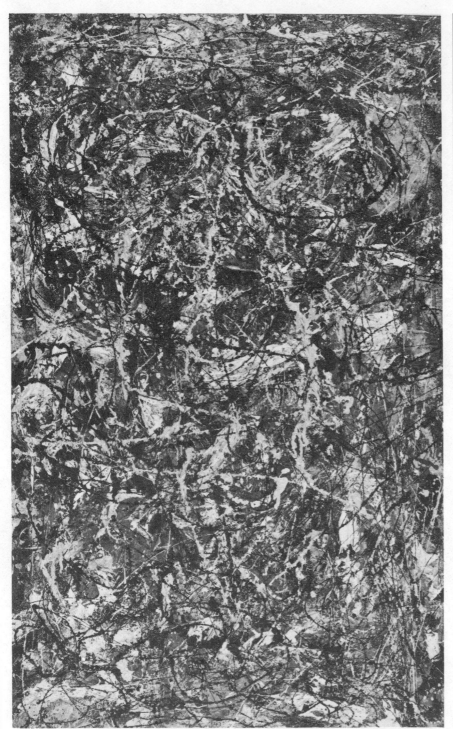

Full Fathom Five (1947), by Jackson Pollock. Courtesy of The Museum of Modern Art, New York, New York. Gift of Peggy Guggenheim.

ACTION PAINTING

This is a process of dripping, pouring, and splashing paint on a canvas that has been laid on the floor. It is the artist's deepest feelings that determine how the paint is applied—big blobs or small splashes, straight drips or curvy lines, and so on—and those feelings he wants the "accidental" drips to capture. This technique gives the artist only limited control over the outcome. In action painting the artist may have little idea of how he wants the finished work to look.

Movement, not surprisingly, is the major element of *Full Fathom Five*. The viewer's eyes explore and move along the lines of paint that crisscross each other. The painting is in some ways a visual puzzle—not to be solved, but only to be explored. In attempting the impossible task of following the drips of paint, the viewer can become as absorbed in viewing the painting as the artist was in creating it.

Project

Try your own action painting. Spread out old newspapers to protect the floor. For a canvas use a piece of cardboard rather than paper—globs of wet paint could cause paper to wrinkle and curl. Drip either poster paints, finger paints, food coloring, or even latex wall paint on your canvas. Don't be too anxious to hang your action painting. It often takes overnight or several days for the globs of paint to completely dry.

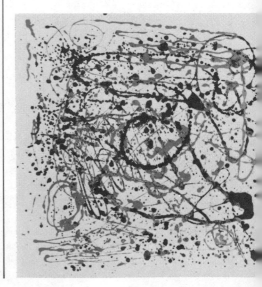

COLLAGE

Collage is the technique of creating an image by pasting various flat materials on a canvas or other surface. The artist often combines several materials: cloth, pieces of printed matter, and fragments of all sorts of objects, even plants. Often just a scrap of an object will suggest the feeling of the whole.

The artist created *Portrait of Ralph Dusenberry* to be a portrait of a man. From the collage we don't know exactly what Mr. Dusenberry looks like, but from the artist's choice of materials there are definite clues as to what kind of man he is. The shape of a fish formed from wood shingles is possibly meant to suggest that Ralph Dusenberry could swim like a fish. The piece of music at the bottom of the collage tells us that he liked to sing. A carpenter's rule is used as a frame, because he was a carpenter by trade. What other clues to descriptions about Ralph Dusenberry can you find in the collage?

Portrait of Ralph Dusenberry (1924), by Arthur G. Dove. Courtesy of The Metropolitan Museum of Art, New York, New York. The Alfred Stieglitz Collection 1949.

Project

Do a collage about yourself, a friend, or the town or city you live in. Do one about an event, your vacation, birthday, hobbies, or other interests. Select the subject for your collage, and then look through magazines and for discarded objects or materials that suggest your subject. Now, using your knowledge of visual language, arrange the material on a stiff piece of cardboard or wood and glue or paste the objects in place.

POP ART

The pop artist creates his images by selecting for his subject things that are common or popular in our everyday lives—hence the name "pop art." The artist redefines the meaning of the subject to give the viewer a new way of seeing familiar objects, and maybe a new understanding of what the objects can also be. Coke bottles, hamburgers, cars, television sets, and beer cans have all been the subject of pop art painting and sculpture. Pop artists do not try to glorify commercial objects the way advertisements do,

Hamburger (1963), by Claes Oldenburg. Courtesy of the Sidney Janis Gallery, New York, New York. Carroll Janis collection.

nor do they try to criticize or satirize the object. The artist simply presents his subject in an art form, as if to say "this is about the world we live in today." It is the viewer who supplies his own personal meaning to the image.

The subject of *Hamburger* is familiar to nearly everyone—what does it mean to you? Early American "still life" images often depicted fruits, vegetables, cheese, and other table foods of the period. This modern pop art still-life sculpture presents a food representative of America today: the hamburger.

Project

What do you think is popular in America now? Or what objects do you think best describe American attitudes? Whatever you choose, mount it on a base and present it as pop art along with the reason you chose it.

ENVIRON-MENTAL SCULPTURE

With an attitude much like that of the pop artist, the environmental sculptor creates works— usually quite large ones—using popular objects; sometimes these sculptures are entire full-scale environments. In experiencing an environmental sculpture, the viewer can physically interact with the work—walk into or around it, touch it, smell it, climb it, or play with it.

Everything in *The Diner* is life-sized. However, the artist presents objects and people with a feeling of loneliness; the ghostly white figures don't interact with each other. By being literally surrounded by the sculpture rather than confronting it head on, the spectator can better sense the feeling of loneliness that the artist was trying to convey.

The Diner (1964–1966), by George Segal. Courtesy of the Walker Art Center, Minneapolis, Minnesota. Gift of the T. B. Walker Foundation.

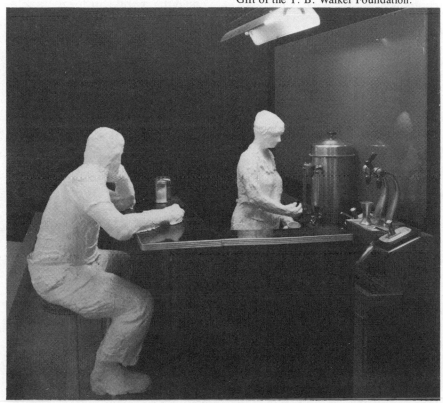

Project

Rearrange your bedroom, or maybe just one corner of your bedroom, into an environmental sculpture that describes what you do there and how you feel about the space. First, decide what feeling or mood you want to create, then collect the objects you decide will help convey the mood. Pajamas, blankets, pillows, beds, bedtime books, and stuffed animals might represent a sleep environment. Books, papers, a desk, and school materials could represent a study; toys might be used for a play environment. To achieve the image you want, you can try stacking objects and furniture or covering them with aluminum foil, colored paper, or ribbon. You might even make an aluminum foil dummy of yourself to put into the sculpture. Experiment until you have arranged the objects in a pleasing composition.

OP ART

The op artist tries to achieve an image and feeling by optical illusion. The viewer's eyes are tricked by the illusion into seeing movement, depth, shape, pattern, or even color where literally there are none.

Stare at *Fall* again, page 214. Do you see this painting as black lines on a white surface or white lines on black? Either way, the result is a wavy, undulating surface (even though the surface is flat) that creates a sense of motion. In which direction do you think the lines are moving?

Project

Create your own op art using ruled paper, graph paper, music notation paper, or even a classified page from the newspaper. Using the lines or grid of the paper, a single color crayon or marker, and what you know about shape, line, motion, and pattern, draw an optical design by alternating dark and light spaces or shapes. Experiment.

MOBILES

Artists usually rely only on visual technique to create the feeling of movement, but the mobile artist actually creates a moving sculpture. The most characteristic mobiles are made from shapes of flat material suspended by string or wire in a delicate state of balance. Slight movements of air cause the shapes to move and turn, loop and swirl, giving the viewer a constantly changing image.

Many early mobiles were motorized so the motion of each element could be controlled. Charles Eames uses solar energy, (power from the sun) to run the *Sun Machine* motor. The motor makes the mobile shapes spin, turn, and play against each other.

Although the shapes of a mobile are often not recognizable as specific objects, the action of *Lobster Trap and Fish Tail* presents a clear image: a lobster, a wire-cage lobster trap, and a fish. The action and association of the three elements make the mobile come to life as it moves. The artist who made this mobile, Alexander Calder, invented the mobile art form.

Sun Machine, by Charles Eames. Collection of Charles Eames.

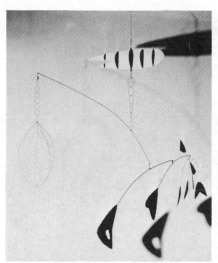

Lobster Trap and Fish Tail (1939), by Alexander Calder. Courtesy of The Museum of Modern Art, New York, New York.

Project

Mobiles can be made in a limitless variety of forms and from many materials. The pattern of elements should present a pleasing design from whichever angle it is viewed. Sticks, dowels, wire coat hangers, and string can be used to hang shapes made from cardboard, foil, paper, or an actual object itself. Just be certain that the hanging objects don't bump into each other as they move. Mobiles often have a mind of their own and don't always turn out as planned. It is usually best to start the mobile at the top and build down using trial and error to get the shapes to balance.

A simple "segmented" mobile can be made by cutting a large recognizable shape from cardboard and then cutting the shape into several pieces. Using string hang them in order along the length of a stick.

AMERICAN KITSCH

This could only be kitsch.

A product whose styling overwhelms its purpose or function is called "kitsch." Kitsch is an American art form of designing an object to look like something other than what it really is. It is making new products look old style, or styling products in a theme.

Kitsch things are often described as "conversation pieces," or "sentimental:" a salt shaker in the shape of the Empire State Building, concrete flamingos on the front lawn, electric and gas fireplace logs, simulated wood wallpaper, tailfins on cars, a bowl of plastic fruit, a Mickey Mouse watch, a Beatles T-shirt, a fake zebra-skin rug, plastic made to look like real wood, epaulets on shirts, and the American eagle on anything. Other familiar examples are ornamental trees and flowers made of plastic. You have probably been fooled—or nearly fooled—by what you thought to be a beautiful healthy house plant or planted tree only to touch or smell it and find the tree was not alive but rather a clever plastic reproduction of the real thing. Maybe you said, "How beautiful" and "How nice it never needs water, feeding, or sunlight" but then maybe you were offended by the idea of counterfeiting Mother Nature. In either case, it is still kitsch; if it fulfills your aesthetic needs, then it is good kitsch, otherwise it is bad kitsch. Only you can decide if a piece of kitsch is good art or bad art for you. You might say, "Why buy a plain kitchen clock when I can buy one in the shape of a pineapple?" To someone else a clock might be considered strictly for telling time and have nothing at all to do with fruit—the plainer the clock, the better.

Look at the objects around you, the products offered in stores and catalogs. Consider their style and function. Consider what you buy. The kitsch that you like is just as much a piece of personal art as it is functional.

Giant Billiard (1970), Haus Rucker Co. Photo courtesy of the N.Y. Daily News, New York, New York.

HAPPENINGS

A happening is a one-time event or environment conceived by the artist and created by everyone who happens to be present at the happening. To see a happening means you have to be a part of it. However, unlike a play performed upon a stage, a happening can take place anywhere: on the street, in the supermarket, in a swimming pool, on a boat, under a pile of coats, anywhere. Also unlike the theater, there is no rehearsal, and no repeat performances—the audience is always a part of the happening itself.

It is an event defined as a piece of art. At this happening, entitled *Giant Billiard*, a New York City street was closed to car traffic so that a huge inflatable mattress-like structure could be placed in the street for those passing by to play on. The artist responsible for this happening wanted to create a spontaneous spirit of participation and play among people who normally just walk the street going about their business.

American art today includes techniques, materials, and subjects limited only by the artist's imagination. Art images can be conceived using copiers, computers, television, lightbulbs, machines, living plants, balloons, and, of course, paint and brush. And yet, whatever the technique or subject all art is created using the same visual language. Understanding the language will help you to better "see" art and create your own art. Anyone can be an artist.

ARTS AND CRAFTS

Most Early Americans were trained to make some essential or decorative craft. To be an Early American was to be a jack-of-all-trades and a master of most. Hands today are just as capable of fine craftsmanship as the hands of the early settlers. And our imaginations can be just as ingenious. Even if the things we want are available in stores, it is sometimes much more satisfying to make them ourselves. The extra work involved seems insignificant when the result is so admired and enjoyed. And in time, handcrafted items can also give pleasure and be an inspiration to future generations of craftsmen.

GRAVE ART

One of the unique and often overlooked art forms in America is gravestone art. Walk through a cemetery, especially an older one with sinking and crumbling tombstones. Look at the designs carved in the stones and read the inscriptions. What information about the people buried there can you discover? To decipher gravestone art you will probably need to understand more about the people of Early America and their beliefs.

The first grave markers in the American wilderness were of necessity only piles of field stone or smooth river rocks. There was little spare time to chisel a design or carve an inscription. At best, only a few words of fact were crudely scratched into the markers. But once Americans began to settle into communities and towns, and the church began to be the religious and social center of the people, funerals became lavish celebrations, as expensive as the "departed" or his relatives could afford. Although Early Americans were plain and simple in their lifestyle, death was considered an event that brought one closer to God. A part of the funeral celebration was to elaborately decorate the gravestone with appropriate symbols and inscriptions to "cheer" the departed "homeward to heaven." The stone was also a permanent marker to celebrate the social event.

Personalized gravestones

All gravestones were cut by hand using only a chisel and mallet. Most Early American gravestone cutters were neither artists nor artisans—just local farmers or stonemasons who had the proper tools and enjoyed the work. Each gravestone cutter had his own style and the designs were recognizable as his signature. Rarely did one gravestone cutter copy the designs of another. In walking through a cemetery you will often notice several stones of the same period using the same elements of design and style of lettering. Chances are they were all made by the same gravestone cutter.

You can "read" the design on a gravestone if you understand the symbolism. Many older gravestones have certain specific graphic themes and each design has a symbolic spiritual meaning. Some symbols represented the future or

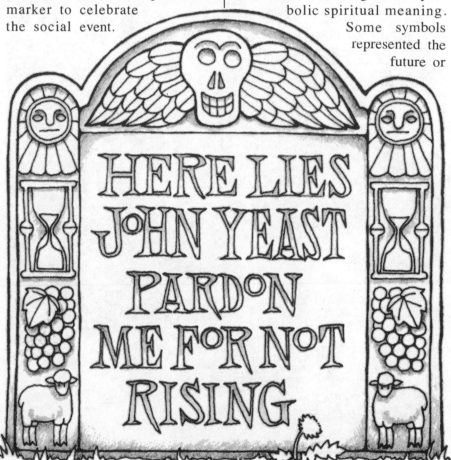

HERE LIES JOHN YEAST PARDON ME FOR NOT RISING

"heavenly home" of the deceased, while other symbols frequently portrayed the deceased's past life on earth.

The "head of death" with wings, and sometimes an entire skeleton, was one of the most popular symbols and is thought to represent the flight of the soul from the body. "Fleeting time" was represented by an hourglass, a bearded man with a scythe, a candlestick resting on the world, and even a hand to show the "hand of time."

Here are a few more of the other common symbols used:

> **Skeleton or crossbones:** mortality and the inevitability of death.
> **Sun:** resurrection of the soul after death.
> **Lamb, grapevine, and squirrel:** sign of a good Christian.
> **Dove:** devotion and innocence.
> **Feathers:** flight of the soul to heaven.

Gravestone design expressed the philosophy of the people in non-symbolic ways as well. Inscriptions or "epitaphs," poems, biographies, and even bits of humor carved into the stones attempted to teach those still living some moral lesson.

Sometimes a person would write his own epitaph long before his death. Most often the inscription was decided upon by the local minister and the gravestone cutter.

These are a few actual epitaphs from Early American gravestones:

Some have children, Some have none,
Here lies the Mother of twenty-one.

Once I wasn't, Then I was,
Now I ain't again.

Friends prepare yourself to follow me,
As I am now you soon will be.

Keep death and judgment always in your eye,
None's fit to live, but who is fit to die.

Gravestone Rubbing

As in all forms of art collecting, there are also collectors of gravestone art. A gravestone collector doesn't actually collect the gravestones, but rather photographs or makes a "rubbing" of the stone design and inscription. Gravestone rubbings often give a crisper, more striking, and easier to read image than do photographs or the actual stone.

Materials

large sheets of paper, such as newsprint, wrapping paper,

Gravestones from the past were intricately carved and make beautiful rubbings.

classified newspaper sections or shelf paper

dark crayons

tape

1. Select the gravestone you wish to copy. Gravestones that are fairly new or well-preserved with clear, sharp letters or designs produce the best rubbings. Many older gravestones made of soft stone or those just worn by years of weather may have inscriptions or designs too shallow to make a clear rubbing.

2. Cut a piece of paper roughly the size of the gravestone or the section of the stone that you wish to copy. The thinner the paper you use, the sharper the rubbing will be. Tape the paper to the face of the stone so that it is flat and smooth. Select a dark-colored crayon. Completely remove the paper from the crayon and, using the broad edge, lightly rub across the surface of the paper until you see the design appear. For a neat appearance, rub with short back and forth strokes, always going either side to side or top to bottom.

If you want the image to be darker, rub the paper with the crayon a second or third time. When the rubbing is as complete as you like it, remove the paper from the stone.

WHITTLING

Whittling is the leisure-time art of shaping a scrap of wood into some sort of model or trinket, practical or not. Though whittling may seem like a craft today, Early Americans considered it more of a "social art." An Early American frontiersman traveled light, but of the few tools he carried none was more frequently used than his pocket-knife. Even when resting from work or travel, the frontiersman would frequently open his knife, pick up a twig, and whittle, just to pass the time. Some pretty famous Americans were dedicated whittlers, including Abraham Lincoln, Calvin Coolidge, and Will Rogers. A common image of rural America even today is that of a group of men sitting around the stove in the village store whittling away at a stick, or even the wooden box they might be sitting on, just passing the time with a little talk.

Don't confuse whittling with wood carving. Wood carvers were usually artisans who had apprenticed and who had become skilled at carving intricate wood designs for chairs, chests, and all types of furniture, as well as carving figures, statues, and other works of fine art. Some whittlers were merely "shaving makers," shaving down a piece of wood with a pocketknife. Sailors, woodsmen, farmers, or anyone who regularly carried a pocketknife was probably also a whittler.

Prevent cutting yourself by whittling away from your body.

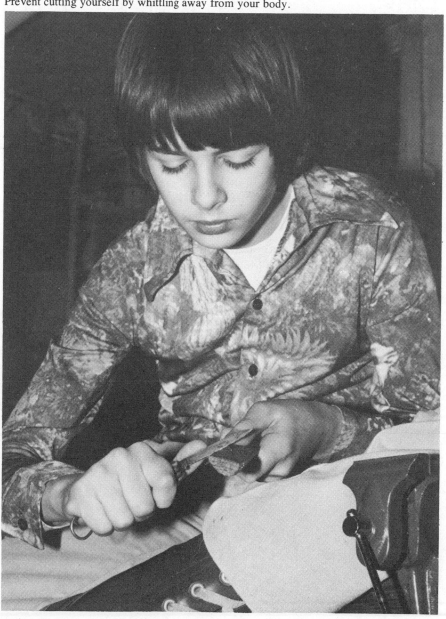

You can whittle too; it's fun and easy, and the only tool you need is a pocketknife. As in any craft, however, it is important that you select the proper tool for the job.

Selecting a knife

There are several styles of penknives available, but no particular one is best for all types of whittling and/or carving. Knives with pointed blades are good for getting into corners and carving intricate designs. There are knife blades for carving holes, making grooves, chipping wood, and several other cuts.

There are three types of knives commonly used for whittling, all being "clasp" knives in which the blade closes into the handle. The smallest is the penknife which usually has two or more blades, none being longer than three inches (eight cm.). Jackknives usually have one large blade between three and a half and five inches long (nine to thirteen cm.), and sometimes one or two smaller blades. The folding hunting knife has just one heavy blade up to eight inches (twenty cm.) long.

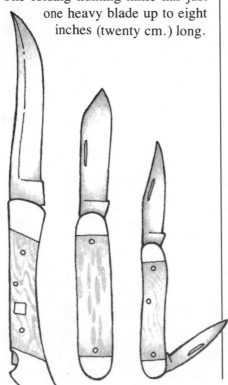

There are also several different designs for pocketknife blades, each designed for a specific type of cutting. The most common whittling blades are the "pen," a larger version with its "spear," the more pointed "B-clip" blade, and the "sabre spear."

Pen   CLIP   SPear   SaBre SPear

Sharpening a knife

A knife used for whittling must be kept sharp. The sharper the blade, the safer it is. Some parents may think that a dull knife blade is safer for kids to use, but a dull blade requires more pressure to cut and is more likely to slip, refuse to cut where you want it to, split the wood, and even possibly snap shut while cutting. (Of course, a knife should only be used by a child who is mature enough to be properly taught how to handle it.) The sharp edge of a knife blade will begin to wear dull as soon as you begin to use it. Even a brand-new knife may require finer sharpening before it can be used for whittling. A blade is made sharp again by wearing down or "grinding" both sides of the blade edge on a sharpening stone.

If a blade has become very dull from neglect, or if a blade has chipped, it may need to be sharpened on a grinding wheel. You had better ask for help from an adult to

do this. But if the blade edge has become slightly dulled from cutting, you can regrind the edge using a stone and oil. There are several types of sharpening stones varying from coarse to smooth, with flat to rounded shapes. If you don't have a sharpening stone, find a smooth, flat rock or stone, and put a few drops of machine oil on the flat surface. Lay the blade almost flat on the stone with the back edge raised slightly. Gently stroke the blade so that the knife edge is pulled across the stone. Turn the blade over and stroke the other edge. Continue stroking and turning the blade over alternately until it is sharp. Don't press the blade hard against the stone—only a gentle, steady pressure is needed. If you ever have the chance, watch a wood craftsman use a sharpening stone. There are several individual hand techniques, and developing a technique for yourself will make sharpening much easier.

To finish the sharpening job, draw the blade several times, as you have been doing, across a piece of leather or cardboard. This technique removes any slightly rough "wire edge" or "burrs" that are sometimes caused by the sharpening stone. To test a whittling blade for sharpness, draw it across the edge of a piece of paper. The blade should cut the paper cleanly and easily. If the paper bends or tears, the blade still needs sharpening. Don't let the blade become dull. Whenever things feel harder to cut, stroke the knife a few times across the stone. Here are a few more tips to help keep your whittling knife sharp and safe:

Never hammer on a knife or use the knife as a hammer. The steel of the knife blade is hard and brittle, and can break or shatter if hit.

Never use a knife on material that is very hard and could dull or break the blade. Also, watch out for knots and nails when whittling in old lumber.

Never heat the blade in a fire. The metal will discolor and loose some of its hardness.

Never use the blade as a screwdriver to pry things open, or for throwing into the ground.

If the blade gets wet, wipe it dry and lightly oil the hinge.

When not using a knife, close the blade with the palm of your hand and put it away. Never carry the knife with the blade open.

Good wood to whittle

The wood you select will greatly determine how hard or easy it is to whittle. For the beginning whittler there are several woods readily found or bought that are soft, straight grained, and free from knots—in other words, easy to cut: These are balsa, northern white pine, basswood, redwood, sugar pine, and willow. Common yellow pine is unsuitable for carving because it is very knotty and splinters easily. After you have become practiced at the art of whittling, you might want to try a harder wood, such as mahogany, oak, birch, or elm.

It is also quite important that the wood you select be "seasoned" and dry. A "green" branch will be most difficult to cut. Wood from downed trees that have naturally dried and seasoned can be excellent for carving unless it is too soft or rotted.

How to Whittle

The general safety rule for whittling is always to cut with the blade moving away from yourself and from the hand holding the wood. If the knife should slip, you won't cut yourself accidentally.

Before starting an ambitious whittling project practice by just chipping away at a scrap of wood. You will soon develop a feel for the knife and the type of wood you are using. If you want to practice whittling, and make something practical at the same time, try to whittle a "fuzz stick." Just make several slices into a length of stick but don't slice the chips entirely off. Fuzz sticks are great for starting camp or fireplace fires.

If you have a specific shape or object you wish to carve, first draw it on the wood. If the shape is complex, also draw the rear and side views. It is easiest when you start

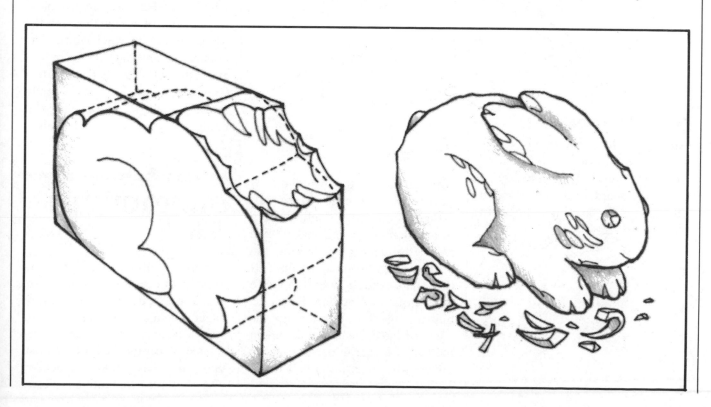

with a piece of wood about the size of the object you want to whittle.

Find a comfortable place to sit and begin to cut away at the wood slowly and carefully removing small chips only—once a chip is whittled off it can't be replaced. Don't try to make big cuts, but gradually "work" the wood down to the line you have drawn. Roughly whittle out the entire shape before carving the details. As you are carving the wood try to keep a mental picture of what you are making.

When roughing-out the object hold the knife in a fist with your thumb on the back edge of the handle. For finer cutting move your thumb out on the dull back edge of the blade.

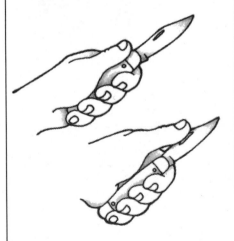

"Relief" carving

Another style of whittling is "relief" carving, done on a flat piece of board. Draw a design directly on a scrap of board, or draw the design on paper and transfer it to the board

using carbon paper. Place the carbon between the drawing and the wood. Redraw over your drawing and the carbon will transfer the design to the wood. Whittle away the wood around the design just deep enough so that it stands out.

One of the classic American whittlings is a ball-in-a-cage, both carved together from a single piece of wood. It takes quite a lot of practice to carve a ball-in-a-cage, but the idea is simple. Start with a square block of wood (balsa is best if this is your first try) and mark out the outline of a cage on four sides. On each of the same four sides in the same relative position, draw a circle indicating the ball, but draw the ball slightly wider than the inside width of the cage bars. Begin

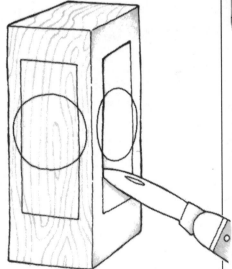

whittling away the wood on all sides between the cage and the ball. So the wood doesn't split or chip further than you want, make "stop cuts" frequently by sinking the blade into the wood along the outline, and cutting with the knife point around the outline. Finish the ball-in-cage by squaring up the edges of the cage and rounding out the ball. Be careful not to trim too much away or else the ball might fall out.

Nothing that you whittle has to be practical, and actually most whittled objects are created more for the fun of doing than for the usefulness. Once you have become hooked on whittling, there are several other classics that you might try: chains, totem poles, fishing lures, propellers, puzzles, ships in bottles, scissors, fans, and so on.

SILHOUETTE ART

Various popular art forms in eighteenth-century America were based on cutting shapes out of paper with a pair of scissors. Paper was scarce, expensive, and never wasted. Paper that had been written upon and was no longer needed was often used for cutting projects.

Simple outline images and whole scenes were carefully cut from scraps of paper: Children cut a string of dolls from folded paper. Even Betsy Ross created the five-pointed star for the first American flag with a few snips of her scissors.

The most popular form of paper cutting, however, especially for making portraits, was silhouette art—at times also known as shadowgraphs, scissors art, shade art, skiagraphy, and profile art. Just as we keep photographs today, Early Americans wanted to keep portraits of themselves and their families as remembrances. Very few Americans could afford the services of a portrait painter, and most Americans were much too busy anyway to sit and model for the painter. So silhouette art be-came a common and inexpensive substitute for painted portraits. The subject to be drawn sat sideways before a candle so that his shadow was cast upon a sheet of paper tacked to the wall. The artist simply traced around the shadow and cut out the image with the scissors.

Scissors artist

To advertise their skills many silhouette artists set up exhibitions of their work in the center of town or in the local merchants' shops. Some silhouette artists prided themselves on the ability to cut a profile freehand by sight alone, giving only occasional glimpses to the subject. Many other silhouettists boasted of detailed accuracy using a machine to make the outlines.

If a family could not afford the services of the traveling silhou-ettist, then they made the silhou-ettes themselves. Only paper, pen, and steady hand were necessary. Most silhouettes were black like a shadow on white paper. The drawn outlines were filled-in with black ink to give a striking contrast. Another technique was to cut the drawn outline from the center of the paper and place a piece of black paper on black silk behind the opening.

Sit perfectly still

It was very important to keep the subject's head quite still while the shadow was being traced. The subject had to remain motionless and be careful not to laugh, sneeze, or cough, as the shadow might move out of place. Silhouette artists in-

A silhouette artist at work.

vented and used various contraptions to hold the head in a steady position. One popular device was called the "silhouette machine." The subject sat in a chair that was attached to an easel. The easel had a piece of glass on which could be mounted a piece of paper that had been oiled to make it translucent. A candle mounted on a stand provided the light, and the artist sat behind the easel drawing the profile outline.

There was also a drawing machine for reducing the size of the silhouette so that the image could be mounted in a locket or brooch.

Silhouette art quickly became popular as a hobby and could be produced even by children, but when photography became popular, silhouette art lost favor.

Making a Silhouette Portrait

Materials
white drawing paper

Tools
lamp (with shade removed)
chair
pencil
tape or tacks
black crayon or marker

1. Place a chair sideways, directly against a blank wall, and seat your subject in the chair so that his head is only a few inches from the wall.

2. Place a light about ten feet (three m.) from the wall and at about the same height as your subject's head so that a strong, sharp shadow is thrown against the wall. A lamp with the shade removed works best; a candle or flashlight propped up with books on a tabletop will do. Hold, tape, or tack a

Fig. 1

piece of drawing paper to the wall directly behind the subject's head and quickly, but carefully, trace the shadow outline while the subject remains motionless, Fig. 1.

3. The silhouette you draw can be completed by filling in the outline with a black crayon or marker, Fig. 2. You can also cut out the silhouette shape and mount either the cut-out or the border on a darker piece of paper. Some silhouette artists prefer to leave the drawing as an outline.

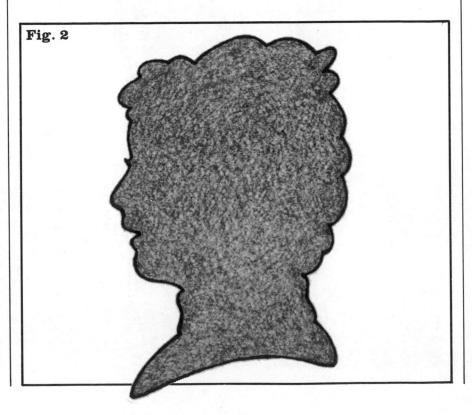

Fig. 2

PAPER DOLL CHAINS

A chain of paper dolls is a classic American craft for children, based on the concept of cutting silhouettes. Only here the silhouettes form a chain with the design repeated again and again.

Materials

length of newspaper or wrapping paper
pencil or felt-tipped marker

Tools

scissors

1. The width of the paper strip will determine the height of the figure you can draw. Accordion-fold the entire length of paper strip, Fig. 3. The width of the folds will determine the width of the doll figures.

2. Draw a simple doll-shape on the front sheet of the paper, being sure to leave arms, dress, or some other figure-part connected to the sides of the paper, Fig. 4.

3. Cut on the doll silhouette and open the doll chain.

If you wish, you can just make random cuts in a folded paper strip. The chain designs that result may be very interesting.

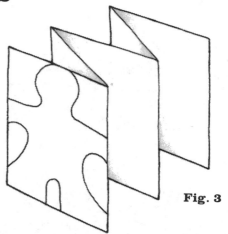

Fig. 3

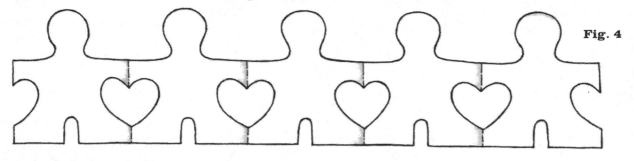

Fig. 4

FLOWER DRYING

One of the methods of food preservation that the Indians taught the settlers was sun drying. When the shriveled-up dried foods were cooked in water they became plump again. In later years it became popular to dry colorful flowers, ferns, and leaves so that their beauty and fragrance would last through the dull winter. These "winter flowers" were often arranged in a jar or hollow gourd, or sometimes just laid in a basket and placed on the table as a decoration and reminder of the spring season to come. By the eighteenth century, flower drying had become a full-fledged art in America, and dried flower arrangements of nearly every available plant species filled American homes. Flower drying as an art is still practiced by some, but we mostly dry flowers for sentiment's sake—to preserve a special memento, like a bridal bouquet or an anniversary rose.

There are several methods of drying flowers, depending on the particular type of foliage, but they all work by Nature's way of drying: evaporation. If you wish to have dried flowers for the winter, you will have to start the drying process in the summer. The flowers, plants, and leaves you wish to dry should be picked when they are perfectly mature; choose a hot sunny day when the humidity is low, and do your gathering at noon. Don't pick flowers when they are damp with dew; if there has been a rain, you should wait about two days before picking. Strip off all the leaves from flower stems and discard other plant parts you don't want to keep. Do not put the cut flowers and foliage in water, but dry them right away. All drying methods hold the plant's original color best when the drying process takes place in the dark, so don't allow the freshly cut plants to remain in strong sunlight too long.

Air Drying

Flowers with delicate stems can be air dried by hanging them in bunches, upside down, in a dark, dry place such as a windowless attic or closet. Your bunches should contain no more than ten flowers or they might mildew. In a week to

more sand until the flower is covered by at least an inch or two. The sand will keep the flower petals separated as they dry so they won't curl up and fall off as might happen when air drying. Sand-dried flowers are usually dry in five or six days, but for plants with thick leaves and other parts that don't dry well, you may have to wait a week or as long as ten days.

Instead of sand, some craftspeople prefer a mixture of five parts yellow or white cornmeal mixed with one part powdered borax. Follow the same drying procedure as with sand but be sure not to use as much meal and borax. As long as the flower is completely covered, everything will be okay. The cornmeal and borax mixture can be reused several times if it is oven dried at a low temperature before each use. Another sand-like material especially good for flower drying is called silica gel and is commercially available at many florist shops and greenhouse nurseries.

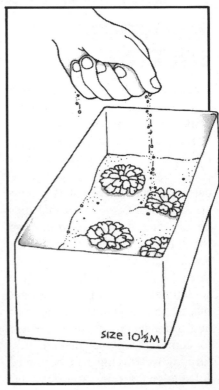

size 10½M

ten days the plants should be completely dry. Some flowers and grasses with sturdy stems and large flower heads can be air dried right-end-up by just standing them in a tall jar or basket.

Sand Drying

Delicate flowers that might be breakable when air dried should be dried in sand. Put an inch or so of sand into the bottom of a shoe box or a container of similar depth. Use only clean, dry, sifted sand, (kitty litter works well also) but not ocean sand which contains salt. Cut the stems of the flowers quite short; other foliage you want to dry should sit flat on the sand. Scoop a shallow depression in the sand and carefully settle the flower or plant into it face-up. Gently mold the sand to support the underside of the flower in its natural position, then trickle a fine stream of sand over the entire blossom. Continue to add

rangement, fill a jar or some other vase-like container with a few inches of sand and poke the dried flower stems into the sand. (You might also add some sheaves of grain, corn tassels, and tall grasses to your arrangement to fill it out.) The finished arrangement must still be protected from humidity, which will cause the dried flowers to wilt almost immediately. The winter season is relatively dry anyway, and in an air-conditioned home the flower arrangement will last through several summers.

Press Drying

Some flowers with relatively flat blossoms, as well as ferns and autumn leaves, can be dried by pressing. Sometimes flowers with special meaning are pressed and left between the pages of a heavy book, like the family Bible. Even after several years the fragrance and color of the fresh flower remains. However, most flower pressing should be done between sheets of newspaper. Put about four thicknesses of newspaper on a hard surface—a table top or floor—where the drying flowers won't be disturbed for several weeks. Lay out the flowers, leaves, or plants to be dried on the newspaper so that none touch each other. Cover the plants with four more thicknesses of newspaper. Now weight the "newspaper and plant sandwich" heavily, using a flat board and several heavy bricks, rocks, large

books, unopened cans of paint, or whatever else heavy you can find. Some people put the newspaper and plant sandwich under a carpet in a frequently used room so that people walking over the plants do the pressing. For the first few days change the newspaper twice a day and then maybe only a few more times during the next two weeks. Each time check the flowers to see if they feel dry. If there is any moisture in the plant, its leaves or petals will begin to curl when exposed to air.

Flower Arrangements

Once the flowers are dried, they may be quite fragile and should be handled with delicate care. If you don't plan to display or arrange the dried flowers right away, store them in an air-tight jar in a dark place. To make a dried flower ar-

You can also arrange dried flowers in a wall decoration. The traditional shape for the arrangement is a circle or wreath. Cut a square or rectangle of poster board or any heavy paper board and draw the rough outline of a wreath on it. Apply white glue to the outline and carefully arrange the dried flowers

PLANTS TO DRY

The following list shows which plants are best for each of the methods of drying.

Air Drying
allium
baby's breath
bittersweet berries
cattail
Chinese lantern
corn tassels
eucalyptus
goldenrod
gourds
heather
hydrangea
milkweed
okra
pussy willow
salvia
strawflower
sumac
yarrow

Press Drying
bluebell
coleus
ferns
ginkgo leaves
huckleberry foliage
maple leaves
oak leaves
pansy poppy violet

Sand Drying
azalea
black-eyed Susan
carnation
chrysanthemum
columbine
daffodil
dahlia
daisy
dogwood blossoms
elder flowers
geranium
gladiolus
hibiscus
hickory leaves
hollyhock
iris
ivy
lilac
marigold
narcissi
peony
Queen Anne's lace
rhododendron
rose
snapdragon
sunflower
zinnia

in a pleasing design. When the arrangement is complete, spray it well with hair spray.

SCRIMSHAW

Scrimshaw is the crafting of objects from the teeth and jaw bone of the sperm whale, as well as the decorative art of carving intricate designs and scenes on individual whale teeth and pieces of bone. All types of simple tools and objects for the home were carved in scrimshaw—cookie cutters, knife, fork, and spoon handles, clothespins, walking sticks, buggy whip handles, door knobs, buttons, checkers, doll house furniture, letter openers, rulers, shoehorns, fancy pins, and all sorts of other jewelry. The

elaborately carved designs usually included scenes of whaling ships, sea animals, and adventures of all descriptions. The American flag, tropical landscapes, eagles, lovers' hearts, flowers, a line or two of verse, and sometimes a picture diary of the sailor's life also appeared in scrimshaw.

A man's craft

Most American handicrafts were made in the home by women. Scrimshaw, however, was strictly a man's craft and most always the handiwork of a whaling seaman. The whale was an important product to growing America in the nineteenth century. Oil melted down from whale blubber was the best oil that could be used to burn for light. The whale that gave the best oil was the sperm whale, but the giant sperm whale was also a fast swimmer, a ferocious fighter, and the most difficult of all whales to catch. When a ship left port to go whaling, it did not return until all the kegs taken on board were completely filled with whale oil. Often that took three or more years.

Even though the work of whaling was hard and busy at times, it could be several weeks or months before a whale was spotted, and the ship's crew had little else to do but wait. Idleness was considered a sin and an invitation to the devil, so to pass the time the ship's crew would play games, sing songs, tell tales, fight with each other, and tinker at handicrafts. The most popular handicraft on a whaling ship was making scrimshaw. The name scrimshaw, in fact, comes from the British word *scrimshank* meaning "to avoid work" or "fool around."

Toothbrushing was never like this

First, all the teeth and bones were cleaned and soaked in hot water to soften the surface. (Sometimes the skin of a shark was used as sandpaper to make the surface even smoother.) Next, a picture was drawn or traced onto the tooth. Designs were either copied from books and magazines or just recalled from memory. The design was then carved or etched into the bone or tooth using a penknife with a blade ground to a fine point. Finally, the carved material was rubbed with black india ink, lampblack, or tobacco juice to darken the etched lines.

Kerosene and other oils for lighting replaced whale oil in the late nineteenth century and whaling eventually died as a commercial industry in America—and so scrimshaw disappeared as a sailor's craft. Today genuine whale teeth and bone scrimshaw are difficult to find. America has declared the whale an endangered species, and no products made from any part of the whale, including scrimshaw, can be transported from one state to another. That means, for example, that by law you cannot buy a piece of whale scrimshaw in Boston and ship it home to Cleveland. It is the hope of those concerned about the remaining whale population that by discouraging people from buying whale scrimshaw fewer whales will be killed throughout the world.

You can still do scrimshaw art today using the bones of animals other than the whale, but you can also make scrimshaw pictures using scrap plastic from around the house. Here is how to do it.

Plastic Scrimshaw

Materials
pencil
carbon paper
black crayon
paper towels

Tools
soft plastic jug
scissors
pocketknife, sharp nail, or large needle

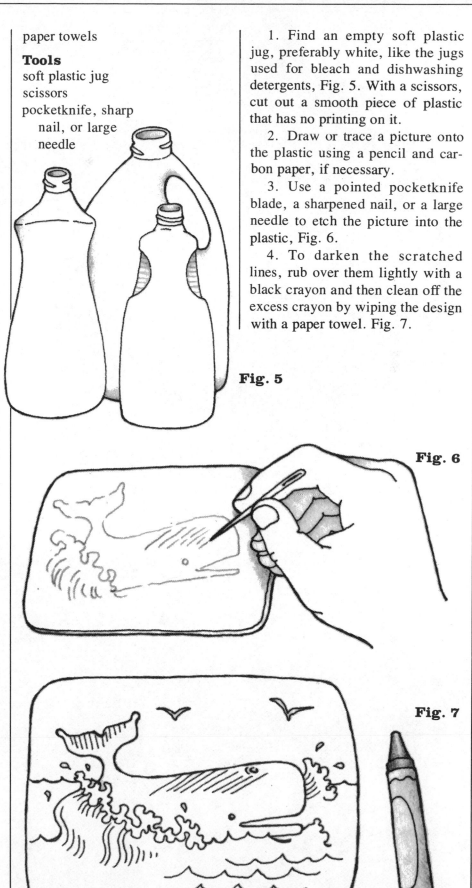

Fig. 5

Fig. 6

Fig. 7

1. Find an empty soft plastic jug, preferably white, like the jugs used for bleach and dishwashing detergents, Fig. 5. With a scissors, cut out a smooth piece of plastic that has no printing on it.

2. Draw or trace a picture onto the plastic using a pencil and carbon paper, if necessary.

3. Use a pointed pocketknife blade, a sharpened nail, or a large needle to etch the picture into the plastic, Fig. 6.

4. To darken the scratched lines, rub over them lightly with a black crayon and then clean off the excess crayon by wiping the design with a paper towel. Fig. 7.

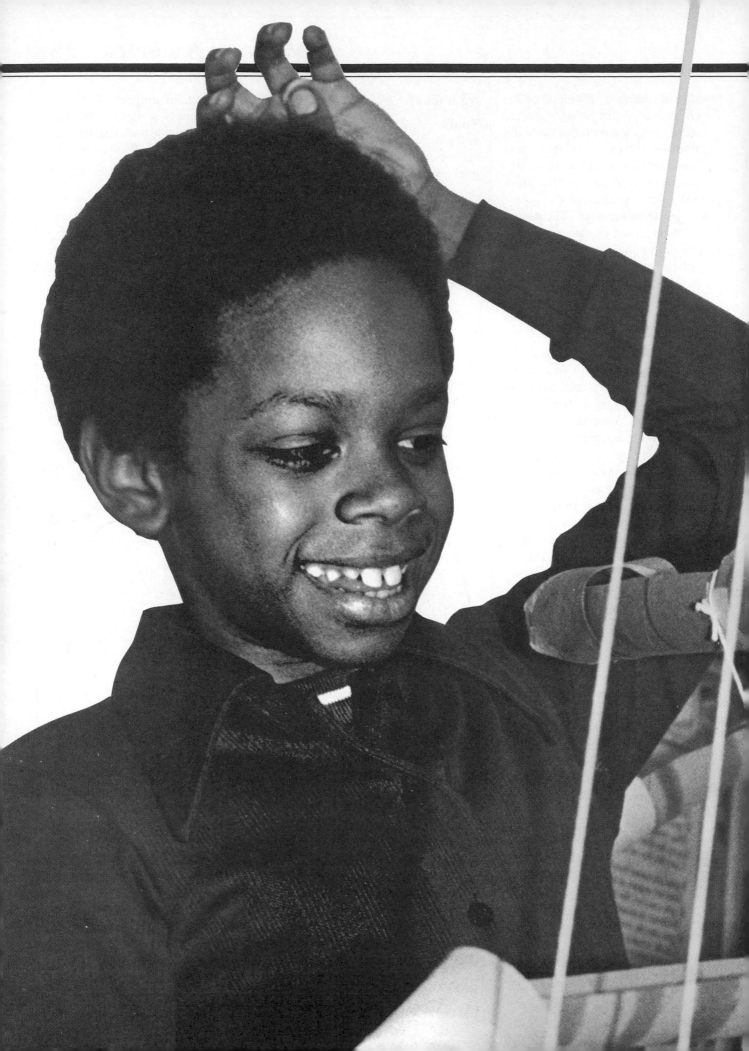

Chapter 9

TOYS, PUZZLES, PLAYPRETTIES, AND GAMES

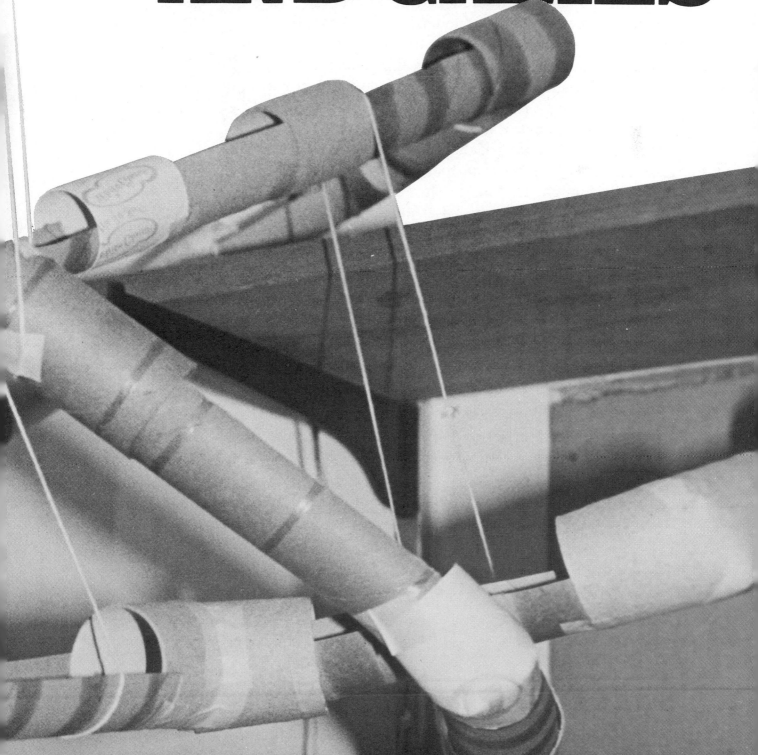

PLAYTHINGS

Children's toys and games are not much different today from the playthings of their parents, grandparents, and great-grandparents. Of course there are always new toy inventions and fads but the play that children enjoy, and the reason play itself is a part of our culture, has always been the same. Children play to prepare for the work of adult life, and toys are their tools. The most popular playthings are usually miniatures of the adult world—dolls or toy trains, for example. These things help a child practice being an adult. All toys are "educational" in the sense that kids at play are trying out skills they will need for the grown-up society of the time.

Toys reflect the culture of the people who make them. Imagine the difference between today's Barbie® doll and the first dolls brought to America by the children of the English colonists! But dolls are basic. Indian children had long played with them before the first settlers arrived, and had a lot to teach the newcomers about doll making. Dolls were among the first presents of friendship presented between Indian and Early American children.

Sometimes the absence of playthings can tell us as much about a people as their presence. Life in Early America was so harsh and busy that there was little time for play. The work of children was essential to the survival of the colony and most parents considered play a waste of time for all but the youngest children.

Girls' dolls from the past.

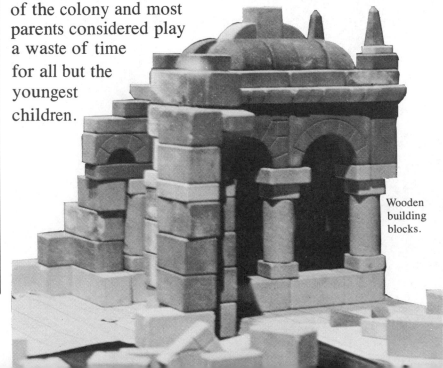

Wooden building blocks.

Little time for fun

Even though playing may have been curbed there were still certain times during the day when children struck up a game or played with whatever was at hand. But other than the dolls and trinkets of very young children, toys and things made just for play were not at all common, and any toys that may have been needed to play games were fashioned from twigs or scraps found around the house. A game "board" would be drawn in the dirt and a few pebbles used as markers.

The best "toy" a boy in Early America had was his pocketknife. Not only was it necessary for doing many chores, but by whittling and carving twigs a boy could make his own toys. Typically, Early American boys learned to carve slingshots, popguns, beanshooters, and bows and arrows. Girls made dolls from corncobs and sewed scraps into doll clothes. Even the wishbone from a turkey was saved and dried to be made into a froglike jumping toy or to make a wish upon.

Some of the games and pastimes from Early American days are still familiar to children today—hopscotch, cat's cradle, hide-and-seek, kite flying, marbles, blindman's bluff, leapfrog, sledding, quoits, and bowling. Some games were in song or rhyme, such as "Here we go 'round the mulberry bush," "Ring-around-a-rosy," "I put my right foot in," or "London Bridge is falling down."

A boy of today on a hobby horse of yesteryear.

Play finally gets a fair shake

During the 1700's, play was still considered a waste of time, even evil. For a while it was against the law in New England for tradesmen or town shops to sell toys. But the struggle to survive on the new land soon became easier and children found more time for just playing. Toys became more common as parents began considering their children's enjoyment of play. Parents and tradesmen crafted dolls, miniature animals, puzzles, and gadgets for children to play with. People of the southern mountain states handcrafted wooden "playpretties" that had silly but descriptive names such as "whimmy diddle," "bull roarer," and "flipper dinger." Some crafted toys of this period were so elaborate and delicate that they seem to have been made by parents for show rather than to be played with.

At the time of America's fight for independence, men and older boys became soldiers so children were once again needed for labor and household chores. Once again there was little time for play and little need for toys. But that didn't last for long. When America celebrated its victory and independence as a new country, toys became more popular than ever. The life was good in a proud America, and play was finally considered a normal part of

Carved playpretties.

A selection of old-fashioned toys for young boys.

growing up. Some parents even became convinced that there was some "teaching value" in toys and that children could learn to read and write and do arithmetic while playing. Concerned and hopeful parents gave their children alphabet blocks, number puzzles, and other "educational toys." And although America still did not have a toy industry, (tradesmen and parents did most of the toy crafting) some city shops and traveling salesmen began to sell manufactured toys brought to America from Europe on trade ships.

Toys become big business

As children's toys became increasingly popular, guilds of toy craftsmen were established in several cities. In a short time the toy guilds grew into factories and the American toy industry was born. By the late 1700's, as the Industrial Revolution was taking hold in America, factories began to make many of the toys that were once crafted at home. In fact, toys were one of the first factory-manufactured items produced by American industry. It did not take long before America became a leading producer of toys in the world.

For a while manufactured toys in America were mostly miniatures of other items the factory produced. A furniture factory might also make miniature doll furniture or a stove company might make miniature stoves or savings banks. Sometimes these miniatures were not made as toys at all but as traveling salesmen's samples to be shown to customers. It was much easier for a stove salesman to carry around a miniature than the real thing! Many of these salesmen's samples were later given to children as playthings.

Early American manufactured toys (as well as toys today) usually followed the interests and trends of the time. Whatever inventions, events, and scientific discoveries affected the life-style of the people, there was sure to be a toy version produced. Children whose parents could afford such toys played with toy steam engines, telegraphs, music boxes, rifles, and dolls of the latest fashion. As America invented or discovered new and faster ways of traveling, toy vehicles became extremely popular with children. Almost as soon as they appeared in the adult world, children had their own toy versions of trains, streetcars, steamboats, passenger cars, and airplanes.

With the steady development of new manufacturing techniques the American toy industry was now able to produce some rather sophisticated playthings including vehicles that could propel themselves with windup spring motors, mechanical banks that performed amusingly for the price of a coin, pull toys with figures that danced, and later, in the early 1900's, all sorts of toys that ran on electricity.

Stacks of games fill a big store's toy department.

As American manufacturing technology quickly grew, so did the sophistication of the toy industry—especially after the invention of plastic. Dolls are now made for boys as well as girls; there are novelty toys and games based on popular television and movie characters; there are toy crazes; craft kits, and a huge number of toys having something to do with outer space. There are even toys and games designed especially for adults. Perhaps in the future, kids will be playing with lifelike robots or androids as playmates—maybe one that will grow up with you!

NEWSPAPER TOYS

Scrap paper has always been a ready plaything for children to fold, tear, roll, glue, tape, or staple into some simple toy or craft. American kids have always made paper hats, paper masks, paper boats, paper baskets, paper pinwheels, and nearly all species of paper animals. Probably the most common scrap paper in America today is newspaper, and so here are two paper toys you can make using only newspapers and a scissors.

Paper Snake

1. Lay out a full-size, double-spread sheet of newspaper, and cut two narrow paper strips from the long edge, Fig. 1. The narrower the paper strips, the longer and more jointed your snake will be.

2. Taper each strip beginning about one-third of the length from the end, Fig. 1.

3. Weave the two paper strips into a snake by first overlapping the wide ends of each strip so they are at right angles to each other, Fig. 1. Now fold the strip on the bottom up and back over the overlap, as shown, and crease, Fig. 1. The other strip has now become the strip on the bottom and is now folded up and back over the overlap. Continue folding strips, in the same manner all the way to the tapered tail ends.

4. Gently stretch out the accordion-folded snake and draw eyes, nose, and tongue on the head, Fig. 2. Whenever you like you can accordion-fold your snake back together and carry him in your pocket. You might also just leave your paper snake somewhere to be found

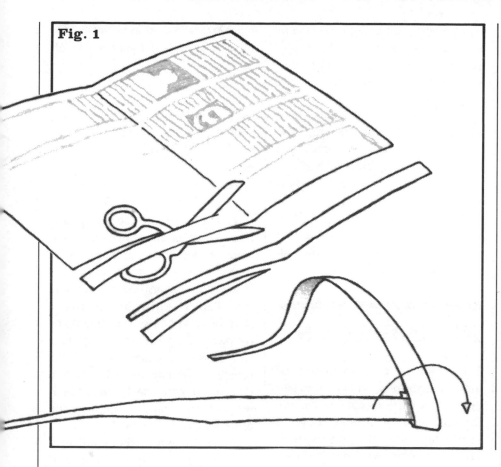

Fig. 1

by an unsuspecting "victim." The ridges of the paper snake folds make it easy to hang the snake from lamps, plants, shelves, or branches.

Paper Tree

1. Lay out a full-size, double-spread sheet of newspaper and begin to roll it up from one narrow end, Fig. 3. The newspaper roll should be about as round as your wrist.

2. Before the newspaper sheet is completely rolled, overlap another full-size sheet on top of the first and continue rolling, Fig. 3. Overlap and roll in a third and fourth newspaper sheet in the same manner to complete the roll. (If the newspaper roll is made from more than four sheets it might get too thick to cut.)

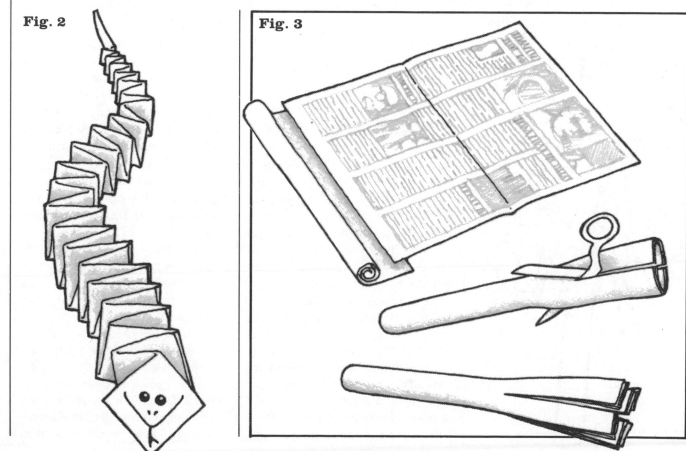

Fig. 2

Fig. 3

Fig. 4

3. Flatten out about one third to one half the length of the newspaper roll, and, using a sharp scissors, make a cut in the center of the folded section, Fig. 3.

4. Refold the flattened section of the roll so that the cuts are at the sides. Flatten the roll again and make a cut in the center so that one end of the roll is now cut in quarters, Fig. 3.

5. Hold the newspaper roll at the uncut end and pull out the tree by gently tugging up at the cut paper "branches," Fig. 4.

FLYING TOYS

Long before the invention of airplanes, rockets, and other spacecraft, kids were fascinated by any toy that could fly. There were just a few flying toys—things like small hot-air balloons or simple winged gliders that imitated the gentle and graceful soaring of large birds. One flying toy, however, was quite different, for it was fashioned after the propeller of a boat.

Flying Propeller

The inventor must have thought that if a boat propeller could "screw" through the water pushing the boat forward then a plain propeller might screw itself through the air. The toy worked—and maybe the flying propeller was an inspiration to airplane and helicopter inventors in later years.

Most flying propellers were not factory-made toys but rather simple novelties hand-carved from wood. These carefully carved propellers mounted on a pencillike stem could fly to a height of twenty feet or more. However, using just a few common scrap materials you can

quickly make a simple version of the flying propeller that works almost as well.

Materials
stiff scrap paperboard
paper clip
plastic drinking straw

Tools
scissors

1. Cut a scrap piece of paperboard so it is about one-half inch wide (thirteen mm.) and four to six inches long (ten to fifteen cm). Exact dimensions are not important. Paperboard strips cut from a shoe box, gift box, mat board, or the back of a paper pad work fine.

2. Fasten a paper clip over the center of the paperboard strip and then insert both the big and small loop of the paper clip into the drinking straw, Fig. 5.

3. To make the paperboard strip into a propeller you must give it "pitch" so that it can screw through the air. Pitch the paperboard strip by grasping it near one side of the paper clip between your thumb and pointer finger, and give the strip a clockwise twist until it is almost flat but pointing slightly up to the right, Fig. 5. Twist the other end of the strip in the same manner, in the same direction.

4. Now you are ready for a test flight of the flying propeller so you can make some fine-tuning adjustments.

First, and before each flight, be certain the paper clip is centered on the propeller and that the pitch angle at both ends of the propeller is equal. Hold the drinking straw stem between the open palms of your hands, then quickly slip your hands past each other so that your right hand pushes forward and your left hand pulls back—and release the spinning propeller. If the propeller flies down instead of up then

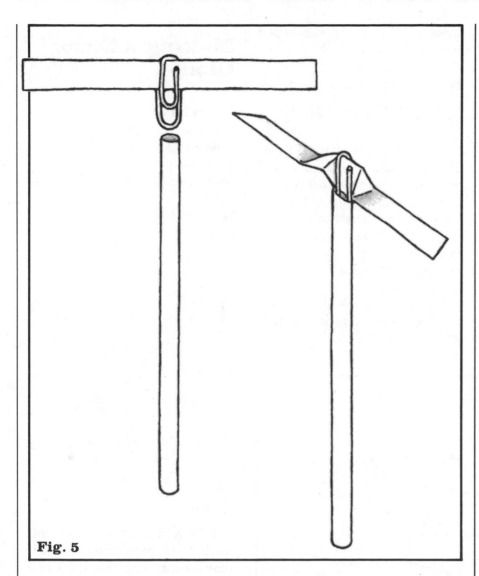

Fig. 5

you have probably spun it in the wrong direction.

A good flying propeller should fly straight up five to ten feet or more. To get the propeller to fly just right you will need to experiment with the pitch by twisting the ends so they point up at more of an angle or less. Depending on the size and weight of the propeller you will sometimes get the highest and smoothest flight by cutting off one third to one half the length of the straw.

Try making several flying propellers using slightly different sizes and weights of paperboard and different-length straws. Now see which ones fly the highest.

Ring Wing Glider

As various flying machines were invented, toy companies kept pace by making miniature flying versions for kids' play. Today kids are still fascinated by flying toys, especially spaceships. During the winter of 1966-67, *Scientific American* magazine sponsored a paper airplane competition. Of the twelve thousand paper planes entered in the competition nearly all were conventional in design—wings, tail, and a body. One design however was quite different from any plane that had ever been seen before, real or paper. The strange

plane with a long skinny body and a ring of paper at either end looked as if it would never fly, but surprisingly it was an excellent glider and competition winner.

Materials
plastic drinking straw
2 paper clips
a notebook-size sheet of heavy paper (8½ x 11 inches)

Tools
scissors

1. Construction paper or a magazine cover work fine for this project. Cut two strips from the long dimension of the paper, Fig. 6. One strip should be about one to one-and-one-half inches wide (two-and-one-half to four cm.) and the other strip about half as wide.

Fig. 6

2. Put one of the paper clips into an end of the straw so that the big wire loop is inside the straw and the smaller loop is on the outside. Put a paper clip in the other end of the straw in the same manner. Align the two smaller loops so that they are facing each other as best as possible.

3. Fold the narrower paper strip in half and make the double strip into a loop with the ends overlap-

ping. Attach the paper loop at the overlap to one of the paper clips as shown, Fig. 7.

4. Now make a loop of the wide paper strip in a similar manner and attach it to the other paper clip.

5. You are ready for your first test flight of the ring wing glider. Be sure the two paper loops are aligned, and hold the straw in the center with the rings overlap-side down and the smaller paper loop facing forward, Fig. 8. Don't throw the glider, just give it a firm push forward.

You can experiment and fine-tune your glider to get the longest and smoothest flights possible by adjusting the size of the larger paper loop. To do this simply pull in the inside end of the loop.

SNOW GLOBE

Lots of kids own snow globes. They are made of heavy glass and usually have a tree or Santa-shape inside surrounded by a colorless liquid. When you shake the globe and then put it down you see wintery "snowflakes" swirl around and then gently fall and stick to the figure in the globe.

You can make a snow globe easily although this version will actually be a snow "jar."

Making a Snow Globe

Materials

clear glass jar with a tight-
   fitting lid, any size
aluminum foil
small piece of an evergreen branch
water
liquid dishwashing detergent

Tools

scissors

1. Any size of glass jar will work from baby food to giant peanut-butter size, but the larger the jar the more "snow" you will have to make. Remove any labels from the jar.

2. Make snow by cutting a piece of aluminum foil into very,

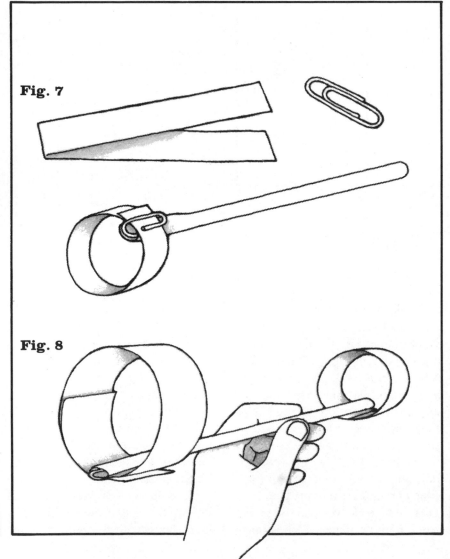

Fig. 7

Fig. 8

Fig. 9

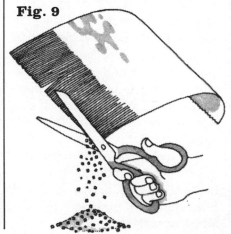

very tiny pieces. You can do this best by first cutting thin strips along one edge of a piece of foil, then cutting off the strips into little pieces, Fig. 9. The smaller the foil pieces, the more realistic the snowfall will be. It takes a lot of foil flakes to make a good snowstorm, so keep cutting until you have enough foil flakes to completely cover the bottom of the jar, at least.

3. For the "tree," cut a small piece of evergreen branch and put it in the jar.

4. Fill the jar with water completely to the top, add just one drop of dishwashing detergent to the water, and tightly screw on the jar lid. The detergent will keep the aluminum flakes from floating.

Now make a winter storm by turning the snow globe upside down, giving it a gentle shake, and setting it down right side up.

NOAH'S ARK

The Sabbath was considered a sacred and holy day to be observed by all family members with dignity and austerity and Colonial children were forbidden to play any games. All toys were put away. However, one special "Bible toy," Noah's ark, was often considered acceptable for Sunday play and was saved for that time.

Even so, play with Noah's ark took place only under the watchful eye of a parent who would relate various Bible stories and moral lessons using wooden ark people and animal figures as illustration. Though play with Noah's ark was more like a school lesson than regular play, hardly any other toy was as favorably accepted by children.

Noah's ark was more than a single toy, actually—it was a collection of toys. Inside the hollow ark (which was almost never seaworthy) there were stored the small, carved figures of Noah, Mrs. Noah, their three sons, and several kinds of animals arranged in identical pairs. It was these small play figures that mostly attracted children. There were the familiar farm animals that most children knew well—pigs, goats, sheep, cows, cats and dogs—but there were several other animal figures that neither children nor their parents had probably ever actually seen—lions, monkeys, camels, giraffes, and elephants. Some Noah's arks of the 1800's had as many as two hundred pairs of animals.

Noah's arks are still being made (in wood, plastic, and paper cutouts) and children are still just as much intrigued by the miniature figures. Kids in America now play on Sunday and every other day of the week, however, so this special Sunday toy is no longer popular.

PUNCH-BOARDS

Punchboards of nearly every size and theme were quite popular not many years ago, but this "game of chance" novelty can hardly be found anywhere today. Most punchboards were about the size of a deck of playing cards and contained anywhere from fifty to five hundred "holes" or "punches." Inside each hole was a small paper scroll with a written message. Using a pencil or a special stick, a player would punch a scroll out through the board, unroll it, read it, and then perform whatever the message commanded, if a command was given. A party punchboard might instruct a player to perform some humorous act; a fortune punchboard might reveal a good or bad omen. There were also gambling punchboards sold to people as a way to earn money. In those punchboards each punch contained a paper slip with a "lucky number." A player would pay the owner of the punchboard five or ten cents for a punch, and if the number on the punched slip he chose matched a list of winning numbers printed on the punchboard, the player won a prize. Of course the punchboard owner collected more money than the value of the prizes he gave out.

Making Punchboards

You can make any of these punchboards following the instructions. Make up your own messages or copy the suggestions that are listed.

Materials
small box, an inch or two deep,

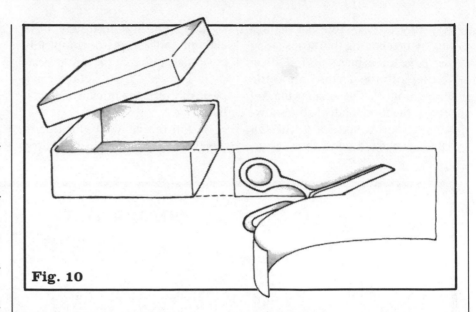

Fig. 10

with or without a lid (note-card box, jewelry box, even the cut-off bottom of a paper milk container)
paper
drinking straws

Tools
scissors
pencil or pen

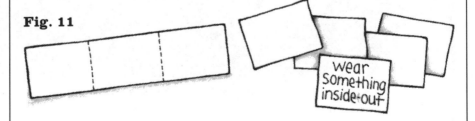

Fig. 11

Fig. 12

1. With scissors, cut paper into strips the width of which is about the same as the depth of the box, Fig. 10. Then cut each strip into three or four smaller paper slips, Fig. 11.

2. Write a message on each slip of paper appropriate to the theme of your punchboard, Fig. 11.

3. Using scissors, cut a few

drinking straws into a lot of short "rings," Fig. 12. Now roll up each message tightly with the printing on the inside, slip a ring over the message to keep it from unrolling, and stand the roll in the small box. Keep writing and rolling messages, and filling the box with them (Fig. 13) until it is full.

How to play with it

To "punch" a message, poke and catch a rolled slip on the tip of a pointed pencil. Read the message aloud, and perform the action it dictates, if one is given. Return the message to the box rolled and banded and in a different space.

Fig. 13

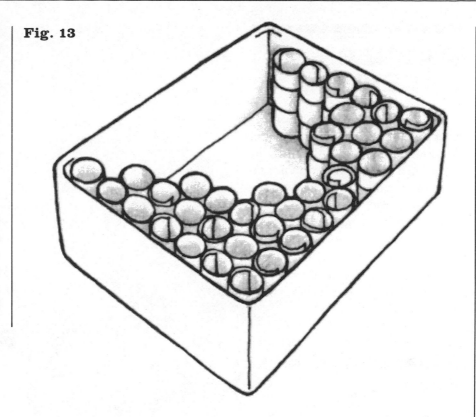

Messages for a party punchboard

Pat your head and rub your tummy at the same time.
Stand on your head.
Say your name spelled backwards.
Name the last person who kissed you.
Draw a picture of yourself.
Eat a banana sandwich.
Have a cool, refreshing ketchup drink.
Swap shoes with someone.
Reveal a long-kept secret.
Touch your toes but don't bend your knees.
Wear something inside out.
Kiss someone wearing blue.
Name all your teachers since first grade.
Dance with the person sitting next to you.
Imitate the sounds of a pet zebra.
Name everything you've eaten today.
Wear something orange in color.

Cross your eyes.
Wiggle your ears.
Bark like a beagle.
Chant a high school cheer.
Sing "The Star-Spangled Banner" in one breath.
Touch your nose with the tip of your tongue.
Eat an invisible lobster.
Name five things that are wet.

Messages for a fortune punchboard

Last night's dream will come true.
Don't quit, your luck will change.
Someone saw what you did.
When the clock strikes three, you will know the answer to your question.
You have made the wrong decision, change your mind.
Follow your plans with confidence.
You will have more luck than you expect.
Someone with the initial *S* is thinking good thoughts about you.

The person who last spoke to you is a true friend.
You will be rich, famous, *and* happy.
Look to yourself for amusement.
Tomorrow will be a better day.
It is only infatuation, not love.
You will live a life of splendor and plenty.
You have been too hasty in your decision.
Your intentions are wrong, try a new plan.
Helping others will help you best.
You will fall into a hole unless you change your direction.
When the moon is full, your stars are favorable.
You have bitten off more than you can chew.
You are hiding your true intentions.
A big opportunity is about to come your way.
You are running away from the truth.
You can't lose. Follow through with your plans.

MARBLE RACEWAY

There have been several popular craft and commercial toys made in America in which little balls or miniature cars slide down and around a raceway. One of the classic raceway toys is the marble roll, in which a marble runs back and forth and down a series of chutes until it rings a bell. Some marble roll toys had two side-by-side raceways so players could have races.

Make a Marble Raceway

Here is how to make a homemade version of the classic marble roll that lets you experiment designing the path and length of the chute.

Materials
several paper tubes (from toilet paper, aluminum foil, waxed paper, plastic wrap, gift wrapping paper, etc.)
tape
marbles

Tools
sharp scissors
small hand-saw (hacksaw, coping saw, keyhole saw, or sharp serrated knife)
pencil

1. Gather together as many paper tubes as you can find. You might ask your parents, friends, or neighbors to save their paper tubes for you. The tubes can be all different lengths but they should all be about the same diameter. The marble raceway is assembled in any configuration you like using components made from the tubes—straight connectors, angle

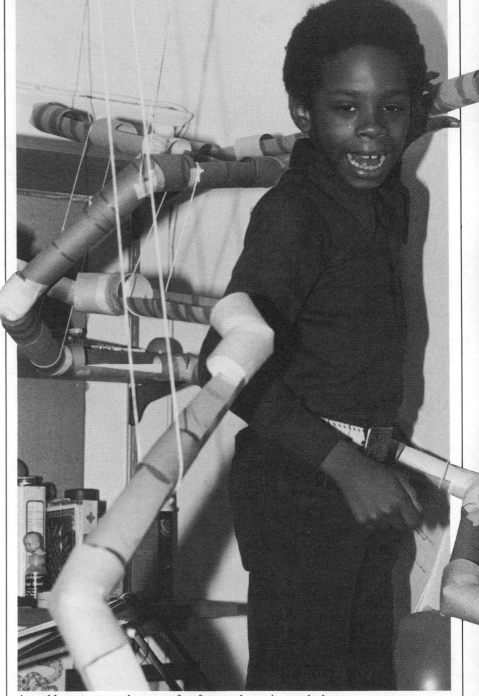

A marble raceway can become a free form sculpture in your bedroom.

connectors, and chutes. A straight connector is just a length of tube, Straight connectors do not need to be very long and toilet paper tubes or sections cut from longer tubes will work just fine.

2. Make angle connectors by cutting out a piece of the tube with a saw blade or sharp serrated knife so that the tube will fold to form an angle, Fig. 14. Follow the example in the illustration drawing cut-lines on the tube. Cut out the section very carefully. Put a piece of tape at the joint of the folded tube to hold it together. With some ex-

Fig. 14

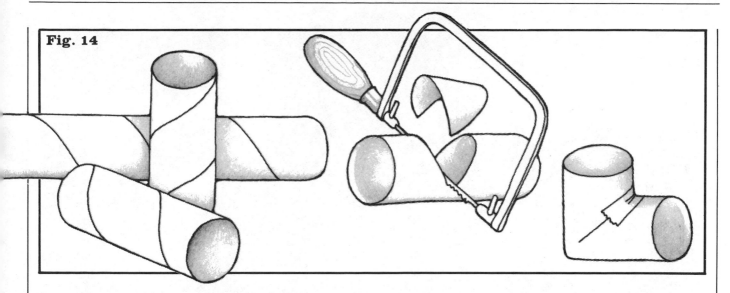

perimentation, you will be able to make these connectors in several different angles.

3. Make chutes by cutting a length of tube in half the long way with a scissors, Fig. 15. Each length of tube will make two chutes.

4. After you have made several connectors and chutes, you can assemble them in any raceway pattern you like, alternating chute, connector, chute, connector, and so on. Push the chutes into the connectors only as far as they need to go to hold them firm.

In order for the marble to roll smoothly down the raceway, all the chutes and connectors, starting from the top, must slant downward to some degree. You will also need a way to support the raceway in its path. Look around the area where you are playing for objects to prop up your raceway or to lean it against. Be inventive. When playing indoors, try pushing a few chairs together, maybe putting a chair on its side or upside down. Weave your raceway through the chairs so it is supported by the chair seats, legs, backs, and rungs.

As you add chutes and connectors to the raceway, keep testing it by rolling a marble through it, and adjust components where the marble gets stuck. For a grand finish to the raceway, put an empty jar or can "bell" at the end of the last chute.

Fig. 15

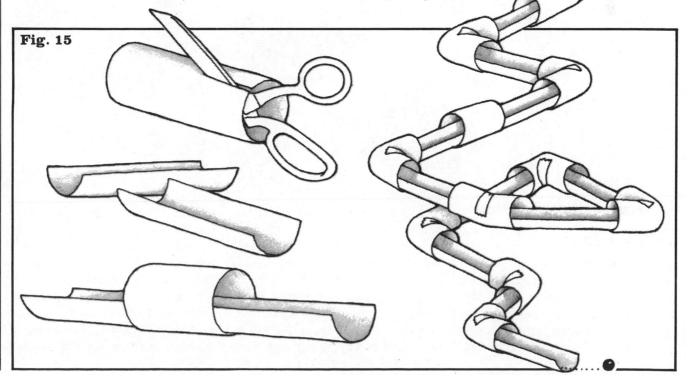

All different kinds of dolls make up a very special play family.

DOLLS

Dolls are and have always been the most popular toy in America. Unlike any other plaything, each and every doll has a personality all its own and the unique ability to become a child's best friend and playmate.

The first children to arrive in America carried simple dolls that had been made for them aboard ship from wood scraps and material. The Indian children whom they met carried dolls carved from wood or cornstalks and dressed in doeskin clothes decorated with beads and porcupine quills. Using what the Indians knew about doll making and adding a bit of inventiveness of their own, Early American children were soon playing with dolls made from gourds, pinecones, dried apples, stones, corn husks, stuffed stockings, and gingerbread. For a very fancy doll, a child's father might carve a wooden head while the mother made a cloth body.

Rag dolls were quite popular and sometimes made by children themselves. Two matching pieces of cloth were cut, stitched partially together, stuffed with rags, sawdust, or beans, and sewn closed. Final touches often included a painted face and maybe small shells, yarn, or needlework for decoration. As rag dolls wore out from use, they were simply re-covered with new material. Dolls frequently survived for several generations, often being kept by their owners well into adulthood, then being passed on to their children.

Doll making moves out of the home

Doll making remained a home craft in America until the early 1800's when some town shops and traveling merchants began to offer a line of imported dolls. Although these dolls were much fancier and elaborate than American home-crafted dolls, the most popular of the imported ones were "penny dolls" crudely carved from wood with jointed arms and legs. They had painted faces —and they cost only a penny each.

By the late 1800's American dolls were being made in factories. Doll heads were constructed of papier-mâché, wax, or glass, and showed fine detail with lifelike painted features. The dresses of these dolls were quite elegant, featuring the fashions and fads of the times. Some dolls were dressed in the latest fashions and sent from town to town so that dressmakers could copy the styles for the clothing they made. When these dolls were no longer needed, or out of fashion, they often became a child's toy. Dolls in America became so popular and elaborate by the early 1900's that many cities had "doll hospitals" equipped to do simple emergency repairs or a complete refurbishing.

Dolls for both sexes

Nearly all dolls made in America were female dolls and almost exclusively the playthings of girls, although boys too have always shown an interest in dolls. Girls were expected to concentrate their play on matters around the house. With a doll to dress, undress, teach, scold, clean, and send to bed, girls could practice playing mother. Since there were no male-figure dolls, boys played with stuffed animals and toy soldiers in their imitation of the father role. It was not until the 1950's that toy companies began to make male-figure dolls that appealed specifically to boys.

With the inventions of mass production, soft plastics, and miniature electronics, dolls have gotten more and more realistic. Dolls today can mimic things that children do: eat, wet, grow, walk, talk, cry, blink, swim, crawl, and write. There are now black dolls as well as white, not to mention dolls in a variety of characters: soldiers, nurses, doctors, ballet dancers, brides, babies, policemen, athletes, politicians, and TV personalities. New sophisticated electronic dolls can obey voice commands, guard your room while you sleep, or wake you up at sunrise. In just a few more years children could be playing with robot dolls that might help with homework, read to them, or be a checkers partner!

Even though these marvelous dolls are fascinating to play with, children also enjoy having a plain, "do-nothing" doll that isn't exactly like every other one on the block. A simple doll with its own personality and name is probably still the most comfortable, cuddly, and appealing doll a child can have.

Yarn Doll

A yarn doll is one of the simplest dolls you can make. Your yarn doll can be small enough to fit in your pocket or much bigger. All you need is yarn and a pair of scissors.

Materials
4-ounce skein of yarn
book, the height you want your doll to be

Tools
scissors

1. The size of a yarn doll is determined by how much yarn you start with. Find a book whose height is about as tall as you would like your doll to be. Wrap the yarn around the book at least seventy-five times to make a thick hank, Fig. 16, considerably more if you want to make a large or chubby doll. (If you want to use scraps of yarn, tie them together end to end.) Be sure to save a few lengths of yarn for tying the doll's body.

2. Slip the hank off the book. To keep the strands together, tie the hank through the top of one end with a length of yarn. Using a pair of scissors, cut the loop at the other end.

3. To make the doll's head and neck, tie another length of yarn tightly around the hank, Fig. 17. All the knots you tie should be made on the same side of the doll. The yarn strands from the knots do not need to be trimmed but can just fall into place along the hank.

4. To make the arms, divide the hank equally in two, and then divide each half in two again. The outside bunches on either side are the arms. Tie each arm at the "wrist" with a length of yarn. With the scissors, trim off any excess yarn, making the doll's hands, Fig. 18.

5. The two bunches of yarn left hanging will form the body and

Fig. 16

Fig. 17

Fig. 18

Fig. 19

legs. Tie a length of yarn at the doll's waist to form the body. If you are making a girl doll, the yarn from the waist down can be considered the doll's skirt and all you need to do is trim it evenly with the scissors, Fig. 19.

6. If you want to make a boy doll, divide the yarn below the waist into two equal bunches for legs and tie each bunch at the ankle. Trim off any excess yarn to form the doll's feet, Fig. 19. Even though your yarn doll can be considered finished as it is, you might want to add buttons or contrasting scraps of yarn to make face and body features.

Roly-Poly Dolls

Not all dolls are serious about play—indeed, some dolls, like the once popular roly-poly can't seem to be anything but funny. The roly-poly is a simple action doll that appears to play with a mind of its own. Just give him a small bump, push, or twirl and the roly-poly will bob, spin, and dance in a very unpredictable and funny fashion. This doll can stand on its head or balance in any position.

Materials
egg or egg-shaped panty hose
    package
sand or salt
tape

Tools
straight pin or needle (if using an
    egg)
felt-tipped markers, crayons,
    poster, or enamel paints

1. If you are using a raw egg, you must empty the contents from the shell by "blowing." An empty eggshell is a lot stronger than you might imagine and makes a fine roly-poly. Brown eggs seem to have somewhat stronger shells than white eggs so they are preferable. To blow an egg, poke a ring of small holes at the top or pointier end of the egg with the pin or needle. Make the ring approximately one-eighth inch (three mm.) round. Now punch out the ring; be careful—you must not shatter the shell. At the middle on one side of the egg, poke out another hole the same size, and in the same manner as the first. Hold the egg over a bowl, pointed end down, and blow hard into the side hole. The white and then the yoke will come out of the first hole, Fig. 20. Carefully rinse the eggshell inside and out.

2. Fill the wider end of the shell with fine sand or salt by pouring it through one of the holes, Fig. 21. Make it about one-eighth to one-quarter full. To see how much sand is in the shell hold the egg up to a bright light. Put a small piece of tape over each of the holes. Adhesive tape works well, Fig. 22.

3. If you are using an egg-shaped panty hose package, separate the two halves of the plastic egg and fill the bottom (the wider half) about half full of sand, salt, or small pebbles, Fig. 23. Snap on the top half and wrap a piece of tape around the seam between the two halves.

4. Now your roly-poly is ready for a face or any decoration you like. A happy clown face is most appropriate for this kind of doll. Use felt-tipped markers, crayons, poster or enamel paint to draw a face and the traditional roly-poly clown costume, Fig. 24.

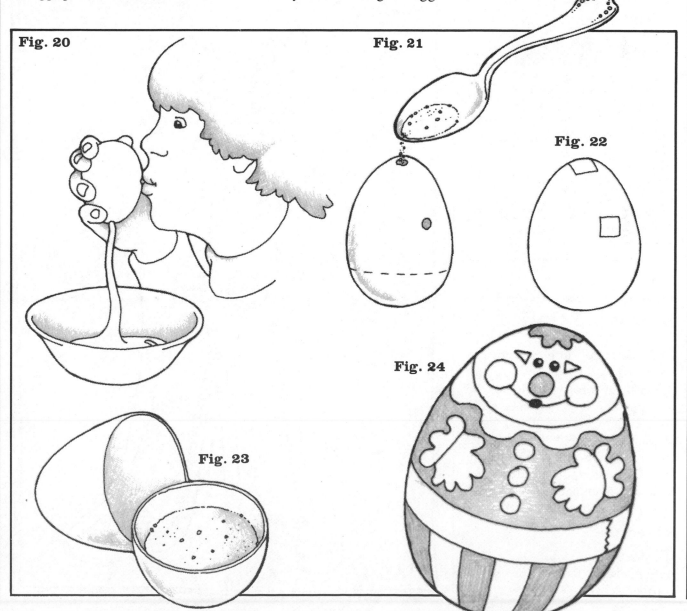

Fig. 20

Fig. 21

Fig. 22

Fig. 23

Fig. 24

Life-Size Doll

What better doll to play with than one that is your own size. A life-size doll can wear your clothes, be a pretend best friend, even be made to look like your twin if you want. Making a life-size doll is easy, and you probably already have the materials and tools needed. You will, however need a real friend to help you do the constructing.

Materials

bed sheet
stuffing: rags, foam chips, newspaper, leaves

Tools

felt-tipped marker
straight pins
sewing scissors
needles and thread (or sewing
  machine or fabric glue)

1. On a clear area of the floor lay out a plain bed sheet and double it over lengthwise. Lie down face up on the sheet, spreading your arms and legs away from your body but not off the sheet, Fig. 25.

2. With a felt marker, have a friend draw an outline around your body on the sheet. Don't crowd the outline, but rather keep it a few inches (or more in places) from your body to allow for body thickness. Don't outline details like fingers, toes, or ears, Fig. 25.

3. You can get up now. Be sure the folded sheet is flat and smooth, then use several straight pins to tack the two halves together. Put the pins inside the outline, Fig. 26.

4. With a sharp pair of sewing scissors and keeping the bed sheet

Fig. 25

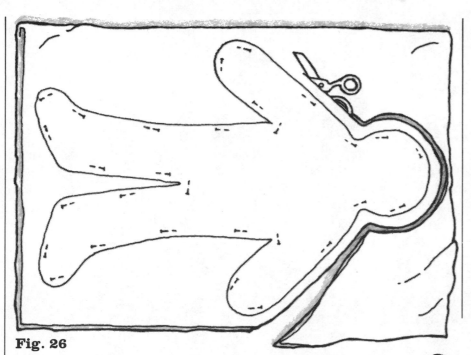

Fig. 26

danger of your doll coming into contact with fire, use crumpled newspaper or dry fall leaves. Whichever stuffing you select, don't use large pieces or your doll will be lumpy. Start by stuffing the feet first and working up, Fig 27. When your doll is filled out and shaped as you like it, sew or glue the head seam closed.

8. The way you decorate and dress your life-size doll depends on who you want it to be. You might draw a face on it with markers or maybe glue on a cutout face from a magazine or newspaper ad. Now try some of your clothes on your doll.

halved, cut out the figure outline. Don't cut right on the outline but stay a few inches to the outside all around.

5. The two figure halves now need to be put together at the outline and there are a few ways to do it. With a needle and strong thread you can sew a tight stitch all around the outline. If you can use a sewing machine, it will make the job go a lot faster. While sewing, be careful not to prick yourself on the pins. You can glue the halves together if you like by laying down a line of fabric glue between the halves along the outline. Whichever method you use, be sure to leave the seam at the top of the open for stuffing.

6. Remove the straight pins. Turn the doll inside out through the opening in the head. It is easy to do if you first reach inside one leg and pull it out through the head. Now pull out the other leg along with the body, and finally pull out the two arms.

7. Your life-size doll is ready to be stuffed. Rags, foam chips, make a good stuffing, or if there is no

Fig. 27

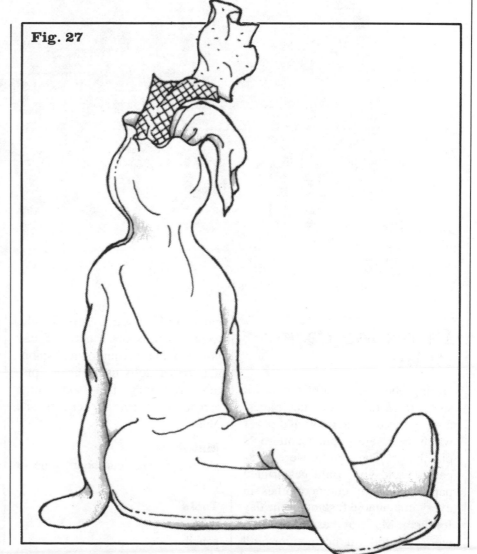

Paper dolls dressed in fashions from long ago.

Dress-Me Paper Dolls

During the early 1900's and for some time thereafter, flat paper-doll figures dressed in printed paper wardrobes were popular children's playthings. These dolls were inexpensive and you could get printed paper sheets of cutout clothes in every imaginable fashion of the day for them. Many of these paper dolls were printed on both sides and came with costume sets for the front and back of an outfit. Today you can make your own fashionable paper dolls using cutout pictures from magazines, some scrap cardboard, a pair of scissors and glue.

Materials
old magazines, cardboard glue or paste

Tools
scissors
pencil

1. First look through several old magazines for full-length pictures of people to be the "body" of your doll. The larger the figure, the easier it will be to make the doll. Look for pictures with figures facing forward and standing straight up with arms out to the side. Magazines that usually carry ads for clothes, like the magazine section of the Sunday newspaper, are good places to look. You might even consider using a full-length photo of yourself. When you have

Fig. 28

Fig. 29

center of the cutout figure. Fit the slits of the stand and the figure together so that their straight bottoms are flush and the doll will stand by itself.

5. Now you will need clothes to make a wardrobe for your dress-me doll. Go through magazines again, this time looking for pictures and ads that show clothes. Hold your doll up to each picture you like to see if the clothes are about the correct size and shape.

6. On each piece of paper clothing you have selected draw a few "hold on" tabs like the ones shown in the illustration, Fig. 30. Carefully cut out the clothes with the tabs attached.

7. Dress your paper doll, by bending the tabs around the back of the figure, Fig. 31. Continue to look in magazines for more doll clothes for your paper doll. Maybe you'd like to make an entire family of doll figures.

found the figure for the doll, cut it out leaving an inch border around the figure's outline, Fig. 28.

2. Find a scrap piece of cardboard (from shirts, shoe boxes, paper-pad backs, etc.) and glue the figure to it using just a thin layer of glue or paste spread over the back of the figure. Wait for the glue to dry.

3. Using sharp scissors, cut out the figure again, now staying as close to the outline as you can. Don't worry about small details like fingers, Fig. 29. Make a straight-across cut below the feet of the figure.

4. Using a leftover scrap of cardboard, draw and cut out a small stand as shown in Fig. 28. Again be sure to cut straight across the bottom. With the scissors, cut a slit halfway down the center of the stand and then cut another slit the same length up from the base in the

Fig. 30

Fig. 31

Teddy Bears

Of all the toys ever made in America probably none is more loved, more popular, or more American than the fuzzy, brown, warm and cuddly teddy bear. Few other doll companions have so generously supplied so much kindness and security to their owners as the teddy bear. But do people know that the first one was accidentally created in honor of the kindly act of a United States president?

In the fall of 1902 then president "Teddy" Roosevelt went to Mississippi to settle a boundary dispute between that state and Louisiana. Having some spare time, and being a sportsman, Teddy Roosevelt went on a bear hunt with the usual group of curious newspaper reporters trailing behind him. As the story goes, President Roosevelt spotted a bear, took aim with his rifle, but refused to shoot when he saw that the bear was only a cub.

One of the newspaper reporters drew a cartoon of the incident showing Roosevelt's humanity in turning away from the frightened cub. Because almost any news about a president seems to be of interest to people, the cartoon was printed in newspapers throughout America, and the bear incident became generally known.

Bears on demand

Morris Michtom, the owner of a small candy and toy shop in Brooklyn, New York, saw the cartoon and had a bright idea. He had his wife sew a stuffed bear cub made of brown plush, with stubby arms and legs, and buttons for eyes, and he put the bear in his shop window along with the cartoon and a sign calling the stuffed toy "Teddy's Bear!" The bear sold quickly and was continually replaced until Michtom's wife could no longer make the bears fast enough to meet the demand.

Realizing that he had created a popular toy, Morris Michtom wrote a letter to President Roosevelt asking permission to use the name Teddy for his stuffed bears. The president replied favorably, and Michtom began a thriving teddy bear factory that was to later become the Ideal Toy Corporation—today one of America's largest toy companies.

Teddy fashions and styles

For the next few years toy manufacturers offered the buying public literally millions of teddy bears in all sizes, designs, and novelties. Besides wardrobes of clothes you could buy for your teddy, there were teddy bear wagons, hammocks, penny banks, games, books, as well as tumbling teddies, whistling teddies, and hand-muff teddies. In just a few years, the teddy bear became the king of toys in America and nearly every child wanted one. Some adults too,

DRAWING THE LINE IN MISSISSIPPI

carried teddy bears about just to be fashionable. There was even a popular joke of the period having to do with teddies: "If Teddy Roosevelt is the president with his clothes on, then what is he with his clothes off?" The answer, of course, is "Teddy bare."

Today the teddy bear is just as famous as ever even if he is not quite as popular. The test of a really good toy is its "play value." A good toy may not be played with every day, but it will certainly be played with again and again long after the first day. Teddy bears have a way of becoming inseparable from their owners, regardless of the age of either. Maybe no other toy has so much play value as your own teddy bear.

"TEDDY BEARS" ARE ALL THE RAGE
The Best Plaything Ever Invented.

THESE BEARS ARE THE MOST SENSIBLE AND SERVICEABLE
toys ever put before the public. Not a fad or campaign article, but something which has come to stay on merit alone. An article which will afford your children and even yourself great amusement and lasting pleasure. Made of the finest quality imported bear plush, they closely resemble the little cubs. They are full jointed and will assume countless different positions (four of which we illustrate). Each bear has a natural voice, produced by slight pressure on the front of body, and they are practically unbreakable. We offer these bears in four sizes. Natural cinnamon color only. The larger the size the better proportioned are the bears. Order one of these bears at once for your boy or girl, and you will find that no toy which you could select would give them more actual pleasure and entertainment.

No.	Size	Shipping Wt.	Price.
18K23358	10 inches high	10 ounces.	$0.75
18K23360	12 inches high	16 ounces.	1.19
18K23362	14 inches high	18 ounces.	1.75
18K23364	16 inches high	24 ounces.	2.38

Teddy bears in many sizes waiting to be picked up and hugged.

Ventriloquism

A doll is a companion—a make-believe friend you can play with. Sometimes that play includes having conversations with your doll with you speaking for both of you, of course. You can, however, make it seem as if the doll itself is talking. That is called ventriloquism.

Ventriloquism is the art of "throwing your voice" so that the words and sounds you speak appear to be coming from a doll or "dummy." A ventriloquist doesn't actually "throw" his voice but he talks for the dummy without moving his lips. The illusion is that the dummy is talking. How well the illusion works depends a lot on the way the ventriloquist manipulates the dummy, moves its head, arms, and mouth. If the audience is involved in watching the dummy, it won't notice any slight movement of the ventriloquist's lips.

Ventriloquism isn't difficult to learn but it does take practice to become good at. If you would like to try, here are some hints and voice exercises to get you started.

First off, you will need a mirror for practicing, to see how well you can keep your lips from moving while talking. Open your lips just enough for your voice to come out clearly and hold them still in that position moving only your tongue to speak. Be sure not to tense up your face—make your expression easy and natural. As you speak, breathe deeply and let your breath and voice come out smoothly and slowly.

Try these exercises

First, keeping your lips still and only slightly parted, say, *ah-ee-oh-ay-oo*. Say it several times remembering to breathe deeply and let the voice out slowly. Watch

your lips in a mirror. You might have some trouble saying *oo* because your lips want to pucker. Keep practicing until you can do it better.

Now without moving your lips try saying this sentence: "Fish and vegetables are a very fine feast." Saying words with the letters *F* and *V* are a bit more difficult. See if you can do it better by moving your lower teeth up against your upper lip without making the move noticeable. Practice saying the above sentence and other *F* and *V* words without moving your lips until you can do it better.

Say the letters of the alphabet with your lips just parted while you are looking in the mirror. You will probably notice that the letters *P*,

B, and *M* are most difficult because their sounds are made by using your lips. Some ventriloquists just move their lips slightly and try not to be noticed. That may work fine if your audience is some distance away, but if you are trying to perform up close to your audience, you should learn a better method.

Substituting letters

Many ventriloquists substitute another letter for the one they have difficulty saying. For the letter *P* substitute *F* or *K*, for *B* use *V* or *G*, and for *M* substitute *N*. It will take a while to get the hang of it, but in time you should be able to say something like "Fass ne the vutter," for "Pass me the butter," and no one will ever notice the switch.

Don't expect to get it all down perfectly right away. Even some professional ventriloquists still have difficulty keeping their lips still for some words. Giving the voice of your dummy some special character like an accent or a deep or high-sounding pitch is another illusion that will help make the dummy appear as if he is doing the talking. Kids are usually quite good at

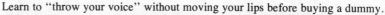

Learn to "throw your voice" without moving your lips before buying a dummy.

mimicking—doing takeoffs on television characters and even their friends. Remember that the voice of your dummy, as well as his general character, should be played stronger and more lively than your own.

The talking hand

The best illusion of all is making the dummy's lips move in rhythm to the words you are speaking for the dummy. Usually only specially made ventriloquist's dummies can do that and they are very expensive. The simplest way to achieve a similar effect is to make a "talking hand" dummy using your own hand, some lipstick, and maybe a few scraps of yarn or cloth for decoration.

First hold your hand in the position shown in the illustration. Your thumb should rest on the side of your pointer finger between the first and second joints. Try moving your thumb up and down to look like lips opening and closing. To complete the effect, draw lips on your thumb and pointer finger, as well as eyes and maybe a nose above the lips, using dark lipstick. A final touch might might be a simple wig made from yarn, or a hat made from a scrap of cloth. You might entertain your audience by applying the makeup and costume in front of them. Now try your ventriloquism using your talking hand dummy. In time you could invent several different talking hand characters, and give each an interesting name.

CRYSTAL RADIO

Once the radio became popular in the 1920's, it wasn't long before toy companies made simple crystal radio receivers for children. These toy radios really worked, but they were powerful enough to receive only one, or at best a few nearby radio stations. The toy crystal radio used no batteries or electrical power of any kind, however. All the energy needed to work it was in the invisible radio signal sent out from the transmitting station and "picked up" by the crystal radio antenna.

Pick up stations on a crystal radio which you can make.

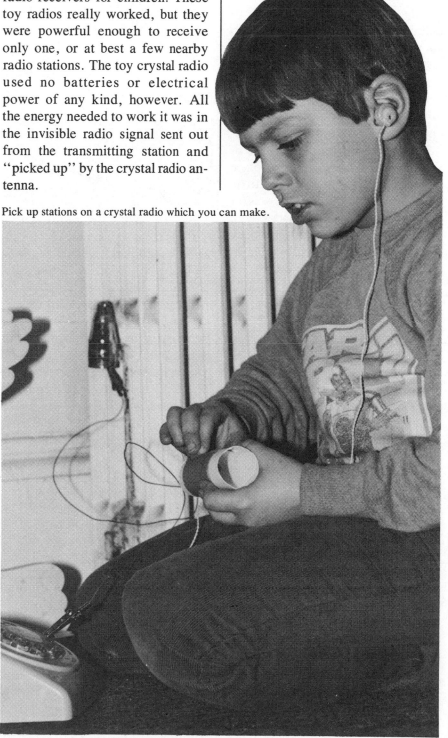

For only a few dollars' worth of common electronic components brought at a radio parts store, and some scrap materials found around the house, you can build a modern version of the old crystal radio toy.

But don't expect it to perform as well as a transistor or table radio. Just like the "old days" you will probably only receive a few stations at most. If you live very far from a city or a radio transmitting station, you may only get a very weak sound or none at all.

Although no special tools or soldering equipment are needed to make this radio, you will have to cut wire and carefully strip the plastic insulation from the wire ends. If you have a wire-stripping tool and you know how to use it, fine. If not, you can use a scissors both to cut the wire and strip the insulation. For stripping, open the tips of your scissors only slightly, place about one inch of the wire end to be stripped in the "V" of the scissor tips, close the scissor blades with only slight pressure, and pull back firmly on the wire. The plastic insulation should come right off.

A crystal radio is safe to build and use. There is no danger of getting an electric shock. And since it uses energy that you don't have to pay for, and there is nothing to wear out, you can leave your crystal radio turned "on" all the time if you like.

Making a Crystal Radio

Materials
toilet paper tube
35 feet (11 m.) No. 22 gauge, solid, insulated wire
germanium diode
2 alligator clips
crystal earphone with wire leads
wide rubber band (to fit snugly around the paper tube)

Tools
scissors
coarse sandpaper
sharp pencil

1. Cut two three-foot (one m.) lengths of wire from the length and put them aside for now.

2. Using a sharp scissors or pencil point, punch three small holes near one end of the paper tube so that the holes are spaced about one inch (twenty-five mm.) from each other, Fig. 32. (To help explain this construction, the holes in the illustration are numbered 1, 2, and 3.)

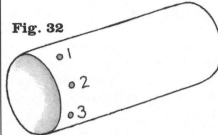

Fig. 32

3. To make the radio tuning coil, first strip about one inch of insulation from one end of the long length of wire, Fig. 33, and put the stripped end through hole 1 in the paper tube. Now wind the entire length of wire around the paper tube carefully and smoothly. The wire should be one layer thick and the coils wound tightly together, Fig. 33. Just before you come to the end of winding the wire, punch another small hole in the tube close to the last winding, insert the wire end, pull the end inside the tube, tightly, Fig. 33, and bend it back over itself so that the end won't pop out. There are no connections to this end of the wire.

4. With a piece of coarse

sandpaper, sand off the plastic insulation across the coil windings so that there is a bare strip of coil wire exposed, Fig. 34a.

5. Strip an inch of insulation from both wire leads of the earphone. Be careful—these wires are very fine and can easily break. Put one of the earphone wires into hole 1 of the tube, Fig. 34b.

6. Strip an inch of insulation from both ends of one of the three-foot "hookup" wires. Insert one end of that wire into hole 1 of the tube, Fig.34c. Now, working with your fingers inside the tube end, tightly twist together all three bare wires coming through hole 1, and then bend them out of the way to the side, Fig. 35a.

7. Bend the wire leads of the diode to form a "U" shape, and insert one lead into hole 2 and the other lead into hole 3 of the tube, Fig. 35b. Put the remaining earphone wire lead into hole 2, Fig. 35c. Twist the two bare wires coming through hole 2 tightly together, then bend them to the side, Fig. 35d. Be certain that the twisted wires coming through hole 2 do not come in contact with the wires coming through hole 1.

8. Strip an inch of insulation from one end of the second hookup wire, and strip about five inches (thirteen cm.) of insulation from the other end. Insert the long stripped end of the hookup wire through hole 3 *up from the inside* of the tube, but not all the way. Leave a

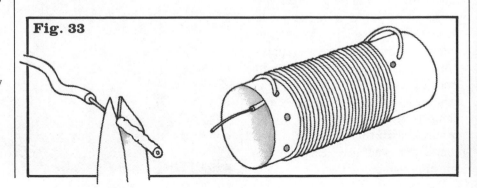

Fig. 33

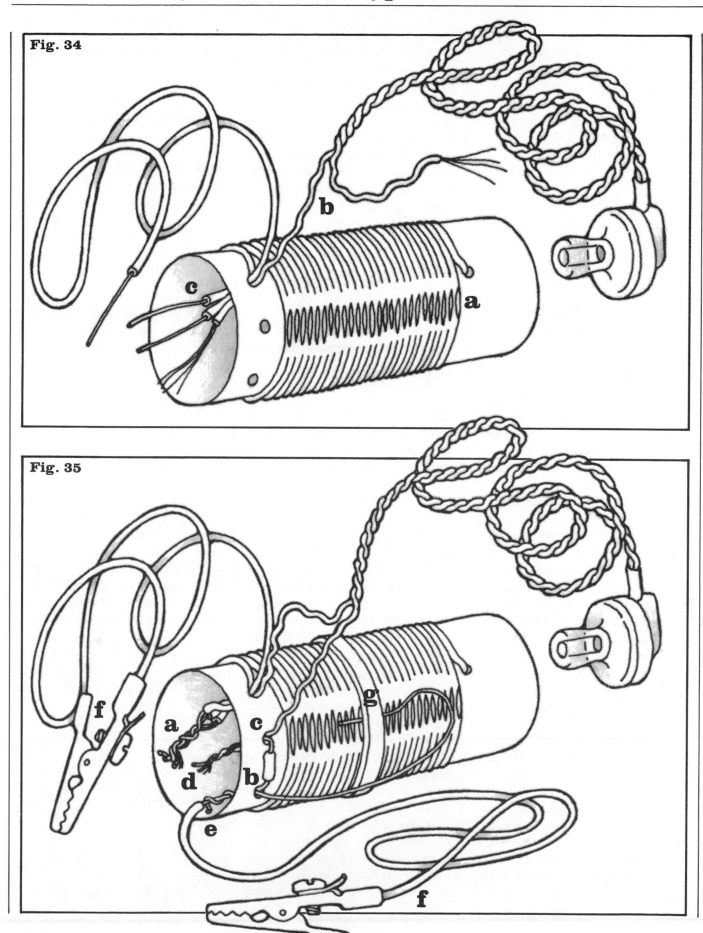

Fig. 34

Fig. 35

bit of the bare wire on the inside of the tube and twist the diode lead in hole 3 tightly around it, Fig. 35e.

9. Attach an alligator clip to the stripped, free end of each hookup wire, Fig. 35f. Your crystal radio is now ready to test.

Tuning the radio

A crystal radio will only receive stations if it is connected to a long antenna. However, you needn't buy one—there are many large metal things around most homes that will work quite well as a crystal radio antenna. The best home antennas are often the metal finger-stop on a telephone dial, a copper cold-water pipe, or the pipe of a hot water radiator. The telephone finger stop is connected to the telephone wiring that runs through your house and the water pipes lead down to the earth which is also a good antenna.

Connect one of the alligator clips to the telephone finger-stop and the other clip to a water pipe or metal faucet. Put the earphone in your ear and listen for a humming sound. Now take the end of the long bare tuning wire that comes out of hole 3 and move it firmly, slowly, across the bared strip of coil wires until you hear a radio station clearly. Slip the rubber band around the tube and over the tuning wire so that it is held firmly in contact with the bare coil wires at the station you have selected, Fig. 35g. To change stations, move the tuning wire along the coil until you find a new station and use the rubber band to hold the wire in place.

If you live in or near a city where there are several radio stations, you may not need to hook up both alligator clips. Instead, hold one of the clips in your hand and attach the other to a telephone finger-stop or water pipe. Your body will then act as an antenna, which

should be sufficient to pull in a station. Other things besides the antenna you use and your distance from a radio broadcasting station will determine which stations you receive and how loud they sound. Whether it is day or night, weather conditions, and the direction you turn the tuning coil all play a part. A crystal radio will usually operate best at night. Under some combination of conditions you might even receive stations from a foreign country. And sometimes—because of conditions—you may receive no stations at all. Be patient, and try again.

PUZZLES

Clever, handmade puzzles were once a favorite after-dinner pastime for children and grown-ups in America. Many are becoming popular again today. Although the origin of these puzzles may be traced to other countries and civilizations, in America we often credit the inventive people of the southern mountain region with the creation of what we now call American folk toys. Indeed, the mountain people of America changed and improved many a traditional hand puzzle as well as inventing their own. And through the years the mountain puzzles have in turn acquired many new names according to their appearance, method of working, or theme.

Construction of the puzzles was out of necessity quite simple using whatever scrap materials and trinkets were available. But even if it took only a few minutes to make a hand puzzle, the solution or explanation of its working was often quite complicated. Solutions are given to most of the hand puzzles which follow, but do try each of

these American favorites first on your own before peeking at the "answers."

Ox-Yoke Puzzle

The object of this hand puzzle is to get two beads (or rings) hanging on separate string loops of a wooden yoke onto the same loop without cutting or untying the string. Unless you know the trick or are very clever and patient, the puzzle will probably seem impossible.

Materials
thin, flat strip of wood, about the size of a tongue depressor
2 large stringing beads or rings
strong string, yarn, or a long shoelace

Tools
drill and bit

1. Make the yoke of the puzzle by drilling three equally spaced holes about as round as your little finger in the strip of wood. Or find another material with three equally spaced holes already drilled. If you look through your drawers and toy collection you will probably find something that will do quite well.

2. Cut a length of strong string, yarn or shoelace to about six times the length of the yoke. Attach the two beads or rings (they should be larger than the drilled holes) and string to the yoke as shown, Fig.

Fig. 36

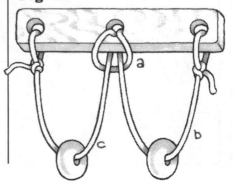

Tangled up in an ox yoke puzzle.

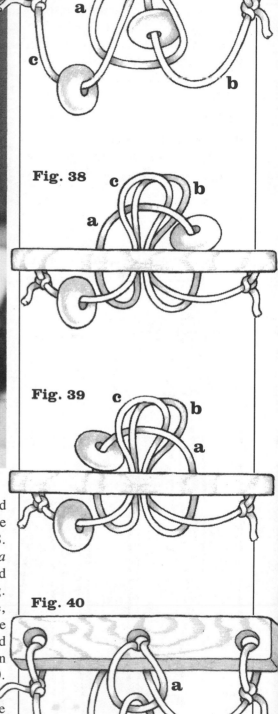

Fig. 37

Fig. 38

Fig. 39

Fig. 40

36. Be sure the string ends are securely knotted to the end holes in the yoke. Now try to get both beads or rings on a single loop without untying the string.

Solution

Carefully study the illustrations, and follow these instructions step by step.

Hold the ox-yoke puzzle so that you are looking at it exactly as shown in Fig. 37. Pull down loop *a* and move the bead on string *b* along the string and through loop *a*, Fig. 37. Reach behind the yoke and pull the two strings coming out the center hole so that both string *b* and *c* are loops pulled through the center hole to the back, Fig. 38. Slide the bead now on string *a* through the loops formed by *b* and *c* on the back side of the yoke, Fig. 39. From the front side of the yoke, pull loop *a* forward through the center hole, bringing strings *b* and *c* with it. Slide the bead now on string *c* through loop *a*, Fig. 40. The puzzle is solved.

Reverse the steps to get the beads back to their original position. If that stumps you, you may untie the string from the yoke and set up the puzzle again.

Buttonhole Puzzle

If you have trouble solving the ox-yoke puzzle, here is another hand puzzle that is not quite so tough. The object of the puzzle is to remove a string with the attached ring through the "buttonholes" in a wood strip, without cutting or untying the string.

Materials

thin, flat strip of wood
1 large stringing bead or ring
string, yarn, or long shoelace

Tools

drill and bit

The strip of wood required for the botton hole puzzle can be the same as that used for the ox-yoke puz-zle, except that you should drill only two holes (instead of three) in it, one at either end, Fig. 41.

Cut a piece of string, yarn, or shoelace about seven times the length of the wood strip. Weave the string through the buttonholes in the wood strip as shown in Fig. 41, then tie both string ends to the bead or string. The ring must be large enough so that it will not pass through the holes.

The puzzle is now ready to be solved, but try it first without looking at the solution.

Solution

Hold the buttonhole puzzle so that you are looking at it as shown in Fig. 42. Grab the small loop coming through the hole at the top, and pull it down then through the bottom hole, Fig. 42. Spread the bottom loop and bring it up and over the top of the wood strip, Fig. 43. Now pull the ring down and the string will separate from the wood strip. Watch what happens as the string is pulled through the buttonholes so you can set up the puzzle again for someone else to try.

Make a simpler version of the

Fig. 41

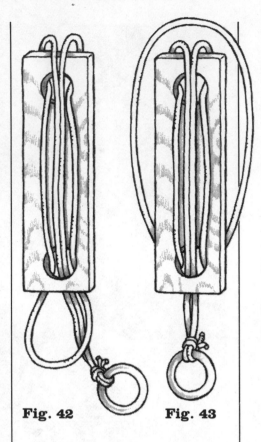

Fig. 42   **Fig. 43**

buttonhole puzzle by threading the string and ring through the finger holes of a pair of scissors, Fig. 44. The solution is very similar to the wooden version, but try to figure it out for yourself.

Fig. 44

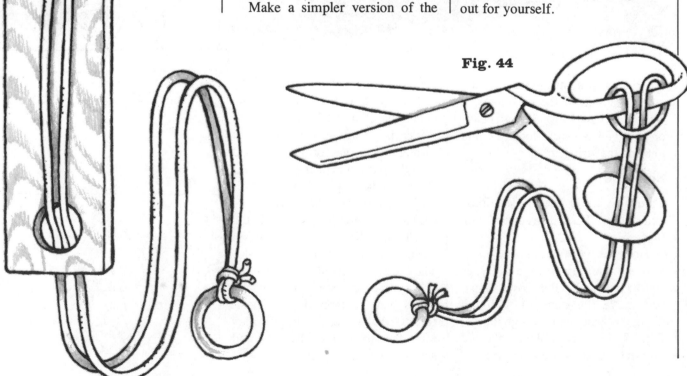

14-15 Puzzle

One of the most prolific puzzle card game inventors in the world was an American whose name was Sam Loyd. Nearly one hundred years ago, Sam Loyd invented a simple number puzzle that became a national craze and has since regained popularity several times. It is called the 14-15 puzzle, and consists of a square box containing fifteen smaller squares, perfectly fitted side by side and numbered 1 through 15. The box contains an empty space without a numbered square. Starting in the upper left corner and going across in rows, all the numbered squares are in numerical order, except that the 14 and 15 squares are reversed, Fig. 45. The object of the puzzle is to move the squares about the box so that the numbers are in their original order, but with the 14 and 15 squares in proper sequence, adjacent to a vacant space. The squares may not be lifted from the box.

Sam Loyd offered one thousand dollars to anyone who could give him the exact order of moves necessary to solve the puzzle. And although the solution was quite possible, no one could seem to remember or set down the moves it took to do it. No one ever claimed the money.

In another version of this puzzle, the player tries to arrange the numbered squares so that all columns of numbers both horizontally and vertically, and the two crisscross diagonals, add up to 30.

Make your 14-15 puzzle either plain or fancy depending on the materials and tools you have. Here is how to make a simple cardboard version.

Fig. 46

Materials
shallow square box or box lid

Tools
crayon or felt-tipped marker
scissors
ruler
pencil

1. If the shallow box or box lid is not square, cut it so that it is. In this case, you will need to add a fourth side to the box. Using paperboard material from the box—or any scrap paperboard—cut a side of the appropriate size and tape it in place. Now cut a paperboard square that will just fit inside the shallow box. With a ruler, pencil, and scissors, divide the paperboard square into sixteen identical smaller squares, and cut them out, Fig.46.

2. Discard one of the small squares, and with a crayon or felt-tipped marker, number the remaining smaller squares 1 through 15.

Now arrange the cards in the box as shown in Fig.45, and try to solve the puzzle.

Fig. 45

Knots-and-Not-Knots

As simple as this pastime appears, it is a real brainteaser that requires much concentration and good visual perception. Knots-and-not-knots was traditionally played between parent or grandparent and child. Some adults felt that perception puzzles like these were a "stimulant to the intelligence" and helped make the player wise. Here is how it was done:

Using a short length of rope, the parent would twist and loop the rope to form what appeared to be a loose knot. But was it a knot or not a knot? The puzzle was simply that—to determine what would happen if the ends of the rope were pulled.

Study the knots in the illustration carefully and see if you can figure which ones are knots and which are not knots. Try to imagine what would happen if you pulled the rope ends of each "knot" in question.

Now, using a piece of rope about eighteen inches (twenty-six centimeters) long — clothesline will work nicely — duplicate the loops shown in the illustration, and see if you were right. You will find that it is now quite simple to make up your own knots-and-not-knots puzzles.

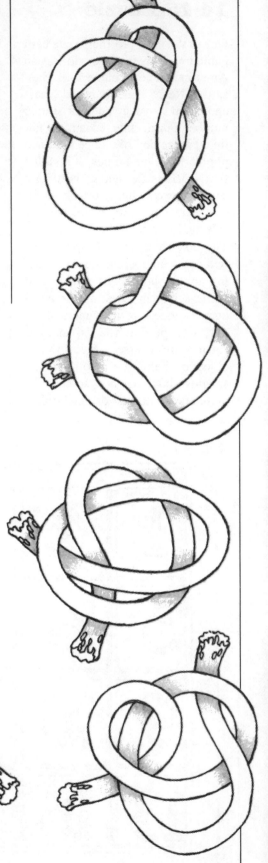

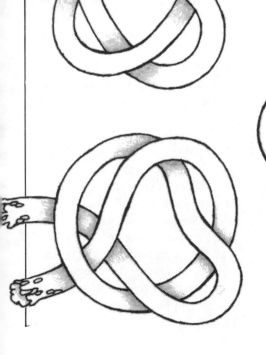

Four Color Cubes

Many puzzles seem to find new popularity over and over again as they are remembered or rediscovered. The four color cube puzzle has been an American favorite a number of times over, at first as a homemade parlor game and later as a store-bought novelty. The four-cube puzzle is most fascinating because no matter how long you work at it the solution seems just about impossible. There are stories told about people who, not being able to solve the puzzle, repainted the faces of the cube with the correct solution just so they could give up trying. But the puzzle can be easily done—once you discover how.

The object of the puzzle

The puzzle consists of four cubes of identical size. Each face of each cube is colored either red, white, blue, or green. The arrangements of the colors in relation to each other on each cube is different. The object of the puzzle is to arrange all four cubes in a row so that one of each of the four colors appears on all four sides in the row. (The colors of the end faces don't count.)

Construction

The cubes can be constructed of various materials. The first thing to do, however, is to try to find four cubes already made. They can be any size, but should be the same size. You might have four identical cubes around the house, like dice, children's blocks, or cardboard boxes. Or construct a set of cubes in one of the following ways:

● Using scissors and eight empty paper milk cartons, cut off the top of the carton so the base is a cube shape which is open on one end. Now insert the base of one carton inside another to make a

Fig. 47

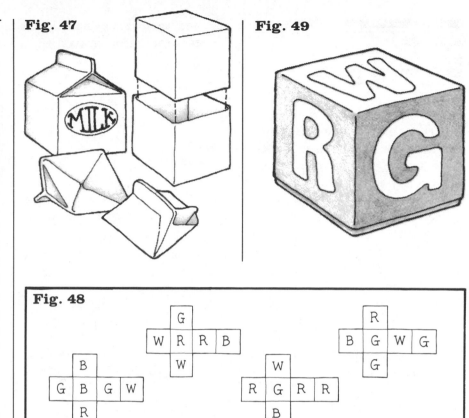

Fig. 49

Fig. 48

closed cube, Fig. 47. Repeat to make four cubes. Half-pint milk cartons from the school cafeteria work well also.

● Or, with a pencil and ruler, lay out the pattern for a box on a piece of scrap cardboard, Fig. 48. Cut out the pattern with scissors, fold up the cube, and glue or tape the edges together, Fig. 49.

● Or, make a pocket version of the four color cube puzzle by cutting up a soft solid material—

sponge, Styrofoam, or balsa wood, for example.

Using crayons, poster paint, or felt-tipped markers, whichever is best suited for the cube material you have chosen, color each of the cubes according to the four color patterns shown in Fig. 48.

Solution

To solve the puzzle, line up the four cubes as shown by the four cubes in Fig. 50. Now mix up the cubes and try to rearrange them again without looking at the solution. Good Luck!

Fig. 50

PLAY-PRETTIES

The settlers from all regions of America, each using their own traditional skills and handicrafts, made simple playthings to amuse and occupy the children. But the folk toys of America that have remained the most popular with kids from each generation to the next are the playpretties of the southern mountain states—Maryland, Kentucky, Tennessee, Alabama, the Carolinas, and Virginias.

These simple inventions, tricks, gadgets, and games were usually hand-carved from wood using bits of whatever scrap material was available. Some families today continue the tradition by teaching their children how to make old-fashioned playpretties as well as a few new ones. And, a few toy companies now produce manufactured versions of the flipper dinger, whimmy diddle, do-nothing machine, climbing bear, and others. But much of the fun of a playpretty is making it yourself, so here are a few simple playpretties both old and new that you can try—and maybe some day pass on to your children.

Finger Trap

Whether at a friend's birthday party or a visit to the local joke shop, nearly every kid has at some time been tricked into putting thumbs, pointers, or pinkies into a finger trap, and finding the fingers caught unable to get them out.

Store-bought or palm-leaf woven finger traps are certainly more elegant and durable than the following, but this "sheet of paper" version is extremely simple, and can always be made up on the spot to amuse or trick a friend.

Materials

paper magazine cover, cut or torn carefully from the magazine
tape

Tools

scissors

1. For the finger trap to really work well you will need to use a magazine cover that is neither too light (thin) nor too heavy. Starting at the middle of one of the narrow sides of the cover, cut a slit about halfway up, Fig. 51.

Fig. 51

2. Roll up each of the paper "legs" you have created as far as the slit, Fig. 52a. You should have made two, small tight tubes.
3. Continue to roll both tubes up together until the entire piece of paper is a tube shape.
4. Very carefully allow the tube to unwind until the holes in both ends are the correct size to fit one of your fingers tightly. Wrap a piece of tape around each end of the tube and the middle, Fig. 52b.

Fig. 52

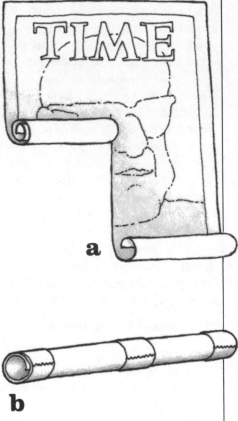

a

b

Now you are ready to try out the finger trap, first on yourself and then on a cooperative victim. See which fingers fit most snugly in the paper tube openings and insert one in each end. The fingers you used to wrap the tube around should fit in the tube past the second joint. Now try to pull them out. If you've made your finger trap well, you'll find it almost impossible to pull your fingers out without removing the tape, cutting or tearing the paper. If you can pull your fingers out easily, the tube may not be snug enough or your fingers are not far enough in. To insure a good trap when pulling this trick on a friend, have him lick his fingers before putting them in the tube. That will hold him for sure. To get yourself (or your friend) out of the finger trap, well, it's up to you!

DOMINO TRAINS

Domino train—up.

Kids frequently find new and sometimes even better ways to play with a toy than the purpose for which it was intended. Dominoes are a good example.

Dominoes have been played in America ever since Colonial days, often using printed cards or crudely carved scraps of wood. In more recent years dominoes have been factory-made of wood or plastic in small rectangular blocks. And these small "bricks" are now also used as toy building blocks as well as for playing the matching game. Someone, at some point, also discovered that a row of dominoes, each standing on its narrow end, made a "domino train." Knocking over the end domino would knock over the next domino, which would knock over the next, and so on with a *click, click, click,* until the entire row was down.

This new way of "playing" dominoes has today become just as popular as the matching game. Sometimes a group of kids will combine all their dominoes to make one super-long train, or arrange them to spell out a name. Experienced players know how to crisscross domino trains, or have one train branch out to form two, three, or more rows which come back together again. Domino pieces can be positioned so the resulting train can "travel" up and down slight inclines.

Make a domino train

If you have never tried making domino trains or if you just want to brush up on your building technique, here are a few helpful hints to get you started.

Set up the domino train on a flat surface, one that isn't too slippery. Wood floors, smooth carpets, sidewalks and most tabletops are fine. On hard, slick surfaces like glass, marble, and shiny kitchen counters, the pieces can slip while falling over, stopping the train before it reaches the other end of the line. Generally speaking stand the domino pieces apart about half the length of a single piece; on curves, or when going up an incline, keep the spacing closer.

Be careful not to knock over a domino accidentally with your hand or clothing while setting up the train pattern. When making really long trains put in a "safety break" every few feet by leaving out two domino pieces. At the end of the pattern go back and carefully fill in the pieces left out.

Now it is up to you to experiment. On a tabletop you might have the last domino positioned near the edge so that when the domino is knocked over it falls off the table and into a cup on the floor. Or you and a friend could have a domino train race. When you are tired of making trains, you might try playing the "regular" game of dominoes.

Domino train —down.

Soggy Ring

This joke ring will surprise even the most cautious. When you wear the soggy ring and shake hands, there is a sudden wet surprise for an unsuspecting victim.

Materials
pipe cleaner
sponge

Tools
scissors

1. Wrap a pipe cleaner around your finger and twist the ends together to make a ring, Fig. 53.

Fig. 53

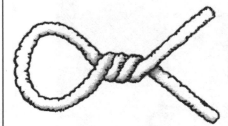

2. Cut a small square from a common kitchen sponge and attach the piece of sponge to the ring using the two ends of the pipe

cleaner, Fig. 54. Be sure to bend back the tips of the pipe cleaner so

Fig. 54

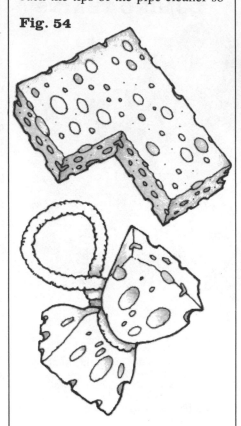

they won't prick you. Now put the soggy ring on the third finger of your right hand with the sponge in your palm, Fig. 55.

3. Wet the sponge so that it is full but not dripping and look about for a good-natured friend. Be sure to keep the sponge hidden and stare your victim straight in the eye when you shake hands. You will both get a soggy wet hand, but your friend gets the surprise!

Fig. 55

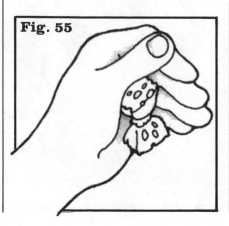

Sky Hook

Some simple amusements, although performed over and over again by generation after generation, still hold their power of amusement. The sky hook—as its name suggests—appears to defy the laws of gravity. You slip a wide leather belt into the slot of the sky hook as shown in the photo, then delicately place the end of the sky hook on the tip of your finger. The sky hook doesn't fall! The appearance of it balancing in midair is astounding but the feeling *you* get when performing this amusement is even more strange.

How to make it

There are several kinds of sky hook you can make from the quick and functional to the painstakingly carved and decorated. A simple sky hook that demonstrates its principle quite well may be made by bending an old spoon or fork as shown, Fig. 56. But the most convincing sky hooks are sawed or carved from a scrap of wood, Fig. 57. Exact dimensions are not necessary.

Fig. 56

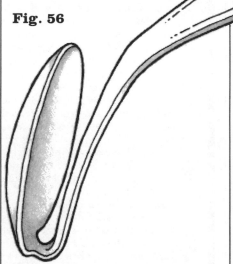

How does it work?

It all has to do with a scientific principle known as "center of grav-

Fig. 57

The mysterious sky hook balancing act.

ity.'' Notice that when the sky hook is balanced on the tip of your finger the belt does not hang straight down, but tilts backward on an angle toward your hand. The angled slot in the sky hook tilts the belt so it does that. You should now notice that about half of the belt and its weight is hanging in front of the tip of your finger, and the other half is actually hanging behind your finger. When the middle of the weight of the belt—the center of gravity—is directly below your fingertip, the sky hook will balance. If this all sounds too confusing, maybe you can ask a science teacher to explain.

String Figures

By weaving and twisting a loop of string about the fingers of both hands you can form different string patterns that very roughly represent familiar objects, or are just interesting in themselves.

Although this idle-time amusement seems to have been played for thousands of years by peoples all over the world, the Navajo Indians of America were the most adept people at making and inventing new string figures. The figures took only a few seconds to construct (once you knew how) and a whole series of different figures could be quickly made—usually to illustrate a song or story being told to children. Sometimes it was the string figure itself that inspired a story.

Literally hundreds of different string figures have been created and passed on to new generations. Museum collections in America have many of the most interesting ones. Although most string figures require only hands to create, more advanced designs use teeth and toes as well. Even a second person can join in working the same string loop.

The instructions which follow guide you through the creation of two basic string figures—cat's cradle and cat's whiskers. The description of how to make them is very wordy, but the doing is really pretty simple. The only material you will need is a piece of heavy string or yarn about four to six feet long. Tie the string ends together to form a closed loop. Don't make the loop too small or your fingers and the figures will be too cramped.

There are three kinds of "moves" in making cat's cradle and cat's whiskers: transferring loops from one finger to the other, dropping loops from fingers, and picking up strings with fingers. After each move, the hands are pulled apart, palms facing each other, so that the strings are taut. Follow the illustrations carefully. They are drawn from the view you will have when making the figures yourself.

Cat's cradle

1. Put the string loop behind your thumb, across your palm, and behind your little finger. Do the same with your other hand, Fig. 58.

Fig. 58

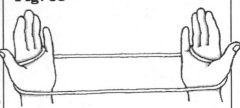

2. Take the pointer finger of either hand and put it under the string that runs across the palm of the opposite hand. Spread your hands pulling the string back, Fig. 59.

3. Repeat the procedure with the pointer finger of your other hand, Fig. 59.

Fig. 59

Two successful attempts at cat's whiskers.

4. After pulling both hands apart, the palms facing you will have the cats cradle, Fig. 60, and the basic position from which to make other string figures.

Fig. 60

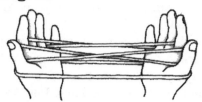

Cat's whiskers

Continue from the cat's cradle position to make cat's whiskers.

1. Curl in both thumbs so that the string slips off them, Fig. 61.

2. Reach down with your thumbs and pick up the bottom string by placing your thumbs under it and pulling up, Fig. 62.

3. Put your thumbs over the top string and pick up the next two strings, Fig. 63.

4. Curl in your little fingers so that the string slips off them, Fig. 64.

5. Put your little fingers over the string next to them and pick it up, Fig. 65. Finally, drop the string from your thumbs and you have cat's whiskers, Fig. 66.

If at any time your string figures end in a tangle, just start again. Once you have reached this point in making string figures you might find a library book on the subject, or experiment with different moves and figures yourself.

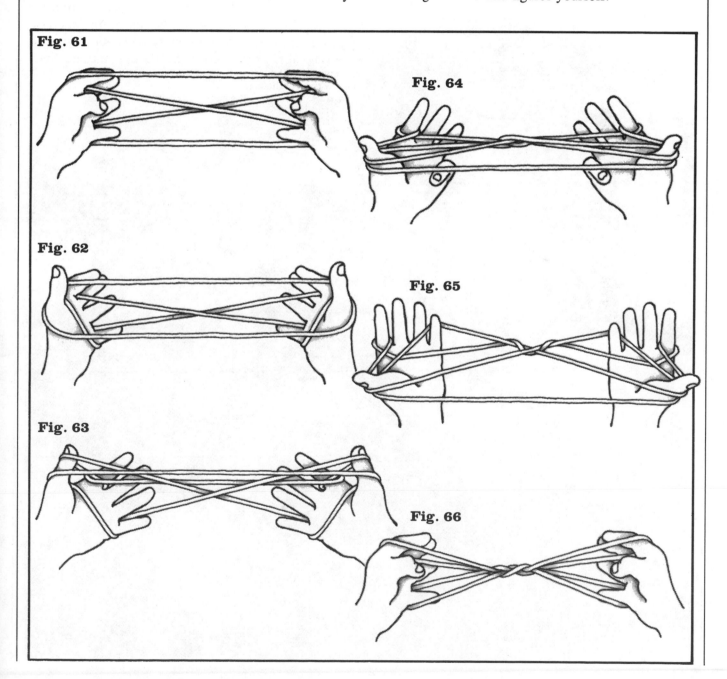

Fig. 61

Fig. 64

Fig. 62

Fig. 65

Fig. 63

Fig. 66

Target Shooting

Target shooting has always been a favorite American pastime. In Early America it was important to learn to shoot well, not only to hunt game for the table, but also for self-protection against would-be robbers and dangerous animals. For adults and older children who had been taught to handle a weapon properly and respect its dangers, target shooting was done with a gun or bow and arrow. Younger children would use less dangerous shooters such as a slingshot, bean shooter or darts, although these could also be considered dangerous weapons.

Today there are many types of shooters sold as toys that are much more dangerous than some of the simple handmade ones children used to make. The United States government has recently established safety standards for some types of manufactured "projectile" toys. These considerations should be applied to all shooting toys, store-bought or homemade. But the most important rule of all is to never, *never* aim or shoot a shooter at another person or any living creature.

When selecting a target make certain that the area all around and beyond it is clear of people or anything that might be injured or broken. You might pick a tree trunk or a post on the fence. You can also set up empty cans for targets or draw a bull's-eye target. Start

You must be careful not to hurt anybody when you play with a peashooter.

shooting from a fairly close distance—about five giant steps away from your target. With experience, gradually increase your range. Shoot for practice or, when target shooting with a friend, keep score by inventing a point system.

PEASHOOTER

A long tube of the proper diameter is all that is needed to make a peashooter. You can make a sturdy tube by rolling a sheet of heavy paper and securing it with a few strips of tape.

Materials
magazine cover
tape
dried peas or other types of small, round—or almost round—dried beans (available at supermarkets)

Tools
pencil
scissors

1. Cut or tear off the front or back cover of a magazine. Put two strips of tape side by side along one long edge of the cover, Fig. 67. The tape makes the inside of the peashooter spit-proof so it won't get soggy.

2. Place a pencil along the taped edge and tightly roll the sheet of paper into a tube around the pencil, Fig. 68.

3. Close the tube with a few strips of tape wrapped around it then punch out the pencil using another pencil.

Fig. 67

How to Shoot

To shoot, put a pea in one end of the shooter, put that end of the tube to your lips, then blow into the tube quickly and very hard. With a little practice you can improve your accuracy somewhat but remember that you can't be a marksman with a peashooter.

Although a peashooter is not very powerful it does shoot a projectile which can be dangerous. So always remember not to shoot or even aim a shooter at any person or breakable possession.

SLINGSHOT

Materials
fork of a small tree
6 or 8 rubber bands of the same size—width, thickness and length
piece of inner tube, old leather belt, or other strong material
small wadded-up paper balls

Tools
saw
penknife

1. Find a fallen forked branch with a stem and arms at least as big around as your thumb. Test the branch to make sure it is strong, not

Fig. 68

dried or rotten. Cut the stem and arms down to size using a small handsaw or penknife, Fig. 69.

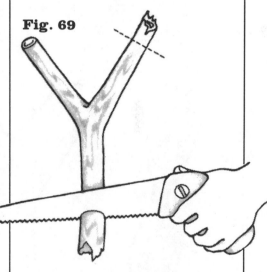

Fig. 69

2. Cut a hole in each end of the strong material, using the penknife, Fig. 70.

3. Make two chains, each three or four rubber-bands long, as shown in Fig. 70. The "heavier" the rubber bands, the more powerful your slingshot will be.

4. Attach one end of the rubber band chain to one of the branch arms near the top, then attach the other end to the material as shown, Fig. 71.

Fig. 70

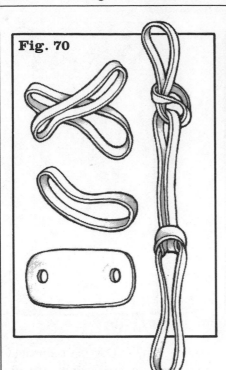

Fig. 71

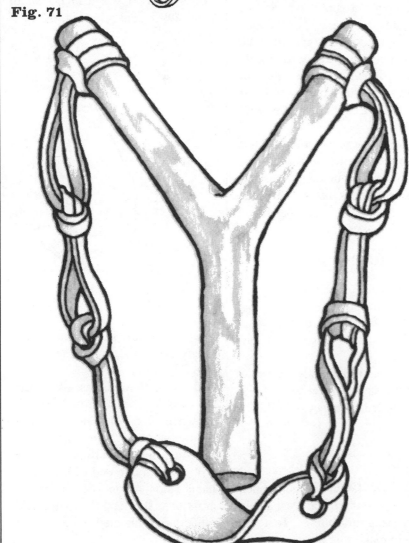

How to Shoot

The slingshot is now ready for a test shooting. Hold the stem of the slingshot tightly in one hand. Place the ammunition—the small wadded-up paper balls—in the center of the rubber band sling, holding it between your thumb and pointer finger. Hold the slingshot straight in front of you, pull back on the sling, then quickly let go of the sling only. The farther back you pull the sling, the harder and farther the shot will go.

And remember not to shoot or even aim your slingshot at any person or other living thing or breakable possession.

GAMES

Any game in which the "men" or game markers move about a surface is called a board game even if the game board is scratched in the dirt, drawn on a scrap of paper, or made from fancy woods or polished stone. Each project that follows calls for a particular kind of game board or markers. Nevertheless, you may substitute one kind of board type for another. You may use whatever is available for playing pieces—marbles, coins, stones, paper clips, buttons, or beans—or make up fancy painted or carved game markers.

You will probably notice that some of the games that follow share the same game board design. The reason is quite simple. Traditional game board patterns were often used as the basis for new board games. However, most of the games fit into one of three categories. Games like Solitaire and How Many Moves are known as "clearance games." In these the players try to remove as many game markers from the board as possible, or remove markers in the least amount of time or moves. In games like Fox and Geese or Indian and Rabbits, players compete by trying to trap or remove each other's markers. These are considered "hunt" games. And finally, there are "point" games, in which players get points for various game solutions.

Fox and Geese
(two players)

This game was first played in this country by the American Indians and called Musinaykah-wanmeto-waywin (pronounce that!)

Materials
paper
13 pennies
1 nickel

Tools
pencil

Cut or tear a piece of writing paper so that it is square, and draw thirty-three circles in the pattern shown in Fig. 72. Arrange the pennies and nickel as shown. The nickel is in the center circle. The pennies represent the geese and the nickel the fox. (A more permanent and portable version of the fox and geese game board can be made from a square scrap of wood that has been drilled with holes of a size to accommodate golf-tee markers, Fig. 73. A wood block about six inches square and one inch thick is ideal, although any size will do. Mark and drill the holes in the pat-

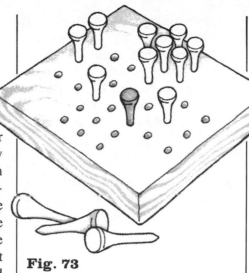

Fig. 73

tern shown in Fig. 73 making sure that the holes go only about three-quarters into the wood. The golf tees should fit snugly in the holes. The "fox" tee should be painted a different color.)

To win

The geese win if they corner the fox so he cannot move. The fox wins if he captures all but one goose.

Rules

1. One player controls all the geese, the other player moves only the fox. The geese make the first move. Players take turns.

2. The fox may move one space at a time, either up and down (vertically) or across, left and right (horizontally) to a vacant space. The geese may move one space at a time downward from their original position, from the top of the board (but not up), or across the board, left and right, to a vacant space.

3. The fox may capture geese (and remove them from the board) by "short jumps," but the geese cannot make jumps or capture the fox. In a short jump, a player jumps his game marker vertically or horizontally over an adjacent marker to the vacant space next to it, Fig. 74. The marker that has been jumped is removed from the

Fig. 72

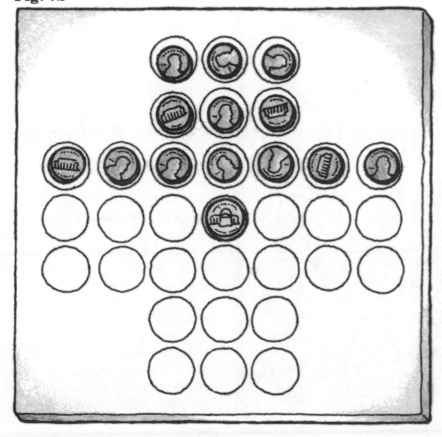

Fig. 74

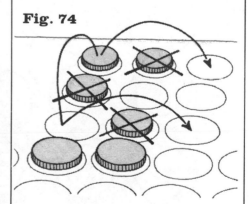

board. Successive jumps are permitted where possible. The illustration also shows a "double" jump in which two markers may be removed from the board in one turn.

Indian and Rabbits

(two players)

This game is very similar to Fox and Geese except for the board layout (and the name of the game, of course). Instead of the fox capturing the geese, the Indian tries to capture the rabbits.

Materials

cardboard scrap
12 identical buttons (size or color)
1 different button

Tools

scissors
pencil or pen

Cut a piece of plain cardboard so that it is square and draw twenty-five circles in the pattern shown in Fig. 75. Depending on the size of the game board, you can draw the circles by tracing around a quarter a half dollar or anything round. Arrange the buttons in the pattern shown. The one different button is the Indian and the rest are rabbits.

To win

The rabbits win if they corner the Indian so he cannot move, and the Indian wins if he captures all but one rabbit.

Rules

1. One player controls all the rabbits and the other player the Indian. The Indian makes the first move.

2. The Indian and the rabbit can move one space at a time either up and down (vertically), or across, left and right (horizontally), to a vacant space.

3. The Indian may capture rabbits by short jumps, (which removes them from the board) but the rabbits cannot make jumps nor capture the Indian. Successive jumps are permitted where possible.

Solitaire

(one player)

The board for this one-person game can be quickly made using the paper-and-pencil methods already described. But you can get hooked on solitaire, so you might want to build a more permanent playing surface. The wood block and golf-tee method (see Fox and Geese) is pretty good for both a traveling or coffee table version. Another quickly made game board can be of clay.

Materials

potter's clay or modeling clay (Plasticine)
32 marbles

Tools

table knife
rolling pin

The solitaire game board can be made using either potter's clay, which will eventually harden and may then be painted, or modeling clay such as Plasticine which is available in several colors and does not harden. Knead a big handful of clay until it is pliable and easy to work, then roll it out into a flat pancake about one-half or three-quarters of an inch thick. Using a table knife, cut away the edges of the pancake to make a square clay slab. Using one of the marbles, make thirty-three impressions or spaces in the clay in the pattern of the game board shown in Fig. 76. The depressions do not have to be

Fig. 75

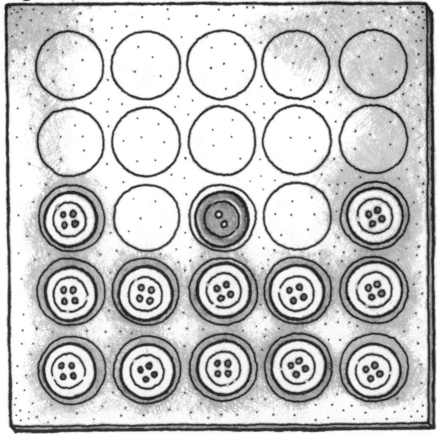

Fig. 76

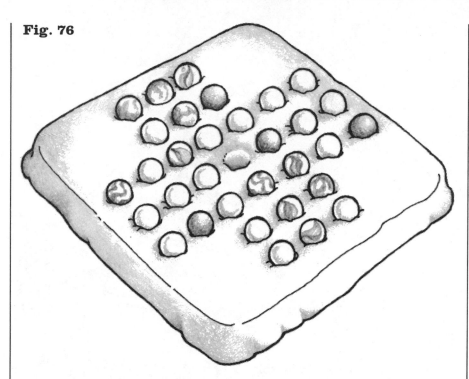

"genius" score, two markers left is "excellent," three markers is "good," and four or more markers remaining is considered only "fair."

How Many Moves
(one player)

The game board layout for How Many Moves is exactly the same as that for the Indian and Rabbits game board. You can use any of the game board construction methods already shown or, for an on-the-spot anywhere game, you can scratch a twenty-five-space pattern in the dirt using your finger or a twig. Nine stones or pebbles can be used for game markers, and are arranged in the nine center spaces as shown, Fig. 78.

To win

The object of the game is to remove eight of the nine markers from the board with the remaining marker

very deep, just enough to keep the marbles in place. Using all thirty-two marbles, put a marble in each of the game board spaces except for the center space.

To win

The object of solitaire is to remove all the markers except one. A super win occurs when the last marker ends up in the center space.

Rules

Moves are made by short jumps *only*, either up and down or across, left and right.

Triangle Solitaire
(one player)

Triangle solitaire is played in exactly the same way as Solitaire except that the game board is triangular and contains only fifteen spaces arranged as shown, Fig. 77. Fourteen game markers are used, and any one space can be left vacant at the start.

Short jumps may be made in any direction, but always in a straight line.

This game is often played with scoring, which depends upon the number of markers left. One marker left gives the player a

Fig. 77

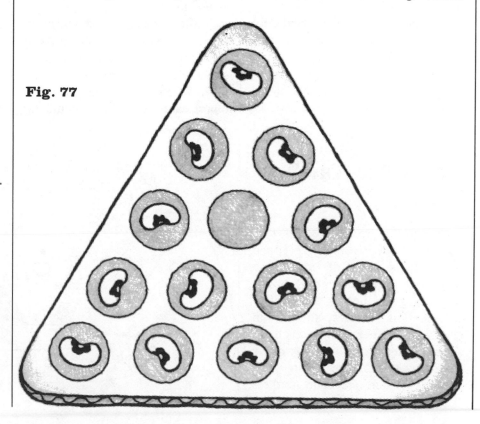

Fig. 78

ending up in the center space, and doing this in as few moves as possible.

Rules

1. Markers may be moved only one space at a time to an adjacent, vacant space: they may be moved up and down, across—left and right—and diagonally.

2. Short jumps are allowed only up and down or across—left and right—but not diagonally.

3. Successive jumps, where possible, are allowed, and count as one turn only.

Point Tic-Tac-Toe
(two players)

This scoring version of tic-tac-toe uses the twenty-five-space square game board of How Many Moves and Indian and Rabbits. Make a game board, and collect two sets of markers, thirteen in each. All markers within each set should be identical, but the two sets should be different from each other. Checkers are good markers if the size of the board permits.

Rules

1. Each player starts with thirteen identical game markers, each set distinguishable from the other.

2. The two players take turns, placing one of their markers on a space in each turn. The object of the game is to place as many of your own markers in straight rows as possible.

3. Rows can be horizontal, vertical, or diagonal. A playing piece can be counted as part of more than one row at a time, Fig. 79.

4. When all spaces on the game board have been filled, count up

Fig. 79

points using the following table to see who has the most points and is the winner.

Three markers in a row = 1 point
Four markers in a row = 3 points
Five markers in a row = 5 points

Tabletop high jumping requires good aim plus several buttons.

Tabletop Olympics

Toys and tabletop games using various sports as themes have long been a favorite activity for kids—especially on a rainy Saturday or some other time when the sport itself can't be played. The sports toys available include action board games for playing hockey, baseball, and football; electronic TV games for playing soccer, Ping-pong, and tennis; as well as several popular homemade games and contests covering a wide range of athletic events.

Tabletop olympics include a few of the more unusual sports games you might have tried. They are all based on official Olympic events although each game can be played sitting at a table, using equipment made from common things you have around the house.

Equipment

toothpicks
spoon or fork
coins
paper tubes
drinking straws
ruler or measuring tape
straight pins
buttons
drinking cup

Rules

1. Before each event the competitors may have a few practice "tries" to become familiar with the sport and develop technique.

2. All players must use similar equipment and a player must share his equipment if another player asks.

3. If there is a non-player, he can be the "official" in case of disputes. Otherwise, majority opinion rules.

4. After each event the winning player and distance should be re-corded in an official Tabletop olympics record book. Players are encouraged to try to break any existing event records.

EVENTS

High Jump. Place a wide-mouth drinking cup on the table. Using flat buttons of various sizes, each player in turn tries to "tiddlywink" a button into the cup. After a set number of rounds—maybe five or ten—only those players who have flipped at least one button into the cup can proceed to compete at the next height. Place a paperback book under the cup to raise it after each round until only one player, the winner, remains. The official height is measured from the tabletop to the lip of the cup.

Here are a few playing hints: It is easiest to flip the buttons tiddlywink-style if you use a launching pad, like a paperback

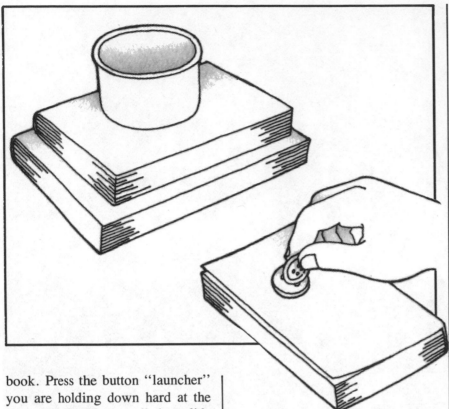

book. Press the button "launcher" you are holding down hard at the center of the "jumper," then slide it back. This will cause the wink to flip up rather than shoot ahead.

Javelin. Each competitor in turn places his elbow at the edge of the table (or the floor). He then tosses a toothpick as far as possible without lifting his elbow. The official distance is measured from the edge of the table to the point where the toothpick first touches the table (or the floor).

Pole Vault. The equipment must first be set up. For "uprights" use long paper tubes. Put a straight pin in each tube at the height you select for vaulting and use a drinking straw as a crossbar. Rest the crossbar on the pins. Make sure the crossbar is on the side of the tubes facing away from the players. To get additional height for the crossbar, you can raise the tubes up on a box or a few books, or attach a few tubes together. Use a common spoon or fork to vault a button, coin, or some other small object up and over the crossbar. The object is placed on the end of the handle and the player strikes the other end with his hand.

After the height of the crossbar is set, each player in turn tries to vault the object he has selected over the crossbar. If the object goes to the side or under the straw, the try is a miss. If the vaulted object knocks the straw off the tubes, the try is also a miss. Three misses in a row and the player is out. After each round of play the crossbar is raised. The player who clears the greatest height over the crossbar is the winner. The official height is measured from the tabletop to the top of the crossbar.

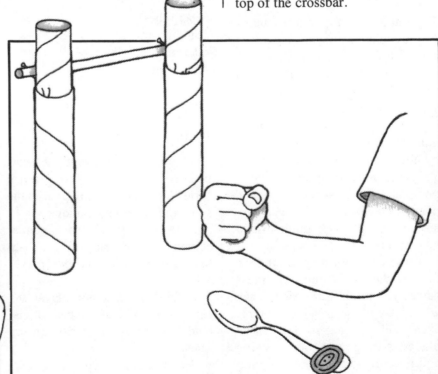

Shot Put. Each competitor in turn places a coin (penny, nickel, dime, or quarter) at the edge of the table and then, blowing hard through a drinking straw, he tries to blow the coin across the table as far as possible. The tip of the straw cannot move past the table edge. Blowing one strong blast through the straw works best. The official distance is measured from the edge of the table to the leading edge of the coin.

In tabletop pole vaulting, you must jump your button over the crossbar without knocking it down.

Calculator Games

One of the most popular electronic inventions of the 1970's is the hand-held or "pocket" calculator. At first these small calculators, capable of performing simple and complex mathematical calculations in only a fraction of a second, were quite expensive and used mostly for business work. Today they are quite inexpensive and as common in homes as radio or television. Even schools are finding that calculators help some students become more interested in numbers and math.

The purpose of a pocket calculator is primarily to do mathematical calculations, but several clever people have discovered or invented interesting ways to use the calculator as a toy for playing games and figuring out number jokes and riddles. The electronic pocket calculator is certainly the beginning of a new generation of children's electronic toys, and in years to come there are bound to be new games which will test your wits against electronic "brains." But you don't need to wait. Here are a few games you can learn to play right now using a simple pocket calculator that can add, subtract, multiply, and divide.

You will need a pocket calculator for these games. First examine it and become familiar with how it works. There are several different models of calculators and many have buttons and switches you won't need for the following games. You *will* need to understand the calculator terms shown in the illustration. Practice doing simple math problems until you are sure what all these buttons do. You will also need to remember some simple mathematics terminology. Numbers are made up of "digits." For example, the number 581 is made up of the digits 5, 8, and 1. A "function" is an operation involving numbers, like addition. For these calculator games you will be using the functions add, subtract, multiply, and divide.

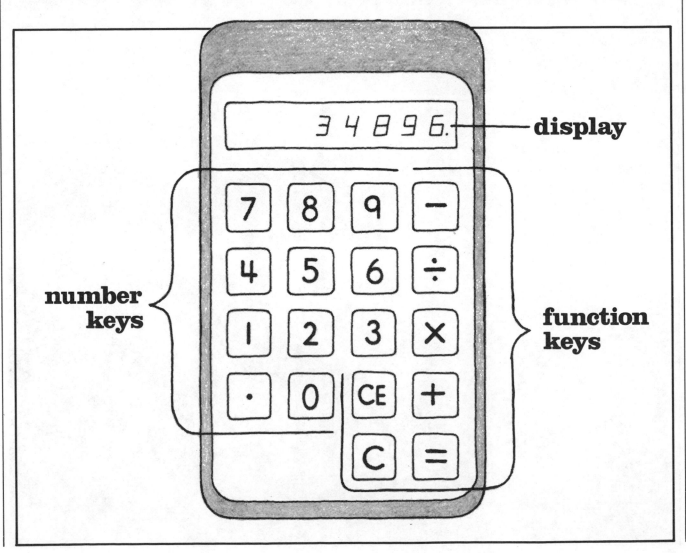

Number-words

If you hold the calculator so that you are reading the display upside down, several numbers will look like letters of the alphabet. The most recognizeable number/letter combinations are: 1/I, 3/E, 4/H, 5/S, 7/L, 8/B, and 0/O. For example, enter the digits 7, 7, 3, 4, and 5, in this order, into your calculator. The display should read 77345. Now turn the calculator upside down and the number becomes the word S-H-E-L-L.

Using the seven letters of the calculator alphabet there are many words you can "write" on the calculator display. To enter a word in the display you must, however, spell it out backward starting with the last letter. For example, the word SHOE would be entered in the order E-O-H-S, as the number 3045.

One other rule is that on some calculators any word ending with the letter O must start with decimal zero (.0). For example the word HELLO would be entered as .O-L-L-E-H or .07734. You will have to experiment with your own calculator to see if this rule applies.

Now see how many words you can make, remembering that each letter can be used more than once in a word but no word can be longer than eight letters (unless your calculator display has more then eight digit positions). Here is a list of words to help you out:

BEE	HOSE
BELL	LESS
BIBLE	LOIS
BLESS	LOSE
BLOB	OBOE
BOO HOO	OIL
EEL	SEE
HEEL	SLOB
HILL	SOIL
HOLE	SOLE

Now that you understand the calculator alphabet you might try to invent a few amusing puzzle rhymes like these:

What do 55 snakes say when there are only 14 bugs for dinner?
Answer: 5514

What happens when the scoreboard reads "Other Team: 35 points" and "Your Team: 07 points"?
Answer: You 3507

Who has 5 suits, 50 ties, and 8 pairs of shoes?
Answer: The 5508

Number-Word Poker
(two or more players)

All players in turn enter digits and functions into the calculator. The object of the game is to be the first player to spell a number-word on the display.

Each player in turn enters a single digit into the calculator and then presses one of the four function keys ($+,-,\times,\div$). The digit 0 is a "wild number" and can be added to another single digit as many times as wanted on each turn with one exception: The first player on his first turn cannot add any 0's to his digit. The player who is first to spell a number-word as the result of his play is the winner of the round.

The number of letters (digits) in the word spelled determines how many points the winning player gets for that round. The first player to score 20 points (or any point total the players agree to) is the winner of the game.

Number-word poker may sound like a simple game, but if any player uses the multiplication or division function, play can get very complicated. Beginners should limit play by using only the addition and subtraction functions.

Here is an example of a simple round:

Player 1 enters digit 9 and function+.
Display reads 9.
Player 2 enters digit 7 plus 00 and function+.
Display reads 709.
Player 1 enters digit 3 plus 000 and function+.
Display reads 3709.
Player 2 enters digit 5 and function−.
Display reads 3704.
Player 2 wins the round with the number 3704 which spells the word H-O-L-E for 4 points.

Goal Number

(two or more players)
Each player secretly writes out a three-digit number on a piece of paper and puts the paper, numberside down, on the playing table. Each player in turn enters a single digit into the calculator then presses any one of the four function keys. The first player to reach his goal number on his turn—and proves it by showing the number he has written—is the winner.

1001 Exactly

(one player)
This is a solitaire game of chance and strategy in which the player tries to display the number 1001 exactly in the least number of turns. A pair of dice is needed.

The player throws the dice to determine which digits and functions he may choose to enter in the calculator. The player can choose to enter the number on either die thrown, or the total value of the dice. For example, if the dice thrown read 6 and 3 then the player can choose to enter 6, 3, or 9. If the number selected is an even number then the player is limited to selecting the addition or subtraction functions only. If the selected number is odd then the player must choose between multiplication or division.

Chapter 10

SATURDAY NIGHT

THE CIRCUS

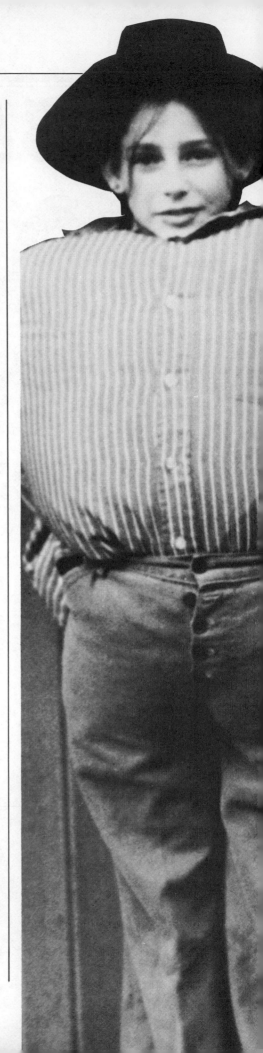

The first circus to "come to town" in America arrived in Philadelphia in 1724. Early circuses in this country consisted usually of a man who, with his wagon, traveled from town to town entertaining people by showing them animals they had never seen before and maybe doing some acrobatics or magic tricks. The most famous circus man was Phineas T. Barnum who began touring parts of America in 1842, showing off a midget he claimed was the world's smallest man—General Tom Thumb. Tom Thumb was a sensation and Barnum added other acts and novelties to his show. Through the years Barnum's circus joined others to become the Ringling Bros., Barnum & Bailey Circus, "The Greatest Show on Earth."

Before circuses came to town on trains and trucks it was common for every kid (and many grown-ups also) to line Main Street on circus day and watch the huge horse-drawn wagons come into town. For several weeks before circus day, town billboards and shop windows would be covered with colorful posters announcing the spectacular acts to come. Everyone talked about the circus; and for some kids it meant more than a show. The circus needed help to set up tents and care for the animals, and if a kid looked strong and was lucky he would be picked to work for the show while it was in town. A circus kid not only got paid but also got to go to the show for free and, even better, he got to meet a lot of interesting people and learn about circus life.

Hurry, hurry, hurry

When the circus was set up and ready for its first performance, all the animals and performers would parade down the main street of town in full costume, accompanied by the circus band and a huge steam calliope that panted and puffed out its own kind of music. As the parade marched into the big tent the audience would follow, pay an admission price and take a seat for the show. Once inside the tent the circus would continue parading around the three rings where the acts would soon take place. When everyone was seated the show began.

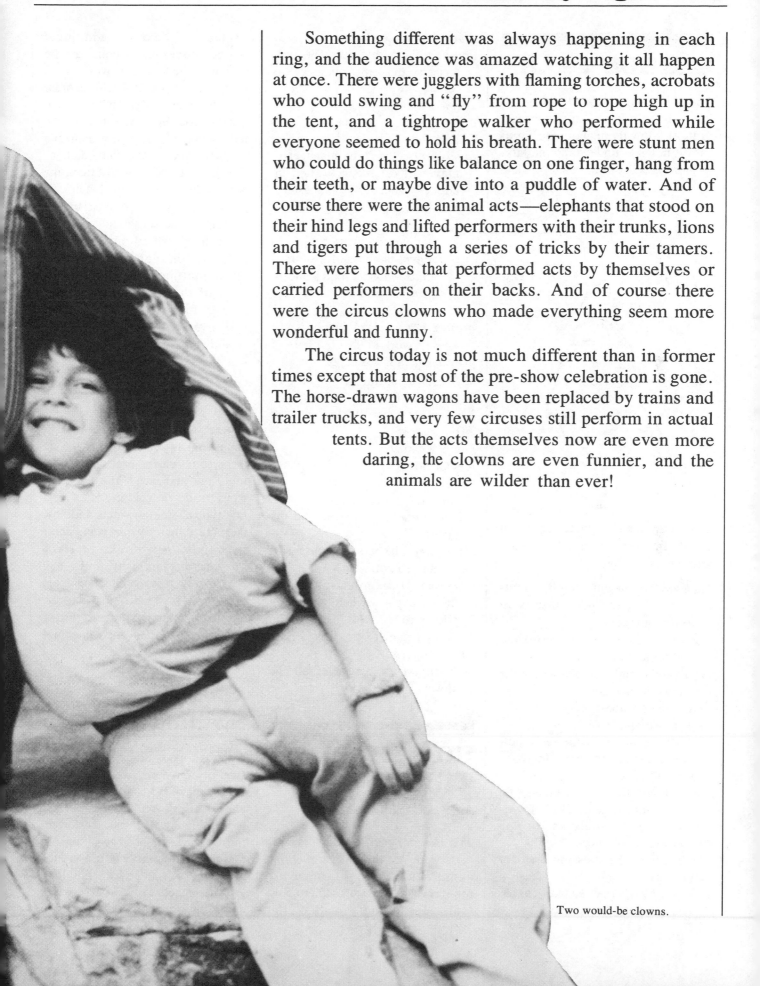

Something different was always happening in each ring, and the audience was amazed watching it all happen at once. There were jugglers with flaming torches, acrobats who could swing and "fly" from rope to rope high up in the tent, and a tightrope walker who performed while everyone seemed to hold his breath. There were stunt men who could do things like balance on one finger, hang from their teeth, or maybe dive into a puddle of water. And of course there were the animal acts—elephants that stood on their hind legs and lifted performers with their trunks, lions and tigers put through a series of tricks by their tamers. There were horses that performed acts by themselves or carried performers on their backs. And of course there were the circus clowns who made everything seem more wonderful and funny.

The circus today is not much different than in former times except that most of the pre-show celebration is gone. The horse-drawn wagons have been replaced by trains and trailer trucks, and very few circuses still perform in actual tents. But the acts themselves now are even more daring, the clowns are even funnier, and the animals are wilder than ever!

Two would-be clowns.

CIRCUS TALK

The circus world has a language all its own and if you want to be a part of it, or know more about the circus life, it helps to understand the talk.

Here is a list of circus terms and

Hey Butcher! Some Grubers Here For my Grunsel!

what they mean. Even if you decide to remain a "private person" it is still fun to know about "kinkers" and their language.

backyard: a place behind the circus entrance where performers wait to do their acts

big cats: lions, tigers, leopards, panthers, and so on

big top: the tent or arena where the circus takes place

blues: the cheapest seats

bull: any elephant

butcher: a person who sells hot-dogs, soda, and other foods to the audience

canvasmen: the men who set up tents. Sometimes called "razor-backs" or "roustabouts"

cherry pie: extra work

clown alley: the dressing area for clowns

dog and pony show: a small circus. Also called a "mud show"

donnicker: the bathroom

doors: a shout that tells the performers that the audience is coming in

deemer: a dime

dry butcher: a person who sells toys and souvenirs

fancy pants: the stage manager or master of ceremonies (often incorrectly called the ringmaster)

first of May: a person new to circus life

fine ways: a quarter

gaffer: the boss of the circus

grease joint: a food stand

grubers: peanuts

grunsel: a child

ground hog: a lazy butcher who doesn't work in the bleachers

greyhound: a fast butcher

hey rube: a call for help in case of danger or trouble

home sweet home: the last show of the season

hump: a camel

joey: a clown

kinker: any circus performer

painted pony: a zebra

private person: anyone not in the circus

ringmaster: the person in charge of the trained horse act

stars and stripes forever: the tune the band plays when something goes wrong. Also called "the disaster march"

stripes: tigers

walk around: a parade of all the clowns

SIDESHOW TRICKS EXPLAINED

The clowns, performers, and animals were not the only attractions at the circus. To the side of the big top there was often a smaller show tent appropriately called the "sideshow." For an additional charge a circus visitor could see the sideshow acts which were, in a way, a live book of world records. If your eyes and stomach could stand it you might see the world's fattest woman, the tallest man, the monkey-faced boy, the chicken-skinned girl, the strongest man, the bearded lady, the tattooed man, and freaks of almost every description. Several of the sensational oddities and acts advertised on the outside of the sideshow often proved to be disappointing once inside. But most of the time what you saw seemed truly amazing. Before your very eyes you might see a man swallowing swords, eating fire, or walking on sharp knife blades or broken glass; you might see a lady being sawed in half, or a man drinking hot molten lead.

Are these acts for real—happening as you see them—or are there some clever tricks used that fools the audience? You can't always trust what you see: Here are a few typical sideshow acts and how they are done. By the way, *don't try any of these tricks yourself.* They can be very dangerous—that is probably why people find them exciting to watch. To do a dangerous trick safely requires a lot of training, and often special equipment too.

Sword Swallowing

Although you might see a sword swallower whose sword is collapsible and folds up into the handle, almost all sword swallowing acts are absolutely real. The performer throws back his head to straighten the path from his mouth to his stomach so that he can put long swords, canes, knives, silverware, and even strings of razor blades in his mouth down and down his throat.

To keep from being cut, a sword swallower develops a tough throat lining by doing certain exercises and using special gargles. The sword swallower must also learn to keep from gagging, which is the body's natural defense against large or non-food items that might be swallowed. Some performers first swallow a thin metal tube into which they then place one or more razor-sharp objects.

Sword Walking

There are many variations to this act but the sword walker usually climbs a ladder with sword blades for ladder rungs, sharp edges up, or walks a path of sharp sword blades. The swords are real and the performer will often demonstrate their sharpness by cutting paper and other things on the blades. What many people don't realize is that a blade cuts best when it is drawn across an object rather than when something is just pressing on it. To prove that to yourself try to cut through a tomato or the edge of thin paper by just pressing down on the blade. It won't work. The sword walker's swords are locked firmly in place so they can't slip; the performer places his feet down on the blades without sliding them at all. Most sword walkers have developed pretty tough-skinned feet as well.

Fire Eating

No act at the side show is more scary and impressive than that of the fire-eater. Before your eyes you watch a performer put flaming torches, molten lead, and burning oil into his mouth; you see him

blow billows of smoke, sparks and flames from between his lips. It does take a lot of nerve and practice to be a fire-eater but the performance is all a trick using special chemicals, materials, and some well-performed illusion.

To breathe out flames the performer shows the audience that his mouth is empty, then he holds a lit candle up to his mouth and blows out on it. Suddenly his breath ignites into flames so he looks like a fire-breathing dragon. Actually the fire-eater's mouth is not empty— tucked up in his cheek there is a sponge filled with a special chemical. When the performer breaths out, the fumes from the chemical are ignited by the candle flame. The fire never actually touches the fire-eater's mouth. However, the fire-eater must be careful to close his lips tightly the instant he stops blowing or else he might breathe in the flames and be seriously burned.

To eat flaming torches, the performer skillfully breaths out to extinguish the flame just an instant before the torch goes into his wet mouth.

In an interesting version of this trick the fire-eater appears to be drinking hot flaming oil. Here the performer fills a bowl with oil and sets it on fire. He then spoons out some of the flaming oil and apparently swallows it, continuing until the bowl is empty. The oil is actually a special liquid that burns away quickly. The fire-eater dips his spoon into the flaming oil to coat it. As he brings the flaming spoon to his mouth the performer extinguishes the flame with his breath. The oil coating on the spoon is burned away by the flame and there is actually no oil left to drink. While the performer repeatedly does this the oil in the bowl burns itself out. The illusion is that the fire-eater has swallowed all the oil.

ROPE SPINNING

The wild-West show was a kind of circus that first became popular in America during the nineteenth century. Just like the regular circus there were clowns, wild animals, and daring acts, but all the performers in the wild-West show were cowboys who demonstrated their skills. There were contests of target and fancy trick shooting using mirrors for aiming, there were bareback riding events to see how long a cowboy could stay mounted on a wild, bucking horse or bull, and—maybe most exciting of all—there were amazing roping and rope-spinning tricks.

A cowboy and his lariat

Like his guns and spurs, the cowboy's lariat or rope was an indispensable tool to be carried everywhere. The lariat could be used to catch a horse, pull a wagon out of the mud, or to whip a stubborn steer. Mostly it was used for catching calves and stray cattle on the drive. In his leisure time the cowboy would practice roping and rope-spinning tricks just for showing off. Often cowboys would pose for their picture holding a gun in one hand and a lariat in the other. A few cowboys toured around the country with wild-West shows giving demonstrations of trick roping and spinning, and teaching kids this new American sport.

The lariat was not just a plain piece of rope. It was made from either grass or rawhide to be exceptionally strong and just the right weight and stiffness. You can make a lariat and do rope-spinning tricks if you have the right materials.

1. Find a piece of rope about ten or twelve feet long and between ¼

and ⅜ inch in diameter. Use only a braided rope often called sash cord, Fig. 1. It is available at most hardware stores. *Don't* use a common "laid rope", Fig. 2, with spiral strands because it kinks and tangles too easily. In a pinch, you can try using a piece of clothesline. If the rope is brand-new it will probably be too stiff and should be worked until the stiffness is gone. Just using the rope for a while will usually soften it up.

Fig. 1
Fig. 2

2. At one end of the rope tie a slip knot known as the "honda," Fig. 3. Be sure to snip off the tail or end of the honda knot or the honda might be too heavy for good rope spinning.

Fig. 3

3. Feed the other end of the rope through the honda, and pull the slip knot tight.

4. Place a large flat washer over the free end of the rope, then tie the end of the rope with a simple knot, Fig. 4.

Fig. 4
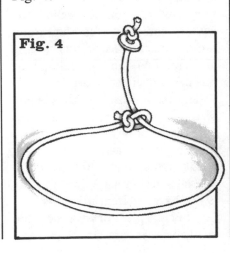

Once you learn to spin a rope, all you'll need is a steer.

How to Spin a Flat Loop

Before you try your first rope spin there are a few "don'ts" to remember: Don't spin ropes inside the house, unless you have a large play area where things are not likely to get bumped and broken. Don't wear a dress or loose clothing that might interfere with the spinning rope. Don't—or rather *never*—put the lariat around anyone's head or body, including your own. And finally, don't be discouraged if the rope doesn't spin a perfect circle right away. Most kids can do a pretty good spin with less than an hour's practice.

1. To adjust the rope for spinning, hold the lariat at the honda; the loop should hang down. The length of rope from the honda to the washer and knot is called the "spoke." When the loop is the proper size, the spoke should hang down from the honda halfway to the bottom of the loop. Adjust the rope so this is so. When you have the rope adjusted properly, be sure the slip knot is pulled tight so that the loop size won't change.

2. The easiest spin to learn is the "flat loop." Find a space where there is plenty of room and stand with your feet slightly apart and your body leaning slightly forward at the waist.

3. Hold the rope at the honda in your left hand. Place the knotted end of the spoke with the washer loosely between the second and third fingers of your right hand so that the knot faces the palm of your hand, Fig. 5. Your right hand is called the "spoke hand."

4. Now bring the loop over to your right hand and let it lie loosely across the fingers of that hand. You're ready to throw out the rope and start spinning.

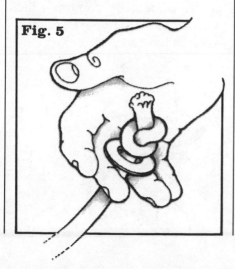

Fig. 5

5. Throw out your right hand in a counterclockwise direction and away from your body. At the same time release the loop from both hands, while still loosely holding the spoke. Your right hand should continue to make counterclockwise movements while the loop spins parallel to the ground and the spoke slips and turns between your fingers. This "slipping" is important if you wish to avoid "wind up" and rope kinking. (Cowboys don't use washers on their ropes, but you should to allow the rope to slip in your fingers.)

Keep trying to throw out the rope and get it spinning before the loop touches the ground. If the rope seems too big or clumsy, you can shorten it or try standing on something sturdy. Don't try to make the rope spin too fast—the secret of good rope spinning is to "get the rhythm." Of course, there are many other rope tricks you can learn, but first get the "flat loop" spin down going in both directions.

BE A STRONGMAN

Circus strongmen usually look muscular and powerful and perform remarkable feats like lifting tables with their teeth, breaking chains and bending horseshoes with their bare hands, challenging volunteers to budge them, or tearing fat telephone books in half. Some strongman stunts do take a lot of strength but you don't have to have large muscles and weigh over two-hundred pounds to do them if you know a little about body mechanics, leverage, and balance. With this knowledge and a little showmanship anyone can appear to be stronger than he really is.

Practice the following strongman tricks in front of a mirror until your act is convincing. Even if the trick comes easy to you try to give a show of great effort and strength. If you make it look too easy your audience may not believe you really did it.

Break a Deck of Cards

This strongman trick is simple to do but you have to prepare the deck in advance. The secret is to bake the cards first. Use an unwanted deck of playing cards, a stack of old file cards, or any scrap cards you might have.

1. Spread the cards out on a pan or tray and put them in the oven (or toaster oven) at 400°F. (205°C.) Depending on the card paper you use and your particular oven it may take fifteen minutes, a half hour, or even longer for the cards to dry out. The longer you heat the cards, the more brittle they will get and the easier they will break. But don't overcook the cards. If the cards begin to brown around the edges you have either made the temperature too hot or the cards have been cooked too long.

2. Remove the cards from the oven using a spatula and spread them out to cool before you restack the deck.

3. Now hold the deck in both hands and flex it back and forth a few times across the middle. If the deck doesn't break in half right away twist it across the middle or try to tear it. At first you might find it easier to practice with only half a deck, but once you get the technique you may be able to break two decks at once. If you are performing this trick for an audience be sure to put on a great show of strength.

Tear a Telephone Book

With some practice you may be able to tear a big-city telephone directory in half. For now however, use a thin out-of-date directory or a paperback novel you no longer want.

1. First, sit down. With both hands hold the book firmly across the long open edge so that your palms are on one side of the book and your fingers on the other. Rest the spine of the book on your knee.

2. Pulling your fingers up and pushing your palms down spread out the long edge of the book in a slanted position so that each page slightly overlaps the one above it. The trick rests in tearing (a little bit) each page individually rather than tearing the whole thickness of the book at once. Once the pages are started the whole tear gets easier.

3. Now try tearing the pages by twisting your hands away from each other. The more you slant the

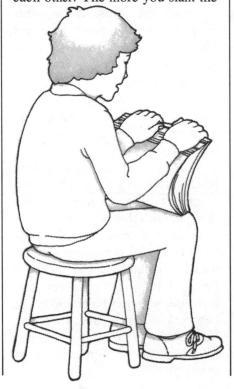

pages the easier they will tear. Your audience can't see the side of the book facing you, so they won't know how you are doing your act of strength. After some practice try tearing a book into strips.

BE A CLOWN

Of all the circus performers the clown is probably America's favorite. A clown's job looks easy enough but it isn't, really. A clown has to be skilled in doing many different circus acts—juggling, acrobatics, balancing, magic, horseback riding, and tightrope walking. Even if the clown appears at times to be doing everything all wrong, he has to learn his act right before he can skillfully do it wrong and be funny. For example a clown might appear to be carefully balancing a ball on the tip of an umbrella. All the clowns moves are very convincing but after a minute or so the clown will show you that the ball was attached to the umbrella all along. Or, there might be a clown who boasts that he can walk on his hands and after several attempts that fail he finally puts his hands on the floor and steps on them.

A clown must also be a good showman and learn to appear eager and excited no matter what. If one of the acts goes wrong for some reason, or if one of the performers should have an accident, the clown must divert the audience's attention and keep the people smiling.

A clown without a circus

You can become a clown without having to join a circus. If you are friendly and have a good sense of humor you've got a head start; you can learn to put on a clown face, dress in a clown costume, and do several clown tricks—just to amuse yourself and friends or maybe to entertain at parties.

First you need to decide what kind of clown you want to be. There are generally three types. A "white-face clown" looks like a puppet with his happy painted face, big red nose, and large exaggerated mouth. He wears loose-fitting, brightly patterned costumes with pom-pom buttons and ruffled collars. A "character clown" is dressed to look like some well-known person— a policeman, fireman, doctor, or maybe the president. His makeup is more natural than that of white-face clowns though certain features are still exaggerated— like a large red nose, bushy eyebrows, or big oversized glasses. The "auguste clown" is usually sad-faced in pink, red, and black makeup, and wears dull, ragged clothes that are much too big for him. The auguste clown makes a mess of everything he does—the harder he tries, the worse things get.

YOU REALLY CAN JOIN THE CIRCUS

At one time nearly every kid in America dreamed of joining the circus. The life of circus people looked glamorous and exciting, especially compared to the everyday world of school and chores. Whenever the circus wagons packed up and pulled out for the next town it was a real temptation for a kid to go along.

If you have the dream of traveling across America, performing in the circus and thrilling crowds of people, and if you have a talent for circus work, you might just consider joining up with a circus for awhile. But remember that although circus life can be everything you dreamed of, it is also routine and very hard work.

During the circus season, from March through October, you would be traveling every few days and probably living in a house trailer. You would be busy with circus life every day of the week, and when you were not actually performing your act you would be needed to help set up or take down the circus. You would also need to spend time practicing your act, to keep in shape and learn new material. During school months you would receive your schoolbooks, assignments, and tests by mail wherever you happened to be. When the circus season ended you would head for home and go back to school until March—then it would be time to join up with the circus again.

Go to Clown College

Probably the best way to join the circus and learn about circus life is by becoming a circus clown. For eight weeks of the winter season, when it is at its winter quarters in Florida, the Ringling Bros., Barnum & Bailey Circus holds a clown college (the only one in the world). Tuition is free and anyone seventeen years old or over can apply. If you are accepted to clown college you will learn how to dress like a clown, do slaps and falls, make your own props, ride a unicycle, walk on stilts, juggle, balance on a rolling ball, do magic, spin plates, even how to ride an elephant. You will also study nutrition and body conditioning. When you graduate from clown college you might get a job with "The Greatest Show on Earth" or some other circus.

If being a circus clown is your heart's desire you can send for an application by writing to:

Clown College
P.O. Box 1528
Venice, Florida 33595

Here are a few of the things you will be asked or asked to do:

What was your very first childhood job for money?

What has given you the most pleasure during the past year?

Describe your first accomplishment?

If you could be someone else, who would you be and why?

What character trait in yourself would you most like to change?

What is your worst hang-up?

What is the most important lesson you have learned to date?

Describe memorable turning points in your life.

Rate your anger "boiling point" on a scale of one to ten.

Name three favorite musical groups and several of their recordings that you consider outstanding.

Name your favorite foods.

List your five all-time favorite movies.

Why do you think you would fit into the circus life-style?

How do you face a new day?

Putting On a Clown Face

Every clown has his own particular face and other clowns are honor-bound not to imitate it. So you can't copy a clown face from a picture—you will have to design one that best fits you, your personality, and the type of clown you want to be.

First get together the materials and makeup you will be using. Don't use wax crayons, felt-tipped markers, or paints. These colors may be bright but the chemicals they contain may harm your skin; you might also have trouble getting the color off. Professional clowns use special theatrical makeup, but for now you can use whatever makeup your mother might have—and let you use. With lipstick, eye shadow crayons, eyeliner pencil, rouge, and powder, you can experiment making different clown features. You will also need cold cream or baby oil to put on your face before the makeup.

This helps protect your skin and makes it easier to get the makeup off. If you want to be a white-face clown, the best makeup to use is zinc oxide salve which you can buy at a pharmacy or theatrical supply store. Otherwise you might try putting baby powder or white flour inside an old sock and "dusting" your face white. If you have a small red hollow ball you can make a good clown nose by cutting a slot in the ball so it will fit snugly but comfortably over your nose. For a character clown face you might want to have a mustache. Cut it out of paper in any size or shape you want with paper "hooks" to attach the mustache to your nose.

Before you start putting on makeup, try to discover which parts of your face you can move the most. One way to find out is to draw a grid of squares lightly over your face, and see which squares twist and move the most. Use an eyeliner pencil to draw the lines. These are the areas of your face that are most flexible and the places you will want to emphasize with makeup.

The smell of the greasepaint

Now you are ready to begin putting on a clown face. Set up a mirror and pull your hair back off your face. Cover your whole face with baby oil or cold cream, then apply a base color of zinc oxide salve, powder or flour. Rub it on smoothly, blend it into your skin at the sides of your face and down your neck. Wherever you decide to

color-on features, carefully rub off the base makeup with a tissue and draw on your design using the lipstick, eye shadow crayons, or an eyeliner pencil. Your clown face might have a large, red, smiling mouth outlined in black; heavy dark eyebrows; a bright blue diamond around each eye; pink circles on either cheek; and maybe a big teardrop next to your nose. If something doesn't look quite right, rub it off with baby oil and try something else. Remember that in putting on a clown face you are not making a mask or putting on a disguise. You are trying to look like the clown you feel inside yourself. Keep trying different clown features until you feel the face is just right.

Clown Clothes

What costume do you think goes with your clown face? Just as you experimented until you found the right clown face, try different costumes until the clown you want to be appears. Any old clothes, especially things too big for you, can be made into a clown costume: mismatched socks; an out-of-fashion hat; your father's shirt, pants, shoes, suspenders, or rope belt. What about a pillow to make you look fat? You might try wearing a yarn wig or a big bow tie made from a scarf. And to hold your costume together, use large safety pins or diaper pins.

When you are satisfied with your face and costume you can begin learning how to act like a clown.

Clown Pantomime

When circuses were small, with only one ring, clowns could talk

and sing to the audience without any difficulty. But as circuses grew larger it became impossible for a clown to be heard clearly by everyone. So clowns began to "speak" in pantomime. Clowns today rarely speak out loud—instead they show feelings, ideas, actions, and even whole stories through facial and body movement. You probably already know a few pantomime gestures. When you put your index finger up to your lips to tell someone to be quiet, or when you cup your hand to your ear to tell someone to speak louder, you are doing pantomime.

To learn other pantomime gestures you should first observe how people perform simple everyday actions. Exactly how does each part of your body move when you take a drink of water, slam a door, or read a newspaper? Practice these and other simple actions without actually touching any objects. It takes experience to convince an audience that you are riding a bicycle when there is no bicycle, or that you are balancing a shaky pile of dishes when there is nothing above your hands but air.

Much of our communication is the result of our facial expressions. Look in the mirror and see how these expressions work for you.

A happy face.

To appear happy, lift all your face muscles up. Raise your eyebrows, your cheeks, and the corners of your mouth.

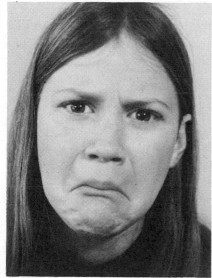

A sad face.

If you want to look sad, do the opposite. Pull down the outer corners of your eyebrows (or raise the inside corners to get the same effect), let your cheeks sag, and lower the corners of your mouth.

A surprised face.

To look surprised, pull your eyebrows up as high as you can, open your eyes wide, and make your mouth into a large *O*.

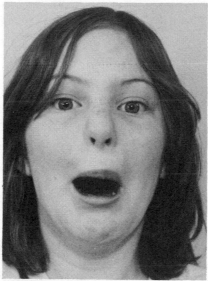

A look of fear.

You can communicate fear by making the top half of your face sad and the lower half happy. Pull down the outer corners of your eyebrows, and open your mouth as though you were going to smile.

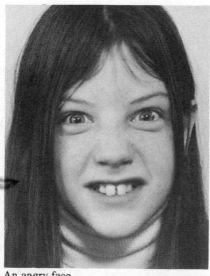

An angry face.

If you want to seem angry, pretend you have the face of a bulldog or that your nose is a magnet pulling the rest of your face toward it. Your nose should wrinkle, your eyes squint, and your eyebrows furrow. To really look mean, turn your mouth into a frown. Keep practicing until you have your gestures down pat.

FORTUNE-TELLING

Have you ever wondered about the future, what fate will bring tomorrow, next week, or next year? Have you ever wondered if you will be rich or famous, who you will marry or where you might travel? Most everyone is curious about his or her future and that is probably why the circus fortune-teller is so popular.

The fortune-teller is often dressed like a mystical gypsy with a long skirt and plenty of golden jewelry. All around her there are mysterious symbols and astrological signs to set the mood in the fortune-teller's dimly lit tent. For a fee the fortune-teller will peer into her crystal ball, consult her deck of cards, or study your palm—all to reveal the secrets of your future.

You will meet a man

A few people have proven to scientific satisfaction that they possess the ability to predict certain things although the scientists don't know why. Some believe that everyone has psychic abilities but that most people have never used and developed them. A fortune-teller may indeed have an uncanny sense for prediction that can't otherwise be explained, but she usually relies on her intuition and imagination, telling you things you would like to hear. It helps if the fortune-teller is a good reader of people's character and personality. What a person wears, how he talks, the way he combs his hair, and even the look in his eyes all tell something about who the person is. From these clues the fortune-teller can make believable predictions.

With some types of fortune-telling the clues already exist and cannot be controlled by the fortune-teller. A palm reader will interpret or read the lines on your palm (as well as several other features of your hand) and tell you what characteristics they represent. Other methods like reading cards and tea leaves provide chance clues which the fortune-teller then reads into a prediction of the the future.

**Gaze into
my crystal ball**

In either case once you learn how to read the clues you too can try to tell a fortune. There is, however, a little more to it than just that. Most fortune-tellers have some type of ritual they perform to help set the mood and create a sense of expectation. The room is usually dimly lit by a candle and the fortune-teller draws out the suspense by deeply concentrating on the clues. Most people enjoy believing the mysterious and unexplained, and the more they believe in your prophecy, the more likely it is to come true.

You may want to test your own psychic abilities or maybe just learn to be a good fortune-teller. But if you do, be aware of this advice: If you get a confused message from the clues, accept it—fortunes are sometimes in a confused state. (And above all, don't re-ask a question or purposely look for a fortune you want to hear simply because you did not like the first message you got. That might bring you bad luck.)

Palmistry

No two hands are exactly alike; even your own hands are not a perfectly matched pair. Look at the lines on your palms and compare them to someone else's. The pattern of lines on your palms are unique to you—and according to palm readers these lines can predict many things such as your health, whether you will be rich or poor, when you might travel, your chances for fame, how many children you will have, and other facts about your personality. Unlike many other methods of fortune-telling that predict only the immediate future, palm reading tells the story of your entire life from birth to death. So you can always check the lines of your palms to see what past predictions have come true. This doesn't mean, however that your entire life is determined by fate and is out of your control.

The spiritual versus the conscious

Look at both your palms and notice the difference in the pattern of lines. According to palm readers the left-hand palm lines represent your spiritual self and the destiny you were born with. Your right hand represents your conscious, active self and what you have chosen to do with your life. Together they communicate the whole picture: what you are given that you can't change, and what you consciously influence, determine, or bring about. It is sort of like the way you look. You can't change the features you were born with—long legs, short neck, or puffy cheeks—but the clothes you choose to wear, whether you smile or frown, if you are generally pleasant or complain a lot, and other aspects of your developed personality influence how you look to others—your "fate." Fortune-tellers have a saying, which

Palmistry gives new meaning to all those lines in your hands.

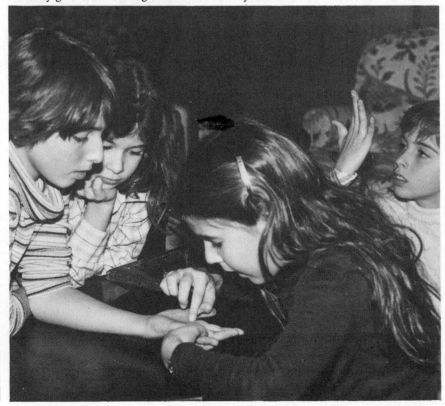

is, "A wise person rules his destiny and is not ruled by it."

Reading palms

A palmist (palm reader) begins by looking at the entire hand—back, front, fingers, and thumb—of the left hand first and then the right, to see what characteristics and differences they show. Even before you study the palm lines there is much you might learn about a person just from the size and shape of his hands. Does the subject have big bold hands, small nervous hands, rough working hands, or smooth delicate hands? What clues might you get from these features?

When you are ready to study the palm lines, hold the subject's hand, palm up, and with the thumb or index finger of your other hand gently rub the middle of your subject's palm. This stimulates the circulation of the hand and sometimes makes the finger lines easier to see. The palm is also considered one of the psychic centers of the body and by touching it and concentrating on your subject you may become more receptive to the subject's true fortune. (If nothing else, lightly rubbing the palm will add to your mystical routine.)

Three important lines

Now look closely at the palm. Of the hundreds of lines on a person's palm, there are three prominent, common ones that nearly everyone has: the "life line," the "heart line," and the "head line." Other lines show a person's health, fate, the possibility of fame and of love, and travel expectations, as well as several other things. These lines may or may not appear. Notice the length, depth, color, breaks, and special markings of each line. These can also be clues.

The length of each line should be viewed as three equal segments each representing about twenty-five years of life. The first segment represents youth, the second middle age, and the third old age.

People are usually most interested in their chances for love, money, success, and travel, so as you read a subject's fortune, try to concentrate your predictions on these topics. Be sure to stress any good fortune you might discover and always end your reading with a positive prediction. "You will have a long life," or "You will enjoy good health," are good enders but if neither of these truly fits you might say, "You will have an interesting life."

Using the following chart and illustration, you can tell a subject's fortune by comparing the size, length, and character of his own particular palm lines. First read your own palms, then mystify your friends by reading theirs.

HANDS

Size:
Small: big ideas
Large: eager to do things alone

Shape:
Square: a worker/earthy/solid values/much physical energy
Pointed: an interest in the arts/must be surrounded by beauty/a feeling for psychic matters
Cone-shaped: creative and imaginative/interested in theory rather than doing
Spade-shaped: a craftsperson/clever, inventive, and mechanically inclined
Mixed hand: versatile/creative and practical/general rather than specific interests

Flexibility:
Relaxed, bends easily at wrist: trustful and easygoing accepting of new ideas
Stiff: a rigid person
Fingers and thumb push back easily: timid or shy
Rigid thumb: a strong will
Fist with thumb out: foolhardy and careless
Fist with thumb under fingers: a strong defender/aggressive

FINGERS

Straight: direct/honest, clear-headed
Crooked: devious
Long and thin: intellectual
Short and heavy: active, physical
Long index finger: dominates others
Long ring finger: artistic/reckless
Long little finger: an ability to talk or sell
With hand spread, little finger stands apart: an independent mind

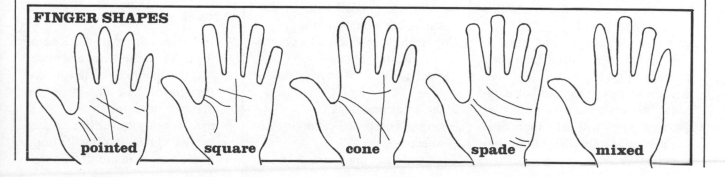

FINGER SHAPES

pointed   square   cone   spade   mixed

Ring and middle fingers close: success is part fate/an artist

Index and middle fingers close: position of authority in work

LINES

Life

This most important line begins at the side of the palm between the thumb and index finger and runs down around the base of the thumb. The life line generally shows vitality as well as length of life.

Long and clearly marked: good health/vitality/average life span

Short and strong: vitality and drive/ the ability to overcome health problems

Thin and wavy: less vitality/many changes in life/variable health

Long and curved around the base: active in older age

Short and shallow: life controlled by another's will

Wide semicircle around base of thumb: strength/enthusiasm/ lucky in love

Straight and close to thumb: a careful life/limited in love

Crosses palm toward other side: travel will affect life/strong imagination

Head

The head line starts at the top of the life line and goes across the middle of the palm. If there is only one crosswise line on the palm it is the head line; if there are two then the lower one is the head line. This line generally shows quality of mind and attitude toward life.

Head and life line joined at start: a thinker/scared and cautious during childhood

Head and life line separated at start: love of adventure/enthusiasm toward life

Long, deep, and straight: logical and direct mind/realistic/good memory

Light and wavy: poor ability to concentrate/lack of interests

Short: more action than thought

Short and upcurved: indecisive/scatterbrained

Long and upcurved: collector of things/good memory

Long and downcurved: creative and imaginative thinking

Heart

If you have two crosslines on your palm, the one above and parallel to the head line is the heart line. It shows emotional attitudes and qualities of love and affection.

No heart line: mind controls emotions completely

Long: idealist/will marry into wealth

Straight and parallel to head line: strong emotional control

Curved and long: warm/affectionate/ romantic nature

Curved upward: will sacrifice all for love

Short: weak emotions

Strong and deep: dedication/loyal in affections

Faint and pale: fainthearted

Fate

This line runs up the middle of your palm, beginning near the wrist and ending under the middle finger. The fate line indicates the degree to which fate controls life. A strong and deep fate line shows fate to be a strong influence, whereas a weak line shows destiny and luck to be self-made. Any breaks in the line can mean a change in jobs or homes.

Fame

Starting at the base of the hand, the fame line goes up the palm, and ends under the ring finger. When it is present, the fame line represents a public life with great success and good fortune. However, if the line is broken it means ups and downs in your career.

Health

Runs from the base of your little finger to the base of your thumb. No health line at all shows good health whereas a strong and straight line indicates a good business sense. Only a wavy line can mean poor health.

Marriage

Look for one or more of these lines on the side of your palm just below the little finger. Light lines show romances and deep ones marriages (the lowest one being the first marriage). Any small lines running down to a marriage line represent children.

Travel

Travel lines appear on the side of the palm, at the base, and opposite the thumb. The length and strength of these lines show the distance and importance of a trip. When a travel line crosses the line of fate, travel will bring a major change in life. If the travel line interesects the line of life, health may be affected when traveling.

Money

Lines that run from the base of the thumb up to any finger show a particular skill for accumulating money. If the line ends at the index finger, a golden touch is the source of wealth; if it ends at the middle finger, good business sense is the source; and a line ending at the little finger shows wealth through inheritance. Another money line may go from the head line to the ring finger, and that indicates money through surprise.

Card Reading

Another method of telling fortunes relies on a person's "chance" selection of particular playing cards from a regular deck. However, the fortune-teller must also be able to tell a good story since the cards give only clues and must be put together and interpreted in a particular sequence to predict a fortune. The more you know about the person whose fortune you are telling, of course, the easier and more personal your interpretation will be. Even without knowing the subject well, you would probably interpret the clues somewhat differently for someone who is married, for example, than for someone who is not; for someone who lives in the country rather than in the city, or for a young girl rather than an older woman.

Shuffle the deck

Begin by sitting at a table across from your subject. Use a regular deck of fifty-two playing cards, shuffle the deck a few times, and put it face down on the table. Ask

your subject to cut the deck just once, which he must do with his *left* hand only. (To cut the deck of playing cards, simply pick up any number of cards from the top of the deck and put that pile under the remaining cards.)

With a bit of flair and mysticism, the fortune-teller now begins to slowly turn the cards face up one by one in rhythm while softly chanting, "Diamond/club/heart/spade/picture/number"—one word for each card. When the card you turn over matches the word you chant—number, suit, or picture—put that card aside. Continue going through the complete deck putting aside the cards that match the chant and lay out the cards in the order they were selected. Once you become familiar with the meanings of specific cards, it will be impressive if you say something about each card as it is selected. For example, if the seven of spades is chosen, you might add the comment, "You have some sorrow."

I see before you great happiness

From the cards and their meanings, you now have to interpret a fortune. In general, hearts represent romance, kindness, and affection; clubs indicate prestige and influence; diamonds show practical traits; and spades are the cards of misfortune, although they can just as well be warnings of things to avoid. Each card in the deck, though, has its own particular meaning, and certain combinations of cards next to each other also predict specific fortunes.

Refer to the chart (next page) to determine the possible meanings of each card. Also check the sequence of cards for the meaning of any special combinations. Using the interpretations of the cards in the order they were selected, weave

an interesting story and predict a fortune. For example, from the following five cards, you might predict this fortune for an older brother:

9 of diamonds:

You will soon need money for something you want very much.

7 of spades:

At first you will not have luck, but avoid quarreling with those who disappoint you.

King of hearts

A man, possibly your father, will offer to help you, but the two of you will not agree to terms. I see an argument.

2 of clubs:

You will take some positive action for yourself and not rely on others.

5 of spades:

Don't be discouraged if things still don't go well. In time, everything you want you will get.

And since the 9 of diamonds and 7 of spades appear next to each other in your sequence, this combination has a special meaning, which might go like this:

However, if you are not careful to avoid future financial problems, you might get into the same unhappy situation again.

	HEARTS	CLUBS	DIAMONDS	SPADES
Ace	happiness at home/ news of family/ perhaps a move	success, wealth, and friends	money or a gift	the "death card"/ bad luck or bad news
King	an important man wishes to help, but it leads to a quarrel	a loyal friend and advisor/ beware of a rival	a ruthless and unfaithful man/ a dangerous rival	ambitious, worthless person who can disrupt business or love
Queen	true love for a man/rival for a woman	a fine woman, close friend, or wife	a very jealous and dangerous woman	a cruel, ruthless woman who may appear friendly
Jack	a long-time friend or relative	a kind and thoughtful friend	bad news from a male friend or relative	a lazy, indifferent partner or friend/ no help
10	good luck card/ success and surprise	very good luck card/happiness and good fortune/ a long journey	money matters/ unexpected journey or romance	very unlucky card/ double your trouble
9	wishes fulfilled/ projects successful/ obstacles can be overcome	disagreements and stubbornness can hurt self and hinder success	unexpected money if next to good cards/bad news if next to bad cards	worst card of all: loss of money/ illness/frustration
8	pleasurable event will happen soon	a desire for money/borrowing	courtship/ marriage/travel	false friends right now/watch out
7	plan won't work out/don't rely on friends	luck and success if next to good cards	bad time to take a chance or start something new/ undeserved criticism	sorrow/avoid quarrels until luck changes
6	be careful with your generosity	success in business/seek advice from friends	an unhappy romance	little or no results from your plans
5	indecision/try a new location	marriage to a wealthy mate/ prosperity	luck in business/ happiness in marriage/life filled with good friends	don't be discouraged/ success despite reverses
4	unmarried person/ a late marriage	unreliable friends can cause misfortune and danger	quarrels with friends/renew an old friendship	jealousy/illness/ money problems
3	slow down/apt to make bad decisions	several romances/ long engagement	serious disputes in business or marriage	unhappiness/ disappointment in love/forget the past
2	good fortune greater than expected	do it yourself and don't depend on others	love or friendship may interfere with future success	loss/separation/ change/journey

Adjacent Combinations: 2 of Hearts/10 of Diamonds: *money and romance work well together*
4 of Hearts/Ace of Spades: *big changes to come from a new influence*
9 of Diamonds/7 of Spades: *a new found happiness but not for long*
5 of Hearts/8 of Diamonds: *the money you wish is coming soon*
9 of Diamonds/7 of Spades: *a new-found happiness but not for long*
2 of Clubs/3 of Diamonds: *expect the unexpected*
8 of Clubs/Ace of Spades: *beware of arguments over nothing*

GRAPHOLOGY

For most people their handwriting is a reflection of their personality. The way they write reveals information about their character traits and aptitudes. The study of how to "read" handwriting is called graphology, or sometimes grapho-analysis. Graphology—discovering people's character or personalities by examining their handwriting—is sometimes used by police in doing detective work, by businesses to help select the right person for a job, or by the doctor to help diagnose illnesses in people. But most of the time grapho-analysis is used to entertain and enlighten. It is an intriguing way for people to find out about themselves. However, you must understand that although handwriting may reveal your true character and personality, it cannot tell details of your past or predict your future.

Even without training most of us can look at a person's handwriting and recognize certain basic features that seem to give a general impression of the writer's personality traits. Handwriting that is simple and clearly legible (A) would seem to indicate a person who is dependable and mature. And you might expect a bold and heavy handwriting (B) to reflect a dynamic and determined person. Using the same sort of judgment, a fancy writing style with ornamental letters (C) might indicate a pretentious or eccentric personality, and an illegible, scrawly handwriting (D) is likely indicative of an inconsistent, tense, and impatient type of person. Look at the handwriting styles of several people you know. Can you see similarities between what you know about an individual's personality and his handwriting?

Get a good sample

If you want to be thorough with your analysis, you must use, first of all, a writing sample that is truly representative of the individual's normal writing style. Notes or postcards that have been hurriedly written with words jammed into a limited writing space might prove deceptive when analyzed. A person's handwriting style changes somewhat, not only over a period of years, but also from one time of the day to another. (After all, if a person's personality is reflected in his handwriting, then it is logical to believe that as a person's mood changes so will his handwriting.) It is a person's general, everyday writing that best reveals his true character and that is the kind of writing sample you should use. Ideally, have the subject you wish to analyze write a few sentences and his signature in pen on an unruled letter-sized piece of paper.

Although a signature alone is insufficient to form a reliable analysis, it is quite important in revealing how the writer wishes others to see him. A signature is the writer's "calling card," and represents the personality he wishes to project. In a sense, a person's normal writing will indicate his inner personality (who he really is), and his signature will represent his outer personality (who he wants us to think he is).

Analyze the elements

There are several elements in a person's handwriting that can be analyzed: base line, slant, margins, line, size of letters, shape of words, spacing between lines and words, connected and disconnected words, and the signature. Each element should be analyzed individually in a complete writing sample. Never base a conclusion on the analysis of a single word or letter. Look for trends and characteristics that appear frequently. Not all the characteristics and traits generally applied to a particular writing style necessarily pertain to your writer. A true characteristic will become evident if it shows up repeatedly in several aspects of the writing sample.

Base line

The base line of someone's writing is an imaginary line that follows the bottom or base of the letters in words and sentences, but excludes the lower loop of letters such as *p* or *g*. The straightness or slant of the base line often reveals a person's dominant emotions.

With a pencil lightly draw a line following the bottom edge of each letter across a sample line of writ-

A *in the sky with diamonds*

B *snow will fall all day*

C *to watch an elephant*

D

E *I'm feeling very good except I*

F *a slant doesn't have to go up cell*

G *Still crazy after all these*

ing. A base line that is relatively straight (E) usually indicates an individual who is dependable, consistent, logical, or self-assured; although in some cases it could reveal someone who is dull or rigid.

A base line that generally slants upward (F) may indicate an imaginative, enthusiastic, ambitious, or optimistic personality; whereas, a downward slanted base line (G) could indicate a tense, sensitive, indecisive, or pessimistic person, or possibly someone who is tired or ill.

Slant

The general slant of the letters in handwriting often reveals the degree to which someone expresses emotion. For a right-handed writer a forward slant (H) expresses strong emotions, someone who responds more with emotions than with reason, or, in other words, someone who is ruled by his feelings. A forward slant also indicates a personality that is determined, impulsive, sociable, kindhearted, or possibly restless or opinionated. A forward slant that is extreme (I) may reveal an irritable, argumentative, or excitable person.

A vertical writing style with no slant (J) can be interpreted to reveal a reserved, logical, or self-sufficient personality; or possibly someone lacking in pity.

A person whose writing slants backward (K) may have strong emotions, but logical reasoning is their dominant characteristic. A backward slant might also reveal someone who is introverted, conservative, withdrawn, critical, or arrogant.

For left-handed writers these interpretations of slant should be read in reverse. For example, a forward slant may indicate inhibition and a backward slant, impulsiveness.

Margin

The margin or borders left blank around the writing on a piece of paper indicate the writer's degree of creativity, consistency, and, sometimes, economy. Narrow to nonexistent margins express a thrifty, cautious, narrow-minded personality. Average margins show a practical and consistent attitude, whereas wide margins can be interpreted as a liberal, tolerant, creative, or maybe an impractical personality.

Line

A heavy or light line in writing caused by the pressure of the writer's pen or pencil is a good indication of energy and aggressiveness. Pen pressure is most easily detected in a sample written in fountain pen or felt-tipped pen, but pen pressure does not usually show up well when using a ballpoint pen or pencil. When a selection of pen points is available, most writers will pick the width point that best reflects their personality.

Writers using a heavy line (L) might be considered energetic, aggressive, sensual, impulsive, stubborn, or reliable.

A writer with a light, delicate line (M) is capable of changing emotions or moods more easily than a heavy-line writer. He is likely to be modest, sensitive, reserved, impressionable, timid, lacking initiative, idealistic, or possibly ill.

A medium line (N) reveals someone who is composed, conforming, and even-tempered.

Writing size

The size of most people's writing is very consistent regardless of the

H *We'r going camping Sam*

I *and all we did today was*

J *Let's get going on the*

K *on a clear day you can*

L *sneaking up silently*

M *I don't want to say anything so I—*

N *Father Byrne is a real sport*

O *a person who respond more emotionally*

P *forget the above*

Q *Love is a many splendored thing*

size of the paper they are writing on. Writing size can be a good indicator of the writer's social habits. Small writing (O) shows an analytical mind or someone who is reserved, scholarly, humble, tolerant, or likes to attend to details. Small writing may indicate someone who feels inferior or lacks self-confidence.

Large-size handwriting (P) may indicate adventurousness, spontaneity, generosity, sociability. It may reveal a personality that is hard working, serious, restless, extravagant, materialistic, persuasive, and inattentive to details. Large writing may also show that a person is arrogant, temperamental, conceited, or boastful.

People who are basically conforming and adaptable to situations usually have a medium-sized handwriting (Q).

Letter forms

Writing in which letter forms are sharp and angular (R) denote a per-

son who is persistent, firm, aggressive, perceptive, impatient, or critical.

Writers who use rounded letter forms (S) might be considered pa-

tient, easygoing, kind, sociable, or maybe indecisive.

Another letter form is "square writing" in which the letters are somewhat box-shaped (T). Writers using this style are considered to have inventive and mechanical abilities.

Letter spacing

Letters within a word that are written close together (U) indicate a critical, economical, introverted, and cautious personality.

An extended writing style with wide spaces between letters (V) shows the writer's personality to be liberal, confident, and sociable.

In addition to these samples, which show fundamental characteristics and traits, there are several individual features of letter formation that help indicate a writer's personality with greater accuracy. Clues to personality can be found in the way a writer dots an *i*, writes capital letters, makes pen strokes at the end of a word, and especially how he crosses his *t*'s.

R *the cat show is next.*

S *Please send me your*

T *the next meeting is on January 25th*

U *Please send all the information.*

V *the sky with diamonds*

HOW DO YOU CROSS YOUR T'S?

There are many ways to cross a *t* and each style has a specific interpretation. However, if a writer is inconsistent within a writing sample and crosses *t*'s in several different ways it may just indicate his versatility or originality. It is the most frequently used manner of crossing *t*'s in the sample handwriting that should be used to analyze true character traits.

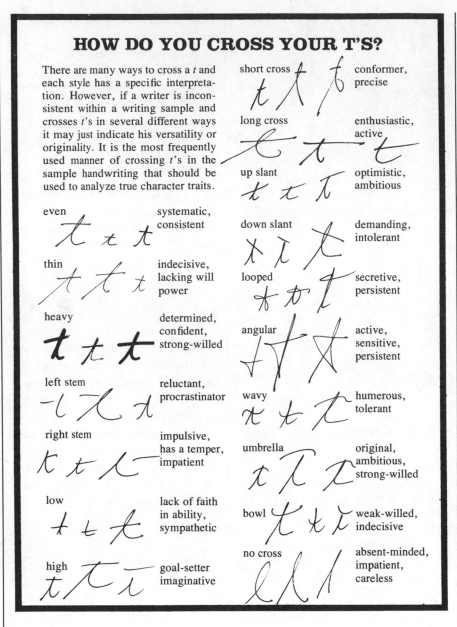

even — systematic, consistent

thin — indecisive, lacking will power

heavy — determined, confident, strong-willed

left stem — reluctant, procrastinator

right stem — impulsive, has a temper, impatient

low — lack of faith in ability, sympathetic

high — goal-setter imaginative

short cross — conformer, precise

long cross — enthusiastic, active

up slant — optimistic, ambitious

down slant — demanding, intolerant

looped — secretive, persistent

angular — active, sensitive, persistent

wavy — humerous, tolerant

umbrella — original, ambitious, strong-willed

bowl — weak-willed, indecisive

no cross — absent-minded, impatient, careless

tunity coming your way.

Use your creative ability to please a friend.

Travel soon but don't chase rainbows.

Contact friends you haven't seen in a long time for an important message.

Do today what you have been putting off.

Be patient, your wish is about to come true.

Whatever you start today may grow in big ways.

Borrow something you really need.

Your reward will be found wrapped in green.

Accept an invitation from a friend today.

Don't complain of the noise when opportunity knocks.

Do it tomorrow, you have made enough mistakes today.

Ingredients

3 eggs
⅛ cup water
½ cup confectioners sugar
½ cup flour
½ tsp. lemon extract

Utensils

mixing bowl
measuring cup and spoons
electric mixer
mixing spoon
griddle
spatula

Tools

plain paper
scissors
pencil or pen

1. First make the fortunes by printing predictions on small strips of paper about ½ × 2 inches (12 × 50mm.).

2. Crack the eggs into a bowl, add the water and beat with the mixer at medium speed for about two minutes.

3. Gradually add the sugar and

The Fortune Cookie

Most Americans have their fortunes told whenever they eat at a Chinese restaurant. The Chinese fortune cookie for dessert has become an American tradition and whether or not we believe the predictions inside the cookie, nearly everyone seems anxious to read theirs.

Here is a recipe for making your own fortune cookies. Make up good or funny fortunes that sound mysterious. Here are a few suggestions to get you started:

There will be good luck for someone you have recently dreamed about.

Someone is planning to give you a big surprise.

Your problems may be mostly imaginary.

The longer you wait, the less chance you have, so do it now.

It is what you learn after you know it all that counts.

Don't hold back on a big oppor-

beat for about ten minutes. Turn off the mixer for now.

4. Gradually add the flour and fold it in with a mixing spoon: gently scoop it down one side of the bowl to the bottom and up the other side until all the flour is well blended.

5. Add the lemon extract and continue to beat the mixture for another two minutes using the electric mixer.

6. Put the flat griddle over a low/medium heat and wait a few minutes while it comes up to temperature. Drop two tablespoons of batter on the griddle and working quickly spread the batter around with the back of the spoon to form a flat pancake about three inches (eight cm.) round.

7. Cook the pancake about one minute on each side or until it becomes golden brown. If the pancake turns dark brown, the heat is too high; if it doesn't turn brown at all the griddle is not hot enough. You will probably have to experiment with your first few cookies to get the cooking temperature just right.

8. Remove the cookie from the griddle, let it cool slightly and while it is still warm and soft, place one of the fortune papers in the center of the cookie circle, fold the cookie over in half with the fortune inside, and bend the two corners of the folded cookie back to make the familiar fortune cookie shape. Put the cookies aside to harden for a half day or so.

Amaze your friends with juggling skills.

JUGGLING

If you have ever watched someone juggling, you probably thought it looked complicated and hard to do. Maybe you have even tried to juggle apples or balls and found it impossible to keep your hands and eyes moving quickly enough to keep the balls from falling. Well, it isn't very difficult to learn to juggle properly, and once your juggling rhythm and coordination become "automatic" you will never forget how to juggle, no matter how long it has been since you last did it.

Jugglers take pride in being able to juggle several kinds of things—

soda cans, eggs, clubs shaped like bowling pins, rolled-up socks, and all kinds of balls. A good juggler can juggle three, four, five, and even more balls or things. However, when you are first learning to juggle it is easiest if you stick to three balls, not too big or too small, and not too heavy or light. Tennis balls will do, but rubber balls like lacrosse balls, Spaldeens®, pinkies, or the rubber balls made for dogs to chew are even better. Some beginning jugglers prefer to use different-colored balls so they can better keep track of the position of each ball.

You can practice your juggling inside or outdoors, but just remember to keep away from anything that might get damaged from falling, flying, rolling balls. Whatever place you choose to practice juggling, be sure it is quiet so you can concentrate easily.

Relaxation first

Before you toss the first ball, take a minute to relax your body. It is almost impossible to learn juggling unless your arms and body are loose and your mind calm and concentrating on what you are doing. Take a few deep breaths, shake your arms and hands, and stretch your neck. Now you are ready to begin juggling.

Don't be too anxious to look like a graceful juggler. First learn and practice each hand-toss and catch exercise until you feel comfortable and can do them well — then go on to the next exercise. If you practice, you may be amazed at how simple it is to juggle.

1. Stand several feet away from a bare wall (which will help you better see the balls in motion). Face the wall squarely and let your arms hang freely at your side. Without changing the position of your upper arms, raise your forearms so they

Fig. 6

Fig. 7

Fig. 8

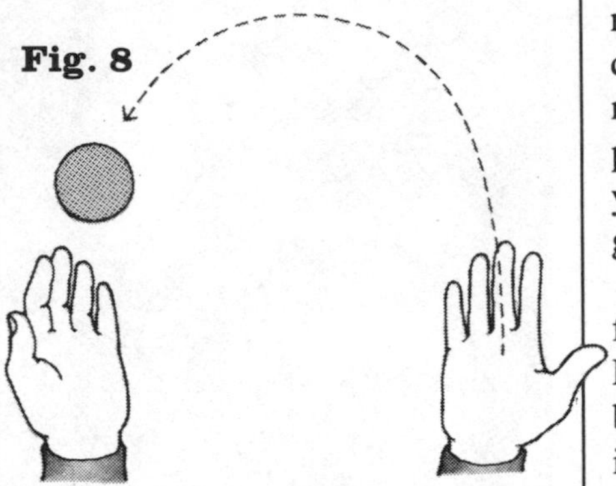

Fig. 9

Fig. 10

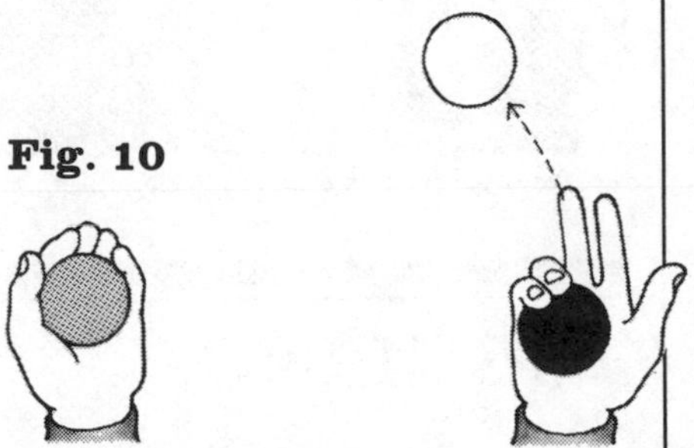

are parallel to the floor, hands in front of you, palms up. You might pretend that you are carrying a tray-load of dishes on your arms. Now make a cup with each hand as

though you were trying to hold water. This is the basic juggling position for beginning and ending all juggling moves, Fig 6 .

2. Standing in the basic position, hold one ball loosely in your right hand. Try to "pop" the ball up out of your hand by quickly flattening out your palm, spreading out your fingers and raising the palm of your hand all in one motion, Fig 7. You can snap your wrist a bit to give the ball some added energy, but try not to move your arm. After each pop of the ball try to catch it in the same hand — with your hand cupped again. The ball should go straight up about as high as your nose or forehead, then straight down so that you don't have to move your arm to catch it. Try popping and catching a ball using your right and left hands until you get good at it.

3. Now try popping the ball from one hand to the other, Fig. 8. Don't change the way you pop the ball, just tip your hand very slightly in the direction that you want the ball to go. A good toss should go up, pass in front of your eyes, and down into your other hand. Practice until you hardly have to move your hands to either throw or catch the ball.

4. Before learning to do a three-ball toss you will need to practice holding, throwing, and catching with two balls in one hand. Hold one ball in your right hand in the basic position. Keeping that ball in the center of your palm, open out your thumb, index finger, and middle finger and put a second ball in your hand resting on those three fingers; this hand position is called a "basket," Fig. 9. Try a basket with your other hand. Practice until the basket feels comfortable in both hands.

5. Now you should be ready to use three balls. Hold a ball in each

hand in the basic position. These balls are called "riders" and for now they are going to stay in your hands while you toss the third ball back and forth between the basket of each hand, Fig. 10. When you pop the ball while holding a rider you can't open all your fingers as you did before (or you may lose the rider ball), so you will need to use a little more wrist and forearm action. Catching the ball in a basket is a little more difficult than throwing it from a basket. As you practice remember to stay relaxed and keep your mind on what you are doing. Is the popped ball passing in front of your face? And are your forearms parallel to the ground?

6. The next step to learn is the two-toss exchange. This exercise is the most difficult so far, but once you can do it you will begin to look and feel like a real juggler. Start with two balls in your right hand and cup the third ball in your left hand. Throw the second ball from the basket of your right hand over to your left hand. Watch the ball go up, pass in front of your face and start downward. But before the ball lands in your left hand, pop the ball from your left hand up and over to your right hand, Fig. 11. Catch the first ball thrown in your left hand, then catch the second ball thrown in the basket of your right hand. The rider ball in your right palm hasn't moved, and you should end up just as you started with two balls in your right hand and one in your left, Fig. 12. Don't be discouraged if at first you have trouble doing the two-toss exchange. Throwing and catching to the proper rhythm is the clue to good juggling. The rhythm you want for the two-toss exchange is "throw . . . throw/catch . . . catch" in three even beats. Try saying the rhythm out loud as you juggle and your hands will follow what you say.

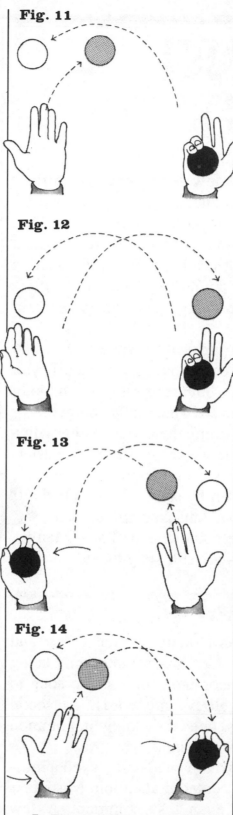

Fig. 11

Fig. 12

Fig. 13

Fig. 14

7. The final step in learning to juggle is keeping all three balls moving continuously in a "cascade." That is the juggling action you are probably most used to see-

ing. Start with a two-toss exchange but just before your right hand catches the ball tossed from your left hand, pop the third ball from your right palm over to your left hand, Fig. 13. Now just keep up the action back and forth and you will be juggling, Fig. 14. The rhythm now should be "throw . . . throw/catch . . . catch/throw/catch . . . throw/catch . . . and so on. While juggling a cascade you will be popping the balls from your palms and you only need a basket to start the juggle and end it.

As you practice the cascade juggle here are some hints to make it easier. Do the juggle slower than you think you should by waiting until you are just ready to catch a ball in a hand before popping the ball you are holding in that hand. If you have trouble with the balls colliding in air, try throwing the balls from your hand moved slightly in then quickly move your hand back out for the catch. In that way the thrown balls will take a different path than the balls coming down for a catch. Most jugglers learn the rhythm of moving their hands slightly back and forth in a small circle for throwing and catching.

Once you have mastered the cascade you can try juggling other objects and doing it in different positions. Try juggling while sitting, kneeling, walking, going up and down stairs, and even lying on your back. When you become a really good juggler you can add some tricks to your juggling routine. You might throw a ball from behind your back, under your leg, or catch one of the balls under your chin. If you practice enough you will become almost automatic without having to concentrate on what you are doing. It won't be long before you can show-off to audiences. You can even teach your friends how to do it.

MAKING MUSIC

As America grew from a few settlements to a strong nation, the people were encouraged and spirited by the words and melodies of their popular music. Music can be more than entertainment—it can bolster courage, ease a pain, help lessen a fear, increase a hope. In Early America life was difficult and often frightening, but the settlers managed to survive. Perhaps singing songs gave them some needed hope.

To sing a song or play a musical instrument was like having a friend to keep you company. It was nice if you could sing or play music well, but the spirit of the melody and the comfort of the words were what really counted. For every tedious job that needed doing there was a song with a melody and a message that made the work seem easier. Even the latest news and gossip of Colonial America was carried from town to town by song. These songs of disasters, romances, Indian attacks, cures, and the ways of pioneer life, were known as ballads. Many of these American folk songs are still sung today.

Memorizing music and lyrics

Songs of Early America were rarely written down and often they were learned as best as possible after only being heard once. So it was not uncommon for a single song to have several versions of melody and words. At social gatherings people often sang songs they knew in common and swapped new verses between them.

Anyone in the Colonies who owned and played a musical instrument was often the center of attention. Musicians were rare and instruments even less common. A few settlers had brought bagpipes or a Jew's harp with them, but most early musical instruments were handmade by the musician who intended to play them. Most popular was the fiddle (which may have been due, in part, to the belief that

fiddle playing frightened away wolves). The banjo and dulcimer, true American inventions, were also popular instruments in the Colonies.

Shall we dance?

When listening to a song with a strong beat, the urge to dance comes naturally to most people. Dancing is fun and a great way to exercise your whole body. But social dancing in America was not always as lively and acceptable as it is today.

In Early America there were of course no radios, or records to play music, and very few farmers played musical instruments. Dancing was usually limited to certain social gatherings and celebrations where a hired musician or a talented neighbor might play the fiddle. After a busy day of corn-husking or barn-raising, it was common for all the helping neighbors to stay around and dance a Virginia reel or the Molly Brooks.

Wealthy Colonial Americans might be invited to a dance at the governor's home where they would politely dance to the music of a string quartet. The black slaves of southern plantations went to few celebrations but danced anyway, doing a "clog" or high-stepping "cakewalk" to the tune of a homemade banjo or the rhythm of clapping hands. In certain religious communities the popular dances of the day were considered sinful, and fiddle players were thought to be agents of the devil; the people still danced, however, but in their own less active style and usually accompanied by a singer.

A fife and drum corps dressed in clothes from the days of the revolution.

MUSIC FOR ALL OCCASIONS

America has had its own special kinds of music and occasions for music listening. When we think of our musical history we think of a fife and drum playing patriotic tunes, accompanying soldiers into battle; gospel hymns and spiritual songs conveying the messages and morals of the Bible; songs of southern plantation life; Civil War bands playing military marches; Sunday concerts in the park; piano recitals of the late 1800's.

Twentieth-century American music continues to both celebrate and represent the varied attitudes of the people who sing and play it. Whether you hum a tune, whistle while you work, sing in a chorus, take music lessons at school, play in a band, or just tap your finger or foot to a tune on the radio, you are making music, and probably making your day a little better. And whether you prefer folk, classical, soft rock, hard rock, jazz, disco, rhythm and blues, country, or electronic music, your music will continue to influence an ever-changing America.

MOTHER GOOSE

Nearly everyone has heard a Mother Goose rhyme—*Little Miss Muffet, There Was an Old Woman, Jack Be Nimble, Patty Cake, Little Boy Blue, Rub-a-Dub-Dub*, and so on. Mother Goose is really the pretend writer of this collection of rhymes, and although the rhymes are English in their origin, the name is thought to have come from France. But surprisingly, there really was an American Mother Goose as well and she lived in Boston during the late 1600's and early 1700's.

Elizabeth Goose was the wife of Isaac Goose and they had a daughter Ann who married Thomas Fleet, a printer. Ann and Thomas Fleet, had six children and Mrs. Goose spent nearly all her time entertaining her grandchildren with silly songs she had learned as a child. The rhymes of her songs were not always original, and strangely —by coincidence—many of her simple rhymes had long been known as children's "goose tales."

However, Mrs. Goose was a loud and boisterous woman who also could not sing very well, and her songs for children often dealt with tales of murder, grave robbing, choking, punishment, and other morbid subjects. After a while the children's father, Mr. Fleet, became annoyed at the woman and her songs, but rather than insult his mother-in-law, Fleet thought he would embarrass her by publishing a book of the silly songs and rhymes.

The book was called *Mother Goose's Melodies*, and contrary to what Mr. Fleet had hoped, the book of songs became an immediate success with both young children and grown-ups. The tune for one of the rhymes, *Lucy Locket Lost Her Pocket* became so popular that it was adopted as a patriotic song of the American Revolution with new words that went, "Yankee Doodle went to town..." You probably know the tune already, so try to sing it now with the words to the original rhyme:

Lucy Locket lost her pocket
Kitty Fischer found it
Nothing in it, nothing in it
But the binding round it.

JUG BANDS

The jug band is an American invention but no one is exactly sure just when or where in America these bands began. During the 1920's a record company asked a country jug band who played snappy rhythms to make a record. The band became a hit and featured a long jug solo which attracted attention. Soon people all over America (but mostly in the South) were listening to the country music of groups like the Memphis Jug Band, Cris Cannon and his Jug Stompers, and the Dixieland Jug Blowers.

There is no typical jug band or jug band music—almost any song can be played in the style. And the style depends on what instruments the band has to play music with: Jug band instruments include nearly any "real" instrument or any household object that can sound a note, beat, click, honk, tap, thump, or buzz. Jug band musicians have been known to play their music on washboards, hubcaps, home radiators, combs, cans, cowbells, spoons, whistles, and bicycle pumps, as well as the more traditional instruments for melody including the banjo, guitar, kazoo, harmonica, and fiddle.

The one necessity

But the one instrument that every jug band has is, of course, a crockery jug. As legend has it, it was common in the late nineteenth century for farmers of the southern states to get together and spend idle time playing music. As they played and sang the farmers got thirsty and the usual refreshment was moonshine whisky kept handy in a crockery jug. As the musicians played they also drank from the jug, and in fun (and to show the others how much he had drunk), someone would "play" the jug by blowing notes to a beat across the jug opening. The emptier the jug, the deeper the note. In time the jug became a regular instrument in a country band.

Jug bands are no longer common to popular music, but there are still plenty of jug bands playing in America, and you can probably still find a few jug band records at the music store. You might also get together with a few friends some afternoon and organize your own jug band. If someone can play a real instrument, that will help, but it is not absolutely necessary. As long as everyone can hum the same tune your band will sound fine.

Playing the Jug

You might as well begin by learning to play the instrument that gives the jug band its name. A crockery jug will certainly look the best, but any jug or bottle with a skinny neck and opening will make a good instrument. Large soda bottles, ketchup bottles, cooking-oil bottles or laundry jugs will also work fine. The larger the jug, the lower the note it will sound, and vice-versa.

To play a note, hold the bottle or

...FOOM!

jug with the rim straight up and against your puckered lips. Your bottom lip should be pressed against the side of the neck and be flush with the opening. Your top lip should arch over the opening a bit. Now blow across the opening, but don't blow too hard; about the way you normally exhale is perfect. Keep adjusting your lips slightly until you get a deep vibrating note. After some practice you will learn exactly how to pucker and place your lips to play any jug or bottle.

To play with the jug band just blow a note in time to each beat of the music. If you want to change the note for a particular song, either use another jug or fill your jug partially with water.

Making a Washtub Bass

The second most common instrument in a jug band, after the jug of course, is a washtub bass. The bass with its deep twangy sound adds a distinctive emphasis to the music, but unlike the one-note jug, you can actually play a melody on the washtub bass.

Materials

washtub—it is best to use a large, round, metal washtub. Washtubs were once very common in American homes, but in recent times they have been almost completely replaced by sinks, bathtubs, and automatic washing machines. However, you might still find one in your basement or maybe at your grandparents' home. You might also buy a new washtub at the hardware store. As a last resort you can look for one at a local garage sale.

Although a washtub will give the clearest, richest sounds, in a pinch you can also make a bass using a metal or plastic bucket, a large dishpan, or even a sturdy corrugated box. These containers probably won't sound as good as a metal washtub but they do work well enough for practice or an impromptu jam session.

old broom handle—a wooden closet rod, or a strong, straight branch will do for the neck of the bass. The exact length of the handle doesn't matter, but when it rests on top of the washtub, the handle should be about as high as your head. If the handle is longer or shorter it could make playing a bit more difficult.

strong nylon cord—or heavy fishing line will make a good bass string. A length of package twine or other cord may sound fine on the bass, but rough cord can make your fingers sore while playing. If you do use a rough cord, wear a glove on your plucking hand.

large washer—or some other object to tie to one end of the string.

Tools
hammer
nail
pocketknife or small saw

1. To assemble the instrument, first turn the washtub upside down and hammer a hole in the bottom center using a fat nail. The bottom is now the top of your washtub. Now thread one end of the cord through the hole and tie a washer, bolt, nut, twig, or anything to it that will prevent the cord from pulling back through the hole.

2. Cut or whittle a small notch in one end of the broom handle or whatever you are using for the neck so that the rim of the washtub fits in this groove. Also cut or whittle a groove in the neck near the top.

3. Stand the neck on the rim of the washtub and lean the neck slightly toward the center of the tub. Hold the neck in that position and tie the free end of the cord tightly around the groove at the top of the neck so that the string is taut. This step is sometimes easier if you have a helper hold the neck while you do the tying. The washtub bass is now complete and ready to play.

Position the tub on the floor so you are standing directly behind the neck. Put one foot on the washtub rim to keep it from slipping, hold the top of the neck in one hand, and pluck the cord with your other hand.

You can raise or lower the pitch of the notes you play by pulling back on the neck to tighten the cord or slacking it slightly. With a little practice you will figure out just how much to tighten or loosen the cord to get the notes you want.

Some washtub bass players use one hand to hold the string tightly against the neck while also keeping the string taut. By moving this hand a bit up and down the neck, the playing part of the string is made shorter or longer so that the other hand can get the notes they want.

Practice playing different notes on the washtub bass and try to play a steady rhythm. Even though you may be able to play a melody, most of the time a jug band bass player plucks out rhythm or bass notes that harmonize with the music being played by the other instruments. Practice some more, and play along to a record on the radio plucking the string in time to the music. As you play, "work" the neck to find what notes sound good with the tune being played. When you have finished playing leave everything connected and just rest the neck across the washtub.

Playing the Washboard

Not only have washtubs almost disappeared since the invention of the modern washing machine, but another popular jug band instrument, the washboard, is fast becoming extinct.

In nearly every jug band song there is the distinctive "ra-ta-ta-tat" sound of thimbled fingers running up and down the washboard slats. Some washboard players add cymbals, bells, and other noisemakers to the top of their washboard so they can make different accent sounds now and then.

The only trouble with learning to play the washboard today is finding one. A few hardware stores still sell washboards, or you might ask your grandparents if they have one stored away somewhere. As a substitute you can try using a wooden, slatted window shutter. Small indoor shutters are about the right size, but an outdoor shutter will need to be cut down to a size that is manageable.

Make yourself comfortable

The easiest way to play the washboard is sitting down. Hold the washboard upside down (legs up), resting in your lap and against one shoulder—just as if you were giving it a hug. If your arms are long enough, you should be able to play the washboard slats with both hands. If the washboard is too big for you, just rest it flat on your lap and play it that way.

Some washboard players prefer to stand while playing and they often wear the washboard hung around the neck by a strap. You might want to try that, but don't use a skinny cord or string that might make your neck hurt. It is best to use an old belt or a piece of rope, adjusting its length so the washboard hangs just below your shoulders and against your chest.

To play the washboard, just run your fingernails up and down the

slats in time to the music. Or even better, put sewing thimbles on your playing fingers. After some practice you might get a little fancy by playing with both hands or just your thumbs; and doing a variety of finger runs, taps, and beats.

Playing the Musical Comb

One of the musicians in the jug band needs to play the actual melody of the song rather than just the beat. If you can hum a tune, you can play the melody on a musical comb. The comb player can also be the leader of the band—he hums the tune and the rest of the band follows.

Materials
fine-tooth comb
waxed paper or any other thin paper
tape (optional)

Making a musical comb is simple. Just wrap a piece of waxed paper (or any thin paper) once around a fine-tooth pocket comb. The paper should cover most of the comb and the middle fold should cover the ridge of the comb teeth. You can tape the waxed paper in place or just hold it with your fingers.

Now hold the comb loosely between your lips with the teeth of the comb pointing up, and hum out a tune. Be sure to hum through your mouth and not your nose. (Just to be sure, try holding your nose closed for a moment while you hum.) Your humming causes the paper and comb teeth to vibrate and sound very much like a kazoo.

Another way to play the musical comb is by singing the tune in "do-do's" and "doodle-oodle's" instead of humming. Try it like this, "do-do-doodle-oodle-do-do-doodle—oodle-do-do." For prac-

tice, you can play the comb along to the music of a record or the radio. To get somewhat different sounds from the musical comb, try using different types of paper over the comb. Even aluminum foil and plastic food wrap will work.

Playing the Spoons

Country bluegrass and jug bands often have at least one spoon player whose clickety-clack solo parts impress audiences as a well-practiced art form. The spoon player clicks his spoons on his knees, hands, chest, feet, head—and then on nearly everything on the stage. It looks so simple and sounds so good that many would-be spoon players are eager to go home and bang out a tune with the family silverware. There are only a few top-notch spoon players left in America and we certainly could use a few more.

Here's how to do it

1. Find two not-so-good tablespoons or soup spoons (do not use the guest silverware). Put the handle of one spoon between the first and middle fingers, and the handle of the other spoon between the middle and third fingers. Arrange the spoons so that the rounded bottoms of the spoons face each other, Fig. 15. Both handles should be tucked loosely in the palm of your hand.

2. Now, holding the spoons in your fingers loosely enough so the spoon bowls are slightly apart, slap the pair of spoons together in the palm of your other hand. Do it a few more times and try to slap out a steady rhythm: clickety, clickety, clickety, click clickety, clickety, clickety, click. The secret of good spoon playing is not holding the spoons too loose or too tight.

3. Once you get the rhythm try a hand-and-knee spoon-slap. Put

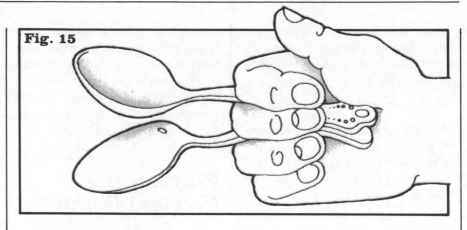

Fig. 15

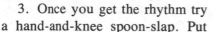

Sing out while accompanying yourself on the spoons.

your free hand between your knees with the palm facing one knee and slap the pair of spoons between palm and knee. This system lets you make up varied and interesting rhythms. Now turn on the radio or put on a record to play along to, and beat the spoons against your foot, the chair, or whatever.

Playing the Tin Can, Flowerpot Wastepaper Basket, Cooking Pot, and Cake Pan

Some kids are naturally good at tapping out a rhythm, using anything that may be handy at the moment. You probably have seen someone tap out a tune on the table with a pencil, maybe play the wastepaper basket with their fingers, or even jingle pocket change to the beat of a song. A friend who is a "born" drum player might like to join your jug band.

But instead of a drum set to beat on, a jug band drummer often uses cans he finds or other drum-sounding objects. Look around to see what "drums" you might have. Try large tin cans like the ones coffee or juice drinks come in. See what sounds you can get from an

GLONK

RING

BanG

JUICE

RaP

empty flowerpot, cooking pot, cake pan or even an old hubcap from a car. Tap each one with your fingers and a pencil "drumstick" to see which make the most pleasant sounds. Usually, the larger the object, the easier it is to play, and the louder the sound it will make.

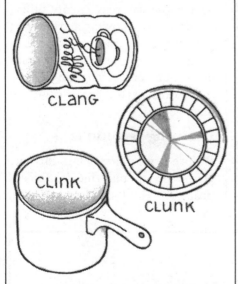

CLanG

CLink

CLunk

If you use a tin can, remove one end completely with a can opener. Experiment with several pots to see if they sound better resting on your lap or being held. Can you get different sounds from the same object by playing it in different spots? What is the sound like when you beat one of these drums with your palms or wearing sewing thimbles on your fingers?

Select the drum sound you like best and practice tapping out rhythms using different drum sounds combined. Now you are ready to play along with the jug band. But do remember that drums can often be the loudest instruments in the band so try not to drown out the music of the other players.

MUSICAL GLASSES

During the 1700's one of the popular musical pastimes for everyone in the family was the playing of musical glasses. Lovely sounding musical notes could be played by simply rubbing a wet finger around the rim of a drinking glass partially filled with water. Nearly any song could be played with several glasses, each tuned to a different note.

It was actually Benjamin Franklin who popularized musical glasses by inventing a musical instrument he called the "armonica." Franklin's musical contraption used bowls of different sizes, a trough of water, and a foot pedal to spin the bowls. As the player pumped on the pedal he put his finger to the rim of a spinning bowl to produce a note.

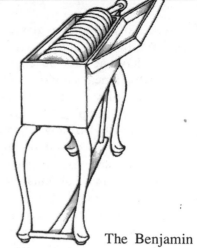

The Benjamin Franklin armonica became quite the rage among America's wealthier families; most people made their own simpler version using just glasses and water.

Materials

8 drinking glasses
cookie sheet or towel
pencil or spoon

You can make your own set of musical glasses the same way. First you will need to borrow several drinking glasses (they can be returned when you are through). Find a messy play place where any spilled water won't cause damage. The kitchen counter is usually convenient. You might also put the glasses on a cookie sheet or a spread-out towel. You can use any kind and size of drinking glass but it must be made of glass and not plastic. The thinner the glass, the nicer the tone

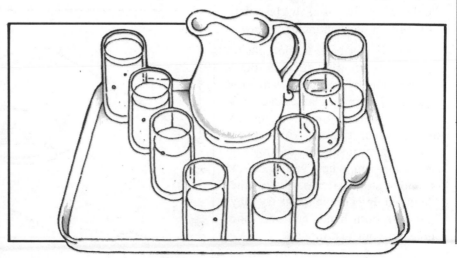

will be. Any number of glasses will do, but to play most songs you should have at least an eight-note scale which means eight glasses.

1. Test-play each of the empty glasses by snapping it with your fingernail or by striking it gently at the rim with a pencil or spoon. Every type and size of glass will produce its own particular sound. Replace any glass that does not produce a clear, one-note tone.

2. Now take one of the glasses and play it over and over again while slowly filling it with water from another glass or pitcher. The more water you pour in the glass the deeper the tone it plays.

3. Now line all the glasses up in a row. First fill the glass on the left end nearly completely full of water and tap it to be sure it sounds a clear, deep note. That glass will be the first note or "do" in the scale. Now pour water into the second glass while tapping it until it is tuned to a clear "re" and the second note in the scale.

4. Continue filling each of the musical glasses, one at a time in order, tuning them up the scale, "do-re-mi-fa-so-la-ti-do."

Play up and down the scale a few times with your pencil or spoon and adjust the water level in any glass the note of which seems a bit flat or sharp. If you do not want to tune the glasses to any particular scale, then just fill each glass until it sounds a pleasant note.

Now if you have a good ear for music, try to play or pick out a simple tune by tapping the musical glasses. For some glasses each note you play will continue to sound for a second or two. If you want a shorter note, just put your finger on the glass rim when you want the sound to stop. After you have practiced playing simple songs try playing with both hands and add more notes to your instrument.

YOU CAN PLAY THE HARMONICA

For over one hundred years, the harmonica (mouth organ, or pocket piano as it is sometimes called) has been one of America's most popular musical instruments. United States presidents Abraham Lincoln, Calvin Coolidge, and Dwight Eisenhower all played the harmonica; and so do Bob Dylan, Mick Jagger, and Stevie Wonder.

Most musical instruments take a lot of learning and practice before you can play music and a good-sounding instrument can also be quite expensive to own. A harmonica, however, is an exception. A professional-quality harmonica can be bought for just a few dollars and you can play your first song on it in an hour or so after you get it. Of course, the more you practice and the more songs you know, the better harmonica player you will become.

Choose your harmonica

When you go to buy a harmonica you will probably find several different types and sizes to choose from. The most common and simplest to play (and what you should ask for) is a ten-hole diatonic harmonica in the key of C. A few harmonicas are made of plastic but most are metal and wood because these materials produce a nicer tone and last longer. Don't be tempted, for now, by harmonicas that have more holes, changeable keys, or other special features—even though some don't cost much more than a simple instrument.

Take a close look at your harmonica to see how it works. Inside each hole there are two reeds—one on top and one on the bottom. When you blow into a hole the air rushing past one of the reeds causes it to vibrate and sound a musical note. When you suck or draw air out of the same hole the other reed sounds a different note. So every hole will give you two notes—one for blow and one for draw; if you have a ten-hole harmonica that means you can play twenty different notes. Try blowing and drawing into the holes to hear what they sound like. (Make sure you don't chew gum or eat anything at the same time or the reeds could be damaged.)

Learning technique

Before trying anything further, learn how to play the instrument properly. Hold the harmonica in

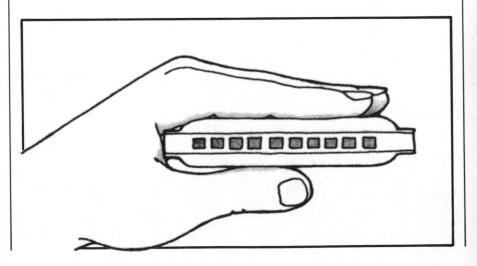

your left hand, resting it on your thumb with one or two fingers on top. The low-note holes should be to your left and the higher-note holes to the right. If the holes are numbered, the harmonica will be in the correct position when the numbers are facing up. Be sure that your thumb and finger are not blocking any holes.

Hold the harmonica up to your mouth, pucker your lips, and blow gently into one of the holes. Don't blow too hard, just normal breathing in and out is fine. Don't be too concerned if at first you have trouble blowing a single note at a time and instead play a chord of two or several notes. With practice you will be able to block off the holes you don't need with your tongue. For now, just try to blow or draw in

on the hole you want. A note will last for as long as you blow or draw it. For a short note try a short breath and for a long note use a longer breath.

Practice what you have learned by playing an eight-note scale (do-re-me-fa-so-la-ti-do). Start with the fourth hole from the left and blow. For the next note draw in on the same hole. Now move your lips to the fifth hole—blow, then draw in. Go to the sixth hole, blow and draw, then to complete the scale play the seventh hole, but this time draw first and then blow. Practice the scale going both up and down the notes.

By now you should be ready to play a song. If you are good at "picking out" simple tunes, then go ahead, or you might try the fol-

lowing songs to get started. The numbers indicate which hole to play and the arrows tell you whether to blow or draw: an up arrow is blow and a down arrow is draw. The length of the arrow tells you how long to hold the note: long arrow, long note; short arrow, short note.

PUSH-BUTTON TELEPHONE SONGS

It is not often that a totally new kind of musical instrument is invented; however, in the 1960's and 70's several musicians began to experiment with instruments that made music electronically. Today there are electronic music "synthesizers" that duplicate the sounds of different musical instruments as well as making unique sounds of their own. You don't have to wait for the future to play electronic music, however, if you already have a push-button telephone in your house.

Each telephone button, when pressed, plays an electronic tone that you can hear when listening at the receiver. Once you figure out which musical note each button plays you can then push-button a simple tune on the telephone.

A limited audience

To play the musical telephone, however, you must first call up someone, and they must stay on the line while you (or they) push buttons. (The two of you can play a duet.) If you just picked up the receiver and started playing music the buttons would still sound tones but you might accidentally dial a real phone number.

If absolutely no one you know is

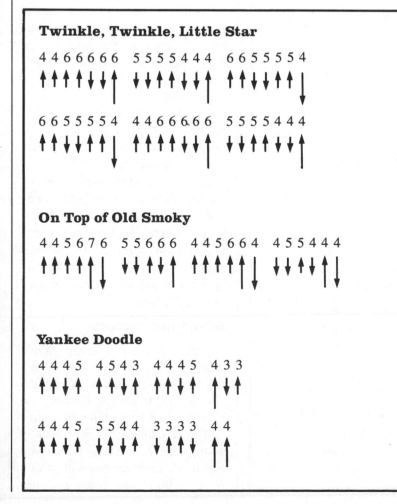

home (or willing to listen) you might call one of the telephone numbers that give the time or weather and practice your push-button songs while listening to the recorded message.

Now here are a few push-button telephone tunes to get you started.

Mary Had a Little Lamb

6 2 1 2 6 6 6
Mar-y had a lit-tle lamb

2 2 2 6 6 6
Lit-tle lamb, lit-tle lamb

6 2 1 2 6 6 6
Mar-y had a lit-tle lamb

6 2 2 6 2 1
Its fleece was white as snow.

Happy Birthday

1 1 2 1 # 6
Hap-py birth-day to you

1 1 2 1 # 3
Hap-py birth-day to you

1 1 # # 8 4 1
Hap-py birth-day dear (na-me)

6 4 2 1
Hap-py birth-day to you

Old MacDonald

6 6 6 7 8 8 7
Old Mac-Don-ald had a farm

9 9 0 0 4
Ee-i-ee-i-oh

4 6 6 6 7 8
And on that farm he had

8   7
some chicks

9 9 0 0 4
Ee-i-ee-i-oh

Swanee River

3   2   1 3 2
Way down up-on the

1   #   4 5
Swan-ee Riv-er

6   1 4 2
Far, far a-way

3   2   1   3 2
That's where my heart is

1   #   1 5
turn-ing ev-er

6   5   4 2 2   4
That's where the old folks stay

America

5   5   6   1 5 9
My coun-try 'tis of thee

0   0 9 0 8 4
Sweet land of lib-er-ty

8   4 2 4
Of thee I sing

Oh Susannah

4 8 6   6   9 # 8 7
Oh I come from Al-a-bam-a

7   8   # # 8 1   8
With my ban-jo on my knee

4 4   8 6   6   9 6 7
I am going to Louis-i-an-a

8   6   6   0 0 4
My true love for to see

By the beginning of the twentieth century dancing had become an accepted social activity in America and people organized special occasions just for dancing. Saturday night became dance night as couples romantically waltzed around the floor to the music of a hired dance band. Dancing quickly became America's favorite social pastime.

Styles and fads in music and dance were changed quickly. Ragtime music and jazz became popular and dances like the fox trot or the turkey trot were introduced to keep pace with the livelier beat.

Dance halls opened in many cities where for a ten-cent admission anyone could spend the evening dancing to the music of a band. Restaurants cleared out back rooms for dancing and hired a band. Schools began to hold dances and proms. And with the invention of the phonograph and the radio, people could dance right in their own living rooms.

One of the dance innovations of the 1930's was the marathon contest. The object was to see how long a couple could continue dancing with only a few hours rest each night. The all-time champions lasted twenty-four weeks, five days or 4,152½ hours.

Brand-new dances

America went dance crazy. While polite society continued to do the fox trot everyone else danced the Charleston, the black bottom, the shimmy, and later on the jitterbug.

The talk of the day was usually about what new daring dance you had tried. Latin dances with strong new rhythms and strange names

In the 1970's America has come back to dance steps. Disco dancing is the latest fad as partners "bump" and "hustle" their way around the floor. What next? Just keep dancing and find out.

Tap Dancing

Tap dancing is a uniquely American art. American blacks were the true inventors of the tap dance, but it quickly became an all-American favorite and nearly every stage entertainer would do a tap dance number as part of his act. Many variations of the dance step were developed and a few dancers became famous for their original tap dance specialties.

A Virginia reel is still fun to dance today.

like the tango, samba, conga, and cha-cha became popular and so did dance lessons to keep pace with the new intricate dance steps. At some dance studios that spread across America it was even possible to sign up for a lifetime of lessons so your dance steps would always be in style.

During the 1950's America invented rock and roll music and the lindy dance to go with it. By the 1960's America was dancing the twist, the stroll, the chicken, the fish, and the watusi, and suddenly "single dancing" became the rage. You no longer needed a partner to dance. Dancing became more than just foot steps, you needed to know "body steps" as well. In dances like the frug, the jerk, or the mashed potato, body style was much more important than what your feet did.

It is not difficult to learn to tap dance, but it does require some pretty fast footwork and a bit of arm swinging. Beginners should do everything slowly at first and then gradually build up speed. You learn basic tap steps and then create dance "routines" using a combination of these steps. One tap routine you can easily learn—and it has a great-sounding tap rhythm—is the waltz clog. You will need to learn three tap steps to do the waltz clog and then practice some more to put the three steps together for the dance routine. But first—do you have a pair of tap shoes?

Tap shoes you can make

Tap dancers wear special shoes that have metal cleats or taps on the heel and toe. These cleats give the dance its sound, and you have to learn to get separate tap sounds from the balls and heels of your feet. After you have learned to tap-dance you may want to buy a pair of tap shoes or have a shoemaker put taps on a spare pair of your own shoes. In the meantime you can make your own tap shoes using common thumbtacks and flat metal washers.

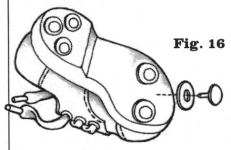

Fig. 16

Select a pair of your shoes that *doesn't* have very thin or worn-out soles and heels. Place a washer over the spike on a thumbtack and push the tack into the heel of a shoe near the back. Put two or three more such "taps" in the heel and three or four more between the ball and the toe of the shoe, Fig. 16. Now do the same to the other shoe. Walking in your tap shoes on a hard surface will help drive in the tacks, but the tacks can easily be pried out anytime you like, and the shoes returned to normal. It is *not* a good idea to try out your tap shoes on a good wood floor—the taps might scratch. Use not-so-good wood floors, tiled floors and concrete surfaces. All will give a nice tap sound.

A word of encouragement

You will learn how to do the waltz clog. To do this routine, you must first master three steps—the slap, the shuffle, and the ball change. But first some general advice and encouragement. Learn to do one step at a time. Practice each step eight times on one foot, then eight times on the other. When the tap step no longer feels awkward, try doing it four times on each foot while counting a steady rhythm—one-two-three-four, one-two-three-four. Once you have the rhythm, try doing the step to music. You can hum, sing, or play music. Two easy-to-tap-to songs are "Tea for Two" and "East Side-West Side."

An important point to work on is switching from one foot to the other while still keeping time. Good arm movements always add a touch of grace to tap dancing and sometimes help balance. For practice, put your hands on your hips or hold your arms straight, and out slightly from your side with palms down. Stay relaxed and keep on the balls of your feet.

Learning a new dance will feel strange at first, but as you practice you will get faster and better. In three or four days you should be able to do a pretty decent waltz clog.

The slap

1. Place your feet side-by-side with your weight on the left foot and hands on hips, or out to the side. Bend your right knee slightly and pick up your right foot so it is a bit behind you, Fig. 17.

2. Swing your right foot forward, toe pointed down, and momentarily "brush" the floor with your toe making a tap sound.

3. Continue to swing your foot forward a bit more, then slap your toe against the floor making another tap, Fig. 18. Swing your foot back to its raised starting position without tapping. To get the rhythm, say to yourself, "tap, tap, swing back, tap, tap, swing back, tap, tap, swing back, tap, tap, swing back." Now switch feet and do a left-foot slap. Try to keep your eyes straight ahead and not stare down at your feet.

The shuffle

1. Start with your feet in the same position as you did for the

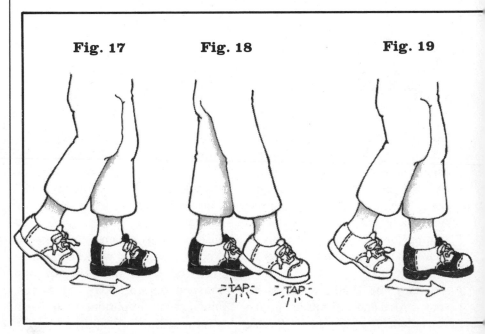

Fig. 17   **Fig. 18**   **Fig. 19**

slap: right foot raised and a bit behind you, Fig. 19. Swing your right foot forward, toe pointed down, so that your toe brushes the floor for a moment making a tap and continue the swing a bit more forward and up, Fig. 20.

2. Now swing your foot backward again, brushing the floor with your toe for a tap, Fig. 21, and bring your foot back to the starting position. The rhythm for the shuffle is "tap, tap, and pause."

The ball change

This step involves nothing more than shifting your weight from the ball of one foot to that of the other giving a tap, tap.

1. Standing with your feet together and your knees slightly bent, raise your right foot and bring it slightly behind your left with your right toe pointing out a bit to the right.

2. Put your right toe down with all the weight on the ball making a tap, Fig. 22. At the same time, lift your left foot. Land on the ball of your left foot and shift your weight to the left foot. Now repeat the step. First step to the side with your

right foot making a tap, bring your left toe behind your right foot making a tap and raising your right foot, Fig. 23. Again, the rhythm is "tap, tap, and pause, tap, tap, and pause."

The waltz clog

Once you have practiced all the steps on both right and left feet and can do them quickly without having always to think what your feet are doing, you are ready to try a routine, the waltz clog. To do the waltz clog you repeat the three steps you just learned as follows: slap, shuffle, ball change; slap, shuffle, ball change.

Starting with your right foot, do a slap step, shift your weight to your right foot, then do a shuffle with your left foot, then with the weight on your left foot do a right foot ball change. Now your left foot is positioned to do a left foot slap, right foot shuffle, left foot ball change, and so on.

Try to get the rhythm by counting, Then add the music.

The waltz clog is just the beginning. By adding a few more simple steps like heel hops, turns,

struts, digs, toe points and scoot backs, you can do all kinds of exciting routines.

Dance the L.A. Hustle

During the mid 1970's disco dancing became the craze in America and the basic disco dance is the hustle. Anybody can hustle—the steps are simple and there is plenty of chance to try out your own moves. You may have watched others dance the hustle but that isn't nearly as exciting as doing it yourself. So have some fun dancing and "get up and hustle with all your muscle."

To get the disco feeling you have to feel loose, keep smiling, and get sweaty. You should also wear loose, comfortable, flat shoes to prevent blisters.

The L.A. hustle is a "line dance" done without partners, and the more dancers the better. All dancers form a line, side by side, and they all move together doing each dance step in order, in rhythm

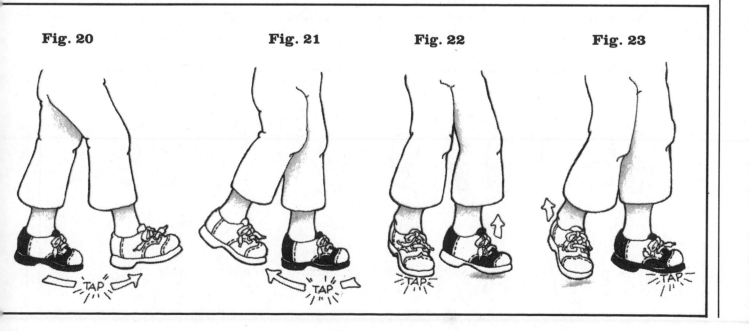

Fig. 20   **Fig. 21**   **Fig. 22**   **Fig. 23**

Part 1

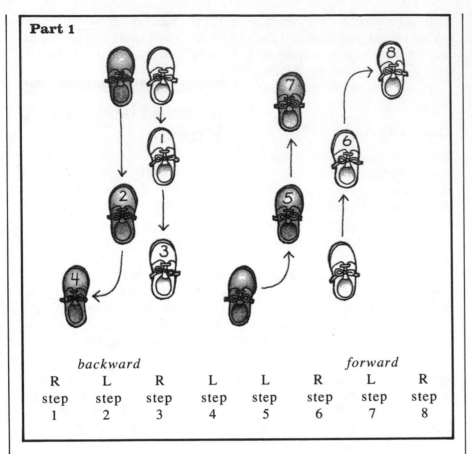

backward					forward		
R	L	R	L	L	R	L	R
step	step	step	step	step	step	step	step
1	2	3	4	5	6	7	8

backward and forward; to the right and the left; then a couple of jumps and chicken flaps; and finally a few toe pokes ending in a kick, a turn, and back to the beginning again. Each part is danced to a steady beat of eight.

Part 1

1. Starting with your feet together take three steps backward —right foot, left foot, right foot.

2. Keeping in rhythm, tap your left foot out to the side and bring it back past your right foot and ready to start three steps forward on the next beat—left foot, right foot, left foot.

3. Without losing a beat of the rhythm, tap your right foot out to the right side and bring it back alongside your left foot. That completes part one of the L.A. hustle. Practice the rhythm of this step and each step you learn before moving to the next.

Part 2

1. Sidestep to the right with your right foot, cross your left foot over in front of your right foot, take another sidestep to the right and tap your left foot alongside of your right.

3. Keeping beat to the music

to the music. So if you learn the L.A. hustle, practice to get the steps down right: If you are the only dancer going the wrong way among a group of nonstop dancers you might get accidentally kicked or poked.

To begin, play some lively disco music and get your body loose. Lift your shoulders and elbows a bit then swing and strut your whole body from side to side in rhythm to the music. Be deliberate and sharp about every move you make.

Now you are warmed-up and ready for the actual steps. The L.A. hustle has four parts danced in order over and over again: first

Part 2

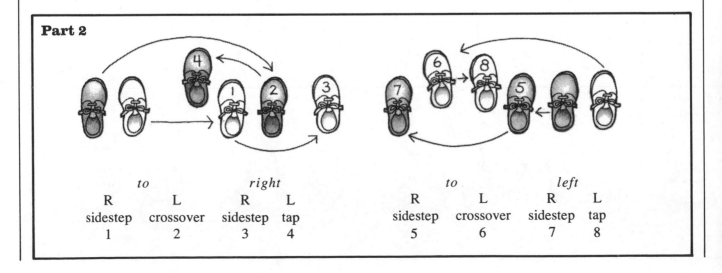

	to		right			to		left	
R	L	R	L		R	L	R	L
sidestep	crossover	sidestep	tap		sidestep	crossover	sidestep	tap
1	2	3	4		5	6	7	8

Part 3

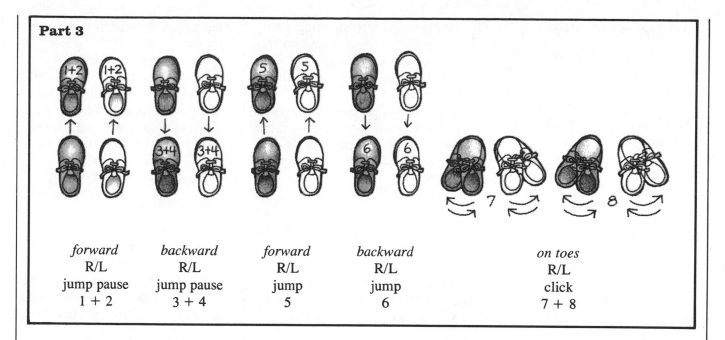

| forward R/L jump pause 1 + 2 | backward R/L jump pause 3 + 4 | forward R/L jump 5 | backward R/L jump 6 | on toes R/L click 7 + 8 |

shift your weight to the left and repeat this step to the left to get back to where you started—left foot sidestep, right foot front crossover, left foot sidestep again, and tap your right foot alongside of your left foot.

Part 3

Now comes the fun. This part is the chicken flap and you need to use your arms as well as feet.

1. With both feet together jump forward and pause, jump back and pause again. Repeat the forward-backward jump again, but faster.

2. Now up on your toes and click your heels together twice while at the same time flapping your arms chicken style—hands at waist, elbows out. As your heels spread out your arms flap up and when your heels click together your arms flap down.

Part 4

1. For the last part, tap your right foot in front two times, then in back two times. Next tap in front once, in back once, and once to the right side. Now kick up your right foot and cross it over your left leg while at the same time turning your entire body one quarter around to the left. Got it? With luck the whole line will have turned the same way and you are ready to start with part one again—this time facing a different direction.

Dance the New York Hustle

Like many older dances the New York hustle is a "touching" dance done with a partner. To help explain the dance steps, assume for now that you are the boy and your partner is the girl (although, of course, boy/boy or girl/girl partners can dance together if they like).

Part 4

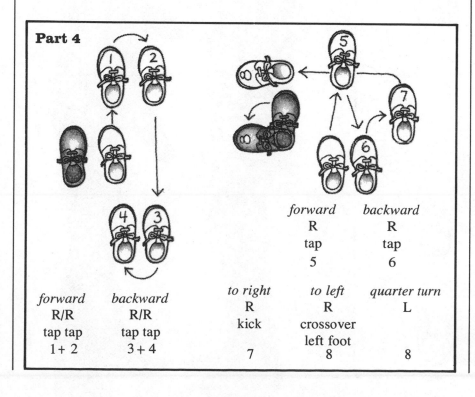

| forward R/R tap tap 1 + 2 | backward R/R tap tap 3 + 4 | to right R kick 7 | to left R crossover left foot 8 | quarter turn L 8 |

forward R tap 5 — backward R tap 6

The correct position

Face your partner in the "standard social-dancing" position, that is:

Her left hand should rest on his right shoulder.

His right hand should rest on the left side of her waist while the other two hands are gently held together, out to the side.

His feet should be side by side and facing his partner's feet.

Do the hustle

1. With your left foot make a short step to the left, Fig. 24 then lift your right foot and bring it over to the left, tapping it and so that your two heels form an "L," Fig. 25. The right foot's heel remains off the floor.

2. Bring your right foot back to its starting position and tap your left heel over to your right heel as you just did on the other side, Figs. 26 and 27.

That's the basic step! You are now back where you started and ready to do it again. Just keep your dance step in time to the beat of the music—step/tap/step/tap. The dance is done pretty fast and taking small steps will make it easier. Your partner should do the same thing as you only starting with the right foot.

Practice until you can do the basic step smoothly. Dance to different disco records. Get your body rocking to the music—side to side in a somewhat smooth glide. When you can New York hustle without thinking of what your feet are doing, try the following variations.

A little variety

Now and then while dancing, step forward and backward rather than sideways, remembering always to bring your heels together in an "L." Add a little style by swinging your clasped hands up high then

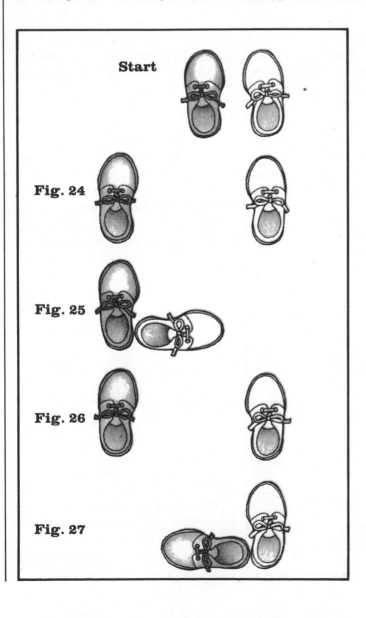

Start

Fig. 24

Fig. 25

Fig. 26

Fig. 27

The New York hustle is one of the many forms of this popular disco dance.

down low in rhythm as you dance. You might also dip a bit as you step to each side, or try to turn your whole body outward in the direction you are stepping. Practice until each new move feels natural.

For a little more variety and style add a few turns to your dance step. Just remember that in dancing the New York hustle you must always keep holding at least one of your partner's hands. Start the turn on a step to the side of your raised, clasped hands. Turn your body toward that side while letting go of your partner's waist (and your partner lets go of your shoulder). Pivot around under your arched hands until you are back facing your partner again. Your partner has meanwhile continued to do the basic step which you pick up at the end of your turn. Now your partner can try making a turn, and after a few practices the two of you can try turning together—at the same time.

In another hustle turn you clasp each of your partner's hands and without letting go, both of you turn completely around at the same time by lifting your hands over you until you are back facing each other.

In still another turn you or your partner make only a half turn or "wrap turn." Both hands are clasped with one pair raised to form an arch. Without letting go of hands, turn under the arch until your back is toward your partner. You both then lower your clasped hands and if the wrap turn worked right both you and your partner are now facing the same direction and still holding hands—with your arms criss-crossed in front of you. To get back to the basic step just reverse the moves.

Practice by mixing the basic step and body motions with turns and variations of your own. The best place to practice and learn new steps is right on the disco dance floor.

AT HOME

Saturday night in America has a very special feeling for most people; it is the one time of the week strictly dedicated to having fun. Saturday night is going to the movies, the school dance, bowling, ice skating, to sleepovers (and telling ghost stories), out to dinner; it's staying up late and eating pizza or hanging out with friends and playing records: it's baby-sitting, watching a special or horror movie on TV; it's seeing a basketball game or rock concert; it's staying with grandparents or camping-out in the yard. It's a time for games, a time to do just plain nothing, a time to write in your diary, a time to relax at home.

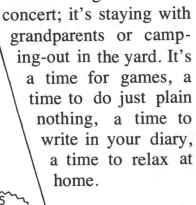

Awarded to
SATURDAY NIGHT
as the
Most Fun
NIGHT OF THE WEEK
KID: *Gwen Agro-Zirn*
KID: *Luis Sierra*
KID: *Katie Butterfield*
KIDS KA America

A radio play taping session.

COMIC BOOKS AND FUNNY PAPERS

The "comics" or "funnies" are a unique American invention. Our favorite comics and comic characters not only entertain but also influence us. When Joe Palooka was shown eating cheese for strength while training for a fight, the sale of cheese in America skyrocketed. And Popeye has sold so much spinach that the farmers of Crystal City, Texas have erected a statue in his honor. There are dolls, games, and costumes having to do with comic characters, as well as TV specials and stage plays that bring the comic characters to life.

The first comic strip appeared in the first color supplement to the *New York World* newspaper in 1894 and was drawn by a staff artist named Richard Fulton Outcault. The strip was titled "Origin of a New Species or the Evolution of the Crocodile Explained" and it poked fun at what was then a very serious controversy over the theory of evolution. The comic strip showed a clown character and his dog picnicking under a tree. The clown takes an after-lunch nap and a huge snake slithers down from a nearby tree, eating the dog whole. The clown wakes up surprised but slits the snake's belly. The dog's four feet pop through the snake and the clown casually walks off leading the dog/snake, now turned crocodile, by a leash.

Comics become popular

The crocodile strip was very popular and much talked about, and the *New York World* began selling more newspapers than ever. It wasn't long before Outcault was regularly

ORIGIN OF A NEW SPECIES, OR . . .

THE EVOLUTION OF THE CROCODILE EXPLAINED.

and offer their own comic strips. The Yellow Kid was soon followed by Hooligan Harry, the Katzenjammer Kids, and Buster Brown.

Newspaper comic strips continued to grow in popularity with new characters and story situations appearing regularly. Some comic strips were serials: Each week the strip would solve the mystery of the previous week and end with yet another unresolved situation. In that way, the reader became "hooked" and would anxiously wait for next Sunday to buy the newspaper and see how things worked out.

And then the comic book

It was some twenty-five years after the first comic strip before someone thought up the idea of the comic book, which presented the entire story all at one time. The first comic books were merely collections of comic strips that had already appeared in the newspaper, but in 1937 Detective Comics published the first original and popular comic book story. Within a year, the first *Superman* comic book was published and its incredible success led the way for a host of other new "super" comic characters.

During the 1940's and into the 50's, comic books became a way of life for most American kids. Bedroom closets held stacks of comic books already read and waiting to be traded; the latest comic book was carried everywhere to be perused at any spare moment until it was finished—and read over again. The Sunday newspaper was hardly in the house before the color comic section was pulled out, divided among the kids, and spread out on the floor.

The popularity of television put a dent in comic book sales but comics never disappeared. Today's

drawing a comic strip for the Sunday paper called *Hogan's Alley*. The main character of this strip was a hairless big-eared kid dressed in a bright yellow nightshirt. The "Yellow Kid" as the character was popularly called, was a smashing success, and the comic strip was here to stay. Other newspapers of the day were quick to hire artists

They aren't the most scholarly reading, but who can resist a good comic book?

comic characters are mostly taken from popular TV shows for kids, but several old-time characters are still around and never seem to lose their appeal. How many of these comics do you know or remember?

Making Shuffle-Deck Comics

Most of the comic strips in the newspapers tell a story in three or four drawn boxes called "frames." The first frame usually introduces the story or the situation; the second frame develops the story or presents some predicament; the third frame usually has the hero meet up with a surprise of some sort; and in the fourth frame— sometimes—everything gets straightened out. Following this pattern or any other sequence of events you wish, you can make up your own original cartoon stories using a shuffle-deck of comic frames.

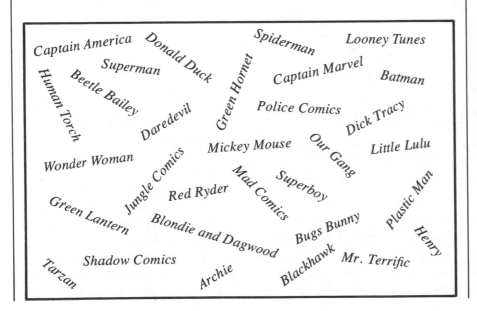

Captain America   Donald Duck   Spiderman   Looney Tunes
Superman   Green Hornet   Captain Marvel   Batman
Human Torch   Beetle Bailey   Police Comics   Dick Tracy
Daredevil   Mickey Mouse   Our Gang   Little Lulu
Wonder Woman   Jungle Comics   Superboy   Plastic Man
Green Lantern   Red Ryder   Mad Comics   Henry
Blondie and Dagwood   Bugs Bunny
Tarzan   Shadow Comics   Archie   Blackhawk   Mr. Terrific

First select one of your favorite comic strips and cut out that strip for a whole week or a number of Sundays. Carefully cut the individual frames apart into "cards" until you have a good stack or deck.

Shuffle the cards to mix up the sequences and then lay the cards out in a strip in order from the deck. Read the words and pictures of the long strip to see if it makes any sense. Sometimes the stories you get by chance are very funny, but you will probably need to rearrange the order of the cards or eliminate some of the cards from the strip to make the new story work. After you make your own shuffle-deck comic strip, gather up the cards, reshuffle, and pass them to a friend. Now see what comic story he or she can make.

AMERICA'S FUNNY BONE

We Americans have a rich sense of humor and can usually laugh at ourselves, poke fun at our politicians, and express feelings of satisfaction, pleasure, disappointment, fear, and friendship with laughter. But it wasn't always that way in America.

Early Americans were mistrustful of laughter and those who did laugh, were not considered very respectful or trustworthy. The settlers believed that a person was either serious-minded, and therefore had no need for laughter, or was foolhardy, in which case the person wasn't expected to be responsible.

Americans were generally a rather somber bunch until the nineteenth century when pioneers traveling west rediscovered their sense of humor almost out of necessity. The pioneers learned that laughing often eased the pain of misfortune and fear, and provided the encouragement to continue. When the journey was finally over, the pioneers found it was better to laugh about it than to recall the many hardships that had to be endured. The American pioneer not only settled the West but introduced America to the humor of tall tales, jokes, riddles, and funny bits of homespun wisdom.

Have you heard this one?

Although everyone likes to think of himself as an individual, people are similar in many ways down to sharing similar experiences. The funniest jokes are often based on our recognition of the way we act in everyday situations. On the other hand, anything about a person or situation that is different can also be the source of a joke. Then there are those personal things we all think in common but rarely talk about. The relief of knowing we think the same thoughts also makes us laugh.

Current events are the subject of much of our humor, but many of the jokes we laugh at today have been around a long time. Some of your favorite jokes were probably just as funny to your older brother or sister or your parents or grandparents when they were your age.

You probably already know several funny jokes and what things make you and your friends laugh. Maybe you like elephant jokes, pickle jokes, banana jokes, grape jokes, monster jokes, or moron jokes. If a joke is clever enough (and Americans do appreciate cleverness) it will probably remain funny for several generations to come. Here are a few typically American jokes and riddles that have passed the test of time. Choose the ones you think are best and try them out on your friends. But watch out! If the joke you tell is a dud you might only get a big "ugh!" If it is a hit your audience will not be able to keep from laughing—and laughter can be quite contagious.

What-is-it jokes

What gets more wet the more it dries? *A towel.*

No matter how smart you are there is one thing you always overlook. What is it? *Your nose.*

What is green, has two legs, eats rocks, and dingle-dangles?

A green, two-legged, rock-eating dingle-dangle.

What is the best thing to put in an apple pie? *Your teeth.*

What is Smokey the Bear's middle name? *The.*

What is the best thing to do when you feel run down? *Get the car's license number.*

What is worse than raining cats and dogs? *Hailing cabs and buses.*

What comes once in a minute, twice in a moment, and never in a hundred years? *The letter M.*

What is it you lose whenever you stand up? *Your lap.*

What is it you have that you can always count on? *Your fingers.*

What is full of holes yet still holds water? *A sponge.*

What is as light as air yet can't be held for long? *Your breath.*

Name me and I'm gone. What am I? *Silence.*

What is the color of a hurricane? *The wind blue and the wave rose.*

Moron jokes

Why did the moron wear his warm fur coat to the basketball game? *He heard there would be a lot of fans there.*

What did the moron say when he was asked why he was wearing one green sock and one orange sock? *"I don't know but I've got another pair just like these at home."*

Did you hear what happened to the moron who walked through the screen door? *He strained himself.*

Why did the moron write so quickly? *He wanted to finish a letter before the pen ran out of ink.*

Did you hear about the moron who wrote himself a letter but forgot to sign it? *When the letter was delivered he didn't know who it came from.*

Why did the moron jump up and down before taking his medicine?

The bottle said "shake well before using."

What is the difference between a dog and a flea?

A dog can have fleas but a flea can't have dogs.

What-is-the-difference jokes

What is the difference between a hill and a pill? *One is hard to get up and the other is hard to get down.*

What is the difference between a glass of water and a glass of soda? *About twenty-five cents.*

What is the difference between an elephant and a loaf of bread? *I'll never send you to the store.*

What is the difference between a jeweler and a jailer? *One sells watches and the other watches cells.*

What is the difference between an Indian-head penny and a buffalo-head nickel? *Four cents.*

What is the difference between a railroad engineer and a school teacher? *One minds the train and the other trains the mind.*

What is the difference between a book and a bore? *You can shut up a book.*

What-did-he-say jokes

What did the pupil say when the English teacher asked him to name two pronouns? *Who me?*

What did the scarf say to the hat? *You go on ahead, I'll hang around.*

What do you say to a two-headed monster? *Hello, hello.*

What did the big rose say to the small rose? *Hi, bud.*

What did General George Washington say to his men before crossing the Delaware? *Men, get in the boat.*

What did Paul Revere say at the end of his famous ride? *Whoa, horse.*

What did one eye say to the other eye?

Something smells between us.

Who, what, why, which, if, and how jokes

Why does Uncle Sam wear red-white-and-blue suspenders? *To hold up his pants.*

What do you get when you cross a cat with a lemon? *A sourpuss.*

How can you lift an elephant? *Put an acorn under him and wait twenty years.*

What animal can jump higher than a house? *Any animal —houses can't jump.*

If an elephant sat on your watch what time would it be? *Time to get a new watch.*

If the blue house is up the street and the brown house is across the street, where is the white house? *In Washington, D.C.*

What building has the most stories? *The public library.*

What U.S. president wore the largest hat? *The one with the biggest head.*

If two wrongs don't make a right, what do two rights make? *The first airplane.*

When is a purple dog most likely to walk into your house? *When the door is open.*

How do you keep a fish from smelling? *Put beans up its nose.*

What goes in one ear and out the other? *A worm in a cornfield.*

If Miss-ouri wears her New Jersey what will Dela-ware? *I don't know but Alaska.*

When is a door not a door? *When it is ajar.*

Who is bigger, Mr. Bigger or Mr. Bigger's baby? *The baby is a little Bigger.*

Why do bumblebees hum?

Hmmm, Hm. Hmm, Hmm. Hm, La-De-Da...

They know the tune but not the words.

PARLOR GAMES

Game-playing in America is a relatively new pastime. The early settlers hadn't much time for play. Sunday was the only "free" day and that time was committed to attending church and practicing lessons of self-betterment. There was usually more work to do than time allowed, and to waste time at frivolous pleasure was considered a sin.

As America was settled and life became easier, some of the wealthier families took up card playing to entertain themselves and guests. The popular card game of the late 1700's was whist; even George Washington was known to be devoted whist player.

America grew rapidly after the Civil War and with Industrial Age machinery to help do the work, families found more time each week to entertain themselves or just relax. By now there was leisure time on Saturday afternoons for many people, and that meant sitting in the parlor or living room, with family or friends, and playing a card game, charades, or a round of twenty questions.

More fun and games

During the decades that followed, Americans continued to find more and more leisure time for play and more games to play. By the early twentieth century the popular parlor games included many board games; newspapers carried a new crossword puzzle every day; and whist gave way to canasta and then bridge.

Kids today have more free time and more games to play than ever. Besides card games and a few ever-popular board games, kids now play electronic television games, simulated sports games, and even sophisticated computer games. The parlor has been replaced by the family room, but games are also played at school, on the front porch, while traveling, and even while waiting for the food at some restaurants. From a rather slow beginning, Americans have become the most ardent game-players in the world.

The next time you and your family or friends have nothing particular to do, but you do have a place for doing, try these typical American parlor (or anyplace) games. They are still just as much fun as ever.

Charades

(two teams of two or more players)

The object of charades is quite simple although playing the game isn't always easy. One player thinks of a famous person, a movie title, a song, or maybe some common expression; he then tries to communicate to the other players that name or title or whatever, using pantomime only. It is no fair moving your lips or writing things out. The first player to correctly guess the charade gets to play out the next one.

The basics

In the game of charades there are certain standard gestures that communicate helpful clues to the players guessing. First you should indicate the general category of the subject you are going to pantomime.

● For a book title, pantomime reading a book.

● For a song title, pantomime singing.

● For a saying or expression, make quotation marks with your fingers.

● For a movie title, pretend to crank an old-time movie camera.

● And for a famous name put a hand inside your shirt like Napoleon.

Next show how many words are in the name, title, or expression by holding up that many fingers.

As you pantomime the charade,

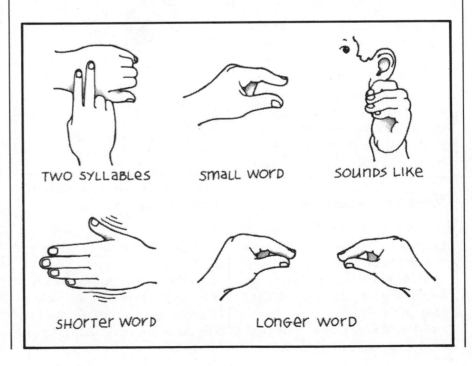

TWO SYLLABLES   SMALL WORD   SOUNDS LIKE

SHORTER WORD   LONGER WORD

indicate by holding up fingers which word you are acting out. If you get to a really tough word you might sound it out in pantomime syllable by syllable. Indicate to the players how many syllables are in the word and which syllable you are acting out by putting fingers across the back of your wrist. If you want to give the entire charade all in one pantomime gesture, indicate so by waving your hands in a circular motion.

To indicate a small word like *a* and *the*, make a small measurement with your thumb and index finger.

To show that a word "sounds like" the pantomime action you will be doing, point to or pull on your ear.

To show that the word is a shorter form of the word last guessed, do up-and-down karate chops with your hand. If the word is longer, pretend to stretch out an imaginary word between your hands.

Charades in action

Here is an example of how a simple round of charades might go: Suppose you wanted to pantomime the song title "Blue Suede Shoes." First indicate the category of things you are pantomiming by pretending to sing until someone calls out "song title." Next hold up three fingers to indicate that there are three words in the title, and then one finger to show you are now going to pantomime the first word. You might point to something blue in the room until someone yells out "blue." Whenever anyone guesses a word correctly point to them and nod your head yes, then continue with the next word. By swaying back and forth, or getting down on your hands and knees like a swayback mule, one of the players might guess the word *sway*. Point "yes" to that player and pull on your ear to indicate that the correct

word sounds like *sway*. Encourage the players by continuing to gesture until someone guesses the word *suede*. And finally point to everyone's shoes to get the response, "Blue Suede Shoes."

Grandmother's Trunk

(any number of players)

This is a simple word game that will test your imagination as well as your memory. The first player names any item to be found in grandmother's trunk, but the name of the item must begin with the letter *a*:

> "In grandmother's trunk, I found an apricot."

The next player in turn names any item that begins with the letter *b* after he has repeated what the first player found:

> "In grandmother's trunk, I found an apricot and a balloon."

The game continues with each player in his turn adding a word beginning with the next letter of the alphabet, in order, reciting each time the entire list from the beginning:

> "In grandmother's trunk I found an apricot, a balloon, and a chicken."

And so on. Any player who misses an item (or can't come up with a word for his letter) is out of the game. The winner is the last remaining player.

To make the game even tougher, you might try playing double grandmother's trunk. The rules are the same except that the name of each item must be preceded by an adjective beginning with the same letter as the name.

> "In grandmother's trunk, I found an awful apple, a brown bear, a crunchy cucumber, a dainty doilie. . ." and so on.

Alphabet Sentences

(any number of players)

The first player makes up the longest sentence he can but every word in the sentence must begin with the letter *a*. Little words such as *a, the, to, at*, etc., are exempted from the rule. For each word in the sentence (little words not counting) the player gets one point.

Now the second player makes up a sentence of words beginning with the letter *b*. The game continues letter by letter through the entire alphabet with each player getting the same number of turns. The player with the most points is the winner.

Here is an example to help you out if you are ever the player to get the letter *z*.

"Zelda zig-zagged on the zoo's zippy zebra."

Twenty Questions

(two or more players)

One player is chosen to be "it" and he thinks of any particular well-known person, place, or thing. He then tells the other players whether the category of what he has chosen is "animal" (such as a person, a dog or a fish), "vegetable" (trees, flowers, food, or anything that grows), or "mineral" (anything made of metal, glass, plastic, rubber, etc.).

Now each of the players, in turn, can ask "it" any yes/no question to either get clues or to take a guess at the mystery subject. "It" must answer the question correctly but can only respond with a "yes," "no," or "maybe." The first

player in his turn to guess the subject correctly is the winner. He now becomes "it" and can try to stump the other players with his own mystery subject.

However, if after twenty questions no one has guessed correctly then the "it" player must reveal his mystery subject and he wins the game, plus a turn to go again with a new subject.

Here is a hint for playing. Try to ask about only one thing in each question. For example, if you asked, "Is it something a girl would wear?" you have actually asked two questions: "Is it something to wear?" and "Is it something for a girl?" The subject might be something to wear but for a boy, or it could be something for a girl but not a thing to wear. In both situations, your question would get a no answer and you would not have gotten any clue. Also, to avoid arguments, one player should agree to be the official counter of questions asked.

Botticelli or the Nope Game

(two or more players)

There is a much more difficult version of twenty questions called botticelli—sometimes known as the nope game. The best way to learn this game is by playing it, so don't expect to remember all the rules after reading them once.

The "it" player thinks of a famous person or someone all the players know, and then he tells the other players the initial of the last name of the mystery person and a clue about what the person does or what made him famous (baseball player, junior high school student, American president, etc.). For example, the "it" player might say, "R is a teacher" and be thinking of

Ms. Ringer who teaches music at the school. Or "it" might say, "J is a rock star" and be thinking of Elton John.

Now each of the players, in turn, can ask "it" a yes/no question to guess who the mystery person is. However, to ask a question the player must have someone particular in mind who fits the description given by "it." The questioner cannot say the name of the person he is thinking of. For example, using Elton John as the mystery person with the clues "J is a rock star" the first player to question might ask, "Is this person the lead singer of the Rolling Stones?" The questioner was obviously thinking of the rock star Mick Jagger whose last name begins with a *J*.

The "it" player must now give an appropriate answer to the question and use a name that also fits the clues. So "it" might answer the question by saying, "Nope, it is not Mick Jagger."

The next player to question might then ask, "Is this a female rock star?" and "it" might answer, "Nope, it is not Olivia Newton-John."

If "it" cannot come up with a name for the answer, or if the answer would actually reveal the mystery person then "it" can say, "Nope, I don't know." That response allows the questioning player to ask directly if the mystery person is the one he is thinking of. For example, the next player to question asks, "Is the first initial of this rock star also a *J*?" Now suppose "it" can't think of a rock star with the initials J.J., so he would answer, "Nope, I don't know." The questioning player could then ask, "Is the star Janis Joplin?"

If the guess is correct then that player wins the game. If the guess is not correct, the player may take a second guess but now he can only ask a yes/no question and "it" only needs to respond with a yes or no.

For example, if the answer to a player's guess was, "Nope—the star is not Janis Joplin," the challenging player might then ask, "Does this star play lead guitar?" and to that "it" would answer no (Elton John plays the piano).

There is one other situation that can occur. In the event that "it" answers a question with "I don't know" and the questioning player cannot come up with a fitting guess, that player is immediately out of the game.

The game continues with the next player asking a question, and so on until someone guesses the correct name. For example, the next player to question might ask, "Does this rock star wear fancy eyeglasses?" Elton John did wear fancy eyeglasses but unless "it" can think of another rock star who wears fancy eyeglasses and whose last name initial is *J*, "it" would answer, "Nope, I don't know." The asking player then gets to guess, "Is the rock star Elton John?" He is correct, and that player wins the game and now gets to be "it."

There is no limit to the number of questions that can be asked, but if after playing a while no one has guessed correctly, just quit and try another name.

Geography
(two or more players)

This game is called geography because it is usually played with the names of cities, states, and countries. But you can also play geography using other categories—the names of people, animals, household objects, or maybe even companies. Just be sure the category you choose is varied enough so you don't get stumped right away.

Once the players choose a category, the first player says a name that fits the category. For example, if the category is states, then a player might say Ohio or Nevada. Now the next player in turn must think of another name that fits the category but it must begin with the last letter of the previous player's choice. The game continues with each player in turn; no name can be repeated. If a player is stumped and can't think of an appropriate name, he is out of the game and the next player in turn begins with a new category. The player remaining when all others have been stumped is the winner.

For example, suppose the category is people's names, then a game might go like this: "Rober*t*"—

"Thoma*s*"—

"Steve*n*"—

"Ne*d*"—

"Davi*d*"—

"Danie*l*"—

"Laur*ie*" ... and so on until someone is stumped.

The bare letters

Instead of whole names you can play geography using initials only. Your category could be famous people's initials, initials of mutual friends, initials of well-known cities and states, or maybe any well-known three-letter initials. In this version of the game a player can be challenged: If that player cannot match the initials to an appropriate name, he is out of the game. For example, if the category is three-letter initials a game might begin like this: "AB*C*"—

"CB*S*"—

"SO*S*"—

"ST*P*"—

"PO*W*"—

"WP*A*"—

"AA*A*" ... and so on until a player or challenged.

Ghost
(two or more players)

To win at ghost it helps to be a good speller. You don't, however, want to be the one who finishes the spelling of a word. Here is how the game is played.

The player to go first picks any letter of the alphabet and announces it. The second player adds a letter to the first. The next player in turn adds a letter, and so forth. Play continues with the object of the game to not be the player who adds a letter that spells a word. Only words of four letters or more count.

The player who does spell a word loses that round and he is penalized with a *g*—the first letter of *ghost*. If that player should lose another round he would then get an *h* and so on. When any player has five losses he is a *g-h-o-s-t* and out of the spelling part of the game.

Haunted by former players

However, there are a few catches. When a player adds a letter he must have a word in mind that he is trying to spell. After adding a letter that player can be challenged; if the player has a word in mind the challenger is penalized with one ghost letter. But if the player has been bluffing and he can't give a word, he gets the penalty ghost letter.

There is one final rule. No player remaining in the game may talk to one who has become a *ghost* (only until the game is over of course). But ghosts are allowed to provoke (no tickling) the remaining players; the penalty for a player caught talking to a ghost is one ghost letter.

The game continues until only the winner is left. Here is a short sample playing for a game with three players.

- The first player says the letter *c*; he can be thinking of any word beginning with that letter.
- The second player adds *a* to make *ca*; he might be thinking of the word *cape* or *candle,* for instance.
- The third player adds *r* to make *car*; he could be thinking of the word *cardinal*. Car is a word, but it doesn't count because it has only three letters.
- It is the first player's turn again and he adds *p* to make *carp*. He was thinking of the word *carpenter* but *carp* is the name of a fish and so it spells a word. This player gets a penalty—the ghost letter *g*.
- The second player who is the next player in turn now says a letter to begin a new round.

Double and quadruple ghost

If you want even more of a challenge, you can try playing double or quadruple ghost. These games are a bit more complex and you should use a pencil and paper to keep track of the play.

Generally the rules are the same as in regular ghost but in double ghost the players can choose to add their letter to either the beginning or end of the word being spelled. For example:

- Player one says *a* thinking of any word beginning with *a*.
- Player two adds *p* before the *a* making *pa*; maybe he is thinking of *paint*.
- Player three adds *s* before the word making *spa* possibly thinking of *spaniel*. Spa is a word, but it is only three letters long so it doesn't count.
- The next player adds *r* after the word to make *spar*, maybe thinking *sparrow*. But spar is a word and he becomes a ghost.

In a game of quadruple ghost

players can add letters on either side of the word as well as up or down from the first letter played. This is what a game might look like with *r* as the starting letter.

```
        P
        A
S  C  R  U  B
        S
```

Whist

(for four players—two teams—and a standard fifty-two-card deck)

The four players sit in a square with partners opposite. Someone is chosen dealer and he deals out all the cards—thirteen to each player. However, before the last card is dealt, it is shown face up and the suit of that card is the "wild" suit for the game.

Each player now holds his cards in a concealed manner and arranges his hand by suit and in order. At this time, each player must show any honor cards he has (picture cards and aces) and then return the cards to his hand.

The player to the dealer's left picks any card from his hand and places it face up on the table. Now each of the other players, in turn clockwise, places a card of the same suit on the table. The player with the card of the highest value wins all four cards, or the "trick," for himself and his partner.

If a player cannot follow in turn by playing the correct suit he may then play a card of the wild suit. If more than one player plays a wild

card then the highest wild card wins. A wild card beats any card of the other three suits.

If a player has neither a card of the correct suit nor a wild card, he can play any card he holds but he has no chance of winning the trick.

The player who wins a trick gets to start off the next round, and the game continues until all the cards have been played.

To determine the winning team, partners combine tricks and count up their score according to this point system:

If a team has all the honors of a suit (jack, queen, king, ace) they score four points.

If a team holds three out of four honors of a suit they score two points.

The first six tricks for a team don't count for score, but each trick over six counts one point.

The team with the highest total point score is the winner.

GHOST STORIES

Try to imagine how scary it might have been living in the lonely wilderness of Early America. The land was strange and unexplored and there were many kinds of animals and plants that had never been seen before. The settlers were often surprised by the unusual new things they discovered, but they were also very frightened by what they imagined they *might* find. It was common for people to fear that imaginary wild beasts or supernatural spirits might be lurking in the dark or hiding around the next corner. And even though people's fears were mostly imagined, they often talked about such things as if they were real. Any strange sound, motion, or occurrence that could not be explained was often attributed to some supernatural spirit or ghost, and in time these explanations became tall tales and ghost stories.

Scared parents tried to warn their children of these dangers by telling them stories about bad children who get dragged away by murderous ghosts and good children who bravely outwit some spooky creature or spirit. Often times these stories about ghosts, witches, beasts, foggy graveyards, and strange happenings were told before bedtime as the flickering evening fire made shadows bounce around the room and the wind whistled through a crack in the front door. The stories usually mixed just the right amount of fact and fiction to make them believable and very scary. Even so, the children looked forward to these ghost stories. They liked getting scared as long as there was the comfort of a blanket to hide under and someone nearby to hold on to.

Often several families would gather at a neighbor's house and swap spooky tales. When the evening ended it took a brave person and all his courage to return home through the dark and not be frightened by the hoot of an owl or the sight of the evening mist rolling through the town graveyard. People had such vivid imaginations that some actually believed they did see a ghost; nothing could make them believe differently. And wherever someone claimed to see a ghost, that place was considered haunted for years to come.

Ghost encounters

According to legend, a person becomes a ghost when he has died violently or unexpectedly. The ghost is usually trying to get revenge or make up for some of his own wrongdoing. Few ghosts if any seem to be particularly evil and supposedly only the wicked have anything to fear. Over the years people have reported seeing or hearing ghosts nearly everywhere in America. Certain places, however, seem to attract an unusually large number of ghosts. According to eyewitness reports, the hillsides and mountain regions of the eastern United States seem to have a large ghost population. Several ghosts have been reported in old abandoned mines and caves. And every chest of buried treasure is supposed to be protected by a ghost.

Ghost facts

In any case, you might like to know what to do should you someday actually meet up with a ghost—or even imagine you have. First of all, no one born at night is supposed to be able to see ghosts, but they can still hear them. Ghosts are afraid of other ghosts, so holding up a mirror will scare one way. Also rarely will a ghost cross over water, so crossing a stream is a sure way to stop a ghost from following you. If you find a treasure and you want to avoid the ghost that protects it, you must not speak, laugh, or sweat while digging or taking the treasure away. And if for whatever reason you actually want to see a ghost, you might try counting nine stars and nine bricks and then quickly look into a dark room. Boo!

If you are not quite ready to actually meet a ghost, maybe you would enjoy being scared by a ghost story. There are hundreds of ghost stories and bogeyman tales that have become popular in America and many of them go back to the time of the settlers. Most of these tales follow the same general story line but the characters and places change to suit the storyteller. Here are three short ghost stories that are quite typically American.

The Ghostly Rider

John Cooke was a fine young man who lived in Boston with his pretty wife and young daughter. John was a good husband and father except for one fault—he had a terrible temper. When things did not go the way John had planned he would often have a fit of rage, swearing, yelling, kicking, and throwing. It was well known in certain parts of Boston that when John Cooke got mad anyone near should stand clear.

One day in the fall of 1765 John Cooke and his young daughter hitched their beautiful black horse to an open carriage and went to visit a friend in the country town of Concord. On the way back that afternoon John and his daughter were overtaken by a heavy rainstorm and they took shelter at a roadside inn. But the longer they waited for the rain to stop the heavier the rain fell.

John began to become impatient with the long delay and decided to continue his journey regardless of the rain, wind, and mud. The kindly innkeeper pleaded with him to stay the night. "It's no weather for a young girl to be riding in an open carriage," the innkeeper told Mr. Cooke, "and it's so dark out there you won't be able to see beyond your horse."

John Cooke lost his temper and yelled back at the innkeeper, "Let it get worse, I'll get home tonight or I'll never get home!"

And with a long string of curses and a vexed look in his eye, John Cooke grabbed his daughter's arm and stomped out of the inn and into the downpour. The two of them climbed up into the carriage and with the rain beating against their

faces John Cooke and his daughter rode off in the direction of Boston town.

But they never got home that night or any other night. Cooke's pretty wife waited and watched by the window for weeks, but her husband and daughter never returned.

Then early one calm evening the next spring the young wife was roused from her chair by the sound of a horse and carriage approaching the house at a furious pace. At last they have returned, she thought, and the woman rushed to the front door and ran out to greet them.

It was indeed her husband John and their daughter sitting side by side atop the carriage. As they approached the house Cooke pulled on the reins to stop the horse, but the horse just kept running full speed right past the house.

John Cooke and his daughter looked longingly at the woman as they quickly passed. There was no time to speak and Mrs. Cooke just watched as the carriage disappeared down the road into the dark. Within minutes the wind began to howl and a terrible rainstorm drenched the land.

From time to time Mrs. Cooke would hear that same carriage approaching, and each time she went to the door only to see her husband and daughter pass quickly in the night. Following them always was a terrible rainstorm.

Mrs. Cooke died a few years later from loneliness and heartbreak. But John Cooke and his daughter have never stopped riding. For several years after the incident travelers at the inn between Concord and Boston reported seeing a young man and his daughter riding rain-drenched and at full speed in an open carriage, and always within a few minutes after they passed a heavy downpour would muddy the road.

In time this same man and his daughter were reported seen in other towns and later in other states—and always the heavy rains and wind would follow the road that they traveled.

Every year the travels of John Cooke wandered farther from Boston, and today he can be seen traveling almost any road in America.

Nobody Here But You

One cool fall evening a wicked old man sat alone by the fire rocking in his chair. He mumbled words to himself and laughed out loud as he remembered all the "foolish" people he had robbed and cheated. The old man was now blind, but he still liked to dream and scheme of ways to make others miserable.

Suddenly the old man could feel the fire get much hotter and he could sense the presence of something else in the room. The blind man just listened, and soon he heard the sound of a chair being dragged across the room to a place next to his. The man silently reached over to feel who this visitor might be. But what he felt was not a human, not even an animal—it was just a thing!

The old man still remained silent but then the thing spoke and said, "Ain't nobody sitting here but you and me."

The blind old man jumped out of his chair in fright, grabbed his cane, and felt his way to the door. He then opened the door just wide enough to slip through and quickly slammed it shut so as to keep that thing, whatever it was, from escaping with him.

The old man stood shaking in the cold night air wondering what to do next. And then he heard the voice of the thing speak again, "Ain't nobody standing out here but you and me."

The old man's heart was pounding faster and faster and he began to run, as best as a blind man could, down the road to town. But as he ran he heard the voice of the thing following closely behind, "Ain't nobody running like this but you and me."

For a moment it seemed as if the old man was getting ahead of the thing, but then he suddenly came to what seemed to be a high stone wall. The blind man could not see which way to turn to go around the wall so he decided to climb over it. The old man used every bit of strength he had to climb to the top of that wall, and he sat on the top resting to catch his breath. Then the voice of the thing spoke again, "Ain't nobody sitting here on this cemetery wall but you and me."

"Cemetery!" the old man screamed and in a frightened panic he fell from the wall into the cemetery and into a freshly dug grave. The thing fell right down on top of him and spoke one last time, "Ain't nobody here in this grave but YOU!"

The wicked old man died of fright—or some "thing."

The Haunted House

VERY SCARY

In a small New England village there was a house that was said to be haunted by a ghost. For ten years time several people had been dared to spend the night alone in the house but always before midnight the ghost would appear and the guest would be scared away.

A preacher in the village decided that he wanted to meet the ghost or dispel the stories that the house was haunted, so with his Bible in hand he locked himself in the haunted house for the night. It was a chilly dark night, so the preacher lit some wood in the fireplace and sat down to read his Bible by candlelight.

Then all at once just before midnight he heard a noise coming from the cellar stairs. It was the deathly sound of a woman trying to scream as she was being choked. Then there was the sound of a struggle and a tumbling down the stairs. Just as suddenly as the noise began everything was quiet again.

The preacher took up his Bible with his shaking hands and he began to pray, but before he had read the first verse he heard a sound from the cellar again. It was the sound of footsteps and they were getting closer and closer to the top of the cellar stairs—step!—step!—step!—step! The preacher sat frozen watching the cellar door. The door knob began to slowly turn and then the door squeaked open.

There in the shadow of the doorway was what appeared to be a young woman. The preacher was so scared he had nearly stopped breathing, but he found the courage to speak and loudly he said, "Who are you? What do you want of me?" The ghostly figure just stood

would have fainted right there on the spot, but he stared at the ghost and again repeated his question, "Wh-a-a-at do you wa-a-ant?"

The girl began to speak, but the voice seemed to be coming from the wind. As the preacher listened he heard the ghost tell the story of how the man she was to marry had killed her hoping to steal her fortune in gold. After he had dug up the cellar unsuccessfully looking for the buried treasure, the man had buried the young girl's body there.

The ghost then begged the preacher to dig up her bones from the cellar and give her a decent Christian burial. Only then could she rest in peace. Then she told him this: "To find the man who murdered me cut off the small finger of my left hand and put it in the collection plate at the next church meeting. And if you do what I ask, the gold I've hidden will be yours for the church." At that the ghost let go of the preacher and vanished into nothing.

The next morning the preacher wasn't sure if the incident he had experienced was real or just a dream, but there on either shoulder of his coat was the unmistakable print of a bony hand burned right into the cloth. The incident had happened all right and, remembering the ghost's request, the preacher went to the cellar, dug up the young girl's bones and buried them in the church graveyard. Then he said a prayer for the girl's tormented soul.

But before he buried the body the preacher, according to his instruction, cut off the little finger of the left hand, and that next Sunday he put the finger bone in the church collection plate. When the plate was passed about the congregation a certain man happened to touch the bone, and it immediately stuck to his hand. No matter how hard

in the doorway motionless. Again the preacher spoke to the figure, this time holding his Bible out in front of him as if it were protection against an evil spirit, "Who are you and what do you want?"

Without an answer the ghost figure slowly moved across the room to where the preacher was now standing and placed her hands on his shoulders. The preacher could see the ghostly girl quite clearly now. She was about twenty years old and she smelled of the damp earth. Her hair was long and tangled and the flesh of her face was decayed so he could see her cheek and jaw bones. She had no eyes but there was a faint glow of light where her eyes had once been. And she had no nose. If it were not for the preacher's great faith he

the man pulled and rubbed and tore at the bone to get it off, it just stuck there. The man screamed and sobbed and the look of a crazy man glowed in his eyes but the finger bone remained stuck to his hand. Finally out of fear and desperation the man confessed to the murder of the young girl, and he was taken to jail and later hanged—with the finger bone still attached to him.

A few days later the preacher returned to the haunted house, and just before midnight he heard the faint echoing voice of the young girl tell him where to find the treasure of gold. And sure enough a large sack of gold coins was found exactly where the ghost had said.

Homemade Ghost Stories

Ghost stories and other tales of the unknown are more popular now than ever and if you have seen a few horror movies or television mysteries you probably recognize certain character types, plots, and special effects that appear in almost every story to make it seem even more spooky. What would a good spine-tingling ghost story be without heavy rain and flashing lightning, rattling chains, wolves howling, strange laboratory experiments, squeaking doors, or odd creatures who live beneath the earth, in the ocean, or in outer space. And the plot often involves some innocent "everyday"—type person who by some strange stroke of chance meets some evil villain or horrible creature. Then just as the worst is about to happen, a hero saves the victim (or the victim saves himself) and evil is destroyed. Whew!

First turn out the lights

Once you are aware of what makes

up a scary story you can try to make up your own. First invent some sinister character and describe him in detail, then put your character into some version of a typical plot. What is even more fun (and scary) is to get together with a few friends or your family and have each person make up a part of the ghost story. Several imaginations are better than one; besides, you may be able to scare others with your story, but it is pretty hard to scare yourself if you already know what is going to happen.

On some dark, rainy, windy night when the thunder is cracking and lightning is flashing (or, really, at any other time) have everyone sit on the floor in a circle, then turn off all the lights. A candle or a flashlight or the flame of a fireplace is all you need to see by.

Someone begins the story by making up absolutely anything at all as long as it is spooky. The more details described the better. The storyteller continues for a minute or two, thickening the plot, and then he abruptly stops—sometimes right in the middle of a sentence.

The next person around the circle must then pick up the story where it left off and continue the telling for another few minutes. Each person in the circle should add at least one part to the story before someone decides to give it an ending—and then that person must begin a new ghost story.

You might want to tape the story as it is being told so you and the other storytellers can hear it through again. Sometimes a scary homemade story can be very funny when you hear it a second time and already know the ending.

WHITE HOUSE GHOSTS

In nearly every town in America there are at least a few houses which claim the reputation of being haunted, but the most well-known haunted house of all is the White House in Washington, D. C. According to "official government records" the ghosts of at least eight well-known people have been seen in various rooms of the White House, and there are many reports of mysterious and unaccountable rapping noises, creaks, and groans.

The oldest White House ghost is Abigail Adams, wife of the second president, John Adams, who is occasionally seen floating in and out of the East Room where she used to hang laundry to dry. And Dolley Madison's ghost is supposed to return each year to look at the roses she planted in the garden. Both Andrew Jackson and Thomas Jefferson occasionally haunt the White House and sometimes Jefferson has been heard playing his violin.

But the most famous White House ghost is Abraham Lincoln. He has frequently been seen standing in his room, gazing out the window. Even Eleanor Roosevelt claimed to have once met Lincoln's ghost. And there is a legend that you can hear Abraham Lincoln's ghost pacing the floor the night before some terrible calamity occurs.

However not all White House ghosts are presidents or their wives. The original owner of the land the White House is built on is sometimes heard (but never seen) announcing himself to guests, and there is a ghostly janitor who is seen wandering through the halls of the mansion dusting the woodwork.

OLD-TIME RADIO

The radio is a part of all of our lives. Where else can you hear the Top Forty songs plus the new releases. Most families have at least one radio at home as well as a portable transistor radio and a car radio; some kids even have radios mounted on their bicycles.

Radio was first invented in the late 1800's but it was not actually perfected for home entertainment until 1920. To most Americans the invention of radio seemed like magic. Families who had spent their leisure time going to the movies or the theater to be entertained, or who spent a typical Saturday night visiting with neighbors or maybe just going to bed early, were now staying home and staying up late gathered around the living room radio receiver listening to their favorite radio shows. With just a turn of the dial you could tune in live broadcasts of famous bandleaders and singers, vaudeville comedians, stories about the drama of life, and the everyday drama of news events.

Watching radio

The 1930's and 40's were called the "golden age of radio" and indeed there was a certain magic unique to the shows of the time that made radio unlike any other entertainment. You did not just listen to the radio broadcast, you also watched it in your mind. Whether you worked at something else while listening, or just stared at the little red light on the front of an old-time radio set, the words and sound effects coming from the radio speaker would create a lifelike scene in your imagination. One of the most famous examples showing the powerful combination of radio and imagination was a radio play called *War of the Worlds* broadcast in 1938 on Halloween eve. The story was a detailed account of the invasion of earth by Martians, and despite repeated announcements by the radio station that the story was only make-believe, thousands of listeners across America believed the Martian invasion was actually happening and were panic-stricken.

Lots to listen to

Until the 1950's most radio programming included shows much like those you see on TV today. In addition to news and music programs there were adventure stories, situation comedies, detective and mystery dramas, as well as variety shows, and listeners soon became addicted to their favorite programs.

During the 1930's the comedy show *Amos 'n' Andy* was so popular with most Americans that some movie theaters would interrupt the picture show at 7:00 p.m. and instead play *Amos 'n' Andy* for the audience. If they hadn't, many moviegoers would probably have stayed home to listen.

Most radio shows on weekday mornings and early afternoons were dramas of romance and heartbreak aimed at the housewife who listened as she cleaned, cooked, and took care of the kids. Because most of these shows were sponsored by soap companies they became known as "soap operas." Your parents or grandparents might remember some of these "soaps" which included *Just Plain Bill, Stella Dallas, Pepper Young's Family, Lorenzo Jones, Road of Life, Helen Trent, Our Gal Sunday,* and *Backstage Wife.*

In the evenings after dinner there was a choice of comedy, drama, and music shows such as the *Eddie Cantor Show, Burns and Allen, The Bob Hope Show, Death Valley Days, Lux Radio Theatre, Gangbusters, Lights Out, Suspense, Inner Sanctum, Baby Snooks,* and *The Great Gildersleeve.*

Kids' favorites

But weekday afternoons and Saturday morning radio programs were reserved just for kids. After school most kids would rush home to listen to *Dick Tracy, Jack Armstrong, Tom Mix, Superman, Charlie Chan, Little Orphan Annie, Terry and the Pirates,* or *The Lone Ranger.* And on Saturday mornings the kids were always the first ones up with the radio tuned to shows like *Buster Brown, Let's Pretend, Adventure Theatre,* and *Henry Aldrich.*

Even radio theme songs and singing commercials were entertaining and some became almost as well known as popular songs of the day. It wasn't uncommon at all for kids then to sing the Halo® shampoo song or "Pepsi-Cola® hits the spot..." And nearly every kid in America learned the classic melody of the *William Tell Overture* by humming *The Lone Ranger* theme song.

Just like kids' TV programs today, kids' radio shows were often sponsored by companies advertising breakfast cereals and all kinds

Radio premiums for kids were once popular.

Meet the competition

In the late 1940's television became the new home entertainment and many of the popular radio shows soon became television shows. Now instead of imagination and fantasy creating the pictures in your mind, the television screen did everything for you. And many people were surprised and sometimes disappointed to see what their favorite radio characters "really" looked like.

After only a few years of television, radio was almost considered obsolete. Nearly all the shows had disappeared, and radio had become a medium of music and news programs. But radio did not die, and today Americans are beginning to rediscover radio drama and the power of their own imaginations. Some evening turn on your radio and dial slowly through the stations. If you are lucky you might find a station that rebroadcasts many of the old popular radio shows or maybe even some brand-new ones. If you have never listened to a radio play, you and your imagination have a wonderful old treat to look forward to.

Radio Plays

Unlike actors in the movies or on stage or television who "show" the story to the audience the radio actor relies on the spoken world alone to tell what the characters look like, the various settings, and the action that is taking place. In some ways that makes radio acting easy. There are no costumes or makeup to wear, no hot stage lights, no props, and you don't even have to memorize your lines. In a radio studio the actors just gather around a microphone holding a script of the story and each actor reads his lines on cue. Of course there is also the sound ef-

of sweet-tasting drinks. To encourage kids to buy and eat even more cereal and drinks, most of these companies offered toy premiums that came inside the box or that you sent away for.

Most of these premiums had something to do with the theme or main character of the radio show. Using your *Captain Midnight* decoder you could figure out the coded secret message given at the end of each program. Or you could blow a warning signal-whistle through the barrel of your six shooter *Lone Ranger* gun ring. There were also telescope rings, rubber stamp rings, decoder rings, and glow-in-the-dark rings—they all left a temporary green stain on your finger. Jack Armstrong, the all-American boy, offered radio listeners a pedometer; by sending ten cents and the inner seal from a chocolate drink mix you could get your very own Little Orphan Annie shake-up mug or "secret society" ring.

fects person who adds a convincing creak, thud, bang, or slam when necessary just to help the listener's imagination a bit.

However, in other ways radio acting is more difficult than performing on stage or in front of a camera. Because the listening audience cannot actually see the character being played, the actor must be able to establish the particular personality of the character he is playing using only his voice. Some radio actors can play two or three different character roles in the same radio play and switch from one voice to another without getting confused. These actors are called "utility men" and frequently they can also imitate regional accents, foreign dialects, and several animal sounds.

"To be or not to be…"

You can pretend to be a radio actor and put on your own radio play. For a studio all you need is a tape recorder and for a script you can narrate a short story—maybe a mystery, a ghost story, a romance, a comedy, or even a musical. Now just add a few appropriate sound effects and you are ready to go on the air.

If the characters in your radio play have spoken lines, try to disguise your voice and speak so that each one has a distinctive personality. Practice your characters on tape and play it back to hear how you sound. Of course, you can also have some of your "would-be" actor friends help you out and play the character roles.

Prepare the script by making notes in the margins of the chosen story where a particular sound effect is needed and maybe how long it should last. For example, if the story calls for a train passing in the night, then write in the margin at that point, "distant train pass-ing—5 seconds." Or if the story describes a horse galloping up to a ranch on a windy, rainy night, with the rider then walking across a porch and knocking on the front door, you might write in the margin next to that part, "wind and rain over hoofbeats then footsteps and knock on door." You can also include appropriate background music as a sound effect, and maybe a theme song to begin the radio play while you announce the story and actors. Now make a copy of the script for each actor and one for the sound effects person.

When the script is prepared and your cast of volunteer actors is ready, turn on the tape recorder and perform the radio play. It will be more fun, and you will probably do a better acting job if you pretend your show is a live broadcast. This means that you can't stop the tape until the show is finished—even if someone should miss a line or the sound effects person rings the phone after you have answered it. And if you really want to get slick, put a few breaks in your radio play and make up commercials.

When there are several actors in a play and maybe lots of sound effects you might want to choose someone to be the studio director. It is the director's job to run the tape recorder, follow the script, and point to each actor or the sound effects person when their line or cue is coming up next.

Making Sound Effects

Most of the sound effects used in radio plays today are recordings of the actual sounds being made; sometimes an electronic synthesizer is used to create interesting noises. However, back in the early days of radio all the sound effects were made right in the studio while the show was being broadcast. Sometimes the actors would create their own sound effects, firing off a blank gun, punching their own palms to sound like a fight, imitating a barking dog, or maybe blowing into the microphone softly to sound like a gentle breeze.

But most often each radio studio had a sound effects person who stood off to the side of the actors with his own microphone and a tableful of common everyday objects that he would bang, drop, rub together, shake, or maybe pluck to make whatever sounds the script called for. A few sound effects were quite easy to accomplish. If the script called for footsteps, the sound technician just stepped in place, or if the sound of a window breaking or a door slamming shut was required, that is exactly what the sound effects person did.

Variations of a sound effect can be created by placing the microphone closer or farther away from the source of the sound. Test the sound effects you plan to use by recording them and listening to the playback. As you listen, close your eyes, let your ears be the judge, and try to imagine what the audience will believe is making the sound.

Try some yourself

It is not difficult to invent ways of making sound effects, but to get you started here are a few tried and tested techniques.

Rain: Roll a handful of dried peas or beans around on a cookie sheet or brownie pan, or spray water from the kitchen sink hose or a watering can into a bucket.

Railroad train: Fill a metal bandage box with paperclips or tacks and shake in the rhythm of a train.

Running water: Pour water from a pitcher into some other container, dripping the water, making a steady stream, or a big splash, depending on the effect you require.

Fire: Use cellophane or plastic and crinkle it in your hand.

Gun shot: Slap a yardstick or flat scrap of wood on a tabletop or floor.

Banging shutters: Open and close a wooden folding chair.

Crash, bang, boom: Fill a cardboard box with lots of noisy junk—cans, old dishes and silverware, stones, glass jars, etc. Close the box and flip it around and around.

Jet plane: Whistle gently, going gradually from a high note to a low note.

Phone conversation: Talk into a hat or a box.

Wind: Blow air gently from a distance into the microphone for a breeze, close to the microphone and with more force for a blizzard.

Motor and engines: Turn your bike upside down and put a piece of cardboard or a blown-up balloon against the spokes of a turning wheel. You can also use the sound of a kitchen blender.

Hissing steam: Spray an empty aerosol can.

Slap: Slap your own hand or leg.

Ringing phone: Ring a bicycle bell.

Galloping horse: Slap your open palms against your chest in a galloping rhythm.

Crickets: In a high-pitched, soft voice say, "Knee-deep, knee-deep, knee-deep, rivit, rivit, knee-deep..."

Buoy bell: Tap a glass bowl with a spoon.

Cork popping: Put your index finger way inside your mouth against your cheek, build up air pressure and quickly curl your finger forward making a mouth pop.

Punch: Punch your fist into the palm of your other hand.

Falling thud: Pound your fist into a pillow.

Crunching bones: Grind hard candy in a plastic bag with a hammer.

Blood-and-guts fight: Squash a bowl of soft spaghetti with a bathroom plunger.

Chapter 11

OPPORTUNITY

AMERICAN FREEDOM

We usually think of laws as things that tell us what we must do or can't do. There are laws that require you to be a certain age to get a driver's license or prohibit you from taking things that don't belong to you. Laws say that you must go to school, tell the truth in court, and get licenses to operate a business. But in America there are also laws that work the other way—laws that give every American citizen certain rights and that say what the government can and cannot do. The most important of these laws make up the Bill of Rights which became a part of our constitution in 1791. Under the protection of these laws, you are guaranteed, among other things, the freedom to say what you like, to practice any religion you choose, to vote and hold public office, to enjoy privacy, and to own property. Newspapers can publish whatever they want so long as it is to the best of their knowledge true, even if what is written doesn't please the government. The people can assemble in a group of any size, for any purpose so long as they do it peacefully. The government can't search your house or take anything from you unless they have a good reason and get permission from a court judge beforehand. And should you be accused of breaking a law, you have the right to know what you are accused of and the right to have a trial. In court, you don't have to say anything that will show that you are guilty, and you can question the person who has accused you. If you are found to be innocent, you cannot be tried again for the same crime.

Rights of children

All Americans have these basic rights, rights that are guaranteed by the Constitution of the United States. There are other rights, however, that are limited to certain people at certain times. As a kid, you must know there are many things you can't do legally until you reach a certain age. The legal ages for working, driving a car, writing a will,

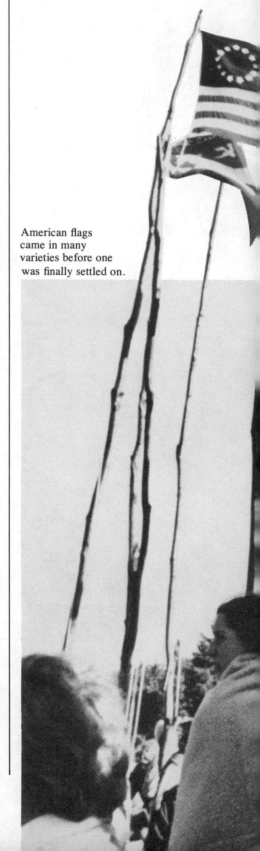

American flags came in many varieties before one was finally settled on.

buying alcoholic beverages, and getting married, among other things, are regulated by each state. Children must also by law go to school until they reach a certain age—usually between sixteen and eighteen years old depending on particular state laws. Children are also considered the responsibility of their parents or legal guardian until they are mature enough to be responsible for themselves. In most states, the legal age for children to be subject to the same rights and laws as adults is eighteen years old but in a few states the age is nineteen and in some as high as twenty-one. However, as a child under the legal age, you have certain special rights guaranteed by law.

Parents can discipline children and even use reasonable force in doing so, but no parent can abuse or mistreat a child by using excessive force. If you know of parents who

are too rough in their discipline, have been rough enough to cause bruises or other physical injuries, tell your school counselor and he will contact the proper state agency which will look into the matter and do something about it.

The right of a schoolteacher or school administrator to discipline a child at school varies from state to state and even among schools in a particular state. However, no teacher can punish a child using unreasonable force, regardless of the cause. If you think a teacher has physically hurt you by some form of punishment, tell your parents. They should contact and discuss the matter with the principal.

Parents are obligated to support their children by supplying food, clothing, shelter, and medical care, usually until the child is twenty-one years old. But that obligation is limited to the parents financial ability. You cannot force your parents to buy you fancy or expensive clothes or more clothing than you actually need. Nor can you make them feed you any food you like. Parents are only obligated by law to give their children minimal support.

As a child, you cannot be forced to work to support yourself or others. And even if you want to work, the younger you are, the more limited are the kinds of work you can do. There are many types of jobs a child under the age of sixteen cannot hold, including jobs in construction, operating power machinery, mining, and other types of employment that might be hazardous. Fourteen- and fifteen-year-olds are allowed to work but only at non-hazardous jobs, and only outside of school hours. Most states do not allow children under the age of fourteen to hold regular jobs, and some states require children under sixteen or eighteen to obtain work permits or "working papers" before they can get a full-time job.

If you do work as a child, your parents are entitled to all the money you make, but usually parents allow children to keep most or all the money they earn for their own use. Any money or property you inherit, however, is completely yours.

As you become older, you will become aware of more laws that protect you and govern what you can and cannot do. Ignorance of the law in America is not a valid excuse for breaking it and it is every American citizen's responsibility to be aware of what laws affect their daily lives.

As times and attitudes in America change, so must the laws that govern the people. Although new laws are made by the government, many obsolete laws dating back to a time when they were deemed necessary remain. Lots of these laws are no longer effective nor enforced, but they are still technically "on the books" until state lawmakers get around to repealing them. Here are some examples:

No one may stop children from jumping over water puddles in the town of Hanford, California.

Growing dandelions in Pueblo, Colorado, is against the law.

It is illegal in Vermont to whistle under water.

In Compton, California, it is against the law to dance cheek to cheek.

Beanshooters are prohibited in the state of Arkansas.

Turtle racing in the city of Key West, Florida, is outlawed.

Geese may not be walked on the main street of MacDonald, Ohio.

IT'S THE LAW!

Roller-skating in the streets of Quincy, Massachusetts, is a punishable offense.

The state of Kentucky prohibits patrons from sleeping in a restaurant.

A hunter cannot shoot a camel in Arizona.

In Kansas, restaurants are not allowed to serve ice cream on a slice of cherry pie.

Milkmen must walk, not run, when delivering in St. Louis, Missouri.

In Lynn, Massachusetts, it is illegal to give coffee to children.

You are not allowed to put pennies in your ears while in Hawaii.

During the months of January through April in the state of Wyoming, it is against the law to photograph a rabbit without first obtaining a special permit.

When a man meets a cow in Pine Island, Minnesota, he is required by law to remove his hat.

In Berea, Ohio, every animal out in the streets after dark must wear a red taillight.

A Florida law makes it illegal to take off your clothes while bathing—even in your own bathtub.

It is against the law in Minnesota to hang men's and women's underwear on the same clothesline.

A hotel guest in California cannot peel an orange in his hotel room.

In Los Angeles, California, a customer at a food market cannot poke his finger into a turkey.

Bathing suits must be inspected by the police before wearing at the beach in Rochester, Michigan.

New Jersey restaurant patrons are not allowed to slurp their soup.

In Huntsville, Alabama, a person cannot move his bed without first getting a permit from the police.

Bicycle riders in Denver, Colorado, may not lift their feet higher than the front wheel while riding.

The mayor of Danbury, Connecticut, says who may or who may not fly a kite on the city streets.

In Atlanta, Georgia, it is illegal for anyone to make strange faces at children in a school classroom.

Taking a bath during the winter is prohibited in Clinton, Indiana.

Bears cannot be disturbed to have their pictures taken in Fairbanks, Alaska.

In Washington, D.C., it is illegal to go fishing while on horseback.

People in Saco, Missouri, cannot wear hats that frighten children.

In Meligh, New Hampshire, bakers are forbidden from selling doughnut holes.

In North Carolina, people are not allowed to sing out of tune.

And baby-sitters in Altoona, Pennsylvania, cannot eat everything in their employers' refrigerator.

Anyone in the state of Maine walking with his shoelaces untied is subject to a fine.

HOW TO BE A POLITICIAN

Try to imagine having a job with thousands of bosses—thousands of people telling you what to do and how to do it. When a politician is elected to a job, he has promised these bosses—the people—that he will represent them and take care of their needs. Often the job isn't easy. It is difficult, if not impossible, to please all the people all the time. Then why do people become politicians? Sometimes a person has a special cause—say, stopping pollution or getting better care for the poor—and they feel that the most effective way to do something about is to become a member of the government. Or someone might just think that they can do the job better than anyone else—including the person who has the job now. And sometimes a person wants to be elected to a government job because, even though it is hard work, it can also be fun and exciting to be in the business of running America.

Someone who runs for an elected government job is called a politician. To be a politician there are no formal requirements except a minimum age for some offices. But the process of getting elected does require certain personal attributes and a serious dedication. It helps a lot if you like people and can talk to them, as well as listen to what they have to say. As a politician, you must represent everyone you are elected to represent, not just your friends.

Can you handle the job?

To be a politician you should be self-confident. If you don't believe that you can do a great job if elected, then no one else will believe that you can either. You will have to be a good organizer. As a political candidate, and if elected, you will have a lot of things that need to be done and somehow never enough time to do them all. You should be able to work well with other people, because you will need their help to get everything accomplished. You should also be able to take criticism without getting upset or discouraged. Not everyone you talk with is going to agree with your views and ideas, and some people may be just plain hostile to your viewpoint. Remember that some people are going to vote for the other candidate, and they have a right to their convictions too.

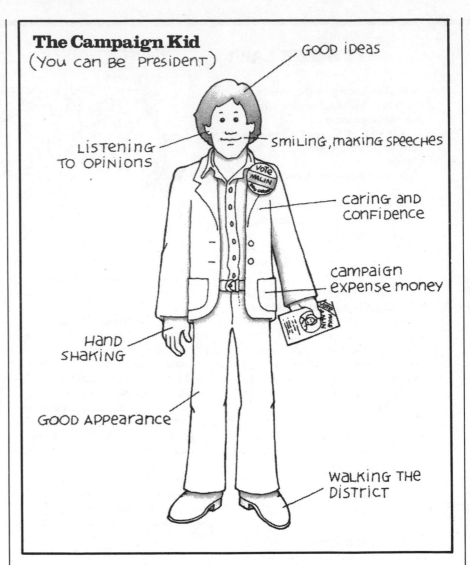

The Campaign Kid
(You can Be President)

GOOD ideas

SMILING, making speeches

caring and confidence

campaign expense money

walking the district

LISTENING TO OPINIONS

Hand shaking

GOOD APPEARANCE

The Campaign

If you want, as an adult, to become a politician, you'll have to run for an elected office and organize a political campaign to get yourself elected. The main idea is to meet as many voters in person as possible and be sure the others at least know who you are, and what you plan to do in the job if elected. Here are a few pointers to remember.

A local campaign

Run first for an elected job in your home town and then work your way up from there to other jobs. In each job, you will be getting more experience in running some part of the government and representing a specific group of people. And, of course, more and more people will have gotten to know you.

It is important that you feel that you can do the job better than the person who is presently doing it. Suppose that you decide to run for the job of town dogcatcher, perhaps an elected office in your town. Let's say the present dogcatcher has decided he is going to run for something else this coming election and there don't seem to be too many other people interested in the job. It seems as though you might have a chance to win. Next find out everything you can about the job. Will you just have to catch stray dogs, or will you have to feed and shelter them also? What will you be paid for your work, and how much time will it take? How is the present dogcatcher doing the job—how can you do it better? Maybe because you are young and a fast runner, you are better at catching dogs then someone older and slower. Maybe you have some good ideas about how to get stray dogs back to their owners or ideas about helping people keep their dogs from getting loose in the first place. Whatever good traits you would bring to the job or good ideas you have about being a dogcatcher, you should make the voters aware of so they will vote for you on election day.

A future in politics?

If you decide some day to run for a major political job, like mayor of the town or state representative from your district, you may want to join a political party so you can get their support to help you win. There are two major political parties in America—the Democrats and Republicans—as well as many smaller ones. A political party is an organization of people who generally have the same ideas about what government should do for the people. If you agree with the ideas of a particular political party and they like your ideas, the party members may decide to support your campaign by handing out brochures, calling people, organizing get-acquainted meetings, and doing whatever they can to convince the voters to vote for you. Or you might choose to run as an "independent" candidate and organize your own group of people to work for your campaign.

You would have to plan your campaign well in advance but start to campaign only about three to four weeks before election day. If you begin too early, the people may not yet be interested in the election, or they might forget about you and your ideas by election time. If you start too late, you may not have time to meet enough people. The most important campaign time is the week before election day when most people are making up their minds who to vote for.

Round up your supporters

During the campaign you'll need to get all the help you can. Have your supporters hand out fliers, put up posters, and write "letters to the editor" recommending your election. Send them to all the newspapers in your voting district. Someone might act as your publicity or public relations manager and he can inform the newspapers, radio, and television when you are planning to make a special announcement—maybe an answer to an opponent's charges against you, or a notice of where you'll be campaigning. Perhaps you and your opponents will have a debate. You'll have to remember to keep the media posted and they might advertise your events and possibly report on them in the news. And while your supporters are making telephone calls, knocking on doors, and handing out literature, you should be busy meeting the people—visiting shopping centers, public functions, and private parties. Your supporters will arrange to have "coffees" in their own neighborhoods to introduce you to their friends so you can answer questions, listen to ideas, and ask the people to vote for you.

As election day approaches, your supporters should call those voters they think will support you to remind them to vote, and ask if they need a ride to the voting polls. On election day, your campaign is nearly over but your campaign people should still be checking to see that people get out and vote. Now you just have to wait for the vote to be counted, then—win or lose—you can relax.

THE PRESIDENT WANTS TO HEAR FROM YOU

After someone has been elected to a political office, it is his job to represent all the people in his district—not just the people who voted for him, but all the people. In order to represent all the people, the representative must always know what the people want and what they think of the job he or she is doing. And that is your job. It is your responsibility to tell your elected officials how you feel about certain issues and what you want done. You communicate your feelings by writing a letter, sending a telegram, or collecting signatures on a petition which you send to your representative. Here is how to go about it.

If you want to get in touch with a state representative, you can usually phone him at his statehouse office. If you are not sure who your state representatives are, then call your state citizen-information or legislature-information phone number listed in the telephone directory. Tell the person who answers where you live and they will be happy to give you the names, addresses and phone numbers of your district representatives.

Let them know your opinion

If your opinion has to do with national or international affairs, you will want to let your U.S. congressman or even the president know. It is not quite so easy to call them directly. Although congressmen spend much of their time in Washington, D.C., they do have local offices equipped to listen to your opinions and answer your questions. Or you can write directly to your congressman. Make your letter brief and to the point, but do say who you are and why you think whatever you do. Then send your letter to:

> The Honorable (U.S. representative's name)
> U.S. House of Representatives
> Washington, D.C. 20515

or

> The Honorable (U.S. senator's name)
> U.S. Senate
> Washington, D.C. 20510

If you don't know who your U.S. congressmen are, call your city hall information telephone or town clerk and they should be able to tell you.

If you wish to write to the president of the United States, send your letter to:

> The President
> The White House
> Washington, D.C. 20500

If you are in a bit of a hurry for some reason, you can send a special telegram to the president called a Personal Opinion Message—it is much cheaper than sending a regular telegram. First think out your message and write it down in fifteen words or less, then call your local Western Union operator and say that you want to send a Personal Opinion Message to the president. The operator will take your message, your name and phone number, and the cost for the telegram will be charged on your next phone bill.

Will they answer?

Once you have called, written a letter, or sent a telegram, the following is what is likely to happen: If your letter just expressed an opinion, you may not get a letter in response. However, representatives do keep count of how many people are for or against a particular issue so they can do what the majority wants them to. If you asked a specific question in your letter, or if you wanted some particular information, you probably will get a letter back in answer. Sometimes the letter will be from the elected official himself, but more often the letter you receive will have been written by one of his staff members who is authorized to sign the official's name. In either case, you can be sure that your letter will be read and your opinion appreciated. The president and your other elected government officials want to hear from you.

PRESIDENTS COME IN ALL SHAPES AND SIZES

Of the thirty-nine presidents, from George Washington to Jimmy Carter, Americans have elected men in all shapes and sizes (from tiny James Madison to an over-three-hundred-pound William Taft), from all areas of the country (Ohio with seven presidents and Virginia with six win out), and from many different backgrounds. Five American presidents were born in log cabins and a few were born to wealthy and socially prominent families. Nine presidents never went to college. George Washington went to school for only six years, and Andrew Johnson never went at all.

There have been lawyers, teachers, merchants, a farmer, an engineer, a journalist, a tailor, and ten army generals elected president as well as several relatives of previous presidents. John Adams and John Quincy Adams were father and son. William Harrison was Benjamin Harrison's grandfather and Theodore Roosevelt and Franklin Roosevelt were cousins. The American people have not yet elected a woman or a member of a minority group as president but that too will undoubtedly someday happen. Even you can be the president of the United States.

HOLIDAYS AND CELEBRATIONS

We Americans have a tradition of working hard, but we also like our holidays and celebrations. We have dozens of special days set aside in honor of one thing or another. We commemorate, inaugurate, honor, observe, memorialize, and celebrate almost anything. But for all our festivity, there is only one holiday permanently established by law: Sunday. And there are only two official national holidays proclaimed each year by the president: Thanksgiving and Independence Day. All other holidays and celebrations are determined by tradition and by yearly proclamations made by the governor of each state.

"We made it" feast

Thanksgiving is the oldest American holiday. It was first celebrated in October of 1621, when the Pilgrims feasted and gave thanks for having survived their first winter in America and having had a plentiful enough harvest to survive yet another. The Pilgrims, along with the Indians who had helped them to cultivate and hunt the new land, celebrated and feasted for three days, eating venison, goose, and duck, and drinking berry wine.

Thanksgiving became an annual fall event in New England and was occasionally celebrated in other regions of America. In 1863, Sarah Josepha Hale, the editor of a then popular magazine, waged an editorial campaign to make Thanksgiving a holiday for all Americans. The people's sentiments were with her and President Lincoln declared the first national Thanksgiving. Since then, and usually on the fourth Thursday of November, the holiday of feasting on turkey, cranberries, and pumpkin pie has been celebrated by all Americans.

Happy Second of July

American Independence Day has been an annual national celebration since the day America was founded in 1776 but the celebration hasn't always been held on the Fourth of July. That first year Independence Day was celebrated on July 2, the day the Colonies officially separated from Great Britain. By the next year, however, the holiday had moved up two days to July 4, the day the Continental Congress accepted the Declaration of Independence. Independence Day was first celebrated only in Philadelphia, but over the next few years the celebration spread to other cities and states, until the holiday was declared a national event and all Americans celebrated America's birthday on the Fourth of July.

All Fourth of Julys, since the first, have been celebrated in much the same way with parades, picnics, speeches, fireworks, bonfires, and bell-ringing. The only Independence Day custom practiced by the Early Americans that we don't observe today was putting lighted candles in house windows to show support for the new American government.

Why not Clown Month?

Some holidays are traditional for all states like Christmas, New Year's Day, and Labor Day, while the date for others like Memorial Day vary from state to state. Also, each state or region of the country has its own special day or days that only it celebrates: Maine and Massachusetts have Patriot's Day on April 19, while Kentucky commemorates Franklin D. Roosevelt's birthday January 30, and Oklahoma celebrates Will Rogers Day on November 4. States also proclaim special days, weeks, or months to honor particular people or events like Clown Week, Peanut Month, or Johnny Appleseed Day. Other days such as Halloween and Valentine's Day are traditional but not official days of celebration. The president or governor don't proclaim them, and banks and official buildings do not close. People celebrate them as special American days anyway.

Make Your Own Official Day of Celebration

How does an ordinary day get to be proclaimed as special? It's really a rather simple process. Anyone can ask the governor of his state to proclaim anything a reason for celebration. Maybe you would like your birthday honored or a week declared in honor of your school. Or maybe you love eating ice cream cones and feel that the ice cream cone needs to be appreciated and recognized by more Americans for the cold, sweet, satisfaction it has given to kids for so many years. If you would like your state to declare an Ice Cream Cone Day, you can have it done—and maybe get to meet the governor as well.

The first thing to think of is all the reasons why ice cream cones should be honored, and then decide on what date you would like to proclaim Ice Cream Cone Day. Now write a letter to the governor of your state telling him who you are, the holiday you would like proclaimed, and when. Give all the reasons you have thought of as well. You might write your reasons in typical proclamation fashion by using the word "whereas" before each reason and concluding with a "therefore," suggesting a way of celebrating.

Ice Cream Cone Day— A Proclamation

Whereas: Ice Cream Cones are a summer institution in this state; and

Whereas: They come in a wide variety of flavors; and

Whereas: Ice Cream Cones provide cheap and cool refreshment to thousands of children and adults each day of the year; and

Whereas: This year will be the seventy-fourth year that Americans have enjoyed this unique frozen treat; and

Whereas: American ingenuity is constantly developing new and more flavorful variations of the Ice Cream Cone; and

Whereas: Without Ice Cream Cones this state would be a less pleasant place to live;

Therefore: I request that the governor of this state proclaim that August 26, 1978 be designated Ice Cream Cone Day and call upon all citizens to remember the Ice Cream Cone and support this American institution by enjoying an Ice Cream Cone on that day in the flavor of their choice.

GUIDE TO THE

In many communities throughout America kids are invited to take part in festive parades and other celebrations in which they decorate and parade their bicycles or doll carriages. Some-

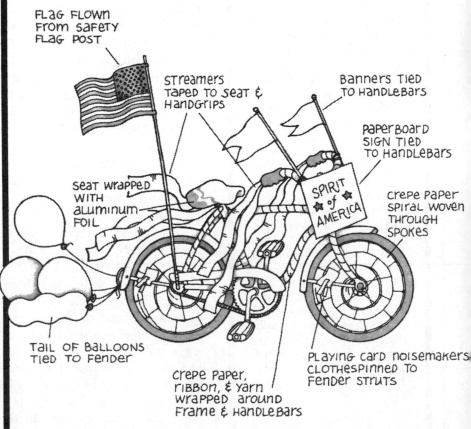

FLAG FLOWN FROM SAFETY FLAG POST

STREAMERS TAPED TO SEAT & HANDGRIPS

BANNERS TIED TO HANDLEBARS

PAPERBOARD SIGN TIED TO HANDLEBARS

SEAT WRAPPED WITH ALUMINUM FOIL

SPIRIT of AMERICA

CREPE PAPER SPIRAL WOVEN THROUGH SPOKES

TAIL OF BALLOONS TIED TO FENDER

CREPE PAPER, RIBBON, & YARN WRAPPED AROUND FRAME & HANDLEBARS

PLAYING CARD NOISEMAKERS CLOTHESPINNED TO FENDER STRUTS

If you can't think of good reasons to celebrate your special day, you can propose a date of celebration, asking that "citizens take cognizance of this event and participate fittingly in its observance." That just means that people may celebrate the day for any reason they like.

Send your letter to the governor at his office in the capitol building of your state. In time, the governor or one of his press secretaries, will review your request. If your proclamation is approved, you will be contacted and told a date and time to come to the statehouse to meet the governor (or sometimes his representative) and participate in the ceremony of your proclamation being signed and made official. You will be given a copy of the legal proclamation document, and in some states you will also receive a photograph of you and the governor together taken during the signing. The proclamation will be good for celebrating the holiday only once during the next twelve months. If you want to celebrate the day again next year, you will have to go through the whole process again. Now that your proclamation is official, you could begin to make your plans to "fittingly participate" in its observance.

Official Whatever Days

If you combined all the national and state holidays with the days of proclamation in America, you would probably find a reason to rejoice literally every day of the year. So if you would like a few more days to celebrate this year, mark down which of these events interests you the most.

January
7:   Millard Fillmore's birthday
second week: Joke Revival Week
16:   National Nothing Day
29:   Common Sense Day

WELL-DECORATED BIKE OR DOLL CARRIAGE

times prizes or awards are given for the best-decorated bike or carriage. Although there is no "right" way to decorate your bike or carriage, the idea is to cover as much of it as possible with a colorful assortment of crepe paper, ribbon, aluminum foil, tissue paper, balloons, string, yarn, and paperboard signs.

However, if you do decorate a bike or doll carriage, you must be absolutely certain that none of the decorations interfere with the function of wheels, chains, brakes, or steering. Hang streamers only where they can't get caught in moving parts, and be sure not to put up any decoration or sign that might block your vision.

When the celebration is over, you may want to display your bike or carriage for a while, but before you put it back to normal use, be sure to remove all the decorations including tape and tied pieces of string and yarn. Except for parades and other supervised celebrations, it is not safe to ride a bike or push a carriage in the street that has been decorated.

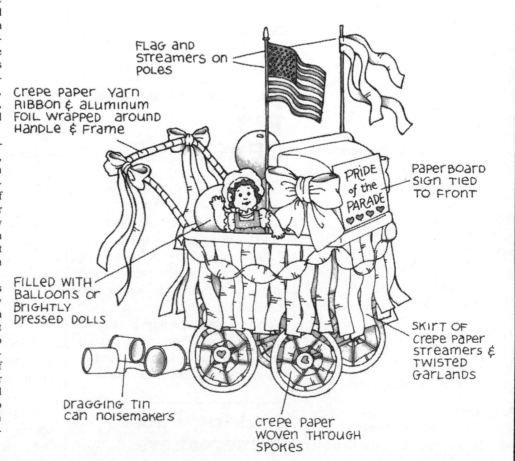

FLaG anD STreamers on POLes

Crepe Paper Yarn RIBBon & aLuminum FOIL WrapPeD arounD HanDLe & Frame

PRIDE of the PARADE

PAPerBoarD SIGn TIeD TO Front

FILLeD WITH BaLLoons or BrIGHTLY DresseD DOLLS

Dragging Tin can noisemakers

crepe paper WoVen THrouGH SPoKes

SKIrt OF Crepe Paper STreamers & TWISTeD GarLanDs

February
National Music Month
1:   National Freedom Day/Robinson Crusoe Day
2:   Groundhog Day
second week: National New Idea Week
29:   Bachelor's Day

March
National Hamburger and Pickle Month
National Dandelion Month
National Peanut Month
second week: National Procrastination Week
15:   Buzzard Day in Ohio

April
National Automobile Month
first week: National Laugh Week
third week: National Coin Week/Bike Safety Week
22:   Earth Day
fourth week: National Baby Week

May
first week: National Family Week/Be Kind to Animals Week
1:   Lei Day in Hawaii
second week: Let's Go Fishing Week
8:   Children Should Be Seen and Not Heard Day
15:   Rooster Day

June
Fight the Filthy Fly Month
second Sunday: Children's Day
third week: National Little League Baseball Week
21:   Flower Day

July
1:   First U.S. Postage Stamp anniversary
20:   Men on the Moon Day

August
National Sandwich Month
first week: Smile Week/National Clown Week
21:   The Queen of Oz's birthday

September
5:   Be Late for Something Day
8:   National Pardon Day
26:   National Good Neighbor Day
fourth Friday: American Indian Day

October
National Pizza Month
first Sunday: Grandparents' Day
second week: National Letter Writing Week
third week: National Joke Telling Week
fourth week: National Cleaner Air Week
27:   Good Bear Day

November
first week: American Art Week
second week: Split Pea Soup Week
12:   National Ding-A-Ling Day
third week: Asparagus Week

December
17:   Wright Brothers' Day
third Friday: Underdog Day

FIRE-CRACKERS

The Fourth of July has traditionally been celebrated in America with colorful displays of fireworks and loud popping firecrackers. However, because they are explosive and potentially dangerous, most states only allow fireworks and firecrackers to be bought and used by adults who have first obtained a special permit from their city or town. Permits are usually limited to *public* displays and celebrations.

Making Paper Firecrackers

Using a plain piece of notebook paper, you can make a paper firecracker that can give you a *bang* just about as loud as the real thing. Instead of lighting a fuse to explode the tiny bit of gunpowder inside, a paper firecracker makes its bang using a quick flick of the wrist.

1. You'll need a sheet of notebook paper, stiff wrapping paper or typewriter paper. Cut out a square about seven or eight inches (eighteen or twenty cm.) square, Fig. 1.

Fig. 1

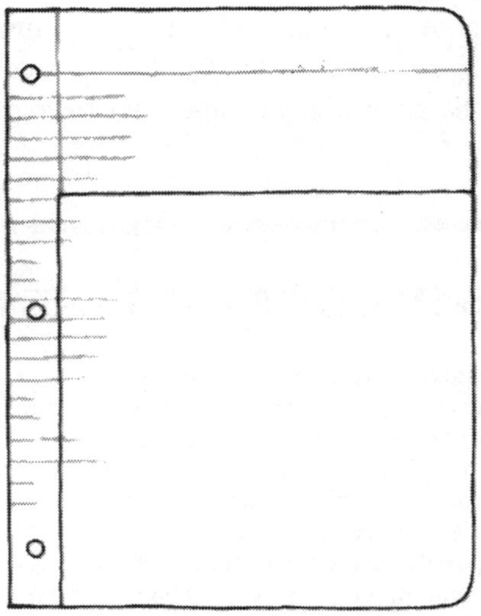

2. Fold the square in half so that the bottom edge of the sheet comes within a half inch (thirteen mm.) of the top edge. Crease the fold well, Fig. 2.

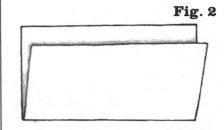

Fig. 2

3. Now fold the sheet in half again from side to side so the flap is on the inside. Crease the fold well, Fig. 3.

4. Hold the paper firecracker tightly between your thumb and index finger at the open corner where the paper is only two thicknesses thick, Fig. 4.

Paper firecrackers make loud "pops" and are harmless.

Fig. 3

Fig. 4

5. To make the firecracker bang, quickly flick your arm and wrist downward. The inside paper flap will pop out and make a loud snap. You may have to practice your wrist flick several times to get a really loud bang. The more flexible the creases of your firecracker become with use, the louder a pop you can make. "Reset" the firecracker by folding the flap back into its original position.

To make the sound of a firecracker rocket, have a group of friends set off paper firecrackers at the same time by popping and resetting them as quickly as possible.

NEED INFORMATION?

The United States government prints and sells books, pamphlets, magazines, posters, and maps concerning nearly anything and everything. Many of these, as you might expect, have to do with government business—legislative debates, reports from Congress and official bills—but there are thousands of others about such subjects as:

Airplanes	Government
Architecture	Growing up
The Arts	Health
Baby-sitting	Home repairs
Bicycles	Insects
Camping	Law
Careers	Music
College	Pets
Commuters	Photography
Cooking	Railroads
Energy	Space
Fishing	exploration
Floods	Sports
Foreign	Stamps and
countries	coins
Fossils	Swimming
Gardening	Weather

To get a complete listing of subjects, write to the government at this address:

Superintendent of Documents
Government Printing Office
Washington, D.C. 20402

Ask for a free copy of the *Consumer's Guide to Federal Publications*. Order forms are included for detailed lists and prices. Many government publications are priced under a dollar and several are free. You can ask to be put on the mailing list for a free monthly (ten times a year) publication called *Selected U.S. Government Publications* which describes the most recent publications, as well as others of interest.

Information stores

The Government Printing Office also operates its own bookstores in many major cities across the country where you can shop and buy many of the more popular government books, pamphlets, and posters. To see if there is a G.P.O. bookstore near you, look in the white pages of the telephone directory under U.S. Government. Look down the listings for Government Printing Office—bookstore.

The Government Printing Office isn't the only U.S. agency eager to give you information. The Consumer Information Center has several how-to-do-it and what-to-buy type booklets. Write to them for a catalog of all subjects covered. The address is:

> Consumer Information Center
> Pueblo, Colorado 81009

If you want a map showing all the geographical features of a particular area, maybe where you live, including hiking trails, old roads, public buildings, and other landmarks, you can write to:

> Defense Mapping Agency
> Topographic Center
> Attention 55500
> Washington, D.C. 20315

They will let you know how you can buy the maps you want directly from them or what retail stores near your area carry them.

Perhaps you would like an authentic reproduction of the Declaration of Independence or some other famous American document. For a list of what is available ask for "documents from America's past" when writing to:

> General Services
>   Administration
> Publications Sales Branch
> NEPS-G
> Washington, D.C. 20408

For more information on science, technology, history or the arts in America, request a catalog of books and pamphlets from:

> The Smithsonian Institution Press
> Publication Distribution Section
> 1111 North Capitol Street
> Washington, D.C. 20002

SYMBOLS OF AMERICA

If by some magic you could change into any animal at all, what particular animal do you think would best represent you? Would you be a lazy lapdog, warm and loving but also wanting someone to take care of you, or a ferocious and cunning tiger? Think about yourself, who you are, and what your strongest characteristics and beliefs might be. Now try to imagine what animal has those similar traits and might best represent you. You might also think about what vegetable or fruit is "you" or what season of the year, month, day of the week, tree, or color. The things

you choose to stand for you might be said to "symbolize" you.

I'm THE KID

Symbols are a kind of shorthand way of informing others who and what you are. For example, sports teams have names and accompanying symbols that often brag about their toughness: The Giants, Eagles, Warriors, and Vikings. Stores, shops, and restaurants may also put out signs with symbols that easily and quickly tell the passerby what the shop offers. Look at the store signs in your town, and you might find symbols in the shape or image of eyeglasses, plants, hamburgers, keys, paint cans, or whatever. Each symbol represents the product or attitude that the owner

Can you tell from these shop signs what businesses they represent?

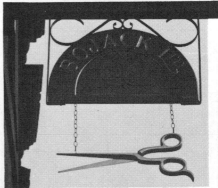

would like you to know him by.

Americans, likewise, have always been proud of what their country stands for, and since Colonial days, America has had its symbols to give notice and warning that America is strong and fearless, yet free and just. The following are some of the symbols that we Americans have chosen to represent our country and our American attitudes.

American Flag

One of the best-known symbols of our country is the American flag. Every day the "Stars and Stripes" fly over government buildings, schools, post offices, American

An Independence Day parade.

ships at sea—anywhere someone wants to display national pride. However, the American flag we know today looked somewhat different when it was first designed, and has had a rather uncertain history.

Before its declaration of independence from Great Britain, America was represented by many different flags, hundreds of them in fact. There were flags for each of the colonies, a flag for each town, flags for army regiments and flags for ships. One flag that was flown

in all thirteen colonies was the Grand Union—a flag of red and white stripes with a small replica of the British flag in its upper left-hand corner. The origin of the stripes is uncertain (perhaps they were copied from one of the flags used by the British navy), but there were thirteen stripes on the Grand Union, one for each colony. The small British flag emblem represented the British king who ruled over the colonies.

A flag of our own

After America declared its independence, the Grand Union was no longer a fitting symbol, but it was not until June 14, 1777, that the American Congress decided on a design for a new flag. The design kept the thirteen red and white stripes of the Grand Union but replaced the British emblem with thirteen white stars on a blue background. The red color of the flag represented earth, hardiness, and courage; blue stood for heaven,

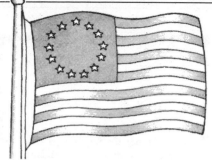

vigilance, and justice; and white for liberty, purity, and innocence.

More confusion

However, in its haste Congress agreed on what symbols would make up the flag but not its actual design. So whoever made a flag designed his own variation. The most popular was a flag with seven red and six white horizontal stripes with thirteen five-pointed white stars on a blue field in the upper-left-hand corner. But there is no record and no one seems to really know who actually designed it first. The most popular legend has it that George Washington made a sketch and gave it to Betsy Ross who then made some changes in the design and sewed up what was to be called the first American flag. We don't even know for sure when the American flag was first officially flown.

After Vermont and Kentucky joined the United States, Congress decided to add another star and stripe for each state. So for a while the American flag had fifteen

stripes and fifteen stars. It was this version of the flag that Francis Scott Key admired as he wrote the "Star Spangled Banner."

Our "Star Spangled Banner"

It soon became obvious that as more territories joined the United States, the flag would become crowded with too many stripes. Finally in 1818, Congress voted on a more specific flag design. From now on the stripes were to be horizontal and the stars five-pointed; only a star would be added to the flag for each new state. The thirteen stripes would remain in honor of the original thirteen colonies.

Again in 1912, the United States Congress reviewed the design of the American flag and determined standards for size and shape of the stars and stripes, as well as the exact colors of red, white, and blue to be used. Congress also established rules for displaying the flag. Some of these are listed in the box, but periodically these are revised to meet new circumstances. For example, the law used to state that the flag could be flown only on "days when the weather permits." With the technological advances made in weather-resistant flag material and outdoor lighting, the law has been changed so that an all-weather American flag can be displayed anytime.

The Donkey and the Elephant

The Democrats and Republicans haven't always used the donkey and elephant as their symbols—in a way, the parties didn't even choose them. It was Thomas Nast, a political cartoonist working for the magazine *Harper's Weekly*, who first drew the Democrats as donkeys and the Republicans as elephants sometime in the 1870's.

First to appear was the donkey. Nast was a Republican and he drew a cartoon making fun of the Demo-crats by showing them as stubborn, lazy donkeys. His Republican readers thought the image was fitting and they encouraged Nast to continue symbolizing the Democrats as donkeys. It didn't take long for the image to stick, and the Democrats had little choice but to accept the donkey as their mascot.

The elephant by popular demand

Three years after the donkey first appeared, Nast drew a political cartoon showing the Republican voters as an elephant. As odd as this may seem now, the Republicans *liked* the image and thought the

power and size of the elephant represented them well; perhaps they were also a bit jealous that the Democrats had a symbol and they didn't. So the elephant, by popular demand, was adopted by the Republicans for their mascot.

The Great Seal of the United States

The official seal of America is our nation's coat of arms, a symbol of American ideals and independence.

The Great Seal of the United States is used not only for display, but it is also placed on certain documents signed by the president, such as government bills and treaties with other nations. In fact, these documents are not considered legal unless the United States Seal is there to authenticate the president's signature.

Traditionally a nation's seal was the coat of arms of its ruler. But America had no royal or ruling family, so a design that represented America had to be created. It took six years, three committees, and countless revisions before the design was finally decided.

The Seal explained

Take a look at the Great Seal; you can find it on the back of a one-dollar bill. The two circles on the bill show the two sides of the seal. On the face side is the American bald eagle with a shield of thirteen stripes (representing the original thirteen colonies) topped by one larger stripe (the nation). In his beak the eagle holds a ribbon with the Latin words, *E Pluribus Unum* meaning "one out of many"; in one claw he holds an olive branch representing peace and in the other a bunch of arrows symbolizing strength and war. Above the eagle's head are thirteen stars breaking out of the clouds (again standing for the thirteen colonies forming a new nation).

On the other side of the seal—the left-hand circle on the bill—there is a pyramid symbolizing strength and endurance. At the base of the pyramid is the date 1776 in Roman numerals and at the top is the all-seeing Eye of Providence (to watch over America). Going around this side of the seal are two Latin phrases. The two words across the top have the meaning "God has favored our undertak-

ings"; the bottom three words mean "a new earthly order."

The American Bald Eagle

How do you think the turkey would do as America's national bird? Or how about the goose? Well, both of these birds were suggested to Congress to represent the United States. Benjamin Franklin especially favored the turkey but it was the majestic American bald eagle that was finally selected.

The eagle has long been a sym-

bol of strength and victory to many people. To the American Indians the bald eagle was known as the sacred "thunderbird" whose wings were so huge it could flap them and cause thunder. Another Indian legend has it that the bald eagle is the only bird that can fly to the sun and push it across the sky.

Everything about the bald eagle seemed to represent some facet of America. It is native to North America, and at that time would fly across the entire continent, soaring at great heights, living in lofty places, and swooping down on its prey with unexpected speed. The bald eagle was the perfect symbol to represent America's freedom, power, and majesty.

In 1782, the American bald eagle was adopted as the national bird and has proudly remained one of America's most respected ambassadors.

Uncle Sam

There are a few different versions of the story of how the white-bearded character known as Uncle Sam became a national symbol of the United States. The most popular one has it that during the war of 1812 a man named Sam Wilson of Troy, New York, had the job of inspecting meat for the U.S. Army. Part of Sam's job was to stamp the barrels of inspected meat with the large initials "U.S." standing for United States. Sam Wilson had the nickname Uncle Sam and people in that area began to joke that the bar-  rels of meat and anything else marked U.S. came from Uncle Sam. In this way, Uncle Sam became symbolically connected to America.

Sam becomes news

A local newspaper reported the story, and as the name Uncle Sam spread across America, newspaper cartoonists in other cities began to conjure up images of what Uncle Sam looked like. During the Civil War, cartoonists drew him as a tall, thin, bearded man resembling the president at that time, Abraham Lincoln. In later years, clowns began dressing the part of Uncle Sam, wearing brightly colored, red, white, and blue costumes with stars and stripes. The image of Uncle Sam that we know today—a white-haired, stern-faced man wearing a jacket and top hat decorated in America's colors—began on a World War I army recruiting poster. The Uncle Sam character drawn for that poster by artist James Montgomery Flagg was so successful in encouraging men to join the army, that the image has stuck ever since.

The Pine Tree (Liberty Tree)

The pine tree that is one of our country's symbols was in fact used by the Iroquois Indians as a symbol for their government long before the first European settlers ever arrived. The pine first appeared as a colonial symbol on coins minted by the Massachusetts Bay Colony and later became popular on flags and coins of other colonies. The pine tree was probably popular in the New England colonies because it was a plentiful and valuable resource for construction. Even the colonial flag of the early colonies featured a pine tree until Britain declared that only the English flag could be used.

During the American Revolution the pine tree was once again used as a symbol of America—particularly by the army regiments of New England and later by the U.S. naval fleet. The pine tree was usu-ally referred to as the Liberty Tree, which was probably just as well, since each flag or seal maker drew his own version of the pine which frequently turned out looking more like an oak, spruce, or willow tree, and in one instance, a cabbage.

After the Revolution, the pine tree was considered too closely associated with New England to be used as a symbol for the whole nation. It is still found, however, as an element in the insignia of New York, Maine, and Massachusetts.

AMERICAN SYMBOLS TO DRAW

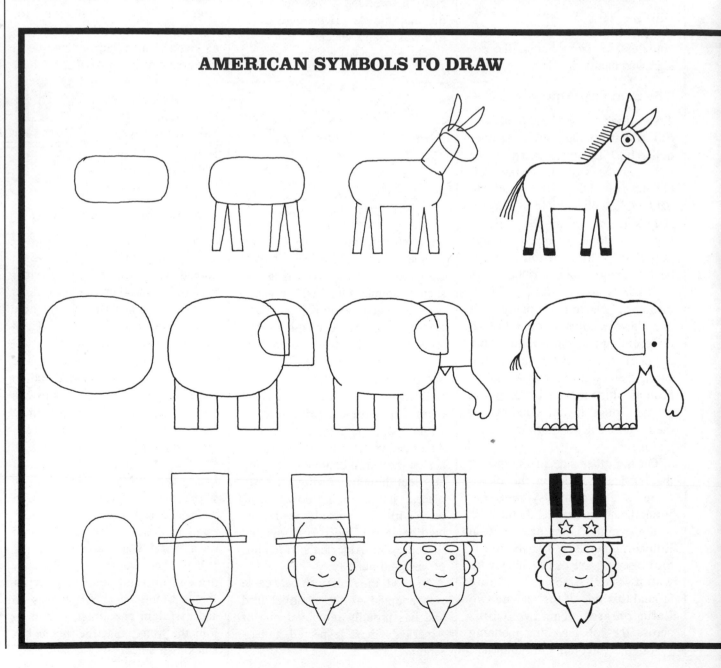

The Rattlesnake

Along with the turkey, the rattlesnake was one of Ben Franklin's suggestions for a national symbol. Not only was the rattlesnake native to North America, but it also possessed many of the same qualities that America stood for. If left alone, the rattlesnake, supposedly like America, is calm and peaceful. But if provoked or stepped on, the rattlesnake is a deadly fighter. The snake always gives warning before striking, never surrenders, and rarely loses a fight. This symbolized our country to a lot of people.

Ben Franklin was more successful in promoting the rattlesnake as an American symbol than the turkey, and the snake soon began appearing as the subject of political cartoons representing the Colonies. During the Revolution, the rattlesnake was an especially popular symbol on flags. Although there were several flag designs, the rattlesnake was most often shown coiled and ready to attack. American mottos of independence, such as "Liberty or Death" or "Don't Tread on Me," were often used with the rattlesnake.

After the Revolution, the rattlesnake lost favor as a national symbol, perhaps because it was too warlike now that the people were trying to build a new country. The United States Defense Department, however, fittingly incorporated the rattlesnake into their official seal.

The Buffalo

Buffalo are native to North America, and at one time (only a hundred years ago or so), they roamed the plains freely in huge herds. Several Indian tribes relied almost entirely on the buffalo, not just for food but for the hide which provided bags, moccasins, tepee coverings, ropes, and clothing. Where the buffalo herds roamed, the Indians would settle.

The settlers hunted the buffalo for food and skins. The buffalo was quite plentiful in those days with over seventy-five million head; and there was little danger of running out of them. But beginning in the 1860's, the buffalo's days were numbered. The railroad began to construct tracks across the plains states and hired professional hunters to provide meat to the workers. The buffalo was large, clumsy, and easy to hunt, and with a powerful rifle a single hunter could kill as many as one hundred fifty buffalos a day. One of those hunters, William Cody, earned his nickname, Buffalo Bill, by killing supposedly no fewer than 4,280 buffalos in a single year.

Industry steps in

At about the same time, commercial leather factories in America, wanting buffalo hides to make into leather, killed off literally millions of buffalo. It became sporting for easterners to go west on hunting expeditions to shoot buffalo for fun.

By 1900 the buffalo population in America had, incredibly enough, dwindled to less than one thousand. The animal that was once native to this country and such a common sight across America for centuries had in a few years become nearly extinct.

Today, even with the efforts of several societies which try to preserve the species, there are only possibly ten thousand buffalos in the country. The animals roam protected land in a few small herds.

To honor the buffalo as a symbol of America's wild west and adventure, the U.S. mint issued the Buffalo nickel in 1913. To date, that is the only official use of the buffalo as an American symbol, but the buffalo should always be a reminder to the American people to conserve our natural resources.

CIGAR STORE INDIAN

It was common in the cities and towns of Early America for trade shops to display eye-catching outdoor signs that advertised what a merchant sold or made. A hatmaker might have the picture of a hat painted on his sign or the entire sign might be cut in the shape of a hat. And likewise, drugstores often had signs displaying large glass bottles filled with colored liquids; an eye-glass store might have a huge pair of spectacles hanging above the shop door; and the cigar and tobacco shops of America usually displayed a brightly painted, life-size wooden Indian. But do you know why the Indian was the symbol for a tobacco store?

Tobacco was a plant native to America and it was first introduced to the settlers by the Indians. Tobacco was more commonly known then as "Indian weed." It was natural for the Indian to become a well-recognized symbol for any tobacco product.

America soon developed a brisk Indian weed trade with England. As an advertising novelty, tobacco shops in England began to display carved Indian figures. Most of these were made by ships' crew members who had been to America and actually seen an Indian. By the mid-eighteenth century, shops in America selling tobacco had also taken up the custom, and the "cigar store Indian" became a well-recognized sight in every town.

Most cigar store Indians were life-size or larger, and often carved from a single tree trunk or hammered in metal. Smaller tobacco shops often had counter-size Indian figures and sometimes only the picture of an Indian painted on the shop window. Indian chiefs and braves were the most popular figures. They were carved wearing head feathers, knee-length skirts, and moccasins; in one raised hand the figure usually held a tomahawk or a bunch of cigars. In later years most cigar store Indians wore a sign that displayed the trademark or brand of tobacco that the store sold.

By the late 1800's many of the cigar store Indians that decorated the sidewalks were being replaced with hanging signs which were much less expensive and didn't take up as much space. One by one the Indian figures became collector's items, but the Indian as a symbol for tobacco is still recognized today.

BUMPER STICKERS

Back in the late 1940's someone got the idea of putting a sign with a personal message on the bumper of his car. Everyone who saw the car got more than one message and the idea of the bumper sticker was born. Today there are millions of bumper stickers on car bumpers as well as bikes, notebooks, windows, fences, doors, lockers, bulletin boards, telephone poles, or anyplace else people are likely to see them.

The first bumper stickers were not stickers at all but only printed strips of paperboard tied or wired onto the car bumper. When the stick-on type first appeared the glue was often so strong that once the sticker was in place, it was on for good. And the printed messages on some early bumper stickers either faded from sunlight or sometimes washed off in the rain. Today most bumper stickers are made from thin vinyl plastic or waterproof paper and they peel right off when you want to change your message.

For many of us Americans the bumper sticker has become a personal advertisement expressing to others what we stand for, showing how we feel about particular issues or political candidates, promoting groups and causes we believe in, telling others about our special interests and pastimes, and very often just giving others a good laugh. There are even bumper stickers that answer questions asked by other bumper stickers. You can tell quite a lot about a person by the one he displays, just as you can get your own ideas and messages across to those people you want to inform.

Make your own bumper sticker

If you can't find a bumper sticker that best expresses your thoughts, there are several ways you can make your own depending on how large you want it to be and where it is going to be placed. To make small bumper stickers (perfect for bike fenders) you can write your messages on blank pressure-sensitive labels using a felt-tip marker. Boxes of these labels are available at most stationery stores and they come in several shapes, sizes, and colors. To make larger bumper stickers, just write your message on a bumper sticker-size piece of paperboard or heavy paper, and then just tape the sign in place. If you plan to display your bumper sticker outdoors, be sure to use waterproof markers or crayons and neatly wrap a piece of clear plastic food wrap around the paperboard before taping it in place.

If you are not quite sure about what you want to say, you might get a few ideas from these actual bumper sticker messages that have been seen in all different parts of America.

WARNING! I BRAKE FOR ANIMALS	UP WITH TREES	DON'T FOLLOW ME I'M LOST TOO
EVERY LITTER BIT HURTS	GOT A LEMON? MAKE LEMONADE	SAVE ON SHOES GO BAREFOOT
EARTH: NO DEPOSIT, NO RETURN	THINK METRIC	DON'T BUMP MY BUMPER
PHOTOGRAPHERS WORK WELL IN THE DARK	HAVE YOU HUGGED YOUR KIDS TODAY?	HAPPINESS IS WINNING
NIGHT IS RIGHT END LIGHT POLLUTION	PITCH IN!	IF YOU CAN READ THIS YOU ARE TOO CLOSE
SPACE IS THE PLACE	AN EVIL MIND IS A GREAT COMFORT	BRAHMS NOT BOMBS
SKY DIVING A NATURAL HIGH	DON'T BE FUELISH	PEACE BEGINS WITH YOU AND ME
FIGHT FOREST FIRES	GIVE A HOOT DON'T POLLUTE	I'D RATHER BE SNORING
FAIR PLAY FOR THE PRESIDENCY	BLESS THIS MESS	BLACK HOLES ARE OUT OF SIGHT
BEAT THE HEATING CRISIS EAT HORSERADISH	TUBA PLAYING IS A LOW BLOW	I WATCH HEAVENLY BODIES
OPEN MINDS SAY MORE THAN OPEN MOUTHS	POLLUTION STINKS	HELP STAMP OUT BUMPER STICKERS

HOBO SIGN LANGUAGE

The hobo, a wanderer, lived by asking for handouts, or offering to trade work for food and a place to sleep. They drifted throughout America during the Depression of the 1930's. Some hobos could sing or dance for a meal, while others might do physical labor. Many hobos did no work at all, but just took what they needed, scrounging food and clothes from people's gardens and clotheslines.

As you might expect, many people were frightened of hobos and would just as soon see them run out of town. It is true that some hobos were dangerous criminals, or maybe just showed a mean disposition, but most hobos, tramps, vagrants, and drifters were people down on their luck looking for work and trying just to get by. Some people were sympathetic and gladly helped the hobo with a handout.

The problem for the hobo was knowing what houses might offer help or who might cause him trouble. So a hobo would look at the corner of the house door, or on a nearby mailbox, fence, sidewalk, or tree for the small written symbol left by other hobos who had previously passed that way. These symbols gave warnings or advice about the house dwellers within or the attitude of the town in general. Of the hundreds of symbols that were used, here is a sampling of the most common.

A kind-hearted woman lives here. The triangles advise to tell her a sad story.

A drink is available. An upside down dipper means no drink is available.

Fresh water and a safe campsite.

This is a good place for a handout.

Home of a kind old lady.

Dangerous drinking water.

Get out of town quick!

This is the place you have been looking for.

No use going in this direction.

The people here beat up hobos.

Home of a dishonest person.

Home of an easy mark, a sucker.

Home of a sympathetic doctor who will treat you for free.

Be prepared to defend yourself.

The owner is in.

The owner is out.

Free telephone here.

Hobos are put in jail in this town.

The police here are on the lookout for hobos.

This town doesn't mind hobos coming through.

This is not a safe place.

Food is available here but you have to work for it.

"OK." or "all right."

The home of a gentleman.

Police here do not welcome hobos.

There has been a crime here and it is not safe for strangers.

A good place to catch the train.

This is a dangerous neighborhood.

A good road to follow.

These people are rich.

You can sleep in the hayloft here.

A well-guarded house.

Look out for a barking dog.

Danger! An ill-tempered man lives here.

AMERICAN MONEY

The very first settlers didn't use money. What they required they got from the land or bartered for with their neighbors. Certain scarce commodities were especially valuable for trading and any colonists who had an extra supply of nails, musket balls, or tobacco could trade them for nearly anything.

The colonists also traded with the Indians and for a while they used the Indian money known as "wampum." Wampum "coins" were made of finely polished shells ground down to a standard size and strung like beads.

British coins were also used for exchange among the settlers and with the Indians (two blue wampum shells equaled one penny). The amount of British money the settlers could have was strictly controlled by England, however, and there just wasn't enough to go around.

Two of yours for three of mine

As the colonies grew, traders and settlers came from several foreign countries, bringing with them their own native currency. Soon, in addition to British coins and wampum, the colonists were trading with Spanish, Dutch, French, German, and Italian coins. The most popular and valuable coin was the Spanish doubloon, or "piece of eight" as it was better known. This silver coin could actually be broken up into eight pieces for making change.

The money situation became quite confusing and so each of the colonies decided to make—or "mint"—its own coins. The best-known colonial money was the Massachusetts tree coin. Each denomination was decorated with a different tree.

The British government didn't like the idea of the colonies minting their own money and declared it illegal for them to make anymore. But that didn't stop the colonists who continued to mint their own coins but dated them with a year previous to the decree to fool the British.

Attractive wallpaper

During the Revolution when America declared its independence from Britain, the United States began to print a national currency to replace the different coins that had been used by the individual colonies. The paper money of that period was called "continentals," and eventually it became worth so little that people sometimes used large bills as wallpaper. Coins were minted from silver, brass, and pewter and they were more highly valued. It was quite common then for people to take their jewelry, silverware, and other metal objects down to the local mint and have them made into coins.

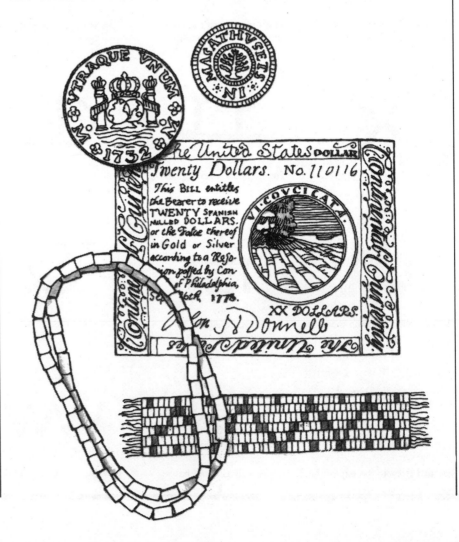

When the Revolutionary War was over and America was at last a free nation, the U.S. Congress decided to establish a more unified and controlled system of money. We still use that system today although during the past two hundred years, our paper bills and coins have often changed in design and denomination.

Why there are ridges in your coins

Today the design and values of coins and paper bills is rather fixed but occasionally changes are made and new denominations added. Check in your pocket and look at the coins and bills you have. There is some interesting information on each if you know what to look for. For example, notice that all of your coins except pennies and nickels have tiny ridges around the edges. When coins were made from gold or silver and worth the precious metal they were made of, some people would cut off the edges of coins before spending them. The edge snippings could be melted down and sold as pure gold or silver. To prevent that dishonest practice, the government mint began putting ridges around the edges of the more valuable coins so that it would be obvious if someone had taken a snip.

Minting coins

Also notice that all American coins are marked with the phrases "In God We Trust" and *"E Pluribus Unum,"* and all are marked with the date of issue, the denomination, and the country identification: the United States of America. If you look closely, you will also see the coin designer's initials and perhaps a mint mark indicating where the coins were made. These marks are usually quite small and almost hidden in the coin design. A mint mark showing a small capital letter *D* shows that the coin was minted in Denver. If a coin has no mint mark at all, it indicates that it was minted in Philadelphia. Coins with the mint letter *S* were made at the San Francisco mint.

Inspecting your fortune

Now take a close look at a dollar bill. What color is the paper? If you look very closely at a bill that isn't too old and dirty, you will see tiny red and blue threads running through the paper. These colored threads are woven into a special paper only used for making money. They help prevent counterfeiting (the making of phony money). All paper money from the one-dollar bill to the one-hundred-dollar bill shows portraits of past presidents or historical American figures on the front sides. The back sides of bills usually show some important government building or event in American history. The serial number that is printed twice on the face of bills is recorded at the United States Treasury Department. The Treasury keeps a record of every bill that has ever been printed. Notice also the date of the bill, printed in small numbers on the face, to the bottom right of the portrait. The date tells the year the bill was designed, not when it was printed.

Coins

At one time America had one-half-cent coins as well as two- and three-cent pieces. For a short time, there was even a twenty-cent piece but it was so close in size and looks to a twenty-five-cent coin that the confusion forced it out of circulation.

Take a closer look at the coins in your pocket. If you have both old and new coins, you might notice a few different symbols or designs for each denomination. You might even be curious about what the symbols mean and why they were chosen to represent America.

Pennies: The Lincoln penny that we use today was first minted in 1909 to commemorate the one hundredth anniversary of Abraham Lincoln's birth. The Lincoln penny was the first common American coin to have a president's portrait on it. Before that we used the Flying Eagle penny (1856 to 1858) and the Eagle Head (1859 to 1909). Both of these looked similar to the Lincoln cent and were generally circulated along with several earlier, very large penny designs. The mint mark on Lincoln cents can be found under the date on the "head" side of some pennies and, if you look closely, you can find there the designer's initials, VDB. Since 1959, the reverse side of the Lincoln penny has carried the image of the Lincoln Memorial in Washington, D.C. This side was done by a different designer with the initials FG. See if you can find them. Lincoln pennies minted before 1959 have two sheaves of wheat on their reverse side—an American symbol for peace and plenty. The penny is made of pure copper and always has been, except for the year 1943 when a war-caused copper shortage forced the mint to make the coins from steel.

Nickels: You would think a nickel would be made mostly of nickel. Actually, the five-cent coin is only one part nickel to three parts copper. The nickel first became an American coin in 1866. Before that another coin worth five cents was minted in silver and called a "half dime." The first nickels carried the image of a shield. Next came the Liberty Head nickel, then the Buf-

Save your coins in an album.

falo nickel (better known for its Indian Head). Since 1938, we have used, for the most part, a nickel with a portrait of Thomas Jefferson. (Again, look closely and see if you can find the designer's initials, FS.) On the nickel's reverse side is an image of Jefferson's home in Virginia known as Monticello. The mint mark may appear on either side of the nickel depending on the year it was minted.

Dimes: Dimes or "dismes" as they were once called, are one of the oldest denominations. They date back to 1796 and have been continuously produced since then except for the single year 1808 when, for some unknown reason, none were issued. Although the design of the dime has undergone several changes, each has in some way shown the head of Liberty or Liberty's torch. Even the dime popularly known as the Mercury Head dime (issued 1916 to 1945) actually depicts the Winged Head of Liberty—not the Roman messenger of the gods. The dimes cur-

rently minted were first designed in 1946 and show a portrait of Franklin Roosevelt, the thirty-second president. This time the designer's initials are JS. The reverse side on the Roosevelt dime shows the Torch of Liberty flanked by laurel and oak branches which symbolize liberty, peace, and good will.

Look at the edge of a dime. All dimes, quarters, half-dollars, and silver dollars were once made from silver, but since 1965 these coins are actually made of copper coated with nickel. The nickel coating wears away quickly from the edges and you can see the copper center showing through. If there is no copper lining around the edge, you have one of the older silver coins still in circulation.

Quarters: Quarters were originally minted with the image of Liberty either standing, sitting, or as a bust. The Liberty image has been carried on all quarters since the first year of issue in 1796. The current George Washington quarter, which first appeared in 1932, commemorates the bicentennial year of Washington's birth. (The designer's initials on the Washington quarter are JF.) The reverse side of this quarter shows an American eagle with an olive branch. To commemorate the two-hundredth birthday of America in 1976, quarters were issued showing the date as 1776–1976, with a portrait on the reverse side of a colonial minuteman and the Flame of Liberty surrounded by thirteen stars. JLA are the designer's initials.

Half-Dollars: There have been several half-dollar designs since the first one was issued in 1794 with Liberty appearing on most. The half-dollar coins still in circulation today include Walking Liberty with the American eagle on the reverse side (1916 to 1947); Benjamin Franklin with the Liberty Bell on the reverse side (1948 to 1963); and the John F. Kennedy half-dollar with the presidental coat of arms on the reverse side (since 1964). Custom has it that the eagle is stamped facing the arrows during wartime and facing the olive branch during peace. There were two designers of the Kennedy half-dollar: GR did the portrait and FG the seal—see if you can find their initials. A special Bicentennial half-dollar was minted during 1976, with the

coin's date presented as 1776–1976 and Independence Hall in Philadelphia on the reverse side.

Silver Dollars: The largest coin minted in the United States is the silver dollar which first appeared in the 1790's. Since then, the silver dollar has had many designs and times during which none were minted at all. One of the first American silver dollars was modeled after the Spanish "pieces of eight," and it too could be broken up into halves or fourths for making change. That is how the old money expressions "two bits" and "four bits" came into use. In 1971, after a lapse of thirty-five years, the present silver dollar with a portrait of Dwight D. Eisenhower was is-

sued. The reverse side commemorates man's first trip to the moon, showing an American eagle, an olive branch in its claws, landing on the surface of the moon. The designer's initials are FG. An American Bicentennial version of the Eisenhower silver dollar was issued only in 1976 and carried the image of the moon and the Liberty Bell on its reverse side. The designer's initials are DRW.

COIN COLLECTING

Many people who are fascinated by coins and their history become coin collectors or "numismatists." If

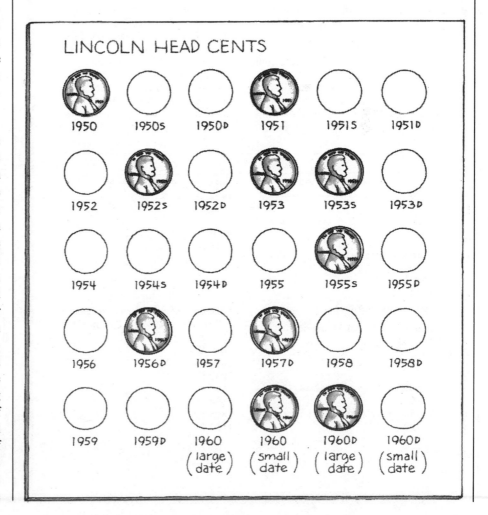

this is your first attempt at coin collecting, don't be too anxious to collect every kind of coin that you can find. It is much more rewarding to start by collecting a coin of a particular denomination and design, and to try to collect all the dates in that series including the various mint marks for specific dates. It is also easiest to start a collection of coins that are mostly still in circulation. Lincoln Head pennies make a fine first coin collection for a number of reasons. The face value of the entire collection will be less than two dollars. (If you were starting a silver dollar collection, your investment just in the coins would have to be well over one hundred dollars.) And you usually have a pocketful of pennies to check over. If your interest and enthusiasm still hold, you can start collecting another more difficult coin series, say Indian Head pennies or Buffalo nickels.

However, you may want to organize a coin collection in another way. You could collect all the American coin styles depicting a particular subject, such as American presidents or the figure of Liberty, or maybe examples of all the coin styles minted of a particular denomination.

Time to get started

Whatever type you decide upon, first make a list of all the coins to be included in your coin collection or you can copy a list from a library book on coin collecting.

Next it helps to have a magnifying lens for seeing detail on coins such as mint marks and designer's initials. But most important of all you need a way to safely store or display your collection. Some collectors place coins in small individual envelopes, but if you wish to display your coins, it is better to

---

VALUABLE CHANGE

The actual value of a coin can be much greater than its face value. Certain pennies, for example, may be worth only one cent each if you spend them, but to a collector of rare coins, a single penny may be worth several hundred or even several thousand dollars. The number of a particular coin made in a year at a particular mint determines how difficult the coin might be to find. And the more difficult a coin is to find, the more money it is worth to a collector.

Another important factor in determining the value of a rare coin is its physical condition. A coin in new, uncirculated condition (just as it left the mint) is worth considerably more than the same coin worn from use. A coin that is very worn or battered is worth little or nothing to a collector unless it is extremely rare.

Sometimes a coin must be more than just rare and in good condition to have a high value to a collector—it must be in demand. There are certain coins that collectors especially want, and the more difficulty they have in finding them, the higher the price they'll pay.

Listed below are a number of coins, many of which are worth no less than twenty dollars; the most valuable in uncirculated condition might bring as much as ten thousand dollars. So go check your change to see if you have any of these coins. If not, maybe you should check again in a few days—you might have more money in your pocket than you think.

Lincoln Head Pennies
1909 S
1914 D
1922
1931 S

Buffalo Nickels
1913 S
1913 D
1914 D
1918 D (only some)

Mercury Head Dimes
1916 D
1921
1921 D

Standing Liberty Quarters
1916
1918 S (only some)
1919 D
1919 S
1921
1923 S

Washington Quarters
1932 D
1932 S

Walking Liberty Half-Dollars
1916 S
1921
1921 D
1938 D

Liberty Head Silver Dollars
1879-1885CC (Carson City mint)
1888 S
1889 S
1889 CC
1892 CC
1893 S
1894
1895 S
1902 S

Fig. 5

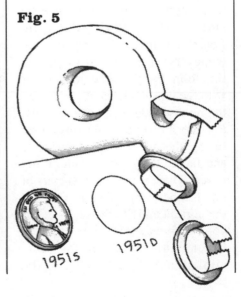

1951S   1951D

mount them in a specially designed coin album that you can buy at most hobby or coin shops.

You can also make your own coin display cards. To do so, find a piece of plain cardboard from a box lid or the back of a paper pad and write in the dates for your particu-lar coin collection under a space designated for each coin. Mount the coins, date side up, using a short loop of tape sticky side out, Fig. 5.

Lincoln head pennies

Here is a list of all the Lincoln Head pennies minted from 1909 through 1977. You don't have to collect the entire series. At first you may decide on only a range of dates—say all the Lincoln pennies minted from 1925–1950. (Remember, S stands for the San Francisco mint, D for the Denver mint,

---

Lincoln Head Pennies

1909 VDB*	1921 S	1935 D	1948	1961 D
1909 S VDB*	1922	1936	1948 S	1962
1909	1922 D	1936 S	1948 D	1962 D
1909 S	1923	1936 D	1949	1963
1910	1923 S	1937	1949 S	1963 D
1910 S	1924	1937 S	1949 D	1964
1911	1924 S	1937 D	1950	1964 D
1911 S	1924 D	1938	1950 S	1965
1911 D	1925	1938 S	1950 D	1966
1912	1925 S	1938 D	1951	1967
1912 S	1925 D	1939	1951 S	1968
1912 D	1926	1939 S	1951 D	1968 S
1913	1926 S	1939 D	1952	1968 D
1913 S	1926 D	1940	1952 S	1969
1913 D	1927	1940 S	1952 D	1969 S
1914	1927 S	1940 D	1953	1969 D
1914 S	1927 D	1941	1953 S	1970
1914 D	1928	1941 S	1953 D	1970 S
1915	1928 S	1941 D	1954	1970 D
1915 S	1928 D	1942	1954 S	1971
1915 D	1929	1942 S	1954 D	1971 S
1916	1929 S	1942 D	1955	1971 D
1916 S	1929 D	1943 steel	1955 S	1972
1916 D	1930	1943 S steel	1955 D	1972 S
1917	1930 S	1943 D steel	1956	1972 D
1917 S	1930 D	1944	1956 D	1973
1917 D	1931	1944 S	1957	1973 S
1918	1931 S	1944 D	1957 D	1973 D
1918 S	1931 D	1945	1958	1974
1918 D	1932	1945 S	1958 D	1974 S
1919	1932 D	1945 D	1959	1974 D
1919 S	1933	1946	1959 D	1975
1919 D	1933 D	1946 S	1960 small date	1975 D
1920	1934	1946 D	1960 large date	1976
1920 S	1934 D	1947	1960 D small date	1976 D
1920 D	1935	1947 S	1960 D large date	1977
1921	1935 S	1947 D	1961	1977 D

*with designers initials VDB

and no letter means the coin was minted in Philadelphia.)

Be on the lookout

Check all of the coins that pass through your hands each day. If you are going to find the missing dates in your collection, you must be consistent about checking coins before spending them. Try to collect the best specimens you can find of a particular coin. Even after you have found your "missing coin," continue to be on the lookout for a better example, so you'll always be upgrading the quality of your collection. Any duplicates of the rarer coins can be kept for trading.

There are also coin shops and coin auctions where you can buy coins that are missing from your collection—especially rare ones—but at first it is usually more fun for a beginning collector to just hunt through pocket change and piggy banks for the coins needed.

Handle with care

Handle your coin collection carefully. Even though your coins may have been in general circulation for some time, there is no need to treat them carelessly. Coins that are left to bang around loose will wear even more and be worth less as collectibles.

Never clean a coin unless it is extremely dirty and then use only mild hand soap and warm water. Don't use a metal polish. Harsh cleaning can damage a coin and take away from its natural aged beauty.

BORROWING MONEY

Everything costs money. To live in our American society you must earn money to pay at least for the necessities of life: food, clothing, and shelter. But you will also want money to pay doctor bills, buy a television set, go on a vacation, or own a car. You probably aren't concerned with such expenses since parents take care of those things while you are still young. But there are times when you want money just for yourself to spend as you like. Maybe your parents give you a weekly allowance or maybe you earn money doing odd jobs around the house. Maybe you have some sort of neighborhood business. However you get your spending money, or no matter how much you save, there will probably be many times when you just don't have enough money to pay for what you need or want right now.

Need a quarter quickly?

Who do you know who will lend you the money as long as you agree to pay it back? The most likely loan-givers are probably your parents or an older—or richer—brother or sister. Before you ask for a loan, you should know exactly how much money you need, what you are going to spend the money for, and how you will pay back the loan. Maybe you can give an amount from your weekly allowance or agree to "work" the loan by doing some job for the lender. In any case, it is your responsibility to pay back the loan as you have arranged. If you are good about paying back a loan, then you can probably go back to the same lender sometime again when you need extra money.

SAVING MONEY

There may be other times, though, when you have extra money that you don't need to spend right away. Maybe you have saved up your allowance, received money for your birthday, or you have a neighborhood business that is doing very well. What are you going to do with that money? You can just save it in some safe place

---

PIGGY BANKS

You most probably and quite logically think that the piggy bank gets its name from its animal shape, but in fact that just isn't so. The piggy bank is named for the clay material it was at one time made from.

In Early America, just as today, kids were encouraged to save any spare change they had by keeping the coins in a kitchen jar or pot. At first, most such containers were made from tin or glass, but during the eighteenth century a new kind of clay called "pygg" clay became popular in America for making kitchen cookware. In time, many colonists began to refer to all clay pots, pans, and jars as pygg. And so the kitchen jar frequently became known as the "pygg jar."

It didn't take long for someone to make the name association between the material pygg and the animal "pig." Soon the family coin bank became known as the "piggy bank." Then, as would be expected, several clay potters began making clay coin banks in the actual shape of a pig.

for something you have in mind to buy, or may want to buy in the future.

Saving money for a specific purchase or just to have when a special want comes along is a good habit to get into. To help develop the habit you might try saving particular coins—all the pennies, quarters, or half-dollars you get. You can get a piggy bank to put your saved money in or a box, envelope, jar, or bag will do, so long as it can be opened and closed.

Piggy banks are fine for saving small amounts of money, but if you have managed to save a lot of money and are planning on continuing to save, you should think about putting your money into a bank savings account.

How savings accounts work

You can open a savings account at most banks with as little as one dollar, although many banks require that a parent or some adult sign the bank application card for kids under a certain age. When you give the bank your money, they will give you a savings account "passbook" with your name and account number printed on it. Inside the passbook there are pages with columns labeled "Date," "Withdrawal," "Interest," "Deposit," and "Balance." If you are withdrawing—taking out—money from your account, that amount will be noted in the Withdrawal column. If you are depositing— putting in—money in your account, that amount will be noted in the Deposit column.

Your money makes money

Interest, in banking, is the amount of money your money has earned for you while sitting in your account. You see, the money doesn't just sit. The bank actually borrows that deposited money and uses it to make more money. It is loaned out to others, invested in land and other business deals. The bank makes money from its business ventures and some of the money it makes is paid back to all the people who have savings accounts at the bank. This extra money added on to a customer's account is called "interest." The amount of interest each customer receives depends on the amount of money each has in his or her account.

The Balance column shows the new money total once the deposit has been added or the withdrawal has been subtracted, and the interest, if any is due, is added on.

Make a Piggy Bank

Today there are several styles and sizes of clay piggy banks you can buy, as well as banks made from papier-mâché, glass, plaster, and plastic. You can easily make your own piggy bank from an empty plastic jug.

Materials
plastic jug
pencil
small butcher knife or penknife
felt-tipped markers or crayons

1. Find an empty plastic jug like a common bleach or fabric softener jug. Thoroughly wash and rinse the jug, then put the screw cap back on.

2. Position the jug on its side with the handle straight up. With a pencil, draw a narrow rectangular slit at the top of the jug as a coin slot. If you want to save different-sized coins in the piggy bank, you will have to make the slot big enough, but not much bigger than a silver dollar, the largest U.S. coin. With a small, pointed kitchen knife or a penknife blade, cut out the coin slot.

3. Using felt-tipped markers or crayons, decorate the jug with eyes, mouth, ears, feet, and a tail to look like a pig. Invent your own design or use the illustration shown here as an example.

4. To have your piggy bank stand up straight, you will have to put in some change to weight the pig's belly. Whenever you want to collect your savings—or just to count it—remove the screw cap and empty the pig.

NUMBER
0192

SHARES
~10~

Atlas Bicycle Company

This Certifies that Nathan B. Diamond is the owner of ~Ten~ Shares of the Capital Stock of *Atlas Bicycle Company*, Incorporated transferable only on the books of the Corporation by the holder hereof in person or by Attorney upon surrender of this Certificate properly endorsed. IN WITNESS WHEREOF, the said Corporation has caused this Certificate to be signed by its duly authorized officers and its Corporate Seal to be hereunto affixed this fifth day of January, A.D. 19 78

If you buy stock in a company, you will be issued a stock certificate.

INVESTING MONEY

Another thing to do with your money is to invest it in a business. If you have your own neighborhood business, you might want to spend money for more supplies, advertising, a tool to make the work easier, or even to hire someone to help run your business so you can possibly even make more money. You can also invest in someone else's business. This is the way many large companies in America get the money they need to expand. People who invest their money in a company are called "investors" or "stockholders,"

and by investing they actually become part-owners of the business. When you invest your money, the company will send you a piece of paper called a stock certificate that shows how much or how many "shares" of the company you own.

When you invest in a company, you are letting them use your money and the company will pay you a share of any profits that they make. That share is called a "dividend" and can be paid to you either in money or in additional shares of stock. Of course, if the company you have shares in doesn't make any money, then you won't get a dividend; if the company loses money in their business, then you might lose some of the money you have invested. You

have to be careful in selecting the companies in which you might invest your money. You should know something about what the company does and have faith that the business will do well.

See your broker

People who buy stock often ask a person called a "stockbroker" to help them decide what companies might be good risks for investing. The stockbroker will also buy the stock for you. Here is how it works. Suppose you have $50 and have decided to invest it in the Atlas Bicycle Co. Your stockbroker would call the stock exchange—a large central marketplace where stocks are bought and sold—and he would tell his representative there what stock to buy for you. The representative at the stock exchange then finds someone who wants to sell stock in the Atlas Bicycle Co. Suppose the seller is asking $5 a share, then for your $50 you could buy ten shares of stock in the company.

Now suppose the Atlas Bicycle Co. makes a 10 percent profit next year. You might then get a dividend of 10 percent of the $50 you invested (which would be $5), or if you wished, the company could give you another $5 share of their stock instead. Then you would have eleven shares.

If you decide at some point to sell your stock to get back your money, you again call your stockbroker and he will repeat the same process, but in reverse. The stockbroker asks his representative at the stock exchange to find someone to buy the stock that you want to sell.

However, there is a risk. If the company you have invested in does well in business, then the chances are that you can sell your stock at the same price you paid for it—or maybe even more. But if the company has done poorly, or isn't growing larger, then you will probably have to sell your stock at a price less than what you paid, and you will lose some money. If the company should fail and go out of business, then your stock in that company might be worth nothing.

Read the financial pages

One way to keep track of how your company is doing and whether you should consider selling your stock or possibly buying more is to read the financial section of the newspaper. Each day, in long complicated-looking columns of names and numbers, are listed America's major companies and price information about their shares of stock. All the companies are listed alphabetically so you can skim through the lists to find the company you are looking for. In the stock market dollars are called "points." And each point is divided into eighths and each eighth point is worth $.12 ½.

• The first column shows the highest price that stock sold for that year (5 ½ points or $5.50).

• The second column lists the lowest price of the year (3 ⅛).

• Next comes the company name and how much of a dividend they paid on each share last year (.50).

• The fourth column tells you how many hundreds of shares in that company were sold that day (13x100=1300 shares).

• The next three columns tell the price that stock was selling for during the day: the highest price (5⅛), the lowest (4⅞), and the price at the end of the day or "closing price" (5).

• The last column shows "net change," or how much the price changed from the closing of the day before (+¼).

From this listing you can see that each of your ten shares of Atlas Bicycle Co. stock is worth one-quarter point more today than yesterday. Therefore, your stock has gained $2.50 in value (¼ point= $.25x10 shares=$2.50).

As in any type of investment, the more experience you have and the more you learn, the less risk you will be taking in possibly losing some of your money. However, you will only learn by trying. To invest in the stock market you must first open an account with a stockbroker. If you are under twenty-one years old, you will have to have a parent open a "custodian account" for you, but all the money that is invested or made from dividends belongs to you.

1978				Sales				
High	Low				High	Low	Close	Net Chg
23½	19⅝	Allied Stor	1.28	94	23	22⅝	22⅝	− ⅛
15¼	12⅝	Am Family	.40	58	13⅞	13⅝	13⅞	+ ¼
61⅞	50	Atl Rich	1.60	374	60⅝	60	60⅜	+ ⅜
5½	3⅛	Atlas Bike	.50	13	5⅛	4⅞	5	+ ¼
23½	19⅜	Avery Int	.36	132	22⅜	22	22	− ⅛

GOING INTO BUSINESS

In Early America trading or "bartering" was the primary means of exchange. Even today it is satisfying to barter. There's a good feeling about sharing or trading with others for the things we need and want. If you have a large vegetable garden, you might want to trade some of your surplus crop with a neighbor for a toy he no longer uses, or maybe you could help paint a friend's house in exchange for guitar lessons. But because of the nature of our economy—the fact that most of us do not make or grow the things we need—it would be very difficult, if not impossible, to barter for everything we wanted. Just try to imagine always needing to find a person who had what you wanted who also needed just what you had to trade. Shopping could get very complicated.

The alternative to the problem of bartering is, of course, money. Money is the common means of exchange between people who are buying and selling. But how do you earn the cash you need so you can get that new bicycle, camera, or model plane? You can sell a service or product that people want. In other words, you can start a business.

You do not need a goal to earn lots of money when you go into business. You may just wish to earn enough for specific things you want to buy. In any case, you shouldn't make the mistake of working just so that you can earn money. Being successful at what you do cannot necessarily be measured by how much money you earn. What is most important is that you enjoy doing your work and you do the job well. You will find rewards in the work you do other than earning money. You will enjoy meeting new people and learning new skills. It feels good to work hard at what you like to do.

CHOOSING A BUSINESS

The first problem is to choose what kind of business you'll want to go into. Many possible businesses might sound interesting at first, but the only business worth sticking with is the one you continue to enjoy. To start your own business you need to have a product or service you can sell. Make a list of all the things you can, and like to do. If you like animals, you might consider a dog walking, washing, or training service. If you enjoy gardening, you could offer lawn care or houseplant watering services. If you enjoy building or making things, there are several products you could make or sell: bird feeders, pot holders, spice racks, jewelry, and so on. Think of the hobbies you most enjoy. What do you like best about school, or what chores do you usually do around your own home?

To be successful in your business it is not only important to do what you enjoy, but you must also supply a product or service that is in demand—someone must want what you have to offer. Make a second list noting the services or products you believe that your neighbors can use—car washing, baby-sitting, weed pulling, garden hose hangers, pincushions, newspaper fireplace logs. Because you

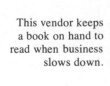

This vendor keeps a book on hand to read when business slows down.

are probably just taking "educated" guesses, it would be helpful, however, if you actually asked your neighbors what they needed. You might begin your survey by asking your parents. Based on your first list of interests, write out several interview questions, and write down the responses during the interview.

Ask the right questions

Try to be very specific with your questions. Don't just ask "What products do you need?" or "What work could I do to help you out?" Ask questions like "If available, would you buy newspaper logs for your fireplace?" "What would you expect to pay for each log?" "How many logs do you think you might use in a month?" "Do you ever need a helper to do your house and yard work?" "What type of help and skills do you need?" "How often do you need a helper?" "What would you expect to pay for such help?" Ask questions about those things your neighbors don't like to do for themselves, or have difficulty getting. Many successful businesses begin with solutions to customers' problems and dissatisfactions. As you continue to ask questions of friends and neighbors, you will probably be given several suggestions for products and services to consider. What you are doing is "surveying" the needs of your prospective customers. So that your responses give you a good average sampling, try to survey at least five neighbors—more if possible. Based upon the responses to your questions, some of the people that you survey may actually become your customers.

Analyze the results

Now analyze carefully both lists of information—what *you* like to do and what your neighbors need.

How many match-ups can you find? What products or services seem to be most needed that you can and would like to supply also? You may have several match-ups to choose from, or none that seem appealing. You may need to go back and expand both lists with more ideas and interviews.

Before making a final decision—especially if you have several businesses to choose from—there are several things you should ask yourself:

● Is there enough demand for my product or service to keep me as busy as I want to be?

● What is the going rate for services in my neighborhood? Can I earn enough money to reach my goal?

● Can I do the job myself or will I need others to help? Are others willing to help me?

● What money do I need for materials or tools to start the business? Do I have the money, or can I borrow it?

● Do I expect to have competition? How am I different or better than my competition?

The business that you choose is probably not going to be a lifelong commitment, but you should consider carefully all the possible choices and base your decision mostly on what you enjoy doing. You should let yourself learn from experience. Your interests might just lead to a business or a profession that you will develop and continue into your adult life—or your experience may show you otherwise.

Once you have made a decision to start a business you should write out a "business plan" describing in details what you plan to do and how you plan to do it. As you write, try to imagine everything that will happen in your business and what you will do to make it successful.

THE BUSINESS FOR YOU

Here are several ideas for starting a neighborhood business and instructions on how to do some of them. But don't limit yourself to the ideas and suggestions in this book. Everyone has their own good ideas for suitable jobs.

Products to make and sell
Greeting cards
Pot holders
Growing worms for bait
Bird feeders
Garden vegetables
Pincushions
Newspaper logs
Kites
Neighborhood newspaper
Seashells
Riddle and joke book
Neighborhood recipe book
Polished stones
Garden flowers
Used records
Garage sale
Cookies and cakes
Houseplants
Lemonade
Decorated T-shirts
Candles

Neighborhood services to sell
Window washing
Car waxing
Dog walking and washing
Errand service; Baby-sitting
Gardening
Snow shoveling
Toy repairing
Fence painting
Berry picking
Dog, fish- and pet-sitting
Newspaper delivery
Taking kids to the movies
Lost-article searcher
Important dates reminder service
Magic shows
On vacation home checking and plant watering
Sidewalk sweeping
Laundromat sitting

JENNIFER'S ECOLOGICAL and ECONOMICAL NEWSPAPER LOG COMPANY

Making a Business Plan

Here is a sample business plan to use as a model.

Give a description of the business

I plan to make newspaper logs and sell them to my neighbors to burn in their fireplaces. I want to earn $125 during the months October through March so I can buy a ten-speed bike next spring. I am going to call my business Jennifer's Ecological and Economical Newspaper Log Company.

Note the need for the product or service

My friends in the neighborhood tell me their parents have fireplaces and use them in the winter—mostly on weekends and snowy nights. Four of the nine adults that I surveyed said they burned fireplace logs, and use about fifteen logs during an average winter month.

Competition

Of the four people surveyed who said they burned logs, two buy their fireplace logs at the food market and pay about $1.25 for each log. One neighbor buys real wood logs at a road stand in the country and pays about $3.50 for a bundle of seven or eight logs. One other neighbor has a crank machine for rolling her own newspaper logs. Everyone except the lady who makes her own logs said that they would try using my newspaper logs.

Production

I will collect old newspapers from my own home, and the superintendent of the apartment building on the next block says I can have all the old newspapers that he accumulates and stores in his basement. I will need three pieces of heavy twine to tie up each log. A roll of twine costs $1.97 and is enough to make about one hundred logs. I have saved $5 from my allowance and the cost of the string can come from there. I will use my brother's wagon to collect the newspapers and deliver the logs.

Labor

I, by myself, will do all of the work: collect the newspapers, make the logs, distribute the advertising brochures, and deliver the product. My younger brother, Tim, says he would like to help so I may let him make the logs when business is busy and pay him eight cents for each one he makes. By myself, I can make about six logs in one hour, and I have enough time to make and sell about twenty-four logs each week, October through March.

Place of business

My mom and dad say they don't want all those newspapers anywhere in the house, but it is OK for me to work and store my materials in the garage as long as I clean up after I am done working.

Sales

There are twenty-two houses on my block, sixteen houses on the block across the street, and eighty-three apartments on the block down the street. Dad says they all have fireplaces, although some people do not use them. I am going to write an advertising leaflet and my mom will make one hundred and fifty copies for me at her office where they have a copy machine. She says it will cost $3 to make the copies and I can use the rest of my savings to cover that expense. I will put an advertising leaflet under the door or in the mail slot of each home. After a day or two I will start going back to each house to show a sample of my fireplace logs and try to get orders. If I need more business, I will print more leaflets and distribute them on two more blocks. I plan to sell my newspaper logs for thirty cents each and collect the money when I deliver the logs.

Sales Projection Chart
Jennifer's Ecological and Economical Newspaper Log Company
Starting Capital $5.00

Expenses	October	November	December	January	February	March
Cost of materials (string)	$1.97	$1.97	$1.97	$1.97	$3.94	—
Cost of labor (brother's help)	—	—	—	2.00	2.00	—
Cost of advertising (leaflets)	3.00	3.00	—	—	—	—
Total Expenses per month	4.97	4.97	1.97	3.97	5.94	—
Income						
Sale of logs	19.80	30.00	30.00	37.50	37.50	19.80
Profit per month (income less expenses)	14.83	25.03	28.03	33.53	31.56	19.80
Cumulative profit	14.83	39.86	67.89	101.42	132.98	152.78

A sales projection chart

After you have written a business plan, there is one more list that you should make to estimate whether your business will be successful or not. By now you know what your expenses will be (string, leaflets, and maybe the cost of your brother helping) and you know how many logs you can produce. From your survey, you can project that you will probably sell all the logs you can make yourself, possibly fewer during the moderate-temperature months of October and March, and possibly more during the colder months of January and February. You will be borrowing money from your parents to start the business and you will need to pay it back from your earned money. If you put all that information into a chart, listing expenses and sales income month by month, you can project approximately how much money you will earn. A "sales projection" chart, as this is called, doesn't guarantee how your business will actually operate. But if you have been thorough and realistic about your business plan, your sales projection will be reasonably accurate.

Advertising

Unless you are able to take sales orders or make agreements for services with enough customers to keep you busy for a while, you will probably need to advertise your product or service to get more customers.

There are several ways to advertise your business, although the best advertising will come from your satisfied customers who recommend your business to their friends. But "word of mouth" advertising can only happen once your business is operating.

Depending on your type of business and your business plan, you might decide to advertise by placing notices or posters in public neighborhood places: the entrances to apartment buildings, at the corner store, on a public information bulletin board at school, the library, or at the local food market. But for most neighborhood businesses it is best to advertise directly, delivering your notice to a specific list of potential customers.

For either type of advertising you will need to write ad copy and design advertising layout. Make your ad brief and to the point (be sure to spell correctly!) describing what you have to offer, what it will cost, and how your customers can reach you. It is also good to praise yourself or your product.

If your advertisement is a poster or a bulletin, it must also be graphically bold to catch the eye of those passing by. Be sure your words are printed large enough to be easily seen at a distance, and use bright colors. A colorful illustration of your product, or a symbol or slogan for your business, are all good "eye-catchers" for your

Every business that is well run should know exactly how much money it is taking in and how much it is spending. Don't try to rely only on your memory, but keep some kind of simple written record. Every business should keep records or "books" that explain how much money has been spent and what for, as well as how much money the business is making (or losing).

A large notebook or just a few sheets of notebook paper will do fine as an "account book" for keeping your business records. Follow the example illustrated and write these five column headings across the top of each page: Date, Explanation, Cash Received, Cash Spent, and Cash on Hand.

At the end of each business day, or whenever spending money, list the business transactions you have made. In the first column write the date; in the second write a brief description of why you received or

poster. Notice billboards and advertising signs on buses and cabs to help you get the idea for a bold, brief, and to-the-point message.

You can be more detailed in describing your business in an advertising flier to be delivered to the homes of potential customers. Include the same information as on the poster, but try also to state the "problem" or "need" as you perceive it, and how your product or service can solve it. Be confident about yourself and what you can do. Praise the merits of your product. Remember that you are in business because others want your product or service, not because your customers are doing you a favor.

> 'For you it makes good sense
> For me to paint your fence.'

Fence Painting

All types: picket fences, chain link fences, stockade fences, rail fences, and ornamental railings.

- Wood posts treated with preservative
- Gate hinge and other small repairs
- Neat and dependable – especially careful of your bushes and plants
- Two summers of experience
- $2.00 per hour — You supply the paint

Call: Billy Belanger
555-3612 (6 to 8 pm)

BUSINESS BOOKS AND RECORDS

spent money; then under the appropriate received or spent column list the proper amount.

In the last column, keep a running account of the cash you have after all transactions have

been made for the day. Try to get into the habit of being a good record keeper.

Date	Explanation	Cash Received	Cash Spent	Cash on Hand
6.17	allowance	$1.50		$1.50
6.20	two batteries		.43	1.07
6.21	install screens for Mrs. Baxter	3.75		4.82
6.22	model boat		2.95	1.87
6.24	paint for model boat		.83	1.04
6.24	allowance	1.50		2.54

PHONE TABS

For the convenience of those seeing your poster or bulletin, you can attach to it a strip of "phone tabs" so the person can be saved the time (and often inconvenience) of copying your name and phone number.

Cut slits across the length of a piece of paper to make several long tabs. Neatly write your name, business, and phone number on each tab. Attach the strip to your poster so that interested people can just tear off a tab and take it with them.

Yard work JOHN Berman 555-4895 (×6)

NEWSPAPER LOGS

Unless people cut their own firewood from their own trees, fireplace logs can be very expensive to buy. And unless the logs are cut from already fallen trees. wood may be needlessly cut and burned that could otherwise be used for construction or some other more permanent and worthwhile purpose.

A log made from a rolled-up newspaper burns just as well as a wood log (although not quite as long) and is an economical, as well as ecologically sound, solution to the problem. Newspaper comes from trees in the first place and is a good fireplace fuel. Also it is ecologically sound to make fireplace logs from old newspapers yourself. You can use these logs for your own fireplace, or sell them to your neighbors. Ask your family, and possibly a few friends and neighbors, to save their old newspapers for you. It will take about four or five weekday newspapers to make one log, or maybe only one Sunday newspaper, if you live in or near a big city with a fat Sunday paper.

Materials
old newspapers
twine
detergent (optional)

Tools
scissors
large washtub, sink or bathtub (optional)

1. Lay out the first newspaper flat and roll it up, making sure the center of the log is hollow. The hollow will allow air to circulate through and it will burn better.
You can make your paper logs

two different lengths, depending on whether you roll the newspaper from the width or the length.

2. Continue to add newspapers to the log being sure to roll them tightly. When the log is about the right size for a fireplace—about a five inch (thirteen cm.) circumference, tie it up using three or four pieces of twine. Your fireplace log is now ready to use.

3. If you want to make the best possible newspaper logs, there is one more thing that you can do, although it can be a bit messy. Thoroughly soak each completed newspaper log in a tub of water with some household detergent added. Use a bit more detergent in the water than you would to do the dishes (or wash). Allow the water solution to drip off the log for a minute, and then put it in a warm place to dry. Be patient, it may take a few days for the paper to completely dry. The water and detergent will allow you to mold and

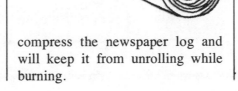

compress the newspaper log and will keep it from unrolling while burning.

BABY-SITTING

Baby-sitting is one of the most common jobs for older kids and one of the jobs requiring the most maturity and responsibility. Baby-sitting is a serious job, but it is also great fun and a good way to earn money.

To be a responsible baby-sitter, first of all, you must like younger children. You must know what the parents and child expect of you and what you expect of them. Above all else, your major responsibility is watching the children you are caring for and keeping them away from danger. You should know the "rules" of the house you'll be sitting in; how and what to play with the children; how to handle trouble situations and emergencies; what courtesies to expect from parents; and what to charge for your service. As a baby-sitter, you are a substitute parent, but you must only do as much as the real parents want you to. For example, you cannot decide yourself to punish a child, or let him or her stay up late. Always be clear about what is expected of you, and enforce all rules.

Preliminaries

Ask parents about bedtimes, watching TV, playing outdoors. Ask also about the rules concerning you: Can you watch TV, play the stereo, raid the refrigerator? What rooms can you use?

If you want to have a friend visit you, ask permission. Make sure, however, that your friend won't interfere with your job. Your first responsibility is to care for the child—remember that! If you do have a friend sit with you, never give that responsibility to your friend. Sometimes it is best to avoid the tempting distractions of a friend, deciding to do the sitting by yourself.

When taking care of small children or infants, you will need to know where clothing is kept, feeding instructions, if any, and what special habits or fears the child may have. For older children, ask about favorite activities and games.

Ask for, and make a list of, important phone numbers to put by the telephone: where the parents can be reached, a neighbor who might be helpful if needed, emergency numbers like those of the family doctor, police, and fire department.

The Carters are with
Bill & Dawn Morton
179 Carlisle Place
555-2914
Nextdoor neighbors
Jerry & Jane Berman
183 Carlisle Place
555-1616
Police: 911
Fire Station: 555-2444

Some parents may seem too strict about rules, while others seem too easy-going. Some parents will make it very clear what they expect you to do, and others will leave that pretty much to you. If you have any uncertainty about what you should do, ask questions. To remember rules and responsibilities, write them down. As you do repeat baby-sitting jobs and develop regular customers, you will become familiar with each family's routine.

Until then, keep a notebook for reference with specific information and about each family and child.

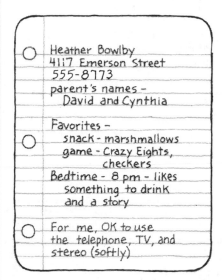

Heather Bowlby
4117 Emerson Street
555-8773
parent's names –
David and Cynthia

Favorites –
snack - marshmallows
game - Crazy Eights,
checkers
Bedtime - 8 pm - likes
something to drink
and a story

For me, OK to use
the telephone, TV, and
stereo (softly)

On the Job

No one can tell you *everything* you must do. Parents will trust you to act in a mature way. There are many responsibilities you must assume yourself.

Be sure to arrive, or be ready to be picked up, on time. Be friendly. Once parents have left, lock all the doors to the house, and don't open them again unless you know who's knocking.

Play with the kids. A good baby-sitter is a good player. Most kids will tell you what they want to do and enjoy teaching you their games. But children enjoy being shown the things you know and can do best. Maybe you can do a few card tricks, make animals from folding paper, play a musical instrument, or tell a good story (but not a scary one). Do you know any funny jokes or good riddles?

Try not to be too rough when playing active games with young children. Many kids will tempt you to play hard, but you should know better. A child that gets too excited

may have trouble falling asleep at bedtime.

Come supplied

Although almost every home will have its supply of games, books, or craft materials, some baby-sitters come to the job prepared for play. You can make a baby-sitter's playbag by filling a tote bag with a variety of playstuff. Things like: crayons and pencils, a deck of cards, storybook, paper, scissors, tape, pipe cleaners, yarn, a rubber ball, a flashlight, checkers, and so on, make good bring-alongs.

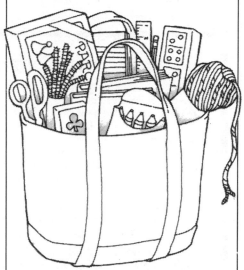

Once a child is asleep, you should *not* fall asleep yourself. If you do feel drowsy, do some homework, play a game by yourself, or get a snack to eat. Keep busy. It's a good idea to look into the child's bedroom at least once an hour. Check to be sure that the child is properly covered and that there are no hard toys on the bed.

If you do have refrigerator privileges, don't overdo it. Unless you are told otherwise, a snack or a sandwich will probably be OK, but don't eat the whole turkey.

Stay off the phone

Don't spend the evening talking to your friends on the phone. Not only are you avoiding your job, but someone may be trying to reach you to leave an important message.

Sometimes little things go wrong that are more embarrassing than serious. An accidentally broken lamp, or a child's skinned knee should be reported to the parents as soon as they return home.

Take care of yourself. You should feel safe going to and from your baby-sitting job no matter how near or far it is to your own home. If you are concerned, or if it is a late-night baby-sitting job, an adult should drive or escort you, even if you only have to go a few

blocks. Be sure to let your parents know where you will be and what time you expect to be coming home.

Don't be timid about charging for your time. Baby-sitting is a valuable service and your responsibility should be rewarded at a fair price. Ask your friends who baby-sit what they charge, and if you think that is fair, then set your rates accordingly. Make it clear before you start the job what you charge per hour. When the sitting job is over, collect your money and be sure you have been properly paid.

It's always nice to get a job and earn some money, but there are times when you shouldn't baby-sit. For instance, if you are sick you might give your illness to the children. If you feel uncomfortable on the job or you don't get along with the children, it is better not to take a job with the same family. Don't take a job when you feel the responsibility is too much for you.

HOUSE PAINTING

Painting a house—or anything for that matter, even a picket fence—requires neat and careful workmanship. (Always cover furniture and areas not to be painted with a paint drop cloth or old sheets to prevent paint getting all over.) You'll find that you get satisfying results for your effort. A coat of paint will make any house look better, and you, the painter, will be able to take the credit.

Of course, there is much more to house painting than just being neat. As in nearly everything you do, "practice makes perfect," and your painting technique and knowledge will improve with every job you do. It's probably best if you start on small painting jobs (like that picket fence, or maybe a porch floor) before tackling a house, or parts of it. Before you begin, you should know about the different paints available, brush types and rollers, the preparation of surfaces to be painted, and so on. Here is most of the information you'll need to help you get started.

Paints

The average hardware or paint store offers a wide variety of

WHAT TO DO IF...

No matter how well prepared you try to be, unexpected problems might come up. You will be expected to handle most situations using your "common sense." But you are not expected to be a doctor, teacher, or parent. If something happens that you can't handle, call the parents. You should be able to handle the more common baby-sitting problems, however.

The baby won't stop crying. Unless you are aware of why the baby is crying and can remedy the situation (feeding, diaper change, or teething), the best solution is to quiet the baby by loving, holding, and gently rocking him back and forth until he is calmed.

The child won't fall asleep. The child may be too excited to sleep or lonely for his parents. Allow the child to get out of bed and spend five or ten minutes of quiet time with you. Then be gentle but firm about going back to bed. You might also spend a few moments with the child in his room as he is falling asleep.

The child has a temper tantrum. Whatever the cause of a temper tantrum, there isn't much you can do until the child calms down, except to be sure that the child doesn't do anything to hurt himself. Tantrums usually don't last long,

and when you see the situation easing, try to calm the child by suggesting several activities or projects to do.

Siblings fight. At times, all siblings (brother and sisters) fight with each other, but most scraps are over as quickly as they begin. If the fighting gets out of hand, however, or if a bigger child is beating-up a smaller child, you should step in and separate the two, organizing separate projects or activities for each child in different areas of the room. Don't try to be the judge as to who is right or wrong.

A child is shy. Some children are naturally shy and others might be shy only with strangers—such as you, the new baby-sitter. Don't push things too quickly. Give the child time to warm up and trust you, then begin a project or activity by yourself. Eventually the child will be curious and trusting enough to join you.

A child gets too excited. Some children become so active and excited it is difficult to quiet them down. If you can't avoid the excitement, gradually reduce the pace by suggesting active, but not wild, play—maybe a sport or game of strength. Active children get hungry, so you might suggest a snack—sitting down at the table.

paints, each for a specific purpose or customer taste. The first consideration is whether you'll be painting indoor or outdoor surfaces. Interior paints should be used only on surfaces protected from the elements of rain, snow, extreme changes in heat and cold; outside paints are mostly resistant to these conditions. Among these paints you will then have to choose whether to use latex, alkyd-base, or oil-base paint.

Paints to choose from

Latex is a "water-thinned" paint that dries quickly, won't crack or peel, has a mild odor, resists dripping, and (most important to amateur painters) can be washed from brushes, rollers, pans, and yourself, using only water and soap. Latex paint is also easy to apply, and because it is quick-drying you will get fewer bugs stuck in the painted surface. It is possible to apply a second coat of latex paint fairly soon after the first.

Alkyd and oil-base paints take longer to dry (oil-base paint takes considerably longer), tend to drip if applied too heavily, and must be cleaned off all tools—and yourself—with turpentine or paint thinner. Alkyd and oil-base paints sometimes have better "hiding power," which means they cover another color better than does latex paint. Oil-base paints can give off strong odors; alkyd paint is almost odorless, but like oil-base paint can produce toxic fumes, and should be used only in well-ventilated areas. You can select whichever type of paint you want. Latex paint will be by far the easiest paint to work with (and possibly the most expensive), while still helping you to do a professional-looking job.

There are several special-purpose paints available: stains for wood, water-repellent paint for

House painting is one business you might consider.

damp walls, cement paints for applying a texture, and paints for concrete and other materials. Many of these paints are available in latex.

Glossy or flat

Paints come in three different finishes or degrees of gloss. A "flat" finish is used mostly for inside walls. The flatness of the finish tends to hide unevenness and imperfections in the walls but is difficult to keep clean.

Semi-gloss, eggshell, and satin finish are all names for a dull-gloss finish paint that is often used on woodwork trim, doors, and walls that tend to get dirty (kitchens, bathrooms, playrooms, and hallways). Semi-gloss painted surfaces will show brush marks and wall imperfections more than flat paint but can be washed and scrubbed.

"Glossy" paints are usually the most difficult to apply but the easiest painted surfaces to clean. Glossy finishes, or enamels as they are sometimes called, must be extra-carefully applied. Glossy paint tends to show and exaggerate brush marks and surface imperfections, and will also drip if applied too heavily. Glossy paints are primarily used for wood trim, doors, and floors. Gloss-finish paints are usually available only in alkyd and oil-base types, so if you can, avoid gloss and use latex or semi-gloss paints instead.

The paint inside a can that has been stored on the shelf will sometimes separate into its various ingredients, and needs to be thoroughly mixed before it can be used. Most paint stores have machines for shaking and mixing fresh cans of paint. Always have the paint store mix the paint in a shaker machine. It will save you a lot of stirring.

Paintbrushes

To do any job well you should use the proper tools. Even the most careful painter can't do a neat job if the hairs of the brush keep coming out, or the paint roller leaves stripes or globs on the wall. The results will always be better, and the job will go more quickly if you use the proper brushes and paint rollers of the best quality you can afford.

When selecting a brush, know which type of paint you will be using and on what surface you will be painting. Nylon and other plastic-bristle brushes work best with latex paint; animal hair and synthetic-bristle brushes are for use with alkyd and oil-base paints. Each type of bristle is best-suited to a particular paint because it holds that type of paint in the brush, lets it flow smoothly on the painted surface, and helps prevent excessive brush marks.

Which brush to use

The shape, length, and size of the brush bristles determine the surface on which it is best used. You would not use a very small brush to paint the side of a house—it would take all day to get the job done—just as you would not use a very large

brush to paint window trim, it would be impossible to do a neat job.

Fig. 6

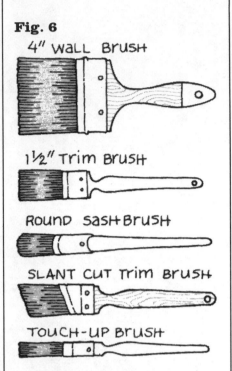

4" WALL BRUSH

1½" TRIM BRUSH

ROUND SASH BRUSH

SLANT CUT TRIM BRUSH

TOUCH-UP BRUSH

Brush size is indicated in inches according to the width of the bristles. A four- or six-inch brush is good only for large areas such as panels, floors, and walls. One- to three-inch brushes are generally used to paint windows and trim. And smaller brushes are best for very delicate painting or touch-up work. Some painters prefer to use round or slant-cut brushes to paint trim, Fig. 6.

A good brush can last for several years and actually feel better the more you use it and break it in. But any brush will only give you good service if you use it properly, clean it well, and keep it in shape. The easiest and best time to clean a paintbrush is just after you have finished painting.

Painting technique

To paint with a brush, dip the brush bristles no more than one-third of their length into the paint, then lightly tap both sides of the brush against the inside wall of the paint can. This will help the brush hold the paint and keep it from dripping. Paint back and forth in long, straight strokes, finally smoothing the overlaps before dipping the brush again. Be sure to brush out any paint runs or sags before the paint begins to dry.

Clean the brush in paint solvent: water for latex, and turpentine or paint thinner for alkyd and oil-base paint. After cleaning the paint from the brush, wash the brush again in warm water and soap. Shake out any excess water, straighten the bristles with your fingers or a comb, and carefully wrap the bristles in a piece of paper toweling, Fig. 7. Wrapping the bristles will keep them from "fanning out" while drying.

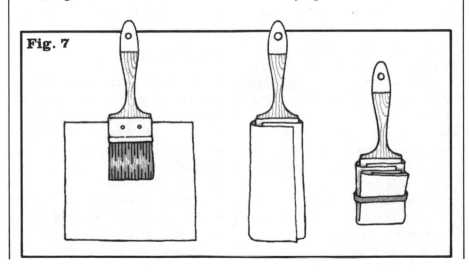

Fig. 7

Paint Rollers

The neatest and fastest way of painting a wall or any other large flat surface is to use a roller. But just as there are various brushes, so there are several kinds of rollers to choose from depending on the paint you are using and the area to be painted.

The size of a roller refers to the length of the roller tube. Although there are several specially shaped rollers for specific painting jobs (like baseboards, for example), you will probably only need a common seven- or nine-inch roller. Roller covers are made of many different materials, which come in different lengths of nap. When buying your roller, it is best to ask the salesman what roller cover would be most suitable according to the paint you intend to use, and the roughness or smoothness of the surface to be painted. The general rule is that short-nap covers are best for smooth surfaces (walls and woodwork), and longer-nap covers for rough or irregular surfaces (brick, fence wood, and concrete).

Paint the corners first

Before painting with a roller, brush-paint corners, edges, or other hard to reach areas. Then fill the trough in a roller pan with paint. Partially dip the roller into the paint and "roll in": Spread the paint on the roller cover evenly by working the roller back and forth a few times on the flat slanted back of the roller pan, Fig. 8. Apply the paint, at first using zigzag strokes of the roller, then smoothing out the painted surface with even parallel up and down strokes while also filling in any skips. Do this without adding more paint. To avoid splashing, never roll paint too quickly or spin the roller at the end of a stroke. And when painting walls, always start each application of a full roller with an upward stroke.

As soon as you have finished painting, remove the roller cover and clean it with the proper solvent. You might save a little cleaning time by first rolling out the extra paint on several thicknesses of old newspaper. It will take a lit-

Fig. 8

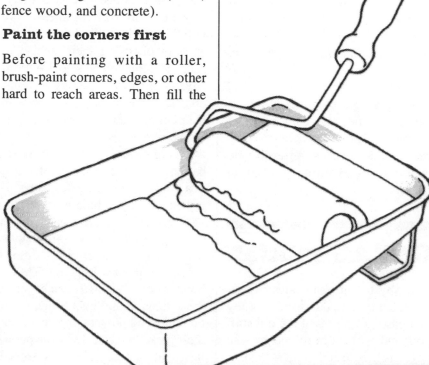

tle scrubbing with your fingers to get the cover really clean. If you have been using a latex paint, keep the cover under a faucet of warm running water while gently squeezing out the paint until the rinse water is clear. Finally, squeeze off as much water as possible and stand the roller on end to dry.

Preparing the Surface

Any surface to be painted must be properly prepared and free of dust, dirt, and grease or the paint job might quickly chip, peel, or discolor. If the surface is just dusty, a cleaning with a cloth will be satisfactory. For dirtier surfaces, use a strong detergent and a scrub brush, and be sure to wipe off all the soap with a damp cloth.

If you are painting over an already painted surface, be sure the old paint is not chipping or peeling—a new paint job won't do anything to help that situation, and in a short time the new paint will chip or peel also. Paint that is chipping, peeling, or badly cracked should be removed completely. Sometimes that is a major job better left to a professional paint contractor who has power equipment and paint removers to do the job. If the old paint is in good shape but glossy, lightly sandpaper the glossy paint until it is dull. That will allow the new paint to stick better and not chip.

Small cracks and other minor imperfections can be filled with a fast-drying latex putty or Spackle®. Squeeze the Spackle® into the crack using a putty knife (a flat-bladed kitchen knife or table knife will do in a pinch), and then scrape off the excess putty using the flat tip of the knife.

If you are repainting a surface in

approximately the same color, one coat of paint will probably do. Two coats are usually needed when painting in a different color, or painting previously unpainted surfaces.

Using Ladders

Nearly all house painting requires the use of a ladder at some time. Don't stand on chairs, boxes, or furniture to paint out-of-reach places. Makeshift ladders too frequently contribute to accidents.

Ladders are designed to be safe, but are safe only if you use them correctly. For most situations a five- or six-foot stepladder will do nicely, especially a stepladder with a folding platform to hold the paint can or roller trough. Open the ladder completely so that it sits firmly on the ground, and always check to be certain that the "spreaders" at the side of the stepladder are locked in place. Never climb to the top step of a stepladder, but leave at least two steps clear at the top to give you steadying and body support. When the area being painted is out of reach, don't lean further to reach, but get down off the ladder and move it to a new position.

Extension ladders

When painting the exterior of a house you may need an extension ladder to reach portions on the second level. Before setting up and climbing a tall ladder you must be fully aware of and practice the rules of ladder safety.

Lean the ladder up against a wall so that its base is about one-quarter the length of the ladder away from the wall, Fig. 9. Be sure the ladder is firmly footed and won't sway to either side. Climb the ladder facing the rungs, and never go all the way to the top. Leave three or more

Fig. 9

rungs at the top to hold onto and help steady you. To keep both hands free, one for painting and one for holding on, use a paint can hook on a ladder rung to hang the paint can.

Always keep both feet firmly on the ladder and your body between the rails of the ladder. Reach out a comfortable distance on each side but *never* lean your body out from the ladder.

GARAGE SALE

One way to get good sales experience, and to make some money (and also get rid of all the old stuff you and your family never use anymore), is to hold a garage sale.

Running a garage sale is like setting up your own business. You will be getting first-hand experience in choosing merchandise to sell, deciding on a sale location, advertising and attracting customers, handling money, dealing with the public, and maybe even managing employees.

Garage sales—or porch sales, barn sales, attic sales, yard sales, flea markets, and tag sales, depending on where you hold it or the particular custom in the part of the country where you live—have long been a part of American tradition, especially in New England. Thrifty Yankees have always been eager to see if they mightn't get some return on their used possessions, and even their junk. In recent years the popularity of garage sales has spread across the country, and on any warm weekend you can probably find one or two right in your own neighborhood.

To you it may be junk

First, snoop around the house and discover what you have that you might want to sell. Anything goes: old toys, the wagon you haven't used in years, your father's broken tools, old books and magazines, plant cuttings and seedlings from the garden, an old set of dishes, even empty jars and interesting old cans. Everyone has stuff that they want to get rid of. Ask your parents, brothers, sisters, and neighbors for suggestions or contributions. If you like, you can sell your friends' stuff for them, or you might decide to have a group garage sale with each of you dividing up the jobs and the profits.

You don't need a garage

Next decide where to hold your sale. Garages work well and are "weatherproof," but other locations you choose might be the lawn, porch, or even the sidewalk. Some communities have special locations for weekend sales or "flea markets" where you can rent a display space, usually for only a couple of dollars. Flea markets are nice because there is plenty of parking space and people already know where to come so you won't have to do much advertising. Another possibility—if you get permission in advance—is a school or shopping-center parking lot. Choose a date and time when people will be around and traffic will be passing by. Good-weather Saturdays and Sundays are best. Don't hold your sale on holidays when people might

Garage sales can bring lots of extra cash.

be out of town. Decide on your hours, giving yourself time to set up at the beginning of the day and clean up at the end of the sale. If you plan to have an all-day sale, start at ten A.M. and end at five P.M.

Once you have a date and place in mind check with your town hall to see if you need a permit. If so, the fee is usually only a dollar or two. You should also ask if you need permission to put up signs for advertising your sale and showing directions to get there.

Bring on the customers

To have a successful garage sale you will need to attract customers. The more people you attract, the more chances you have of selling everything. To interest people in your sale, you will need to advertise. Start about one week before the sale and tell everyone you know—your friends, the kids at school, and neighbors. Make up advertising fliers and hand them out, as well as posting them on bulletin boards around town. The fliers should tell the time, date, and place of your sale; what kinds of things you are selling; and give directions or a map to the site of your sale. Check with your local radio stations—some will announce garage sales for free. You might also put a classified ad in your local paper—many people look there for garage sales. The best time to run an ad is one or two days before the sale. The morning of your sale, put up large, readable signs and arrows directing the way. If you want people to park in a certain spot, make a sign to show them where. Trees, telephone poles, and sides of buildings are all good places to put signs, but do check first before you put up a sign on someone else's property.

Collecting inventory

Now start collecting things to sell. As you collect objects, make sure they are clean and—if necessary—in working order. You may want to offer a box of broken stuff at a special price. Group similar things together: Put all the books and magazines in one group; dolls, doll furniture, doll clothes in another group, and so on.

As you sort through items, price them. Everything should be clearly marked. Small tags or peel-off stickers work well. If you are having a group sale, use a different colored sticker for each person's merchandise. When an item is sold, peel off the sticker, save it, and at the end of the day add up the stickers of each color to see how much money each person has made. If you have a lot of small items selling for a single price, you can put them all in the same box with one large price tag.

Cheap, cheap, cheap

Pricing the merchandise might involve some detective work and even some guessing. One general

rule of thumb is to charge one-quarter to one-half the original price for items which are in good condition. If something is badly worn or broken, price it much lower, or offer it in a box of bargains: "Anything here for ten cents." If you aren't sure of the original price, check a Sears or Montgomery Ward catalog (or a local department store) for the price of similar items. If you have been to another garage sale, you can get an idea for prices for "trash and treasures." During the sale, you can always reprice items that don't seem to be selling or attracting attention.

Decide how to display your merchandise. You might use chairs or portable tables, or make your own display counters by laying boards or sheets of wood across chairs or cardboard boxes. Large boxes alone make good displays, or you can put your stuff on spread-out blankets and sheets. Be sure to display items so that people can easily spot them.

Cash and carry

Save boxes and bags, or collect them from local stores (food markets and liquor stores are great sources for cardboard boxes), so you will have wrapping and containers for people to carry things home in. While you are collecting boxes, look for one to use as a cash-box—something shoe-box-size will do. Also be sure to have paper and pencils for those people who ask for a sales receipt. If you are selling electrical appliances, connect an extension cord from the house to the grounds so that people can try the appliances out. And provide a mirror if you are going to be selling clothes or jewelry.

A little help from friends

Your garage sale will be even more fun if you have a friend or two help out. You will have to decide with them whether they will work for free or how much you can afford to pay them. One person should be in charge of the cashbox to take money and make change, as well as just keep an eye on it. And don't forget to start the day with some change—about ten dollars in bills or coins should do it.

Talk to your customers and try to answer their questions. Lots of people will probably come to see what you have, and if you are friendly they will stay longer and maybe buy more. (If it's a hot day, you may want to have another friend selling iced tea or lemonade to your customers.) Some people at garage sales like to bargain. If you see someone looking at an object he can't seem to decide on, offer it to him at a lower price, or offer to throw in something extra at the same price. A customer may offer to buy something at a lower price, maybe even at half price. Bargain with him, and usually you can agree at a price somewhere in between what you're asking and what he is willing to pay.

When the garage sale is over, pack up all the unsold items and save them for another sale, or maybe give them to the Good Will store or the Salvation Army in your area. Return anything you may have borrowed, and don't forget to take down all the signs you put up.

OVERWORKED CHILDREN

Kids in Early America helped to plant fields, harvest crops, feed the animals, milk the cow, and do anything that might contribute to the family welfare. Most kids today still have odd jobs or help around the house, but we now consider good play and school to be the primary jobs of children.

Unfortunately, that was not always the concern for American youngsters. Only seventy-five years ago children were often employed as factory workers—corking bottles, packing crates, working machines, sifting, sorting, carrying, and sweeping up. Many parents, also working in factories, did not get paid enough to support their families, so children were forced to work. Sometimes children wanted to work, like their parents, and sometimes parents wanted children to work to keep them out of trouble. Children mostly did the lighter work while adults did the heavier "muscle work." But the hours were extremely long and the pay very little. Often children would start work as soon as they were old enough (or looked old enough) for factories to hire them—about age eight. It was not uncommon for a child of ten or twelve to work from sunrise until sundown without even a break for lunch, six or seven days a week, for only a few cents pay per hour. A child might be fired or part of his pay held back if he was caught talking or laughing. And if a child fell asleep on a job, he might be harshly awakened with a sharp smack of the foreman's hand or by a bucket of cold water poured on his head.

Working in a factory was sometimes very dangerous, especially for children. The large noisy equipment was not designed for safety, and there were frequent accidents in which hair or fingers got caught in machinery. Gradually we became aware of these situations and the government passed laws which forbade children less than sixteen years old from doing certain types of work. It also limited the hours that children could spend on the job. Machinery and factory operations were improved, in general, to reduce injuries and make the work easier. Training programs, job advancement, vacations, medical care, retirement pay, and other benefits have vastly lightened the factory worker's job. A modern factory in America today depends on and values its employees; and children, thankfully, no longer have to toil in them.

INDEX

Note:
Page numbers in boldface refer to activities and projects.

A

abstract art, 213–15
acorns, cooking, **178**
acorn-top finger puppets, **109**
action painting, **216**
Adams, Abigail, 347
Adams, John, 361
Adams, John Quincy, 361
Adams, Thomas, Sr., 174–75
Adventure Theatre, 348
advertising, 389–90, 400
air drying of flowers, **231–32**
  plants best for, 234
Airedales, 116
Alaskan malamutes, 116
Alaskan dishes, 150
almanac as source of weather predictions, 54–55
alphabet sentences game, **340**
America, 324
American cheese, 155–56
  making soft, **157**
American foxhounds, 116
American freedom, 354–401
Amish people, 77
Amos 'n' Andy, 348
Amour, Philip, 149
ancestry, tracing your, *see*
  genealogy
animal miniatures, 240
apple peeler, 75
apples, 152–55
  American apple pie, **152–53**
  candy, **153–54**
  dried apple rings, **154**
  Johnny Appleseed, 155

art, 202–35
  action painting, **216**
  collage, **217**
  color, 203–**204**
  composition, 209–**10**
  environmental sculpture, **219**
  flower drying, 231–**34**
  framing, **210**
  grave, 223–**25**
  happenings, 222
  kitsch, 221
  light, **206**
  line, 204–**206**
  mixed media, **215**
  mobiles, 220–**21**
  modern, in America, 211–222
  motion, 207–**208**
  op art, **220**
  paper doll chains, 229, **231**
  scrimshaw, 234–**35**
  shape, **203**
  silhouette, 228–**30**
  texture, **207**
  whittling, 225–28
athlete's foot, home remedies for,
  63
aunt, 29, 30
autograph verses, 194–96

B

baby-sitting, 392–94
  tips for, 394
Baby Snooks, 348
Backstage Wife, 348
backyard fun, 96–126
  bird feeders, 119–20
  bottles, digging for, 123–25
  compost, making, **100–101**
  frog jumping, 110–13
  gardens, 96–100
  nature games, 107–10
  peanuts, 103–106
  pets, family, 113–18
  scarecrows, 101–103
  time capsules, 121–22
  water, dowsing for, 126
ball-in-a-cage, whittling a, **228**

bangs and bruises, home remedies
  for, 63
banjo, 315
barns, 70
  hex signs on, 77
Barns, 207
Barnum, Phineas T., 292
bartering, 386
Bash-Bish Falls, 213–14
Basset hounds, 116
Beagles, 116
bears, *see* teddy bears
beaver "cap," 140
beds:
  four-poster canopy, making,
    82–83
  "trundle," 82
berry ink, **184–85**
Bible, 182
bicycle, guide to the well-
  decorated, 361–62
Bill of Rights, 354
bird feeders, 119–20
  food for, 119
  making, **119**
birdhouses, 120
Birdseye, Clarence, 149
black bottom (dance), 324
Blibber Blubber®, 175
blindman's bluff, 239
blocks, alphabet, 241
Bloodhounds, 116
Bob Hope Show, The, 348
boll weevil, 103, 104
bonnets, 141
boot warmers, 74
borrowing money, 382
Boston terriers, 116
Botticelli or the nope game,
  340–41
bottles, glass, 123–25
  digging for, **124–25**
  poison, 125
  uses of, 124
bowler (hat), 140
bowling, 239
Boxers, 116
buffalo as an American symbol,
  372
Bulldogs, 116
"bull roarer," 240
bumper stickers, **373**

Bureau of Land Management, U.S., address of, 61
Burnett, Frances, 138
Burns and Allen, 348
burr building, **108**
business, going into, 386–401
   advertising, 389–90
   baby-sitting, 392–94
   business books and records, 390–91
   choosing a business, 386–87
   garage sale, 398–401
   housepainting, 394–98
   ideas for, 387
   making a business plan, 388
   making newspaper logs, **392**
   phone tabs, 391
   sales projection chart, 389
Buster Brown, 333, 348
bustle, making a, **136**
butter, 42–44
   making, **43–44**
butter-churning rhymes, 43
butter churns, 42–43
   making, **43**
butter molds, 43
buttonhole puzzle, **268**

C

cake pans as drums, playing, **321**
"cakewalk," 315
calculator games, 288–**89**
Calder, Alexander, 220
California Gold Rush, 59
"calash," 140
campaign, political, 358–59
candle(s), 48–52
   clocks, making, **52**
   collecting fat for, 48
   dipping and molding, 48
   history of, 48
   making dipped, **50**
   making molded, **48–49**
   making a tin lantern for, **51–52**
   materials for making, 49, 50
   sweet smelling, 48
candlemaker, 46, 48

candy:
   chewing gum, 174–**76**
   vanilla molasses taffy, **173–74**
candy apples, **153–54**
canes, 144–45
   materials for, 145
canopy bed, four-poster, making, **82–83**
cap, making the basic, **144**
cape, making a, **136**
cape style homes, 67
Captain Midnight, 349
"captain's walk," 70
card reading, 305–306
   chart of card meanings, 306
cards, breaking a deck of, **297**
Carter, Jimmy, 361
Carver, George Washington, 103–104
cat's cradle, 239, **276–77**
cat's whiskers, **277**
cattails, pancakes made with, **179**
Caverly Family, 211
Celebrated Jumping Frog of Calaveras County, The (Twain), 110, 113
celebrations, *see* holidays and celebrations
cellar, 70
chairs:
   ladder-back, 84
   rockers, 84
   Shaker, 85
charades, **338–39**
Charleston (dance), 324
Charlie Chan, 348
cigar store Indian, 372
cheeses, American, 155–57
   "Big Cheese,"157
   cottage cheese, making, **156**
   pot cheese, making, **156–57**
   processed, 156
   soft American cheese, making, **157**
chewing gum, 174–76
   history of, 174–75
   making spruce, **175–76**
Chihuahuas, 116
children:
   fashion of, 131, 138–39, 145
   overworked, 401
   playthings of, 238–39

rights of, 354–56
chores of Early America, 40–63
   as a family effort, 40–42
circus, 292–93
   the clowns, 298–301
   fire eating, 295
   first, in America, 292
   fortune-telling, 301–306
   joining the, 299
   juggling, 311–**13**
   language of the, 294
   sideshow tricks, 294–95
   strongman tricks, **297–98**
   sword swallowing, 294–95
   sword walking, 295
claws, maple-seed, **109**
clocks, 52
   candle, making, **52**
"clog," 316
clothing, *see* fashion
clowns, 298–301
   "auguste clown," 298
   "character," 298
   clothes, **300**
   college for, 299
   pantomime, **300–301**
   putting on a clown face, **299–300**
   "white-face," 298
coat of arms, your, 34–**35**
Cocker spaniels, 116
Cody, William, 372
coins, American, 379–82
   collecting, 379–82
   dimes, 378–79, 380
   half-dollars, 379, 380
   minting, 377
   nickels, 377–78, 380
   pennies, 377, 379, 380, 381
   quarters, 379, 380
   ridges in, 377
   silver dollars, 379, 380
   valuable, 380
cold, common, home remedies for, 63
collage, **217**
collar, making a Puritan or Victorian, **136**
Collies, 116
colonial style home, 67
color, 203–**204**
colors of natural dyes, origin of, 137

comb, playing the musical, **319**
comic books and funny papers, 332—**35**
   history of, 332–34
   making shuffle-deck comics, **334–35**
   see also jokes and riddles
composition (art), 209–**10**
compost, making, **100–101**
Congressman, how to contact your, **360**
Consumer Information Center, 366
Consumer's Guide to Federal Publications, 365
cooking pots as drums, playing, **321**
"continentals," 376
cooking of Early America, 148–49
   see also food of Early America
Coolidge, Calvin, 225, 322
corn, 96, 148
   popcorn balls, 166
   popper for, 165
   popping, 166
corncribs, 70
cottage cheese, making, **156**
cotton, 103
coughing, home remedy for, 63
cousins, and cousins once removed, 30
Covering the Earth, 215
cow:
   manure, 44, 45
   milking a, 44–**45**
   tail holder, 74
cravat, making a man's, **136**
cricket thermometer, 58
Crum, George, 163
crystal radio, 263–**66**
   tuning the, 266
cubes, four color, **271**
cures and remedies, home, 61–63
Curtis, John, 174
cuts, small, home remedies for, 63

D

Dachshunds, 116
dairying, 44

daisy chains, **108**
Dalmatians, 116
dancing and dances, 315, 324–**31**
   brand-new, of the twentieth century, 324–25
   L.A. hustle, 327–**29**
   New York hustle, 329–**31**
   tap, 325–**27**
dandelions, eating and preparing, **178–79**
day lilies, cooking, **177–78**
Death Valley Days, 348
deed for a tree house, 93
Defense Mapping Agency, 366
Democratic party, 359, 368
derby, 140
Detective Comics, 333
Dick Tracy, 348
diet, *see* food of Early America
dimes, 378–79
   valuable, 380
Diner, 219
"dirt carpet," 69
Doberman pinschers, 116
Does Your Chewing Gum Lose Its Flavor on the Bedpost Over Night?, 176
dogs, 115–18
   breeds of, 116–18
   bringing up a puppy, 115
   selecting, 115
dog tongs, 75
doll carriage, guide to the well-decorated, 361–62
doll hospitals, 253
doll making, 252–53
dolls, 238–42, 252–**59**
   dress-me paper, **258–59**
   of Early America, 238–41, 252–53
   fashion for, 253, 258–59
   life-size, **256–57**
   rag, 253
   roly-poly, **254–55**
   for both sexes, 253
   today's, 253
   yarn, **253–54**
domino trains, **273**
doughnuts, 167–68
   history of, 167
   making, **167–68**
dowsing for water, **126–27**

dress-me paper dolls, **258–59**
drums, household items as, **320–21**
dulcimer, 315
dunce cap, making a **143**
Dutch settlers, homes of, 67
dyes, color, 136–38
   making your own, **137–38**

E

eagle, American bald, 369
Eames, Charles, 220
earache, home remedies for, 63
Eddie Cantor Show, 348
education, 182–99
   toys used in, 238, 241
Eisenhower, Dwight D., 322, 379
elocution, 193
emblems for coats of arms, 35
England, clothing styles of, 131, 132
English setters, 116
English settlers, homes built by, 67
English springer spaniels, 116
Enterprise, Alabama, 104
entertainment, *see Saturday night; toys*
Environmental sculpture, **219**
epitaphs, 224
etiquette, 196–99
   for a formal tea party, 196–98
   table accidents, 199
evergreen trees, 110

F

Fall, 213–14, 220
family group sheets, **26–28**, **29**
   family facts, 26–27
   rooting out clues, 27–28
family treasure notebook, **36**
family treasures, 36
"family tree or circle," 26, **28**, **29**
   sorting out family relationships, 29–30

Faneuil Hall, Boston, weathervane atop, 56
fashion:
  for automobile riding, 133, 141
  for beach attire, 133, 134
  children's 131, 138–39, 145
  color dyeing, 136–38
  for dolls, 253, 258–59
  dressing up in a costume, **135–36**
  hats, 139–44
  imitation of French and English, 131, 132
  late 19th century, 132–33
  making hats, **142–44**
  making your own dye, **137–38**
  in the 1920's, 133–34
  in the 1930's, 134
  post-Revolutionary War, 132
  post-World War II, 134
  Puritan and Pilgrim, 131
  of the settlers, 130, 140
  of a tea party, 197
  of tradesmen, 131
  walking sticks, 144–45
felt hats, 140–41
fiddle, 314–15
finger trap, **272**
firecrackers, making paper, **364–65**
fire eating explained, 295
fireplaces, 68–69
first cousins, 30
flag, American, 367–68
  code for the, 368
Flagg, James Montgomery, 369
Flapper Era of the 1920's, 134
Flax Scutching Bee, 212
"flipper dinger," 240
floors in Early American homes, 69
flower drying, 231–**34**
  air drying, **231–32**
  and arrangement, **233–34**
  plants to dry, 234
  press drying, **233**
  sand drying, **232**
flowerpots as drums, playing, **321**
fly-catcher, making a, **113**
flying toys, **244–46**
  flying propeller, **244–45**
  ring wing glider, **245–46**
fly trap, 74, 75

folklore, weather, 54–55
food of Early America, 148–79
  all-American dishes, 150–51
  apple dishes, making, **152–55**
  cheese dishes, 155–**57**
  chewing gum, 174–**76**
  cooking methods, 148–49
  doughnuts, **167–68**
  foraging for, 177–79
  graham cracker dishes, 168–**69**
  hamburgers, 157–**59**
  hot dogs, 159–**60**
  ice cream, 172–**73**
  ketchup, spicy, 162–**63**
  kitchen rules and hints, 151
  peanut butter, **168**
  popcorn, **165–66**
  potato chips, **163–64**
  pretzels, 169–**71**
  refrigeration and freezing's effects on, 149
  soft drinks, **172**
  submarine sandwiches, 160–**62**
  sweets, 171–**76**
  vanilla molasses taffy, **173–74**
"Fool's Gold," 61
foraging, **177–79**
fortune cookies, **310–11**
fortune telling, **301–11**
  card reading, 305–306
  crystal ball, 302
  fortune cookies, **310–11**
  graphology, 307–10
  palmistry, 302–305
four-poster canopy bed, making a, **82–83**
14-15 puzzle, **269**
Fourth of July, 361, 364
Fox and Geese, **280–81**
foxtrot, 324
framing, **210**
France, clothing styles of, 132
Franklin, Benjamin, 54, 56, 148, 369, 371, 379
  rocking chair of, 84
freckles, home remedies to remove, 62
freezing methods, 149
French settlers, homes of, 67
frog jumping, 110–13
  catching a frog, **111–13**
  contest, holding a, **111**

feeding the frog, **112–13**
  hints and rules for, 110–11
Full Fathom Five, 216
funny papers, *see* comic books and funny papers
furniture, 82–85
  four-poster canopy bed, 82–83
  rocking chairs, 84
  Shaker, 84, 85

gadgets, old-fashioned, 74–75
games:
  calculator, 288–**89**
  "clearance," 280
  fox and geese, **280–81**
  how many more, 280, **283–84**
  "hunt," 280
  Indian and rabbits, 280, **282**
  nature, 107–10
  "point," 280
  point tic-tac-toe, **284**
  solitaire, 280, **282–83**
  tabletop olympics, **285–87**
  triangle solitaire, **283**
  see also dolls; parlor games; playpretties; puzzles; toys
Gangbusters, 348
gardens, 96–99
  caring for, **99**
  crops of Early America, 96–97
  growing a kitchen, **98–99**
  harvesting, **99**
  kitchen, 97–99
  planning the, **98**
  planting the seeds, **99**
  preparing the soil, **98–99**
genealogy, 26–37
  coats of arms, 34–35
  discovering your pedigree, 26–30
  family treasures, 36
  meaning of surnames, 30–34
  knock, knock names, 37
German settlers, homes of, 67, 68
garage sales, 398–401
General Services Administration, 366

geography game, **341**
German shepherds, 116–17
ghost (game), **341–42**
ghost stories and ghosts, 342–47
   ghost encounters, 343
   ghost facts, 343
   The Ghostly Rider, 343–44
   The Haunted House, 345–47
   homemade, 347
   Nobody Here But You, 344–45
   White House, 347
Giant Billiard, 222
glass:
   bottles, 123–25
   lanterns, 51
glassblower, 124
glasses, musical, **321–22**
goal number game, **289**
gold:
   location of, in the United States, 59
   panning for, **59–61**
   staking a claim, **61**
Golden retrievers, 117
Goose, Elizabeth and Isaac, 316
Government Printing Office, U.S., 365, 366
government publications, how to receive, **365–66**
Graham, Sylvester, 168–69
graham crackers, 168–69
   making s'mores, **169**
Grahamite Society, 169
grandaunts and granduncles, 29
grandchild, 29
grandfather, 29
Grandma's Lye Soap, 46
grandmother, 29
grandmother's trunk game, **339**
grandnieces and grandnephews, 29
graphology, 307–10
   base line, 307–308
   crossing your t's, 310
   letter forms, 309
   letter spacing, 309
   line, 308
   slant, 308
   writing size, 308–309
grass-blade whistle, **109**
grave art, 223–25
   epitaphs, 224
   gravestone rubbing, **224–25**

   personalized gravestones, 223–24
   symbols, 224
Great danes, 117
Great Gildersleeve, The, 348
great-grandaunts and great-granduncles, 29
great grandchild, 29
great-grandnieces and great-grandnephews, 29
great-grandparents, 29
Great Plains Indian tepee, 85–88
   etiquette of, 86–87
   inner lining of, 86
   making a five-pole, two-kid, **87–88**
Great pyrenees, 117
Gregory, Hanson Crockett, 167
Greyhounds, 117
Groundhog Day, 54

H

Hale, Sarah Josepha, 361
half-dollars, 379
   valuable, 380
hamburgers, 157–59
   making, **158–159**
   origins of, 157–58
Hamburger, 218
Handball, 208
Hancock, John, 186
hand bellows fog horn, 75
handwriting analysis, 307–309
happenings, 222
Happy Birthday, 324
harmonica, playing the, **322–23**
Harper's Weekly, 368
Harrison, Benjamin, 361
Harrison, William, 361
hats, 139–44
   for automobile riding, 141
   basic cap, **144**
   beaver "cap," 140
   bonnets, 141
   bowler or derby, 140
   "calash," 140
   dunce cap, **143**
   felt, 140–41

   making, **142–44**
   "merry widow," 141
   Panama, 141
   "stovepipe" or high, 140
   straw, 141
Hawaiian dishes, 150
Helen Trent, 348
Henry Aldrich, 348
"here we go 'round the mulberry bush," 239
hex signs, 76–77
   making, **77**
   meaning of, 76
hiccups, home remedies for, 62
hide-and-seek, 239
high hat, 140
High Noon, 203–204
hobo sign language, 374–75
Hogan's Alley, 333
holidays and celebrations, 361–65
   making paper firecrackers for, **364–65**
   make your own, **362–63**
   national, 361
   official whatever days, 363–64
   state, 361–62
homes, 66–93
   adding on buildings, 70
   changes from early, 71–73
   construction materials of settlers, 66–67, 68
   "dirt carpet," 69
   dirt floors, 69
   fireplaces in, 68–69
   furniture, 82–85
   of the future, 71
   gadgets, old-fashioned, 74–75
   hex signs, 77–78
   nails for, 76
   second-floor lofts, 69
   stenciled walls, 79–81
   tepees, Great Plains Indian, 85–88
   tree houses, 89–93
   types of, 67
   windows, 69–70
Hooligan Harry, 333
hopscotch, 239
horses, snow shoes for, 74–75
hot dogs, 159–60
   batter-dipped corn dogs, making, **159–60**

origins of, 159
house painting, 394–98
    paintbrushes, 396
    paint rollers, 397
    paints, 394–96
    preparing the surface, 397–98
    using ladders, 398
houses, *see* homes
humidity, hygrometers to measure, 57
humor, American, 335–37
    see also comic books and funny papers
hunting knives, 226
hustle, the:
    L.A., 327–**29**
    New York, 329–**31**
hygrometer(s), 57–58
    making a, **57–58**

I

ice box, 172
ice cream, 172–73
    cones, 172–73
    easy vanilla, making, **173**
    history of, in America, 172–73
ice cream freezer, 172
ice shoes, 75
Ideal Toy Corporation, 260
I'm My Own Grandpaw, 30
Incense of a New Church, 203
Independence Day, 361
Indian, cigar store, 372
Indian and rabbits, 280, **282**
Indians, American, 376
    cooking methods, 149
    crops, 96, 97, 148
    cures and remedies, 61
    dolls of, 252
    tepee, 85–88
    weather folklore, 54
Industrial Revolution, 132, 241
infants, clothing of, 131, 138
information, writing to the government for, **365–66**
ink, making, **184–85**
Inner Sanctum, 348

insect bites, stings, and itches, home remedies for, 62
investing money, 384–85
invitations and replies for a tea party, 197
"I put my right foot in," 239
Irish setters, 117

J

Jack Armstrong, 348
jackknives, 226
Jackson, Andrew, 157, 347
Jaffe, Moe, 30
Jefferson, Thomas, 100, 148, 157, 172, 347, 348
jitterbug, 324
Johnny Appleseed, 155
Johnson, Andrew, 361
jokes and riddles, 336–37
jug, playing the, **317**
jug bands, 317
juggling, 311–**13**
Just Plain Bill, 348

K

Katzenjammer Kids, 333
Kennedy, John, 379
ketchup, spicy:
    history of, 162–63
    making, **163**
Key, Francis Scott, 367
kitchen gardens, 96–99
kitchen rules and hints, 151
kite flying, 239
kitsch, 221
knee nutcracker, 74, 75
knives, 239
    proper handling of, 227
    selection of, for whittling, 226
    sharpening, 226–27
knock, knock names, 37
knots-and not-knots puzzles, **270**

L

L. A. hustle, 327–**29**
Labrador retrievers, 117
ladders:
    for tree houses, 92–93
    using, when painting, 398
lanterns:
    glass, 51
    tin, making, **51–52**
lariats, **295–96**
Latham, Dwight, 30
laws, American, 354–57
    obsolete, 356–57
    protecting children, 354–56
leapfrog, 239
Let's Pretend, 348
life-size dolls, **256–57**
light, **206**
Lights Out, 348
Lincoln, Abraham, 84, 225, 332, 347, 361, 369
    and Lincoln head pennies, 377, 379, 380, 381–82
line, 204–**206**
Little Lord Fauntleroy, 138
Little Orphan Annie, 348, 349
leaves, why they change color, 110
Lititz, Pennsylvania pretzel factory, 169
Lobster Trap and Fish Tail, 220
lofts, 70
log cabins, 66
"London Bridge is falling down," 239
Lone Ranger, The, 348, 349
Lorenzo Jones, 348
Louisiana Purchase Exposition in 1904, 158, 159, 173
Loyd, Sam, 269
Lucy Locket lost her pocket, 316
lunch counter lingo, 167
Lux Radio Theatre, 348
lye flakes, 47

M

Madison, Dolley, 347

Madison, James, 361
Maltese, 117
manufacturing of toys, 241–42
maple-seed claws and noses, 109
marathons, dance, 324
marble raceway, **250–51**
marbles, 239
Mary Had a Little Lamb, 324
media, mixed, **215**
Mennonites, 77
"merry widow" hats, 141
Michtom, Morris, 260
Mid-Atlantic states, dishes of the, 150
Midwestern states, dishes of, 151
milking a cow, 44–**45**
"milking parlors," 45
miniatures, 238, 241
mixed media, **215**
mobiles, 220–**21**
modern art in America, 211–22
  photography and, 212–13
molasses, 166
Molly Brooks, 315
money, American, 376–85, 386
  borrowing, 382
  coin collecting, 379–82
  coins, 377–82
  investing, 384–85
  paper, 376, 377
  piggy banks, 382, **383**
  of the Revolutionary period, 376–77
  saving, 382–83
  of the settlers, 376
mordants, 137, 138
Mother Goose, 315
Mother Goose's Melodies, 316
motion in art, 207–**208**
motto for coat of arms, 35
muff, making a hand, **136**
mules, contraptions to hitch to, for farm work, 74
music making, 314–**31**
  for all occasions, 316
  dancing, 315, 324–**31**
  in Early America, 314–15
  musical instruments, 314–24
musical comb, playing the, **319**
musical instruments, playing, 314–24
  in Early America, 314–15

harmonica, **322–23**
the jug, **317**
musical comb, **319**
musical glasses, **321–22**
push-button telephone songs, **323–24**
spoons, **319–20**
tin can, flowerpot, wastepaper basket, cooking pot, and cake pan as drums, **320–21**
washboard, **318–19**
washtub bass, **317–18**

N

nails, 76
names:
  knock, knock, 37
  meaning of surnames, 30–34
Nast, Thomas, 368
nature games, 107–109
  burr building, **108**
  daisy chains, **108**
  finger puppets, acorn-top, **109**
  grass-blade whistle, **109**
  maple-seed claws and noses, **109**
  seed-head shooters, **109**
nephews, 29, 30
New England, foods of, 149, 150
New England Primer, 188
Newfoundland (dog), 117
newspaper logs, making, **392**
newspaper toys, **242–44**
  paper snake, **242–43**
  paper tree, **243–44**
New York hustle, 329–**31**
New York World, 332–33
New York World's Fair:
  1939 time capsule, 121
  1964, 157
nickels, 377–78
  valuable, 380
nieces, 29, 30
Nighthawks, 206
Noah's ark, 247
Northwestern states, dishes of the, 151
nosebleed, home remedies for, 63

noses, maple-seed, **109**
number-word poker, **289**
nursery rhymes, 316
nutcracker, knee, 74, 75
nut ink (brown), **184**

O

Oh Susannah, 324
Old English sheep dog, 117–18
Old MacDonald, 324
Old Models, 209–10
olive oil soap, making, **46–48**
1001 exactly, **289**
op art, **220**
Our Gal Sunday, 348
Outcault, Richard Fulton, 332–33
outhouses, 70
ox-yoke puzzle, **266–67**

P

pains, home remedies for, 63
paintbrushes, 396
paint rollers, 397
paints, 394–96
palmistry, 302–305
  fingers, 303–304
  hands, 303
  lines, 304–305
  reading palms, 303
Panama hats, 141
panning for gold, 59–61
  locations for, in the U.S., 59
  method for, **59–61**
  staking a claim, **61**
  tools for, 59
pantomime, clown, **300–301**
paper currency, American, 376, 377
paper dolls:
  chains, 229, **231**
  dress-me, **258–59**
parfleche, 86
parlor games, **338–42**
  alphabet sentences, **340**

Botticelli or the nope game, **340–41**
charades, **338–39**
geography, **341**
ghost, **341–42**
grandmother's trunk, **339**
twenty questions, **340**
whist, 338, **342**
Peaceful Village, 211
peanut butter, making, **168**
peanuts, 103–106
   growing a plant, **104–105**
   recipes for a dinner using, 106
   roasting, 105
peashooter, 279
pedigree, discovering your, 26–30
pedigree chart, **26–29**
   charting, **28–29**
   preparing the information for, **26–28**
Pekingese, 118
pen(s), 185–86
   for fancy writing, 186, 188
   making a quill, **185–86**
   making a wood-nib, **185**
penmanship, 186–88
   fancy writing, 186–**88**
pennies, 377
   Lincoln head, 379, 380, 381–82
   valuable, 380
Pepper Young's Family, 348
pets, family, 113–118
   America's, list of, 118
   dogs, 115–18
   naming, 115
   you don't own, 114–15
Philadelphia, Pennsylvania:
   pretzels, making, **170–71**
   submarine sandwiches, 161
phone tabs, 391
photography, 212–13
pigeons, 114
pie, American apple, **152–53**
piggy bank(s), 382
   making a, **383**
Pilgrims:
   diet, 148
   fashion, 131
pine tree as American symbol, 370
Plains states, dishes of the, 151
plants best for drying, 234
plastic scrimshaw, **235**

playpretties, **272–77**
   domino trains, **273**
   finger trap, **272**
   origin of, 272
   sky hook, **274–75**
   soggy ring, **274**
   string figures, 275–**77**
playthings, 238–89
pocketknives, 226, 239
poetry, *see* rhymes
Pointers, 118
poison bottles, 125
poison ivy, home remedies for, 63
political parties, 359
   symbols of American, 368
politicians, 358–60
   the campaign, 358–59
   how to contact your representatives, **360**
   qualities of, 358
Poodles, 118
pop art, 217–**18**
popcorn, 165–66
   making a corn popper, **165–66**
   popping, **166**
popcorn balls, making, **166**
Portrait of Ralph Dusenberry, 217
portraits, 211
   silhouette, 228–**30**
potato chips, making, **163–64**
potatoes, 100
pot cheese, making, **156–57**
Power of Music, 210
President of the United States:
   background of past presidents, 361
   how to write the, **360**
press drying of flowers, **233**
   plants best for, 234
pressing irons, electric, 132
pretzels, 169–71
   history of, 169
   Philadelphia soft, making, **170–71**
   without salt, 169
   varieties of, 169–70
primers, 188
primitive art, 211
propellers, flying, **244–45**
prospecting for gold, 59–61
"pudding cap," 138
Pugs, 118

pumpkin, 96
punchboards, **248–49**
   how to play with, 249
   messages for a fortune, 249
   messages for a party, 249
puppets, acorn-top finger, **109**
Puritan fashion, 131
push-button telephone songs, playing, **323–24**
puzzles, 240, 241, **266–71**
   buttonhole, 268
   four color cubes, **271**
   14-15, **269**
   ox-yoke, **266–67**

quarters, 379
   valuable, 380
quill pens, **185–86**
quoits, 239

raccoons, 114–15
radio:
   crystal, 263–**66**
   history of, 348–49
   old-time, 348–51
   plays, 349–50
   sound effects, making, **350–51**
rag dolls, 253
rattlesnake as American symbol, 371
rat trap, 74–75
rebus, 190–**92**
   dictionary, 192
recipes, *see* food of Early America
refrigeration of transported food, 149
"relief" carving, 228
remedies and cures, home, 61–63
Republican party, 359, 368
rhymes:
   autograph verses, 194–96
   nursery, 316
   weather folklore, 55

riddles and jokes, 336–37
Riis, Jacob, 213
"Ring-arround-a-rosy," 239
Ringling Bros., Barnum &
    Bailey Circus, 292, 299
ring wing glider, **245–46**
Road of Life, 348
rockee, 84
rocking chairs, 84
Rogers, Will, 225
roly-poly dolls, **254–55**
Roosevelt, Eleanor, 347
Roosevelt, Franklin Delano, 157,
    361
Roosevelt, Theodore, 260, 261,
    361
rope, 52–53
    for humidity measurement, 57
    making, **53**
    materials for, 53
    uses of, 52–53
rope spinning, 295–**97**
    making a lariat, **295–96**
ropemakers, 53
ropewalks, 53
rose petals for tea, **179**
Ross, Betsy, 229

S

St. Bernard dogs, 118
sales projection chart, 389
Salisbury, Dr. James, 158
saltbox style homes, 67
Samoyed, 118
sand drying of flowers, **232**
    plants best for, 234
sandwich, submarine, 160–62
    making a, **162**
Saratoga Springs, New York, 163
Saturday night, 292–351
    the circus, 292–93
    comic books and funny papers,
        332–37
    ghost stories, 342–47
    making music, 314–31
    parlor games, 338–42
    radio, 348–51
saving money, 382–83

sawmills, 68
scarecrows, 101–103
    clothing on, 102
    making your own, **102–103**
Schauzers, 118
schoolhouses, 183
schools, 182–83
Scientific American, 245
scrimshaw, 234–**35**
    plastic, **235**
sculpture, environmental, **219**
seal of the United States, 369–70
second cousins, 30
seed-head shooters, **109**
setting the table for a tea party,
    197–98
*Selected U.S. Government Publi-
    cations*, 366
Senator, how to contact your, **360**
sewing bees, 131
Shakers:
    furniture, 84, 85
    inventions of, 85
shape in art, **203**
shield emblems, tracing, **35**
shimmy (dance), 324
Siberian husky, 118
sign language, hobo, 374–75
silhouette art, 228–**30**
    making a portrait, **230**
silver dollars, 379
    valuable, 380
sky hook, **274–75**
slingshot, **279–80**
sledding, 239
Smelt Brook Falls, 213–14
Smithsonian Institution Press, 366
smokehouse, 70
s'mores, 169
snake, making a paper, **242–43**
sneezing, how to stop, 63
snow globes, **246–47**
snow shoes for horses, 74, 75
soap, 45–48
    ingredients for, 45, 46, 47
    making olive oil, **46–48**
    molds for, 48
    uses of, 46
soda pop, making, **172**
sod "bricks," 66
soft drinks, 172
soggy ring, **274**

solitaire, 280, **282–83**
songs:
    of Early America, 314–15
    for the harmonica, 323
    for the push-button telephone,
        324
sore throat, home remedies for, 63
sound effects, making, 350–51
Southern dishes, 150–51
Spackle®, 397
Spanish settlers, homes of, 67
Spanish terriers, 118
speech, clear, 193
spelling, 188–89
    commonly misspelled words,
        190
spelling bee, 188–89
splinters, home remedy for, 63
spoons, playing the, **319–20**
sprains, home remedies for, 63
spruce gum, 174, **175–76**
squirrels, 115
Stag at Sharkeys, 209
"Star Spangled Banner," 267
stencil prints, 79–81
    making, **79–80**
    materials for, 79
    sample patterns, 80–81
    themes of, 79
Stella Dallas, 348
"stepped roof" colonial homes, 67
stock, buying and selling of,
    384–85
stockbrokers, 384, 385
"stovepipe" hat, 140
straw hats, 141
string figures, 275–**77**
    cat's cradle, **276–77**
    cat's whiskers, **277**
strongman tricks, **297–98**
submarine sandwich, 160–62
    making a, **162**
sugar, 171
    recipes for sweet foods,
        172–76
sugar loaf cutter, 74
sunburn, home remedies for, 62
Sun Machine, 220
Superintendent of Documents,
    U.S., 365
Superman comic books, 333
Superman radio show, 348

surnames, 30–34
Suspense, 348
Swanee River, 324
Swedish settlers, homes of, 67, 68
sweets, recipes for, **172–76**
Swift, Gustav, 149
sword swallowing explained,
    294–95
sword walking explained, 295
symbols of America, 366–75
    drawing, **370–71**

T

table accidents, etiquette and, 199
tabletop olympics, **285–87**
    high jump, **285–86**
    javelin, **286**
    pole vault, **286**
    shot put, **287**
taffy, vanilla molasses, **173–74**
Taft, William, 361
talking hand, **263**
tap dancing, 325–27
    the ball change, **327**
    the shuffle, **326–27**
    the slap, **326**
tap shoes, making, **326**
target shooting, 278–**80**
tea(s), 196–97
    how to make, 198–99
    rose-petal, **179**
    serving, 199
teachers, 183, 186, 356
tea party, the formal afternoon,
    196–99
    invitations and replies, 197
    setting the table, 197–98
    what to wear, 197
teddy bears, 260–61
telephone book, how to tear a, **298**
telephone songs, push-button,
    323–24
television, 349
temperature, cricket thermometer
    and, 58
tepees, Great Plains Indian, 85–88
    etiquette of, 86–87

inner lining of, 86
    making a five-pole, two-kid,
    87–88
Terry and the Pirates, 348
texture, **207**
Thanksgiving, 361
thorns, home remedy for, 63
Three R's, 182–83
time, telling, 52
    candle clocks for, 52
time capsules, 121–22
    making your own, **122**
tin cans as drums, playing, **320,
    321**
tin lanterns, making, **51–52**
toaster, old-fashioned, 74, 75
tobacco, 96–97, 372
tomatoes, 100
Tom Mix, 348
Tom Thumb, 292
tongue twisters, 193–94
toothache, home remedies for, 63
toy guilds, 241
toys, 238–42
    in Early America, 238–41
    flying, **244–46**
    manufactured, 241–42
    marble raceway, **250–51**
    newspaper, **242–44**
    Noah's Ark, 247
    punchboards, **248–49**
    snow globes, **246–47**
    today's, 242
    see also dolls; games; playpret-
        ties, puzzles
tradesmen, clothing of, 131
treasure hunt for family treasures,
    36
tree, making a paper, **243–44**
tree house(s), 89–92
    building, **90–92**
    "deed" for, 93
    ladders, 92–93
    legal restrictions, 90
    safety precautions, 89–90
    selecting a tree for, 91
triangle solitaire, **283**
"trundle" beds, 82
Tuskegee Institute, Alabama, 103
Twain, Mark, 54, 110, 112
twenty questions, **340**
Twinkle, Twinkle, Little Star, 323

U

uncle, 29, 30
Uncle Sam, 369
United States Defense Department
    seal, 371
United States Government Assay
    Office, 61
United States Treasury Depart-
    ment, 377

V

vanilla ice cream, making, **173**
vanilla molasses taffy, making,
    173–74
ventriloquism, 262–63
Virginia reel, 315, 325

W

walking sticks, 144–45
    materials for, 145
waltz clog, 325–27
War of the Worlds, 348
washboard, playing the, **318–19**
Washington, Booker T., 103–104
Washington, George, 172, 338,
    361, 379
washtub bass, making and playing
    the, **317–18**
wastepaper baskets as drums, play-
    ing, **321**
water, dowsing for, **126–27**
watermelon, 96
weather forecasting, 54–58
    almanac for, 54–55
    cricket thermometer, 58
    folklore, 54–55
    hygrometers for, **57–58**
    weather clues, 58
    weathervanes for, 55–**56**

weathervane(s), 55–56
  famous, 56
  making a, **56**
  for weather forecasting, 55–56
weaving machines, automatic, 132
well, locating a, 126
whaling, 234
  scrimshaw and, 234–35
"whimmy diddle," 240
whist, 338, **342**
whistle, grass-blade, **109**
White Castle hamburgers, 158
White House ghosts, 347
whittling, 225–28, 239
  good wood for, 227
  how to whittle, 227–28
  "relief" carving, 228
  selecting a knife for, 226

sharpening a knife, 226–27
"widow's walk," 70
wild-West show, 295
William Tell Overture, 348
Wilmington, Delaware, submarine
  sandwiches, 161, **162**
Wilson, Sam, 369
wind direction, weathervanes for
  telling, 55–**56**
wind flags, 55–56
windows in Early American
  homes, 69–70
windsor-chair rocker, 84
Wirehaired fox terrier, 118
Wisconsin cheddar cheese, 157
wood, for whittling, 227
wood carving, 225
wood-nib pens, **185**

writing, fancy, 186–**88**

yarn dolls, **253–54**
Yellow Kid, 333
Yorkshire terrier, 118

Z

zoning laws, 93
zoot suit, 134